Big S

on dining,

Les Routiers, universally known ... blue symbol of quality and value, now bring you the ultimate travel and leisure club ***"Club Bon Viveur"***

Annual membership brings you more of the good things in life for much less outlay. You can enjoy up to 50% discount on dining in some 700 restaurants throughout the country, save £££'s on weekend breaks in Routiers approved hotels, superb value golf breaks and the chance to buy the famous Les Routiers guides at knockout prices. In addition, you can enjoy discounts on all major 'package' brochure holidays abroad*, savings on charter and schedule airline tickets, car hire and access to the best cross Channel fares available. Too good to be true?

Normally membership costs £30 a year, but because we know you will like what you see, as a reader of this guide you can take the chance to spoil yourself without spending a fortune by 'sampling' Club Bon Viveur for 3 months for just £3! This allows you to try discount dining and accommodation by using the free vouchers included in your 'trial' pack.

The good things in life are seldom free, but sometimes they come very close!

Complete the coupon and send it off to us today.

* Les Routiers Travel Services are operated by High Flyers, the travel agent, ABTA A7462

Club Bon Viveur **Application Form**

TO: Club Bon Viveur, 11 Mayland Green Industrial Estate, Steeple Road, Mayland Chelmsford, Essex CM3 6AU

Please send me my Club Bon Viveur trial pack, at the special introductory price of just £3.00. COMPLETE IN BLOCK CAPITALS PLEASE

Mr/Mrs/Ms/Miss Surname

Address

Postcode Telephone no.

I enclose my cheque for £3.00 made payable to Club Bon Viveur OR charge my Access/Visa/Amex/Mastercard

Card Number:- - - -

Expiry date: Signature

If you have any further queries do not hesitate to contact us on: Telephone: 0171 385 6644 Fax: 0171 385 7136

Ways Across The Channel

"To travel hopefully is a better thing than to arrive," wrote a great traveller, Robert Louis Stevenson. Crossing the Channel to France is not in quite the same league as Stevenson's sailings in the South Pacific, but the excitement of a continental holiday starts on the journey out. And, in the case of France, it starts either at a ferry port or with Eurostar.

Eurostar has revolutionised cross-Channel travel on the shortest crossing. This year, it carried over 6m passengers and has presented such fierce competition to the ferry companies that it has driven the two major ferry companies – Stena Line and P & O European Ferries – into a merger. Unfortunately, at the time of writing, it's not clear what effect this merger will have on the frequency and timing of sailings, although, hopefully, frequency will increase even further.

What is almost certain is that there will be less competition (which means higher fares are likely). At present, all we know is that P & O has pulled out of the Southampton-Cherbourg route for 1997 and the small 7,000 tonne Pride of Bruges, which covers the Dover to Calais route, will not be commissioned in 1997 leaving four large 20,000 tonne ships on this service. For other developments and 1997 sailings, readers will have to consult their travel agent or the ferry companies direct.

However, although fares will probably increase, the competition between Eurostar/Le Shuttle and the ferry companies means that prices will remain keen in a market which is very buoyant – in 1995/96 the number of passengers crossing the Channel by ferry and tunnel increased by 20 per cent and this growth – though perhaps not at the same rate – is likely to continue for as long as fares stay competitive.

Ferry companies are competing with the Tunnel by pouring millions of pounds into new, faster and bigger ships. In August 1996, for example, Stena, introduced what it claims is the largest ship on the Dover-Calais run – the 28,559 tonne Stena Empereur; this followed the earlier launch of two fast catamarans to run alongside its four traditional ferries.

Stena Empereur is able to carry 2,000 passengers and 550 cars and even has a casino on board for its 90 minute crossing.Stena is also introducing the Stena HSS – its fast ferry – on the Newhaven-Dieppe route in 1997. This carries 1,500 passengers and 375 passengers for a two hour journey – half the normal ferry time.

P&O, which has invested over £600m in ship and shore improvements since 1988, launched two new ships in 1995 – the Pride of Dover and the Pride of Calais, both 26,000 tonnes. Carrying 2,290 passengers and 650 cars, the two flagships are twice as large as those they replaced and offer extensive retail, catering and children's amenities on board. Their restaurants have been inspected and approved by Les Routiers in common with seven other P&O ships – the Pride of Bilbao, Pride of Le Havre, Pride of Portsmouth, Pride of Burgundy and Kent, European Pathway and Seaway.

Of course, if you don't like a traditional ferry, both Stena and Hoverspeed operate a catamaran service – Stena, the Stena Lynx from Dover to Calais and Hoverspeed a SeaCat service four times a day from Folkestone to Boulogne (a journey of only 55 minutes). Hoverspeed also runs a hovercraft service 12 times a day from Dover to Calais which takes only 35 minutes.

In 1996, P&O, Stena and Hoverspeed provided not far off 60 sailings a day each way on the most

popular run – Dover-Calais; from most other ports, there are up to half a dozen sailing a day, so there is great flexibility in your choice.

When it comes to investment, of course, everything pales into insignificance in comparison to Eurostar. Its troubled financial history is only matched by its engineering triumph. One train can take as many people as two jumbo jets and, with a 35 minute journey time by the car-carrying Le Shuttle from Folkestone to Calais, it offers a fast and very frequent service.

If you aren't taking your car, Eurostar is probably as quick, central London to central Paris (or Brussels) as flying. At present, there are 16 daily departures to Paris from London's Waterloo station, the trip taking three hours. Some of these departures also stop at Ashford International, Calais and Lille. A recently introduced Friday service to Disneyland Paris (returning Sunday) is proving popular. Eurostar is planning to schedule dedicated regional daytime services for 1997 from Manchester, Birmingham Newcastle and and the West Coast, providing technical track and signalling problems can be overcome.

If you're taking a car, Le Shuttle offers a regular service three times an hour every day, from 07.00hrs to 24.00hrs. Before 07.00, there's a service every 75 minutes. Each shuttle can take 180 cars and the idea is for motorists to turn up and drive on. Obviously, at peak times, there are more cars than capacity so it's best to book in advance. Higher vehicles, such as camper vans, four-wheel drive vehicles and coaches can also be carried.

Given the fact that fares will stay competitive with each other, the key factor in your choice is whether you like a sea crossing or an underground rail journey. For many, the sea crossing is an adventure in itself, particularly for children. Although the quickest journey is a mere 45 minutes, the ferry companies are promoting the journey as a mini cruise – with plentiful opportunities to buy duty-free goods and have a meal. But some people hate sea travel and, for them, the tunnel has been a life-safer. Travelling through the tunnel is quicker – 35 minutes – and there's no question of being sea-sick. In addition, the tunnel isn't affected by bad weather so there's no fear of cancellations.

Of course, if you want to go to parts of France west of Dunkerque, the tunnel is a rather long way around. In this case, it would be easier to take the longer sea crossings to Dieppe, Le Havre, St Malo and Roscoff rather than take the tunnel and drive west. But, if you aren't in a hurry, an unhurried day or two travelling through France can be a holiday in itself.

But before you start your journey, make sure you are fully prepared. Here's a quick checklist:

PASSPORTS

You need to carry a full passport valid until the completion of your trip abroad. The one year British Visitors passport is no longer available. Remember that the recommended application time for getting a new passport is six weeks.

MEDICAL INSURANCE

A very useful government leaflet "Health Advice for Travellers" is available from all the main post offices. Generally speaking, most European Economic Area countries have reciprocal health agreements with the UK, so that you can receive medical treatment if you need it on your holiday, You will have to produce E.111 form should either your children or yourself require medical treatment in a country in the European Economic Area. "Health Advice for Travellers" is also available, freephone 0800 555777.

It is always advisable to take out extra medical insurance in this country for your trip abroad – the premium may be an extra cost, but you could save yourself many hundreds of pounds if you need to have expensive treatment or be flown home in an air ambulance.

MOTOR INSURANCE

It is advisable to apply for an International Motor Insurance Certificate (Green Card). However, you should check with your own motor insurance company in order to know exactly to what extent you are covered. Both the AA and the RAC have special European motoring assistance schemes.

CAR DOCUMENTS

You will need your current full driving licence and the original Vehicle Registration Document – a photocopy will not be accepted. You cannot drive in most European countries under the age of 18 years. If your car is a company car, leased or hired, be sure you have a letter of authority from the registered owner and the original Vehicle Registration Document. Always have your car documents available as you will be expected to produce them immediately, if asked. Don't forget – provisional licences are not generally accepted on the continent

PREPARING THE CAR

The car must have a "GB" sticker displayed as near as possible to the rear number plate. As you are driving on the other side of the road, your car headlamps will need to be adjusted – any motor shop or garage will provide the necessary 'beam benders'. You should also have a first-aid kit, fire extinguisher and a triangular advance warning sign in case you break down on the road and need to warn traffic.

Obviously, it makes sense to ensure that the car has been properly serviced before you leave; be particularly careful about your brakes (you will need to use them constantly on the continent!) and tyre pressure. Don't forget, many continental countries are hotter than the UK and put greater pressure on a car's cooling system.

If you have not planned your accommodation or found it wanting on arrival, carry a Les Routiers guide in your car – you may be grateful of it!

HEALTH, SAFETY AND SECURITY

Always be conscious of car security and lock the car with no windows open or valuables on display. Be wary of strangers on the highway as robberies are not unknown. A phrase book or language guide in French may prove indispensible in the case of a car breakdown or any incidents in which you become involved.

MOTORWAY TOLLS

There are mandatory motorway tolls in France so be prepared and make sure that you have plenty of change available. The tolls vary greatly according to the many motorway companies regulating them. Tolls begin for as little as 19F but can go as high as 343F, depending on the distance travelled. Don't forget – to travel down to the South of France on the motorway system from northern France will cost about £70.

...And enjoy your visit to France – remember Les Routiers' Guide will help you along your way.

Taking Your Car

The nightmare of any traveller taking a car to the continent is to have an accident or breakdown. Are you insured? How do you get help? How do you get home?

Under these circumstances, it really does pay to be a member of one of the motoring organisations and to take out a special insurance which covers your travel in Europe and assistance back, if necessary. In fact, under any circumstances abroad, it pays to have the protection of one of these policies. The cover varies according to the type of policy you take out but you can drive away in confidence knowing that, if your car is stolen or an accident befalls you, help is near at hand.

Generally speaking, these policies provide assistance, towing, storage and labour if you break down on the continent, or have a road traffic accident. If your car needs replacement parts, they can also be provided (but you generally have to pay for them when you get back home).

If the car is stolen and cannot be recovered, or if it cannot be repaired within a day, there is also assistance in finding hotel accommodation or in covering the cost of return travel by rail or hire car.

In addition, some policies cover the cost of seeking legal advice if, by some mischance, you are prosecuted for breach of traffic regulations and uninsured loss claims.

The benefits of these comprehensive European motoring policies are so great that it makes no sense not to be insured. The premium is unlikely to much more than £50 or so for a vehicle.

Similar policies exist for personal travel insurance – again available through the motoring organisations. It is possible, however, to be over-insured in this area as many personal insurance policies have a travel provision and there is no point in insuring twice. Check your existing policy. If you are not covered for travel abroad, ask your insurance company for a quote and compare it with those provided by other companies.

Without taking out one of these special policies, you will have to check with existing motor policy whether your car insurance extends to the continent. This is not always the case by any means and, unless you tell your insurance company, your comprehensive insurance may be reduced to third party only – not a wise move.

Your car insurance company will provide an international motor insurance certificate (Green Card) which will provide cover for the duration of your holiday. A Green Card is not compulsory except in a few countries, but it is strongly recommended; in Spain, a bail bond is also important – available from your insurer.

If you break down, contact the telephone number provided by your motoring organisation. If you haven't joined one of these schemes, then the nearest garage is your only alternative – preferably one handling your make of car. As in the UK, not all garages are open 24-hours a day, so the local police may be able to help you find one. If you break down on a motorway, or in a motorway service area, you have to use the emergency telephone system – and wait patiently.

In the unfortunate event of having an accident, immediately report it to the police – essential if there is a personal injury. If there is an accident with a third party, tell the insurance bureau (the number is on the Green Card) and your own insurance company. It's a good idea to take a photograph of the accident or to make a rough sketch and record as many details as you can. As in the UK, don't admit anything to anyone without the advice of a lawyer.

When you take your car abroad, its good advice to insure for the worst. Make sure you are fully insured, drive carefully – and enjoy the many Les Routiers establishments throughout the country. If you are in trouble, you will find that they will help you along your way.

How to use this Guide

Les Routiers establishments can be located quickly and easily using the guide.

Regional Sections

France has been divided into eight regional sections:

- Paris and nearby
- Northern France
- North-West France
- North-East France
- Central France
- The Loire Valley
- South-West France
- South-East France

Entries Listed Alphabetically

Within each regional section, individual establishments are listed alphabetically by town name. The department and the post code for each town are also given. Each entry gives details of the establishment, its cuisine and specialities, accommodation, prices, opening hours and facilities, as well as road numbers and directions.

Colour Maps

At the rear of the guide are full colour regional maps of France, with every location that has a Les Routiers establishment plotted to allow ease of journey planning.

Index

The index at the back of the guide is an A-Z of all the towns and villages included in the guide. If you know the name of a town but not its department, look in the index – if it is not shown, it has no Relais Routiers.

Symbols used in the guide

🛏	Establishment with accommodation
🛏 🍴	Establishment with accommodation and dining
🍴	Restaurant
👨‍🍳	Establishments offering 'above average' meals (Relais Casserole)
☆	Official French Tourist Board Rating
🏰	Sights and places of interest

Relais Routiers 👨‍🍳

Some Les Routiers establishments offer a more elaborate menu, still at a reasonable price. They are denoted within individual entries by the inclusion of the above symbol.

WHEN IN FRANCE

Always keep your Les Routiers guide with you when visiting restaurants or hotels in France, to let owners know that you have chosen their establishment from the guide, and you are expecting a high standard of food, service and hospitality.

The French mostly take their holidays in July and August, and you may find some hotels and restaurants closed during this time. You should book well ahead if you plan to travel in France during this time and it is especially busy on the roads on during the July and August bank holidays – so avoid travelling on those days.

Understanding the Menu

Meat (les viandes):

abats .... offal
agneau .... lamb
boeuf .... beef
boudin .... black pudding
charolais .... best cut
chateaubriand .... double fillet steak
contrefilet .... sirloin
cuisses (de grenouille) .... (frogs') legs
daube .... stew
entrecote .... rib steak
escargot .... snail
faux filet .... sirloin steak
filet .... fillet
foie .... liver
foie gras .... goose liver
gigot .... leg of mutton
jambon .... ham
jambon cru .... raw smoked ham
langue .... tongue
petit sale .... pickled pork
porc .... pork
quenelle .... meatball
ris .... sweetbreads
rognons .... kidneys
tripes .... tripe
veau .... veal

Poultry/game (la volaille/le gibier):

caille .... quail
canard .... duck
caneton .... duckling
cassoulet .... goose/pork bean casserole
chevreuil .... venison
dindon .... turkey
faisan .... pheasant
gibelotte .... hare/rabbit
lapin .... rabbit
oie .... goose
perdrix .... partridge
pintade .... guinea fowl
poulet .... chicken

Fish/shellfish (les poissons/les coquillages):

anguille .... eel
cabillaud .... cod (fresh)
calmar .... squid
coquille St Jacques .... scallop
crabe .... crab
crevette rose/grise .... prawn/shrimp
daurade .... sea bream
espadon .... swordfish
fletan .... halibut
fritures .... whitebait
fruits de mer .... seafood
gamba .... large prawn
homard .... lobster
huitre .... oyster
langouste .... crayfish
limande .... lemon sole
lotte de mer .... monkfish
loup (de mer) .... sea bass
maquereau .... mackerel
morue .... cod (salt)
mouclade .... mussels (in curry sauce)
moule .... mussel

plie .... plaice
sandre .... zander (freshwater fish)
saumon .... salmon
seiche .... cuttlefish
Saint-Pierre .... John Dory
thon .... tuna
truite .... trout

fruit/vegetables/herbs/spices
(les fruits/les legumes/les herbes/les epices:

ail .... garlic
ananas .... pineapple
aneth .... dill
abricot .... apricot
artichaut .... artichoke
asperge .... asparagus
avocat .... avocado
banane .... banana
basilic .... basil
cassis .... blackcurrant
cep .... vine-stock
cep/cepe .... flat mushrooms
cerise .... cherry
champignon .... mushroom
chou .... cabbage
choufleur .... cauliflower
ciboulette .... chive
citron .... lemon
citron vert .... lime
concombre .... cucumber
coriandre .... coriander
cornichon .... gherkin
courgette .... courgette
couscous .... North Africa semolina dish
cresson .... watercress
endive .... chicory
epinards .... spinach
estragon .... tarragon
fenouil .... fennel
feve .... broadbean
fraise .... strawberry
framboise .... raspberry
gingembre .... ginger
groseille .... gooseberry
haricot vert .... French bean
laitue .... lettuce
menthe .... mint
morille .... (flat) mushroom
mure .... blackberry
muscade .... nutmeg
myrtille .... blueberry
oignon .... onion
oseille .... sorrel
pamplemousse .... grapefruit
peche .... peach
persil .... parsley
petit pois .... pea
poire .... pear
poireau .... leek
poivre .... pepper
pomme .... apple
pomme de terre .... potato
prune .... plum
pruneau .... prune
radis .... radish
raisin .... grape
romarin .... rosemary
safran .... saffron
thym .... thyme
tomate .... tomato
trugge .... truffle

Au Restaurant

EATING OUT IN FRANCE

The French consider eating well as an essential part of their national birthright and there are few other places where people are as passionately knowledgeable about their food and wine.

The traditional large meal at noon survives mainly in rural areas and nowadays, lunch is increasingly likely to consist of an omelette, sandwich or a selection of cold meats. Usually lunch is from noon to 2pm and dinner from 8pm to 10pm, although this will vary depending on whether you are in a rural, town or city restaurant. You will also note from browsing the guide that many cafes and bars are closed for part or whole of the weekend and your hotel may be the best place to eat at this time. When travelling in rural areas out of season you will find that many restaurants and hotels are closed for lengthy periods and it is recommended that you plan your journey carefully before setting off.

In every region of France you will find menus will nearly always include local specialities which reflect local products and agriculture, from cassoulet, a rich stew of white beans, tomatoes, sausage and duck, favoured in the province of Alsace to bouillabaisse, a rich fish soup from Marseille.

On a number of the meal prices in the guide you will find that a drink or wine is included in the price of the meal and when you visit a restaurant you will find this denoted on the menu in the following ways;

Vin Compris – means that a pitchet (jug) of ordinary or house wine is included in the price. These wines are often good quality as few restaurants will risk their reputations on an inferior house wine.

Boisson compris (BC) – means that a drink is included. This can often vary, from a pitchet of wine, a beer or a bottle of mineral water.

Tap water is provided with your meal free of charge, on request, but of course the French pride themselves on the quality and variety of their bottled mineral water.

Useful expressions you may need when you are eating out

Have you got a table ....Avez-vous une table libre

I'd like to reserve a table ....Je voudrais réserver une table

menu ....le menu, la carte

fixed price menu...le menu à prix fixe

rare ....saignant

medium..à point

well done ....bien cuit

A L'Hotel

STAYING IN A HOTEL IN FRANCE

French Hotels de Tourisme are officially classified with one to four star ratings according to the level of comfort. The stars are displayed on a blue plaque by the main entrance. There are many unclassified hotels in France, where standards are equally acceptable.

Accommodation prices are normally for the room, not the number of occupants, and only a small extra charge is made if more than two people share. Always check the room rate at the time of booking – even though, by law, the rates are displayed on a card on the back of the room door.

If you are likely to arrive at your hotel after 6pm you should let the hotel know as soon as possible, without a reservation, your chances of finding a room after this time are slight. Many small hotels lock their doors quite early at night and it is recommended that you advise the proprietors if you are going out in the evening to ensure arrangements to re-admit you can be made.

Useful expressions you may need when you are staying in a hotel

Do you have a room available ....Avez-vous une chambre libre

How much does the room cost ....Combien coute la chambre

I have a reservation ....J'ai fait une réservation

double room with double bed ....la chambre a deux personnes avec un grand lit

twin room ....la chambre à deux lits

single room ....la chambre à une personne

room with a bath, shower ....la chambre avec salle de bains, une douche

key ....la clef

Could you prepare my bill please ....Pouvez-vous me preparer la note

How much do I owe you..Combien je vous dois

Paris and Nearby

This chapter covers the Ile-de-France and Paris itself, and includes the following départments:

Essone (91)
Hauts-de-Seine (92)
Seins-St-Denis (93)
Val-de-Marne (94)

ABLIS
Yvelines, 78660

AUBERGE DE LA CLEF DES CHAMPS
(Mr Joël Henault) Route Nationale 10
TEL: 01.30.59.01.45 FAX: 01.30.59.01.45
DIRECTIONS: RN10, between Chartres and Rambouillet.
LANGUAGES: English, Spanish.
MENU: 62 Frs (drink included).
RESTAURANT: Snacks from 4.30
CLOSED: Sat and Sun.
SPECIALITIES: home-cooking.
OTHER POINTS: credit cards accepted.

ALFORTVILLE
Val-de-Marne, 94140

LA TERRASSE
(Mr Boualem Belamri) 173, rue Etienne Bolet
TEL: 01.43.75.17.02
LANGUAGES: English.
RESTAURANT: Dinner up to 20.00
CLOSED: Sun, and in Sept.
OTHER POINTS: bar.

ANTONY
Hauts-de-Seine, 92160

LES ROUTIERS
(Mme Ginette Laurence) 86, avenue de la Division Leclerc
TEL: 01.46.66.02.62
DIRECTIONS: RN20.
MENU: 50 Frs.
RESTAURANT: Snacks from 7.30, lunch 12.00-14.00
CLOSED: Sat and Sun.
SPECIALITIES: home-cooking.
OTHER POINTS: bar.

AUBERVILLIERS
Seine-St-Denis, 93300

AU RENDEZ-VOUS DES CAMIONNEURS
(Mr Akli Ayadi) 17, rue de la Haie Coq
TEL: 01.48.34.78.35
DIRECTIONS: Porte d'Aubervilliers.
MENU: 53 Frs (drink included).
RESTAURANT: Snacks from 6.00, lunch 11.30-15.30, dinner 19.00-23.00
CLOSED: Sat evening and Sun evening.
SPECIALITIES: regional menu,
HOTEL: 16 rooms.
FACILITIES: shower, private bathroom
OTHER POINTS: bar.

LE TEICH
(Mr Henri Labayle) 5, rue de la Haie Coq
TEL: 01.48.33.42.82
LANGUAGES: Spanish, Portuguese.
MENU: 64 Frs.
RESTAURANT: Snacks from 8.00, lunch 12.00-14.15, dinner 19.00-21.45
CLOSED: Sat and Sun.
SPECIALITIES: cassoulet, home-cooking.
OTHER POINTS: bar.

AUFFERVILLE
Seine-et-Marne, 77570

AUBERGE DE LA DILIGENCE
(Mr Bernard Vincent) 9, route Nationale
TEL: 01.64.28.75.91
DIRECTIONS: RD403, between Nemours and Orléans.
MENU: 55 to 75 Frs.
ROOMS: 120 Frs.
RESTAURANT: Snacks from 7.00, lunch 11.00-15.00, dinner 18.00-21.00
SPECIALITIES: couscous, paella, home-cooking.
HOTEL: 2 rooms.
FACILITIES: shower, bath
OTHER POINTS: credit cards accepted.

Fontainebleau (23km); Château-Landon (11km); Nemours (9km); prehistory museum; forêt de Poligny.

BANNOST
Seine-et-Marne, 77970

LA PETITE GARE
(Mme Martine Klein et Patrice RENAUDIN)
Route Nationale 4
TEL: 01.64.01.02.07
DIRECTIONS: RN 4, RN4, between Rozay-en-Brie and Beton-Bazoche.
MENU: 60 Frs (wine included).
RESTAURANT: Snacks from 5.00
CLOSED: Sat, Sun and public holidays.
SPECIALITIES: home-cooking.
OTHER POINTS: credit cards accepted.

BERNES SUR OISE
Val-d'Oise, 95340

LE BEL AIR
(Mr Hubert Ansevin) 1, rue de Creil
TEL: 01.34.70.04.00
MENU: 59 Frs (wine included).
RESTAURANT: Snacks from 5.00, lunch 12.00-14.00, dinner 20.00-21.00
CLOSED: Sun.
SPECIALITIES: home-cooking.
OTHER POINTS: credit cards accepted.

BLANC MESNIL
Seine-St-Denis, 93150

HOTEL DU PARC
(Mohand et Abdellah Ayadi)
Avenue Charles Floquet
TEL: 01.45.91.19.92
DIRECTIONS: RN916, between Mont-Saint-Michel and Brittany.
LANGUAGES: English, German.
MENU: 50 Frs.
ROOMS: 80 to 110 Frs.
RESTAURANT: Snacks from 5.30, lunch 11.30-15.00, dinner 19.00-23.00
CLOSED: Sun.
SPECIALITIES: ris de veau Vallée d'Auge, coquelet au cidre, anguilles (eels) au cidre, regional menu, home-cooking.
HOTEL: 9 rooms.
FACILITIES: shower, bath, private bathroom
OTHER POINTS: bar.
la Suisse normande; Bagnoles-de-l'Orne; le haras (stud-farm) du Pin; châteaux de Sassy and de Carrouges.

AU BON ACCUEIL
(Mr André Seban) 58, avenue du 8 mai 1945
TEL: 01.48.67.19.88
DIRECTIONS: RN2, Le Bourget.
LANGUAGES: English.
MENU: 59 to 79 Frs.
RESTAURANT: Snacks from 5.30, dinner up to 24.00
CLOSED: Sun.
SPECIALITIES: home-cooking.
OTHER POINTS: credit cards accepted.
Bourget: musée de l'air (aviation museum).

LA TRAVERSEE DE L'ATLANTIQUE
(Mr Blaïd Makkeb)
178, boulevard du 8 Mai 1945
TEL: 01.48.67.25.97
LANGUAGES: English, Italian, Portuguese.
MENU: 55 to 78 Frs.
RESTAURANT: Lunch 11.30-14.30, dinner 18.30-22.00
OTHER POINTS: bar.

LA CARAVELLE
(Mr Madgid Ayadi) 206, avenue du 8 Mai 1945
TEL: 01.48.67.83.71
DIRECTIONS: RN2, RN2.
LANGUAGES: English, Spanish.
MENU: 55 Frs(1/2 wine included).
RESTAURANT: Snacks from 5.00
CLOSED: Sun.
SPECIALITIES: home-cooking, couscous (Wednesday and Friday).
OTHER POINTS: credit cards accepted.

BOISSY SOUS ST YON
Essonne, 91790

LE RELAIS DE TORFOU
(Mr Mohamed Toufahi) 52, avenue de Paris
TEL: 01.64.91.30.50
DIRECTIONS: RN20.
LANGUAGES: English, German, Spanish.
MENU: 51 Frs.
ROOMS: 70 to 80 Frs.
RESTAURANT: Snacks from 6.30, lunch 12.00-15.00, dinner 19.00-22.30
CLOSED: Sat afternoon and Sun.
SPECIALITIES: home-cooking.
HOTEL: 4 rooms
OTHER POINTS: credit cards accepted.
Arpajon (3km); Saint-Sulpice (11thc church).

BOURGET (LE)
Seine-St-Denis, 93350

LE SPOUTNICK
(Mr Karim Ayadi) 70, rue de Verdun
TEL: 01.48.38.32.87
LANGUAGES: English, German.

MENU: 43 to 62 Frs.
RESTAURANT: Snacks from 5.00, lunch 11.00-16.00, dinner 19.30-23.00
CLOSED: Sun.
SPECIALITIES: home-cooking, couscous.
OTHER POINTS: credit cards accepted.

BRIIS SOUS FORGES
Essonne, 91640

L'ARCHE DE LIMOURS JANVRY
(Mr Gaston Bisson) A10 – Aire de Limours Janvry Accessible sens Paris/Province
TEL: 01.64.90.77.18 **FAX:** 01.64.90.89.81
RESTAURANT: Open 24h.
OTHER POINTS: credit cards accepted.

BROSSE MONTCEAUX (LA)
Seine-et-Marne, 77940

LE PETIT PERICHOIS
(Mr Aimé Vollereau) 33, rue de la Vallée
TEL: 01.60.96.25.75 **FAX:** 01.64.70.29.41
DIRECTIONS: RN6, between Fontainebleau and Sens.
LANGUAGES: English, German.
MENU: 59 to 140 Frs.
RESTAURANT: Snacks from 5.00, lunch 11.00-14.30, dinner 19.00-23.00
SPECIALITIES: regional menu, home-cooking.
OTHER POINTS: credit cards accepted.
Orvanne valley; château at Brie; pottery museum at Montereau.

CHAMARANDE
Essonne, 91730

RELAIS DE MONTFORT
(Mr Daniel Cottin) Route Nationale 20
TEL: 01.60.82.20.80
DIRECTIONS: RN20, between Arpajon and Etampes.
LANGUAGES: English.
MENU: 52 Frs (drink included).
ROOMS: 70 to 180 Frs.
RESTAURANT: Snacks from 3.30, lunch 12.00-15.00, dinner 19.30-23.00
CLOSED: Sat afternoon, Sun, in Aug and during the last week of Dec.
SPECIALITIES: home-cooking.
HOTEL: ☆ 34 rooms.
FACILITIES: shower, private bathroom
OTHER POINTS: credit cards accepted.

CHAPELLE LA REINE (LA)
Seine-et-Marne, 77760

LA SALAMANDRE
(Mme Micheline Bourlier)
5, rue du Docteur Battesti
TEL: 01.64.24.30.03
DIRECTIONS: RN1 52, Fontainebleau/Orléans road.
MENU: 60 to 66 Frs.
ROOMS: 120 to 180 Frs.
RESTAURANT: Snacks from 6.30, lunch 11.30-14.30, dinner 19.00-21.00
CLOSED: Sat, Sun, and between Christmas Day and New Year's Day.
SPECIALITIES: home-cooking.
HOTEL: 6 rooms.
FACILITIES: shower, bath, private bathroom
OTHER POINTS: credit cards accepted.
forêt de Fontainebleau; Saint-Pierre basilica; leisuretime base at Buthiers; glassworks at Noisy.

CHARENTON LE PONT
Val-de-Marne, 94220

L'ALLIANCE AUVERGNE NORMANDIE
(Mr Albert Series) 121, rue de Paris
TEL: 01.43.68.03.71
DIRECTIONS: From Porte de Cahrenton towards Charenton Bridge.
MENU: 54 to 95 Frs.
RESTAURANT: Snacks from 6.30, lunch 12.00-14.30
CLOSED: Wed, Aug and 1st week in Sept.
OTHER POINTS: credit cards accepted.

LE PARIS/LISBONNE
(Mr Jacinto Duarte) 195, rue de Paris
TEL: 01.43.68.32.29
LANGUAGES: Spanish, Portuguese.
MENU: 50 Frs.
RESTAURANT: Snacks from 7.00, lunch 12.00-15.00, dinner 19.00-23.00
CLOSED: in Aug.
SPECIALITIES: home-cooking, Portuguese dishes, regional menu.
OTHER POINTS: bar.

CHAUFOUR LES BONNIERES
Yvelines, 78270

AU BON ACCUEIL
(Mr Gérard Magne) Route Nationale 13
TEL: 01.34.76.11.29
DIRECTIONS: RN13, Paris/Deauville road.
MENU: 60 to 170 Frs.
ROOMS: 110 to 200 Frs.
RESTAURANT: Snacks from 5.30, lunch 11.30-14.30, dinner 19.55-22.00
CLOSED: Sat, and from mid-July to mid-Aug.
SPECIALITIES: regional menu, home-cooking.
HOTEL: 15 rooms.
FACILITIES: shower, bath, private bathroom
OTHER POINTS: credit cards accepted.
Claude Monet's house at Giverny.

CHELLES
Seine-et-Marne, 77500

LA PETITE VITESSE
(Mme Ngo Sun-Taï) 32, avenue du Marais
TEL: 01.64.21.09.47
DIRECTIONS: RN34, the Meaux/Paris road.
MENU: 56 Frs.
ROOMS: 160 to 210 Frs.
RESTAURANT: Snacks from 5.00, lunch 12.00-14.00, dinner 19.00-21.30
CLOSED: Sat afternoon and Sun.
SPECIALITIES: home-cooking,
HOTEL: 7 rooms
OTHER POINTS: credit cards accepted.

CLAYE SOUILLY
Seine-et-Marne, 77410

LE RELAIS DE LA ROSEE
(Mme Claude Blom) Chemin Départemental 212
TEL: 01.60.26.17.74 FAX: 01.60.27.02.28
DIRECTIONS: CD212.
MENU: 67 Frs.
RESTAURANT: Snacks from 10.00, lunch 11.00-14.30, dinner 18.30-22.00
CLOSED: Sat, Sun.
SPECIALITIES: home-cooking.
OTHER POINTS: credit cards accepted.
EuroDisneyland; la Mer des Sables theme park at Ermenonville.

CLERY EN VEXIN
Val-d'Oise, 95420

AUBERGE DE CLERY
(Mr Serge Prevot) Route Nationale 14
TEL: 01.34.67.44.15
DIRECTIONS: RN14, Pontoise/Rouen road.
MENU: 60 Frs.
RESTAURANT: Snacks from 6.30, lunch 11.00-15.30, dinner 19.00-21.30
CLOSED: Sat and Sun.
SPECIALITIES: home-cooking.
OTHER POINTS: credit cards accepted.
Cité archéologique, musée de l'outil (museum of the tool) at 3km.

CLICHY
Hauts-de-Seine, 92100

AU SOLEIL
(Mr Roger Queyraud) 105, boulevard Victor Hugo
TEL: 01.47.37.15.45
OTHER POINTS: bar.

COURNEUVE (LA)
Seine-St-Denis, 93120

L'AUBERGE DES SEPT COEURS
(Mr Khaled Naïet Liman) 27, avenue Jean Jaurès
TEL: 01.48.36.43.78
DIRECTIONS: Porte de la Villette exit.
LANGUAGES: English, Italian, Arabic.
MENU: 55 Frs.
RESTAURANT: Snacks from 6.30, lunch 12.00-15.00, dinner 19.30-24.00
CLOSED: Sun.
SPECIALITIES: couscous, pizzas, home-cooking,
HOTEL: 14 rooms.
FACILITIES: shower, bath, private bathroom
OTHER POINTS: credit cards accepted.
Parc de la Courneuve; Paris sights.

LE CYNODROME
(Mr Patrick Mimouni)
22, avenue Roger Salengro
TEL: 01.48.36.72.73
DIRECTIONS: between Aubervilliers and Stains.
LANGUAGES: Arabic.
MENU: 55 Frs (wine included).
RESTAURANT: Snacks from 7.30, lunch 12.00-14.30, dinner 19.00-22.00
CLOSED: Sun.
SPECIALITIES: couscous, paëlla and choucroute on Thursday, home-cooking.
OTHER POINTS: credit cards accepted.

CRESPIERES
Yvelines, 78121

AUBERGE DES ROUTIERS
(Mme Magdeleine Glatigny) Route Nationale 307
TEL: 01.30.54.44.28
DIRECTIONS: Versailles/Maule
MENU: 60 to 85 Frs.
SPECIALITIES: gibier (game), regional menu, home-cooking.
OTHER POINTS: bar.
Versailles; Thoiry.

DEUIL LA BARRE
Val-d'Oise, 95170

AU COQ HARDI
(Mr Gérard Lantinier)
62bis, avenue de la Division Leclerc
TEL: 01.39.64.16.81
DIRECTIONS: RN328, towards Saint-Denis-Taverny.
MENU: 50 to 70 Frs.
RESTAURANT: Snacks from 9.00, lunch 11.30-15.00
CLOSED: Sat, Sun and in Aug.
SPECIALITIES: home-cooking.
OTHER POINTS: bar.

DOMONT
Val-d'Oise, 95330

LA VIEILLE AUBERGE
(Mr Roger Badaire) 7, rue de l'Europe
TEL: 01.39.91.01.66
LANGUAGES: Spanish.
MENU: 60 Frs.
ROOMS: 125 to 175 Frs.
RESTAURANT: Snacks from 6.30, lunch 11.00-15.00
CLOSED: Sat, Sun and in Aug.
SPECIALITIES: home-cooking.
HOTEL: 5 rooms.
FACILITIES: shower
OTHER POINTS: bar.

EPINAY CHAMPLATREUX
Val-d'Oise, 95270

AUBERGE DU CHEVAL NOIR
(Mme Annick Muscat) Route nationale 16
TEL: 01.34.71.01.70
DIRECTIONS: RN16, the Paris/Chantilly road.
MENU: 55 to 95 Frs.
RESTAURANT: Snacks from 7.00
SPECIALITIES: regional menu, home-cooking.
OTHER POINTS: credit cards accepted.
museum at Ecouen; musée du cheval (riding) at Chantilly.

EPONE
Yvelines, 78680

REST'AU VERT
(Mme Assunta Artier) Route de Gargenville
TEL: 01.30.95.60.20
DIRECTIONS: RN13, Paris/Caen autoroute, exit at Epône towards Gargenville.
LANGUAGES: Italian.
MENU: 60 Frs.
ROOMS: 120 Frs.
RESTAURANT: Snacks from 6.00, lunch 11.30-14.30, dinner 19.00-22.00
CLOSED: Sat, Sun.
SPECIALITIES: home-cooking.
HOTEL: 14 rooms.
FACILITIES: telephone
OTHER POINTS: credit cards accepted.
Collégiale at Mantes-la-Jolie; zoo at Thoiry; château at Versailles; Paris sights.

ESSARTS LE ROI (LES)
Yvelines, 78690

A LA GRACE DE DIEU
(Mr Daniel Bigot) Route Nationale 10
TEL: 01.30.41.60.04
DIRECTIONS: RN10, Paris/Chartres road.
MENU: 50 to 61 Frs.
RESTAURANT: Snacks from 5.00, lunch 11.30-15.00, dinner 18.30-22.30
CLOSED: Sat, Sun, public holidays and in Aug.
SPECIALITIES: home-cooking.
OTHER POINTS: credit cards accepted.
châteaux at Rambouillet and Versailles; the Chevreuse valley.

LE RELAIS D'ARCOAT
(SARL Arcoat) 39, route Nationale 10
TEL: 01.30.41.60.53
DIRECTIONS: RN10, between Rambouillet and Paris.
LANGUAGES: English.
MENU: 60 Frs.
RESTAURANT: Snacks from 6.00, lunch 10.00-15.00, dinner 19.00-22.00
CLOSED: Sat after 3pm, Sun, public holidays and in July.
SPECIALITIES: home-cooking.
OTHER POINTS: credit cards accepted.

FERTE GAUCHER (LA)
Seine-et-Marne, 77320

LE CONTRE-TEMPS
(Mr Hervé Langle) 4, avenue de la Gare
TEL: 01.64.04.01.90
DIRECTIONS: RN34, Sézanne.
LANGUAGES: English.
MENU: 60 to 120 Frs.
RESTAURANT: Snacks from 8.00, lunch 12.00-14.00, dinner 19.30
CLOSED: Sat evening, Sun.
SPECIALITIES: home-cooking.
OTHER POINTS: credit cards accepted.

GUILLERVAL
Essonne, 91690

RELAIS DE MONDESIR
(Mr Jean Picq) Hameau de Mondésir
TEL: 01.64.95.60.76 FAX: 01.64.95.60.76
DIRECTIONS: RN20, Orléans.
LANGUAGES: Spanish, Italian, Portuguese.
MENU: 50 to 60 Frs.
RESTAURANT: Snacks from 6.00
CLOSED: Sat, Sun, and 1 week in Aug.
SPECIALITIES: chili con carne, tripes maison, regional menu, home-cooking.
OTHER POINTS: credit cards accepted.
château at Chaloux-sur-Mars; la Tour Blanche.

ISLE ADAM (L')
Val-d'Oise, 95290

AU RALLYE
(Mme Paulette Combes) 71, rue de Pontoise

TEL: 01.34.69.08.24
DIRECTIONS: RN322.
OTHER POINTS: bar.

LIMAY
Yvelines, 78520

LA MARMITE
(Mr Michel Blanchard) 1, route de Meulan
TEL: 01.34.78.65.52 FAX: 01.34.78.47.32
DIRECTIONS: RN190;A13, exit Mantes Est (East)/Limay.
LANGUAGES: English.
MENU: 62 Frs (1/4 wine included).
RESTAURANT: Snacks from 6.00, lunch 11.45-16.00, dinner 19.30-22.30
CLOSED: Sat evening, Sun.
SPECIALITIES: cassoulet, choucroute, couscous, paella, home-cooking.
OTHER POINTS: credit cards accepted.
château at Versailles; Mantes-la-Jolie (12thc Collégiale); Paris sights.

MAGNY EN VEXIN
Val-d'Oise, 95420

HOTEL DE LA GARE
(Mme Fabienne Degoul Alves) 65, rue de Beauvais
TEL: 01.34.67.20.70
ROOMS: 150 to 160 Frs.
RESTAURANT: dinner up to 22.00
CLOSED: Sun, last week in Dec.
SPECIALITIES: couscous, home-cooking.
HOTEL: 10 rooms.
FACILITIES: shower
OTHER POINTS: credit cards accepted.

MANTES LA VILLE
Yvelines, 78200

LE HOUDAN BAR
(Mr Hocine Ouhab) 43, route de Houdan
TEL: 01.34.77.06.11
DIRECTIONS: RN13, Houdan.
LANGUAGES: English.
MENU: 58 Frs (¼ wine included).
RESTAURANT: Snacks from 9.00, lunch 12.00-15.00, dinner 19.00-2.00
SPECIALITIES: couscous (at weekends), home-cooking.
OTHER POINTS: credit cards accepted.
Collégiale at Mantes-la-Jolie (2km); château d'Anet (20km); zoo at Thoiry (30km).

MONTLHERY
Essonne, 91310

LE SOLOGNE
(Mr Jacques Cheron) 65, route d'Orléans
TEL: 01.69.01.00.98
DIRECTIONS: RN20.
MENU: 52 Frs.
ROOMS: 120 Frs.
RESTAURANT: Snacks from 7.00, lunch 11.30-14.00, dinner 19.30-21.00
CLOSED: Sun, and in Aug.
SPECIALITIES: home-cooking.
HOTEL: ☆ 7 rooms.
FACILITIES: shower, bath, private bathroom, telephone
OTHER POINTS: credit cards accepted.
tower at Montlhéry; animal park at Saint-Vrain; Chevreuse valley; automobile competition circuit.

MONTREUIL
Seine-St-Denis, 93100

LE RELAIS DES ROUTIERS
(Mmes Sol et Puech) 70, rue de Lagny
TEL: 01.48.51.54.41
OTHER POINTS: bar.

NONVILLE
Seine-et-Marne, 77140

AU RENDEZ-VOUS DES AMIS
(Mme Renée Chambille) 8, rue grande
TEL: 01.64.29.02.12
DIRECTIONS: RD403, Nemours/Montereau axis.
MENU: 52 Frs (wine included).
RESTAURANT: Snacks from 7.30, lunch 12.00-15.00, dinner 19.00-21.30
CLOSED: Sun evening and Mon evening.
SPECIALITIES: home-cooking.
OTHER POINTS: credit cards accepted.

PARIS
Paris, 75018

AUX ROUTIERS
(Mr Bernard Dubreuil) 50bis, rue Marx Dormoy
TEL: 01.46.07.93.80
DIRECTIONS: Porte de la Chapelle; on main road north from Gare du Nord.
MENU: 70 to 100 Frs.
RESTAURANT: Snacks from 7.30, lunch 12.00-14.15, dinner 19.15-22.15
CLOSED: Sun.
SPECIALITIES: couscous, paella, choucroute, home-cooking.
OTHER POINTS: credit cards accepted.
Parc de la Villette; Paris sights.

CHEZ LEON
(Mme Grange) 5 Rue de l'Isly
TEL: 01.43.87.42.77
DIRECTIONS: between Gare St-Lazare and boulevard Haussmann.
RESTAURANT: dinner up to 21.00
CLOSED: Sun, and in Aug.
SPECIALITIES: couscous, home-cooking.
OTHER POINTS: bar.

L'ETOILE DE LISBONNE
(Mr Duarte Ferras Arlindo) 139, boulevard Davout
TEL: 01.40.30.22.13
LANGUAGES: Spanish, Portuguese.
MENU: 50 Frs.
RESTAURANT: Snacks from 7.00, lunch 12.00-14.30, dinner 19.00-23.00
CLOSED: in August.
SPECIALITIES: home-cooking.
OTHER POINTS: bar.

AU PALAIS DE CHAILLOT
(Mr Cyrille Pien) 35, avenue Raymond Poincarré
TEL: 01.53.70.09.09 **FAX:** 01.53.70.09.08
OTHER POINTS: bar.

PAVILLONS SOUS BOIS (LES)
Seine-St-Denis, 93320

LES ROUTIERS
(Mr Mohand Iguerbousbane) 186, avenue Aristide Briand
TEL: 01.48.02.07.82
DIRECTIONS: RN3, between Bonay and Livry Gargan.
MENU: 50 Frs.
ROOMS: 180 Frs.
RESTAURANT: Snacks from 7.00, lunch 12.00-15.00, dinner 19.00-21.00
SPECIALITIES: couscous, home-cooking.
HOTEL: 8 rooms
OTHER POINTS: bar.

PIERREFITTE SUR SEINE
Seine-St-Denis, 93380

LE NORMANDIE
(Mme Marcelline Vidal) 105, avenue du Général Galliéni
TEL: 01.48.26.55.62
DIRECTIONS: RN1, Porte de la Chapelle towards Beauvais.
MENU: 57 to 59 Frs
RESTAURANT: Snacks from 6.00, lunch 11.30-15.00, dinner 19.00-21.00
CLOSED: Sat, Sun, and in Sept.
SPECIALITIES: confit de canard, paella, escalope Normande, home-cooking.
OTHER POINTS: credit cards accepted.
château at Ecouen (5km); Royaumont abbey; château at Chantilly (15km).

PLAINE SAINT DENIS (LA)
Seine-St-Denis, 93210

LE CHRISTAL
(Mme Marie-Louise Rigolet) 101, avenue du Président Wilson
TEL: 01.42.43.75.58
DIRECTIONS: Porte de la Chapelle,
LANGUAGES: English, German.
MENU: 55 Frs (drink included).
RESTAURANT: Snacks from 8.00
CLOSED: Sat and Sun.
SPECIALITIES: home-cooking,
OTHER POINTS: credit cards accepted.
Saint-Denis basilica.

LE RELAIS DU FRET
(Mr Joseph Dahan) 53-55, avenue du Président Wilson
TEL: 01.48.09.41.22
LANGUAGES: English.
MENU: 50 Frs (drink included).
RESTAURANT: Snacks from 9.00, lunch 12.00-14.30, dinner 19.00-23.00
CLOSED: Sun.
SPECIALITIES: home-cooking.
OTHER POINTS: credit cards accepted.

PONTAULT COMBAULT
Seine-et-Marne, 77340

L'ALBHOTEL
(Mr Michel Brugerolle) 9, route de Paris
TEL: 01.60.28.95.96 **FAX:** 01.64.43.94.09
DIRECTIONS: RN 3, RN3, the Ozoir/La-Queue-en-Brie axis.
LANGUAGES: English, Portuguese.
MENU: 53 Frs.
ROOMS: 145 to 330 Frs.
RESTAURANT: Snacks from 5.30, lunch 12.00-14.30, dinner 19.00-22.00
CLOSED: Sun.
SPECIALITIES: home-cooking, portuguese specialities.
HOTEL: ☆☆ 44 rooms.
FACILITIES: shower, bath, private bathroom, television, telephone
OTHER POINTS: credit cards accepted.

QUINCY SOUS SENART
Essonne, 91480

A LA BONNE TABLE
(Mr Pierre Walter)
3Bis, avenue Henri Chasles
TEL: 01.69.00.93.81

MENU: 50 to 75 Frs.
ROOMS: 100 to 180 Frs.
RESTAURANT: Snacks from 5.30, lunch 11.30-14.30, dinner 19.45-21.30
CLOSED: Sun, and in Feb.
SPECIALITIES: dishes from Normandy and Alsace, home-cooking.
HOTEL: 5 rooms.
FACILITIES: shower, bath
OTHER POINTS: credit cards accepted.
Paris sights; Corbeil; Melun; Fontainebleau; forêt de Senart.

RUNGIS
Val-de-Marne, 94582

LES MARAICHERS
(Mr Jacques Chiche) 3, avenue de l'Orléanais
TEL: 01.46.86.47.76 FAX: 01.46.87.81.98
DIRECTIONS: at the "centre routier Sogaris".
LANGUAGES: English, Spanish.
MENU: 60 Frs (wine and coffee included).
RESTAURANT: Open 24h.
CLOSED: Sat evening and Sun lunchtime.
SPECIALITIES: home-cooking.
OTHER POINTS: credit cards accepted.

SAINT DENIS
Seine-St-Denis, 93200

LA CHEMINEE
(Mr Jacques Lebas) 56, rue Ambroise Croizat
TEL: 01.48.20.98.58
MENU: 65 Frs.
RESTAURANT: Snacks from 7.00, lunch 11.30-14.30, dinner 19.00-22.00
CLOSED: Sat, Sun, and in Aug.
SPECIALITIES: home-cooking.
OTHER POINTS: credit cards accepted.

SAINT GRATIEN
Val-d'Oise, 95210

LES ROUTIERS
(Mr Amar Negaa) 57, boulevard Foch
TEL: 01.39.89.29.74
OTHER POINTS: bar.

SAINT LEGER EN YVELINES
Yvelines, 78600

LE RELAIS DE LA VESGRE
(Mr Daniel Benrais) 1, rue de la Harpe
TEL: 01.34.86.34.40
DIRECTIONS: Rambouillet/Houdan or Rambouillet/Montfort-Lamaury.
MENU: 65 Frs (wine included) to 135 Frs.
ROOMS: 160 to 240 Frs.
RESTAURANT: Snacks from 8.00, lunch 12.00-14.30, dinner 19.00-21.30
SPECIALITIES: home-cooking, grillades (summer), game and fish (winter).
HOTEL: 20 rooms.
FACILITIES: shower, bath, private bathroom
OTHER POINTS: credit cards accepted.

SAINT MAUR DES FOSSES
Val-de-Marne, 94100

LA PASSERELLE
(Mr Jean Dias) 45, boulevard du Général Férrié
TEL: 01.42.83.21.75
LANGUAGES: Spanish, Italian, Portuguese.
MENU: 55 Frs.
RESTAURANT: Snacks from 6.30, lunch 11.30-15.30, dinner 19.00-22.00
CLOSED: Sun and public holidays.
SPECIALITIES: home-cooking.
OTHER POINTS: credit cards accepted.

SAINT OUEN
Seine-St-Denis, 93400

AUX ROUTIERS SYMPAS
(Mr Bernard Delouvrier)
93, boulevard Victor Hugo
TEL: 01.40.11.00.31
DIRECTIONS: bridge of Saint-Ouen.
MENU: 53 Frs (wine included).
ROOMS: 90 Frs.
RESTAURANT: Snacks from 6.00, lunch 11.45-15.00, dinner 18.30-20.00
CLOSED: Sun, and in Aug.
SPECIALITIES: home-cooking.
HOTEL: 9 rooms.
FACILITIES: shower, bath
OTHER POINTS: bar.
Paris sights.

SURVILLIERS
Val-d'Oise, 95470

LE COQ CHANTANT
(Mme Edith Resslen) Route Nationale 17
TEL: 01.34.68.24.65
DIRECTIONS: RN17, Senlis.
LANGUAGES: German, Portuguese.
MENU: 59.50 Frs.
RESTAURANT: Snacks from 6.00, lunch 11.45-14.30, dinner 19.00-22.15
CLOSED: Fri evening, Sat evening, Sun, and the first two weeks in Aug.
SPECIALITIES: home-cooking.
OTHER POINTS: credit cards accepted.

abbey at Royaumont; château at Chantilly; riding museum; Parc Astérix; EuroDisneyland at Marne-la-Vallée; Ermenonville; Senlis.

VALENTON
Val-de-Marne, 94460

AU BON ACCUEIL
(Mr Marc Roméro) 46, avenue Henri Barbusse
TEL: 01.43.89.06.70
DIRECTIONS: RN 6, RN6, at the Pompadour/Villeneuve-Saint-Georges crossroads.
LANGUAGES: Spanish.
MENU: 62 Frs (drink included).
RESTAURANT: Snacks from 7.30
CLOSED: Sun.
SPECIALITIES: home-cooking.
OTHER POINTS: bar.

VARENNES SUR SEINE
Seine-et-Marne, 77130

SARL LE PETIT FOSSARD
(Mr José Da Silva) Route Nationale 6
TEL: 01.64.32.17.47
DIRECTIONS: RN6, Paris/Sens road.
LANGUAGES: Portuguese.
MENU: 57 to 80 Frs.
ROOMS: 100 to 120 Frs.
RESTAURANT: Snacks from 4.30, lunch 11.30-15.00, dinner 19.00-23.00
CLOSED: Sun.
SPECIALITIES: home-cooking.
HOTEL: 6 rooms
OTHER POINTS: credit cards accepted.
Montereau cathedral; pottery museum; château at Fontainebleau.

VILLE SAINT JACQUES
Seine-et-Marne, 77130

LE RELAIS FLEURI
(Mr Jean-Luc Bernier) 37, rue Grande
TEL: 01.60.96.66.00 FAX: 01.64.70.91.77
DIRECTIONS: RD 403, RD403, on the Nemours/Montereau axis.
LANGUAGES: English.
MENU: 40 to 98 Frs.
RESTAURANT: Snacks from 7.30, lunch 12.00-14.00, dinner 19.00-21.30
CLOSED: Sun.
SPECIALITIES: home-cooking.
OTHER POINTS: credit cards accepted.

VIRY CHATILLON
Essonne, 91170

LES ROUTIERS
(Mr Stéphane Rouillon) 100, route de Fleury
TEL: 01.69.24.28.46
DIRECTIONS: RN7 and RD91, exit Viry-Châtillon or Crigny.
MENU: 55 Frs.
RESTAURANT: Snacks from 6.30, lunch 12.00-14.30, dinner 19.00-22.00
CLOSED: Sat and Sun.
SPECIALITIES: home-cooking.
OTHER POINTS: credit cards accepted.

VOISINS PAR MOUROUX
Seine-et-Marne, 77120

LE RELAIS DU SOMMET
(Mr Robert Devillers) 968 avenue du Général de Gaulle – Route Nationale 34
TEL: 01.64.03.05.47
DIRECTIONS: Coulommiers.
LANGUAGES: English.
MENU: 57 Frs (drink included).
ROOMS: 220 Frs (full-board).
RESTAURANT: Snacks from 4.30
CLOSED: Sun.
SPECIALITIES: tripoux à l'auvergnate, home-cooking.
HOTEL: 6 rooms.
FACILITIES: shower, private bathroom, television
OTHER POINTS: bar.
the Morin valley.

VOULX
Seine-et-Marne, 77940

LA BRUYERE
(Mr Alban Baldran) 72, Grande Rue
TEL: 01.64.31.92.41
DIRECTIONS: RD219, beyond Montereau towards Montargis.
MENU: 59 to 140 Frs
RESTAURANT: Lunch 12.00-14.00, dinner 19.00-21.30
CLOSED: Sun and Aug.
SPECIALITIES: huitres, escargots, tête de veau, grillades (grills), home-cooking.
OTHER POINTS: credit cards accepted.

Northern France

The following départments are included in this chapter:

Aisne (02)
Nord (59)
Oise (60)
Pas-de-Calais (62)
Some (80)

ABBEVILLE
Somme, 80100

AUBERGE FLEURIE
(Mr Michel Rubin) 294, côte de la Justice
TEL: 03.22.24.73.68
DIRECTIONS: RN1, Abbeville/Dunkerque/Rouen road.
MENU: 55 Frs.
RESTAURANT: Snacks from 5.00, lunch 11.30-15.00, dinner 19.00-23.00
CLOSED: Sat, Sun.
SPECIALITIES: home-cooking.
OTHER POINTS: credit cards accepted.
museums and churches at Abbeville (15km).

LE CHEVAL NOIR
(Mr Boussad Boukela) Route départementale 925 – Petit Miannay
TEL: 03.22.24.20.17
DIRECTIONS: RD925, Abbeville/Le Tréport road.
LANGUAGES: English.
MENU: 55 Frs.
RESTAURANT: Snacks from 6.30
SPECIALITIES: couscous, home-cooking.
OTHER POINTS: credit cards accepted.
Baie de Somme; ornithology reserve; château d'Eu; Abbeville; Vallée de la Bresle.

ABBEVILLE SAINT LUCIEN
Oise, 60480

LE BEAUVAIS BRETEUIL
(Mr Raymond Julen) 5, rue du Bois Saint Martin
TEL: 03.44.79.13.09
DIRECTIONS: RN1, between Beauvais and Amiens.
MENU: 56 to 98 Frs.
RESTAURANT: Snacks from 7.00, lunch 11.30-15.00, dinner 19.00-21.30
CLOSED: Sat and in Aug.
SPECIALITIES: home-cooking.
OTHER POINTS: credit cards accepted.
cathedral at Beauvais; museum; place Jeanne-Hachette; parc Saint-Paul.

AMBLAINVILLE
Oise, 60110

L'ETAPE
(Mme Marie Sylla) 40, rue Nationale
TEL: 03.44.52.03.10
DIRECTIONS: RN327, the Pontoise/Beauvais axis.
LANGUAGES: English.
MENU: 55 Frs (wine included).
RESTAURANT: Snacks from 7.00, lunch 12.00-14.00, dinner 19.00-20.30
CLOSED: Sunday.
SPECIALITIES: home-cooking,
OTHER POINTS: bar.

ARBRET (L')
Pas-de-Calais, 62158

HOTEL DE LA GARE
(Mr Rabah Belhadef) Route Nationale 44
TEL: 03.21.48.24.33
DIRECTIONS: RN44, between Arras and Doullens.
LANGUAGES: German.
MENU: 60 and 65 Frs.
ROOMS: 100 to 150 Frs.
RESTAURANT: Snacks from 6.00
SPECIALITIES: couscous, home-cooking.
HOTEL: 12 rooms.
FACILITIES: shower, bath, private bathroom
OTHER POINTS: credit cards accepted.
château at Grand-Rullecourt.

ARMENTIERES
Nord, 59280

AUBERGE DE LA LYS
(Mme Jacqueline Leflon) 110, rue des Résistants
TEL: 03.20.77.21.83
DIRECTIONS: RN42, Dunkerque/Lille road.
MENU: 36 to 72 Frs.
RESTAURANT: Snacks from 9.30, lunch 11.30-14.30, dinner 19.00-21.00
CLOSED: Sun, and from 16th to 31st Aug.

SPECIALITIES: regional menu, home-cooking.
OTHER POINTS: credit cards accepted.
base of Prés du Hem.

A LA TERRASSE
(Mr Fitouri Meddeb) 112, rue des Résistants
TEL: 03.20.48.24.80
DIRECTIONS: RN42, opposite the customs, near the Prés du Hem.
LANGUAGES: English.
MENU: 45 to 65 Frs.
RESTAURANT: Snacks from 6.00, lunch 11.00-16.00, dinner 18.00-24.00
SPECIALITIES: regional menu, home-cooking.
OTHER POINTS: credit cards accepted.
base of Prés du Hem.

AVELIN
Nord, 59710

A L'EMBUSCADE
(Mme Geneviève Lemoine) 14, route de Seclin
TEL: 03.20.32.90.33
DIRECTIONS: RD949, exit at Seclin, towards Valenciennes.
MENU: 35 to 70 Frs.
RESTAURANT: Snacks from 6.00, lunch 11.30-15.00, dinner 19.00-21.00
CLOSED: Sat afternoon, Sun.
SPECIALITIES: home-cooking.
OTHER POINTS: credit cards accepted.

BAILLEUL
Nord, 59270

AUBERGE DU SEAU
(Mr Joël Dequidt) Chemin Départemental 933 – Le Seau
TEL: 03.20.48.62.00
DIRECTIONS: CD933 from Dunkerque, exit 10, towards Nieppe-Argentières.
MENU: 70 Frs (drink included).
ROOMS: 130 to 200 Frs.
RESTAURANT: Lunch 12.00-14.30, dinner 19.00-22.00
SPECIALITIES: steack de veau de la mer, côte à l'os, couscous de poissons, home-cooking.
HOTEL: ☆ 11 rooms.
FACILITIES: shower, bath, private bathroom, television, telephone
OTHER POINTS: credit cards accepted.
Mont des Flandres; Mont Noir.

CHEZ ANDRE
(Mr André Noorenberghe) Route Nationale 4671 – Route de Lille
TEL: 03.28.49.29.14
DIRECTIONS: RD933.
RESTAURANT: dinner up to 21.00
OTHER POINTS: bar.

BAILLEULVAL
Pas-de-Calais, 62123

RELAIS BAC DU SUD
(Mr Yves Sanson) Route Nationale 25
TEL: 03.21.58.79.12
DIRECTIONS: RN25, between Arras and Doullens.
LANGUAGES: Dutch.
MENU: 62 Frs.
ROOMS: 120 to 170 Frs.
RESTAURANT: Snacks from 5.30, lunch 12.00-14.30, dinner 18.45-21.45
CLOSED: Sun, 1st 2 weeks in Aug.
SPECIALITIES: home-cooking.
HOTEL: 6 rooms.
FACILITIES: shower
OTHER POINTS: credit cards accepted.
caves at Naourc; Mont Saint-Eloi; Arras; Notre-Dame-de-Lorette at Vimy.

BAPAUME
Pas-de-Calais, 62450

L'ESCALE
(Mr Evelyne Owezarek) 45, faubourg de Péronne
TEL: 03.21.07.12.78
DIRECTIONS: RN17, Arras/Paris or Amiens/Cambrai road.
MENU: 55 Frs.
ROOMS: 110 to 150 Frs.
RESTAURANT: Snacks from 7.00, lunch 11.45-14.00, dinner 19.00-21.00
CLOSED: Sun and last 2 weeks in Aug.
SPECIALITIES: home-cooking.
HOTEL: 8 rooms.
FACILITIES: telephone
OTHER POINTS: credit cards accepted.
Arras: belfry, squares and monuments.

LE RELAIS
(Mr Jean-Franáois Fogietta) 32, faubourg d'Arras
TEL: 03.21.07.11.01
DIRECTIONS: RN17, between Arras and Douai.
LANGUAGES: Italian.
MENU: 61 Frs (coffee included).
ROOMS: 100 Frs.
RESTAURANT: Snacks from 6.00, lunch 11.00-15.00, dinner 18.00-22.30
CLOSED: Sat, Sun and in August.
SPECIALITIES: home-cooking.
HOTEL: 4 rooms
OTHER POINTS: credit cards accepted.

BAVAY
Nord, 59570

ETANG DU PRAY
(Mr Patrick Delbove) Route Nationale 49 – Route de Valenciennes
TEL: 03.27.39.83.93 FAX: 03.27.39.89.46
DIRECTIONS: RN49, between Valenciennes and Maubeuge.
LANGUAGES: English.
MENU: 60 Frs (drink included).
RESTAURANT: Snacks from 5.30
CLOSED: During Feb school holidays.
SPECIALITIES: home-cooking.
OTHER POINTS: credit cards accepted.

BEAULENCOURT
Pas-de-Calais, 62450

LE RELAIS DE BEAULENCOURT
(Mr Maurice Pontonnier) 24, route Nationale 17
TEL: 03.21.07.68.81
DIRECTIONS: RN17, between Péronne and Bapaume.
MENU: 58 Frs (drink included).
RESTAURANT: Snacks from 7.30
CLOSED: Sun and in Aug.
SPECIALITIES: home-cooking.
OTHER POINTS: credit cards accepted.
1914-18 war museum.

BEAUVAIS
Oise, 60000

LA TOUR EIFFEL
(Mr Michel Lorusso) 72, rue des Cheminots
TEL: 03.44.02.47.40
DIRECTIONS: RN1, Zone Artisanale No. 1.
MENU: 60 Frs.
RESTAURANT: Snacks from 6.00
CLOSED: Sat afternoon.
SPECIALITIES: couscous (on Thurs), home-cooking.
OTHER POINTS: bar.
Gerberoy (village in bloom); Beauvais cathedral; leisure park at Saint-Paul.

BERCK SUR MER
Pas-de-Calais, 62600

AU RELAIS D'ARTOIS
(Mr Pascla Taisne) 20, rue Alfred lambert
TEL: 03.21.09.29.35
DIRECTIONS: the Arras/Dunkerque/Abbeville axis.
MENU: 58 to 95 Frs.
RESTAURANT: Snacks from 8.00, lunch 12.00-14.00, dinner 19.00-21.00
CLOSED: from Sun morning till Mon 17.00 (Oct to April).
SPECIALITIES: home-cooking.
HOTEL: 11 rooms
OTHER POINTS: credit cards accepted.

BEUVRY LA FORET
Nord, 59310

A LA VIEILLE FRANCE
(Mme Jacqueline Lasser) 2895, rue Albert Ricquier
TEL: 03.20.71.06.93
DIRECTIONS: RN49, between Lille and Valenciennes.
MENU: 70 Frs.
ROOMS: 120 to 200 Frs.
RESTAURANT: Snacks from 7.00, lunch 12.00-15.00, dinner 19.00-21.00
SPECIALITIES: home-cooking.
HOTEL: 11 rooms.
FACILITIES: shower, bath, private bathroom
OTHER POINTS: credit cards accepted.
casino at Saint-Amand; forêt de Marchiennes (Belgium).

BOULOGNE SUR MER
Pas-de-Calais, 62200

LE MARIANY
(Paulette Witkowski et son fils, David) 54, avenue John Kennedy
TEL: 03.21.91.12.96
DIRECTIONS: RN1.
LANGUAGES: English.
MENU: 70 to 82 Frs.
ROOMS: 110 to 230 Frs.
RESTAURANT: Snacks from 7.00, lunch 12.00-15.00, dinner 19.00-21.00
CLOSED: Sun after breakfast and 2 weeks over Christmas/New Year.
SPECIALITIES: home-cooking.
HOTEL: 11 rooms.
FACILITIES: shower, private bathroom, television
OTHER POINTS: credit cards accepted.
old town and cathedral; Nausicaa (journey to the centre of the sea).

BOURNEVILLE MAROLLES
Oise, 60890

LES ROUTIERS
(Mme Huguette Picard-Mathias) 7, rue de Meaux
TEL: 03.23.96.72.11
DIRECTIONS: RD936, between la Ferté-Milon and Meaux.
MENU: 60 to 75 Frs.
RESTAURANT: Snacks from 7.00, lunch 11.00-15.00, dinner 18.00-20.00
SPECIALITIES: home-cooking.
OTHER POINTS: bar.

BOVES
Somme, 80440

LA GRENOUILLERE
(Mr Bouhou Ouannoune) Route Nationale 334
TEL: 03.22.09.31.26
DIRECTIONS: RN334, on the Amiens-Roye expressway.
LANGUAGES: English.
MENU: 55 to 68 Frs.
RESTAURANT: Snacks from 6.00, lunch 11.00-15.00
CLOSED: Sun (except for functions), and in Aug.
SPECIALITIES: couscous, home-cooking.
OTHER POINTS: credit cards accepted.
Amiens: cathedral, belfry.

CAMBRAI
Nord, 59400

AUX CHANTS DES OISEAUX
(Mr Jean-Pierre Plouquet) 3, route du Cateau
TEL: 03.27.78.77.05
DIRECTIONS: RN43, between Cambrai and Le Cateau, Caudry/Le-Cateau/Charleville road.
MENU: 70 to 100 Frs.
ROOMS: 110 Frs.
RESTAURANT: Snacks from 7.00
CLOSED: Sun.
SPECIALITIES: home-cooking, tripes maison, moules, entrecôte à l'échalote, regional menu.
HOTEL: 11 rooms.
FACILITIES: shower, bath, private bathroom
OTHER POINTS: credit cards accepted.

LA GARGOTE
(Mr Jean Claude Massines) 136, boulevard Jean Bart
TEL: 03.27.81.07.18
DIRECTIONS: A2 and A23, along the canal.
MENU: 60 Frs.
RESTAURANT: Snacks from 6.30, lunch 11.30-15.30, dinner 19.00-23.00
CLOSED: Sun.
SPECIALITIES: andouillettes de Cambrai, clafoutis (cherry tart) maison, home-cooking.
OTHER POINTS: credit cards accepted.
Rue des Vignes; area of archeological interest; abbey at Vaucelle.

CAPPELLE EN PEVELE
Nord, 59242

L'AS VEGAS
(Mme Eliane Duquesnoy) 13 Rue de l'Obeau
TEL: 03.20.61.83.10
MENU: 60 Frs (drink included).
RESTAURANT: Snacks from 8.30, lunch 12.00-14.30, dinner 19.00-20.30
CLOSED: Sun.
SPECIALITIES: home-cooking.
OTHER POINTS: credit cards accepted.
windmill at Vertain.

CHAMBLY
Oise, 60230

LE RELAIS DE CHAMBLY
(Mme Franáoise Violette) 660, avenue Aristide Briand
TEL: 03.34.70.50.37
DIRECTIONS: RN1, Paris/Beauvais road via Beaumont-sur-Oise.
MENU: 70 Frs (wine and coffee included).
ROOMS: 130 Frs to 280 Frs.
RESTAURANT: Snacks from 7.00, lunch 12.00-15.30, dinner 19.00-20.30
CLOSED: Sat, Sun, and from 20th Dec to 20th Jan.
SPECIALITIES: bourguignon, coq au vin, boeuf mode, home-cooking.
HOTEL: 14 rooms.
FACILITIES: shower, bath, private bathroom, television
OTHER POINTS: bar.
Chantilly (20km); Senlis (28km); L'Ile Adam (10km); abbey at Royaumont (35km); abbey at Maubuisson; Beauvais; archeological museum at Guiry-en-Vexin; musée de l'outil (tools and implements).

CHEPY
Somme, 80210

RELAIS SANS BOIRE
(Mr Jacky Sueur) 40, route de Oisemont – La Croix de Pierre
TEL: 03.22.26.26.67
DIRECTIONS: RD29, between Le Tréport and Oisemont.
MENU: 60 to 133 Frs.
RESTAURANT: Snacks from 6.30, lunch 11.30-14.30, dinner 19.00-22.00
SPECIALITIES: ficelle picarde, ragoñt, regional menu, home-cooking.
OTHER POINTS: credit cards accepted.
château at Rambtres; bay of the Somme; park at Marquantaire.

COLEMBERT
Pas-de-Calais, 62142

CAFE HOTEL DU COMMERCE
(Mr Jacques Delannoy) 38, route Nationale
TEL: 03.21.33.31.11
DIRECTIONS: RN42, between Boulogne-sur-Mer and Saint-Omer.
MENU: 58 Frs.
ROOMS: 140 to 180 Frs.
RESTAURANT: Snacks from 6.30, dinner 19.00-22.00

SPECIALITIES: home-cooking.
HOTEL: 8 rooms.
FACILITIES: shower, bath, private bathroom, television
OTHER POINTS: credit cards accepted.
maritime museum; 1939-45 war museum; leisure park at Bagatelle.

COMPIEGNE
Oise, 60200

BAR DE LA MARINE
(Mr Aimé Logghe) 17, rue de l'Estacade
TEL: 03.44.40.26.37
MENU: 60 Frs (wine included).
RESTAURANT: Snacks from 6.00
CLOSED: Sat, Sun and public holidays.
SPECIALITIES: home-cooking.
OTHER POINTS: credit cards accepted.
château; Napoleonic museum.

COUCY LE CHATEAU
Aisne, 02380

LE LION ROUGE
(Mr Patrick Clavet) 62, avenue Altenkessel
TEL: 03.23.52.70.13
DIRECTIONS: RN1, between Soissons and Saint-Quentin.
LANGUAGES: English, German.
MENU: 52 to 180 Frs.
ROOMS: 86 to 92 Frs.
RESTAURANT: Snacks from 7.00, lunch 11.30-14.30, dinner 18.30-21.30
SPECIALITIES: flamiche picarde, magrets picards, foie gras, grillades, papillottes de poissons, cassoulet, regional menu.
HOTEL: 13 rooms
OTHER POINTS: credit cards accepted.
ruins and ramparts of the château at Coucy (tower and museum with model of the fortified town); forêt de Saint-Cobain; château and Franco-American museum at Blérancourt.

COURCELLES LES GISORS
Oise, 60240

AU RENDEZ VOUS DES BONS ENFANTS
(Mme Liliane Masurier) 27, rue d'Inval
TEL: 03.32.55.25.00
DIRECTIONS: D181, Gisors/Vernon axis.
MENU: 55 Frs (1/4 wine included).
RESTAURANT: Snacks from 6.30, lunch 11.00-15.00, dinner 19.00-20.30
CLOSED: Sun afternoon.
SPECIALITIES: home-cooking.
OTHER POINTS: bar.
Gisors Les Templiers; La Roche Guyon; Bourg en Vexin; Mortemer; Les Andelys.

CROIX
Nord, 59170

LE RELAIS CHEZ ALAIN
(Mme Georgette Caufriez) 53, avenue Georges Hannart
TEL: 03.20.72.59.08
DIRECTIONS: RD14, Lille/Tourcoing expressway, near station at Croix-Wasquehal.
LANGUAGES: Spanish.
MENU: 35 to 60 Frs.
ROOMS: 100 to 150 Frs.
RESTAURANT: Snacks from 4.00, lunch 12.00-15.00, dinner 19.00-22.00
CLOSED: Sun afternoon.
SPECIALITIES: home-cooking.
HOTEL: 9 rooms.
FACILITIES: shower, bath, private bathroom, television, telephone
OTHER POINTS: credit cards accepted.
Parc Barbieux; orgues de Wasquehal.

CUVILLY
Oise, 60490

RELAIS ROUTIERS LA CAMPAGNARDE
(Daniel et Anne-Maryse Hillion Nicol) 5, route des Flandres
TEL: 03.44.85.00.30
DIRECTIONS: RN17, Paris/Lille road.
LANGUAGES: English.
MENU: 57 Frs (1/4 wine included).
ROOMS: 95 to 160 Frs.
RESTAURANT: Snacks from 5.00, lunch 11.00-15.00, dinner 19.00-23.00
CLOSED: Sat evening and SUn.
SPECIALITIES: home-cooking.
HOTEL: 9 rooms.
FACILITIES: shower, bath, private bathroom
OTHER POINTS: credit cards accepted.
Compiègne; valley of the Somme; Noyon.

DESVRES
Pas-de-Calais, 62240

LE RELAIS DE LA BELLE CROIX
(Mr Jean-Claude Grumelart) 1, rue du Bidet
TEL: 03.21.91.65.81
DIRECTIONS: RN342, between Boulogne-sur-Mer and Longfossé.
LANGUAGES: English.
MENU: 58 Frs.
ROOMS: 85 Frs.
RESTAURANT: Snacks from 7.00
CLOSED: Sun.
SPECIALITIES: regional menu.
HOTEL: 5 rooms.

FACILITIES: shower
OTHER POINTS: bar.
Nausicaa (journey to the centre of the sea); pottery and maritime museums.

DIZY LE GROS
Aisne, 02340

LES ROUTIERS FRANCE EUROPE
(Mr Jean-Claude Dubois) 78, Grande Rue
TEL: 03.23.21.23.15
DIRECTIONS: RD366, to Reims/Vervins/Beigium.
MENU: 55 Frs.
RESTAURANT: Snacks from 6.00, lunch 11.00-14.30, dinner 19.00-21.00
CLOSED: Sun and last 2 weeks in August.
OTHER POINTS: credit cards accepted.

DREUIL LES AMIENS
Somme, 80730

CHEZ JEAN-MARIE ET CHRISTIANE
(Mr Jean-Marie Dumeige) 285, avenue Pasteur
TEL: 03.22.54.10.72
DIRECTIONS: RN235, Picquigny.
MENU: 56 Frs (drink and coffee included).
RESTAURANT: Snacks from 6.30, lunch 11.45-14.00, dinner 19.30-21.00
CLOSED: Sun, and in Aug.
SPECIALITIES: home-cooking.
OTHER POINTS: traditional decor.
Picard capital (1km).

DUNKERQUE
Nord, 59640

LA BECASSINE
(Mme Suzanne Quarré) 26, rue des Scieries
TEL: 03.28.64.74.00
LANGUAGES: English.
MENU: 49.90 Frs.
RESTAURANT: Snacks from 6.30
CLOSED: Sun.
SPECIALITIES: home-cooking.
OTHER POINTS: bar.

ECLAIBES
Nord, 59330

LE ROBINSON
(Mr El Hadi Manseur) Route Nationale 2
TEL: 03.27.57.81.26
DIRECTIONS: RN2.
MENU: 56 Frs.
RESTAURANT: Snacks from 6.00, lunch 11.30-15.30, dinner 18.30-24.00
SPECIALITIES: home-cooking,
OTHER POINTS: bar.

ESTREES DENIECOURT
Somme, 80200

AUBERGE DE LA MAIRIE
(Mme Claudette Demuynck Dehenry)
TEL: 03.22.85.20.16
DIRECTIONS: RN336, exit At Péronne, on the right towards Amiens.
MENU: 55 to 65 Frs.
ROOMS: 100 to 225 Frs.
RESTAURANT: Dinner 19.00-23.00
CLOSED: Sat, Sun, and in Aug.
SPECIALITIES: home-cooking.
HOTEL: 7 rooms.
FACILITIES: shower, bath, private bathroom
OTHER POINTS: bar.

ESTREES MONS
Somme, 80200

A LA POMME D'API
(Mr Albert Gras) 28, route Nationale
TEL: 03.22.85.60.04
DIRECTIONS: RN29, exit Péronne, towards Saint-Quentin.
MENU: 65 Frs (wine included).
RESTAURANT: Snacks from 6.30, lunch 11.30-14.30, dinner 19.00-21.30
CLOSED: Sun, and in Aug.
SPECIALITIES: home-cooking.
OTHER POINTS: credit cards accepted.

ETROEUNGT
Nord, 59219

AU RELAIS DES COLOMBES
(Mr Patrick Kucharski) Route Nationale 2
TEL: 03.27.59.22.11 **FAX:** 03.27.59.24.69
DIRECTIONS: RN2, between Avesnes-sur-Helpe and La Capelle.
LANGUAGES: English, Italian, Polish.
MENU: 54 Frs. Set menu at 40 Frs.
ROOMS: 130 Frs.
RESTAURANT: Snacks from 5.00, lunch 11.45, dinner 18.45
CLOSED: Sun.
SPECIALITIES: home-cooking.
HOTEL: 4 rooms
OTHER POINTS: credit cards accepted.
the Avesnois area.

FLAVY LE MARTEL
Aisne, 02520

LE RELAIS ROUTIERS
(Mme Gilberte Brière) 17, rue André Brulé
TEL: 03.23.52.51.31

DIRECTIONS: RD937, between Ham, Saint-Quentin and Chauny.
MENU: 58 Frs (weekdays) 110 Frs (weekend).
RESTAURANT: Snacks from 7.00, lunch 12.00-14.00, dinner 19.00-21.00
CLOSED: Sat and last 2 weeks in Aug.
SPECIALITIES: home-cooking.
OTHER POINTS: bar.

FORMERIE
Oise, 60220

CAFE DE LA PAIX
(Mme Franáoise Merlin) 8, rue Dornat
TEL: 03.44.46.17.08
DIRECTIONS: between Beauvais and Forges-les-Eaux.
MENU: 50 to 65 Frs.
ROOMS: 80 Frs.
RESTAURANT: Snacks from 4.30, lunch 11.30-15.00, dinner 19.30-21.30
SPECIALITIES: couscous, paella, home-cooking.
HOTEL: ☆ 5 rooms.
FACILITIES: shower, bath, private bathroom, television, telephone
OTHER POINTS: credit cards accepted.
Gerberoy; casino at Forges-les-Eaux.

GONDREVILLE
Oise, 60117

LE RELAIS DU VIRAGE
(Mr Salem Graine) 6, rue Nationale 2
TEL: 03.44.88.20.01
DIRECTIONS: RN 2, RN2, on the Paris/Soissons axis.
LANGUAGES: English, Arabic.
MENU: 53 Frs.
RESTAURANT: Snacks from 7.00, lunch 11.30-14.30, dinner 19.00-22.00
CLOSED: Sun and the last 2 weeks in Aug.
SPECIALITIES: home-cooking, couscous.
OTHER POINTS: credit cards accepted.

GROISE (LA)
Nord, 59360

LE CHAPEAU ROUGE
(Mr Roger Jumelet) Route Nationale 43
TEL: 03.27.77.68.33
DIRECTIONS: on the Charleville/Cambrai axis.
LANGUAGES: English.
MENU: 60 Frs (wine included).
RESTAURANT: Snacks from 5.30, lunch 11.30-14.30, dinner 19.00-22.00
CLOSED: Sun.
SPECIALITIES: home-cooking.
OTHER POINTS: credit cards accepted.

HALLUIN
Nord, 59250

AU ROUTIER
(Mr Richard Kozior) 196, rue de la Lys
TEL: 03.20.23.88.20
DIRECTIONS: RD945, in Le Col Bras Industrial Zone (Z.I.).
LANGUAGES: Dutch, Polish.
MENU: 65 Frs.
RESTAURANT: Snacks from 6.30, lunch 11.30-14.00, dinner 19.30-21.00
CLOSED: Sat afternoon, Sun, in Aug and 1 week XMas/Boxing Day.
SPECIALITIES: couscous (on Fri), home-cooking.
OTHER POINTS: credit cards accepted.

HIRSON
Aisne, 02500

CHEZ JULIANO
(Mr Juliano Corsini) 151, avenue Joffre
TEL: 03.23.58.14.03
DIRECTIONS: RN43, at the Hirson exit for Paris or Lille.
LANGUAGES: English, Italian.
MENU: 60 Frs.
RESTAURANT: Snacks from 7.00
CLOSED: Sun.
SPECIALITIES: lasagne, pizza, spaghetti bolognaise, home-cooking.
OTHER POINTS: credit cards accepted.
abbey; forest; waterfalls; fountain.

HOUSSOYE (LA)
Oise, 60390

LE CHEVAL BLANC
(Mr Luis Martins) 5, route de Gisors
TEL: 03.44.81.40.40 **FAX:** 03.44.81.44.25
DIRECTIONS: RN181.
MENU: 60 Frs (drink included).
ROOMS: 120 to 150 Frs.
RESTAURANT: Snacks from 7.00, lunch 12.00-14.30, dinner 19.00-21.00
CLOSED: Sat afternoon and SUn.
SPECIALITIES: filet de daurade à la provenáale, home-cooking.
HOTEL: 5 rooms.
FACILITIES: shower
OTHER POINTS: credit cards accepted.
Saint-Germer-de-Fly abbey; Beauvais; Gisors.

LE RELAIS DE LA HOUSSOYE
(Mme Christine Sachot) 300, route Nationale
TEL: 03.22.40.57.29
DIRECTIONS: RD929, between Albert and Amiens.
MENU: 45 to 55 Frs.

RESTAURANT: Snacks from 7.00
CLOSED: Sun.
SPECIALITIES: home-cooking,
OTHER POINTS: credit cards accepted.
Albert: Notre-Dame de Brebière, 1914-18 museum; Amiens; Villers-Bretonneux.

HUMIERES
Pas-de-Calais, 62130

RELAIS ROUTIERS
(Mr José Ternisien) 6, route Nationale 39
TEL: 03.21.41.85.77
DIRECTIONS: RN39, between Saint-Pol and Hesdin.
MENU: 48 Frs.
RESTAURANT: Snacks from 5.00, lunch 11.00-15.00, dinner 19.00-21.00
CLOSED: Sun.
SPECIALITIES: home-cooking.
OTHER POINTS: credit cards accepted.

LABROYE
Pas-de-Calais, 62140

CHEZ NATHALIE
(Mme Nathalie Joly) Route Nationale
TEL: 03.21.86.83.10
DIRECTIONS: RD928, between Abbeville and Hesdin.
MENU: 50 to 85 Frs.
RESTAURANT: Snacks from 7.00, lunch 11.30-14.00, dinner 18.00-20.00
CLOSED: 1 week in Oct and 1 week in Feb.
SPECIALITIES: regional menu, home-cooking.
OTHER POINTS: credit cards accepted.
river Authie valley.

LANDRECIES
Nord, 59550

LE SAMBRETON
(Mme Evelyne Vins) 38, route de Guise
TEL: 03.27.77.17.99
DIRECTIONS: on the Laon/Valenciennes axis.
MENU: 50 Frs.
RESTAURANT: Snacks from 5.00, lunch 11.00, dinner up to 24.00
CLOSED: Sun.
SPECIALITIES: home-cooking.
OTHER POINTS: bar.

LAVERSINES
Oise, 60510

LE RELAIS ROUTIER
(Mr Marceau Forestier) 90, rue Saint Germain
TEL: 03.44.07.75.80
DIRECTIONS: RN31, between Reims and Rouen.
MENU: 65 Frs.
RESTAURANT: Snacks from 6.00, lunch 11.30-14.30, dinner 19.30-21.30
CLOSED: Sat, Sun, last 2 weeks in Aug and 1 week at Christmas.
SPECIALITIES: paella (to order), home-cooking.
OTHER POINTS: credit cards accepted.
historic sites; Beauvais cathedral; angora factory tours.

LOCON
Pas-de-Calais, 62400

AU RENDEZ-VOUS DES COPAINS – Chez Jeanine
(Mme Magali Pedro) 1376, rue du 8 Mai
TEL: 03.21.27.82.31
DIRECTIONS: RD945, between Béthune and Lestrem.
MENU: 59.50 Frs (wine included).
RESTAURANT: Snacks from 6.00, lunch 11.00-16.00, dinner 19.00-23.00
CLOSED: Sat, Sun and 3 first weeks in August.
SPECIALITIES: couscous on Friday, home-cooking.
OTHER POINTS: credit cards accepted.

LOUVIGNIES QUESNOY
Nord, 59530

LE RELAIS
(Mme Denise Pruvost) 53, route Nationale
TEL: 03.27.27.60.73
DIRECTIONS: between Valenciennes and Landrecies.
LANGUAGES: English.
MENU: 50 to 115 Frs.
RESTAURANT: Snacks from 5.00, lunch 11.30-15.00, dinner 19.00-21.00
CLOSED: Sat afternoon.
SPECIALITIES: home-cooking, coquilles Saint-Jacques, entrecôtes poivre et cognac.
OTHER POINTS: credit cards accepted.

LUMBRES
Pas-de-Calais, 62380

HOTEL MODERNE
(Mr Pierre Fichaux) 18 rue Franáois Cousin
TEL: 03.21.39.62.87
DIRECTIONS: opposite the station.
RESTAURANT: dinner up to 21.00
CLOSED: Sun and in AUg.
HOTEL: 6 rooms
OTHER POINTS: bar.

MAIRIEUX
Nord, 59600

AUBERGE DU COCHER
(Mme Hélène Barrier) 27, rue de Mons
TEL: 03.27.64.23.25

DIRECTIONS: between Maubeuge and Mons.
LANGUAGES: English, German.
MENU: 55 Frs.
RESTAURANT: Snacks from 5.00
SPECIALITIES: home-cooking.
OTHER POINTS: bar.
zoological gardens at Maubeuge; Mons; Baval: Gallo-Roman remains; Belgium.

MARAIS (AUX)
Oise, 60000

AU GRAND R
(Mr Marcel Boutoille) 12, route de Gisors
TEL: 03.44.48.18.66
DIRECTIONS: RN981, between Mantes and Gisors.
MENU: 54 Frs.
RESTAURANT: Snacks from 5.30, dinner up to 21.30
CLOSED: Sun, and in Aug.
SPECIALITIES: home-cooking.
OTHER POINTS: credit cards accepted.
Le Vexin; Beauvais.

MAZINGARBE
Pas-de-Calais, 62670

AU RELAIS DES ROUTIERS
(Mme Geneviève Marcinkowski) 85 Route Nationale 43
TEL: 03.21.72.00.09
DIRECTIONS: RN43, between Lens and Béthune
LANGUAGES: German, Polish.
MENU: 55 Frs.
RESTAURANT: Snacks from 8.00, lunch 12.00-14.00
CLOSED: Sun, and from 1st to 20th Aug.
SPECIALITIES: lapinaux aux pruneaux, canard, regional menu, home-cooking.
OTHER POINTS: bar.
Lorette; Vimy.

MERLIMONT
Pas-de-Calais, 62155

LE CURACAO
(Mr Guy Arpin) 611, rue Auguste Biblocq
TEL: 03.21.09.45.45
DIRECTIONS: RD940, between Berck and Etaples.
MENU: 65 to 135 Frs.
RESTAURANT: Snacks from 9.00, lunch 12.00-15.00, dinner 19.30-22.00
CLOSED: Mon and Tues evening (out of season)
SPECIALITIES: fondue savoyarde, fruits de mer, espadon (swordfish) à l'oseille, truite aux amandes, émincé de canard aux groseilles, regional menu, home-cooking.
OTHER POINTS: credit cards accepted.
leisure park at Bagatelle; Côte d'Opale beaches; le Touquet; Berck.

MONTDIDIER
Somme, 80500

LE RELAIS DU MOUTON D'OR
(Mr Christian Parmentier) 10, boulevard Debeney
TEL: 03.22.78.03.43
MENU: 55 to 85 Frs.
ROOMS: 75 Frs.
RESTAURANT: Snacks from 7.00, lunch 12.00-14.00, dinner 19.00-21.00
CLOSED: Sun, and in Aug.
SPECIALITIES: regional menu, home-cooking.
HOTEL: 5 rooms
OTHER POINTS: credit cards accepted.

NEUVILLE SAINT AMAND
Aisne, 02100

LA CREMAILLERE
(Mr Alexandre Dupuis) 134, rue de la Fere
TEL: 03.23.68.26.79
DIRECTIONS: RN 44, RN44, between Saint-Quentin and Laon.
LANGUAGES: English.
MENU: 60 Frs (drink included).
RESTAURANT: Snacks from 8.00, lunch 11.30-14.30, dinner 19.00-22.30
CLOSED: Sat and Sun.
SPECIALITIES: home-cooking, entrecôte sauce poivre.
OTHER POINTS: credit cards accepted.

NOEUX LES MINES
Pas-de-Calais, 62290

LE 421
(Mr Norbert Michaud) 402, route Nationale
TEL: 03.21.27.28.11
DIRECTIONS: RN 37, RN37, on the Béthune/Arras axis.
LANGUAGES: English.
MENU: 60 Frs (drink included).
RESTAURANT: Snacks from 8.00
CLOSED: in August.
SPECIALITIES: home-cooking, tagliatelles au saumon, english breakfast.
OTHER POINTS: bar.

OMIECOURT
Somme, 80320

AU BON ACCUEIL
(Mr Rabia Betroune) 2, route Nationale 17
TEL: 03.22.85.42.49
DIRECTIONS: RN17, between Péronne and Roye.
MENU: 56 to 85 Frs.
RESTAURANT: Open 24h.
CLOSED: Sun.
SPECIALITIES: couscous, paella, regional menu, home-cooking.

OTHER POINTS: credit cards accepted.
historial (wax museum) at Péronne.

OVILLERS LA BOISSELLE
Somme, 80300

LE POPPY
(Mr Georges Vandenbulke) 4, route de Bapaume
TEL: 03.22.75.45.45 FAX: 03.22.74.75.65
DIRECTIONS: RD329, between Bapaume and Albert.
MENU: 50 to 95 Frs.
RESTAURANT: Snacks from 6.30, lunch 12.00-15.00, dinner 19.00-22.30
CLOSED: Sat, Sun, and in Aug.
SPECIALITIES: home-cooking.
OTHER POINTS: credit cards accepted.
Battle of the Somme memorial; basilica at Albert; other mementoes of the 1914-18 war.

PERONNE
Somme, 80200

LA CHAPELETTE – Chez Claude et Nicole
(Claude et Nicole Charpentier) 61, route de Paris
TEL: 03.22.84.10.82
DIRECTIONS: RN17, between Roye and Péronne.
MENU: 60 Frs (wine and coffee included).
RESTAURANT: Snacks from 7.00, lunch 11.30-15.00, dinner 19.00-22.30
CLOSED: Sat afternoon and Sun.
SPECIALITIES: home-cooking.
OTHER POINTS: credit cards accepted.
bay of the Somme.

PERONNE ASSEVILLERS
Somme, 80200

LES AS DU VOLANT
(Mme Magali Crappier) A1 – Aire d'Assevillers Ouest – Accessible sens Lille/Paris
TEL: 03.22.85.23.56 FAX: 03.22.85.23.56
DIRECTIONS: ont the service area at Assevillers East
RESTAURANT: Open 24h.
OTHER POINTS: credit cards accepted.

PONT REMY
Somme, 80580

LE CONTINENTAL
(Mme Ginette Thérasse) 9, rue Robert Bordeux
TEL: 03.22.27.12.89
DIRECTIONS: main Paris/Boulogne-sur-Mer road.
MENU: 55 to 100 Frs.
RESTAURANT: Snacks from 8.30, lunch 12.00-14.30
CLOSED: in Aug.
SPECIALITIES: regional menu, home-cooking.
OTHER POINTS: bar.

POULAINVILLE
Somme, 80260

LE RELAIS DE POULAINVILLE
(Mr Jean-Pierre Hennebert) 2, route Nationale
TEL: 03.22.43.05.00
DIRECTIONS: RN25, between Amiens and Arras.
MENU: 61 Frs.
RESTAURANT: Snacks from 5.00, lunch 12.00-15.00, dinner 19.00-22.00
CLOSED: Sat, Sun, and the last 2 weeks in Aug.
SPECIALITIES: home-cooking.
OTHER POINTS: credit cards accepted.
cathedral at Amiens; les Hortillons.

QUAEDYPRE
Nord, 59380

L'GITANT
(Mr José Lermytte) Chemin Départemenatal 916
TEL: 03.28.68.69.87
DIRECTIONS: CD916, exit 16, towards Wormhout.
MENU: 35 to 160 Frs.
RESTAURANT: Snacks from 7.00, lunch 12.00-15.00, dinner 19.00-22.00
CLOSED: Sat, and the 1st 2 weeks in Aug.
SPECIALITIES: carbonnade flamande, Potche Uleech, regional menu.
OTHER POINTS: credit cards accepted.
ramparts at Bergues; circuit of villages in bloom; port of Dunkerque.

ROLLOT
Somme, 80500

LE RELAIS DE LA MADELEINE
(Mr Franáois Baja) 88, rue de la Madeleine
TEL: 03.22.78.02.81
DIRECTIONS: RD935, between Compiègne and Amiens.
MENU: 50 to 60 Frs.
RESTAURANT: Snacks from 7.00, lunch 12.00-15.00, dinner 19.00-21.00
CLOSED: Mon (Sept to June), Sun (July and Aug).
SPECIALITIES: home-cooking.
OTHER POINTS: bar.
Compiègne; valley of the Somme.

ROUBAIX
Nord, 59100

LE CALAIS
(Mme Josette Vaze) 2 quai de Calais
TEL: 03.20.26.00.35
LANGUAGES: English, German, Dutch.
MENU: 50 Frs (wine included).
RESTAURANT: Snacks from 8.00, lunch 12.00-14.30, dinner 19.30-22.00

CLOSED: Sat afternoon, Sun, in Aug and end Dec.
SPECIALITIES: home-cooking.
OTHER POINTS: credit cards accepted.

SAINT INGLEVERT
Pas-de-Calais, 62250

LA MURAILLE
(Mme Jocelyne Salmon) Route Nationale 1
TEL: 03.21.33.75.44
DIRECTIONS: between Calais and Boulogne-sur-Mer.
LANGUAGES: English.
MENU: 68 to 98 Frs.
RESTAURANT: Snacks from 6.30, lunch 11.00-15.00
CLOSED: Sat, Sun, and in Aug.
SPECIALITIES: petit salé (pickled pork), home-cooking.
OTHER POINTS: credit cards accepted.

SAINT LEU
Oise, 60850

RELAIS DE SAINT LEU
(Mr Jean-Claude Laude) 20, rue de Saint Leu – Cuigy en Bray
TEL: 03.44.82.53.17
DIRECTIONS: RN31, between Beauvais and Gournay.
LANGUAGES: English.
MENU: 50 to 75 Frs.
RESTAURANT: Snacks from 6.30
CLOSED: Sun.
SPECIALITIES: poissons en sauce, patisseries maison (home-made pastries), home-cooking.
OTHER POINTS: bar.
Bosquentin : musée de la ferme et des vieux métiers (farm and old crafts museum); abbaye de Saint Germer de Fly; Gerveroy and its remparts.

SAINT OMER
Pas-de-Calais, 62500

LA RENAISSANCE
(SARL Vanyper) 10, place du 11 Novembre
TEL: 03.21.38.26.55
DIRECTIONS: RN43.
LANGUAGES: English, German.
MENU: 55 Frs.
ROOMS: 130 to 150 Frs.
RESTAURANT: Snacks from 6.00, lunch 12.00-14.00, dinner 20.00-21.00
SPECIALITIES: regional menu, home-cooking.
HOTEL: 18 rooms
OTHER POINTS: credit cards accepted.
Marais Audomarois; cathedral; museums.

SAINT QUENTIN
Aisne, 02100

LE NAUTIQUE
(Mr Jean-Claude Tabacznyj) 29, rue du Vieux Port
TEL: 03.23.67.64.02
DIRECTIONS: RN29/D930/N44, crossroads Amiens/Paris/Laon/Cambrai direction.
LANGUAGES: German, Polish.
MENU: 48.50 Frs to 65 Frs.
RESTAURANT: Snacks from 7.30, lunch 11.00-15.00, dinner 18.30-21.30
CLOSED: Sun.
SPECIALITIES: poulet basquaise, bourguignon, lapin, langue de boeuf, home-cooking.
OTHER POINTS: credit cards accepted.

LE VASCO DA GAMA
(Mme Adelaïde Augusto) 30, place Cordier (prés de la gare)
TEL: 03.23.68.22.84 **FAX:** 03.23.68.22.84
LANGUAGES: Spanish, Italian, Portuguese.
MENU: 55 Frs (wine included).
ROOMS: 90 to 100 Frs.
RESTAURANT: Snacks from 6.30, lunch 12.00-14.00, dinner 19.00-22.30
SPECIALITIES: home-cooking.
HOTEL: 11 rooms
OTHER POINTS: credit cards accepted.

SAINT QUENTIN LAMOTTE
Somme, 80880

A GROS JACQUES
(Mr Pascal Niel) Route Départementale 925
TEL: 02.22.60.41.14
DIRECTIONS: RD925, between Eu, towards Abbeville.
MENU: 58 to 90 Frs.
RESTAURANT: Snacks from 6.00, lunch 11.30-14.00, dinner 19.00-21.00
CLOSED: Sun, and public holidays.
SPECIALITIES: home-cooking.
OTHER POINTS: credit cards accepted.
Eu; le Tréport; coast of Picardy.

SAINT QUENTIN URVILLERS
Aisne, 02690

L'ARCHE DE SAINT QUENTIN URVILLERS
(Mme Isabelle Inigo) A26 – Aire d'Urvillers Saint Quentin – Accessible dans les deux sens
TEL: 03.23.08.87.08 **FAX:** 03.23.08.96.49
OTHER POINTS: credit cards accepted.

SAINT RIQUIER
Somme, 80135

LE CENTULOIS
(Mr Raymond Saguez) 70, rue du Général de Gaulle
TEL: 03.22.28.88.15
DIRECTIONS: on the Abbeville/Arras road.
LANGUAGES: English.
MENU: 59 Frs.
RESTAURANT: Snacks from 7.00
CLOSED: Wed and last week in Dec.
SPECIALITIES: regional menu, home-cooking,
OTHER POINTS: credit cards accepted.

SERIFONTAINE
Oise, 60590

LE RELAIS FLEURI
(Mme Annick Fontaine) 22, rue Hacque
TEL: 03.44.84.89.17
DIRECTIONS: between Gournay-sur-Bray and Gisors.
MENU: 62.50 to 90 Frs.
ROOMS: 90 to 160 Frs.
RESTAURANT: Lunch 12.00-14.00, dinner 19.00-21.00
CLOSED: Sat, Sun.
SPECIALITIES: home-cooking.
HOTEL: 9 rooms.
FACILITIES: shower, bath, private bathroom
OTHER POINTS: bar.
cathedral and tapestry museum at Beauvais (40km); abbey at Saint-Germer-de-Fly (10km).

STEENVOORDE
Nord, 59114

CAFETERIA DE STEENVOORDE SAINT ELOI
(Mr Alain Bara) A25 – Aire de Saint Eloi – Accessible sens Dunkerque/Lille
TEL: 03.28.49.71.33 FAX: 03.28.49.70.22
OTHER POINTS: credit cards accepted.

CAFETERIA DE STEENVOORDE SAINT LAURENT
(Mr Alain Bara) A25 – Aire de Saint Laurent – Accessible sens Lille/Dunkerque
TEL: 03.28.49.71.33 FAX: 03.28.49.70.22
OTHER POINTS: credit cards accepted.

THIEULOY SAINT ANTOINE
Oise, 60210

LE SAINT ANTOINE
(Mme Franáoise Joly) 10, route Nationale
TEL: 03.44.46.73.00
DIRECTIONS: RN 901, RN901, between Beauvais and Le Tréport.
LANGUAGES: English.
MENU: 60 Frs (wine included).
RESTAURANT: Snacks from 6.30, lunch 12.00-14.00, dinner 19.00-21.00
CLOSED: Sun.
SPECIALITIES: home-cooking.
OTHER POINTS: bar.

TOURCOING
Nord, 59200

AU SIGNAL D'ARRET
(Mr Michel Guilbert) 28, rue des Francs
TEL: 03.20.26.56.74
DIRECTIONS: exit 15: les Francs, turn right at the lights.
MENU: 65 Frs.
ROOMS: 95 to 145 Frs.
RESTAURANT: Snacks from 6.00, lunch 12.00-14.00, dinner 19.30-21.00
CLOSED: Sat, Sun, and the middle 2 weeks in Aug.
SPECIALITIES: home-cooking.
HOTEL: 6 rooms.
FACILITIES: shower, private bathroom, television
OTHER POINTS: credit cards accepted.

TROSLY BREUIL
Oise, 60350

LA TERRASSE
(Mr Enso Dal Sacco) 47, route de Reims
TEL: 03.44.85.70.39
DIRECTIONS: RN31, between Compiègne and Soissons.
MENU: 58 Frs (drink included).
RESTAURANT: Snacks from 4.30, lunch 11.30-14.30, dinner 19.00-22.30
CLOSED: Fri evening, Sun, and 2 weeks over Christmas/New Year.
SPECIALITIES: goulash, regional menu, home-cooking.
OTHER POINTS: credit cards accepted.
château and forest at Compiègne (10km); château at Pierrefonds (8km); Armistice railway-carriage.

VALENCIENNES
Nord, 59300

AUBERGE DE LA POTERNE – Café des Routiers
(Mr Jean Demolle) 9, boulevard Eisen
TEL: 03.27.46.44.98
DIRECTIONS: RN29, exit Valenciennes Sud (South).
MENU: 60 Frs.
ROOMS: 90 to 160 Frs.
RESTAURANT: Snacks from 7.00, lunch 12.00-14.00, dinner 19.30-21.00
CLOSED: Sat, Sun and public holidays.
SPECIALITIES: home-cooking.

HOTEL: 12 rooms.
FACILITIES: shower
OTHER POINTS: bar.
museum; fortifications; basilica.

VENDIN LEZ BETHUNE
Pas-de-Calais, 62232

LA MOTTE DOREE
(Mme Marie-France De Greef) 18, route de Saint Venant
TEL: 03.21.57.25.24
DIRECTIONS: RD937, between Béthune and Dunkerque.
MENU: 50 Frs.
RESTAURANT: Snacks from 7.00, lunch 11.00-15.00, dinner 19.00-24.00
CLOSED: Sat and Sun morning.
SPECIALITIES: regional menu, flamiche flamande, couscous, home-cooking.
OTHER POINTS: credit cards accepted.
belfry at Béthune.

VILLE AUX BOIS LES PONTAVERTS (LA)
Aisne, 02160

LE RELAIS SAINTE MARIE
(Mme Claudie Soudant) 10, route Nationale 44
TEL: 03.23.20.74.34
DIRECTIONS: RN 44, RN44, on the Laon/Reims road.
LANGUAGES: English, German, Italian.
MENU: 49.50 Frs.
RESTAURANT: Snacks from 5.00, lunch 11.30-15.00, dinner 18.30-23.00
SPECIALITIES: home-cooking, boeuf bourguignon, blanquette, pizzas au feu de bois.
OTHER POINTS: credit cards accepted.

VILLERS COTTERETS
Aisne, 02600

AU BOUT DU MONDE
(Mme Michèle Dorge)
Route de la Ferté Milon
TEL: 03.23.96.07.12
DIRECTIONS: RD936, Meaux.
MENU: 55.50 to 120 Frs.
ROOMS: 95 to 130 Frs.
RESTAURANT: Snacks from 6.30, lunch 11.30-15.00, dinner 19.00-22.00
CLOSED: Sun, public holidays, Christmas Day for 2 weeks, and 2 weeks in Aug.
SPECIALITIES: confit, pierre gourmande confit, escargots 'Alexandre Dumas', regional menu, home-cooking.
HOTEL: 5 rooms.
FACILITIES: shower, bath, private bathroom
OTHER POINTS: credit cards accepted.
Alexandre Dumas museum; château of Franáois 1er; musée du bois (woodcraft).

WORMHOUT
Nord, 59470

CAFE DE LA FORGE
(Mme Claudine Macker) 84, Grand'Place
TEL: 03.28.65.62.33
DIRECTIONS: RD916, Dunkerque.
MENU: 30 to 50 Frs.
RESTAURANT: Snacks from 6.00, lunch 11.30-15.00
CLOSED: mon, and last 2 weeks in Aug to end 1st week in Sept.
SPECIALITIES: home-cooking,
OTHER POINTS: children's menu.
museum; windmill.

North-East France

The following départements are included in this chapter:

Ardennes (08)
Aube (10)
Bas-Rhin (67)
Côte-d'Or (21)
Douds (25)
Haut-Rhin (68)
Haute-Marne (52)
Haut-Saône (70)
Jura (39)
Marne (51)
Meuthe (54)
Meuthe-et-Moselle (54)
Meuse (55)
Moselle (57)
Nièvre (58)
Saône-et-Loire (71)
Territoire-de-Belfort (90)
Vosges (88)
Yonne (89)

ANCERVILLE
Meuse, 55170

LE RELAIS
(Mme Renée Lange) 59, route de Saint Dizier
TEL: 03.29.75.30.13
DIRECTIONS: RN4, the Paris/Strasbourg road.
LANGUAGES: Italian, Polish.
MENU: 55 to 75 Frs.
ROOMS: 110 to 160 Frs.
RESTAURANT: Snacks from 7.00, lunch 12.00-14.00, dinner 19.00-21.00
CLOSED: Sat afternoon, Sun afternoon and mid-Sept.
SPECIALITIES: tête de veau, andouillettes, choucroute, regional menu, home-cooking.
HOTEL: ☆ 12 rooms.
FACILITIES: shower, bath, private bathroom
OTHER POINTS: credit cards accepted.
Lac du Der-Chantecoq; Vaucouleurs; Domrémy; Colombey-Les-Deux-Eglises; Bar-le-Duc; Saint-Dizier.

ARC LES GRAY
Haute-Saône, 70100

BAR RESTAURANT DE LA CROISEE
(Mme Rina Stella Rozanski) 4, place Aristide Briand
TEL: 03.84.65.37.23
DIRECTIONS: Langers/Dijon/Besanáon.
LANGUAGES: Italian.
MENU: 60 Frs.
RESTAURANT: Snacks from 7.00, lunch 12.15-15.00, dinner 19.30-22.30
SPECIALITIES: home-cooking,
OTHER POINTS: credit cards accepted.

ARCES
Yonne, 89320

RELAIS DE LA FORET D'OTHE
(Mme Yolande Misura) 15, place de l'Eglise
TEL: 03.86.88.10.44
DIRECTIONS: RD905.
MENU: 55 to 150 Frs.
ROOMS: 90 to 150 Frs.
RESTAURANT: Snacks from 6.30, lunch 12.00-14.00
CLOSED: Wed.
SPECIALITIES: jambon au Chablis, caneton au cidre, regional menu.
HOTEL: ☆ 7 rooms.
FACILITIES: shower, bath
OTHER POINTS: bar.
cider route; Saint-Florentin; Sens.

ARCHES
Vosges, 88380

LA TRUITE RENOMMEE
(Mme Josseline Hagenauer) 1, rue d'Epinal
TEL: 03.29.32.79.13 FAX: 03.29.32.61.00
DIRECTIONS: Epinai-Remiremont.
LANGUAGES: English, German, Italian.
MENU: 60 Frs (wine and coffee included).
ROOMS: 190 to 240 Frs.
RESTAURANT: Snacks from 6.00, lunch 11.15-15.00, dinner 19.15-21.00
SPECIALITIES: truite 'Fumée-Vosgien' (smoked), regional menu, home-cooking.
HOTEL: ☆☆ 10 rooms.
FACILITIES: shower, bath, private bathroom, television, telephone
OTHER POINTS: credit cards accepted.
Musée de l'imagerie (printing) at Epinal; Gerardmer; Thann.

ARNAY LE DUC
Côte-d'Or, 21230

RELAIS ROUTIERS LE SAINT PRIX
Sivry
TEL: 03.80.84.81.74
DIRECTIONS: RN6, towards Chalon-sur-Saône.
LANGUAGES: English, Italian.
MENU: 54 to 70 Frs.
ROOMS: 120 to 140 Frs.
RESTAURANT: Snacks from 6.00, lunch 11.45-14.00,

dinner 19.30-22.00
CLOSED: Sun.
SPECIALITIES: boeuf bourguignon, home-cooking.
HOTEL: 6 rooms.
FACILITIES: shower
OTHER POINTS: credit cards accepted.
châteaux at Neufchâteau and Rochepot; hospice de Beaune.

ATHIS
Marne, 51150

AU BON ACCUEIL
(Mr Daniel Bourscheidt) 12, Route Départementale
TEL: 03.26.57.62.61
DIRECTIONS: between Epernay and Châlons-sur-Marne.
MENU: 53 Frs.
ROOMS: 160 to 200 Frs.
RESTAURANT: Snacks from 6.30, lunch 11.30-14.30, dinner 19.30-21.00
CLOSED: Sun, public holidays and in Aug.
SPECIALITIES: home-cooking.
HOTEL: 4 rooms.
FACILITIES: shower, bath, private bathroom, television, telephone
OTHER POINTS: credit cards accepted.
tours of the wine-cellars and hills of the Champagne region (Reims, Epernay 13km); Marne valley.

ATTIGNY
Ardennes, 08130

CHEZ NICOLE
(Mme Nicole Pienne) 16, place Charlemagne
TEL: 03.24.71.20.69
MENU: 40 to 70 Frs.
RESTAURANT: Snacks from 5.00, lunch 11.00-15.00, dinner 19.30-23.30
SPECIALITIES: home-cooking.
HOTEL: 3 rooms.
FACILITIES: shower, bath, private bathroom
OTHER POINTS: bar.

AUBETERRE
Aube, 10150

LES TILLEULS
(Mr Raymond Mielle)
TEL: 03.25.37.51.11
DIRECTIONS: RN77.
MENU: 55 to 62 Frs.
RESTAURANT: dinner up to 22.00
SPECIALITIES: home-cooking.
OTHER POINTS: credit cards accepted.
lake and forêt d'Orient; Troyes: cathedral.

AUMETZ
Moselle, 57710

CAFE HOTEL RESTAURANT DE LA POSTE
(Mme Linda Cossa) 15, rue Foch
TEL: 03.82.91.91.71
DIRECTIONS: RN52, the Hayange/longwy road.
LANGUAGES: Italian.
MENU: 50 Frs.
ROOMS: 120 to 150 Frs.
RESTAURANT: Snacks from 6.00, lunch 12.00-14.00, dinner 19.00-21.00
CLOSED: Tues afternoon.
SPECIALITIES: Italian dishes, regional menu, home cooking.
HOTEL: 6 rooms.
FACILITIES: shower
OTHER POINTS: credit cards accepted.
Musée de la mine (mining); metallic church.

AUTECHAUX
Doubs, 25110

RELAIS DE L'AUTOROUTE – Chez Simone
(Mme Simone Courtial)
TEL: 03.81.84.01.14
DIRECTIONS: Baume-les-Daffies exit, towards Lure/Vesoul.
LANGUAGES: English, Spanish.
MENU: 58 to 62 Frs (drink and coffee included).
RESTAURANT: Snacks from 9.00, lunch 11.00-15.00, dinner 19.00-24.00
CLOSED: Sun, public holidays, and 2 weeks in Aug.
SPECIALITIES: croates aux champignons, 3-cheese fondue, canard à l'ananas, choucroute garnie, home-cooking.
OTHER POINTS: bar.
caves at La Glacière; gouffre (abyss) de Poudrey; saut (falls) du Doubs (Villers-le-Lac); lac de Bonnal;

AUTUN
Saône-et-Loire, 71400

PIZZERIA RESTAURANT IL COSENZA
(Mme Eva Rizzo) 13, route de Beaune
TEL: 03.85.52.27.72
LANGUAGES: English, German, Spanish, Italian.
MENU: 65 Frs.
RESTAURANT: Snacks from 6.30, lunch 11.30-14.00, dinner 19.00-21.30
CLOSED: Sun, and in Aug.
SPECIALITIES: Italian and Calabrian dishes, regional menu, home-cooking.
OTHER POINTS: credit cards accepted.
Gallo-Roman town: Roman theatre, temples; Gothic cathedral; son et lumière at the Roman theatre (in summer).

AUVILLERS LES FORGES
Ardennes, 08260

L'ARRET DES ROUTIERS
(Mme Nicole Bonnaire)
TEL: 03.24.54.32.77
DIRECTIONS: Charleville-Mézières/Hirson.
MENU: 50 Frs.
ROOMS: 75 to 110 Frs.
RESTAURANT: Snacks from 6.00, lunch 12.00-15.00, dinner 19.00-21.00
CLOSED: Sat afternoon.
SPECIALITIES: home-cooking.
HOTEL: 5 rooms.
FACILITIES: shower
OTHER POINTS: credit cards accepted.
Meuse and Semoy valleys.

AUXERRE
Yonne, 89000

LE SAINTE NITASSE
(Mme Corinne Courault) Route de Chablis
TEL: 03.86.46.95.07
DIRECTIONS: RN65, Auxerre South.
LANGUAGES: English.
MENU: 56.50 to 87 Frs.
ROOMS: 100 to 130 Frs.
RESTAURANT: Snacks from 6.30, lunch 12.00-14.30, dinner 19.30-22.30
CLOSED: Sat, Sun and last week in Dec.
SPECIALITIES: home-cooking.
HOTEL: ☆ 31 rooms.
FACILITIES: shower, bath, private bathroom
OTHER POINTS: credit cards accepted.
medieval monuments in Auxerre; Avallon; Vézelay; Joigny.

AVALLON
Yonne, 89200

LE RELAIS SAINT CHRISTOPHE
(Mr Oscar Casado) 13, route de Paris
TEL: 03.86.34.07.17
LANGUAGES: Spanish.
MENU: 63 Frs (wine included).
RESTAURANT: Snacks from 7.00, lunch 11.30-14.00, dinner 18.30-21.30
CLOSED: Sat evening, Sun and from 10th Dec to 1st Jan.
SPECIALITIES: regional menu, home-cooking, escargots de Bourgogne.
OTHER POINTS: bar.

BEAUMONT SUR VESLE
Marne, 51360

LA MAISON DU CHAMPAGNE
(Mr Marc Boulard) 2, rue du Port
TEL: 03.26.03.92.45 FAX: 03.26.03.97.59
DIRECTIONS: RN44, between Reims and Châlons-sur-Marne.
LANGUAGES: English, German.
MENU: 76 to 250 Frs.
ROOMS: 110 to 300 Frs.
RESTAURANT: Snacks from 7.00, lunch 12.00-14.15, dinner 19.00-21.00
CLOSED: Sun evening, Mon and 2 weeks in Nov.
SPECIALITIES: terrine du chef, rognons de veau au ratafia, canard aux griottes (duck with cherries), soufflé au Marc, regional menu, home-cooking.
HOTEL: ☆☆ 13 rooms.
FACILITIES: shower, bath, private bathroom, television, telephone
OTHER POINTS: credit cards accepted.
champagne cellars; vineyards; remains of 1914-18 war; Fort de la Pompelle; Faux de Verzy; cathedral at Reims; Le Thau palace.

BEAUREPAIRE EN BRESSE
Saône-et-Loire, 71580

LE RELAIS DES PLATANES
(Mme Thérèse Cornet)
TEL: 03.85.74.11.01
DIRECTIONS: RN78, between Lons-le-Saunier and Louhans.
LANGUAGES: English.
MENU: 55 Frs.
ROOMS: 90 to 100 Frs.
RESTAURANT: Snacks from 7.00, lunch 11.30-14.00, dinner 19.00-21.00
SPECIALITIES: poulet aux écrevisses, saumon à l'oseille, grenouilles fraiches, regional menu, home-cooking.
HOTEL: 6 rooms.
FACILITIES: shower, bath, private bathroom
OTHER POINTS: bar.

BELLEVILLE
Meuse, 55430

LE FRANCO/BELGE
(Mr Roland Buffello) 164, rue du Général de Gaulle
TEL: 03.29.84.57.85
DIRECTIONS: on the Verdun/Sedan axis.
MENU: 44 to 125 Frs.
RESTAURANT: Snacks from 5.00, dinner 17.00-22.00
SPECIALITIES: home-cooking, paëlla, choucroute, couscous, cassoulet, poté indienne.
OTHER POINTS: bar.

BLAGNY
Ardennes, 08110

BAR LES ROUTIERS
(SNC Biagio/Cailleux) 37 Route Nationale
TEL: 03.24.22.00.23
DIRECTIONS: RN43, between Sedan and Charleville-Mézières.
MENU: 52 Frs. Dish of the day at 39 Frs.
RESTAURANT: Snacks from 6.30, lunch 12.00-14.00, dinner 19.00-21.00
CLOSED: Sat, and in Aug.
SPECIALITIES: home-cooking.
OTHER POINTS: bar.

BOUILLY
Aube, 10320

AU RELAIS MONTAIGU
(Mr René Braux) 300, rue au Fébvres – Souligny
TEL: 03.25.40.20.20
DIRECTIONS: RN77, Auxerre, at the Charmont exit.
MENU: 52 to 60 Frs.
ROOMS: 85 to 150 Frs.
RESTAURANT: Snacks from 6.30, lunch 12.00-14.00, dinner 19.00-21.00
SPECIALITIES: regional menu, home-cooking.
HOTEL: ☆ 13 rooms.
FACILITIES: shower, bath, private bathroom, telephone
OTHER POINTS: credit cards accepted.
Troyes: museums; lake and forêt d'Orient; churches.

BRIENNE
Saône-et-Loire, 71290

LA PETITE ROUTE
(Mr Carlo Busca) Route Nationale 975
TEL: 03.85.40.08.85
DIRECTIONS: RD 975, RD975, Tournus/Bourg en Bresse.
LANGUAGES: Italian.
MENU: 70 Frs.
RESTAURANT: Snacks from 6.30, lunch 12.00-14.30, dinner 19.00-22.00
CLOSED: Sun.
SPECIALITIES: home-cooking, italian specialities.
OTHER POINTS: credit cards accepted.

BRIENON SUR ARMANCON
Yonne, 89210

HOTEL DE BOURGOGNE
(Mr Christian Dussart) 21, route de Joigny
TEL: 03.86.43.00.63
DIRECTIONS: the Joigny/Saint-Florentin road.
LANGUAGES: English, Polish.
MENU: 59 Frs.
ROOMS: 80 to 120 Frs.
RESTAURANT: Snacks from 5.00
CLOSED: Sat and Sun.
SPECIALITIES: home-cooking.
HOTEL: 9 rooms.
FACILITIES: shower
OTHER POINTS: credit cards accepted.
Joigny (22km); Auxerre (20km); Chablis (20km).

BRUAILLES
Saône-et-Loire, 71500

RELAIS DES QUATRE CHEMINS
(Mr Thierry Rousse) Les Quatre Chemins – Louhans
TEL: 03.85.75.15.81
DIRECTIONS: RD972.
MENU: 60 Frs.
ROOMS: 140 to 180 Frs.
RESTAURANT: Snacks from 7.00, lunch 12.00-14.30, dinner 19.00-21.30
CLOSED: Wed afternoon.
SPECIALITIES: home-cooking.
HOTEL: 5 rooms.
FACILITIES: shower
OTHER POINTS: credit cards accepted.

BUCEY LES GY
Haute-Saône, 70700

CAFE DE LA GARE
(Sté BMO) Rue de la Gare
TEL: 03.84.32.92.02
DIRECTIONS: between Dijon/Vesoul and Dole/Vesoul.
MENU: 64.50 Frs.
RESTAURANT: Snacks from 5.00, lunch 11.00-14.00, dinner 18.30-22.00
CLOSED: Sun.
SPECIALITIES: home-cooking.
OTHER POINTS: credit cards accepted.

CARIGNAN
Ardennes, 08110

LE RELAIS
(Mr Fabrice Fossani) 33, avenue Charles de Gaulle
TEL: 03.24.22.08.78
DIRECTIONS: RN 43, RN43, between Seban and Montmédy.
MENU: 48 to 75 Frs.
RESTAURANT: Snacks from 11.45, lunch 11.45-14.30, dinner 19.00-22.00
SPECIALITIES: home-cooking, couscous (week-end).
OTHER POINTS: credit cards accepted.

CELLE SUR LOIRE (LA)
Nièvre, 58440

LA BELLE ETOILE
(Mme Brigitte Foucher) Route Nationale 7
TEL: 03.86.26.05.10 FAX: 03.86.26.04.34
DIRECTIONS: RN7, the Paris/Nevers road.
LANGUAGES: English, Spanish.
MENU: 59 to 79 Frs.
RESTAURANT: Snacks from 6.00, lunch 11.00-15.00, dinner 18.30-22.30
CLOSED: 1 week at Christmas.
SPECIALITIES: home-cooking.
OTHER POINTS: credit cards accepted.
Sancerre; Saint-Firgeau; Potteries at Saint-Amand.

CHALLUY
Nièvre, 58000

RELAIS DU PONT CARREAU
(Mme Fernande Taillemitte)
TEL: 03.86.21.00.02
DIRECTIONS: RN7.
HOTEL: 4 rooms
OTHER POINTS: bar.

CHALONS SUR MARNE
Marne, 51000

LE BOEUF MODE DU MONT SAINT MICHEL
(Mme Huguette Legrand)
TEL: 03.26.68.05.08 FAX: 03.26.65.59.71
DIRECTIONS: on the Troyes road.
MENU: 65 Frs (drink and coffee included).
RESTAURANT: Snacks from 5.00, lunch 11.45-14.00, dinner 19.00-22.00
CLOSED: Sat until 10th Sept.
SPECIALITIES: poulet aux écrevisses, boeuf mode, escargots, cuisses de grenouilles, regional menu, home-cooking.
OTHER POINTS: credit cards accepted.
champagne cellars; Reims: cathedral; Notre-Dame Lépine.

CHAMPAGNOLE
Jura, 39300

LES ROUTIERS
(Mr Guy Chagre) La Billaude – Commune du Vaudioux
TEL: 03.84.51.60.33
DIRECTIONS: RN5, the Paris/Geneva road.
MENU: 60 to 120 Frs.
RESTAURANT: Snacks from 7.00, lunch 12.00-14.00
CLOSED: Sun, and 2 weeks in Aug.
SPECIALITIES: home-cooking.
OTHER POINTS: bar.
waterfalls at La Billaudel; Le Hérisson; lakes; Frasnois; Ilay; Bonlieu; Chalain.

CHAMPLOST
Yonne, 89210

AU BON ACCUEIL
(SNC Duteriez – Le Leuch) 23, route Nationale 5
TEL: 03.86.43.14.71
DIRECTIONS: RN5, between Sens and Dijon.
MENU: 55 to 70 Frs.
RESTAURANT: Snacks from 6.00, lunch 11.00-14.00, dinner 19.00-21.00
CLOSED: Sun.
SPECIALITIES: home-cooking.
OTHER POINTS: bar.
Mont-Avrollot (archeological site).

CHATELET SUR RETOURNE
Ardennes, 08300

LE RELAIS PONT ROYAL
(Mr Yves Detruiseaux) Chatelet sur Retourne
TEL: 03.24.38.93.27
MENU: 52 to 150 Frs.
RESTAURANT: Snacks from 6.00, dinner up to 24.00
CLOSED: Tues.
SPECIALITIES: regional menu, home-cooking.
OTHER POINTS: credit cards accepted.
Champagne region.

CHAUDENEY
Meurthe-et-Meuselle, 54200

LE MIRABELLIER
(Mr John Frères) Aire de Service de Toul-Dommartin – Dans les deux sens
TEL: 03.83.64.64.01 FAX: 03.83.64.51.37
DIRECTIONS: A31, the Luxembourg/Metz/Nancy/Dijon road.
LANGUAGES: English.
MENU: 66 Frs (drink and coffee included).
RESTAURANT: Snacks from 6.00, lunch 10.30, dinner up to 23.00
OTHER POINTS: credit cards accepted.
Nancy: place Stanislas; Toul region wine route.

CHELSEY
Côte-d'Or, 21430

LES ROUTIERS
(Mr Bernard et Ursula Sentein) Route Nationale 6 – Liernais
TEL: 03.80.84.40.42
DIRECTIONS: RN6, midway between Saulieu and Arnay-le-Duc.
LANGUAGES: English, German.

MENU: 64 Frs.
ROOMS: 90 to 210 Frs.
RESTAURANT: Snacks from 5.00, lunch 12.00-15.00, dinner 19.00-24.00
CLOSED: Sat and Sun.
SPECIALITIES: pintade rotie, home-cooking.
HOTEL: 5 rooms.
FACILITIES: shower
OTHER POINTS: bar.
Musée de l'Art de la Table (culinary arts) at Arnay-le-Duc; Saulieu.

CHENEVIERES
Meurthe-et-Meuselle, 54122

L'ALCATO
(Mr Philippe Poupon) Route Nationale 59
TEL: 03.83.72.62.75
DIRECTIONS: RN 59*, RN59, between Luneville and Saint-Dié.
MENU: 55 to 85 Frs.
RESTAURANT: Snacks from 5.00, lunch 11.00-15.00, dinner 18.00-21.00
CLOSED: Sat and Sun evening.
SPECIALITIES: regional menu, home-cooking, poisson, choucroute.
OTHER POINTS: credit cards accepted.

CLAIRVAUX LES LACS
Jura, 39130

LES ROUTIERS
(Mr Luc Durand) 4, route de Lons le Saunier
TEL: 03.84.25.85.57
DIRECTIONS: the Besanáon/Genève axis.
LANGUAGES: English.
MENU: 60 to 90 Frs.
RESTAURANT: Snacks from 7.00, lunch 11.30-15.00, dinner 19.00-22.00
CLOSED: Sun morning.
SPECIALITIES: home-cooking.
OTHER POINTS: credit cards accepted.

CLUNY
Saône-et-Loire, 71250

AUBERGE DU CHEVAL BLANC
(Elvire Bouillin) 1, rue Porte de Mâcon
TEL: 03.85.59.01.13 FAX: 03.85.59.13.32
DIRECTIONS: RN980, between Mâcon and Chalon-sur-Saône.
MENU: 77 to 185 Frs
RESTAURANT: Lunch 11.45-14.00, dinner 18.45-21.00
CLOSED: Fri evening, Sat, and from Dec to Feb.
SPECIALITIES: pavé charolais sauce morilles (mushrooms), cuisses de grenoullies à la crème, noix de veau au crémont de Bourgogne, regional menu.
OTHER POINTS: credit cards accepted.
Cluny: abbey, musée Hochier, stud-farm (haras), Norman buildings; château at Cormatin; Roche de Solutré.

COLLONGES LES PREMIERES
Côte-d'Or, 21110

A LA BONNE AUBERGE
(Mr Michel Garnier) 8, rue de la Gare
TEL: 03.80.31.32.01
DIRECTIONS: RN5, between Genlis and Auxonne.
MENU: 57 Frs.
RESTAURANT: Snacks from 6.00, lunch 11.00-15.00, dinner 19.00-21.00
CLOSED: Sun, and between Christmas and Boxing Day.
SPECIALITIES: home-cooking.
OTHER POINTS: credit cards accepted.
Musée de Bonaparte at Auxonne; Mont-Roland.

COLOMBEY LES BELLES
Meurthe-et-Meuselle, 54170

AUBERGE LORRAINE
(Mr Claude Arnould) 71, rue Carnot
TEL: 03.83.52.00.23 FAX: 03.83.52.85.66
DIRECTIONS: RN74, Neufchâteau.
MENU: 54.50 to 116 Frs.
RESTAURANT: Snacks from 7.00, lunch 11.30-14.30, dinner 19.00-22.00
CLOSED: 1 week at Christmas.
SPECIALITIES: home-cooking.
OTHER POINTS: credit cards accepted.
Domrémy; Nancy; Toul; Baccarat crystal-works; Vannes-le-Châtel.

COMBLANCHIEN
Côte-d'Or, 21700

AUBERGE DU GUIDON
(Mr André Vauchez) Route Nationale 74
TEL: 03.80.62.94.39
DIRECTIONS: RN74, between Beaune and Dijon.
MENU: 60 Frs.
ROOMS: 70 to 120 Frs.
RESTAURANT: Snacks from 6.00, lunch 12.00-14.30, dinner 19.00-22.00
CLOSED: Sat, Sun, and mid-Aug.
SPECIALITIES: home-cooking.
HOTEL: 8 rooms
OTHER POINTS: bar.
Nuits-Saint-Georges; Beaune.

CONSENVOYE
Meuse, 55110

L'AUBERGE LORRAINE
(Mr Olivier Florentin) 16, grande Rue
TEL: 03.29.85.80.19
DIRECTIONS: RD964, Verdun/Sedan/Charleville.
LANGUAGES: English, German.
MENU: 49 to 150 Frs.
ROOMS: 85 to 150 Frs.
RESTAURANT: Snacks from 7.00, lunch 12.00-14.00, dinner 19.00-21.30
CLOSED: Mon and 1 week at Christmas.
SPECIALITIES: potée lorraine, couscous, choucroute, tarte à l'oignon, quiche lorraine, regional menu, home-cooking.
HOTEL: 6 rooms.
FACILITIES: shower
OTHER POINTS: credit cards accepted.
Verdun: battlefield memorial, remains of military cemetery, relics of the 1914-18 war.

CORBIGNY
Nièvre, 58800

LES AMIS DES ROUTIERS
(Mme Colette Perini) 8, rue de Clamecy
TEL: 03.86.20.19.77
DIRECTIONS: RD985.
MENU: 55 Frs.
RESTAURANT: Lunch 12.00-15.30
CLOSED: Sat afternoon, Sun, public holidays and 15th Aug to 8th Sept.
SPECIALITIES: home-cooking.
OTHER POINTS: bar.
Parc régional du Morvan (14km); musée du Septennat (President Mitterrand's term of office) at Château-Chinon (30km).

COSNE SUR LOIRE
Nièvre, 58200

LA TASSEE
(Mr Maurice Chet) Route Nationale 7
TEL: 03.86.26.11.76
DIRECTIONS: RN7, Nevers southern (Sud) exit.
LANGUAGES: English.
RESTAURANT: Snacks from 6.00, lunch 12.00-13.30, dinner 20.00-21.30
CLOSED: Sun and public holidays, and in Aug.
SPECIALITIES: home-cooking.
OTHER POINTS: credit cards accepted.
Sancerre; Pouilly-sur-Loire.

LES 3 COULEURS
(Mrs Jean & Pierre Morfaux) 21, rue Saint Agnan
TEL: 03.86.28.23.50
DIRECTIONS: RN7, Nevers.
MENU: 54 to 150 Frs.
ROOMS: 110 to 200 Frs.
RESTAURANT: Snacks from 7.00, lunch 12.00-15.00, dinner 19.00-20.30
CLOSED: 2nd week of Dec to 1st week of Jan.
SPECIALITIES: coq au vin, cuisses de grenouilles à la provenáale, regional menu, home-cooking.
HOTEL: ☆ 13 rooms.
FACILITIES: shower
OTHER POINTS: credit cards accepted.
Sancerre; Pouilly-sur-Loire; banks of the Loire; musée de la Loire.

COURCELLES CHAUSSY
Moselle, 57530

AUBERGE DE LA GARE – Chez Pino
(Mr Joseph Russo) 6, avenue de la Libération
TEL: 03.87.64.08.77
DIRECTIONS: RN 3, RN3, between Metz and Saint-Avold.
LANGUAGES: English, German, Italian.
MENU: 48 to 99 Frs.
RESTAURANT: Snacks from 6.00, lunch 11.45-14.30, dinner 18.45-23.00
SPECIALITIES: regional menu.
OTHER POINTS: credit cards accepted.

COURGIVAUX
Marne, 51310

LE CHAPERON ROUGE
(Mr Pascal Fouques) Place de la République – Route nationale 4
TEL: 02.26.81.57.09
DIRECTIONS: RN4.
MENU: 60 to 100 Frs.
ROOMS: 100 to 120 Frs.
RESTAURANT: Lunch 11.30-14.30, dinner 18.30-22.30
CLOSED: Sun.
SPECIALITIES: red meats, home-cooking.
HOTEL: ☆ 14 rooms
OTHER POINTS: credit cards accepted.
Espernay: champagne region.

COURSON LES CARRIERES
Yonne, 89560

LE RELAIS DE COURSON
(Mr José Carvalho) Route Nationale 151
TEL: 03.86.41.52.58
DIRECTIONS: RN151, between Auxerre and Clamecy,
LANGUAGES: Spanish, Portuguese.
MENU: 65 Frs.
RESTAURANT: Snacks from 6.30
SPECIALITIES: home-cooking.
OTHER POINTS: credit cards accepted.
abbey at Vézelay (30m); caves at Aray (25km); Avallon (35km).

CRENEY
Aube, 10150

CAFE DU CENTRE
(Mr Jacques Jeandon) 29, route de Brienne
TEL: 03.25.81.39.79
DIRECTIONS: RD960, Troyes/Brienne/Saint-Dizier.
MENU: 60 Frs.
RESTAURANT: Snacks from 7.00, lunch 11.00-15.00, dinner 19.00-22.00
SPECIALITIES: home-cooking.
OTHER POINTS: credit cards accepted.
lake and forêt d'Orient; Brevonne; Dienville.

CREUSOT (LE)
Saône-et-Loire, 71200

LE RELAIS
(Mr Guy Beauclair) 26, rue de l'Yser
TEL: 03.85.55.03.34
DIRECTIONS: RN80.
MENU: 48 to 110 Frs.
ROOMS: 100 to 170 Frs.
RESTAURANT: Lunch 12.00-13.45, dinner 19.00-20.45
CLOSED: Sat afternoon.
SPECIALITIES: home-cooking.
HOTEL: 12 rooms.
FACILITIES: shower
OTHER POINTS: credit cards accepted.

CUSSY LES FORGES
Yonne, 89420

LE RELAIS 6
(Mr Hamid Adjaoud) Route Nationale 6
TEL: 03.86.33.10.14
DIRECTIONS: RN6, Avallon exit, towards Lyon.
LANGUAGES: Arabic.
MENU: 54 to 70 Frs.
RESTAURANT: Snacks from 5.00
CLOSED: Sun.
SPECIALITIES: couscous maison, paella, home-cooking.
OTHER POINTS: credit cards accepted.
Marvan region; Vézelay, Bourgogne wine-cellars; caves at Arcy (75km); Vallée du Cousin; Avallon: ramparts.

DANJOUTIN
Territoire-de-Belfort, 90400

LE CHALET FLEURI
(Mme Janine Toesca) 2, rue du Bosmont
TEL: 03.84.28.56.12
DIRECTIONS: the Lyon/Germany/Switzerland road.
MENU: 48 to 56 Frs (wine included).
RESTAURANT: Snacks from 6.30, lunch 11.00-15.00, dinner 19.00-23.00
CLOSED: Sun.
SPECIALITIES: home-cooking.
OTHER POINTS: credit cards accepted.
Belfort.

DANNEMOINE
Yonne, 89700

A LA BONNE AUBERGE
(Mme Nicole Verdin) Route Départementale 905
TEL: 03.86.55.54.22
DIRECTIONS: RD905, the Paris/Geneva road.
MENU: 55 to 65 Frs.
ROOMS: 70 to 110 Frs.
RESTAURANT: Snacks from 7.00, lunch 12.00-14.00, dinner 19.30-21.00
SPECIALITIES: home-cooking.
HOTEL: 13 rooms.
FACILITIES: shower, private bathroom
OTHER POINTS: credit cards accepted.
la Fosse Dionne at Tonnerre; château de Tanlay at Ancy-le-Franc.

DECIZE
Nièvre, 58300

LE BEL AIR
(Mr Dominique Rocq) 164, avenue de Verdun
TEL: 03.86.25.01.86
DIRECTIONS: RN81, the Nevers/Mâcon road.
MENU: 58 Frs (wine included).
RESTAURANT: Snacks from 5.45, lunch 11.00, dinner up to 21.30
CLOSED: Sun.
SPECIALITIES: regional menu, home-cooking.
OTHER POINTS: bar.

DEVAY
Nièvre, 58300

L'ETRIER
(Mr Jean-Marc Boutet) Route Nationale
TEL: 03.86.50.37.77
LANGUAGES: German.

RESTAURANT: dinner up to 22.00
OTHER POINTS: bar.

DORLISHEIM
Bas-Rhin, 67120

HOTEL RESTAURANT LE FORUM
(Mr Serge Jost) 4, avenue de la Gare
TEL: 03.88.38.14.28 FAX: 03.88.38.88.94
LANGUAGES: English, German.
ROOMS: 90 to 120 Frs.
RESTAURANT: Snacks from 6.15, lunch 12.00-13.30, dinner 19.00-20.30
CLOSED: Sun afternoon, end Aug/beginning Sept.
SPECIALITIES: home-cooking.
HOTEL: 7 rooms.
FACILITIES: shower
OTHER POINTS: credit cards accepted.

ECROUVES
Meurthe-et-Meuselle, 54200

LE RELAIS MATHY – Les Routiers
(Mr Paul Wan Dorsselaere) 825, avenue du 15ème Génie – Toul
TEL: 03.83.43.04.27
DIRECTIONS: RD400, Toul Centre/Saint-Mihiel/Ecrouves.
MENU: 42 to 82 Frs.
ROOMS: 98 to 156 Frs.
RESTAURANT: Snacks from 6.00, lunch 12.00-14.00, dinner 19.00-21.30
CLOSED: from Fri 15.00 to Sun 10.00, and 1 week at Christmas.
SPECIALITIES: tête de veau, coq au vin, cervelle (brains), ris de veau (sweetbreads), gibier (game – in season), home-cooking.
HOTEL: 16 rooms
OTHER POINTS: credit cards accepted.
cathedral and ramparts at Totil; church at Ecrouves; fort at Villey-le-Sec; Saint-Gengoult cloister.

EINVILLE
Meurthe-et-Meuselle, 54370

LE RELAIS FLEURI
(Mme Annie Peignier-Bruant) 1, grande Rue
TEL: 03.83.72.90.07
DIRECTIONS: RD 914, RD914, between Luneville and Château-Salins.
LANGUAGES: German.
MENU: 50 Frs.
ROOMS: 130 to 210 Frs.
RESTAURANT: Snacks from 6.30, lunch 11.30-14.30, dinner 19.00-21.30
CLOSED: Sun.
SPECIALITIES: regional menu, home-cooking, quiche lorraine, paté lorrain.
HOTEL: 6 rooms
OTHER POINTS: credit cards accepted.

EPERNAY
Marne, 51200

LES ROUTIERS – Chez Madame Préjent
(Mme Marie-Louise Préjent) 13, rue Jean-Jacques Rousseau
TEL: 03.26.55.23.29
DIRECTIONS: RN3.
MENU: 65 to 95 Frs.
ROOMS: 120 to 175 Frs.
RESTAURANT: Snacks from 6.00
CLOSED: Sat evening, Sun, public holidays and in Jan.
SPECIALITIES: regional menu home-cooking.
HOTEL: 15 rooms.
FACILITIES: shower, bath, private bathroom
OTHER POINTS: bar.
champagne cellars; musée du vignoble (vineyards).

EPINAL
Vosges, 88000

LE RELAIS DE L'ABATTOIR
(Mr Gérard Didier) 63, rue de Nancy
TEL: 03.29.82.32.13
DIRECTIONS: RN57.
RESTAURANT: Snacks from 7.00, dinner 19.00-24.00
CLOSED: Sun, and from mid-July to mid-Aug.
SPECIALITIES: home-cooking.
OTHER POINTS: credit cards accepted.
Musée de l'imagerie (printing) at Epinal.

EPINEAU LES VOVES
Yonne, 89400

RELAIS DES SIX BOULES
(Mr Ahmed Betroune) 2, route de Chambery
TEL: 03.86.91.20.45
DIRECTIONS: RN6.
LANGUAGES: German, Arabic.
OTHER POINTS: bar.

ETOGES
Marne, 51270

LE CAVEAU DE L'ANCIENNE FORGE
(Mme Duchateau) Grande Rue
TEL: 03.26.59.32.79
DIRECTIONS: RD33, Châlons-sur-Marne
MENU: 60 Frs (drink included).
RESTAURANT: Snacks from 8.30, lunch 12.00-14.00, dinner 19.00-20.30

CLOSED: Wed and last 2 weeks in Aug.
SPECIALITIES: home-cooking,
OTHER POINTS: credit cards accepted.

EVANS
Jura, 39700

RELAIS 73
(Mme Yvette Arbey) Route Nationale 73
TEL: 03.84.81.37.29 **FAX:** 03.84.81.38.57
DIRECTIONS: RN73, west of Lyon, north of Mulhouse.
MENU: 60 Frs.
RESTAURANT: Snacks from 5.30
CLOSED: Sun and in Aug.
SPECIALITIES: home-cooking.
OTHER POINTS: credit cards accepted.

FRAIZE
Vosges, 88230

AUBERGE VOSGIENNE
(Mr Michel Gense) 14, rue du Général Ingold
TEL: 03.29.50.30.46
DIRECTIONS: RN415, Colmar via the Col-du-Bonhomme.
MENU: 55 Frs (wine included) to 120 Frs.
ROOMS: 100 to 160 Frs.
RESTAURANT: Snacks from 8.00, lunch 12.00-14.00, dinner 19.00-21.00
CLOSED: Wed, and last 2 weeks in Sept.
SPECIALITIES: home-cooking.
HOTEL: 7 rooms.
FACILITIES: shower, bath
OTHER POINTS: credit cards accepted.
Col-du-Bonhomme.

FRASNE
Doubs, 25560

L'ARC EN CIEL
(Mr Walter Poulain) 94, grande rue
TEL: 03.81.49.83.68
DIRECTIONS: between Champagnole and Pontarlier.
LANGUAGES: English.
MENU: 60 Frs.
RESTAURANT: Snacks from 7.30
CLOSED: Wed afternoon.
SPECIALITIES: regional menu, home-cooking.
OTHER POINTS: credit cards accepted.
château at Joux (17km); gouffre (abyss) de Poudrey; lake at Saint-Point; Salins-les-Bains.

FROUARD
Meurthe-et-Meuselle, 54390

LA GRANDE CHOPE
(Mme Christiane Pallagi) 4, rue de la Gare
TEL: 03.83.49.05.64 **FAX:** 03.83.49.04.65
DIRECTIONS: RN57, Metz.
MENU: 47 Frs, dish of the day at 36 Frs.
RESTAURANT: Snacks from 7.00, lunch 11.30-14.00
CLOSED: Sat, Sun, and in Aug.
SPECIALITIES: home-cooking.
OTHER POINTS: bar.
Moselle valley; Nancy: place Stanislas.

LA PRAIRIE
(Mr Bernard Ban Der Weckene) 6, rue de l'Embanie
TEL: 03.83.49.31.02
DIRECTIONS: between Pompey and Frouard.
MENU: 50 Frs.
RESTAURANT: Snacks from 8.00, lunch 12.00-14.30, dinner 19.00-21.00
CLOSED: Sun.
SPECIALITIES: regional menu, home-cooking, choucroute, quiches.
OTHER POINTS: credit cards accepted.

FUMAY
Ardennes, 08170

HOTEL LION
(Mme Edith Potier) 41, rue de la Céramique
TEL: 03.24.41.10.27
DIRECTIONS: RN51, opposite the station.
MENU: 65 Frs (coffee at 5 Frs).
ROOMS: 100 to 140 Frs.
RESTAURANT: Snacks from 7.00, lunch 12.00-14.00, dinner 19.00-21.00
CLOSED: Sun afternoon, and Sept.
SPECIALITIES: couscous and cassoulet, home-cooking.
HOTEL: ☆ 7 rooms.
FACILITIES: shower, bath, private bathroom
OTHER POINTS: bar.
Musée de l'ardoise (slate).

GENELARD
Saône-et-Loire, 71420

LE PROVENCAL
(Mme Pascale Rizard) Place du Champ de Foire
TEL: 03.85.79.28.90
DIRECTIONS: RN70, between Montceau-les-Mines and Digoin.
LANGUAGES: English.
MENU: 55 Frs.
RESTAURANT: Snacks from 8.00, lunch 11.30-14.00, dinner 19.00-21.00
SPECIALITIES: home-cooking.
OTHER POINTS: bar.
foie gras production at La Noie; marché aux puces (flea market); ferronnerie d'art (craft blacksmith).

GERMIGNY
Yonne, 89600

RELAIS DES ROUTIERS
(Mme Maria Lecoutre) 24, route de Saint Florentin
TEL: 03.86.35.06.39
LANGUAGES: Italian.
MENU: 55 Frs.
RESTAURANT: Snacks from 5.30, lunch 11.30-14.00, dinner 19.00-20.30
SPECIALITIES: regional menu.
HOTEL: 5 rooms.
FACILITIES: shower, bath, private bathroom
OTHER POINTS: credit cards accepted.

GUEMAR
Haut-Rhin, 68970

A L'ANGE
(Mr Michel Schwariz) 16, route de Selestat
TEL: 03.89.71.83.03
DIRECTIONS: Colmar.
LANGUAGES: English, German.
MENU: 55 to 120 Frs.
ROOMS: 130 to 140 Frs.
RESTAURANT: Snacks from 7.00, lunch 11.30-15.00, dinner 18.30-22.00
CLOSED: Sat and Sun afternoon.
SPECIALITIES: Alsace dishes, regional menu.
HOTEL: 10 rooms.
FACILITIES: shower, bath, private bathroom
OTHER POINTS: credit cards accepted.
wine route; Colmar.

GUERIGNY
Nièvre, 58130

HOTEL DU COMMERCE
(Mr Gérard Page) 2 Grande Rue
TEL: 03.86.37.32.77
DIRECTIONS: RD977, the Nevers/Auxerre road.
LANGUAGES: German.
MENU: 63 to 85 Frs.
ROOMS: 160 to 215 Frs.
RESTAURANT: Snacks from 6.30, lunch 11.30-14.00, dinner 19.00-20.30
CLOSED: Sat afternoon and Sun (out of season), and from 20th Dec to 5th Jan.
SPECIALITIES: regional menu.
HOTEL: 8 rooms.
FACILITIES: shower
OTHER POINTS: credit cards accepted.
museum of old Guérigny; duke's palace at Nevers; musée du septennat (President Mitterrand's term of office) at Château-Chinon (60km)

GUMBRECHTSHOFFEN
Bas-Rhin, 67110

AU SOLEIL – Chez Bernard et Lili
(Mme Liliane Peifer) 30, rue Principale
TEL: 03.88.72.90.77
DIRECTIONS: RN62 and RD242, between Niederbronn and Haguenau.
LANGUAGES: German.
MENU: 38 to 100 Frs.
ROOMS: 130 Frs.
RESTAURANT: Snacks from 6.00, dinner 18.30-22.00
CLOSED: Sun afternoon, and in Aug.
SPECIALITIES: gibier, choucroute à l'alsacienne, couscous, pigeonneau, regional menu, home-cooking.
HOTEL: 3 rooms.
FACILITIES: shower, private bathroom, telephone
OTHER POINTS: bar.
parc régional des Vosges du Nord; châteaux; museums; distilleries; potteries.

GUMERY
Aube, 10400

AU RELAIS
(Mme Evelyne Visse) 3, route de Sens
TEL: 03.25.39.16.01
DIRECTIONS: RD439, between Sens and Nogent-sur-Seine.
LANGUAGES: English.
MENU: 57 Frs.
ROOMS: 100 to 140 Frs.
RESTAURANT: Snacks from 6.00, lunch 11.30-14.00, dinner 19.00-21.00
CLOSED: Sat, and 2 weeks in Aug.
SPECIALITIES: home-cooking.
HOTEL: 5 rooms.
FACILITIES: shower, bath
OTHER POINTS: credit cards accepted.
château at La Motte-Tilly; museum at Nogent-sur-Seine; Provins: ramparts.

HAGONDANGE
Moselle, 57300

LES ROUTIERS
(Mme Martine Bognolo) 36, Rue de Mezt
TEL: 03.87.71.46.63
DIRECTIONS: RN53, Metz.
MENU: 54 Frs (¼ wine included).
ROOMS: 115 to 165 Frs.
RESTAURANT: Snacks from 8.00, lunch 12.00-14.00
CLOSED: Sat afternoon, Sun afternoon, and in Aug.
SPECIALITIES: home-cooking.
HOTEL: 9 rooms.
FACILITIES: shower, bath, private bathroom

OTHER POINTS: credit cards accepted.
Annéville-les-Thermes; parc Bing-Bang Strouchps.

HYEVRE PAROISSE
Doubs, 25110

HOTEL RESTAURANT ZISS
(Mrs Claude Krieger et Olivier Yoessle)
TEL: 03.81.84.07.88
DIRECTIONS: RN83, exit A36 Baume-les-Dames (10km)/Isle-sur-le-Doubs/Clerval (15km).
LANGUAGES: German.
MENU: 55 to 160 Frs.
ROOMS: 230 to 250 Frs.
RESTAURANT: Snacks from 10.30, lunch 12.00-14.00, dinner 19.00-23.00
CLOSED: Sat lunch.
SPECIALITIES: coq au vin, canard à l'orange, fritures (whitebait), carpes, regional menu, home-cooking.
HOTEL: ☆☆☆ 21 rooms.
FACILITIES: shower, bath, private bathroom, television, telephone
OTHER POINTS: credit cards accepted.
Jura mountains; grotte (cave) de La Glacière; saut (fails) du Doubs; Besanáon: citadel.

IS SUR TILLE
Côte-d'Or, 21120

CAFE DU MIDI
(Mr Philippe Chalopet) 2, place Villeneuve Motet
TEL: 03.80.95.07.51
MENU: 60 Frs.
RESTAURANT: Snacks from 6.00, lunch 11.30-14.30
SPECIALITIES: home-cooking.
OTHER POINTS: bar.

ISLE SUR LE DOUBS (L')
Doubs, 25250

LE CHAPAGOYE
(Mme Franáoise Hausermann) 14, rue Delattre de Tassigny
TEL: 03.81.96.32.60
DIRECTIONS: RN83, between Besanáon and Belfort.
LANGUAGES: English, German.
MENU: 50 Frs to 120 Frs.
ROOMS: 80 to 240 Frs.
RESTAURANT: Snacks from 5.45, lunch 11.30-14.00, dinner 18.30-21.30
CLOSED: Sat (out of season) and 15th Dec to 15th Jan.
SPECIALITIES: regional menu, home-cooking.
HOTEL: 5 rooms.
FACILITIES: shower
OTHER POINTS: credit cards accepted.
caves; château; springs; glass-works.

JOUDES CUISEAUX
Saône-et-Loire, 71480

LE FRANC COMTOIS
(Mr Gilles Borges) Route Nationale 83
TEL: 03.85.72.57.09
DIRECTIONS: Besanáon Bourg.
MENU: 55 Frs (wine included).
RESTAURANT: Snacks from 6.15, lunch 11.30-14.30, dinner 19.00-22.00
CLOSED: Sun afternoon.
SPECIALITIES: home-cooking.
OTHER POINTS: credit cards accepted.
Jura wine route; church at Brou; Ecomusée at Cuiseaux.

JOUVENCON
Saône-et-Loire, 71290

LA CHAUMIERE
(Mr Jean-Paul Michel) Le Bourg
DIRECTIONS: Tournus/Louhans.
MENU: 58 to 120 Frs.
RESTAURANT: Snacks from 6.30, lunch 12.00-14.30, dinner 19.00-22.00
SPECIALITIES: home-cooking.
OTHER POINTS: bar.
Route des Moulins (windmills road); Aphoticairie de Louhans (old chemistry); Musée de la Chaise (chair museum).

KOGENHEIM
Bas-Rhin, 67230

A L'ETOILE
(Mr Robert Rapp) 36, route de Strasbourg
TEL: 03.88.74.70.02 FAX: 03.88.74.03.45
DIRECTIONS: RN83, between Selestat and Benfeld.
LANGUAGES: German.
MENU: 37 to 100 Frs.
ROOMS: 110 to 160 Frs.
RESTAURANT: Snacks from 7.15
CLOSED: Mon evening, and mid-Jan to mid-Feb.
SPECIALITIES: regional menu, couscous, cheval braisé, home-cooking.
HOTEL: ☆ 9 rooms.
FACILITIES: shower, bath, private bathroom, telephone
OTHER POINTS: credit cards accepted.
leisure park at Rust; la montagne des singes (monkey mountain); Germany (15km).

LANGRES
Haute-Marne, 52200

LA BONNE AUBERGE
(Mme Christine Ruffier) Faubourg de la Collinière
TEL: 03.25.87.09.18
DIRECTIONS: RN74, the Chaumont/Dijon road.
MENU: 60 Frs (wine and coffee included).
ROOMS: 100 to 160 Frs.
RESTAURANT: Snacks from 5.00, lunch 12.00-14.00, dinner 19.00-22.00
CLOSED: Sun.
SPECIALITIES: home-cooking.
HOTEL: 5 rooms
OTHER POINTS: credit cards accepted.

LE RELAIS DE LA COLLINIERE
(Mme Annick Gallier) Faubourg de la Collinière
TEL: 03.25.87.03.27
DIRECTIONS: RN19, the Chaumont/Dijon road.
MENU: 58 Frs (wine included).
ROOMS: 75 to 175 Frs.
RESTAURANT: Snacks from 6.00, lunch 12.00-15.00, dinner 19.00-22.30
CLOSED: Sun afternoon.
SPECIALITIES: couscous, home-cooking.
HOTEL: 7 rooms
OTHER POINTS: bar.
Langres (Roman town).

LOISY PONT A MOUSSON
Meurthe-et-Meuselle, 54700

RESTAURANT DU RELAIS DE L'OBRION
(Mme Jacqueline Frères) Aire de Service de l'Obrion
TEL: 03.83.81.18.89 **FAX:** 03.83.84.01.85
DIRECTIONS: A31, Luxembourg/Nancy/Dijon.
LANGUAGES: English, German.
MENU: 59.50 Frs.
RESTAURANT: Snacks from 6.00, lunch 11.00, dinner up to 23.00
OTHER POINTS: credit cards accepted.
Prémontrées abbey; Pont-à-Mousson; Nancy: place Stanislas.

LONGEAU
Haute-Marne, 52250

CAFE DES ROUTIERS Chez Nanard
(Mr Bernard Denis) Route Nationale
TEL: 03.25.88.40.51 **FAX:** 03.25.90.71.91
DIRECTIONS: RN74, between Langres and Dijon, exit Langres South (Sud).
MENU: 40 to 100 Frs.
ROOMS: 90 to 160 Frs.
RESTAURANT: Snacks from 6.00, lunch 12.00-14.00, dinner 19.00-22.00
CLOSED: Sun afternoon.
SPECIALITIES: terrine maison, steack à l'ail, home-cooking.
HOTEL: 8 rooms
OTHER POINTS: credit cards accepted.
Langres: fortifications; Villegusien lake; Gallo-Roman excavations at Andilly; caves at Sabinus; source of the Marne; forêt and lac de Liez.

LOUHANS
Saône-et-Loire, 71500

CHEZ ALEX
(Mr Eric Alexandre) 19, rue Lucien Guillemaut
TEL: 03.85.75.11.75
DIRECTIONS: RN78, Chalon sur Saône/Lons-le-Saunier.
MENU: 56 to 70 Frs.
RESTAURANT: Snacks from 6.30, lunch 11.30-13.30, dinner 19.00-21.30
CLOSED: Sun.
SPECIALITIES: poulet de Bresse, tête de veau, home-cooking.
OTHER POINTS: bar.

LUGNY
Saône-et-Loire, 71260

L'ARCHE DE MACON PORTE DE BOURGOGNE
(Mr Hervé Lenfroit) A6 – Aires de Mâcon Saint Albain, Mâcon La Salle – Accessible dans les deux sens
TEL: 03.85.33.19.80 **FAX:** 03.85.33.12.98
RESTAURANT: Open 24h.
OTHER POINTS: credit cards accepted.

LUSIGNY SUR BARSE
Aube, 10270

AUBERGE DES PRAIRIES
(Mme Monique Mireux) Route Nationale 19
TEL: 03.25.41.20.32
DIRECTIONS: RN19.
MENU: 55 Frs.
ROOMS: 80 Frs.
RESTAURANT: dinner up to 22.00
SPECIALITIES: home-cooking.
HOTEL: 4 rooms.
FACILITIES: shower, bath, private bathroom
OTHER POINTS: credit cards accepted.
lake and forêt d'Orient; tour of Troyes with its nine churches.

MAILLY LE CAMP
Aube, 10230

HOTEL DU CENTRE
(Mr Denis Barvidat) 64, rue du Général de Gaulle
TEL: 03.25.37.30.08
DIRECTIONS: RN77, Mailly centre.
MENU: 62 to 125 Frs.
ROOMS: 100 to 170 Frs.
RESTAURANT: Snacks from 6.00, lunch 12.00-14.30, dinner 19.00-23.00
CLOSED: Fri afternoon.
SPECIALITIES: andouillettes de Troyes, home-cooking.
HOTEL: 14 rooms.
FACILITIES: shower, bath, private bathroom
OTHER POINTS: credit cards accepted.

MARGUT
Ardennes, 08370

RESTAURANT DE LA MARCHE
(Mr Philippe Lavoisier) 3, rue de Lorraine
TEL: 03.24.60.66
DIRECTIONS: RN 43, RN43, between Seban and Montmédy.
LANGUAGES: English.
MENU: 60 to 120 Frs.
ROOMS: 135 to 185 Frs.
RESTAURANT: Snacks from 7.00, lunch 12.00-14.00, dinner 18.30-20.30
CLOSED: Sat and the 1st 2 weeks in Feb.
SPECIALITIES: regional menu, home-cooking, joue de boeuf, fricassée d'escargots.
HOTEL: 4 rooms
OTHER POINTS: credit cards accepted.

MENIL SUR BELVITTE
Vosges, 88700

LES ROUTIERS
(Mme Nelly Nicolas-Jacquot)
TEL: 03.29.65.15.02
DIRECTIONS: RN 435, between Sarrebourg and Epinal.
MENU: 65 Frs (wine and coffee included).
RESTAURANT: Snacks from 7.30, lunch 11.00-15.00
CLOSED: Sat (in winter)
SPECIALITIES: tête de veau, home-cooking.
OTHER POINTS: bar.
Baccarat crystal-works; medieval buildings at Rambervillers.

MERCUREY
Saône-et-Loire, 71640

LE MERCUREY
(Mme Roselyne Goy) Grande Rue
TEL: 03.85.45.13.56
DIRECTIONS: RD978, on the Autun road.
MENU: 54 to 120 Frs.
ROOMS: 120 to 200 Frs.
RESTAURANT: Snacks from 6.30, lunch 11.00-15.00, dinner 18.00-22.00
SPECIALITIES: coq au vin, poissons, cuisses de lapin, bourguignon, home-cooking.
HOTEL: 8 rooms.
FACILITIES: shower, private bathroom
OTHER POINTS: credit cards accepted.
Touches and environs.

MESGRIGNY
Aube, 10170

LA BELLE ETOILE
(Mme Sylvie Schmutz) La Belle Etoile – Route Nationale 19
TEL: 03.25.21.15.70
DIRECTIONS: RN19, Paris.
MENU: 60 Frs.
RESTAURANT: Snacks from 4.30, lunch 11.00-16.00, dinner 18.00-22.00
CLOSED: Sun.
SPECIALITIES: home-cooking.
OTHER POINTS: credit cards accepted.
Troyes; Champagne region.

MESSIA SUR SORNE
Jura, 39570

LA CHARMILLE
(Mr Patrick Vaucher) 570 Route de Lyon
TEL: 03.84.24.65.92
DIRECTIONS: RN83, Lons-le-Saunier exit, towards Lyon.
MENU: 60 Frs.
RESTAURANT: Snacks from 8.00, lunch 11.00-14.00
CLOSED: Sun.
SPECIALITIES: home-cooking.
OTHER POINTS: bar.
Baume wine-cellars; waterfalls at Le Hérisson; le pont (bridge) de la Pyle.

MONETEAU
Yonne, 89470

AU RENDEZ-VOUS DES PECHEURS
(Mr Michel Rabuat) 14, route d'Auxerre
TEL: 03.86.40.63.32 FAX: 03.86.40.58.25
DIRECTIONS: D84, Moneteau.
MENU: 58 to 130 Frs.
RESTAURANT: Snacks from 7.00, lunch 11.45-15.00, dinner 19.45-22.00
SPECIALITIES: regional menu, poissons, grillades (grills).
HOTEL: 6 rooms.
FACILITIES: shower
OTHER POINTS: credit cards accepted.

MOREY SAINT DENIS
Côte-d'Or, 21220

LE RELAIS DE MOREY
(Mme Maryline Thomas) 71, route Nationale 74
TEL: 03.80.51.80.54
DIRECTIONS: RN74, Beaune/Dijon axis.
LANGUAGES: English.
MENU: 60 Frs (wine and coffee included).
RESTAURANT: Snacks from 7.30, lunch 11.30-14.30, dinner 19.00-21.30
CLOSED: Sun.
SPECIALITIES: pizzas, regional menu, home-cooking.
OTHER POINTS: credit cards accepted.

MOUCHARD
Jura, 39330

LA TONNELLE
(Mr Christian Faivre-Picon) Pagnoz
TEL: 03.84.37.81.17
DIRECTIONS: RN83.
MENU: 60 to 110 Frs.
ROOMS: 100 to 200 Frs.
RESTAURANT: Snacks from 6.30, lunch 12.00-14.00, dinner 19.00-22.30
CLOSED: Sat evening, Sun, 7th to 21st Aug and last week in Dec.
SPECIALITIES: regional menu, home-cooking.
HOTEL: 8 rooms.
FACILITIES: shower, bath
OTHER POINTS: credit cards accepted.

MOULIN DES MALADES
Jura, 39700

AU RENDEZ-VOUS DE LA MARINE
(Mlle Josette Bullet) 73 route nationale
TEL: 03.84.71.32.10
DIRECTIONS: RN73, between Dole and Besanáon.
MENU: 55 to 75 Frs.
RESTAURANT: Open 24h.
CLOSED: Sat evening.
SPECIALITIES: croñte forestière, coq au vin, regional menu.
HOTEL: 2 rooms
OTHER POINTS: credit cards accepted.

MYENNES
Nièvre, 58440

LE RANCH
(Mr Roger Dufour) 68, rue de Paris
TEL: 03.86.28.00.98
MENU: 50 Frs.
RESTAURANT: Snacks from 6.00
OTHER POINTS: bar.

NAVILLY
Saône-et-Loire, 71270

AU BOIS DE BOULOGNE
(Mr André Grapinet)
TEL: 03.85.49.10.40
DIRECTIONS: RN83 bis.
OTHER POINTS: bar.

NEUVY SAUTOUR
Yonne, 89570

AU BON COIN – Chez Gérard
(Mr Gérard Charpignon) 29, route de Troyes
TEL: 03.86.56.35.52
DIRECTIONS: RN77, between Troyes and Auxerre.
MENU: 47 Frs.
RESTAURANT: Snacks from 4.00, lunch 12.00-14.00, dinner 19.00-21.00
CLOSED: Sat afternoon, Sun, and in Aug.
SPECIALITIES: home-cooking.
OTHER POINTS: bar.
listed church.

NOCLE MAULAIX (LA)
Nièvre, 58250

HOTEL DE LA POSTE
(Mr Marcel Senotier)
TEL: 03.86.30.80.32
DIRECTIONS: Autun.
MENU: 38 to 120 Frs.
RESTAURANT: Snacks from 7.00, lunch 12.00-13.30
CLOSED: Mon, and in Sept.
SPECIALITIES: home-cooking.
OTHER POINTS: bar.

NOIREFONTAINE
Haut-Rhin, 6831

LES ROUTIERS
(Mr Michel Maqua) 5, route de Bouillon
TEL: 061.466.374
DIRECTIONS: Sedan-Recogne.
RESTAURANT: Snacks from 6.30
CLOSED: Sun.
SPECIALITIES: home-cooking.
OTHER POINTS: à la carte menu.

NOUZONVILLE
Ardennes, 08700

RESTAURANT DE LA PLACE
(Mme Annie Boquillon) 15, place Gambetta
TEL: 03.24.53.80.43
DIRECTIONS: Charleville-Mézières/Nouzonville 7km
MENU: 50 Frs.
ROOMS: 90 to 130 Frs.

RESTAURANT: Snacks from 7.00, lunch 12.00-13.30, dinner 19.30-20.30
CLOSED: Sat afternoon and Sun afternoon.
SPECIALITIES: home-cooking.
HOTEL: 6 rooms.
FACILITIES: shower, bath, private bathroom
OTHER POINTS: credit cards accepted.
Meuse and Semoy valleys; Belgium (10km).

NOVION PORCIEN
Ardennes, 08270

LE FRANCO BELGE
(Mlle Simone Boniface) Place de la Gare
TEL: 03.24.38.70.06
DIRECTIONS: RN985, Rocroi.
MENU: 48 Frs.
RESTAURANT: Snacks from 7.00, lunch 12.00-14.30, dinner 19.00-21.30
CLOSED: Sun morning.
SPECIALITIES: home-cooking,
OTHER POINTS: bar.

OGEVILLER
Meurthe-et-Meuselle, 54450

LE RELAIS DE LA VERDURETTE
(Michel et Lydie Martin) 22, route de Strasbourg
TEL: 03.83.72.24.65
DIRECTIONS: RN4, the Paris/Strasbourg road.
LANGUAGES: German.
MENU: 59 Frs (wine included).
RESTAURANT: Snacks from 8.30
CLOSED: Sat, Sun, and in Aug.
SPECIALITIES: home-cooking.
OTHER POINTS: bar.

ORNANS
Doubs, 25290

LE PROGRES
(Mr Louis Perriot-Comte) 11, rue Jacques Gervais
TEL: 03.81.62.16.79 FAX: 03.81.62.19.10
DIRECTIONS: RD67, between Besanáon and Lausanne.
LANGUAGES: English, German.
MENU: 70 to 160 Frs.
ROOMS: 200 to 280 Frs.
RESTAURANT: Snacks from 7.00, lunch 11.30, dinner 19.00-23.00
CLOSED: Sun evening.
SPECIALITIES: truite, terrine maison, escargots maison, filet de poissons, home-cooking.
HOTEL: ☆ 19 rooms.
FACILITIES: shower, bath, private bathroom, telephone
OTHER POINTS: credit cards accepted.
Loue valley; lakes; national fishing centre at Ornans; Trépot; musée de la fromagerie (cheese-making); musée de la vigne et du vin (wine-making and viticulture); musée Courbet; musée de l'eau et de la pêche (fishing).

PETIT REDERCHING
Moselle, 57410

AUBERGE DE LA FROHMUHL
(Mr Antoine Bach) 33, route de Strasbourg
TEL: 03.87.96.43.52
DIRECTIONS: Bitche.
LANGUAGES: English, German.
MENU: 60 to 130 Frs.
RESTAURANT: Snacks from 7.00, lunch 11.30-14.00, dinner 18.00-22.00
SPECIALITIES: pierrade, pizzas, tartes flambées, home-cooking.
OTHER POINTS: credit cards accepted.
the Maginot line; citadel at Bitche (10km); Fort Casso at Rohrbach; musée du verre et du sabot (glass/clogs).

RESTAURANT DE LA GARE
(Mr Bernard Vogel) 6, rue de Strasbourg
TEL: 03.87.09.81.09
DIRECTIONS: RN62, near the station.
LANGUAGES: German.
MENU: 55 to 90 Frs.
RESTAURANT: Snacks from 6.00, lunch 12.00-14.00, dinner 19.00-20.30
CLOSED: Sat and in July.
SPECIALITIES: estomac de porc farci, tête de veau, backeoffe, choucroute, fresh fish, regional menu, home-cooking.
OTHER POINTS: credit cards accepted.
citadel at Bitche; Maginot line; Roman remains at Bliesbruck; faïencerie (pottery) at Sarreguemines; museum and crystal factory at Meisenthal.

PETIT RUMONT
Meuse, 55000

AUBERGE DES QUATRE CHEMINS
(M Christophe Calais) 4, voie Sacrée
TEL: 03.29.75.02.32
DIRECTIONS: RN 35, RN35, Bar-le-Duc/Verdun/Saint-Mihel.
LANGUAGES: English.
MENU: 65 Frs (drink included).
RESTAURANT: Snacks from 8.00
CLOSED: Wed evening.
SPECIALITIES: home-cooking.
OTHER POINTS: bar.

PLOMBIERES LES BAINS
Vosges, 88370

STRASBOURGEOIS TOURING
(Mr Alain Robert) 3, place Beaumarchais
TEL: 03.29.66.00.70 FAX: 03.29.66.01.06
DIRECTIONS: RN57.
MENU: 78 to 140 Frs.
ROOMS: 110 to 195 Frs.
RESTAURANT: Snacks from 7.00, lunch 12.00-13.30, dinner 19.00-20.30
CLOSED: Sat evening and Sun (from 1st Oct to 30th Apr), and in Dec.
SPECIALITIES: terrine maison, truite à la crème, vacherin (meringue dessert) glacé, regional menu, home-cooking.
HOTEL: ☆☆ 44 rooms.
FACILITIES: shower, bath, private bathroom, television, telephone
OTHER POINTS: credit cards accepted.
thermal resort; private pond (fishing for guests).

POIX TERRON
Ardennes, 08430

LE GODILLOT
(Mr José Michel) 26, place de la Gare
TEL: 03.24.35.61.46
DIRECTIONS: opposite the chemist.
MENU: 58 Frs (drink included).
ROOMS: 90 Frs.
RESTAURANT: Snacks from 6.30, lunch 11.30-14.00, dinner 19.30-21.00
CLOSED: Fri afternoon, Sat, Sun, between Christmas Day and New Year's Day.
SPECIALITIES: couscous, lasagne maison, home-cooking.
HOTEL: 6 rooms.
FACILITIES: bath, private bathroom
OTHER POINTS: credit cards accepted.
Meuse valley (30km); lac de Bairen (15km).

PONT DE ROIDE
Doubs, 25150

LA CLEF D'OR
(Mr Christian Torrente) 37, rue de Besanáon
TEL: 03.81.92.26.24
DIRECTIONS: RD437, the Montbéliard/Pontarlier axis.
LANGUAGES: English, Italian.
MENU: 50 to 60 Frs.
RESTAURANT: Snacks from 7.30
CLOSED: Sun (from 23rd September).
SPECIALITIES: home-cooking.
OTHER POINTS: credit cards accepted.

PREMERY
Nièvre, 58700

LE ROUTIER
(Mr Jean-Jacques Lemarié) 8, route de Lurcy
TEL: 03.86.37.97.59
DIRECTIONS: RD977, between Clamecy and Nevers.
LANGUAGES: English, German.
MENU: 55 Frs.
RESTAURANT: Snacks from 6.00, lunch 12.00-14.30, dinner 19.30-21.00
SPECIALITIES: home-cooking.
HOTEL: 2 rooms.
FACILITIES: shower, bath, private bathroom, television
OTHER POINTS: credit cards accepted.
Le Morvan: museums, château.

PREZ SOUS LAFAUCHE
Haute-Marne, 52700

LES 3 VALLEES
(Mme Eliane Trommenschlager)
TEL: 03.25.31.57.84
DIRECTIONS: the Chaumont/Nancy road.
MENU: 60 to 150 Frs.
RESTAURANT: Open 24h.
CLOSED: Sat evening, Sun evening, and in Aug.
SPECIALITIES: home-cooking.
OTHER POINTS: credit cards accepted.

PROSNES
Marne, 51400

RELAIS CONSTANTINE
(Mr René Roselet) Lieu dit "Constantine" – Route Nationale
TEL: 03.26.61.70.70
DIRECTIONS: RD31, A4 Reims exit, towards Sainte-Menehould.
MENU: 50 to 100 Frs.
ROOMS: 90 to 240 Frs.
RESTAURANT: Snacks from 6.30, lunch 12.00-13.30, dinner 19.00-21.00
CLOSED: Sat, Sun, and last 2 weeks in Aug.
SPECIALITIES: tête de veau, home-cooking.
HOTEL: 3 rooms.
FACILITIES: shower, bath, private bathroom
OTHER POINTS: credit cards accepted.
wine-cellars and champagne vineyards; museum; 1914-18 cemeteries; cathedral at Reims; windmill at Valmy; Faux-de-Verzy.

RACHECOURT SUR MARNE
Haute-Marne, 52170

L'AURORE
(Mr Marius Narat) Avenue de Belgique
TEL: 03.25.04.41.58
DIRECTIONS: RN67, Saint-Dizier/Chaumont.
MENU: 55 to 70 Frs.
ROOMS: 107.50 to 200 Frs.
RESTAURANT: Snacks from 8.30, lunch 12.00-14.00
SPECIALITIES: cabillaud (cod) sauce hollandaise, andouillette, home-cooking.
HOTEL: 4 rooms.
FACILITIES: shower, bath, private bathroom
OTHER POINTS: credit cards accepted.
château at Joinville; lac du Der.

REGUISHEIM
Haut-Rhin, 68890

RESTAURANT A L'ANGE
(Mr Raymond Bertrand) 90 Grand Rue
TEL: 03.89.81.12.66
DIRECTIONS: RD201, Meyenheim.
LANGUAGES: German.
MENU: 40 to 60 Frs.
RESTAURANT: Snacks from 6.00, lunch 12.00-13.30, dinner 19.00-21.30
CLOSED: Sat, Sun, and in Aug.
SPECIALITIES: home-cooking.
HOTEL: 5 rooms
OTHER POINTS: credit cards accepted.

REVIN
Ardennes, 08500

CHEZ ALEX
(Mme Josepha Mahut) 6 Rue Voltaire
TEL: 03.24.40.12.91
DIRECTIONS: RN388.
RESTAURANT: dinner up to 21.00
HOTEL: 4 rooms
OTHER POINTS: bar.

RIOZ
Haute-Saône, 70190

CHEZ SOPHIE ET DIDIER
(Mr Didier Bonfils) Maison Neuve Quenoche
TEL: 03.84.91.80.54
DIRECTIONS: RN57, between Vesoul and Besanáon.
LANGUAGES: English, German.
MENU: 55 Frs (wine included).
ROOMS: 190 Frs.
RESTAURANT: Snacks from 6.00, lunch 12.00-14.00, dinner 19.00-21.30
CLOSED: Sun.
SPECIALITIES: regional menu, home-cooking.
HOTEL: 9 rooms
OTHER POINTS: credit cards accepted.
Rioz: lake; medieval village of Fondermand.

RIVIERES DE CORPS (LA)
Aube, 10300

LA QUEUE DE LA POELE
(Mme Gaby Barbier) Rue Lafontaine
TEL: 03.25.74.47.94 FAX: 03.25.49.84.01
DIRECTIONS: RN60, Sens.
MENU: 60 to 120 Frs.
RESTAURANT: Snacks from 6.30, lunch 11.30-14.30, dinner 19.00-22.00
CLOSED: Sun evening, and 3 weeks in Aug.
SPECIALITIES: andouillette de Troyes, regional menu, home-cooking.
OTHER POINTS: credit cards accepted.
Troyes: cathedral, maison de l'outil (tools), old quarters; forêt d'Orient and de Dienville; Nigloland leisure park.

ROCHE VINEUSE (LA)
Saône-et-Loire, 71960

RELAIS ROUTIERS – Chez France
(Mme Patricia Randier) Place du Chaucher
TEL: 03.85.37.71.51
DIRECTIONS: RN79, between Mâcon and Charolles, via the tourist route.
LANGUAGES: English.
MENU: 60 Frs.
RESTAURANT: Snacks from 6.00, lunch 11.30-14.30, dinner 19.00-22.00
CLOSED: Sat and Sun afternoon.
SPECIALITIES: regional menu, home-cooking.
OTHER POINTS: credit cards accepted.
Roche de Solutré; prehistoric sites; château; Cluny: abbey and stud-farm (haras).

RONCHAMP
Haute-Saône, 70250

A LA POMME D'OR
(Mme Lucette Cenci) Rue le Corbusier
TEL: 03.84.20.62.12 FAX: 03.84.63.59.45
DIRECTIONS: RN19, between Belfort and Vesoul.
LANGUAGES: English, German, Italian.
MENU: 50 to 200 Frs.
ROOMS: 130 to 230 Frs.
RESTAURANT: Snacks from 6.00, lunch 12.00-14.30, dinner 19.00-22.30
SPECIALITIES: regional menu, home-cooking.
HOTEL: ☆☆ 35 rooms.

FACILITIES: shower, bath, private bathroom, television, telephone
OTHER POINTS: credit cards accepted.
Le Corbusier chapel; musée de la mine (mining); pools (étangs).

ROSOY
Yonne, 89100

LA MAISON BLANCHE
(Mme Martine Boire) 31, route Nationale 6
TEL: 03.86.97.14.52
DIRECTIONS: RN6.
MENU: 55 to 98 Frs.
RESTAURANT: Snacks from 6.00, lunch 11.45-14.00, dinner 19.00-22.00
CLOSED: Sun evening.
SPECIALITIES: moules à la chablisienne, couscous, rognons de boeuf maison, home-cooking.
HOTEL: 5 rooms.
FACILITIES: shower
OTHER POINTS: credit cards accepted.
Sens: cathedral; museum; windmill/garden at Tan.

RUPT SUR MOSELLE
Vosges, 88360

L'ETAPE
(Mme Catherine Lemonnier) Les Meix
TEL: 03.29.24.35.17
DIRECTIONS: RN 66, RN66, between Epinal and Mulhouse.
LANGUAGES: German.
MENU: 60 Frs (wine and coffee included).
RESTAURANT: Snacks from 6.30, lunch 12.00-14.00, dinner 19.00-20.30
CLOSED: Wed and Sun afternoon.
SPECIALITIES: home-cooking.
OTHER POINTS: credit cards accepted.

RYE
Jura, 39230

CHEZ LUCETTE
(Mme Lucette Cambazard)
TEL: 03.84.48.61.60
DIRECTIONS: RD468, between Dijon and Lons-le-Saunier.
RESTAURANT: Snacks from 6.30, lunch 11.00-14.00
CLOSED: Thurs afternoon, first 2 weeks in Aug and 20th Dec to 2nd Jan.
SPECIALITIES: regional menu, home-cooking.
OTHER POINTS: credit cards accepted.
vineyards; Jura countryside; château.

SAINT AUBIN SUR LOIRE
Saône-et-Loire, 71140

RESTAURANT DE L'AMITIE
(SNC Maison-Gaumard) Le Bourg
TEL: 03.85.53.91.09
DIRECTIONS: RD979, between Mâcon and Nevers.
MENU: 55 to 105 Frs.
RESTAURANT: Snacks from 7.00, lunch 11.30-14.00, dinner 19.00-21.30
CLOSED: Mon afternoon, and 1 week at Christmas.
SPECIALITIES: tripes, coq au vin, home-cooking.
OTHER POINTS: bar.
'le Vieux Bourbon', wine-cellars.

SAINT DENIS LES SENS
Yonne, 89100

LES CERISIERS
(Mr Michel Ferrière) 1, rue de Paris
TEL: 03.86.65.28.52
DIRECTIONS: RN360: A6, Sens exit.
LANGUAGES: English.
MENU: 66 Frs.
RESTAURANT: Snacks from 7.00, lunch 11.00-14.00, dinner 19.00-21.00
CLOSED: weekends (except bookings minimum of 30 people), and in Aug.
SPECIALITIES: home-cooking.
OTHER POINTS: credit cards accepted.
Sens: cathedral, museums and gardens.

SAINT DIE
Vosges, 88100

LA CROISETTE
(Mr Bernard Roumier) 41, avenue de Verdun
TEL: 03.29.56.14.37
DIRECTIONS: RN59.
MENU: 58 Frs.
RESTAURANT: Snacks from 8.00, dinner up to 22.00
CLOSED: for the New Year.
SPECIALITIES: couscous (Sat), Vosges regional meal (Sun), home-cooking.
OTHER POINTS: credit cards accepted.

SAINT DIZIER
Haute-Marne, 52100

LE MOLIERE
(Mr Gérard Delaporte) 10, rue Molière
TEL: 03.25.56.63.05
DIRECTIONS: 400 metres from the RN4.
MENU: 65.50 Frs (drink and coffee included).
RESTAURANT: Snacks from 7.00, lunch 11.30-14.00, dinner 18.30-21.30

CLOSED: From Sat 15.00 to Mon 8.30.
SPECIALITIES: moules/frites, couscous, paella, choucroute, regional menu, home-cooking.
OTHER POINTS: credit cards accepted.
lac du Der.

SAINT EUSEBE
Saône-et-Loire, 71120

LE PONT DES MORANDS
(Mme Joëlle Martin) Pont des Morands
TEL: 03.85.78.46.45
DIRECTIONS: Le Creusot/Paray-le-Monial expressway.
MENU: 60 Frs.
ROOMS: 85 Frs.
RESTAURANT: Snacks from 5.30, lunch 11.45-14.30, dinner 19.30-22.00
CLOSED: Sat.
SPECIALITIES: home-cooking.
HOTEL: 9 rooms
OTHER POINTS: credit cards accepted.
Musée de la mine (mining) at Blanzy; étang (pond) Berthaud.

SAINT HIPPOLYTE
Doubs, 25190

LE GRAND CLOS
(Mme Martine Lepême)
TEL: 03.81.96.51.12
DIRECTIONS: RN437, Belfort/Pontarlier/Besanáon.
LANGUAGES: German.
MENU: 60 to 90 Frs.
ROOMS: 130 to 160 Frs.
RESTAURANT: Snacks from 6.00, lunch 11.00-14.00, dinner 18.00-22.00
CLOSED: Sat (out of season).
SPECIALITIES: jambon de montagne, regional menu, home-cooking.
HOTEL: 6 rooms.
FACILITIES: shower, bath, private bathroom
OTHER POINTS: credit cards accepted.
château; saut (falls) du Doubs, caves.

SAINT LOUP DE VARENNES
Saône-et-Loire, 71240

LA PETITE AUBERGE
(Mme Sonia Gaudillat) Route Nationale 6
TEL: 03.85.44.21.87
DIRECTIONS: RN6, the Chalon/Mâcon road.
MENU: 62 Frs.
RESTAURANT: Snacks from 6.30, lunch 9.00-15.00, dinner 18.00-21.30
CLOSED: Sun, and in Dec.
SPECIALITIES: home-cooking.
OTHER POINTS: credit cards accepted.
lakes at Loives; musée de la photographie.

SAINT LOUP SUR SEMOUSE
Haute-Saône, 70800

HOTEL DE LA TERRASSE
(Mr Jean Ballot) Rue de la Gare
TEL: 03.84.49.02.20
DIRECTIONS: RN64.
HOTEL: 4 rooms
OTHER POINTS: bar.

SAINT MIHIEL
Meuse, 55300

LE RELAIS DES ROUTIERS
(Mr Philippe Carbillet) 19, rue de Verdun
TEL: 03.29.89.00.44
DIRECTIONS: RD964, Verdun.
LANGUAGES: English.
MENU: 55 Frs.
ROOMS: 110 to 160 Frs.
RESTAURANT: Snacks from 7.30, lunch 12.00-14.30, dinner 19.00-21.30
CLOSED: Sat and Sun.
SPECIALITIES: couscous, regional menu, home-cooking.
HOTEL: 8 rooms.
FACILITIES: shower, bath, private bathroom
OTHER POINTS: credit cards accepted.
lac de Madine; Meuse region; Verdun.

SAINT PHAL
Aube, 10130

RESTAURANT DU COMMERCE
(Mr Daniel Godefroy) 16, rue des Cafés
TEL: 03.25.42.16.39 **FAX:** 03.25.42.14.65
DIRECTIONS: RN77, the Auxerre/Troyes road.
LANGUAGES: German.
MENU: 58 to 145 Frs.
RESTAURANT: Snacks from 8.00, lunch 11.00-13.30, dinner 19.00-20.45
CLOSED: Mon afternoon, and in Aug.
SPECIALITIES: ris de veau, terrines maison, regional menu.
OTHER POINTS: credit cards accepted.
forêt d'Othe; lake and forêt d'Orient; forêt de Troyes.

SAINT PIERRE LE MOUTIER
Nièvre, 58240

RELAIS SAINT IMBERT
(Mlle Pia Fressle) Route Nationale 7 – Saint Imbert
TEL: 03.86.38.61.65
DIRECTIONS: RN7, between Nevers and Moulins.
LANGUAGES: English, German.
MENU: 28 to 120 Frs.
RESTAURANT: Snacks from 5.00, lunch 12.00-14.30,

dinner 19.00-22.30
CLOSED: Sat and Sun.
SPECIALITIES: choucroute, potée, boeuf stroganoff, poissons, roti de porc à la bière, regional menu, home-cooking.
OTHER POINTS: credit cards accepted.
Boleine arboretum; châteaux.

SAINT PIERREMONT
Vosges, 88700

LE RELAIS VOSGIEN
(Mme Christiane Thénot-Prévost)
TEL: 03.29.65.02.46 **FAX:** 03.29.65.02.83
DIRECTIONS: RD414, between Luneville and Rambervillers.
LANGUAGES: German, Polish.
MENU: 65 to 220 Frs.
ROOMS: 180 to 330 Frs.
RESTAURANT: Snacks from 7.00, lunch 12.00-13.30, dinner 19.00-21.00
CLOSED: Sat morning, and last 2 weeks in Dec.
SPECIALITIES: home-cooking.
HOTEL: ☆☆ 17 rooms.
FACILITIES: shower, bath, private bathroom, television, telephone
OTHER POINTS: credit cards accepted.
Lunéville ('le petit Versailles'); Baccarat crystalworks; springs and ponds.

SAINT SAUVEUR
Haute-Saône, 70300

CHEZ MAXIM
(Mr Joël Lack) 10, avenue Georges Clémenceau
TEL: 03.84.40.02.91 **FAX:** 03.84.93.65.45
DIRECTIONS: RN57, between Nancy and Besanáon.
LANGUAGES: German.
MENU: 52 Frs.
ROOMS: 90 to 130 Frs.
RESTAURANT: Snacks from 6.30, lunch 11.30-14.30, dinner 19.00-22.30
CLOSED: Sun evening, and in Feb.
SPECIALITIES: jambon de Luxeuil, kirsch de Fougerolies, cancoillotte (goat's cheese), regional menu, home-cooking.
HOTEL: 5 rooms.
FACILITIES: shower, bath, private bathroom
OTHER POINTS: credit cards accepted.
Luxeuil: basilica, maison du cardinal, tour des Echevins, tour du Bailly; kirsch distilleries at Fougerolles; glass-works (verrerie) at La Rochère; hermitage de Saint-Valbert.

SAINTE MARGUERITE
Vosges, 88100

LE RELAIS DES AMIS
(Mme Josiane Bonhomme) 486, rue d'Alsace
TEL: 03.29.56.17.23
DIRECTIONS: RN59, the road to the Sainte-Marie-Mines tunnel.
ROOMS: 100 to 160 Frs.
RESTAURANT: Snacks from 7.00, lunch 12.00-14.00, dinner 19.00-21.00
CLOSED: Sat, Sun.
SPECIALITIES: backeoffe and other regional dishes, home-cooking.
HOTEL: ☆ 16 rooms.
FACILITIES: shower
OTHER POINTS: bar.
Alsace region 20 minutes away.

SALINS LES BAINS
Jura, 39110

BAR RESTAURANT DES SPORTS
(Mme Liliane Vacelet) 107, avenue de la République
TEL: 03.84.73.11.18
MENU: 32 to 65 Frs.
RESTAURANT: Snacks from 6.00, lunch 11.00-14.00, dinner 18.00-21.00
CLOSED: Sun.
SPECIALITIES: fondue savoyarde, truite aux amandes, regional menu, home-cooking.
OTHER POINTS: bar.
casino; museum; church.

SARREGUEMINES
Moselle, 57200

HOTEL RESTAURANT RELAIS ROUTIERS
(Mr Camille Fasel) 19, rue du Bac
TEL: 03.87.98.15.39
DIRECTIONS: Bitche or Forbach-St-Avold.
LANGUAGES: German.
MENU: 38 to 60 Frs.
ROOMS: 80 to 120 Frs.
RESTAURANT: Snacks from 5.00, lunch 12.00-14.00, dinner 19.00-21.00
CLOSED: Sat afternoon, Sun, and 1 week in Aug.
SPECIALITIES: choucroute garnie, home-cooking.
HOTEL: 11 rooms.
FACILITIES: shower, bath, private bathroom
OTHER POINTS: bar.
pottery (faïencerie); Bliesbruck: archeological site; citadelle at Bitche; parc régional des Vosges du Nord.

SAULIEU
Côte-d'Or, 21210

AUX POIDS LOURDS
(Mme Michèle Godet) 12, rue Courtépée
TEL: 03.80.64.19.83 FAX: 02.80.64.19.83
DIRECTIONS: RN6, Lyon.
MENU: 57 Frs.
ROOMS: 75 to 105 Frs.
RESTAURANT: Snacks from 8.00, lunch 12.00-14.00
CLOSED: Sat, Sun, and in Aug.
SPECIALITIES: home-cooking.
HOTEL: 6 rooms.
FACILITIES: shower
OTHER POINTS: credit cards accepted.
museum; basilica; lakes.

SEDAN
Ardennes, 08200

CHEZ LOULOUTE
(Mme Thérèse Varloteaux) 56, avenue de la Marne
TEL: 03.24.27.16.62
DIRECTIONS: RN43, Charleville-Mézières.
MENU: 53 Frs (wine included).
ROOMS: 170 to 200 Frs.
RESTAURANT: Snacks from 5.30
SPECIALITIES: home-cooking.
HOTEL: 3 rooms
OTHER POINTS: credit cards accepted.
château-fort (fortified castle); musée de l'aviation; musée du feutre (felt); Maginot line.

SELTZ
Bas-Rhin, 67470

A L'HOMME SAUVAGE
(Mr Philippe Hoerd) 40, rue principale
TEL: 02.88.86.50.60
DIRECTIONS: the Strasbourg/Frankfurt road.
LANGUAGES: German.
MENU: 60 Frs (wine included).
ROOMS: 110 to 160 Frs.
RESTAURANT: Snacks from 6.00, lunch 11.00, dinner up to 23.00
CLOSED: Sat until 15.00
SPECIALITIES: regional menu, home-cooking.
HOTEL: 7 rooms
OTHER POINTS: bar.
Maginot line; Germany.

SENAN
Yonne, 89710

LA CROIX BLANCHE
(Mr Pascal Plessis) 16, rue d'Aillant
TEL: 03.86.63.41.31
DIRECTIONS: RD955.
LANGUAGES: English.
MENU: 55 Frs (wine included) to 75 Frs.
ROOMS: 90 to 150 Frs.
RESTAURANT: Snacks from 6.30, lunch 11.30-14.30, dinner 19.00-23.00
CLOSED: Sun evening.
SPECIALITIES: regional menu, home-cooking,
HOTEL: 6 rooms
OTHER POINTS: credit cards accepted.

SENNECEY-LE-GRAND
Saône-et-Loire, 71240

L'ARCHE DE CHALON SAINT AMBREUIL
(Mr Bruno Brenez) A6 – Aire de Saint Ambreuil – Accessible sens Lyon/Paris
TEL: 85.44.20.64 FAX: 85.44.13.12
RESTAURANT: Open 24h.
OTHER POINTS: credit cards accepted.

SOMMESSOUS
Marne, 51320

LE MIRABELLIER
(SARL SG2R) A26 – Aire de Service de Sommessous Axe Chalons/Troyes
TEL: 03.26.70.17.04 FAX: 03.26.70.42.10
MENU: 64 Frs.
RESTAURANT: Snacks from 6.00, lunch 10.00, dinner up to 23.00
SPECIALITIES: home-cooking.
OTHER POINTS: credit cards accepted.

STENAY
Meuse, 55700

BAR DES SANGLIERS – La Mangeoire
(Mr Daniel Demacon) 1, rue Carnot
TEL: 03.29.80.60.06 FAX: 03.29.80.33.99
DIRECTIONS: RD947, Reims road.
LANGUAGES: German.
MENU: 60 to 150 Frs.
ROOMS: 120 to 150 Frs.
RESTAURANT: Snacks from 6.30, lunch 11.30-14.00, dinner 19.30-21.00
CLOSED: Sat, and in Aug.
SPECIALITIES: home-cooking.
HOTEL: 4 rooms.
FACILITIES: shower, bath, private bathroom
OTHER POINTS: credit cards accepted.
Musée de la bière (beer).

SUBLIGNY
Yonne, 89100

LE RELAIS DE SUBLIGNY
(Mr Jean-Pierre Closier) 17, route de Courtenay
TEL: 03.86.88.83.22

DIRECTIONS: RN60, between Troyes and Orléans.
MENU: 60 Frs (wine included).
RESTAURANT: Snacks from 6.30, lunch 11.30-14.30, dinner 18.30-22.00
CLOSED: Sun evening and Mon.
SPECIALITIES: Burgundian dishes, regional menu, home-cooking.
OTHER POINTS: credit cards accepted.

TIL CHATEL
Côte-d'Or, 21120

LE RELAIS DES PEUPLIERS
(Maleck Ezzedine) Route Nationale 74
TEL: 03.80.95.20.14 **FAX:** 03.80.95.38.11
DIRECTIONS: RN74, the Dijon/Langres road.
MENU: 60 Frs (wine and coffee included).
RESTAURANT: Snacks from 7.00, lunch 11.30-14.30, dinner 18.30-22.00
CLOSED: Sun.
SPECIALITIES: home-cooking.
OTHER POINTS: credit cards accepted.
Til-Chatel; caves at Bèze.

TORCY
Saône-et-Loire, 71210

LA SPIAGGIA
(Mr Salvatore Lotito) Route Expresse – Montchanin
TEL: 03.85.55.35.45
DIRECTIONS: RN80
LANGUAGES: English, Italian.
MENU: 60 Frs.
RESTAURANT: Snacks from 7.00, lunch 12.00-14.00, dinner 19.00-23.00
SPECIALITIES: Italian dishes.
OTHER POINTS: credit cards accepted.

TOUR DU MEIX (LA)
Jura, 39270

AUBERGE DU PONT DE LA PYLE
(Mr Jacques Berger) Route Nationale 470
TEL: 03.84.25.41.92 **FAX:** 03.84.25.42.16
DIRECTIONS: RN470, between Lons-le-Saunier and Saint-Claude, via Orgelet.
MENU: 60 to 180 Frs.
RESTAURANT: Snacks from 8.00, lunch 12.00-15.00, dinner 19.00-22.00
CLOSED: Wed (1st Nov till 15th June) and in Oct.
SPECIALITIES: filets de perches au beurre, cuisses de grenouilles, home-cooking.
OTHER POINTS: credit cards accepted.
lake at Vouglans; waterfalls at Le Hérisson; caves at Osselles and Moidon; dam at Vouglans; musée du jouet (toys).

TREMBLOIS LES ROCROI
Ardennes, 08150

RELAIS ROUTIERS DU PIQUET
(Mr Gérard Clérice) Le Piquet
TEL: 03.24.35.13.86
DIRECTIONS: RN43, Charleville-Mézières/Lille road.
LANGUAGES: Spanish, Portuguese.
MENU: 56 Frs.
RESTAURANT: Snacks from 6.00, lunch 11.30-14.30, dinner 19.00-21.00
CLOSED: Sat, Sun, and in Aug.
SPECIALITIES: home-cooking.
OTHER POINTS: credit cards accepted.
Meuse valley; Vieilles-Forges lake; Rocroi.

TRONSANGES
Nièvre, 58400

L'AUBERGE DU SOLEIL LEVANT
(Mr Jacky Vacher) Route Nationale 7
TEL: 03.86.37.84.02
DIRECTIONS: RN7, La Charité sur Loire.
LANGUAGES: English, Spanish, Italian.
MENU: 60 Frs (drink and coffee included).
RESTAURANT: Snacks from 7.30, lunch 11.30-15.00, dinner 19.00-22.30
SPECIALITIES: home-cooking.
OTHER POINTS: credit cards accepted.

SARL DE LA CROIX DU PAPE – Chez l'Auvergnat
(Mme Agnès Dumaine) Barbeloup
TEL: 03.86.37.84.03
DIRECTIONS: RN7, Nevers.
MENU: 57.50 to 100 Frs.
ROOMS: 120 to 136 Frs.
RESTAURANT: Snacks from 5.00
HOTEL: 6 rooms.
FACILITIES: shower, bath, private bathroom
OTHER POINTS: credit cards accepted.
La Charité-sur-Loire; Vaux; the Loire.

TROYES
Aube, 10000

HOTEL LE SPLENDID
(Mr Dominique Gilles) 44, boulevard Carnot (proximité gare)
TEL: 03.25.73.08.52 **FAX:** 03.25.73.41.04
ROOMS: 135 to 240 Frs.
HOTEL: ☆☆ 16 rooms

UCKANGE
Moselle, 57270

LE PRESSOIR
(Mr Silvio Piccin) 22 rue Jeanne d'Arc
TEL: 03.82.86.25.44
DIRECTIONS: RD952.
MENU: 56 Frs
RESTAURANT: Snacks from 5.30
CLOSED: Sat, Sun, in Aug and 2 weeks from Christmas Day.
SPECIALITIES: regional menu,
OTHER POINTS: bar.

UNIENVILLE
Aube, 10140

CHEZ CHRISTIANE ET MARCEL
(Mme Christiane Saget)
TEL: 03.25.92.70.80
MENU: 50 Frs (drink and coffee included).
RESTAURANT: Snacks from 7.30, lunch 11.30-13.30, dinner 19.00-20.00
SPECIALITIES: home-cooking.
OTHER POINTS: bar.

VANDOEUVRE
Meurthe-et-Meuselle, 54500

LE PERIGORD
(Mme Mari-Sol Lefèbvre) Rue Jean Mermoz
TEL: 03.83.56.77.38 FAX: 03.83.53.35.56
DIRECTIONS: Marché-de-Gros.
LANGUAGES: Spanish.
MENU: 59 to 250 Frs.
RESTAURANT: Snacks from 8.00, lunch 11.00
SPECIALITIES: regional menu, home-cooking, confits, foie gras.
OTHER POINTS: credit cards accepted.

VARENNES LE GRAND
Saône-et-Loire, 71240

HOTEL RESTAURANT DU COMMERCE
(Mr Bertrand Chavanis – SARL Fidem) Route Nationale 6
TEL: 03.85.44.22.34
DIRECTIONS: RN6, between Chalon-sur-Saône and Lyon.
LANGUAGES: English.
MENU: 60 Frs (wine and coffee included) to 80 Frs.
RESTAURANT: Snacks from 5.00
SPECIALITIES: regional menu, home-cooking.
OTHER POINTS: credit cards accepted.
Chalon; Tournus; Cluny.

VARENNES LES MACON
Saône-et-Loire, 71000

LA HALTE DES ROUTIERS
(Mr René Massonneau) Route Nationale 6
TEL: 03.85.34.70.44 FAX: 03.85.29.29.03
DIRECTIONS: RN6, exit at Mâcon Sud (south).
ROOMS: 100 to 150 Frs.
RESTAURANT: Snacks from 5.30
CLOSED: Sat from 10.00, Sun, and last 2 weeks in Aug.
HOTEL: 24 rooms
OTHER POINTS: credit cards accepted.
Roche-de-Solutré.

VERDUN
Meuse, 55100

A LA BONNE AUBERGE
(Mme Yolande Gaïotti-Morano) 11 avenue Garibaldi
TEL: 03.29.86.05.16
DIRECTIONS: RN3, near railway station (SNCF).
LANGUAGES: English, German.
MENU: 49.90 to 75 Frs.
ROOMS: 65 to 91 Frs.
RESTAURANT: Snacks from 5.30, dinner up to 24.00
SPECIALITIES: home-cooking.
HOTEL: 7 rooms
OTHER POINTS: bar.
battlefields.

BAR DU COMMERCE
(Mme Marie-Odile Vincent) Route Nationale 3 – Eix Abaucourt
TEL: 03.29.88.31.94 FAX: 03.29.88.37.16
DIRECTIONS: RN3, Luxembourg/Metz/Longwy.
LANGUAGES: English.
MENU: 55 to 65 Frs.
RESTAURANT: Snacks from 5.00
CLOSED: Sun evening.
SPECIALITIES: escalope à la crème, home-cooking.
OTHER POINTS: credit cards accepted.
battlefield at Verdun; cemetery at Douaumont; Fort de Vaux; 1914-78 war sites; Maginot line.

L'ARCHE DE VERDUN SAINT NICOLAS
(Mr Vincent Gérard) A4 – Aire de Saint-Nicolas – Accessible dans les deux sens
TEL: 03.29.86.41.18 FAX: 03.29.86.64.65
RESTAURANT: Open 24h.
OTHER POINTS: credit cards accepted.

VILLENEUVE AU CHEMIN
Aube, 10130

LE PETIT SAINT JEAN
(Mr Nafaa Nait Mohand) 19, route Nationale 77
TEL: 03.25.42.10.51
DIRECTIONS: RN77, between Troyes and Auxerre.
LANGUAGES: Arabic.
MENU: 58 Frs.
RESTAURANT: Snacks from 8.00, lunch 11.00, dinner up to 23.00
SPECIALITIES: couscous, home-cooking.
OTHER POINTS: credit cards accepted.

VILLEVALLIER
Yonne, 89330

RELAIS 89
(Mme Yvette Petit) 9, rue de la République
TEL: 03.86.91.11.17
DIRECTIONS: RN89, between Joigny and Sens.
MENU: 58 Frs.
ROOMS: 85 to 140 Frs.
RESTAURANT: Snacks from 6.00
CLOSED: Sat, Sun.
SPECIALITIES: home-cooking.
HOTEL: 6 rooms.
FACILITIES: shower, bath, private bathroom
OTHER POINTS: credit cards accepted.
Yonne valley.

VILLOTTE SUR AIRE
Meuse, 55260

LE BRULOT
(Mr Daniel Jeandinot) 35, rue de Mont
TEL: 03.29.75.04.36
DIRECTIONS: RD901, RD901, between Bar-le-Duc and Metz.
LANGUAGES: Dutch.
MENU: 58 to 130 Frs.
ROOMS: 90 to 140 Frs.
RESTAURANT: Snacks from 8.00, lunch 12.00-14.00, dinner 19.00-21.00
CLOSED: Sat and Sun evening.
SPECIALITIES: home-cooking, tête de veau, mirabelle flambée, cervelle d'agneau aux capres.
HOTEL: 5 rooms
OTHER POINTS: credit cards accepted.

VITRY EN CHAROLLAIS
Saône-et-Loire, 71600

TOM BAR
(Mme Ginette Collin) Route Nationale 79
TEL: 03.85.81.02.85
DIRECTIONS: between Paray-le-Monial and Digoin.
LANGUAGES: Spanish.
MENU: 50 to 100 Frs.
RESTAURANT: Snacks from 5.00, lunch 11.30-14.30, dinner 19.00-22.30
CLOSED: Sun.
SPECIALITIES: home-cooking, Italian dishes, regional menu.
OTHER POINTS: credit cards accepted.
basilica at Paray-le-Monial (4km); aqueduct at Digoin (4km).

VITTEAUX
Côte-d'Or, 21350

RELAIS DE LA ROUTE BLANCHE
(Mr Roger Le Gall) Rue de Verdun
TEL: 03.80.49.60.13
DIRECTIONS: RN5, Dijon.
MENU: 60 Frs (drink included).
RESTAURANT: Snacks from 7.00, lunch 12.00-14.30, dinner 19.00-21.00
CLOSED: Sun, and from mid-Aug to mid-September.
SPECIALITIES: boeuf bourguignon, jambon persillé, home-cooking.
OTHER POINTS: credit cards accepted.
Dijon; Semur-en-Auxois; Alésia.

VITTONVILLE
Meurthe-et-Meuselle, 54700

L'AIGLE D'OR
(Eliane et Eric Lanzi) Route Nationale 57 – Pont à Mousson
TEL: 03.83.81.04.08
DIRECTIONS: RN57, between Metz and Nancy.
LANGUAGES: Italian, Dutch.
MENU: 65 Frs.
RESTAURANT: Snacks from 6.00, lunch 11.30-13.30, dinner 19.00-22.30
CLOSED: Sat and Sun.
SPECIALITIES: home-cooking.
OTHER POINTS: bar.
Buttes-de-Mousson: historic château; lac de Madine.

WASSELONNE
Bas-Rhin, 67310

AU ROCHER
(Mr André Hecker) 18, route de Strasbourg
TEL: 03.88.87.06.72
DIRECTIONS: RN4, between Saverne and Strasbourg.
LANGUAGES: English, German.
MENU: 60 to 100 Frs.
ROOMS: 130 to 250 Frs.
RESTAURANT: Snacks from 6.30, lunch 11.30-14.30, dinner 19.00-21.00
SPECIALITIES: choucroute paysanne, cuisses de grenouilles à la provenáale, boeuf bourguignon,

home-cooking.
HOTEL: 8 rooms.
FACILITIES: shower, bath, private bathroom
OTHER POINTS: credit cards accepted.
Haut-Koenigsbourg: château; Strasbourg: cathedral; Mont-Saint-Odile; Saveme.

WITTELSHEIM
Haut-Rhin, 68310

HOTEL DES VOSGES
(Mr Doris Riedle) 137, rue de Reiningue
TEL: 03.89.55.10.20
DIRECTIONS: RN83, between Mulhouse and Thann.
LANGUAGES: German, Italian.
MENU: 60 to 130 Frs.
ROOMS: 130 to 170 Frs.
RESTAURANT: Snacks from 5.00, lunch 12.00-14.00, dinner 19.00-21.00
CLOSED: Sun.
SPECIALITIES: choucroute, carpes, regional menu, home-cooking.
HOTEL: 13 rooms.
FACILITIES: shower, bath, private bathroom, telephone
OTHER POINTS: credit cards accepted.
miner's house; musée de l'automobile et du chemin de fer (cars and railways).

WOIPPY
Moselle, 57140

CHARDON LORRAIN
(Mme Franáoise De Cecco) 58, rue de Metz
TEL: 03.87.30.46.61 FAX: 03.87.32.67.68
LANGUAGES: German.
MENU: 57 Frs.
ROOMS: 110 to 130 Frs.
RESTAURANT: Snacks from 5.00, lunch 11.30-14.30, dinner 19.00-20.00
CLOSED: Wed afternoon, and 20th Dec to 5th Jan.
SPECIALITIES: choucroute, home-cooking.
HOTEL: 3 rooms.
FACILITIES: shower, bath, private bathroom
OTHER POINTS: credit cards accepted.
Metz; Saint-Quentin; pool (étang).

XONRUPT
Vosges, 88400

LES CASCADES
(Mme Dany Godart) Route du Saut des Cuves
TEL: 02.29.63.31.88 FAX: 02.29.63.18.31
DIRECTIONS: D417.
LANGUAGES: German.
MENU: 50 Frs.
RESTAURANT: Snacks from 7.00, lunch 11.30-14.30, dinner 18.30-21.00
SPECIALITIES: choucroute, couscous, home-cooking.
HOTEL: 16 rooms.
FACILITIES: shower, bath, private bathroom, television
OTHER POINTS: credit cards accepted.
Route des vins (the wine road).

XONRUPT LONGEMER
Vosges, 88400

LA PIERRE CHARLEMAGNE - Chez Dédé
(Mr André Caël) Le Saut des Cuves
TEL: 03.29.63.03.86
LANGUAGES: English, German.
MENU: 55 to 80 Frs.
ROOMS: 130 to 180 Frs.
RESTAURANT: Snacks from 9.00, lunch 12.00-14.30, dinner 19.00-22.00
CLOSED: Mon, last 2 weeks in June and Oct.
SPECIALITIES: choucroute, quiche, truite meunière, regional menu, home-cooking.
HOTEL: 8 rooms.
FACILITIES: shower, bath, private bathroom, telephone
OTHER POINTS: credit cards accepted.

North-West France

The following départments are included in this chapter:

Calvados (14)
Côtes-d'Amor (22)
Eure (27)
Finistère (29)
Ille-de-Vilaine (35)
Loire-Atlantique (44)
Maine-et-Loire (49)
Manche (50)
Mayenne (53)
Morbihan (56)
Orne (61)
Sarthe (72)
Seine-Maritime (76)
Vendée (85)

AIGUILLON SUR VIE (L')
Vendée, 85220

RELAIS LA GREVE
(Mr Jean-Pierre Alfonsi) 5, rue des Sables
TEL: 02.51.22.86.23
DIRECTIONS: between Challans and Les Sables d'Olonne.
LANGUAGES: English.
MENU: 50 Frs (wine included) to 70 Frs.
RESTAURANT: Snacks from 7.30, lunch 11.30-14.30, dinner 19.00-21.30
CLOSED: Sun.
SPECIALITIES: home-cooking.
OTHER POINTS: credit cards accepted.
Les Sables d'Olonne (20km); Challans (22km).

AIZENAY
Vendée, 85190

LE SAINT BENOIST
(Mr Frédéric Bastide) 35, rue du Maréchal Leclerc
TEL: 02.51.94.60.17 FAX: 02.51.48.30.91
DIRECTIONS: RD948, between La Rochelle and Saint-Nazaire.
LANGUAGES: English.
MENU: 47 to 170 Frs.
ROOMS: 110 to 160 Frs.
RESTAURANT: Snacks from 6.30, lunch 12.00-14.00, dinner 19.00-21.00
SPECIALITIES: home-cooking.
HOTEL: ☆ 21 rooms.
FACILITIES: shower, bath, private bathroom, television, telephone
OTHER POINTS: credit cards accepted.
La Roche-sur-Yon; Les Sables d'Olonne.

AMBENAY
Eure, 27250

HOTEL DE LA RISLE
(Mr Jean-Louis Marcilly) 9, rue Guy Lacombe
TEL: 02.32.24.63.45
DIRECTIONS: RD830, Rugles.
MENU: 52 Frs.
ROOMS: 100 to 150 Frs.
RESTAURANT: Snacks from 6.00, lunch 12.00-14.00, dinner 19.30-21.30
CLOSED: Sun.
SPECIALITIES: home-cooking.
HOTEL: 6 rooms.
FACILITIES: shower
OTHER POINTS: credit cards accepted.

AMBRUMESNIL
Seine-Maritime, 76550

LE TORTILLARD
(Mme Gilberte Dolbec) Hameau Ribeuf
TEL: 02.35.83.17.00
DIRECTIONS: RD152.
MENU: 50 Frs.
SPECIALITIES: cassoulet, couscous, home-cooking.
OTHER POINTS: bar.
le manoir d'Ango.

ANETZ
Loire-Atlantique, 44150

LE RELAIS DE LA BARBINIERE
(Mme Sylvie Dronet) Route Nationale 23 – La Barbinière
TEL: 02.40.83.11.25
DIRECTIONS: RN23, the Nantes/Angers road.
MENU: 50 Frs.
ROOMS: 160 Frs.
RESTAURANT: Snacks from 6.00, lunch 11.30-14.00, dinner 19.30-21.30
CLOSED: Sat, Sun, 1 week in Aug, 1 week at Christmas.
SPECIALITIES: home-cooking.
HOTEL: 4 rooms.
FACILITIES: shower, bath, private bathroom, television, telephone
OTHER POINTS: credit cards accepted.
Saint-Florent-le-Vieil: church, observatory.

ANGERS
Maine-et-Loire, 49100

LA HAUTE CHAINE
(Mr Jean-Claude Derouet)
7, boulevard Ayrault – Place Saint Serge
TEL: 02.41.43.88.99
DIRECTIONS: the Paris/Nantes road, Saint-Serge exit.
LANGUAGES: English.
MENU: 58.50 Frs (wine included) to 78 Frs.
ROOMS: 120 to 160 Frs.
RESTAURANT: Snacks from 5.00, lunch 11.30-14.30, dinner 19.00-23.00
CLOSED: Sat and Sun, 2 weeks in Dec and 2 weeks in July.
SPECIALITIES: tripes à la mode de Caen, poulet basquaise, home-cooking.
HOTEL: 10 rooms.
FACILITIES: television
OTHER POINTS: credit cards accepted.
Angers: château, jardin des plantes, palais des congrès.

LE RELAIS DE L'ARCEAU
(Mr Bruno Hérant) 47, rue Guillaume Lekeu
TEL: 02.41.43.86.25
DIRECTIONS: at the St Barthélémy/Gaston Birgé crossroad.
LANGUAGES: English.
MENU: 55 Frs.
RESTAURANT: Snacks from 6.00, lunch 11.30-14.30
CLOSED: Sun.
SPECIALITIES: couscous, home-cooking.
OTHER POINTS: credit cards accepted.
Château du Roi René; Cointreau factory.

AUBE
Orne, 61270

LE PETIT QUEBEC
(Mr Jean-Claude Rialland) 47, route de Paris
TEL: 02.33.24.55.34
DIRECTIONS: RN26, between L'Aigle and Argentan.
LANGUAGES: English, Spanish.
MENU: 50 Frs.
RESTAURANT: Snacks from 5.00, lunch 11.00-14.00, dinner 19.00-21.00
CLOSED: Sat, Sun and the 1st 2 weeks in Aug.
SPECIALITIES: home-cooking.
OTHER POINTS: credit cards accepted.
the old forge (biggest hammer in the world); Comtesse de Ségur's museum (children's author).

AUMALE
Seine-Maritime, 76390

HOTEL DE LA GARE
(Mr Bernard Mauquit) 9, place de la Gare
TEL: 02.35.94.61.00
DIRECTIONS: RN29, between Rouen and Amiens.
MENU: 61 Frs.
ROOMS: 125 to 165 Frs.
RESTAURANT: Snacks from 7.00, lunch 12.00
CLOSED: Sun.
SPECIALITIES: home-cooking.
HOTEL: 5 rooms
OTHER POINTS: credit cards accepted.
château at Rambures.

AUTHEUIL AUTHOUILLET
Eure, 27490

CHEZ PIERROT
(Mr Pierre Denoitte) 17, rue de Pacy
TEL: 02.32.34.67.67
DIRECTIONS: RD316 and 836, exit at Gaillon towards Evreux.
RESTAURANT: Snacks from 6.30, lunch 12.00-14.00, dinner -21.00
CLOSED: Sun afternoon, and mid-Aug.
SPECIALITIES: home-cooking.
OTHER POINTS: bar.
Eure valley.

AUVERSE
Maine-et-Loire, 49490

LES ROUTIERS
(Mme Evelyne Lejeune) Le Bourg
TEL: 02.41.82.20.13
DIRECTIONS: RD766, the Angers/Tours road.
LANGUAGES: English.
MENU: 57 Frs.
RESTAURANT: Snacks from 6.00, lunch 11.30-15.00, dinner 18.30-23.30
CLOSED: Sat and Sun.
SPECIALITIES: home-cooking.
OTHER POINTS: credit cards accepted.
Loire châteaux.

BAGNEUX
Maine-et-Loire, 49400

RELAIS DE BOURNAN
(Mme Jeanine Sanzay) 288, rue du Pont Fouchard
TEL: 02.41.50.18.02
DIRECTIONS: RN160, between Cholet and Niort.
MENU: 58 Frs.
RESTAURANT: Snacks from 6.30, lunch 11.30-14.00, dinner 19.00-21.00
CLOSED: Sun (out of season).
SPECIALITIES: home-cooking.
OTHER POINTS: bar.
caves à champignons (mushroom cellars); château.

BAINS SUR OUST
Ille-et-Villaine, 35600

LES QUATRE VENTS
(Mme Cristelle Bonhomme) Carrefour des Quatre Vents
TEL: 02.99.91.61.62
DIRECTIONS: Redon/La Gacilly/Ploërmel.
MENU: 50 Frs (drink included).
RESTAURANT: Snacks from 7.00
CLOSED: Sun afternoon.
SPECIALITIES: home-cooking.
OTHER POINTS: credit cards accepted.

BARRE EN OUCHE (LA)
Eure, 27330

CHEZ JACKY ET CORINNE
(Mr Jacky Scipion) Grande Rue
TEL: 02.32.44.35.28
DIRECTIONS: RN833, the Paris/Evreux road.
MENU: 52 Frs.
RESTAURANT: Snacks from 7.30, lunch 11.30-15.00, dinner 19.00-21.00
CLOSED: Sun afternoon, 2 weeks in Aug and 2 weeks in Dec.
SPECIALITIES: escalope normande, home-cooking.
OTHER POINTS: bar.
château at Beaumesnil (8km).

BAYEUX
Calvados, 14400

LA COLOMBE
(Mr Gérard Hardy) 13, route de Caen
TEL: 02.31.92.13.65 FAX: 02.31.21.12.26
DIRECTIONS: RN13, Cherbourg.
MENU: 49 to 140 Frs.
RESTAURANT: Snacks from 7.00, lunch 12.00-15.00, dinner 18.00-21.00
CLOSED: Sat evening and Sun (out of season).
SPECIALITIES: fruits de mer, regional menu, home-cooking.
OTHER POINTS: credit cards accepted.
landing beaches; cathedral; museums.

BEAUCE
Ille-et-Villaine, 35133

AUX BECS FINS
(Mr Pierrick Roux) 19, route de Paris
TEL: 02.99.99.08.00
DIRECTIONS: RN12, the Paris/Brest road, 3km before Fougères.
MENU: 54 Frs.
RESTAURANT: Snacks from 6.30, lunch 12.00-14.00, dinner 19.30-21.30
CLOSED: Sun, public holidays, and in Aug.
SPECIALITIES: home-cooking.
OTHER POINTS: credit cards accepted.
château at Fougères.

BEAUVOIR EN LYONS
Seine-Maritime, 76220

RELAIS NORMAND – Chez Franáoise et Julien
(Mr Julien Jue) Les Carreaux – Route Nationale 31
TEL: 02.35.90.17.20
DIRECTIONS: RN31, the Rouen/Reims road.
MENU: 61 Frs (coffee included).
RESTAURANT: Snacks from 5.00, lunch 11.30-14.00, dinner 19.00-21.00
CLOSED: Sat, Sun, public holidays, 1 week in May, 3 weeks in Aug and 1 week in Dec.
SPECIALITIES: home-cooking.
OTHER POINTS: credit cards accepted.
Les Andelys; Lyons-la-Forêt; châteaux de Vascoeuil and de Martainville.

BEAUVOIR SUR MER
Vendée, 85230

AU RELAIS DU GOIS
(Mr Gilles Grondin) Route Nationale 148
TEL: 02.51.68.70.31
DIRECTIONS: RN148, between Noirmoutier and Le Gois.
MENU: 55 to 160 Frs.
RESTAURANT: Lunch 12.00-14.00
CLOSED: in Dec.
SPECIALITIES: fruits de mer, poissons, regional menu.
OTHER POINTS: credit cards accepted.
passage du Gois (a low-tide causeway, unique in Europe, across to l'Ile de Noirmoutier).

BEDEE
Ille-et-Villaine, 35137

HOTEL DU COMMERCE
(Mme Odette Rigoreau) 14, place de l'Eglise
TEL: 02.99.07.00.37
DIRECTIONS: RN12, between Rennes and Saint-Brieuc.
LANGUAGES: English.
MENU: 65 to 115 Frs.
ROOMS: 115 to 150 Frs.
RESTAURANT: Snacks from 6.30, lunch 12.00-14.00, dinner 19.30-21.00
CLOSED: Sat evening, Sun, 3 weeks in Aug and last week in Dec.
SPECIALITIES: coquilles Saint-Jacques à la Bretonne, gibelotte (hare or rabbit) au cidre, poissons, home-cooking.
HOTEL: ☆ 22 rooms.
FACILITIES: shower, bath, private bathroom, television, telephone

OTHER POINTS: credit cards accepted.
🏰 ètang (pool) de Blavon; Neo-Gothic church.

BELLENGREVILLE
Calvados, 14370

LE BELLEN
(Mr Christophe Deschamps) 16, route de Paris
TEL: 02.31.23.61.50
DIRECTIONS: RN 13, RN13, theCaen/Lisieux axis.
LANGUAGES: English.
MENU: 55 Frs (wine and coffee included).
RESTAURANT: Snacks from 6.30
CLOSED: Sun.
SPECIALITIES: home-cooking.
OTHER POINTS: credit cards accepted.

BERNAY CARSIX
Eure, 27300

L'ESCALE
(Mr Michel Silliau) Carrefour de Malbrouck
TEL: 02.32.44.79.99
DIRECTIONS: RN13, Lisieux.
MENU: 58 Frs.
ROOMS: 110 to 160 Frs.
RESTAURANT: Snacks from 4.30, lunch 11.00-15.00, dinner 19.00-21.00
CLOSED: Sat, Sun, 1st 2 weeks in Aug.
SPECIALITIES: home-cooking.
HOTEL: 6 rooms.
FACILITIES: shower, bath, private bathroom
OTHER POINTS: credit cards accepted.
🏰 Abbaye du Bec-Hellouin; Château-Gaillard; Giverny; Vernon.

BERUS
Sarthe, 72610

LE RELAIS DE LA ROUTE D'OR
(Mme Josette Le Pabic) Route Nationale 138
TEL: 02.33.26.83.34
DIRECTIONS: RN 138, RN138, on the Alenáon/Le Mans road.
MENU: 55 Frs.
RESTAURANT: Snacks from 7.00, lunch 12.00-14.00, dinner 19.00-20.30
CLOSED: Sun.
SPECIALITIES: home-cooking.
OTHER POINTS: bar.

BESSE SUR BRAYE
Sarthe, 72310

LES ROUTIERS
(Mme Nadine Lenoir) 19, avenue de la Gare
TEL: 02.43.35.30.22
MENU: 52 to 57 Frs.
ROOMS: 150 to 170 Frs.
RESTAURANT: Snacks from 8.00, lunch 12.00-14.00, dinner 19.30-21.30
CLOSED: Sun, end Aug/beginning of Sept.
SPECIALITIES: home-cooking.
HOTEL: ☆ 13 rooms.
FACILITIES: shower, bath, private bathroom, television, telephone
OTHER POINTS: credit cards accepted.
🏰 château at Courtanvaux (2km).

BEUZEVILLE
Eure, 27210

CAFE DE L'ESPERANCE
(Mme Josiane Kampynck) 4, rue Pasteur
TEL: 02.32.57.70.60
DIRECTIONS: Honfleur or Caen.
MENU: 55 Frs.
RESTAURANT: Snacks from 6.30
CLOSED: Sat afternoon, Sun afternoon.
SPECIALITIES: couscous, choucroute, escalope viennoise, lapin chasseur, home-cooking.
OTHER POINTS: bar.
🏰 Honfleur; Deauville; Trouville.

BIVILLE LA BAIGNADE
Seine-Maritime, 76890

LA CUILLERE EN BOIS
(Mme Yvette Guerillon)
TEL: 02.35.32.88.81
DIRECTIONS: RN27, Dieppe.
MENU: 50 Frs.
RESTAURANT: Snacks from 7.30, lunch 12.00-14.00, dinner 19.00-18.30
CLOSED: Wed and Sept.
SPECIALITIES: home-cooking,
OTHER POINTS: bar.

BLAIN
Loire-Atlantique, 44130

LE RELAIS DU CHATEAU
(Mlle Francesca Bonhomme) Lieu dit : Le Gravier
TEL: 02.40.79.97.11
DIRECTIONS: RN171, between Saint-Nazaire (40km) and Rennes (80km).
MENU: 48 Frs.
RESTAURANT: Snacks from 6.00, lunch 11.30-15.00, dinner 19.00-21.30
CLOSED: Sat and Sun.
SPECIALITIES: home-cooking.
OTHER POINTS: credit cards accepted.
🏰 château at La Groulais; forêt du Gavres.

BOISNEY
Eure, 27800

CHEZ BILL
(Mr Jean-Jacques Billy) Route Nationale 13
TEL: 02.32.46.23.43
DIRECTIONS: RN13, the Evreux/lisieux road.
MENU: 50 Frs.
RESTAURANT: Snacks from 5.00
CLOSED: Sat, Sun.
SPECIALITIES: home-cooking.
OTHER POINTS: credit cards accepted.
Le Bec-Hellouin; zoo at Cerza.

BOISSY LAMBERVILLE
Eure, 27300

LE RELAIS DE LA BRETAGNE
(Mr Philippe Sauvage) Carrefour de la Bretagne – Route Nationale 13
TEL: 02.32.44.00.57
DIRECTIONS: RN 13, RN13, on the Lisieux/Evreux and Le-Havre/Alenáon axis.
MENU: 58 Frs (drink included).
RESTAURANT: Snacks from 4.30, lunch 11.00-14.30, dinner 18.00-22.30
CLOSED: Sat afternoon and Sun.
SPECIALITIES: home-cooking.
OTHER POINTS: credit cards accepted.

BOLBEC
Seine-Maritime, 76210

AUBERGE NORMANDE
(Mr Gérard Baudribos) Route Nationale 15 – Trouville-Alliquerville
TEL: 02.35.31.15.21
MENU: 59 Frs.
ROOMS: 90 Frs.
RESTAURANT: Snacks from 5.45, lunch 11.30-14.30, dinner 19.00-21.30
CLOSED: Sat, Sun, and last 2 weeks in Aug.
SPECIALITIES: home-cooking.
HOTEL: 5 rooms.
FACILITIES: shower, bath, private bathroom
OTHER POINTS: credit cards accepted.

BONNEVILLE SUR ITON (LA)
Eure, 27190

LE CAFE DES SPORTS
(Mr Roland Fontaine) 45, rue Jean Maréchal
TEL: 02.32.37.10.16
DIRECTIONS: RN830, Conches via Vallée de I'Iton.
MENU: 50 Frs.
RESTAURANT: Snacks from 6.30
CLOSED: last week in Dec.
SPECIALITIES: home-cooking.
HOTEL: 6 rooms.
FACILITIES: shower, bath, private bathroom, television
OTHER POINTS: bar.
étang de la Noé.

BOSGUERARD DE MARCOUVILLE
Eure, 27520

LA TETE D'OR
(Mr Serge Vannier) Route Nationale 138
TEL: 02.35.87.60.24
DIRECTIONS: RN138, between Bernay and Rouen.
MENU: 55 to 130 Frs.
ROOMS: 110 to 250 Frs.
RESTAURANT: Snacks from 6.30, lunch 11.00-14.30, dinner 18.30-21.30
CLOSED: Sun evening, mon and last 2 weeks in Dec.
SPECIALITIES: boeuf bourguignon, regional menu, home-cooking.
HOTEL: ☆ 10 rooms.
FACILITIES: television, telephone
OTHER POINTS: credit cards accepted.
Le Bec-Hellouin.

BOUGUENAIS
Loire-Atlantique, 44340

A LA FERME
(Mr Yvon Burlot) 65, rue de la Pierre
TEL: 02.40.65.23.58
DIRECTIONS: RN751, in the Cheviré industrial zone (Z.I.).
MENU: 52 to 57.50 Frs.
RESTAURANT: Snacks from 7.00
CLOSED: Sat, Sun.
SPECIALITIES: home-cooking.
OTHER POINTS: bar.
Loire valley; Nantes.

BOURG BEAUDOUIN
Eure, 27380

AU PECHE MIGNON
(Mr Pascal Lenoir) 19, route de Paris
TEL: 02.32.49.05.20
DIRECTIONS: RN14, 20km from Rouen, towards Pontoise.
MENU: 53 Frs.
RESTAURANT: Snacks from 7.00, lunch 11.00-15.00, dinner 19.00-21.00
CLOSED: Sun, and in Aug.
SPECIALITIES: home-cooking.
OTHER POINTS: credit cards accepted.
châteaux de Martinville and de Vascoeuil; abbaye de Mortemer; Rouen: cathedral; Ry: musée des automates (automata).

BOURGNEUF EN MAUGES
Maine-et-Loire, 49290

RELAIS DE LA BOULE D'OR
(Anne-Marie et Thierry Véron) 6, rue Notre Dame
TEL: 02.41.78.03.61
DIRECTIONS: RD762.
MENU: 50 to 160 Frs.
ROOMS: from 100 to 150 Frs.
RESTAURANT: Snacks from 6.30, lunch 12.00-14.00, dinner 19.00-20.00
CLOSED: Wed afternoon (hotel closed the week-end).
SPECIALITIES: home-cooking.
HOTEL: 5 rooms.
FACILITIES: shower, bath, private bathroom
OTHER POINTS: bar.

BOURNEZEAU
Vendée, 85480

LE RELAIS DU CHEVAL BLANC
(Mme Sylvia Demesy) 29 rue Jean Grolleau
TEL: 02.51.40.71.54
DIRECTIONS: RD949 and 948, La Roche-sur-Yon/Fontenay-le-Comte toad.
LANGUAGES: Spanish.
MENU: 47 Frs.
RESTAURANT: Dinner -22.00
SPECIALITIES: home-cooking.
OTHER POINTS: credit cards accepted.
La Roche-sur-Yon (20km); le Puy du Fou (35km); beaches (20km).

BREAL SOUS MONTFORT
Ille-et-Villaine, 35310

LE RELAIS RENNES/LORIENT
(Mr André Tardif) Echangeur RN24/RD62 – Bellevue
TEL: 02.99.60.04.20
MENU: 50 to 115 Frs.
RESTAURANT: Snacks from 7.00, lunch 11.30-15.30, dinner 18.00-23.30
SPECIALITIES: choucroute, jambon de pays grillé, poisson, bavette, regional menu, home-cooking.
OTHER POINTS: credit cards accepted.
Forêt de Paimpont/Brocéliande; pays de Monfort; Ecomusée; Saint-Cyr-Coëtquidan; moulin de la Roche; châteaux of Artois, Chesnais and Haute Forêt; Mordelles.

BRECE
Mayenne, 53120

LE DOMINO – Maître Traiteur
(Mr Jean-Marc Dethyre) 1, rue du Lavoir – Le Bourg
TEL: 02.43.08.62.72
DIRECTIONS: Mayenne.
LANGUAGES: English, Portuguese.
MENU: 50 to 105 Frs.
RESTAURANT: Snacks from 8.00, lunch 11.30-14.30, dinner 19.00-21.00
SPECIALITIES: regional menu, home-cooking.
OTHER POINTS: credit cards accepted.

BRECOURT DOUAINS
Eure, 27120

LE PACY VERNON
(Mr Alain Cote) Route Nationale 181
TEL: 02.32.52.44.67
DIRECTIONS: RN181, between Pacy-sur-Eure and Vernon.
MENU: 59 Frs.
RESTAURANT: Snacks from 5.00, dinner -21.00
CLOSED: Sat and Sun.
SPECIALITIES: home-cooking.
OTHER POINTS: credit cards accepted.
Claude Monet museum at Giverny; bird park at Bernay; château de Bizy.

BRETEUIL SUR ITON
Eure, 27160

LE RELAIS DES MARES
(Mr Danick Guiot) Le Chesne
TEL: 02.32.29.85.09
DIRECTIONS: RD840, Rouen.
MENU: 52 Frs.
RESTAURANT: Snacks from 5.00, lunch 11.00-15.00, dinner 19.30-22.00
CLOSED: Sat and Sun.
SPECIALITIES: regional menu.
OTHER POINTS: bar.
BRETTEVILLE-SUR-DIVES

BRETTEVILLE SUR DIVES
Calvados, 14170

LE BRETTEVILLAIS
(Mme Patricia Dufailly)
TEL: 02.31.20.13.31
DIRECTIONS: RD16, Crêvecoeur-en-Auge/Saint-Pierre-sur-Dives road.
MENU: 55 Frs.
RESTAURANT: Snacks from 6.30
CLOSED: Sat, Sun, and 3 weeks in Aug.
SPECIALITIES: home-cooking.
OTHER POINTS: terrace.
basilica at Lisieux; château at Crêvecoeur-en-Auge; abbatiale (abbey-church) at Saint-Pierre-sur-Dives.

BRIX
Manche, 50700

LE CLOS NORMAND
(Mme Josiane Germain)
TEL: 02.33.41.94.35
DIRECTIONS: RN13.
OTHER POINTS: bar.

BROGLIE
Eure, 27270

LES TOURISTES ET LES ROUTIERS
(Mr Jean-Louis Bunel) 47, rue Augustin Fresnel
TEL: 02.32.44.60.38
DIRECTIONS: RN138, the Rouen/Alenáon road.
MENU: 55 to 83 Frs.
ROOMS: 100 to 140 Frs.
RESTAURANT: Snacks from 11.00, lunch 12.00-14.00, dinner 19.30-21.30
CLOSED: Wed, and end Sept/beginning of Oct.
SPECIALITIES: côte de veau normande, rognons au Porto, home-cooking.
HOTEL: 5 rooms.
FACILITIES: shower, bath, private bathroom
OTHER POINTS: credit cards accepted.
Charenton valley; jardin aquatique de Broglie; basilica at Lisieux.

BUEIL (LE)
Eure, 27730

AUBERGE DE LA TRUITE
(Mr Jean Curtelin) 3, grande Rue – Route d'Anet
TEL: 02.32.26.22.35
DIRECTIONS: between Pacy-sur-Eure and Ivry-la-Bataille.
MENU: 59.50 to 160 Frs.
ROOMS: 120 to 150 Frs.
RESTAURANT: Snacks from 6.30, lunch 12.00-15.00, dinner 19.30-21.00
CLOSED: Mon and Sun evening, and in Aug.
SPECIALITIES: filet de canard aux morilles, home-cooking.
HOTEL: 9 rooms.
FACILITIES: bath, private bathroom
OTHER POINTS: credit cards accepted.
Eure valley; château d'Anet; Giverny; château de Bizy at Vernon.

CABOURG
Calvados, 14490

L'AUBERGE DES VIVIERS
(Mr Jean-Louis Delatte) Avenue Charles de Gaulle
TEL: 02.31.91.05.10 FAX: 02.31.24.77.72
DIRECTIONS: RD514.
LANGUAGES: English, German, Spanish, Italian.
MENU: 60 to 180 Frs.
ROOMS: 200 to 350 Frs.
RESTAURANT: Snacks from 8.00, lunch 11.00-16.00, dinner 19.00-24.00
CLOSED: 10th Jan to 10th Feb.
SPECIALITIES: crevettes grises sautées à la Trouvillaise, planche de poissons grillés, langoustines et gambas grillées, magret de canard aux deux pommes, regional menu, home-cooking.
HOTEL: ☆☆ 7 rooms.
FACILITIES: shower, bath, private bathroom, television, telephone
OTHER POINTS: credit cards accepted.
Honfleur; pays d'Auge; landing beaches.

LE COLOMBIER
(Mr Gérard Baudel) Petiville
TEL: 02.31.78.00.67
DIRECTIONS: RD513, between Caen and Cabourg.
MENU: 60 Frs.
RESTAURANT: Snacks from 6.30
CLOSED: Sun.
SPECIALITIES: home-cooking.
OTHER POINTS: credit cards accepted.

L'EDELWEISS – Chez Nino
(Mr Dominique Goulle) 10, avenue d'Isabelle
TEL: 02.31.91.17.46
DIRECTIONS: on the Caen/Cabourg axis, Dozulé exit.
LANGUAGES: English.
MENU: 55 Frs (drink included).
RESTAURANT: Snacks from 7.30
SPECIALITIES: regional menu, home-cooking.
OTHER POINTS: bar.

CAEN VENOIX
Calvados, 14350

LE VELODROME
(Mr Daniel Levigoureux) 9, avenue Henry Cheron
TEL: 02.31.74.40.71
DIRECTIONS: RN175, on the road to Vire, towards Mont-Saint-Michel.
MENU: 56 Frs (coffee included).
ROOMS: 120 to 145 Frs (60 Frs for extra bed).
RESTAURANT: Snacks from 7.00, lunch 11.30-14.00, dinner 19.00-20.30
CLOSED: Sat evening, Sun, and in Aug.
SPECIALITIES: home-cooking.
HOTEL: 9 rooms.
OTHER POINTS: bar.
landing beaches; Caen.

CAGNY
Calvados, 14630

HOTEL DE LA POSTE
(Mme Annick Robenard) 32, route de Paris

TEL: 02.31.23.41.26
DIRECTIONS: RN13, between Caen and Lisieux.
MENU: 54 Frs.
ROOMS: 120 to 150 Frs.
RESTAURANT: Snacks from 6.00, lunch 12.00-15.00, dinner 19.00-20.30
CLOSED: Sat afternoon and Sun.
SPECIALITIES: regional menu, home-cooking.
HOTEL: 5 rooms.
OTHER POINTS: credit cards accepted.

CALIGNY
Orne, 61100

RELAIS DU PONT DE VERE
(Mr Henri Vivier) Le Pont de Vère
TEL: 02.33.65.65.60
DIRECTIONS: RD962, Caen.
MENU: 61 Frs (coffee included).
RESTAURANT: Snacks from 6.30, lunch 11.30-14.30, dinner 19.00-21.30
CLOSED: weekends (reserved to functions), and 3 weeks in Aug.
SPECIALITIES: tripes, home-cooking.
OTHER POINTS: credit cards accepted.
la Suisse normande; Bagnoles-de-I'Orne; le Mont de Cerisy-Belle-Etoile.

CALLAC DE BRETAGNE
Côtes-d'Armor, 22160

LE KERGUIVIOU
(Mme Muriel Aubry) Zone Artisanale
TEL: 02.96.45.92.08
DIRECTIONS: RD787, between Guingamp and Carhaix.
MENU: 54 to 150 Frs.
RESTAURANT: Snacks from 6.30
SPECIALITIES: fruits de mer, regional menu, home-cooking.
OTHER POINTS: credit cards accepted.
Gorges du Corong.

CAMBES EN PLAINE
Calvados, 14610

LA FOURCHETTE
(Mr Claude Schwalm) 4, rue du Bourg
TEL: 02.31.43.73.54
DIRECTIONS: RD7, RD7, between Caen and Courseulles.
LANGUAGES: English, German.
MENU: 55 Frs, dish of the day at 35 Frs.
RESTAURANT: Snacks from 7.00, lunch 12.00-14.30, dinner 18.30-23.00
CLOSED: Sun afternoon.
SPECIALITIES: home-cooking, grill.
OTHER POINTS: credit cards accepted.

CAMPODARSEGO
Ille-et-Villaine, 35011

LES ROUTIERS
(Mr Diégo Favaretto) Via Antonina 230
TEL: 049.556.41.13
DIRECTIONS: between Padou and Venise.
LANGUAGES: Italian.
MENU: 70 Frs.
RESTAURANT: Snacks from 10.00, lunch 12.00-15.00, dinner 18.30-23.00
CLOSED: Tues and in August.
SPECIALITIES: fondue savoyarde et bourguignonne, home-cooking.
OTHER POINTS: bar.
Padoua and Venise (40km).

CARCAGNY
Calvados, 14740

AUX JOYEUX ROUTIERS
(Mr Michel Pacary) Le Hameau Saint Léger
TEL: 02.31.80.22.01
DIRECTIONS: D82, between Caen and Bayeux.
LANGUAGES: English, Italian.
MENU: 54 Frs.
RESTAURANT: Snacks from 7.30, lunch 11.30-14.00
CLOSED: Sat, SUn and 3 weeks in July.
SPECIALITIES: boudin noir, tripes, petit salé, patisseries maison, regional menu, home-cooking.
OTHER POINTS: bar.
Bayeux: tapestry (8km); Caen: peace memorial (20km); landing beaches (15km).

CARENTAN
Manche, 50500

LE DERBY
(Mme Elisabeth Lepelletier) 12, rue de la 101ème Air Borne
TEL: 02.33.42.04.77
DIRECTIONS: RN13, between Cherbourg and Caen.
LANGUAGES: English.
MENU: 55 Frs.
RESTAURANT: Snacks from 6.45, lunch 12.00-16.00
CLOSED: Sat afternoon, Sun and last 2 weeks in July..
SPECIALITIES: tripes maison, home-cooking.
OTHER POINTS: bar.
landing beaches; listed church and town hall (mairie); marina.

CAST
Finistère, 29150

LE RELAIS SAINT GILDAS
(Mme Marie Philippe et Mr Patrice Philippe) 11-13, rue du Kreisker
TEL: 02.98.73.54.76

DIRECTIONS: between Châteaulin and Douarnenez.
LANGUAGES: English.
MENU: 50 to 195 Frs.
ROOMS: 120 to 190 Frs.
RESTAURANT: Snacks from 7.00, lunch 12.00-14.30, dinner 19.00-22.00
CLOSED: Sat, and from 15th Oct to 15th Nov.
SPECIALITIES: fruits de mer, couscous maison, regional menu, home-cooking.
HOTEL: 12 rooms.
FACILITIES: shower
OTHER POINTS: credit cards accepted.
chapels and calvaires (crosses); Locronan (ancient town, 7km); Douarnenez fishing port (18km); Pointe du Raz (40km); Châteaulin: fishing, canal (7km); beaches.

CAUDAN
Morbihan, 56850

LE BOUTON D'OR
(Mr Aimé Le Bail) Z.A. Kergoussel
TEL: 02.97.81.16.01
DIRECTIONS: RD81, exit at Lanester – parc des expositions.
LANGUAGES: English.
MENU: 45 Frs.
RESTAURANT: Snacks from 7.00, lunch 11.30-14.30
CLOSED: Sat, Sun, and 3 weeks in Aug.
SPECIALITIES: couscous de poisson, regional menu, home-cooking.
OTHER POINTS: bar.
marina; Lorient.

CAUDEBEC LES ELBEUF
Seine-Maritime, 76320

LE TIVOLI BAR
(Mme Claudette Touchard) 43, rue Félix Faure
TEL: 02.35.77.16.94
DIRECTIONS: Elbeuf, on the road to Pont-de-l'Arche.
MENU: 50 Frs (wine included).
RESTAURANT: Snacks from 6.00, lunch 11.30-14.30, dinner 18.30-20.00
CLOSED: Sun.
SPECIALITIES: home-cooking.
OTHER POINTS: bar.

CAULNES
Côtes-d'Armor, 22350

LES ROUTIERS
(Mme Marie-Thérése Gaudrel) 40, rue de la Gare
TEL: 02.96.83.94.14
DIRECTIONS: D166/700, Dinan/Saint-Brieuc by the RN12.
MENU: 55 Frs.
RESTAURANT: Snacks from 7.00, lunch 11.30-14.30, dinner 19.00-21.00
CLOSED: Sun and 3 weeks in Aug.
SPECIALITIES: home-cooking,
OTHER POINTS: bar.

CEAUCE
Orne, 61330

LE RELAIS DE L'ETAPE
(Mme Michèle Gérault) 21, rue de Domfront
TEL: 02.33.30.84.04
DIRECTIONS: RD962, the Laval/Caen road, between Domfront and Mayenne.
MENU: 50 Frs.
RESTAURANT: Snacks from 7.45, lunch 12.00-14.00
CLOSED: Sun.
SPECIALITIES: fruits de mer (to order), home-cooking.
OTHER POINTS: credit cards accepted.
Bagnoles-de-l'Orne; Saint-Fraimbault (village in bloom).

CHAIGNES
Eure, 27120

AUBERGE MA NORMANDIE
(Mr Yves Holliger) Route Nationale 13
TEL: 02.32.36.95.52 FAX: 02.32.36.82.13
DIRECTIONS: RN13, Chauffour towards Caen, on the Paris/Lisieux road.
LANGUAGES: English.
MENU: 63 to 75 Frs.
RESTAURANT: Snacks from 4.30, lunch 10.00, dinner - 23.00
CLOSED: Sat evening and Sun (except bookings).
SPECIALITIES: regional menu, home-cooking.
OTHER POINTS: credit cards accepted.
Giverny; châteaux d'Anet and de Bizy at Vernon.

CHAILLE LES MARAIS
Vendée, 85450

AU CHTI-MI
(Mr Jean-Pierre Tison) 13, rue Principale – Le Sableau
TEL: 02.51.56.70.87
DIRECTIONS: RN137, the Nantes/La Rochelle road.
RESTAURANT: Snacks from 5.00
CLOSED: Sat and Sun (out of season).
SPECIALITIES: home-cooking.
OTHER POINTS: credit cards accepted.
La Venise Verte ('Green Venice') marshlands.

CHALLANS
Vendée, 85300

RELAIS DE LA NOUE
(Mme Monique Menez) Place Victor Charbonnel

TEL: 02.51.93.20.20
DIRECTIONS: RN148.
MENU: 48.50 to 56 Frs.
RESTAURANT: Snacks from 7.00, lunch 11.30-14.30, dinner 19.30-21.00
CLOSED: Sat, Sun, and 3 weeks in Aug.
SPECIALITIES: home-cooking.
OTHER POINTS: bar.

CHAMBRETAUD
Vendée, 85500

AUBERGE BEL'AIR
(Mme Jacqueline Martin) Route du Puy du Fou
TEL: 02.51.67.51.61
DIRECTIONS: RN160, between Les Herbiers (7km) and Cholet (18km).
MENU: 59 to 183 Frs.
RESTAURANT: Snacks from 7.00, lunch 12.00-15.00, dinner 19.00-22.00
SPECIALITIES: Provenáal dishes, regional menu, home-cooking.
OTHER POINTS: credit cards accepted.
le Puy du Fou; le Mont des Allouettes.

CHAMPAGNE
Sarthe, 72470

LE RELAIS DES FOUGERES
(Mr Jean-Marie Peeters) Route de Saint Calais
TEL: 02.43.89.50.96
DIRECTIONS: RN157, between Le Mans and Saint-Calais.
MENU: 60 to 90 Frs.
RESTAURANT: Snacks from 5.00, lunch 11.30-14.30, dinner 19.00-23.30
CLOSED: Sun.
SPECIALITIES: regional menu, home-cooking.
OTHER POINTS: credit cards accepted.

CHANGE
Mayenne, 53810

LE RELAIS DE NIAFLES
(Mme Marie-Franáoise Carret) 25, rue de Tisserants
TEL: 02.43.53.76.15
DIRECTIONS: A81, exit 3, towards Laval.
MENU: 52 Frs.
RESTAURANT: Snacks from 5.00
CLOSED: Sat, Sun, and in Aug.
SPECIALITIES: home-cooking.
OTHER POINTS: credit cards accepted.
château at Laval; abbaye de Clermont; river Mayenne.

CHANGE LES LAVAL
Mayenne, 53810

CHEZ CHRISTIANE
(Mme Christiane Pouteau) Les Chênes Secs
TEL: 02.43.56.16.06 **FAX:** 02.43.56.16.06
DIRECTIONS: RN30; A81, 2km from exit 4 in the direction of Fougères.
MENU: 56 to 76 Frs.
ROOMS: 110 to 150 Frs.
RESTAURANT: Snacks from 6.00, lunch 12.00-14.30, dinner 19.00-22.30
CLOSED: Sun evening and evenings of public holidays.
SPECIALITIES: fruits de mer, home-cooking.
HOTEL: 9 rooms.
FACILITIES: shower, bath, private bathroom, telephone
OTHER POINTS: credit cards accepted.
abbaye de Clermont; musée des Chouans (militant Breton royalists of 1793).

CHAPELLE CARO (LA)
Morbihan, 56460

HOTEL DE LA GARE
(Mme Marie-Claire Boulvais) La Gare
TEL: 02.97.74.93.47
DIRECTIONS: RN166, Vannes.
RESTAURANT: Snacks from 7.00, lunch 11.00-15.00, dinner 19.00-22.00
CLOSED: from 25th Dec to 2nd Jan.
SPECIALITIES: home-cooking.
HOTEL: 4 rooms
OTHER POINTS: bar.

CHAPELLE CRAONNAISE (LA)
Mayenne, 53230

LE RELAIS DES ROUTIERS
(Mr Jean-Franáois Littée) Le Bourg
TEL: 02.43.98.81.80 **FAX:** 02.43.98.53.93
DIRECTIONS: RN171, the Châteaubriant/Laval/Nantes road.
RESTAURANT: Snacks from 7.30
SPECIALITIES: home-cooking,
OTHER POINTS: bar.
musée de Tatin; château at Craon.

CHAPELLE DU BOIS (LA)
Sarthe, 72400

LE RELAIS
(Mr Jean-Claude Lhérault) 3, rue de la Poste
TEL: 02.43.93.18.69 **FAX:** 02.43.93.18.69
DIRECTIONS: RD59, between La Ferté-Bernard and Mamers.
MENU: 52 to 155 Frs.

ROOMS: 100 to 150 Frs.
RESTAURANT: Snacks from 7.30, lunch 11.30-14.30, dinner 19.00-21.00
CLOSED: Sun afternoon.
SPECIALITIES: regional menu, home-cooking.
HOTEL: 3 rooms.
FACILITIES: shower, bath, private bathroom
OTHER POINTS: credit cards accepted.
belvedere in the Forêt de Perseigne; pool.

CHAPELLE SAINT AUBERT (LA)

Ille-et-Villaine, 35140

LE RELAIS PARIS/BREST

(Mr Denis Potrel) Lieu dit : La Salorgue
TEL: 02.99.98.82.04
DIRECTIONS: RN12, between Fougères and Rennes.
MENU: 53 to 75 Frs.
RESTAURANT: Snacks from 7.00, lunch 11.30-14.30, dinner 18.30-21.00
CLOSED: Sun (in winter).
SPECIALITIES: paella, couscous, home-cooking.
OTHER POINTS: credit cards accepted.
château at Fougères.

CHASSILLE

Sarthe, 72540

LE PETIT ROBINSON

(Mr Olivier Fournigault) Le Petit Robinson
TEL: 02.43.88.92.01
DIRECTIONS: RN157, Le Mans/Lava] road.
MENU: 55 Frs.
ROOMS: 95 to 110 Frs.
RESTAURANT: Snacks from 5.00, lunch 11.30-14.00, dinner 18.30-23.00
CLOSED: Sat, Sun, public holidays and in Aug.
SPECIALITIES: regional menu, tête de veau sauce ravigote, tarte tatin, home-cooking.
HOTEL: 3 rooms.
FACILITIES: shower, bath, private bathroom
OTHER POINTS: credit cards accepted.
grottes (caves) de Saulges (20km).

CHATEAU GONTIER

Mayenne, 53200

L'ETOILE

(Mr Norbert Corvé) 43, rue Garnier
TEL: 02.43.07.20.80
DIRECTIONS: RN162, the Angers/Laval road.
MENU: 48 Frs (wine included).
RESTAURANT: Snacks from 8.00, lunch 11.45-14.30, dinner 19.00-21.00
CLOSED: Sun, public holidays, and in Aug.
SPECIALITIES: home-cooking.
OTHER POINTS: credit cards accepted.
châteaux; mayenne river trips.

CHATEAU L'HERMITAGE

Sarthe, 72510

LA BELLE CROIX

(Mr Sylvie David) La Belle Croix
TEL: 02.43.46.35.73
DIRECTIONS: RD307, Le Lude.
MENU: 53 Frs.
RESTAURANT: Snacks from 7.00
CLOSED: Sat, Sun (except functions) and Aug.
SPECIALITIES: home-cooking.
OTHER POINTS: bar.
Le Lude; Le Mans.

CHATEAUBRIANT

Loire-Atlantique, 44110

SARL LE TUGNY

(Mr Jean-Louis Boisgard) Rue du Général Eisenhower – ZI – Centre Leclerc
TEL: 02.40.28.29.58
DIRECTIONS: RN171, the Châteaubriant/Saint-Nazaire road.
RESTAURANT: Snacks from 8.00
CLOSED: Sun evening.
SPECIALITIES: home-cooking.
OTHER POINTS: credit cards accepted.
château; carrière des fusillés.

SARL PARIS/OCEAN

(Mme Maryse Gelée) 25, rue d'Ancenis
TEL: 02.40.81.21.79
DIRECTIONS: Route de Laval, behind the station.
LANGUAGES: English, Spanish.
MENU: 35 to 125 Frs.
ROOMS: 100 Frs.
RESTAURANT: Snacks from 6.30, lunch 12.00-15.00, dinner 19.30-23.00
CLOSED: Sun.
SPECIALITIES: rognons de veau flambés, truite 'Paris-Océan', regional menu.
HOTEL: ☆ 7 rooms
OTHER POINTS: credit cards accepted.
château.

CHATEAUTHEBAUD

Loire-Atlantique, 44690

LA SAUCISSE VOLANTE

(Mme Janine Roy) Route Nationale 137 – Lieu dit : Le Butay
TEL: 02.40.06.63.55 FAX: 02.40.06.60.59
DIRECTIONS: RN137, the Nantes/La Rochelle road.
MENU: 56 to 71 Frs.
ROOMS: 110 Frs.
RESTAURANT: Snacks from 5.00, lunch 9.00, dinner - 23.00
CLOSED: Sat evening and Sun.

SPECIALITIES: home-cooking.
HOTEL: 5 rooms
OTHER POINTS: credit cards accepted.
Nantes; African safari (35km).

CHEMERE
Loire-Atlantique, 44680

LES TOURISTES
(Mr André Arnoult) 40, rue de Nantes
TEL: 02.40.21.31.06
DIRECTIONS: D751, Nantes/Pornic road.
MENU: 51 Frs.
RESTAURANT: Snacks from 7.00, lunch 11.30-14.30, dinner 17.30-22.00
SPECIALITIES: home-cooking.
OTHER POINTS: bar.
african Safari (12km).

CHERBOURG
Manche, 50100

LES ROUTIERS
(Mme Viviane Couvrie) 8/10, rue de l'Onglet
TEL: 02.33.53.08.15
LANGUAGES: English, Spanish.
MENU: 55 to 85 Frs.
ROOMS: 80 to 190 Frs.
RESTAURANT: Snacks from 5.30, lunch 12.00-13.45, dinner 19.00-22.00
SPECIALITIES: fruits de mer, poissons, regional menu, home-cooking.
HOTEL: 20 rooms.
FACILITIES: shower, bath
OTHER POINTS: credit cards accepted.
Le Cotentin.

CHERBOURG TOURLAVILLE
Manche, 50110

A LA BONNE ASSIETTE
(Mr Michel Colas) 400, rue Jean Goubert
TEL: 05.33.20.43.80
LANGUAGES: English.
MENU: 53 to 65 Frs.
RESTAURANT: Snacks from 9.00
CLOSED: Sat and Sun.
SPECIALITIES: home-cooking.
OTHER POINTS: credit cards accepted.

CHOLET
Maine-et-Loire, 49300

HOTEL RESTAURANT LES ROUTIERS
(Mr Michel Dubillot) 13, place de la République
TEL: 02.41.62.11.09
MENU: 50 Frs.
ROOMS: 85 to 120 Frs.
RESTAURANT: Snacks from 6.45, lunch 12.00-14.00, dinner 19.30-21.00
CLOSED: Sun, and from 13th July to 16th Aug.
SPECIALITIES: home-cooking.
HOTEL: 19 rooms
OTHER POINTS: bar.

LE RELAIS DES PRAIRIES
(Mr Claude Albert) 3, boulevard du Pont de Pierre – Parc des Prairies
TEL: 02.41.58.09.39
DIRECTIONS: RN160, opposite the aerodrome.
LANGUAGES: English, German.
MENU: 49 to 160 Frs.
RESTAURANT: Snacks from 6.30, lunch 12.00-14.00, dinner 19.30-21.00
CLOSED: Sat (except bookings), and from 25th Dec to 2nd Jan.
SPECIALITIES: onglet (beef) à l'échalotte, côte de boeuf, tête de veau, home-cooking.
OTHER POINTS: credit cards accepted.
lac de Ribou (7km); lac du Verdon (7km); le Puy du Fou (25km).

CLERMONT CREANS
Sarthe, 72200

LE CREANS
(Mme Marie-France Rouault) 19, rue Nationale
TEL: 02.43.45.20.13
DIRECTIONS: RN23, Le Mans/Angers/Saumur road.
MENU: 52 Frs.
RESTAURANT: Snacks from 7.00
CLOSED: Sat and SUn.
SPECIALITIES: home-cooking.
OTHER POINTS: credit cards accepted.
zoo at La Flèche (3km); Mareil village; châteaux at Créans and Le Lude.

COEMONT-VOUVRAY
Sarthe, 72500

LE BON COIN
(Mme Jouanneau)
TEL: 02.43.44.04.17
DIRECTIONS: RN158.
RESTAURANT: Snacks from 7.00, lunch 11.30-15.00
CLOSED: Sun, and in Aug.
SPECIALITIES: home-cooking.
OTHER POINTS: bar.
Loir valley.

COETQUIDAN
Morbihan, 56380

L'UNION
(Mr Olivier Guérin) 3, avenue Brocéliande
TEL: 02.97.75.71.46

DIRECTIONS: Ecole militaire de St Cyr Coetquidan.
MENU: 47 to 52 Frs.
ROOMS: 90 to 130 Frs.
RESTAURANT: Snacks from 7.00, lunch 12.00-14.00, dinner 19.00-21.00
CLOSED: Sun, and in Aug.
SPECIALITIES: home-cooking.
HOTEL: 6 rooms.
FACILITIES: shower
OTHER POINTS: credit cards accepted.
Coëtquidan: military academy museum (1km), 70km from Paimpont.

COLOMBELLES
Calvados, 14460

LES VIKINGS
(Mr Jean-Claude Musson) 3, route de Cabourg
TEL: 02.31.72.18.8
DIRECTIONS: RD513.
MENU: 51 to 90 Frs.
ROOMS: 95 to 130 Frs.
RESTAURANT: Snacks from 6.30, dinner 19.00-21.30
CLOSED: Sun, and in Aug.
SPECIALITIES: home-cooking.
HOTEL: 32 rooms.
FACILITIES: shower, bath, private bathroom
OTHER POINTS: credit cards accepted.

COLOMBY
Manche, 50700

LA TAVERNE
(Mr Yves Moulin) Le Bourg
TEL: 02.33.40.10.59
DIRECTIONS: on the Cherbourg/Le-Mont-Saint-Michel road.
LANGUAGES: English.
MENU: 50 Frs (drink included).
RESTAURANT: Snacks from 8.00
CLOSED: Mon evening.
SPECIALITIES: home-cooking, couscous (Thursday).
OTHER POINTS: credit cards accepted.

COLPO
Morbihan, 56390

AUX DELICES DE L'OCEAN
(Mr Jean-Claude Le Guillan) 1, avenue de la Princesse
TEL: 02.97.66.82.21
DIRECTIONS: the Vannes/Saint-Brieuc road.
LANGUAGES: English, Spanish.
MENU: 50 to 150 Frs.
RESTAURANT: Snacks from 8.00, lunch 12.00-14.30
CLOSED: In July.
SPECIALITIES: fruits de mer, home-cooking.
OTHER POINTS: credit cards accepted.
Forêt de Lanvaux; Gulf of Morbihan.

CONCOURSON SUR LAYON
Maine-et-Loire, 49700

AUBERGE DU HAUT LAYON
(Mr Bernard Battais) 7 Route Nationale
TEL: 02.41.59.27.60
DIRECTIONS: RD160, the Tours/Nantes road.
LANGUAGES: English.
MENU: 64 to 115 Frs.
RESTAURANT: Snacks from 5.00, lunch 12.00-14.30, dinner 19.00-21.00
CLOSED: Sun evening.
SPECIALITIES: home-cooking.
OTHER POINTS: credit cards accepted.
zoo (3 km); troglodyte village (10km); rose garden.

CONLIE
Sarthe, 72240

LE CENTRE
(Mr Michel Cossonnet) 27, grande rue
TEL: 02.43.20.50.30
LANGUAGES: English.
MENU: 66 Frs (wine and coffee included).
ROOMS: 95 to 190 Frs.
RESTAURANT: Snacks from 7.30
CLOSED: from Sun afternoon to Mon afternoon and the 3 last weeks in Aug.
SPECIALITIES: home-cooking.
HOTEL: 8 rooms.
FACILITIES: shower
OTHER POINTS: bar.

CONNERRE
Sarthe, 72160

LA BICHE DOREE
(Mr Dominique Hérault) Route Nationale 23 – La Belle Inutile
TEL: 02.43.76.70.45
DIRECTIONS: RN23, Le Mans/Paris road.
MENU: 53.50 Frs.
ROOMS: 110 to 130 Frs.
RESTAURANT: Snacks from 5.00, lunch 12.00, dinner 19.00-22.00
CLOSED: Sat, Sun and public holidays.
SPECIALITIES: couscous (Thurs), home-cooking.
HOTEL: 10 rooms.
FACILITIES: shower, bath
OTHER POINTS: credit cards accepted.
automobile museum; Le Mans 24-hour-race circuit; animal reserve at Pescheray (7km); étang (pool) de Tuffé.

CORBON
Calvados, 14340

LE RELAIS SAINT JEAN
(Mr Jean-Hugues Neveu) Route Nationale 13 – Carrefour Saint Jean
TEL: 02.31.63.05.33
DIRECTIONS: RN13, between Lisieux and Caen.
MENU: 50 Frs.
RESTAURANT: Snacks from 6.00
SPECIALITIES: home-cooking.
OTHER POINTS: bar.
basilica at Lisieux (20km).

CORNE
Maine-et-Loire, 49250

LE RELAIS DE LA CROIX BLANCHE
(Mr Jean-Noël Pignard) Route Nationale 147
TEL: 02.41.45.01.82 FAX: 02.41.54.87.19
DIRECTIONS: RN147, the Tours/Nantes road, via Saumur.
MENU: 57 Frs.
RESTAURANT: Snacks from 6.30, lunch 11.45-13.45, dinner 19.30-21.30
CLOSED: Sat evening, Sun, 1 week in Aug, 1 week at Christmas.
SPECIALITIES: home-cooking.
OTHER POINTS: credit cards accepted.
château de Montgeoffroy at Maze; château at Pignerolle; musée de la communication at Saint-Barth.

CORNEVILLE SUR RISLE
Eure, 27500

RELAIS DU BOULANGARD
(Mr Francis Egret)
TEL: 02.32.57.01.27
DIRECTIONS: RN180, between Pont-Audemer and Rouen or Brionne.
MENU: 49.50 to 55 Frs.
RESTAURANT: Snacks from 7.30
CLOSED: Sat and Sun.
SPECIALITIES: home-cooking.
OTHER POINTS: bar.
les cloches (clocks) de Corneville; pont de Tancarville.

CORPS NUDS
Ille-et-Villaine, 35150

LES ROUTIERS
(Mme Solange Piel) 7, place de l'Eglise
TEL: 02.99.44.00.25
DIRECTIONS: the Rennes/Châteaubriant road.
MENU: 50 Frs.
RESTAURANT: Snacks from 7.00, lunch 12.00-13.30
CLOSED: Sat, Sun, and in Aug.
SPECIALITIES: home-cooking.
OTHER POINTS: credit cards accepted.

COUDEVILLE
Manche, 50290

LA POMME D'ARGENT
(Mr Abdel Ben Mustapha) Lieu dit : La Plesse
TEL: 02.33.90.03.33
DIRECTIONS: between Coutances and Granville.
LANGUAGES: English.
MENU: 55 to 100 Frs.
RESTAURANT: Snacks from 8.00, lunch 12.00-14.30, dinner 19.00-21.00
CLOSED: Wed (out of season) and Feb.
SPECIALITIES: couscous, tagine, home-cooking.
HOTEL: 6 rooms
OTHER POINTS: credit cards accepted.
Granville: haute ville, port, Aquarium du Roc; Coutances: cathedral; Abbaye de la Luceme; Mont-Saint-Michel; zoo at Champrepus.

COUTANCES
Manche, 50202

LE RELAIS DU VIADUC
(Mr Jean-Marc Harau) 25, avenue de Verdun
TEL: 02.33.45.02.68 FAX: 02.33.45.69.86
DIRECTIONS: RN171, between Granville and Saint-Lô.
LANGUAGES: English.
MENU: 55 to 180 Frs.
ROOMS: 150 to 200 Frs.
RESTAURANT: Snacks from 7.00, lunch 12.00-14.00, dinner 19.00-21.00
CLOSED: Fri evening and Sat (in winter), and 3 weeks in Feb.
SPECIALITIES: langouste gratinée, tripes maison, gigot d'agneau, calmars à l'américaine, filet de merlu sauce moutarde, confit de manchons de canard, émincé de dinde normande, regional menu.
HOTEL: 7 rooms.
FACILITIES: shower, bath, private bathroom, television, telephone
OTHER POINTS: credit cards accepted.
cathedral at Coutances; château du Grato.

COUVILLE
Manche, 50690

LE BOURG NEUF
(Mr Yves Anquetil) Le Bourg Neuf
TEL: 02.33.52.01.76 FAX: 02.33.52.01.76
DIRECTIONS: between Cherbourg and Valognes.
MENU: 48 to 55 Frs.
RESTAURANT: Snacks from 6.00, lunch 12.00-16.00, dinner 19.00-22.00
CLOSED: Tues afternoon, and in Aug.

SPECIALITIES: home-cooking.
OTHER POINTS: credit cards accepted.

CROISILLES
Calvados, 14220

RELAIS DE LA FORGE – Tabac
(Mme Monique Gibon) Le Bourg à Cambro
TEL: 02.31.79.71.80
DIRECTIONS: RD962, the Caen/Flers road.
MENU: 50 to 65 Frs.
RESTAURANT: Snacks from 6.00, lunch 11.00-15.00, dinner 18.00-20.00
CLOSED: Sun (out of season) and 24th Dec to 3rd Jan.
SPECIALITIES: riz cauchois, home-cooking.
OTHER POINTS: credit cards accepted.
pont du Hom; aquatic centre at Thury-Harcourt.

CROISY SUR ANDELLE
Seine-Maritime, 76780

LE RELAIS DU COMMERCE
(Mr Francis Dubois) Route Nationale 31
TEL: 02.35.23.61.82
DIRECTIONS: RN31, the Rouen/Beauvais road.
MENU: 58 Frs.
RESTAURANT: Snacks from 5.00
CLOSED: Sun (out of season), and Christmas holidays.
SPECIALITIES: regional menu, home-cooking,
OTHER POINTS: credit cards accepted.
château at Vascoeuil; Forêt de Lyons.

CROIX BEAUCHENE (LA)
Maine-et-Loire, 49490

RELAIS DE LA CROIX BEAUCHENE
(Mr Jean-Louis Metzger) Route Départementale 767
TEL: 02.41.82.14.63
DIRECTIONS: RD767, between Le Lude and Noyant.
MENU: 48.50 Frs.
RESTAURANT: Snacks from 6.00
SPECIALITIES: home-cooking.
OTHER POINTS: bar.
châteaux at Saumur and Le Lude; Loire wine-cellars.

CUON
Maine-et-Loire, 49150

LA POMME DE PIN
(Mme Yvette Pécot) Route Nationale 938 – Le Bourg
TEL: 02.41.82.75.74
DIRECTIONS: RN938.
MENU: 55 to 171 Frs.
RESTAURANT: Snacks from 7.00, lunch 11.30-14.30, dinner 19.00-21.30
CLOSED: Mon afternoon, and last 3 weeks in Aug.
SPECIALITIES: home-cooking.
HOTEL: 4 rooms.
FACILITIES: shower, bath, private bathroom
OTHER POINTS: credit cards accepted.

DENEE
Maine-et-Loire, 49190

LE PENALTY
(Mr Alain Saulgrain) Place Muller
TEL: 02.41.78.72.03
LANGUAGES: German.
RESTAURANT: Dinner -22.00
CLOSED: Sun afternoon, and 1 week at Christmas.
OTHER POINTS: bar.

DERVAL
Loire-Atlantique, 44590

LE RELAIS DE DERVAL
(Mr Jean-Joseph Bonnet) Carrefour Industriel des Estuaires
TEL: 02.40.07.77.77 FAX: 02.40.07.77.78
DIRECTIONS: RN171, the Nantes/Rennes road.
MENU: 55 to 138 Frs.
RESTAURANT: Snacks from 5.00, lunch 11.30-14.00, dinner 19.00-22.30
SPECIALITIES: beurre blanc, home-cooking.
OTHER POINTS: credit cards accepted.

DIEPPE
Seine-Maritime, 76200

CAFE DE L'AVENIR
(Mr Benoît Pan) 10 cours de Dakar – Port de Commerce
TEL: 02.35.84.18.10
DIRECTIONS: RN15.
MENU: 51 Frs.
RESTAURANT: Snacks from 4.30, lunch 11.00-14.00
CLOSED: Sun, and in Aug.
SPECIALITIES: home-cooking.
OTHER POINTS: bar.
Dieppe.

DINAN
Côtes-d'Armor, 22100

LA MARMITE
(Mr Gérard Bouillet) 91, rue de Brest
TEL: 02.96.39.04.42
DIRECTIONS: RN176, Saint-Brieuc.
LANGUAGES: English.
MENU: 50 to 80 Frs.
ROOMS: 180 to 250 Frs.
RESTAURANT: Snacks from 8.00, lunch 12.00-14.00,

dinner 19.30-21.00
SPECIALITIES: blancs de seiches à l'armoricaine, regional menu, home-cooking.
HOTEL: 5 rooms.
FACILITIES: shower, private bathroom, television, telephone
OTHER POINTS: credit cards accepted.
Mont-Saint-Michel; Cap-Fréhel; Dinan (medieval city); Saint-Malo.

DINARD
Ille-et-Villaine, 35800

L'EPICURIEN
(Mr Marc Arnoult) 28, rue de la Corbinais
TEL: 02.99.46.10.84
MENU: 50 to 95 Frs.
ROOMS: 120 to 190 Frs.
RESTAURANT: Snacks from 10.00, lunch 12.00-14.30, dinner 19.30-22.00
CLOSED: Sat and Sun evening (out of season).
SPECIALITIES: home-cooking.
HOTEL: 9 rooms.
FACILITIES: shower, private bathroom
OTHER POINTS: credit cards accepted.
Dinard; Saint-Malo; Dinan.

DOL DE BRETAGNE
Ille-et-Villaine, 35120

LE RELAIS DE LA BELLE LANDE
(Mr Thierry Honoré) 23bis, rue de Rennes
TEL: 02.99.48.06.14
DIRECTIONS: RN12, between Combourg and Rennes.
LANGUAGES: English.
MENU: 50 Frs (wine included).
RESTAURANT: Snacks from 7.00, lunch 12.00-14.00, dinner 19.00-21.00
CLOSED: Sun.
SPECIALITIES: mussel dishes: moules marinières, bouchots de la baie, moules de bouchots; paella, couscous, home-cooking.
OTHER POINTS: credit cards accepted.
Mont-Saint-Michel; Saint-Malo; Dinan; Combourg,

DOLO
Côtes-d'Armor, 22270

LES VALLEES
(Mme Paulette Hervé) ZA Les Vallées
TEL: 02.96.31.64.62
DIRECTIONS: RN12, between Rennes and Saint-Brieuc.
LANGUAGES: English.
MENU: 54 Frs (drink and coffee included).
RESTAURANT: Snacks from 7.00, lunch 11.30-14.30, dinner 19.00-22.00
CLOSED: Sun.
SPECIALITIES: home-cooking.
OTHER POINTS: credit cards accepted.
Abbaye de Boquen; lakes at jugon; château at La Hunaudaye.

DONGES
Loire-Atlantique, 44480

CAFE RESTAURANT DE LA POSTE
(Mr Eric Madiot) 5, place de la Gare
TEL: 02.40.45.73.20
DIRECTIONS: between Nantes and Saint Nazaire.
LANGUAGES: English, German, Spanish.
MENU: 52 Frs (drink included).
RESTAURANT: Snacks from 5.30, lunch 11.30-14.30, dinner 19.30-21.30
CLOSED: Sat and Sun.
SPECIALITIES: paella, couscous, choucroute, fruits de mer, cassoulet toulousain, beakoffa, potée bretonne.
OTHER POINTS: credit cards accepted.

DOUE LA FONTAINE
Maine-et-Loire, 49700

EUROROUTE – CHEZ PAUL
(Mme Marie-Hélène Dousset) Zone Industrielle – Route de Montreuil
TEL: 02.41.59.03.33 **FAX:** 02.41.59.00.34
DIRECTIONS: Angers/Poitiers or Cholet/Saumur road.
LANGUAGES: English.
MENU: 58 Frs (drink included).
ROOMS: 170 to 230 Frs.
RESTAURANT: Snacks from 4.30, lunch 11.00-15.00, dinner 18.30-22.00
CLOSED: Sun (out of season), and from 24th Dec to 2nd Jan.
SPECIALITIES: regional menu, home-cooking.
HOTEL: ☆☆ 20 rooms.
FACILITIES: shower, bath, private bathroom, television, telephone
OTHER POINTS: credit cards accepted.
troglodyte dwellings; 16thC sculpted cavern; rose gardens; musée des vieux métiers (ancient crafts); Anjou vineyards; zoo; Saumur; Cadre Noir, musée des blindés (armoured tanks).

DOZULE
Calvados, 14430

CHEZ MICHEL
(Mr Michel Martin) Route de Rouen – Putot en Auge
TEL: 02.31.79.20.29
MENU: 60 Frs.
RESTAURANT: Snacks from 5.00, lunch 11.30-15.00, dinner 19.00-22.00
CLOSED: Sat, Sun, and in Aug.

SPECIALITIES: regional menu, home-cooking.
OTHER POINTS: credit cards accepted.
basilica at Lisieux; Croix Delande.

DUCEY
Manche, 50220

LE MONTGOMERY
(Mme Marie-Thérèse Brosset) 44, rue du Genie
TEL: 02.33.48.51.36
DIRECTIONS: RN176, between Saint-Hilaire-du-Harcouët and Avranches.
MENU: 35 to 55 Frs.
ROOMS: 90 to 190 Frs.
RESTAURANT: Snacks from 7.30, lunch 11.00, dinner - 20.30
CLOSED: Sun afternoon (from Jan to end March).
SPECIALITIES: regional menu, home-cooking.
HOTEL: 7 rooms.
FACILITIES: shower
OTHER POINTS: credit cards accepted.
Mont-Saint-Michel; darn at Vezins; Avranches museum; zoo at Champrepus; Saint-Symphorien; falls at Mortain.

DURANVILLE
Eure, 27230

LES ARCADES
(Mme Geneviève Boga) Route Nationale 13
TEL: 02.32.46.83.01
DIRECTIONS: RN13, between Evreux and Lisieux.
MENU: 50 to 60 Frs.
RESTAURANT: Snacks from 5.30, lunch 11.30-15.30, dinner 19.00-24.00
CLOSED: from Sat 15.00 to Sun 22.00.
SPECIALITIES: home-cooking.
OTHER POINTS: credit cards accepted.
Lisieux.

ECARDENVILLE LA CAMPAGNE
Eure, 27170

AUBERGE DU RELAIS
(Mr Lionel Fouchard) Route Nationale 13
TEL: 02.32.35.05.32
DIRECTIONS: RN13, the Paris/Lisieux/Caen road.
MENU: 57.50 to 99 Frs.
ROOMS: 90 to 110 Frs.
RESTAURANT: Snacks from 5.00, lunch 11.00-14.00, dinner 18.30-22.00
CLOSED: Sat evening and Sun (out of season), Sat evening (in season) and Christmas Day.
SPECIALITIES: coquilles Saint-Jacques, home-cooking.
HOTEL: 10 rooms.
FACILITIES: shower
OTHER POINTS: credit cards accepted.
château du champs de bataille; château d'Harcourt; abbaye du Bec-Hellouin.

ECORPAIN
Sarthe, 72120

LE RELAIS DE LA JAGOTIERE
(Mme Mireille Gaborit) La Jagotière
TEL: 02.43.35.12.00
DIRECTIONS: RN157, between Bouloire and Saint-Calais.
MENU: 54 to 65 Frs.
RESTAURANT: Snacks from 7.00
CLOSED: Sun after 16.00.
SPECIALITIES: home-cooking.
OTHER POINTS: bar.

ELVEN
Morbihan, 56250

LE RELAIS DE L'ARGOET
(Mr André Le Douarin) 36, avenue de l'Argoët
TEL: 02.97.53.32.98
DIRECTIONS: RN166.
LANGUAGES: English.
MENU: 52 to 160 Frs.
ROOMS: 135 to 225 Frs.
RESTAURANT: Snacks from 6.30, lunch 12.00-14.00, dinner 19.30-21.30
CLOSED: Sat (out of season), and 2 weeks in Nov.
SPECIALITIES: fruits de mer, poissons, regional menu.
HOTEL: ☆ 12 rooms.
FACILITIES: shower, bath, private bathroom, telephone
OTHER POINTS: credit cards accepted.
tours de l'Argoët (highest dungeon in France); grottes (caves) de Callac; Gulf of Morbihan.

EMONDEVILLE
Manche, 50310

LE COUP DE FREIN
(Mr Albert Jean) Route Nationale 13
TEL: 02.33.41.22.74
DIRECTIONS: RN13, Cherbourg.
RESTAURANT: Snacks from 6.30, lunch 11.30-14.30, dinner 19.30-22.30
CLOSED: Sat, Sun, and 3 weeks in Aug.
SPECIALITIES: home-cooking.
HOTEL: 3 rooms.
FACILITIES: private bathroom
OTHER POINTS: credit cards accepted.
Sainte-Mère L'Egllse; landing beaches; Cherbourg; Saint-Vaast-le-Hague; Sarre valley; Ile de Tatihou.

EQUEURDREVILLE
Manche, 50120

RESTAURANT DE LA HAGUE
(Mr Claude Lamy) 120, rue de la Paix
TEL: 02.33.93.88.46
DIRECTIONS: RD901.
LANGUAGES: English.
MENU: 42 Frs.
ROOMS: 100 to 200 Frs.
RESTAURANT: Snacks from 6.30, lunch 12.00-14.30, dinner 19.30-20.45
CLOSED: Sat, Sun, and last 2 weeks in Aug.
SPECIALITIES: boeuf bourguignon, home-cooking.
HOTEL: 20 rooms.
FACILITIES: shower, bath
OTHER POINTS: credit cards accepted.

ERBRAY
Loire-Atlantique, 44110

LE SAINT HUBERT
(Mr Bernard Bellanger) 1, place du Calvaire – La Touche
TEL: 02.40.55.08.37
DIRECTIONS: RD163, between Châteaubriant and Angers.
MENU: 52 to 120 Frs.
ROOMS: 180 to 250 Frs.
RESTAURANT: Snacks from 6.00, lunch 11.00-14.30, dinner 19.00-22.30
CLOSED: Fri evening.
SPECIALITIES: fruits de mer and poisson au beurre blanc (to order), regional menu, home-cooking.
HOTEL: ☆☆ 8 rooms.
FACILITIES: shower, bath, private bathroom, telephone
OTHER POINTS: credit cards accepted.
château at La Motte-Glain and La Chapelle-Glain; château at Châteaubriant; carrière des fusillés.

ESSARTS (LES)
Vendée, 85140

LE RELAIS DU PINIER
(Mr Joseph Brunelière) Route Nationale 160 – Lieu dit : Le Pinier
TEL: 02.51.62.81.69 **FAX:** 02.51.48.40.85
DIRECTIONS: RN160, La Roche-sur-Yon.
LANGUAGES: English, Spanish.
MENU: 55 Frs (drink included).
RESTAURANT: Snacks from 5.00
SPECIALITIES: home-cooking.
OTHER POINTS: credit cards accepted.

EXMES
Orne, 61310

HOTEL DU COMMERCE
(Mme Fernande Simon) Grande Rue
TEL: 02.33.39.93.04
DIRECTIONS: CD14, the Rouen/Granville road.
MENU: 57 Frs.
ROOMS: 100 to 145 Frs.
RESTAURANT: Snacks from 7.00, lunch 11.00-14.00
SPECIALITIES: Norman dishes, home-cooking.
HOTEL: 4 rooms.
FACILITIES: shower, bath
OTHER POINTS: bar.
Haras du Pin (deer-breeding).

EZY SUR EURE
Eure, 27530

HOTEL TERMINUS – Chez Annie
(Mme Annie Veisen) 16, boulevard Ulysse Lavertue
TEL: 02.37.64.73.24
LANGUAGES: English, Spanish.
MENU: 58 to 100 Frs (drink included).
ROOMS: 120 to 170 Frs.
RESTAURANT: Snacks from 6.15, lunch 12.00-14.00, dinner 19.00-20.30
CLOSED: Sat, and in Aug.
SPECIALITIES: boeuf bourguignon, cassoulet, home-cooking.
HOTEL: 11 rooms.
FACILITIES: shower, bath, private bathroom, television
OTHER POINTS: bar.
château d'Anet; musée du Peigne.

FALAISE
Calvados, 14700

L'ESCALE
(Mr Claude Russeau) 16, rue du Pavillon
TEL: 02.31.90.12.67
DIRECTIONS: between Argentan and Caen.
MENU: 50 to 70 Frs.
RESTAURANT: Snacks from 6.00
CLOSED: Sun, and in Aug.
SPECIALITIES: regional menu, home-cooking.
OTHER POINTS: bar.
château at Falaise; la Suisse normande.

LE RELAIS DES ROUTIERS
(Mr Christian Durand) 33, avenue D'Hastings
TEL: 02.31.90.04.67
DIRECTIONS: RN158, Caen exit, towards Le Mans.
MENU: 50 Frs.
RESTAURANT: Snacks from 7.00, lunch 12.00-13.30, dinner 17.30-20.30
CLOSED: Sun and in July.
SPECIALITIES: home-cooking.

OTHER POINTS: credit cards accepted.
Falaise; châteaux (including that of William the Conqueror); churches.

FALLERON
Vendée, 85670

LE RELAIS VENDEEN
(Mr Jacques Herbert) 54, rue Nationale
TEL: 02.51.35.50.22
DIRECTIONS: RD753, between Cholet and Chalans.
LANGUAGES: English.
MENU: 51 Frs.
RESTAURANT: Snacks from 6.45, lunch 11.30-14.30
CLOSED: Sun.
SPECIALITIES: home-cooking.
OTHER POINTS: credit cards accepted.
Ile de Noirmoutier and Ile d'Yeu (35km).

FAOUET (LE)
Morbihan, 56320

LE RELAIS DES HALLES
(Mr Armel Le Puil) 19, rue du Soleil
TEL: 02.97.23.07.66
DIRECTIONS: RN782, between Lorient and Roscoff.
LANGUAGES: English.
MENU: 50 Frs.
ROOMS: 100 to 180 Frs.
RESTAURANT: Snacks from 7.00, lunch 12.00-14.00, dinner 19.30-21.00
CLOSED: Sun, and in Sept.
SPECIALITIES: home-cooking.
HOTEL: 8 rooms.
FACILITIES: shower, bath, private bathroom, telephone
OTHER POINTS: bar.
15thC market and chapels.

RELAIS ROUTIER 769
(Mr Jean-Yves Bourhis) Ty Cravic
TEL: 02.97.23.07.04
DIRECTIONS: RD769, the Lorient/Roscoff road.
MENU: 48 to 150 Frs.
RESTAURANT: Snacks from 6.00, lunch 11.30-14.00, dinner 19.30-21.30
CLOSED: Sat 15.00 to Mon 6.00 (except in June and Sept).
SPECIALITIES: regional menu, home-cooking.
OTHER POINTS: credit cards accepted.
15thC markets; chapels of Sainte-Barbe and Saint-Fiacre.

FERRIERES EN BRAY
Seine-Maritime, 76220

HOTEL DU CHEMIN DE FER
(SARL Jumeaux) 26, avenue de la Gare
TEL: 02.35.90.01.61
DIRECTIONS: RN31, Rouen or Beauvais.
LANGUAGES: Spanish, Arabic.
MENU: 58 Frs (drink and coffee included).
ROOMS: 100 to 150 Frs.
RESTAURANT: Snacks from 6.30
CLOSED: Sun.
SPECIALITIES: home-cooking.
HOTEL: 10 rooms.
FACILITIES: shower
OTHER POINTS: bar.
Saint-Germer-de-Fly; Gerberoy.

FLEURY SUR ORNE
Calvados, 14123

LA POMME D'OR
(Mme Emilienne Franáois) 20, route d'Harcourt
TEL: 02.31.82.36.87
DIRECTIONS: RD562, Caen-Flers, towards Laval.
MENU: 48 to 50 Frs.
RESTAURANT: Snacks from 7.00, lunch 12.00-15.00
CLOSED: Sun, public holidays, and in Aug.
SPECIALITIES: home-cooking,
OTHER POINTS: credit cards accepted.

FONTAINE SAINT MARTIN (LA)
Sarthe, 72330

LE CHENE VERT
(Mme Marie-Louise Flameygh) Le Chêne Vert
TEL: 02.43.87.80.84
DIRECTIONS: RN23, Nantes.
MENU: 55 to 65 Frs.
RESTAURANT: Snacks from 7.00, lunch 11.00-15.00, dinner 19.00-22.00
CLOSED: Sat and Sun.
SPECIALITIES: andouillette grillée, regional menu, home-cooking.
OTHER POINTS: credit cards accepted.
château at Le Lude; zoo at La Flèche; museum and Le Mans 24-hour-race circuit.

FOUCARMONT
Seine-Maritime, 76340

CAFE DU MARCHE – Chez Régine
(Mme Régine Recoquillon) 35, rue Douce
TEL: 02.35.94.83.14
DIRECTIONS: RN28, the Rouen/Abbeville road.
MENU: 49 Frs.
RESTAURANT: Snacks from 7.00, lunch 12.00-15.00, dinner 19.00-20.30
CLOSED: Sat, Sun, and 3 weeks in Aug.
SPECIALITIES: home-cooking.
OTHER POINTS: bar.
Côte d'Opale; bay of the Somme (35km).

FOUGERES
Ille-et-Villaine, 35300

AUX AMIS DE LA ROUTE
(Mr Michel Bastien) 6, boulevard Saint Germain
TEL: 02.99.99.07.62
DIRECTIONS: RN12, the Rennes/Saint-Malo road.
LANGUAGES: English, German.
MENU: 60 Frs (drink included).
ROOMS: 140 to 150 Frs.
RESTAURANT: Snacks from 7.00, lunch 12.00-14.00, dinner 19.30-21.00
CLOSED: Sun, and 1 week at Christmas/New year.
SPECIALITIES: couscous, choucroute, coq au vin, regional menu, home-cooking.
HOTEL: ☆ 12 rooms.
FACILITIES: shower, bath, private bathroom
OTHER POINTS: credit cards accepted.
Saint-Malo; Mont-Saint-Michel; Fougères: park, forest and château.

GAEL
Ille-et-Villaine, 35290

LES ROUTIERS
(Mme Annick Rebillard) Place des Tilleuls
TEL: 02.99.07.72.39
DIRECTIONS: the Dinan/Lorient road.
MENU: 50 Frs.
ROOMS: 83 to 126 Frs.
RESTAURANT: Snacks from 7.00, lunch 11.30-14.30, dinner 19.00-21.00
CLOSED: Fri after 15.00.
SPECIALITIES: tête de veau à l'ancienne (Wed), couscous and choucroute (Thurs), regional menu, home-cooking.
HOTEL: 5 rooms.
FACILITIES: shower, bath, private bathroom, telephone
OTHER POINTS: credit cards accepted.
forêt de Paimpont.

GIBERVILLE
Calvados, 14730

LE STOP BAR
(Mr Maurice Pilon) 47, rue de la Liberté
TEL: 02.31.84.52.63
DIRECTIONS: RN175, Cabourg.
LANGUAGES: English.
MENU: 48 Frs.
RESTAURANT: Snacks from 8.00, lunch 12.00-14.00
CLOSED: Sun.
SPECIALITIES: tripes à la mode de Caen, couscous, choucroute, home-cooking.
OTHER POINTS: credit cards accepted.
landing beaches.

GISORS
Eure, 27140

LA BONNE FOURCHETTE – Chez Mado et Daniel
(Mr Daniel Mercier) 95, route de Dieppe
TEL: 02.32.27.52.73
DIRECTIONS: on the Paris/Dieppe road.
MENU: 60 Frs (drink and coffee included).
RESTAURANT: Snacks from 5.00, lunch 11.00-15.00, dinner 18.30-22.00
CLOSED: Sun.
SPECIALITIES: home-cooking.
OTHER POINTS: credit cards accepted.

GLACERIE (LA)
Manche, 50470

LE RELAIS DE LA GLACERIE
(Mr Paul Roupsard) Route Nationale 13
TEL: 02.33.44.13.54
DIRECTIONS: RN13, Cherbourg.
MENU: 55 Frs, dish of the day at 35 Frs.
RESTAURANT: Snacks from 6.00, lunch 12.00-14.00, dinner 19.30-21.00
CLOSED: Sat, Sun, and from 14th July to 7th Aug.
SPECIALITIES: regional menu, home-cooking.
OTHER POINTS: credit cards accepted.
landing beaches; Cherbourg; cap La Hague.

GOUESNIERE (LA)
Ille-et-Villaine, 35350

LE RELAIS ROUTIERS
(Mme Marie-Thé Bourgalais) 2, rue d'Halet
TEL: 02.99.58.80.57
DIRECTIONS: Dol-de-Bretagne/Dinard/Saint-Malo.
MENU: 50 Frs.
ROOMS: 150 to 200 Frs.
RESTAURANT: Snacks from 7.00, lunch 11.30-14.00, dinner 19.00-21.30
CLOSED: Sun.
SPECIALITIES: home-cooking.
HOTEL: 13 rooms.
FACILITIES: shower
OTHER POINTS: bar.
Saint-Malo; Cancale; Mont-Saint-Michel; Dinan; Dinard.

GOULET (LE)
Eure, 27950

LE TERMINUS
(Mr Claude Hard) 30, route de Rouen
TEL: 02.32.52.50.07
DIRECTIONS: RN15, the Vernon/Rouen road.
MENU: 62 Frs.
ROOMS: 120 to 150 Frs.

RESTAURANT: Snacks from 5.00, dinner 19.00-23.00
CLOSED: Sat, Sun, 3 weeks in Aug and 1 week from Christmas Day.
SPECIALITIES: home-cooking.
HOTEL: 18 rooms.
FACILITIES: shower, bath, private bathroom
OTHER POINTS: credit cards accepted.
Claude Monet's house and garden at Giverny; Château-Gaillard; les Andelys.

GOUSTRANVILLE
Calvados, 14430

LE RELAIS DU BON ACCUEIL
(Mr Claude Pommereul) Route de Rouen – Route Nationale 175
TEL: 02.31.79.21.90
DIRECTIONS: RN175, Dozulé exit, towards Caen.
LANGUAGES: Spanish.
MENU: 55 to 60 Frs.
RESTAURANT: Snacks from 6.30
CLOSED: Sat afternoon, Sun (public holidays).
SPECIALITIES: home-cooking.
OTHER POINTS: credit cards accepted.
landing beaches; Beuvron-en-Auge; Croix Glorieuses at Dozulé; Norman village at Dives-sur-Mer.

GRAINVILLE
Eure, 27380

LE RELAIS DE GRAINVILLE
(Mr Leblanc) 40, Route Nationale
TEL: 02.32.48.06.28
DIRECTIONS: RN14, the Paris/Rouen/Le Havre road.
LANGUAGES: English, German.
MENU: 53 Frs.
RESTAURANT: Snacks from 4.30, lunch 11.30
CLOSED: Sat afternoon, Sun.
SPECIALITIES: home-cooking.
OTHER POINTS: credit cards accepted.
Château-Gaillard (15km); Rouen (25km); les Andelys.

GRAVIGNY
Eure, 27930

HOTEL DES SPORTS
(Mr Tarik Senouci) 109, avenue Aristide Briand
TEL: 02.32.33.16.19
LANGUAGES: English, Spanish, Arabic.
MENU: 49 Frs.
ROOMS: 80 Frs.
RESTAURANT: Snacks from 7.00, lunch 12.00-14.30, dinner 19.30-21.30
CLOSED: Sun.
SPECIALITIES: Oriental dishes, couscous.
HOTEL: 7 rooms.
FACILITIES: shower, bath, private bathroom
OTHER POINTS: bar.

GREMONVILLE
Seine-Maritime, 76970

LA CHAUMIERE
(Mr Christian Le Masurier) Place de l'Eglise
TEL: 02.35.56.45.65
DIRECTIONS: RN15, between Rouen and Saint-Valery-en-Caux.
LANGUAGES: English.
MENU: 50 to 120 Frs.
RESTAURANT: Snacks from 7.00
CLOSED: Sun and public holidays.
SPECIALITIES: regional menu, lapin au cidre, langue à la sauce piquante, rognons en sauce, home-cooking.
OTHER POINTS: bar.
Yvetot: round church (5km); Saint-Valery: beach (25km); le chêne (oak-tree) d'Allouville-Bellefosse.

GUE DE LA CHAINE (LE)
Orne, 61130

LE GUE ROUTIER
(Mme Marylène Disztl) 3, route de Mamers
TEL: 02.33.73.02.66
DIRECTIONS: between Mamers and Bellême.
MENU: 53 Frs.
RESTAURANT: Snacks from 7.00, lunch 11.30-14.00, dinner 19.00-20.30
CLOSED: Sun and Aug.
SPECIALITIES: home-cooking.
OTHER POINTS: bar.
Forêt de Bellême; golf course.

GUE ORY
Sarthe, 72130

AUBERGE DU GUE ORY
(Mr Gérard Gahagnon) Le Bourg -
TEL: 02.43.33.32.18
DIRECTIONS: RN 15, RN15, on the Fresnay/Vilaines-la-Juhel axis.
LANGUAGES: English.
MENU: 50 Frs (drink included)) to 148 Frs.
RESTAURANT: Snacks from 7.00, lunch 12.00-14.30, dinner 19.00-21.00
CLOSED: Wed evening.
SPECIALITIES: regional menu, home-cooking, coq au vin, lapin au cidre, poisson.
OTHER POINTS: credit cards accepted.

GUENIN
Morbihan, 56150

LE RELAIS DE BON VALLON
(Mr Joël Le Hazif) Z.I. de Bon Vallon
TEL: 02.97.39.10.40
DIRECTIONS: between Lorient and Rennes.
LANGUAGES: English.
MENU: 52 Frs.
RESTAURANT: Snacks from 6.00
CLOSED: Sun.
SPECIALITIES: regional menu.
OTHER POINTS: credit cards accepted.

GUERCHE DE BRETAGNE (LA)
Ille-et-Villaine, 35130

LE RELAIS DU PONT D'ANJOU
(Mr André Moussu) 11, faubourg d'Anjou
TEL: 02.99.96.23.10
DIRECTIONS: RN176, the Rennes/Angers road.
MENU: 44.50 to 125 Frs.
RESTAURANT: Snacks from 6.45, lunch 11.00-15.00, dinner 19.00-22.00
CLOSED: Sun evening.
SPECIALITIES: fruits de mer, couscous, paella, regional menu, home-cooking.
HOTEL: ☆ 12 rooms
OTHER POINTS: bar.

GUILBERVILLE
Manche, 50160

RESTAURANT LE POTEAU
(Mr Frédy Menant) Le Poteau
TEL: 02.33.56.73.10
DIRECTIONS: RN175.
LANGUAGES: English, Italian.
MENU: 59.50 (wine and coffee included).
RESTAURANT: Snacks from 5.00
CLOSED: Sat and Sun, and Christmas holidays.
SPECIALITIES: regional menu, home-cooking,
OTHER POINTS: credit cards accepted.

GUINGAMP
Côtes-d'Armor, 22200

AU RELAIS DE BELLEVUE
(Mr Jacques Yvinec) 1, rue Bellevue – Bel Orme Saint Agathon
TEL: 02.96.43.80.53 FAX: 02.96.43.97.04
DIRECTIONS: RN12, Brest/Rennes road.
LANGUAGES: English.
MENU: 44 to 58 Frs.
ROOMS: from 170 to 200 Frs.
RESTAURANT: Snacks from 5.30
CLOSED: Sat afternoon and Sun.
SPECIALITIES: home-cooking.
HOTEL: ☆ 20 rooms.
FACILITIES: shower, bath, private bathroom, television, telephone
OTHER POINTS: credit cards accepted.
pink granite coast, old medieval prison.

GURUNHUEL
Côtes-d'Armor, 22390

CHEZ GILBERTE
(Mr Yves Georgelin) Kérambellec
TEL: 02.96.21.81.00
DIRECTIONS: RN787.
RESTAURANT: Snacks from 7.30, lunch 12.00-14.00
CLOSED: Sat lunch, Sun lunch, and in July.
SPECIALITIES: home-cooking.
OTHER POINTS: credit cards accepted.

HAVRE (LE)
Seine-Maritime, 76600

AU TELEPHONE
(Mr Jean-Claude Bouillon) 173, boulevard Amiral Mouchez
TEL: 02.35.53.24.76
DIRECTIONS: in the l'Eure district.
LANGUAGES: English.
MENU: 54 Frs (wine included).
RESTAURANT: Snacks from 7.00
CLOSED: Sat, Sun, and in July.
SPECIALITIES: home-cooking.
OTHER POINTS: credit cards accepted.

LE P'TIT COMPTOIR
(Mr Philippe Levitre) 31, rue du Général Faidherbe
TEL: 02.35.42.78.72
DIRECTIONS: in the Saint-Franáois district.
LANGUAGES: English.
MENU: 63 to 88 Frs.
RESTAURANT: Snacks from 9.00, lunch 12.00-14.30, dinner 19.00-23.00
CLOSED: Sun.
SPECIALITIES: choucroute aux 3 poissons, home-cooking.
OTHER POINTS: credit cards accepted.

LE RELAIS
(Mr Didier Eudes) 128, boulevard de Graville
TEL: 02.35.24.54.48
DIRECTIONS: RN15, Autoroute towards Le-Havre, 1st traffic lights on the left.
LANGUAGES: English.
MENU: 55 to 120 Frs.
RESTAURANT: Snacks from 6.30, lunch 11.45-14.30, dinner 18.45-22.30

CLOSED: Sun.
SPECIALITIES: regional menu, fruits de mer, home-cooking.
OTHER POINTS: credit cards accepted.
Le Havre port; seaside.

LES ROUTIERS
(Mme Marie-Pierre Priser) 57, rue Marceau
TEL: 02.35.25.06.44
MENU: 52 to 55 Frs.
RESTAURANT: Snacks from 6.30, lunch 11.30-15.00, dinner 19.00-23.00
CLOSED: from 24th Dec to 7th Jan.
SPECIALITIES: home-cooking.
HOTEL: 11 rooms.
FACILITIES: shower, private bathroom
OTHER POINTS: bar.

LE WELCOME
(Mr Eric Maniguet) 55, quai Southtampton
TEL: 02.35.43.17.84
LANGUAGES: English.
MENU: 50 Frs (wine included).
ROOMS: 90 to 150 Frs.
RESTAURANT: Snacks from 7.00, lunch 12.00
SPECIALITIES: home-cooking.
HOTEL: 8 rooms
OTHER POINTS: bar.

HAYE DU PUITS (LA)
Manche, 50250

RESTAURANT DU CHATEAU
(Mr André Maleuvre) 16, rue du Château
TEL: 02.33.46.03.42
DIRECTIONS: between Coutances and Cherbourg.
MENU: 50 Frs.
RESTAURANT: Snacks from 7.00, lunch 11.30-14.30, dinner 19.00-22.00
CLOSED: Sat evening, Sun and 3 weeks in Aug.
SPECIALITIES: home-cooking.
OTHER POINTS: credit cards accepted.

HAYE PESNEL (LA)
Manche, 50320

CHEZ ARMELLE
(Mme Yolande Bourrel) Rue de la Libération
TEL: 02.33.61.50.83
LANGUAGES: English.
MENU: 59.50 to 100 Frs.
RESTAURANT: Snacks from 7.30
CLOSED: Sat, Sun, in Dec and 1 week in July.
SPECIALITIES: coquilles Saint-Jacques, escalope de veau à la crème, regional menu, home-cooking.
OTHER POINTS: credit cards accepted.
Abbaye de la Lucerne; zoo at Champrepus.

HERBERGEMENT (L')
Vendée, 85260

LES ROUTIERS
(Mr Michel Bretin) 17, rue Georges Clémenceau
TEL: 02.51.42.80.71
DIRECTIONS: RD763, between Nantes and La Roche-sur-Yon.
MENU: 50 Frs.
RESTAURANT: Snacks from 7.30, lunch 11.45-14.30
CLOSED: Sun, and in Aug.
SPECIALITIES: home-cooking.
OTHER POINTS: credit cards accepted.
château de La Chabotterie: memorial of 1793 Vendée uprising.

HERBIERS (LES)
Vendée, 85500

L'OREE DES BOIS VERTS
(Mr René Joulin) Route des Sables
TEL: 02.51.91.00.18 FAX: 02.51.64.97.70
DIRECTIONS: RN160, between Angers and La Roche-sur-Yon.
MENU: 49 to 100 Frs.
ROOMS: 130 to 250 Frs.
RESTAURANT: Snacks from 7.00, lunch 12.00-14.00, dinner 19.30-21.15
CLOSED: Sun, All Saints' Day (1st Nov) and first 2 weeks in May.
SPECIALITIES: home-cooking.
HOTEL: ☆ 11 rooms.
FACILITIES: shower, bath, private bathroom, television, telephone
OTHER POINTS: credit cards accepted.
le Puy du Fou; l'étang de la Tricherie; Abbaye de la Grainetière.

HERIC
Loire-Atlantique, 44810

LE CANAL
(Mme Catherine Jallais) Route Nationale 137 – Bout de Bois
TEL: 02.40.57.60.54
DIRECTIONS: RN137, the Nantes/Rennes road.
LANGUAGES: English.
MENU: 53 Frs (drink included).
RESTAURANT: Snacks from 6.00, lunch 12.00-14.30, dinner 19.00-20.30
CLOSED: SUn.
SPECIALITIES: home-cooking.
OTHER POINTS: credit cards accepted.
Nantes; Brest; pool.

HERMITAGE (L')
Ille-et-Villaine, 35590

LE VILLAGE
(Mr Christian Laillé) 23, rue de Rennes
TEL: 02.99.64.03.31
DIRECTIONS: RD125, between Montfort and Rennes.
MENU: 52 Frs.
RESTAURANT: Snacks from 7.00, lunch 11.45-14.00
CLOSED: Sun, and in Aug.
SPECIALITIES: couscous, tripes, regional menu, home-cooking,
OTHER POINTS: credit cards accepted.

HERMITAGE LORGE (L')
Côtes-d'Armor, 22150

RESTAURANT DE LA PLACE
(Mr Dominique Georgeot) Le Paly
TEL: 02.96.42.12.26
DIRECTIONS: RD 700, RD700, on the Loudéac/Saint-Brieuc road.
LANGUAGES: English.
MENU: 52 Frs (drink and coffee included).
ROOMS: 130 to 175 Frs.
RESTAURANT: Snacks from 6.45, lunch 11.30-14.00, dinner 18.30-21.00
SPECIALITIES: regional menu, home-cooking, coucous (Friday).
HOTEL: 9 rooms.
FACILITIES: shower, private bathroom
OTHER POINTS: credit cards accepted.

HINGLE LES GRANITS (LE)
Côtes-d'Armor, 22100

LES ROUTIERS
(Mr Rémy Pessel) Rue de la Gare
TEL: 02.96.83.58.45
DIRECTIONS: RN166.
LANGUAGES: English.
MENU: 44 Frs.
RESTAURANT: Snacks from 6.30, lunch 11.30-14.00
CLOSED: Sun.
SPECIALITIES: home-cooking.
OTHER POINTS: bar.
Dinan; the northern coast.

HONFLEUR
Calvados, 14600

LES OISEAUX DE MER
(Mr Pascal Quesney) 28, route des 4 Francs – La Rivière Saint Sauveur
TEL: 02.31.89.11.62
DIRECTIONS: in the industrial zone (Z.I.).
MENU: 49 Frs (drink included).
RESTAURANT: Snacks from 5.30, lunch 11.00, dinner - 22.00
CLOSED: Sun, and 3 weeks in Aug.
SPECIALITIES: home-cooking.
OTHER POINTS: bar.
Honfleur; Deauville; Trouville.

HOTEL LA DILIGENCE
(Mme Teeraya Blais) 53, rue de la République
TEL: 02.31.14.47.47 FAX: 02.31.98.83.87
ROOMS: 250 to 750 Frs.
HOTEL: 30 rooms.
FACILITIES: shower, bath, private bathroom, television, telephone
OTHER POINTS: credit cards accepted.

HOPITAL CAMFROUT (L')
Finistère, 29460

LES ROUTIERS
(Mr Bernard Hamery) 68, rue Emile Salaun
TEL: 02.98.20.01.21 FAX: 02.98.20.06.62
DIRECTIONS: RN170, Brest/Quimper autoroute, Daoulas exit.
MENU: 57 to 180 Frs.
RESTAURANT: Snacks from 7.30, lunch 12.00-14.00
CLOSED: 1 week in Feb and 2 weeks in Oct.
SPECIALITIES: fruits de mer, regional menu, home-cooking.
OTHER POINTS: credit cards accepted.
abbey at Daoulas (2km); parc régional d'Armorique (10km); beaches and presqu'île de Crozon (peninsula) (30km).

HOTTOT LES BAGUES
Calvados, 14250

LE RELAIS DE LA MANCHE
(Mr Roland Jeanne) Route de Caumont
TEL: 02.31.80.81.72
DIRECTIONS: D9, Granville.
MENU: 53 Frs.
RESTAURANT: Snacks from 6.00, lunch 11.30-14.00
CLOSED: Sat (in winter), and in June.
SPECIALITIES: home-cooking.
OTHER POINTS: credit cards accepted.

HYENVILLE
Manche, 50660

LE RELAIS DE LA SIENNE
(Mr Guy Defontaine) Le Pont
TEL: 02.33.45.82.22
DIRECTIONS: RD73, between Coutances and Granville.
MENU: 50 Frs (wine and coffee included).
RESTAURANT: Snacks from 4.30

SPECIALITIES: home-cooking.
HOTEL: 3 rooms.
FACILITIES: shower
OTHER POINTS: credit cards accepted.
bell foundry at Villedieu-les-Poëles; Granville; zoo at Champrepus.

IRAI
Orne, 61190

LE CAFE DE LA GARE
(Mme Jeannine Lenoir) La Cernetterie
TEL: 02.33.34.21.13
DIRECTIONS: between Loingny and Saint-Anne.
MENU: 60 Frs (wine and coffee included).
RESTAURANT: Snacks from 7.00, lunch 12.00-14.00
CLOSED: Sun, Mon afternoon and in Aug.
SPECIALITIES: home-cooking, terrine maison.
OTHER POINTS: bar.

JALLAIS
Maine-et-Loire, 49510

LA CROIX VERTE – LE VERT GALANT
(Mr Pierre Gaillard) Centre Ville
TEL: 02.41.64.20.22 **FAX:** 02.41.64.15.17
DIRECTIONS: 15km from Cholet.
LANGUAGES: English.
MENU: 82 to 200 Frs
ROOMS: 220 to 300 Frs.
RESTAURANT: Snacks from 7.00, lunch 12.00-14.00, dinner 19.30-22.00
CLOSED: Fri evening and Sun evening (out of season).
SPECIALITIES: salade rillauds d'Anjou chauds, pavé de boeuf au Chinon, brochet au beurre blanc, civet de porcelet ivre de vin, regional menu.
HOTEL: ☆☆ 21 rooms.
FACILITIES: shower, bath, television, telephone
OTHER POINTS: credit cards accepted.
le Puy du Fou; Muscadet and Anjou wine regions; handkerchief museum at Cholet; musée de la guerre (war) de Vendée; the banks of the Loire; zoo at Doué-la-Fontaine and amphitheatre.

JANZE
Ille-et-Villaine, 35150

HOTEL RESTAURANT BAR METAYER
(Mr Michel Métayer) 5, rue Jean-Marie Lacire
TEL: 02.99.47.05.10
ROOMS: 140 to 160 Frs.
RESTAURANT: Snacks from 7.00, lunch 12.00-14.00, dinner 19.00-20.30
SPECIALITIES: home-cooking.
HOTEL: 7 rooms.
FACILITIES: shower, bath, private bathroom, television, telephone
OTHER POINTS: bar.

JOSSELIN
Morbihan, 56120

LA ROCHETTE – Les Routiers
(Mme Annie Le Corre) 128 rue Glatinier – Z.I. La Rochette
TEL: 02.97.22.27.29
LANGUAGES: English.
MENU: 45 to 70 Frs.
RESTAURANT: Snacks from 8.00, lunch 12.00-14.00, dinner 19.00-21.30
CLOSED: Sat and Sun (out of season).
SPECIALITIES: home-cooking.
OTHER POINTS: credit cards accepted.
château at Josselin; musée des poupées (dolls).

JOUE DU BOIS
Orne, 61320

LE RELAIS DU MANOIR
(Mme Jeanine Laidet) Le Bourg
TEL: 02.33.37.96.83
DIRECTIONS: RN12, Alenáon.
MENU: 55 Frs (wine included).
RESTAURANT: Snacks from 7.00
SPECIALITIES: home-cooking, regional menu.
OTHER POINTS: credit cards accepted.
manoir (manor) of Joué-du-Bois; Forges; château at Carrouges; casino at Bagnoles-de-l'Orne.

JUILLEY
Manche, 50220

LE GERMON
(Mme Gilberte Horel) Le Guermon
TEL: 02.33.60.66.46
DIRECTIONS: on the Avranches/Fougères axis.
LANGUAGES: English.
MENU: 55 to 105 Frs.
RESTAURANT: Snacks from 7.30
CLOSED: Sun evening and Mon (out of season).
SPECIALITIES: home-cooking, terrine de saumon, huitres au cidre, grillades au feu de bois.
OTHER POINTS: credit cards accepted.

JUMELLIERE (LA)
Maine-et-Loire, 49120

LA BOULE D'OR
(Mme Janine Sécher) 2, rue du Val de Loire
TEL: 02.41.64.33.23
DIRECTIONS: RD961, the Cholet/Angers road – exit at Chemillé, then 5km on the left.

MENU: 54 to 170 Frs.
ROOMS: 110 to 180 Frs.
RESTAURANT: Snacks from 7.15, lunch 11.45-14.00, dinner 19.00-20.15
CLOSED: Sun.
SPECIALITIES: saumon au beurre blanc, home-cooking.
HOTEL: 6 rooms.
FACILITIES: shower, bath, private bathroom, television
OTHER POINTS: credit cards accepted.
musée des vieux métiers (ancient crafts) (9km); musée de la vigne (vineyards) (8km); jardin des plantes médicinales (6km); Angevin coastline (13km); château at Serrant (17km).

JURQUES
Calvados, 14260

AU BON ACCUEIL
(Mr Christian Lesage) Route de Vire
TEL: 02.31.77.81.17
DIRECTIONS: RD577 – exit at bypass (déviation) if coming from Caen, at Vire interchange.
MENU: 50 Frs (wine included).
RESTAURANT: Lunch 11.45-14.00, dinner 19.00-21.30
CLOSED: Sun (from 15.00 til 17.00).
SPECIALITIES: regional menu, home-cooking.
OTHER POINTS: credit cards accepted.
zoo at Jurques (3km); Bungy (10km); gorges of the Vire.

KERFAVEN
Finistère, 29230

RESTAURANT DE KERFAVEN
(Mr Vincent Pronost)
TEL: 02.98.20.41.26
DIRECTIONS: RD712, between Landivisiau and Landernau.
LANGUAGES: English.
MENU: 50 Frs (coffee included).
RESTAURANT: Snacks from 6.00
CLOSED: Sat, Sun, 2 weeks in July and 1 week in Aug.
SPECIALITIES: home-cooking,
OTHER POINTS: credit cards accepted.

KERGONAN LANGUIDIC
Morbihan, 56440

LE RELAIS KERGONAN
(Mr André Le Garrec) 9, rue du Commerce
TEL: 02.97.85.90.69
DIRECTIONS: RN24, the Rennes/Lorient road.
MENU: 45 Frs.
RESTAURANT: Snacks from 8.00, lunch 11.30-14.00
CLOSED: Sat, and last 2 weeks in Dec.
SPECIALITIES: home-cooking.
OTHER POINTS: credit cards accepted.
Ecomusée at 16thC Breton village of Poul-Fetan; Blavet valley.

KERHOSTIN
Morbihan, 56510

LA CHALOUPE
(Mlle Christiane Bouvrande) 10, rue Hoche
TEL: 02.97.30.91.54
DIRECTIONS: Quiberon.
MENU: 50 to 75 Frs.
ROOMS: 150 Frs.
RESTAURANT: Snacks from 8.00, lunch 12.00-14.00
CLOSED: Mon afternoon and Sun.
SPECIALITIES: regional menu, home-cooking.
HOTEL: 6 rooms.
FACILITIES: shower, bath
OTHER POINTS: credit cards accepted.

LAMBALLE
Côtes-d'Armor, 22400

LA TOUR D'ARGENT
(Mr Claude Mounier) 2, rue du Docteur Lavergne
TEL: 02.96.31.01.37 **FAX:** 02.96.31.37.59
DIRECTIONS: RD12, between Rennes and Saint-Brieuc.
LANGUAGES: English.
MENU: 52 to 100 Frs.
ROOMS: 180 to 350 Frs.
RESTAURANT: Snacks from 7.30, lunch 12.00-14.30, dinner 19.00-21.30
CLOSED: Sat (out of season).
SPECIALITIES: crevettes grillées, canard à l'orange, blancs de seiches, fruits de mer, regional menu, home-cooking.
HOTEL: ☆☆ 31 rooms.
FACILITIES: shower, bath, private bathroom, television, telephone
OTHER POINTS: credit cards accepted.
Saint-Malo; Mont-Saint-Michel; Dinan; Cap Fréhel; the coast; haras (stud-farm) national; Ile de Bréhat.

LANDEBIA
Côtes-d'Armor, 22130

AU RENDEZ-VOUS DES AMIS
(Mme Michèle Abbé) 17, rue de la Gare
TEL: 02.96.84.48.22
DIRECTIONS: RD768, between Lamballe and Plancoët.
LANGUAGES: English, Spanish.
MENU: 45 to 150 Frs.
ROOMS: 100 to 130 Frs.
RESTAURANT: Snacks from 7.00, lunch 11.00-15.00, dinner 19.00-22.00
SPECIALITIES: poissons, paella, couscous, regional menu, home-cooking.
HOTEL: 12 rooms.

FACILITIES: shower, bath, private bathroom
OTHER POINTS: credit cards accepted.
Mont-Saint-Michel; Saint-Malo; Côte d'Emeraude (Emerald coast); forêt la Hunaudaye and medieval château.

LANDIVISIAU
Finistère, 29400

LE TERMINUS
(Mr Serge Médelec) 94, avenue Foch
TEL: 02.98.68.02.00
DIRECTIONS: RN12, Brest, exit Ouest (west).
LANGUAGES: English, Spanish.
MENU: 80 to 120 Frs.
ROOMS: 120 to 150 Frs.
RESTAURANT: Snacks from 6.30, lunch 11.45-15.00, dinner 18.30-22.00
CLOSED: Fri evening, Sat lunch, Sun evening.
SPECIALITIES: regional menu, fruits de mer, poissons, home-cooking.
HOTEL: ☆ 23 rooms.
FACILITIES: shower, television
OTHER POINTS: credit cards accepted.
Brest; Breton calvaires (crosses); the coastline; les 'enclos', Roscoff.

LANISCAT
Côtes-d'Armor, 22570

AUBERGE DU DAOULAS
(Mme Marie-Claude Quemener) Rue de Bon Repos
TEL: 02.96.36.94.64
DIRECTIONS: RN164, between Rostrenen and Mur-de-Bretagne.
MENU: 52 to 200 Frs.
ROOMS: 120 to 170 Frs.
RESTAURANT: Snacks from 7.00, lunch 12.00-14.00, dinner 20.00-21.00
CLOSED: Mon and Sun from 14.30 till 17.00.
SPECIALITIES: regional menu, home-cooking.
HOTEL: 7 rooms.
FACILITIES: shower, private bathroom, television
OTHER POINTS: credit cards accepted.
Lac de Guerlédan; abbaye de Bon-Repos; Les Forges-des-Salles; Daoulas valley.

LANNION
Côtes-d'Armor, 22300

LA CROIX ROUGE
(Mr Claude Brozec) La Croix Rouge Ploumilliau
TEL: 02.96.35.45.08
DIRECTIONS: Lannion, towards Morlaix.
MENU: 55 to 165 Frs.
RESTAURANT: Snacks from 6.30, lunch 11.30-14.30, dinner 19.00-21.30
CLOSED: last 2 weeks in Aug.
SPECIALITIES: fruits de mer (Sunday), home-cooking.
HOTEL: 16 rooms.
FACILITIES: shower, private bathroom, television, telephone
OTHER POINTS: credit cards accepted.

LAPENTY
Manche, 50600

LE RELAIS DU BOIS LEGER
(Mme Sylvie Tirard) Le Bois Léger
TEL: 02.33.49.01.43
DIRECTIONS: RN 176, RN176, on the Paris/Mont-Saint-Michel axis.
LANGUAGES: English.
MENU: 50 to 120 Frs.
ROOMS: 100 to 170 Frs.
RESTAURANT: Snacks from 6.00, lunch 12.00-14.00, dinner 19.00-21.00
CLOSED: Sat.
SPECIALITIES: regional menu, terrines du chef, magret de canard.
HOTEL: 9 rooms.
FACILITIES: shower, bath, private bathroom
OTHER POINTS: credit cards accepted.

LAVAL
Mayenne, 53000

BAR DE LA GARE
(Mme Claudia Helbert) 107 Avenue Robert Buron
TEL: 02.43.53.94.88
DIRECTIONS: RN162 and RD53.
OTHER POINTS: bar.
old Laval.

LIGNOL
Morbihan, 56160

LE RELAIS DES VOYAGEURS
(Mr Bernard Le Solliec) 4, rue de la Mairie
TEL: 02.97.27.03.48
DIRECTIONS: RD782, the Pontivy/Quimper road via Le Faouet.
LANGUAGES: English.
MENU: 52 Frs.
ROOMS: 100 to 140 Frs.
RESTAURANT: Snacks from 7.00, lunch 12.00-14.00, dinner 19.00-21.00
CLOSED: Mon afternoon and 2 weeks in Feb.
SPECIALITIES: home-cooking.
HOTEL: 7 rooms.
FACILITIES: shower, television
OTHER POINTS: credit cards accepted.
Kemascleden: church (5km); étang (pool) at Priziac; zoo at Le Harlay (20km).

LOCMARIA GRAND CHAMPS
Morbihan, 56390

LA MARMITE
(Mr Jean-Pierre Joulaud) Collec
TEL: 02.97.66.66.80
DIRECTIONS: RD767, 10km from Vannes, towards Pontivy.
MENU: 45 to 200 Frs.
RESTAURANT: Snacks from 5.30, lunch 11.30-15.00, dinner 18.30-22.00
SPECIALITIES: home-cooking, regional menu.
OTHER POINTS: credit cards accepted.
Gulf of Morbihan

LOIRE
Maine-et-Loire, 49440

AU RENDEZ-VOUS DES ROUTIERS
(Mr Philippe Audouin) 24, rue de la Libération
TEL: 02.41.94.10.83
DIRECTIONS: RD923, the Nantes/Laval road.
MENU: 53 Frs (wine included).
RESTAURANT: Snacks from 6.30, lunch 11.30, dinner 19.00-20.00
CLOSED: first 2 weeks in July.
SPECIALITIES: canard au muscadet, beurre blanc, pintade (guinea-fowl) aux raisins, home-cooking.
OTHER POINTS: credit cards accepted.
la Mine Bleue.

LONGUE
Maine-et-Loire, 49160

LE RELAIS DES SOUVENETS – Chez Réjane
(Mme Réjane Taugourdeau) Les Souvenets
TEL: 02.41.52.13.86
DIRECTIONS: RN147.
RESTAURANT: Snacks from 7.30
CLOSED: Sat, Sun, and in Aug.
SPECIALITIES: home-cooking.
OTHER POINTS: credit cards accepted.
Saumur: château.

SARL LE RELAX
(Mr Chevré) Route Nationale 147
TEL: 02.41.52.68.81
DIRECTIONS: RN147, between Saumur (15km) and Angers (40km).
MENU: 55 (wine included) to 135 Frs.
RESTAURANT: Snacks from 6.00
CLOSED: Sun.
SPECIALITIES: regional menu, home-cooking.
OTHER POINTS: credit cards accepted.
Saumur: vineyards; Loire châteaux.

LORIENT
Morbihan, 56100

L'ALBATROS
(Mme Marie Legouic) 56, avenue de la Perrière
TEL: 02.97.37.55.76
DIRECTIONS: RN162, Vannes/Lorient, towards the fishing harbour.
MENU: 48 Frs (wine included).
RESTAURANT: Snacks from 9.00, lunch 11.30-14.00, dinner 19.00-21.30
CLOSED: Sat and Sun.
SPECIALITIES: home-cooking.
OTHER POINTS: credit cards accepted.
marina and fishing port.

LOUDEAC
Côtes-d'Armor, 22600

LES ROUTIERS
(Mr Dominique Le Cozannet) 7, rue Lavergne
TEL: 02.96.28.01.44
DIRECTIONS: RN164.
LANGUAGES: English.
MENU: 50 to 60 Frs.
ROOMS: 90 to 160 Frs.
RESTAURANT: Snacks from 7.00, lunch 12.00-14.00, dinner 19.00-21.00
CLOSED: Sun.
SPECIALITIES: fruits de mer, regional menu, home-cooking.
HOTEL: ☆ 40 rooms.
FACILITIES: shower, bath, private bathroom, television, telephone
OTHER POINTS: credit cards accepted.
lac de Guerlédan (75km).

LUCEAU
Sarthe, 72500

LA CROIX DE PAILLE
(Mr Jacques-Yves Moreau) Route du Mans – Château du Loir
TEL: 02.43.44.05.50
DIRECTIONS: RN138, between Le Mans and Tours.
RESTAURANT: Snacks from 6.00
CLOSED: Sat evening and Sun, and in Aug.
SPECIALITIES: home-cooking.
OTHER POINTS: credit cards accepted.

MACHECOUL
Loire-Atlantique, 44270

LA BICYCLETTE D'ARGENT
(Mme Marie-Joseph Baudry) 6, place du Pont
TEL: 02.40.78.50.48
LANGUAGES: English.
MENU: 45 to 120 Frs.

ROOMS: 90 to 180 Frs.
RESTAURANT: Snacks from 6.00, lunch 11.45-14.00, dinner 19.00-21.00
CLOSED: Sat (out of season), 1st week in May and 1st week in Nov.
SPECIALITIES: beurre blanc, anguilles (eels), cuisses de grenouilles, regional menu, home-cooking.
HOTEL: 9 rooms.
FACILITIES: shower, bath
OTHER POINTS: credit cards accepted.
châteaux; churches; wine-cellars.

MAGNY LA CAMPAGNE
Calvados, 14270

LA VALLEE D'AUGE
(Mme Marie-Thérése Sevin)
TEL: 02.31.20.04.20
DIRECTIONS: RD40, between Caen and Saint-Pierre-sur-Dive.
MENU: 50 to 105 Frs.
RESTAURANT: Snacks from 7.30
CLOSED: Tues, and in Jan.
SPECIALITIES: escalope Vallée d'Auge, poulet aux écrevisses, regional menu.
OTHER POINTS: children's menu.
châteaux; historic monuments; markets.

MALE
Orne, 61260

LA BELLE RENCONTRE
(Mr André Carle) Le Gibet
TEL: 02.37.49.68.85
DIRECTIONS: RN23, the Paris/Le Mans road.
MENU: 56 Frs.
ROOMS: 190 Frs.
RESTAURANT: Snacks from 6.00, lunch 11.00-14.00, dinner 19.00-22.00
CLOSED: Sat evening, Sun and in Aug.
SPECIALITIES: home-cooking.
HOTEL: ☆ 17 rooms.
FACILITIES: shower, bath, private bathroom, television
OTHER POINTS: credit cards accepted.
château; Perche valley.

MARIGNE LAILLE
Sarthe, 72220

AUBERGE DU BON ACCUEIL
(Mr Jean-Louis Loudière) Route Nationale 138 – Laillé
TEL: 02.43.42.12.01
DIRECTIONS: RN138, the Le Mans/Tours road.
MENU: 49 to 150 Frs.
RESTAURANT: Snacks from 7.00, lunch 12.00-14.30, dinner 19.00-21.30
CLOSED: Wed afternoon.
SPECIALITIES: home-cooking.
OTHER POINTS: credit cards accepted.

MARTIGNE FERCHAUD
Ille-et-Villaine, 35640

LE POT D'ETAIN
(Mme Yvonne Bouteiller) 10, grande rue
TEL: 02.99.47.90.12
DIRECTIONS: RN178.
SPECIALITIES: home-cooking.
OTHER POINTS: children's menu.

MARZAN
Morbihan, 56130

LES RIVES DE VILAINE
(Mr Gilles Jouan) 13, rue de la Fontaine
TEL: 02.99.90.63.22
DIRECTIONS: RN165, Vannes, on the right after bridge at La Roche-Bernard.
MENU: 50 to 180 Frs.
RESTAURANT: Snacks from 7.30, lunch 12.00-14.00
CLOSED: 3 weeks in Aug and last week end Dec.
SPECIALITIES: fruits de mer, poissons au beurre blanc (to order), regional menu, home-cooking.
OTHER POINTS: credit cards accepted.
zoo at Branféré; La Roche-Bernard; La Baule; Gulf of Morbihan.

MATHIEU
Calvados, 14920

LE COTE DE NACRE
(Mr Marc Bedeau de l'Ecochère) 4, rue Augustin Fresnel
TEL: 02.31.44.10.17
DIRECTIONS: RD7, Douvres-la-Délivrande.
MENU: 56 to 70 Frs.
ROOMS: 120 to 150 Frs.
RESTAURANT: Snacks from 7.00, lunch 12.00-15.00, dinner 19.30-21.00
CLOSED: Sun, public holidays and from 12th to 28th Jan.
SPECIALITIES: home-cooking.
HOTEL: 2 rooms.
FACILITIES: shower, bath
OTHER POINTS: bar.

MAY SUR ORNE
Calvados, 14320

L'AMMONITE
(Mme Maryvonne Horel) 2, rue du Canada
TEL: 02.31.79.80.27
DIRECTIONS: RD562, the Caen/Laval road (8km from Caen).
LANGUAGES: English.

MENU: 50 to 130 Frs.
ROOMS: 130 to 170 Frs.
RESTAURANT: Snacks from 8.00, lunch 11.30-14.30, dinner 19.30-21.30
CLOSED: Sun (out of season).
SPECIALITIES: escalope normande, côte de porc au cidre, regional menu, home-cooking.
HOTEL: 8 rooms.
FACILITIES: shower, bath, private bathroom
OTHER POINTS: credit cards accepted.
Orne valley; Caen; la Suisse normande; landing beaches; route des fromages.

AU BON MAY
(Mr Guyon Alain) 6, rue des Ursulines
TEL: 02.31.79.81.39
DIRECTIONS: RD 562, RD562, on the Caen/Laval axis.
LANGUAGES: English.
MENU: 55 Frs (drink and coffee included).
ROOMS: 185 Frs.
RESTAURANT: Snacks from 8.00, lunch 11.30-14.30, dinner 18.30-20.30
CLOSED: from Sat 14.00 till Sun 16.30 and 1st 2 weeks in July.
SPECIALITIES: regional menu, home-cooking, blanquette de jambon.
HOTEL: 4 rooms
OTHER POINTS: credit cards accepted.

MAYENNE
Mayenne, 53100

L'ESCALE
(Mr Dominique Fortin) Route du Mans
TEL: 02.43.04.19.14
DIRECTIONS: CD35, Le Mans.
MENU: 55 Frs (wine and coffee included).
ROOMS: 100 to 200 Frs.
RESTAURANT: Snacks from 5.30, lunch 11.00-14.00, dinner 19.00-21.00
CLOSED: Sat evening and Sun.
SPECIALITIES: home-cooking.
HOTEL: 9 rooms
OTHER POINTS: credit cards accepted.
Mayenne: château, basilica, church, chapel; Gallo-Roman site at Jublains; musée de l'ardoise (slate) at Renazé; musée Robert Tatin at Cossé-le-Vivien.

LE RELAIS DES BRUYERES
(Mr Jean-Pierre Bordas) Route d'Alenáon – Aron
TEL: 02.43.04.13.64
DIRECTIONS: RN12, between Alenáon and Mayenne.
LANGUAGES: German.
MENU: 55 to 138 Frs.
ROOMS: 120 to 180 Frs.
RESTAURANT: Snacks from 5.00
CLOSED: Sat, and in Aug.
SPECIALITIES: regional menu, home-cooking.
HOTEL: 9 rooms.
FACILITIES: shower, bath, television
OTHER POINTS: credit cards accepted.
Bagnoles-de-l'Orne (30km).

MEILARS
Finistère, 29790

LA CREMAILLERE
(Mme Franáoise Guivarch') Bourg de Confort
TEL: 02.98.74.51.97 FAX: 02.98.74.58.75
DIRECTIONS: between Audierne and Douarnenez.
LANGUAGES: English.
MENU: 47 Frs (wine included).
RESTAURANT: Snacks from 7.30, lunch 11.30-14.00
SPECIALITIES: regional menu, home-cooking, ragoñt de homard.
OTHER POINTS: credit cards accepted.

MENIL BROUT (LE)
Orne, 61250

CHEZ GHISLAINE
(Mme Ghislaine Gautier) Route Nationale 12
TEL: 02.33.27.10.03
DIRECTIONS: RN12, between Alenáon and Dreux.
MENU: 53 Frs.
ROOMS: 100 to 120 Frs.
SPECIALITIES: home-cooking.
HOTEL: 8 rooms.
FACILITIES: shower, bath, private bathroom
OTHER POINTS: bar.
Alenáon; 'les Alpes Manselles'; lake at Le Mêle-sur-Sarthe.

MESNIL DURAND (LE)
Calvados, 14140

LE RELAIS DE LA FORGE – Chez Chantal
(Mme Chantal Le Rosier) Les Forges Mézières
TEL: 02.31.63.52.79
DIRECTIONS: RD579, between Lisieux and Livarot.
MENU: 60 Frs.
RESTAURANT: Snacks from 6.00, lunch 12.00-14.30, dinner 19.00-21.00
CLOSED: Sat, Sun and 2 weeks at Christmas.
SPECIALITIES: home-cooking.
OTHER POINTS: credit cards accepted.
Lisieux: basilica (12km); Auge valley.

MINIAC SOUS BECHEREL
Ille-et-Villaine, 35190

LE RELAIS DES CHATEAUX
(Mr Yvonnick Trochet) Le Bourg
TEL: 02.99.66.78.57
DIRECTIONS: on the Rennes/Dinan road.

LANGUAGES: English.
MENU: 55 Frs (wine and coffee included).
RESTAURANT: Snacks from 9.00, lunch 12.00-14.00, dinner 19.00-20.30
CLOSED: Tues afternoon and Sun evening.
SPECIALITIES: home-cooking.
OTHER POINTS: credit cards accepted.

MIRE
Maine-et-Loire, 49330

L'ESPERANCE
(Mr Jean-Pierre Pourias) 4, place Jean Bourré
TEL: 02.41.32.82.08
DIRECTIONS: on the Angers/Château-Gontier axis.
MENU: 52 Frs (wine included).
RESTAURANT: Snacks from 7.30, lunch 12.00-14.00, dinner 19.00-20.00
CLOSED: Wed afternoon and last 2 weeks in Aug.
SPECIALITIES: regional menu, home-cooking.
OTHER POINTS: credit cards accepted.

MOLAY LITTRY (LE)
Calvados, 14330

LA TAVERNE
(Mr Alain Marie) 32, rue de Balleroy
TEL: 02.31.22.96.36
DIRECTIONS: Balleroy/Isigny and Bayeux/Lison.
MENU: 50 Frs.
RESTAURANT: Snacks from 8.00, lunch 11.30-14.30
CLOSED: Wed afternoon.
SPECIALITIES: home-cooking.
OTHER POINTS: bar.
forêt de Balleroy; Potteries at Noron; moulin (windmill) at Marcy, musée de la mine (mining).

MONNAI
Orne, 61470

LE CHEVAL BAI
(Mr Gilbert Roussel) Route Nationale 138
TEL: 02.33.39.42.00
DIRECTIONS: RN138.
RESTAURANT: Snacks from 5.00
CLOSED: Sun.
HOTEL: 6 rooms
OTHER POINTS: bar.

MONT SAINT MICHEL (LE)
Manche, 50116

HOTEL MOTEL VERT
(Mr Philippe Franáois) Route du Mont Saint Michel
TEL: 02.33.60.09.33 FAX: 02.33.68.22.09
DIRECTIONS: RD976, at the last crossroads before the causeway.
LANGUAGES: English, German, Italian.
MENU: 59 to 205 Frs.
ROOMS: 210 to 500 Frs.
RESTAURANT: Open 24h.
CLOSED: Dec and Jan.
SPECIALITIES: agneau (lamb), fruits de mer, omelette du Mont-Saint-Michel, regional menu.
HOTEL: ☆☆ 113 rooms.
FACILITIES: shower, bath, private bathroom, television, telephone
OTHER POINTS: credit cards accepted.
Mont-Saint-Michel; Cancale; Saint-Malo; château at Fougères; Island of Jersey; Dinan.

MONTAUBAN DE BRETAGNE
Ille-et-Villaine, 35360

HOTEL DE FRANCE
(Mr Gabriel Le Metayer) 34, rue du Général de Gaulle
TEL: 02.99.06.40.19
DIRECTIONS: The Rennes/Brest axis.
LANGUAGES: English, Spanish.
MENU: 65 to 160 Frs.
ROOMS: 120 to 220 Frs.
RESTAURANT: Snacks from 7.00, lunch 11.30-14.00, dinner 19.00-21.30
CLOSED: Mon (out of season), and from 20th Dec to 20th Jan.
SPECIALITIES: fruits de mer, coq au Muscadet, far breton (biscuits), poissons, regional menu, home-cooking.
HOTEL: ☆☆ 10 rooms.
FACILITIES: shower, bath, private bathroom, television, telephone
OTHER POINTS: credit cards accepted.
forêt de Brocéliande; medieval château.

RELAIS DE LA HUCHERAIS
(Mr Alain Meheust) La Hucherais
TEL: 02.99.06.54.31
DIRECTIONS: RN12 and 164bis.
LANGUAGES: English.
MENU: 52 to 120 Frs.
ROOMS: 210 to 230 Frs.
RESTAURANT: Snacks from 5.00, lunch 11.00-15.01, dinner 18.30-22.00
CLOSED: Sun.
SPECIALITIES: regional menu,
HOTEL: ☆☆ 14 rooms
OTHER POINTS: bar.

MONTAUDIN
Mayenne, 53220

HOTEL DE PARIS
(Mr Daniel Doudard) Route d'Ernée
TEL: 02.43.05.30.79
DIRECTIONS: RN799.

LANGUAGES: English.
MENU: 44 to 67 Frs.
ROOMS: 155 to 205 Frs.
RESTAURANT: Snacks from 7.00, dinner -21.00
CLOSED: Mon, and in Aug.
SPECIALITIES: brochet au beurre blanc, home-cooking.
HOTEL: 4 rooms.
FACILITIES: shower, bath, private bathroom, television
OTHER POINTS: credit cards accepted.
Mont-Saint-Michel; château at Fougères (17km); Pontmain (9km).

MONTFIQUET
Calvados, 14490

LE RELAIS DE LA FORET
(Mr Christian Desobeaux) Balleroy
TEL: 02.31.21.39.78 FAX: 02.31.21.44.19
DIRECTIONS: RD572, between Bayeux and Saint-Lô.
MENU: 56 Frs.
ROOMS: 198 to 240 Frs.
RESTAURANT: Snacks from 5.00, lunch 11.00-15.30, dinner 19.00-24.00
SPECIALITIES: regional menu, home-cooking.
HOTEL: ☆ 19 rooms.
FACILITIES: shower, bath, private bathroom, television, telephone
OTHER POINTS: credit cards accepted.
château at Balleroy; musée de la mine (mining); Bayeux tapestry.

MONTMARTIN SUR MER
Manche, 50590

HOTELLERIE DU BON VIEUX TEMPS
(Mr Erick Bourbonnais)
TEL: 02.33.47.54.44 FAX: 02.33.46.27.12
DIRECTIONS: RD20, Granville.
LANGUAGES: English.
MENU: 60 to 200 Frs.
ROOMS: 145 to 260 Frs.
RESTAURANT: Snacks from 8.00, lunch 12.00-14.00, dinner 19.30-21.00
CLOSED: Sun evening (from 1st Nov to Easter).
SPECIALITIES: cider and cream-based cuisine, regional menu.
HOTEL: ☆☆ 20 rooms.
FACILITIES: shower, bath, private bathroom, television, telephone
OTHER POINTS: credit cards accepted.
Baie de la Sienne; lime-kilns; nearby manor-houses; Granville; Channel Islands excursions.

MONTOIR DE BRETAGNE
Loire-Atlantique, 44550

LES NOES
(Mme Brigitte Liberge) Route Nationale 171 – Les Noës
TEL: 02.40.45.55.67
DIRECTIONS: RN171, the Nantes/Saint-Nazaire expressway.
MENU: 50 Frs.
RESTAURANT: Snacks from 6.30, lunch 11.45-14.00, dinner 19.00-21.00
CLOSED: Sat and Sun.
SPECIALITIES: home-cooking.
OTHER POINTS: credit cards accepted.
Montoir: port; Saint-Nazaire; parc regional de Brière.

RELAIS DU BOSCO
(Mr Jean-Michel Valain) Centre International de Frêt
TEL: 02.40.90.18.80
DIRECTIONS: between Nantes and Saint-Nazaire.
MENU: 50 Frs.
RESTAURANT: Snacks from 6.00, dinner -22.00
CLOSED: Sat and Sun.
SPECIALITIES: home-cooking.
OTHER POINTS: credit cards accepted.
Montoir: port; Saint-Nazaire.

MONTREUIL LE CHETIF
Sarthe, 72130

AU RENDEZ-VOUS DES CHASSEURS
(Mme Franáoise Bordeau) Le Grand Gué
TEL: 02.43.33.39.90
DIRECTIONS: RD310, Sillé-le-Guillaume, at Fresnay, on the edge of the forest.
MENU: 52 to 82 Frs.
RESTAURANT: Snacks from 7.00, lunch 12.00-14.00, dinner 19.00-21.00
SPECIALITIES: regional menu, home-cooking.
OTHER POINTS: credit cards accepted.
château at Sainte-Suzanne; grottes (caves) de Sauges; Fresnay; musée des coiffes (head-dresses); abbaye de Champagne.

MORDELLES
Ille-et-Villaine, 35310

LE RELAIS DE MORDELLES
(Mr Michel Cavalier) La Croix Ignon
TEL: 02.99.60.02.50
DIRECTIONS: RN24, between Rennes and Lorient.
MENU: 55 to 100 Frs.
RESTAURANT: Snacks from 7.30, lunch 12.00-14.00
CLOSED: Sat, Sun, and in Aug.
SPECIALITIES: home-cooking.

OTHER POINTS: credit cards accepted.
forêt de Brocéliande.

MOREAC
Morbihan, 56500

LE RELAIS DU BARDERFF
(Mr Jean Lamour) Z.I. du Barderff
TEL: 02.97.60.18.60 **FAX:** 02.97.60.25.55
DIRECTIONS: RN24, between Rennes and Lorient or Vannes and Saint-Brieuc.
LANGUAGES: English.
MENU: lunch at 50 Frs, dinner at 54 Frs.
ROOMS: 220 to 360 Frs.
RESTAURANT: Snacks from 5.00, lunch 12.00-14.00, dinner 19.00-22.00
CLOSED: Sun (out of season).
SPECIALITIES: regional menu, home-cooking.
HOTEL: ☆☆ 20 rooms.
FACILITIES: shower, bath, private bathroom, television, telephone
OTHER POINTS: credit cards accepted.
the sea (30km).

MOREILLES
Vendée, 85450

LE CHEVAL BLANC
(Mr Christian Sarraud) 9, route Nationale
TEL: 02.51.56.11.02
DIRECTIONS: RN137, the Nantes/Bordeaux road.
LANGUAGES: English, Spanish.
MENU: 59 to 72 Frs.
ROOMS: 105 to 145 Frs.
RESTAURANT: Snacks from 6.00, lunch 11.30-14.00, dinner 19.00-21.30
CLOSED: Sun (out of season), and from 25th Jan to 10th Feb.
SPECIALITIES: mojettes (beans), jambon vendéen (Vendée ham), regional menu, home-cooking.
HOTEL: 5 rooms.
FACILITIES: shower, private bathroom
OTHER POINTS: credit cards accepted.
Poitou marshlands; La Rochelle; Ile de Ré; Vendée coast.

MORLAIX
Finistère, 29600

POIVRE ET SEL
(Mme Marie-Catherine Daniel) Zone d'Activités La Boissière
TEL: 02.98.88.02.66
DIRECTIONS: on the Rennes/Brest axis, motorway La Boissière exit.
LANGUAGES: English.
MENU: 55 Frs (wine included).
RESTAURANT: Snacks from 9.00, lunch 12.00-15.00, dinner 19.00-21.00
CLOSED: Sun.
SPECIALITIES: home-cooking.
OTHER POINTS: credit cards accepted.

MORTAGNE (SAINT LANGIS)
Orne, 61400

HOTEL DE LA GARE
(Mr Belaïd Leroul) Avenue de la Gare
TEL: 02.33.25.16.10
DIRECTIONS: the Bellème/Le Mans road.
MENU: 49 to 55 Frs.
ROOMS: 100 to 130 Frs.
RESTAURANT: Snacks from 6.00, lunch 12.00-14.30, dinner 19.00-21.30
CLOSED: Sat afternoon, Sun, and in Aug.
SPECIALITIES: home-cooking.
HOTEL: 6 rooms.
FACILITIES: shower, bath, private bathroom, telephone
OTHER POINTS: bar.
Chapelle Montlugeon.

MORTAGNE SUR SEVRE
Vendée, 85290

LE PUY NARDON
(Mr Gérard Duval) Z.A. du Puy Nardon – Route de Poitiers
TEL: 02.51.65.19.14 **FAX:** 02.51.65.19.12
DIRECTIONS: RN149, the Nantes/Poitiers road.
LANGUAGES: English.
MENU: 45 Frs.
RESTAURANT: Snacks from 6.00, lunch 11.30-14.30, dinner 19.00-22.00
SPECIALITIES: home-cooking.
OTHER POINTS: credit cards accepted.
le Puy du Fou; château Barbe-Bleue; la maison de l'eau at Mallièvre; musée paysan (peasant life); musée des arts at Cholet.

LE RELAIS DE LA GARE
(Mr Jean-Luc Arrouet) 52, route de Cholet
TEL: 02.51.65.11.56
DIRECTIONS: RN160.
RESTAURANT: Snacks from 6.30
CLOSED: Sat, Sun, and in Aug.
OTHER POINTS: bar

MORTREE
Orne, 61570

LE POINT DU JOUR
(Fabienne et Jacky Huette) 139, Grande Rue
TEL: 02.33.35.35.22
DIRECTIONS: RN158, between Argentan and Sées.
LANGUAGES: English.

MENU: 55 Frs.
RESTAURANT: Snacks from 6.30, lunch 11.45-14.00, dinner 19.00-21.00
CLOSED: Sat afternoon and Sun (except functions), and in Aug.
SPECIALITIES: bourguignon maison, émincé de volaille au calvados, regional menu, home-cooking.
OTHER POINTS: credit cards accepted.
châteaux at Mortrée and Sassy; cathedral at Sées.

MOSLES
Calvados, 14400

RESTAURANT DE LA POSTE
(Mr Jacques Lerosier) Route Nationale 13
TEL: 02.31.22.33.79
DIRECTIONS: RN13, the Bayeux/Cherbourg road.
MENU: 54 to 80 Frs.
RESTAURANT: Snacks from 6.00, lunch 11.00-15.00, dinner 19.00-22.00
CLOSED: Sat afternoon and Sun.
SPECIALITIES: home-cooking.
OTHER POINTS: credit cards accepted.
landing beaches and museum; Bayeux tapestry.

MOULT
Calvados, 14370

LE MILLE PATTES
(Mme Chantal Hervieu) Route de Saint Pierre – La Gare de Moult
TEL: 02.31.23.53.83
LANGUAGES: English.
MENU: 54 Frs (drink included) to 69 Frs.
RESTAURANT: Snacks from 5.00, lunch 11.00-15.00, dinner 18.00-23.30
CLOSED: Sat afternoon, Sun and from 1st to 23rd July.
SPECIALITIES: regional menu, home-cooking.
OTHER POINTS: credit cards accepted.

MOUZEUIL SAINT MARTIN
Vendée, 85370

CENTRAL ROUTIERS
(Mr Jean-Marie Guilbaud) 33, rue Louis Apraille
TEL: 02.51.28.72.44
DIRECTIONS: RN148, between Niort and Les Sables d'Olonne.
MENU: 55 Frs (coffee included).
ROOMS: 100 to 240 Frs.
RESTAURANT: Snacks from 6.30, lunch 12.00-15.00, dinner 20.00-22.00
SPECIALITIES: anguilles (eels), couscous, regional menu, home-cooking.
HOTEL: 10 rooms.
FACILITIES: shower, bath, private bathroom, television
OTHER POINTS: credit cards accepted.
Poitou marshlands; le Puy du Fou; baie de l'Aiguillon; dam; forêt de Mervent.

NANTES
Loire-Atlantique, 44200

A L'ANCRE D'OR
(Mlle Pascale Camier) 55, boulevard Gustave Roch
TEL: 02.40.35.39.30
DIRECTIONS: RN43, M.I.N.
LANGUAGES: English.
MENU: 43 Frs (wine included).
ROOMS: 75 to 85 Frs.
RESTAURANT: Snacks from 4.30
CLOSED: Sat and Sun.
SPECIALITIES: home-cooking.
HOTEL: 5 rooms.
FACILITIES: shower
OTHER POINTS: credit cards accepted.
Nantes: cathedral, château des ducs de Bretagne; Muscadet wine route.

CAFE RESTAURANT DE L'AVENIR
(Mme Viviane Baron) 1, rue de la Pompe
TEL: 02.40.43.46.03
DIRECTIONS: RN23, Nantes Ouest (West), La Januraie exit.
MENU: 47 to 55 Frs.
RESTAURANT: Snacks from 5.30, lunch 11.30-14.30, dinner 19.00-22.30
CLOSED: Sat, Sun, and mid-Dec.
SPECIALITIES: home-cooking.
OTHER POINTS: credit cards accepted.
Lac de Grand-Lieu (20km); pont de Cheviré; African safari; Port-Saint-Père.

NASSANDRES
Eure, 27550

LE PARIS/CAEN/CHERBOURG
(Mr Laurent De Nave) Route Nationale 13
TEL: 02.32.45.00.26
DIRECTIONS: RN13, the Evreux/Lisieux road.
MENU: 54 Frs.
RESTAURANT: Snacks from 3.30
CLOSED: from Sat afternoon to Sun 22.00.
SPECIALITIES: pieds de veau, regional menu, home-cooking.
HOTEL: 4 rooms
OTHER POINTS: credit cards accepted.
abbaye du Bec-Hellouin; château d'Harcourt.

NEUBOURG (LE)
Eure, 27110

LE PROGRES
(Mme Colette Fournier) Le Tremblay Omonville
TEL: 02.32.35.41.80 FAX: 02.32.34.88.00
DIRECTIONS: Verneuil/Le Neubourg road, Evreux-Lisieux.
MENU: 55 to 75 Frs.
RESTAURANT: Snacks from 6.00, lunch 11.30-14.30, dinner 19.00-22.00
CLOSED: Sun and in Aug.
SPECIALITIES: regional menu, home-cooking.
OTHER POINTS: credit cards accepted.
Château du Champ de Bataille; château d'Harcourt; Abbaye du Bec.

NEUFBOURG (LE)
Manche, 50140

LE MERCURY
(Mme Mauricette Bertrand) 13, route de Vire
TEL: 02.33.59.92.17
DIRECTIONS: RD577, Mortain/Vire axis.
MENU: 50 Frs (drinks included).
ROOMS: 100 to 150 Frs.
RESTAURANT: Snacks from 6.30, lunch 12.00-14.00, dinner 19.00-21.00
CLOSED: Sun.
SPECIALITIES: pizzas, home-cooking.
HOTEL: 4 rooms
OTHER POINTS: credit cards accepted.

NEUFCHATEL EN BRAY
Seine-Maritime, 76270

RELAIS DES HAYONS
(Mr Jean-Claude Piednoël) Esclavelles
TEL: 02.35.93.13.15
DIRECTIONS: A28, towards Forges-les-Eaux.
MENU: 50 Frs.
RESTAURANT: Snacks from 5.30, lunch 11.30-15.00, dinner 18.30-22.00
CLOSED: Sat and Sun.
SPECIALITIES: Normand dishes, home-cooking.
OTHER POINTS: credit cards accepted.
Neufchâtel-en-Bray; château at Mesnières.

NEUVE LYRE (LA)
Eure, 27330

LE RELAIS DES AMIS
(Mr Jean-Claude Guyot) Hameau de Chagny
TEL: 02.32.30.50.60
DIRECTIONS: between Evreux and L'Aigle.
ROOMS: 49 Frs.
RESTAURANT: Snacks from 6.30
CLOSED: Sun, and the 1st 2 weeks in Aug.
SPECIALITIES: home-cooking.
HOTEL: 5 rooms.
FACILITIES: shower
OTHER POINTS: bar.

NEUVILLE (PHILIPPEVILLE)
Morbihan, 5600

LE RELAIS DE LA FORET
(Mme Christiane Lothier) 47, route de Mariembourg
TEL: 071.667.203 FAX: 060.312.985
DIRECTIONS: RN 5, RN5, between Charleroi and Rocroi.
MENU: 250 to 550 FB.
RESTAURANT: Snacks from 8.00, lunch 12.00-14.30, dinner 18.00-20.00
CLOSED: Tues and in Jan.
SPECIALITIES: regional menu, home-cooking, rabbit à Shendy, game, meats et fish.
OTHER POINTS: credit cards accepted.

NIEUL LE DOLENT
Vendée, 85430

CHEZ JACQUES
(Mr Jacques Pinel) 8, rue de Lattre de Tassigny
TEL: 02.51.07.93.71
DIRECTIONS: RD36, between La Roche-sur-Yon and Les Tranches-sur-Mer.
MENU: 45 to 55 Frs.
RESTAURANT: Snacks from 7.30, lunch 11.30-14.30
CLOSED: Sun.
SPECIALITIES: fraise de veau, home-cooking.
OTHER POINTS: credit cards accepted.
Les Sables d'Olonne.

NOTRE DAME DE GRAVENCHON
Seine-Maritime, 76330

AU COUP DE FREIN
(Mme Marie-Josée David) Rue Claude Bernard
TEL: 02.35.38.61.35
DIRECTIONS: town centre, towards Norville.
MENU: 48 Frs.
RESTAURANT: Snacks from 6.30, lunch 11.30-14.30, dinner 19.00-20.30
CLOSED: Sat afternoon and Sun afternoon.
SPECIALITIES: home cooking
HOTEL: 4 rooms
OTHER POINTS: modern decor.

NOYAL SUR BRUTZ
Loire-Atlantique, 44110

LE CUIRASSE
(Chez Bernadette et Bernard Bichet)
2, rue de la Mairie

TEL: 02.40.81.32.50
RESTAURANT: Snacks from 6.30, lunch 11.45-15.00, dinner 18.30-21.30
SPECIALITIES: sea-food, potée auvergnate, home-cooking.
OTHER POINTS: credit cards accepted.

NOYAL SUR VILAINE
Ille-et-Villaine, 35530

LE RELAIS 35
(Mme Pascale Sefelin) 20, avenue du Général de Gaulle
TEL: 02.99.00.51.20
DIRECTIONS: RN157, the Paris/Rennes road.
LANGUAGES: English.
MENU: 49.50 to 85 Frs.
ROOMS: 100 to 115 Frs.
RESTAURANT: Snacks from 6.00, lunch 11.00-15.00, dinner 18.00-22.00
CLOSED: Sat afternoon, Sun and 3rd week of Aug.
SPECIALITIES: pizza, home-cooking.
HOTEL: 12 rooms
OTHER POINTS: credit cards accepted.

OISSEAU LE PETIT
Sarthe, 72610

HOTEL DE L'ESPERANCE
(Mme Andrée Besnard)
TEL: 02.33.26.81.97
DIRECTIONS: RN138, between Le Mans and Alenáon.
MENU: 55 to 70 Frs.
ROOMS: 80 to 110 Frs.
RESTAURANT: Snacks from 6.00, lunch 12.00-14.00, dinner 19.30-21.00
CLOSED: Sat, Sun, and in Aug.
SPECIALITIES: home-cooking.
HOTEL: 6 rooms.
FACILITIES: shower
OTHER POINTS: credit cards accepted.

OSMANVILLE
Calvados, 14230

AUX AMIS DE LA ROUTE
(Mr Jacques Duchêne) Route Nationale 13
TEL: 02.31.22.14.84 FAX: 02.31.51.88.29
DIRECTIONS: RN13, the Caen/Cherbourg axis.
MENU: 58 to 110 Frs.
ROOMS: 149 Frs.
SPECIALITIES: home-cooking.
HOTEL: 2 rooms.
FACILITIES: shower, private bathroom, television
OTHER POINTS: credit cards accepted.

OUISTREHAM
Calvados, 14150

AU COIN DU PORT
(Claude et Andrée Morin Notamy) 90, avenue Michel Cabieu
TEL: 02.31.97.15.22
LANGUAGES: English.
MENU: 58 Frs.
RESTAURANT: Snacks from 7.30, lunch 12.00-15.00, dinner 19.00-22.00
CLOSED: Sun (out of season), and last week in Dec.
SPECIALITIES: regional menu, home-cooking.
OTHER POINTS: credit cards accepted.
museums; landing beaches and military cemetery.

PACE
Orne, 61250

LE RELAIS DU CHENE
(Mr Gilles Boutinon) Route Nationale 12
TEL: 02.33.27.72.06
DIRECTIONS: RN12, between Alenáon and Mayenne.
MENU: 49 Frs.
RESTAURANT: Snacks from 5.00
CLOSED: Sat afternoon, Sun, and 1 week from Christmas Day.
SPECIALITIES: truite normande, home-cooking.
OTHER POINTS: credit cards accepted.
forêt d'Ecouve; Mancelles.

PACE PAR ALENCON
Orne, 61250

LE RELAIS DES ROUTIERS
(Mr Marcel Bruneau) Damigni
TEL: 02.33.27.70.69 FAX: 02.33.28.82.45
DIRECTIONS: RN12, the Saint-Malo/Rennes/Alenáon road.
MENU: 65 to 130 Frs.
RESTAURANT: Snacks from 6.30, lunch 11.30-15.00, dinner 19.00-21.00
CLOSED: Fri evening, Sat evening, Sun and from 15th Nov to 15th Dec.
SPECIALITIES: home-cooking, rillettes, paté du chef, regional menu.
OTHER POINTS: credit cards accepted.

PARIGNE
Ille-et-Villaine, 35133

LE FRANCK'ELLE
(Mr Franck Rousset) 12, rue de la Mairie
TEL: 02.99.97.22.90
DIRECTIONS: RD108, Flers, Fougères exit.
MENU: 51 to 120 Frs.
RESTAURANT: Snacks from 8.00, lunch 12.00-15.00,

dinner 19.00-21.00
CLOSED: Mon afternoon, and 1st 2 weeks in Aug.
SPECIALITIES: poulet aux écrevisses, truite hussarde, fruits de mer, regional menu.
OTHER POINTS: credit cards accepted.
forêt de Fougères and château; Mont-Saint-Michel (23km); château at Fretay (2km); Rocher de Monthault; Saint-James American cemetery; Parigné: tourbière (peat-bog); Pontmain (pilgrimage).

PARIGNE LE POLIN
Sarthe, 72330

LE RELAIS FLEURI
(Mr Bruno Servain) Route Nationale 23
TEL: 02.43.87.95.04
DIRECTIONS: RN23, between Le Mans and La Flèche.
MENU: 56.50 to 92.50 Frs.
RESTAURANT: Snacks from 5.30
CLOSED: Sat and Sun.
SPECIALITIES: home-cooking.
OTHER POINTS: credit cards accepted.

PEDERNEC
Côtes-d'Armor, 22540

LE MAUDEZ
(Mr Denis Dutillet) Maudez
TEL: 02.96.45.31.28
DIRECTIONS: Lannion.
MENU: 36 to 85 Frs.
RESTAURANT: Snacks from 6.45, lunch 11.30-14.00, dinner 19.00-21.00
CLOSED: Sun, and 2 weeks in Aug.
SPECIALITIES: home-cooking.
OTHER POINTS: bar.
Perrier valley; leisure park (Armoripark); Ménez-Bré.

PERCY
Manche, 50410

LE RELAIS DE L'ANCIENNE GARE
(Mr Henri Yhuello) 4, rue de l'Ancienne Gare
TEL: 02.33.61.94.60
DIRECTIONS: RD999, on the left as you reach Percy, coming from Saint-Lô.
MENU: 55 Frs (wine and coffee included).
ROOMS: 100 Frs.
RESTAURANT: Snacks from 7.00, lunch 12.00-14.00, dinner 19.00-21.00
CLOSED: Sat afternoon, Sun, last 2 weeks in Aug and 1 week for Christmas/New Year.
SPECIALITIES: home-cooking.
HOTEL: 4 rooms.
FACILITIES: shower, bath, private bathroom
OTHER POINTS: bar.
Villedieu-les-Poëles (9km); Mont-Saint-Michel (55km).

PIACE
Sarthe, 72170

LES DEUX RENARDS
(Mr Jérôme Brilliet) Route Nationale 138 – Le Bourg
TEL: 02.43.97.02.16
DIRECTIONS: RN138, between Alenáon (20km) and Le Mans (30km).
MENU: 50 to 55 Frs.
RESTAURANT: Snacks from 5.00, lunch 11.00-14.30, dinner 19.00-22.00
CLOSED: Sat, Sun, and in Aug.
SPECIALITIES: home-cooking.
OTHER POINTS: credit cards accepted.
'les Alpes Manselles'(20km).

PICAUVILLE
Manche, 50360

HOTEL DES VOYAGEURS
(Mme Fabienne Franáoise) 43, rue de Périers
TEL: 02.33.41.00.59
DIRECTIONS: RN13, Cherbourg.
LANGUAGES: English.
MENU: 53 to 125 Frs.
ROOMS: 115 to 172 Frs.
RESTAURANT: Snacks from 6.30, lunch 11.45-14.30, dinner 19.15-22.00
CLOSED: Sun (out of season), and 2 weeks for Christmas school holidays.
SPECIALITIES: moules marinières, soupe de poisson, home-cooking.
HOTEL: 9 rooms
OTHER POINTS: credit cards accepted.
Sainte-Mère-Eglise; landing beaches.

PIPRIAC
Ille-et-Villaine, 35550

HOTEL DE LA TOUR D'AUVERGNE
(Mr Michel Gérard) 7, rue de l'Avenir
TEL: 02.99.34.41.34
MENU: 52 to 180 Frs.
ROOMS: 120 to 200 Frs (extra bed for children).
RESTAURANT: Snacks from 7.00, lunch 12.00-14.30, dinner 19.00-21.30
CLOSED: Mon afternoon, and 2 weeks in Feb.
SPECIALITIES: poissons au beurre blanc, regional menu.
HOTEL: ☆ 10 rooms.

FACILITIES: shower, bath, private bathroom, television, telephone
OTHER POINTS: credit cards accepted.
châteaux; glass-blowing demonstrations; craft village; excursions on the Oust; boats for hire; chapels.

PLAINTEL
Côtes-d'Armor, 22940

LE SEBASTOPOL
(Mme Marie Hervé) Route de Sébastopol
TEL: 02.96.32.52.77
DIRECTIONS: between Saint-Brieux and Lorient.
LANGUAGES: English.
MENU: 50 Frs (coffee included).
RESTAURANT: Snacks from 6.00, lunch 11.30-15.30, dinner 19.30-21.30
CLOSED: Sun.
SPECIALITIES: choucroute, cassoulet, fer de mer, regional menu, home-cooking.
OTHER POINTS: credit cards accepted.
Quintin (7km); Saint-Brieuc (12km); Loudéac (32km).

LA DESCENTE DES CHAOS
(Mme Micheline Perrein) Gare de Plaintel
TEL: 02.96.32.16.05
DIRECTIONS: RD 700, RD700, between Saint-Brieux and Loudéac.
LANGUAGES: English, Spanish.
MENU: 52 Frs (wine and coffee included).
ROOMS: 60 to 190 Frs.
RESTAURANT: Snacks from 5.00, lunch 11.30-15.00, dinner 18.30-24.00
SPECIALITIES: regional menu, home-cooking, cassoulet, couscous, choucroute (Friday), croissants maison.
HOTEL: 6 rooms
OTHER POINTS: credit cards accepted.

PLEBOULLE
Côtes-d'Armor, 22550

LE WELCOME
(Mr Stany Poulain) La Ville Abbé
TEL: 02.96.41.04.35
DIRECTIONS: RD 13, RD13, on the Lamballe/Matignon axis.
LANGUAGES: English.
MENU: 48 Frs (drink included) to 60 Frs.
ROOMS: 100 Frs.
RESTAURANT: Snacks from 7.30, lunch 11.30-15.00, dinner 18.30-22.00
CLOSED: Mon afternoon.
SPECIALITIES: home-cooking, pizzas.
HOTEL: 4 rooms
OTHER POINTS: credit cards accepted.

PLENEE JUGON
Côtes-d'Armor, 22640

RELAIS LES GARENNES
(Mr Grant Shannon)
TEL: 02.96.34.52.11
DIRECTIONS: RN12, between Rennes and Brest.
LANGUAGES: English, Dutch.
MENU: 51 Frs.
RESTAURANT: Snacks from 5.00, lunch 11.30-15.00, dinner 18.00-24.00
CLOSED: Sat evening, Sun and the 3rd week in Aug.
SPECIALITIES: truite farcie aux cêpes, paella, couscous, cassoulet, home-cooking.
OTHER POINTS: credit cards accepted.
abbaye de Bacquin; lakes at lugon; Dinan.

PLESLIN TRIGAVOU
Côtes-d'Armor, 22490

GRILL MILL'PATT
(Mr Loïc Renault) Le Bourg
TEL: 02.96.27.84.14
MENU: 50 to 110 Frs.
ROOMS: 120 to 200 Frs.
RESTAURANT: Snacks from 7.00, lunch 12.00-14.30, dinner 19.30-21.30
CLOSED: Sun (out of season), and 15th Dec to 1st Jan.
SPECIALITIES: grillades au feu de bois, saucisse du pays, regional menu, home-cooking.
HOTEL: 6 rooms
OTHER POINTS: bar.

PLEUMEUR GAUTIER
Côtes-d'Armor, 22740

L'AUBERGE DE LA CROIX NEUVE
(Mr Michael Frébault) Route de Tréguier – La Croix Neuve
TEL: 02.96.92.42.19
DIRECTIONS: Tréguier/Paimpol.
LANGUAGES: English.
MENU: 52 to 75 Frs.
RESTAURANT: Snacks from 8.00, lunch 11.30-14.30, dinner 19.00-21.30
CLOSED: Sun evening and Mon evening.
SPECIALITIES: regional menu, home-cooking.
OTHER POINTS: bar.

PLOERMEL
Morbihan, 56800

LES ROUTIERS
(Mme Solange Rio) Avenue Georges Pompidou – Sorite Est, vers Dinan
TEL: 02.97.74.00.48
DIRECTIONS: RN24, after the roundabout at the

entrance to Ploermel.
MENU: 52 to 150 Frs.
ROOMS: 90 to 150 Frs.
RESTAURANT: Dinner -22.00
CLOSED: Sat, and in Sept.
SPECIALITIES: home-cooking.
HOTEL: 11 rooms
OTHER POINTS: credit cards accepted.

PLOEUC SUR LIE
Côtes-d'Armor, 22150

LE RELAIS DU SQUARE
(Mme Sylviane Lafon-Sagory) 5, rue d'Enfer
TEL: 02.96.28.70.47
DIRECTIONS: RN168.
RESTAURANT: Dinner -21.00
CLOSED: Sat, Aug.
OTHER POINTS: bar.

PLOUAGAT
Côtes-d'Armor, 22170

CHEZ PIERRETTE
(Mr Pierre Drouin) ZA de Fournello
TEL: 02.96.74.28.13 **FAX:** 02.96.74.25.42
DIRECTIONS: RN12, exit at Quintin-Châtelaudren.
MENU: 58 Frs.
ROOMS: from 190 Frs.
RESTAURANT: Snacks from 5.00
CLOSED: From Sat 15.00 to Mon 5.00 and public holidays.
SPECIALITIES: home-cooking.
HOTEL: ☆☆ 12 rooms.
FACILITIES: shower, bath, private bathroom, television, telephone
OTHER POINTS: credit cards accepted.

AU TRISKEL
(Mr Serge Depre) ZA de Fournello
TEL: 02.96.74.25.35 **FAX:** 02.96.74.25.42
DIRECTIONS: RN 12, RN12, on the Saint-Brieuc/Brest axis, Quintin exit.
LANGUAGES: English.
MENU: 60 Frs (drink included).
ROOMS: 170 to 290 Frs.
RESTAURANT: Snacks from 5.00, lunch 11.30-14.30, dinner 19.00-23.00
CLOSED: Sun.
SPECIALITIES: regional menu, home-cooking, paëlla and couscous (Wednesday), choucroute, potée et pot au feu (winter).
HOTEL: 12 rooms.
FACILITIES: shower, private bathroom, television, telephone
OTHER POINTS: credit cards accepted.

PLOUEDERN
Finistère, 29800

LE RELAIS KERIEL
(Mme Marie Gac) Keriel-Landerneau
TEL: 02.98.20.82.53
DIRECTIONS: RN12, the Paris/Brest road.
LANGUAGES: English.
MENU: 54 to 130 Frs.
RESTAURANT: Snacks from 6.30, lunch 11.30-14.00, dinner 19.00-21.00
CLOSED: from 15th Sept to 8th Oct.
SPECIALITIES: fruits de mer, regional menu, home-cooking.
OTHER POINTS: credit cards accepted.
coast of Brittany.

PLOUER SUR RANCE
Côtes-d'Armor, 22490

LE BON ACCUEIL
(Mr Théophile Yris) La Gourbanière
TEL: 02.96.86.91.67
DIRECTIONS: RD366, between Dinan and Saint-Malo.
MENU: 58 to 135 Frs (weekdays), 135 to 190 Frs (Sunday).
RESTAURANT: Snacks from 7.30, lunch 12.00-14.00
CLOSED: Mon afternoon, and in Aug.
SPECIALITIES: fruits de mer, saumon fumé maison, regional menu, home-cooking.
OTHER POINTS: credit cards accepted.
Rance bridge; Dinan; Saint-Malo: marina.

PLOUGOUMELEN
Morbihan, 56400

LE KENEAC'H
(Mr Joël Boriller) Zone commerciale du Kenyah
TEL: 02.97.56.25.37
DIRECTIONS: RN165, the Vannes/Lorient road.
LANGUAGES: English.
MENU: 55 Frs (all included).
RESTAURANT: Snacks from 6.00, lunch 12.00-14.00, dinner 19.00-21.00
CLOSED: Sat evening and Sun.
SPECIALITIES: grillades au feu de bois, regional menu, home-cooking.
OTHER POINTS: credit cards accepted.
Auray, Vannes; Gulf of Morbihan; Quiberon; Carnac.

PLOUNEVEZ MOEDEC
Côtes-d'Armor, 22810

RELAIS DU BEG AR C'HRA
(Mr Jean-Marie Rubeus)
TEL: 02.96.38.61.08
DIRECTIONS: RN12, between Morlaix and Guingamp,

expressway exit at Beg Ar C'Hra.
MENU: 53 Frs.
ROOMS: 120 to 170 Frs.
RESTAURANT: Snacks from 6.30, lunch 12.00-14.00, dinner 19.30-22.00
CLOSED: Sat, Sun, public holidays, 1st week in May and mid-Aug to mid-Sept.
SPECIALITIES: home-cooking.
HOTEL: 11 rooms.
FACILITIES: shower, bath
OTHER POINTS: credit cards accepted.
château at Rosambo (10km); Côte de Granit Rose (25km).

PLOUNEVEZ QUINTIN
Côtes-d'Armor, 22110

LES ROUTIERS
(Mme Gildas Martin) 1, place de l'Eglise
TEL: 02.96.24.54.05
DIRECTIONS: RN790, Saint-Brieuc.
MENU: 55 to 120 Frs.
RESTAURANT: Snacks from 7.00, lunch 11.30-14.00, dinner 19.00-21.00
CLOSED: Sat, and from 15th Aug to 15th Sept.
SPECIALITIES: home-cooking,
OTHER POINTS: credit cards accepted.
lakes; the valley.

PLOURAY
Morbihan, 56770

BAR RESTAURANT LES ROUTIERS
(Mme Léandre Le Lain) 2 rue de l'Ellé
TEL: 02.97.34.81.39
DIRECTIONS: the Rennes/Quimper road.
MENU: 50 Frs.
RESTAURANT: Snacks from 8.00, lunch 12.00-14.00, dinner 19.30-20.00
CLOSED: Sat.
SPECIALITIES: home-cooking.
OTHER POINTS: bar.

POLIGNE
Ille-et-Villaine, 35320

LE TIROUANEZ
(Mr Philippe Petit)
TEL: 02.99.43.73.06
DIRECTIONS: RN137, the Nantes/Rennes road.
LANGUAGES: English.
MENU: 50 Frs.
RESTAURANT: Snacks from 7.00, lunch 11.30, dinner - 24.00
CLOSED: Sun.
SPECIALITIES: home-cooking.
OTHER POINTS: credit cards accepted.
Le Tertre Gris; animal park.

PONT AUDEMER
Eure, 27500

AU DEPANN'EURE
(Mr Franck Lapierre) Route de Saint Paul – Quartier Les Saulniers
TEL: 02.32.41.16.17
DIRECTIONS: RN 13, RN13, on the road to Bernay after the Intermarché supermarket.
LANGUAGES: English.
MENU: 59 Frs.
RESTAURANT: Snacks from 7.30, lunch 12.00-15.00, dinner 19.00-22.00
CLOSED: Thurs afternoon (open the evening).
SPECIALITIES: regional menu, home-cooking, moules-frites (Friday), grillades (summer).
OTHER POINTS: bar.

PONT HEBERT
Manche, 50880

LE MADRILENE
(Mme Marie-Thérèse Hamet) Quartier du Pont la Meauffe
TEL: 02.33.56.44.18
MENU: 58 Frs.
ROOMS: 95 to 110 Frs.
RESTAURANT: Snacks from 7.00, lunch 12.00-14.00, dinner 19.30-20.30
CLOSED: from Sat afternoon to Mon morning.
SPECIALITIES: home-cooking.
HOTEL: 7 rooms.
FACILITIES: shower, bath
OTHER POINTS: credit cards accepted.

PONT SAINT MARTIN
Loire-Atlantique, 44860

LE RELAIS COTE OUEST
(Mr Jean-Louis Vrignaud) Parc d'Activité de Viais
TEL: 02.40.32.72.40
DIRECTIONS: the Nantes/La Roche-sur-Yon road.
MENU: 50 to 185 Frs.
RESTAURANT: Snacks from 6.15, lunch 12.00-14.30, dinner 19.00-21.30
CLOSED: Sun evening and Mon evening.
SPECIALITIES: cuisses de grenouilles, poissons au beurre blanc, home-cooking.
OTHER POINTS: credit cards accepted.
Lac de Grand-Lieu.

PONTCHATEAU
Loire-Atlantique, 44160

L'AUBERGE DU CALVAIRE
(Mme Gabrielle Couvrand) 6, route de la Brière – Lieu-dit "Le Calvaire
TEL: 02.40.01.61.65 **FAX:** 02.40.01.64.68

DIRECTIONS: RD33, 4km from the centre of Pontchâteau, towards Herbignac.
LANGUAGES: English.
MENU: 60 to 120 Frs.
ROOMS: 180 to 250 Frs.
RESTAURANT: Snacks from 9.00, lunch 12.00-14.00, dinner 19.00-21.00
SPECIALITIES: anguilles (eels) au muscadet, merlan au beurre blanc, regional menu, home-cooking.
HOTEL: ☆☆ 12 rooms.
FACILITIES: shower, bath, private bathroom, television, telephone
OTHER POINTS: credit cards accepted.
Calvaire de Pontchâteau; parc régional de Brière; Côte d'Amour; pont Saint-Nazaire; La Baule; La Roche-Bernard.

LE RELAIS DE BEAULIEU
(Mr André Briand) Beaulieu
TEL: 02.40.01.60.58 **FAX:** 02.40.45.60.82
DIRECTIONS: RN165, the Nantes/Vannes road.
LANGUAGES: English.
MENU: 71 to 165 Frs.
ROOMS: 130 to 270 Frs.
RESTAURANT: Snacks from 5.00, lunch 12.00-15.00, dinner 19.00-22.00
CLOSED: Sat evening and Sun evening. The hotel stays open.
SPECIALITIES: anguilles au cidre, saumon grillé au beurre blanc, langoustes, soupe de poissons, regional menu, home-cooking.
HOTEL: 15 rooms.
FACILITIES: shower, bath, private bathroom
OTHER POINTS: credit cards accepted.
Calvaire de Pontchâteau; parc régional de Brière; La Baule; La Roche-Bernard; château de la Bretesche at Missillac.

PONTIVY
Morbihan, 56300

L'ESCALE
(Mr Jean Tison – SA Pondinal) Intermarché – Route de Lorient
TEL: 02.97.25.48.68 **FAX:** 02.97.25.13.70
DIRECTIONS: Saint-Brieuc/Loudéac/Lorient.
LANGUAGES: English.
RESTAURANT: Lunch 11.30-14.00, dinner 18.30-20.30
SPECIALITIES: home-cooking, pizza maison, couscous (week-end).
OTHER POINTS: credit cards accepted.

PONTORSON
Manche, 50170

LE RENOVE
(Mme Marie-Claire Pépin) 4, rue de Rennes
TEL: 02.33.60.00.21
DIRECTIONS: RN175.
MENU: 55 to 120 Frs.
ROOMS: 145 to 260 Frs.
RESTAURANT: Snacks from 7.00, lunch 11.30-15.00, dinner 19.00-22.00
CLOSED: Sun (out of season).
SPECIALITIES: home-cooking.
HOTEL: 10 rooms.
FACILITIES: shower, private bathroom
OTHER POINTS: credit cards accepted.
Mont-Saint-Michel.

QUIMPERLE
Finistère, 29300

LA FOURCHE
(Mme Solange Philipot) Route de Lorient
TEL: 02.98.39.11.45
DIRECTIONS: Quimperlé, the Kerfleury exit.
MENU: 55 to 60 Frs.
RESTAURANT: Snacks from 6.30, lunch 12.00-14.00, dinner 19.30-22.00
CLOSED: Sat and Sun.
SPECIALITIES: choucroute, couscous, andouillette chaude, home-cooking.
OTHER POINTS: credit cards accepted.
Forêt de Carnoët; beaches; zoo.

TI LANIG
(Mr Alain Minec) ZA de Keringant
TEL: 02.98.39.16.07 **FAX:** 02.98.39.01.28
DIRECTIONS: RN165, exit at Manoir-de-Kernault.
LANGUAGES: English.
MENU: 38 to 115 Frs.
RESTAURANT: Snacks from 6.00, lunch 11.00-14.30, dinner 19.00-21.45
CLOSED: Fri evening, Sat evening, Sun.
SPECIALITIES: regional menu, home-cooking.
OTHER POINTS: credit cards accepted.
Forêt de Clohars-Carnoët; beaches.

RANES
Orne, 61150

HOTEL RESTAURANT DU PARC
(Mr Benoît Jeanne) 9, rue du Parc
TEL: 02.33.39.73.85
DIRECTIONS: La Ferté-Mace/Argentan.
LANGUAGES: English
MENU: 50 to 130 Frs.
ROOMS: 140 to 170 Frs.
RESTAURANT: Snacks from 7.30, lunch 12.00-14.00, dinner 19.30-21.00
CLOSED: Sun evening.
SPECIALITIES: regional menu, home-cooking, tripes.
HOTEL: 6 rooms.
FACILITIES: shower, private bathroom
OTHER POINTS: credit cards accepted.

RENAC
Ille-et-Villaine, 35660

RESTAURANT CREPERIE BEAUREGARD
(Mme Marie-Annick Bonno) Beauregard
TEL: 02.99.72.07.83
DIRECTIONS: RD177, between Rennes and Redon.
MENU: 46 to 108 Frs.
RESTAURANT: Snacks from 9.00, lunch 12.00-14.00, dinner 19.00-21.00
CLOSED: Mon, and 1 Week in Feb.
SPECIALITIES: home-cooking.
OTHER POINTS: credit cards accepted.
megalithic site at Saint-Just, Redon: church.

REORTHE (LA)
Vendée, 85210

LES ROUTIERS
(Mr Pascal* Renaud) 4, rue Nationale – Lieu dit : La Leue
TEL: 02.51.94.41.46
DIRECTIONS: RN137.
LANGUAGES: English.
MENU: 55 Frs.
ROOMS: 60 to 100 Frs.
RESTAURANT: Snacks from 5.00, lunch 11.30-15.00, dinner 18.30-23.00
CLOSED: Sat evening and Sun.
SPECIALITIES: home-cooking.
HOTEL: 8 rooms.
FACILITIES: shower, television, telephone
OTHER POINTS: credit cards accepted.
dam at l'Angle-Guignard; maison de-Lattre-de-Tassigny, le Puy du Fou; château de Clemenceau; seaside.

REZE
Loire-Atlantique, 44400

RESTAURANT DES AMIS
(Mme Irène Richard) 4, place Saint Pierre
TEL: 02.40.75.53.29
DIRECTIONS: between Pornic and Nantes.
MENU: 52 to 130 Frs.
RESTAURANT: Snacks from 7.00, lunch 12.00-14.30, dinner 19.00-22.00
CLOSED: SUn and in July.
SPECIALITIES: home-cooking,
OTHER POINTS: credit cards accepted.
Nantes: château des Ducs de Breligne, old town; route du Muscadet.

RIAILLE
Loire-Atlantique, 44440

LE RELAIS DE L'ERDRE
(Mr Joël Aspot) Route de Joué sur Erdre – Les Fuseaux
TEL: 02.40.97.80.95 FAX: 02.40.97.85.28
DIRECTIONS: D178 and 33, Candé/Nort sur Erdre.
MENU: 48.50 Frs (drink included).
RESTAURANT: Snacks from 6.00, lunch 11.30-14.30, dinner 19.00-22.00
SPECIALITIES: regional menu, fruits de mer, home-cooking.
OTHER POINTS: credit cards accepted.
châteaux and monuments.

RICHEVILLE
Eure, 27420

LE BALTO RESTO
(Mme Pouillart) 4, route Nationale 14
TEL: 02.32.27.10.55
DIRECTIONS: RN14, the Paris/Rouen road.
MENU: 55 Frs (drink included).
RESTAURANT: Snacks from 5.00
CLOSED: Sun.
SPECIALITIES: escalopes normandes, filet au poivre, home-cooking.
OTHER POINTS: bar.
Château-gaillard; les Andelys; Vernon; Claude Monet's house at Giverny; Gisors.

ROCHE SUR YON (LA)
Vendée, 85000

HOTEL SULLY
(SA Le Sully) Boulevard Sully
TEL: 02.51.37.18.21 FAX: 02.51.46.09.63
DIRECTIONS: RN137, Noirmoutier.
LANGUAGES: English, Spanish.
MENU: 57 Frs.
ROOMS: 170 Frs.
RESTAURANT: Snacks from 6.00, lunch 11.30-15.00, dinner 19.00-22.30
SPECIALITIES: jambon de Vendée aux haricots blancs, home-cooking.
HOTEL: ☆☆ 34 rooms.
FACILITIES: shower, bath, private bathroom, television, telephone
OTHER POINTS: credit cards accepted.
haras (stud-farm); dam; moulin Papon; Ecomusée de la Vendée; le Puy du Fou; Poitou marshlands.

ROE (LA)
Mayenne, 53350

AUBERGE DE L'ABBAYE – Chez Dominique et Lydia
(Mr Dominique Fischbach) 20, rue Robert d'Abrissel
TEL: 02.43.06.63.26
DIRECTIONS: Angers/Rennes/Craon-la-Guerche.
LANGUAGES: English, Spanish.
MENU: 53 Frs (drink included) to 143 Frs.
RESTAURANT: Snacks from 7.00
CLOSED: Thurs evening, Fri, 1st 2 weeks in July and 1 week for Christmas/New Year.
SPECIALITIES: home-cooking, farm products grilled 'au feu de bois'.
OTHER POINTS: credit cards accepted.

ROMAGNY
Manche, 50140

AUBERGE DES CLOSEAUX
(Mr Bernard Clouard) Les Closeaux
TEL: 02.33.59.01.86 **FAX:** 02.33.69.41.02
DIRECTIONS: RD977, between Rennes and Caen, towards Saint-Hilaire-du-Harcouët.
LANGUAGES: English.
MENU: 57 to 120 Frs.
ROOMS: 180 to 230 Frs.
RESTAURANT: Snacks from 7.00, lunch 11.45-13.45, dinner -20.30
CLOSED: Sun, and 10th Dec to 15th Jan.
SPECIALITIES: home-cooking, pintade (guinea-fowl) au cidre, crustacés (shellfish), poissons, regional menu.
HOTEL: ☆☆ 10 rooms.
FACILITIES: shower, bath, private bathroom, television, telephone
OTHER POINTS: credit cards accepted.
Mont-Saint-Michel (20km); côte de Granville.

ROMAZY
Ille-et-Villaine, 35490

LE RELAIS
(Mr Jean-Claude Moncel) Le Bourg
TEL: 02.99.39.50.83
DIRECTIONS: RN175, between Rennes and Mont-St-Michel.
MENU: 53 Frs.
RESTAURANT: Snacks from 6.30, lunch 11.00-14.30, dinner 19.00-22.00
CLOSED: Sat and Sun.
SPECIALITIES: escalope Normande, home-cooking.
OTHER POINTS: credit cards accepted.
Mont-Saint-Michel (30km); châteaux at Combourg (20km) and Fougères (30km); leisure park (30km).

RONAI
Orne, 61160

LE PIERREFITTE
(Mr Stéphane Duclos)
TEL: 02.33.35.95.06
DIRECTIONS: RN158, the Caen/Argentan road,
LANGUAGES: English.
MENU: 55 Frs (drink and coffee included).
RESTAURANT: Snacks from 5.30
CLOSED: Sat, SUn and public holidays.
SPECIALITIES: home-cooking.
OTHER POINTS: credit cards accepted.
château at Falaise; memorial at Caen.

RONCEY
Manche, 50210

AU BON ACCUEIL
(Mr Rabah Benakli) 32, rue de la Liberté
TEL: 02.33.46.88.73
DIRECTIONS: on the Saint-Lo/Granville road.
LANGUAGES: English, Spanish, Portuguese, Arabic.
MENU: 49 Frs (drink included) to 70 Frs.
RESTAURANT: Snacks from 7.00, lunch 11.30, dinner -24.00
SPECIALITIES: regional menu, home-cooking, couscous, paëlla.
OTHER POINTS: credit cards accepted.

ROSPEZ
Côtes-d'Armor, 22300

LE HANNETON D'OR
(Mr Thierry Lignereux) Le Hanneton d'Or
TEL: 02.96.38.05.54
DIRECTIONS: Lannion/Tréguier road.
MENU: 52 to 92 Frs.
RESTAURANT: Snacks from 7.30, lunch 11.30-15.00, dinner 19.00-23.00
SPECIALITIES: home-cooking.
OTHER POINTS: credit cards accepted.
Perros Guinée; Tréguier; Paimpol; la côte de Granit (the Granite Coast).

ROSPORDEN
Finistère, 29140

LES ROUTIERS
(Mme Maryvonne Michal) 9, pont Biais
TEL: 02.98.59.20.40
DIRECTIONS: RN165, Quimper.
MENU: 54 Frs.
ROOMS: 170 Frs.
RESTAURANT: Snacks from 6.00, lunch 12.00-13.30, dinner 19.30-20.15
CLOSED: Sat and Sun
SPECIALITIES: home-cooking.

HOTEL: 17 rooms
OTHER POINTS: bar.
Concarneau (13km).

ROTS
Calvados, 14980

LE RELAIS DU COUP DE POMPE
(Mr Yannick Groult) 22, route de Caen
TEL: 02.31.26.63.56
DIRECTIONS: RN13, Cherbourg.
MENU: 56 Frs (drink and coffee included).
ROOMS: 90 to 120 Frs.
RESTAURANT: Snacks from 5.30, lunch 11.30, dinner -21.30
CLOSED: Sat afternoon and Sun.
SPECIALITIES: home-cooking.
HOTEL: 5 rooms
OTHER POINTS: credit cards accepted.
Bayeux.

ROUEN
Seine-Maritime, 76100

LES PLATANES
(Mr Roger Sannier) 57, avenue du Mont Riboudet
TEL: 02.35.71.01.52 **FAX:** 02.35.71.01.52
DIRECTIONS: A15, Rouen/Le-Havre exit, towards Barentin.
MENU: 53 to 60 Frs.
ROOMS: 73 to 93 Frs.
RESTAURANT: Snacks from 6.00, lunch 12.00-15.00, dinner -19.30
CLOSED: public holidays, first 2 weeks in Aug and 1 week at Christmas.
SPECIALITIES: regional menu, home-cooking.
HOTEL: 20 rooms.
FACILITIES: shower, bath
OTHER POINTS: credit cards accepted.
Rouen and the Seine valley; museums.

ROUFFIGNY
Manche, 50800

LE RATELIER
(Mme Franáoise Durand) Route Nationale 175
TEL: 02.33.61.08.06
DIRECTIONS: RN175, between Villedieu and Avranches.
LANGUAGES: English.
MENU: 53 to 70 Frs.
RESTAURANT: Snacks from 6.00
CLOSED: Sat, Sun, 2 weeks in August and 10 last days of the year.
SPECIALITIES: home-cooking.
OTHER POINTS: credit cards accepted.

ROUGEMONTIER
Eure, 27350

LE LUDO
(Mr Jean-Claude Duboc) 175 Route Nationale
TEL: 02.32.56.85.22
DIRECTIONS: RN175, the Rouen/Caen road.
MENU: 58 Frs (wine included).
RESTAURANT: Snacks from 5.00
CLOSED: Sat from 14.30, Sun, public holidays and in Aug.
SPECIALITIES: home-cooking.
OTHER POINTS: bar.
Parc de Brotonne; four à pain (baker's oven) at Haye-de-Routout; musée du sabotier (clog-maker); moulin de pierre at Hauville; maison des métiers (trades) at Bourneville.

SABLES D'OLONNE (LES)
Vendée, 85100

AU COQ HARDI
(Mlle Franáoise Pajot) 7, avenue Alcide Cabaret
TEL: 02.51.32.04.62
DIRECTIONS: RD949, La Rochelle.
MENU: 55 to 100 Frs.
ROOMS: 160 to 200 Frs.
RESTAURANT: Snacks from 9.00, lunch 12.00-15.00
CLOSED: Sat, Sun (out of season), and from 20th Sept to 10th Oct.
SPECIALITIES: fruits de mer, poissons, home-cooking.
HOTEL: 8 rooms
OTHER POINTS: credit cards accepted.
ports; beach and coastline; Atlantic coast.

LES VOYAGEURS
(Mr Clément Pacory) 17, rue de la Bauduère
TEL: 02.51.95.11.49 **FAX:** 02.51.21.50.21
DIRECTIONS: RN160 and 149.
MENU: 47 to 118 Frs.
ROOMS: 170 to 230 Frs.
RESTAURANT: Snacks from 7.00, lunch 12.00-14.00, dinner 19.15-21.00
CLOSED: Fri evening and Sat (out of season), and 3 weeks from Christmas Day.
SPECIALITIES: regional menu, poissons, fruits de mer, home-cooking.
HOTEL: 15 rooms.
FACILITIES: shower, bath, private bathroom, television, telephone
OTHER POINTS: credit cards accepted.

SAINT AUBIN SUR SCIE
Seine-Maritime, 76550

LE RELAIS DE LA SCIE
(Mr Roger Burgot) Rue du Gouffre
TEL: 02.35.85.44.60

DIRECTIONS: RN27, between Tôtes and Dieppe.
MENU: 58 Frs (wine included).
RESTAURANT: Snacks from 6.30, lunch 11.30-14.30
CLOSED: Sun and in Aug.
SPECIALITIES: home-cooking.
OTHER POINTS: credit cards accepted.
Dieppe; Côte de Nacre.

SAINT BERTHEVIN
Mayenne, 53940

L'INTERNATIONAL
(Mr Henri Garnier) Lieu dit "L'Aulne" – Route Nationale 157
TEL: 02.43.69.31.74 **FAX:** 02.43.69.31.74
DIRECTIONS: RN157, Rennes.
LANGUAGES: English.
MENU: 57 to 110 Frs.
ROOMS: 100 to 145 Frs.
RESTAURANT: Snacks from 6.00, lunch 12.00-15.00, dinner 19.30-23.00
CLOSED: Sun.
SPECIALITIES: home-cooking.
HOTEL: ☆☆ 22 rooms.
FACILITIES: shower, bath, private bathroom, television, telephone
OTHER POINTS: credit cards accepted.
château at Laval; gardens at La Périne.

SAINT BRANDAN
Côtes-d'Armor, 22800

RELAIS ROUTIERS
(Mr Pierre Jacob) 47, rue de Launay
TEL: 02.96.74.88.19
DIRECTIONS: RD790, on the road to Saint-Brieuc.
MENU: 51 to 80 Frs.
RESTAURANT: Snacks from 8.00, lunch 11.00-15.00, dinner 19.00-21.00
CLOSED: Sat afternoon, Sun, and in Aug.
SPECIALITIES: regional menu, home-cooking.
OTHER POINTS: bar.
Marhalach; lac de Bosmeliac; le Chaos du Gouet.

SAINT BREVIN L'OCEAN
Loire-Atlantique, 44250

LA DUCHESSE ANNE
(Mme Rose-Annie Laloue) 82, avenue du Président Roosevelt
TEL: 02.40.27.23.38 **FAX:** 02.40.39.03.81
DIRECTIONS: between Saint-Nazaire and Pornic.
LANGUAGES: English.
MENU: 54 to 110 Frs (crêperie).
RESTAURANT: Snacks from 11.00, lunch 12.00-14.00, dinner 19.00-21.00
CLOSED: Mon/Tues after 14.30 (out of season).
SPECIALITIES: noix de Saint-Jacques à la provenáale, poisson au beurre blanc, magrets de canard, home-cooking.
OTHER POINTS: credit cards accepted.
Saint-Nazaire; dolmen du Rossignol; jardin aux Moines; musée de la marine.

RESTAURANT LA POTINIERE
(Mme Colette Mellerin) 124, avenue du 11 Novembre
TEL: 02.40.27.23.36
DIRECTIONS: Saint Nazaire/Pronic, Saint-Brévin southern entrance.
MENU: 50 Frs (drink included).
RESTAURANT: Snacks from 8.00, lunch 12.00-14.30, dinner 19.00-21.00
SPECIALITIES: regional menu.
OTHER POINTS: bar.

SAINT BROLADRE
Ille-et-Villaine, 35120

LE FLORIDA
(Lulu et Eliane Lecoq) Le Bourg
TEL: 02.99.80.26.41
DIRECTIONS: RD797, between Pontorson and Saint-Malo.
MENU: 49 to 70 Frs.
ROOMS: 110 to 180 Frs.
RESTAURANT: Snacks from 6.00, lunch 12.00-14.00, dinner 19.00-21.00
CLOSED: Mon afternoon (in winter).
SPECIALITIES: moules, viandes grillées, home-cooking.
HOTEL: 9 rooms.
FACILITIES: shower, bath
OTHER POINTS: bar.
Saint-Malo; Mont-Saint-Michel.

SAINT COME DU FRESNE
Calvados, 14960

LE SANTA DE A
(Mme Andréa Boquet) 3, rue Panoramique
TEL: 02.31.21.15.70
MENU: 52 to 140 Frs.
RESTAURANT: Snacks from 9.00
CLOSED: Mon afternoon.
SPECIALITIES: fruits de mer, home-cooking.
OTHER POINTS: credit cards accepted.
landing beaches; Bayeux tapestry; maison de la mer; château at Saint-Côme.

SAINT CYR EN PAIL
Mayenne, 53140

LES ROUTIERS
(Mme Antoinette Dupont) Le Bourg
TEL: 02.43.03.03.21

DIRECTIONS: RN12, between Alenáon and Mayenne.
MENU: 48 to 50 Frs.
RESTAURANT: Snacks from 6.30, lunch 11.30-14.30, dinner 18.30-21.00
CLOSED: Sun, and in Aug.
SPECIALITIES: home-cooking.
OTHER POINTS: bar.
Mont des Avaloirs (2km); château at Carrouges (20km); Pierre-au-Loup (2km); la Corniche de Pail (2km).

SAINT DENIS DE MAILLOC
Calvados, 14100

LA FORGE
(Mr Bruno Morin)
TEL: 02.31.63.73.19
DIRECTIONS: RD519, between Lisieux and Orbec.
MENU: 59 Frs.
RESTAURANT: Snacks from 7.00, lunch 11.30-14.00
CLOSED: Sat, Sun, and last 2 weeks in Aug.
SPECIALITIES: regional menu, home-cooking.
OTHER POINTS: bar.
basilica at Lisieux; château at Saint-Germain-de-Livet; Deauville; zoo at Cerza.

SAINT DENIS DE MERE
Calvados, 14110

LE RELAIS DES LANDES
(Mr Emmanuel Ranguet)
TEL: 02.31.69.97.60
DIRECTIONS: between Caen and Condé-sur-Noireau.
MENU: 55 Frs.
ROOMS: 110 Frs.
RESTAURANT: Snacks from 5.30, lunch 11.00-14.30, dinner 18.30-21.30
CLOSED: Sat afternoon and Sun.
SPECIALITIES: regional menu, home-cooking.
HOTEL: 3 rooms.
FACILITIES: shower
OTHER POINTS: credit cards accepted.

SAINT DENIS DES MONTS
Eure, 27520

LE LAMA
(Mr Christian Chuette) Route Nationale 138
TEL: 02.32.42.60.10
DIRECTIONS: RN138, between Rouen and Brionne.
MENU: 58 Frs.
RESTAURANT: Snacks from 6.00, lunch 11.00-15.00
CLOSED: Sat, SUn and 3 weeks in Aug.
SPECIALITIES: home-cooking.
OTHER POINTS: bar.
Le Bec-Hellouin.

SAINT DENIS SUR SARTHON
Orne, 61420

HOTEL DE LA GARE – AUX BONS AMIS
(Mme Patricia Descroix) La Gare
TEL: 02.33.28.68.14
DIRECTIONS: RN 12, RN12, on the Alenáon/Rennes axis.
LANGUAGES: English, Spanish.
MENU: 48 to 55 Frs (wine included).
ROOMS: 100 Frs.
RESTAURANT: Snacks from 5.00
SPECIALITIES: home-cooking, Méridionales.
HOTEL: 10 rooms
OTHER POINTS: credit cards accepted.

SAINT ETIENNE DE BRILLOUET
Vendée, 85210

LE STEPHANOIS
(Mme Marie-Thérèse Dugas) Route Nationale 148
TEL: 02.51.27.63.37
DIRECTIONS: RN148, the Niort/Saint-Hermine/Nantes road.
LANGUAGES: English.
MENU: 60 Frs (wine included).
RESTAURANT: Snacks from 6.30, lunch 11.30-14.30, dinner 19.00-22.00
CLOSED: Thurs, 1 week in Feb and 1 week from Christmas Day.
SPECIALITIES: fruits de mer, regional menu, home-cooking,
OTHER POINTS: bar.
Poitou marshlands; le Puy du Fou (40km); châteaux.

SAINT EVARZEC
Finistère, 29170

AU BON REPOS
(Mr Roger Guillou) Poullogoden
TEL: 02.98.56.20.09
DIRECTIONS: RD783, between Quimper and Concarneau.
MENU: 60 to 100 Frs.
ROOMS: 130 to 200 Frs.
RESTAURANT: Snacks from 6.30, lunch 12.00-14.00, dinner 19.00-20.30
CLOSED: Sat (out of season), and in Dec.
SPECIALITIES: coquilles Saint-Jacques, fruits de mer, home-cooking.
HOTEL: 20 rooms.
FACILITIES: shower, bath, private bathroom, television, telephone
OTHER POINTS: credit cards accepted.
Bénodet; beaches; Port la Forêt; Concarneau.

SAINT EVROULT DE MONTFORT
Orne, 61230

HOTEL DU RELAIS
(Mr Daniel Conan) Le Bourg
TEL: 02.33.35.60.58
DIRECTIONS: RN138, between Rouen and Alenáon.
MENU: 49 Frs.
ROOMS: 80 to 150 Frs.
RESTAURANT: Snacks from 7.00, lunch 11.00-15.00, dinner 19.00-22.00
CLOSED: Sun.
SPECIALITIES: home-cooking.
HOTEL: 5 rooms.
FACILITIES: shower
OTHER POINTS: bar.

SAINT FROMOND
Manche, 50620

LE FLAMANT ROSE
(Mr Jean-Pierre Lemarchand) 5, porte des Marais
TEL: 02.33.56.24.49
DIRECTIONS: Bayeux/Périers axis.
LANGUAGES: English.
MENU: 51 Frs (1/4 wine included).
ROOMS: 100 to 150 Frs.
RESTAURANT: Snacks from 7.00, lunch 12.00-14.30, dinner 19.00-21.00
CLOSED: 3 last weeks of September.
SPECIALITIES: home-cooking.
HOTEL: 5 rooms
OTHER POINTS: credit cards accepted.

SAINT GEORGES DE ROUELLEY
Manche, 50720

AUBERGE DU LION D'OR
(Mme Nadia Desgaroins) Route de Domfront
TEL: 02.33.59.35.14
DIRECTIONS: RD907, between Domfront and Saint-Mortain.
MENU: 50 Frs.
RESTAURANT: Snacks from 7.30, lunch 12.00-14.00
SPECIALITIES: home-cooking.
OTHER POINTS: credit cards accepted.
Fosse Arthour; Saint-Frimbault; waterfall at Mortain; abbaye de Lonlay.

SAINT GERMAIN DES PRES
Maine-et-Loire, 49170

LE RELAIS DE CHANT'PAILLE
(Mr Jean-Pierre Hontès) Route Nationale 23 – La Janière
TEL: 02.41.39.35.63
DIRECTIONS: on the Angers/Nantes axis.
LANGUAGES: English, Portuguese.
MENU: 55 to 145 Frs.
RESTAURANT: Snacks from 7.00, lunch 11.30-14.00, dinner 18.00-23.00
CLOSED: Sun.
SPECIALITIES: regional menu, home-cooking.
OTHER POINTS: credit cards accepted.

SAINT GERMAIN SUR MOINE
Maine-et-Loire, 49230

LE TAILLIS DU VERGER
(Mr Paul Eraud) Carrefour du Petit Lapin – Route de la Renaudière
TEL: 02.41.64.64.61
DIRECTIONS: RN249, on the Nantes/Cholet expressway.
MENU: 55 Frs (coffee included).
RESTAURANT: Snacks from 6.30, lunch 11.30-14.30, dinner 19.00-22.00
CLOSED: Sun.
SPECIALITIES: regional menu, home-cooking.
OTHER POINTS: credit cards accepted.

SAINT GILDAS DES BOIS
Loire-Atlantique, 44530

RELAIS CASSEROLE LES ROUTIERS
(Mr Michel Gaidano) 27, rue du Pont
TEL: 02.40.01.42.15 **FAX:** 02.40.19.60.32
DIRECTIONS: RD773, between Redon and Pontchâteau.
MENU: 74 to 300 Frs.
ROOMS: 120 to 135 Frs.
RESTAURANT: Snacks from 7.30, lunch 12.00-14.30, dinner 20.00-21.00
SPECIALITIES: fruits de mer, homard (lobster) grillé, beurre blanc, regional menu.
HOTEL: 10 rooms.
FACILITIES: shower, bath, private bathroom, television, telephone
OTHER POINTS: credit cards accepted.
calvaire at Pontchâteau; château at La Bretèche.

SAINT GILLES
Manche, 50180

CARREFOUR SAINT GILLES
(Mr Yannik Toutain) Le Bourg
TEL: 02.33.05.74.50
DIRECTIONS: between Saint-Lô and Coutances.
MENU: 50 Frs.
RESTAURANT: Snacks from 6.30
CLOSED: Sat, Sun.
SPECIALITIES: home-cooking.
OTHER POINTS: credit cards accepted.
Saint-Lô: ramparts (7km); les vieux métiers (trades) at Remilly-sur-Lozon (10km).

SAINT GILLES CROIX DE VIE/LE FENOUILLER
Vendée, 85800

LA MADELON
(Mme Christine Poupart) 64, rue du Centre
TEL: 02.51.55.17.37
DIRECTIONS: RN754, from Saint-Gilles-Croix-de-Vie, towards Nantes.
LANGUAGES: English.
MENU: 49 to 110 Frs.
ROOMS: 90 to 210 Frs.
RESTAURANT: Snacks from 8.00, lunch 12.00-14.00, dinner 19.30-21.00
CLOSED: in Jan.
SPECIALITIES: fruits de mer, home-cooking.
HOTEL: 15 rooms.
FACILITIES: shower, bath
OTHER POINTS: bar.
Saint-Gilles-Croix-de-Vie; the Vendée coast: fishing ports, marinas, beaches.

SAINT GREGOIRE
Ille-et-Villaine, 35760

RESTAURANT DE L'ETANG
(Mr Michel Hubert) Rue de l'Etang au Diable
TEL: 02.99.38.49.43 FAX: 02.99.63.09.49
MENU: 51 to 200 Frs.
RESTAURANT: Snacks from 6.00, lunch 11.30-15.00, dinner 19.00-21.00
CLOSED: Sat, Sun.
SPECIALITIES: home-cooking.
OTHER POINTS: credit cards accepted.

SAINT HELEN
Côtes-d'Armor, 22100

RELAIS DE LA CROIX DU FRENE
(Mr Guy Gabillard) La Croix du Frene
TEL: 02.96.83.25.02
RESTAURANT: Snacks from 7.00, lunch 11.30-14.30, dinner 19.00-22.30
CLOSED: Sat (after 15.00), Sun, and public holidays.
SPECIALITIES: home-cooking.
OTHER POINTS: bar.

SAINT HILAIRE DE LOULAY
Vendée, 85600

LE RELAX
(Mr Luc Van Wanghe) Les Landes de Roussais
TEL: 02.51.94.02.44 FAX: 02.51.94.27.25
DIRECTIONS: RN137, between Nantes and La Rochelle, 30km from Nantes.
LANGUAGES: English, German.
MENU: 62 to 154 Frs.
ROOMS: 180 to 210 Frs.
RESTAURANT: Snacks from 6.00, lunch 11.30-15.00, dinner 19.00-24.00
CLOSED: Sat lunch, and last week in Dec.
SPECIALITIES: grillades au feu de bois, poissons au beurre blanc, regional menu.
HOTEL: ☆☆ 11 rooms.
FACILITIES: shower, bath, private bathroom, television, telephone
OTHER POINTS: credit cards accepted.
château; Muscadet wine-cellar.

SAINT IGNEUC
Côtes-d'Armor, 22270

LES 4 ROUTES – Chez Chantal
(Mme Chantal Durand) Route Nationale 76
TEL: 02.96.31.68.40
DIRECTIONS: RN76, the Saint-Malo/Saint-Brieuc road.
MENU: 51 Frs.
RESTAURANT: Snacks from 5.30
CLOSED: Sat, Sun.
SPECIALITIES: couscous, Breton patisseries, regional menu, home-cooking.
HOTEL: 5 rooms.
FACILITIES: shower, bath, private bathroom, television, telephone
OTHER POINTS: credit cards accepted.
château at La Hunaudaye; Lugon; ferme d'antan (farm of yesteryear); old Dinan.

SAINT JACQUES DE LA LANDE
Ille-et-Villaine, 35136

LA GAITE
(Mr Yannick Echelard) 26, boulevard Roger Dodin
TEL: 02.99.31.27.56
DIRECTIONS: RD177, 'La Gaité' interchange on the Redon road.
LANGUAGES: English.
MENU: 51 Frs.
ROOMS: 100 Frs.
RESTAURANT: Snacks from 7.00, lunch 12.00-14.30, dinner 19.30-22.00
CLOSED: Sat, Sun, and public holidays (except group bookings).
SPECIALITIES: regional menu.
HOTEL: 3 rooms.
FACILITIES: shower, bath, private bathroom
OTHER POINTS: credit cards accepted.
étangs (ponds) d'Apigné; Rennes town centre.

SAINT JEAN DE BEUGNE
Vendée, 85210

L'OASIS
(Mme Louisette Le Joncour)
61, Route Nationale 137
TEL: 02.51.27.38.80 FAX: 02.51.28.87.48

DIRECTIONS: RN137, the Nantes/La Rochelle road.
MENU: 55 Frs.
RESTAURANT: Snacks from 4.00, lunch 11.30-14.30, dinner 18.30-23.00
CLOSED: Sun and Christmas to the new year.
SPECIALITIES: regional menu, home-cooking.
OTHER POINTS: credit cards accepted.
le Puy du Fou; château at Fontenay-le-Comte; dam at Longuignard.

SAINT JEAN DE DAYE
Manche, 50620

LE P'TIT TROT
(Mme Christiane Marie) Rue de la Libération
TEL: 02.33.55.48.00
DIRECTIONS: RN174, between Saint-Lô and Carentan.
MENU: 50 Frs (75 Frs on Saturday).
RESTAURANT: Snacks from 7.00, lunch 11.30-14.30, dinner 19.00-21.00
CLOSED: Sun.
SPECIALITIES: home-cooking,
OTHER POINTS: credit cards accepted.
Graignes racecourse and riding school; château at La Rivière.

SAINT JEAN DE LA MOTHE
Sarthe, 72510

CHEZ FRANCOISE
(Mme Franáoise Coutouis) Le Point du Jour
TEL: 02.43.45.72.02
DIRECTIONS: RN23, between Le Mans and Angers.
MENU: 55 Frs (drink included).
RESTAURANT: Snacks from 5.00, lunch 11.00-15.00, dinner 19.00-22.00
CLOSED: Sat and Sun.
SPECIALITIES: home-cooking.
OTHER POINTS: credit cards accepted.
Le Lude (25km); Le Mans circuit (30km); Malicorne: Potteries.

SAINT JULIEN LE FAUCON
Calvados, 14140

LE CAFE DE LA GARE
(Mr Robert Gallais)
TEL: 02.31.63.62.91
DIRECTIONS: RD511, between Lisieux and Saint-Pierre-sur-Dives.
MENU: 49.50 Frs (wine included).
RESTAURANT: Snacks from 7.00, lunch 12.00-15.00, dinner 20.00-23.00
CLOSED: Sun.
SPECIALITIES: home-cooking.
OTHER POINTS: bar.
Lisieux (14km); abbey at Saint-Pierre-sur-Dives; château at Saint-Germain-de-Livet.

SAINT LEGER DES PRES
Ille-et-Villaine, 35270

LE RELAIS DE SAINT LEGER
(Mr Jean-Pierre Dupuy) Le Bourg
TEL: 02.99.73.63.32
DIRECTIONS: between Combourg and Vitré.
LANGUAGES: English.
MENU: 53 Frs (drink and coffee included).
RESTAURANT: Snacks from 7.30, lunch 12.00-14.30, dinner 19.00-21.00
CLOSED: Mon afternoon and last 2 weeks in Aug.
SPECIALITIES: home-cooking, couscous (Thursday).
OTHER POINTS: credit cards accepted.

SAINT LO
Manche, 50000

LE DEVERSOIR
(Mme Clotilde Daireaux) 35, rue Valvire
TEL: 02.33.57.96.41
DIRECTIONS: on the Coutances/Caen road.
MENU: 55 Frs (drink and coffee included).
RESTAURANT: Snacks from 7.00, lunch 11.30-14.30, dinner 19.00-21.00
CLOSED: Sat evening and Sun (bar open).
SPECIALITIES: home-cooking, petit salé frites.
OTHER POINTS: credit cards accepted.

SAINT MALO
Ille-et-Villaine, 35400

RESTAURANT LE PERROQUET VERT
(Mr Michel Fraboulet) 2, rue Amiral Protet
TEL: 02.98.81.64.19
DIRECTIONS: Saint-Servan exit.
LANGUAGES: English.
MENU: 50 Frs.
RESTAURANT: Snacks from 6.30, lunch 11.30-17.00, dinner 17.00-23.00
CLOSED: Sat from 16.00, Sun, and 2 weeks in Aug.
SPECIALITIES: home-cooking.
OTHER POINTS: bar.
Saint-Malo.

SAINT MARS LA BRIERE
Sarthe, 72740

AUBERGE DU MARAIS
(Mr Rémy Tressy) Route Nationale 157
TEL: 02.43.89.87.30 **FAX:** 02.43.89.87.30
DIRECTIONS: RN157, between Le Mans and Orléans.
MENU: 55 to 200 Frs.
RESTAURANT: Snacks from 6.00, lunch 11.30-15.00, dinner 19.00-22.30
CLOSED: Sat after 15.00, Sun.
SPECIALITIES: home-cooking.
OTHER POINTS: credit cards accepted.

animal park; crystalline spring; château; forest.

SAINT MARTIN DES BESACES
Calvados, 14350

LA RENAISSANCE
(Mme Renée Lehericey) Route Nationale 175 – Le Bourg
TEL: 02.31.68.72.65
DIRECTIONS: RN175, between Avranches and Caen.
LANGUAGES: English.
MENU: 70 to 90 Frs.
ROOMS: 150 to 180 Frs.
RESTAURANT: Snacks from 7.30, lunch 12.00-14.30, dinner 19.00-21.30
CLOSED: Mon (out of season), and from 15th Jan to 15th Mar.
SPECIALITIES: coquilles Saint-Jacques, rognons au vieux calvados, faux filet au poivre, regional menu.
HOTEL: 8 rooms.
FACILITIES: shower, bath, private bathroom
OTHER POINTS: bar.

SAINT MARTIN DES CHAMPS
Manche, 50300

LE GRAND CHIEN
(Mr Michel Boittin)
TEL: 02.33.58.04.52
DIRECTIONS: between Pontorson and Avranches.
MENU: 50 Frs (coffee included).
RESTAURANT: Snacks from 5.30, lunch 11.30-15.00, dinner 19.00-22.00
CLOSED: Sat afternoon, 2 weeks in Aug and last week in Dec.
SPECIALITIES: home-cooking.
OTHER POINTS: credit cards accepted.
musée de la 2ème guerre mondiale (Second World War); jardin des plantes; Mont-Saint-Michel.

SAINT MATHURIN
Vendée, 85150

LE DAUPHIN
(Mr Michel Neau) Route des Sables
TEL: 02.51.22.71.81
DIRECTIONS: RN160, Nantes/Les Sables road.
MENU: 55 to 140 Frs.
RESTAURANT: Snacks from 7.00, lunch 11.00-15.00, dinner 18.00-20.00
CLOSED: Sun (except bookings).
SPECIALITIES: regional menu, home-cooking.
OTHER POINTS: credit cards accepted.
Les Sables.

SAINT MEEN LE GRAND
Ille-et-Villaine, 35290

LE RELAIS DU MIDI
(Mr Christian Posnic) 25, place Patton
TEL: 02.99.09.60.02
DIRECTIONS: RN164, Rennes/Vannes/Saint-Malo/Loudéac.
MENU: 53 Frs.
RESTAURANT: Snacks from 8.00, lunch 12.00-14.00
CLOSED: Sat afternoon, Sun afternoon, and last 2 weeks in Aug.
SPECIALITIES: home-cooking.
HOTEL: 3 rooms.
FACILITIES: bath, private bathroom, television, telephone
OTHER POINTS: credit cards accepted.

SAINT MESMIN
Vendée, 85700

LE RELAIS
(Mr Henry Thibault) La Boutinerie
TEL: 02.51.91.95.00
DIRECTIONS: RD960, La Roche-sur-Yon.
MENU: 54 Frs (wine included) to 65 Frs.
RESTAURANT: Snacks from 7.00, lunch 11.30, dinner 19.00-21.00
CLOSED: from Fri evening to Sat evening (out of season).
SPECIALITIES: crêperie (at weekends), home-cooking.
OTHER POINTS: credit cards accepted.
château at Saint-Mesmin; le Puy du Fou.

SAINT NAZAIRE
Loire-Atlantique, 44600

LE LAFAYETTE
(Mr Gilles Criaud) 7, avenue de Penhoët
TEL: 02.40.22.53.82
DIRECTIONS: chantiers de l'Atlantique (Atlantic dockyards).
MENU: 45 Frs.
RESTAURANT: Snacks from 5.20
CLOSED: Sat , Sun, and July.
SPECIALITIES: home-cooking.
OTHER POINTS: bar.
Saint-Nazaire; La Baule.

SAINT NICOLAS DE REDON
Loire-Atlantique, 44460

LES ROUTIERS
(Mme Marie-Annick Hemery) 84, avenue Jean Burel
TEL: 02.99.71.01.96
DIRECTIONS: the Nantes/Redon or Rennes/Redon road.
MENU: 52 Frs.

RESTAURANT: Snacks from 7.30, lunch 11.30-15.00, dinner 19.00-22.00
CLOSED: Sat and Sun (1/11 to 30/04).
SPECIALITIES: couscous, home-cooking.
OTHER POINTS: bar.
Redon; la Gacilly; Rochefort-en-Terre; forêt de Brocéliande.

SAINT NOLFF
Morbihan, 56250

LE RELAIS DE BELLEVUE
(Mme Edith Hureau) Bellevue
TEL: 02.97.45.44.04
DIRECTIONS: RN164, via the old Rennes road.
MENU: 49 Frs (coffee included).
RESTAURANT: Snacks from 6.30, lunch 11.45-15.00, dinner 19.00-21.30
CLOSED: Sun, and in Aug.
SPECIALITIES: home-cooking.
OTHER POINTS: bar.

SAINT PELLERIN
Manche, 50500

LE RELAIS DE LA FOURCHETTE
(Mr Frédéric Poupaux) Village de la Fourchette
TEL: 02.33.42.16.56
DIRECTIONS: RN 13, RN13, between Isigny and Carentan.
LANGUAGES: English, German.
MENU: 50 Frs (wine included).
RESTAURANT: Snacks from 6.00, lunch 11.30-15.00, dinner 18.30-22.00
CLOSED: Sat and Sun.
SPECIALITIES: home-cooking, pied de veau.
OTHER POINTS: credit cards accepted.

SAINT PHILBERT DE GRAND LIEU
Loire-Atlantique, 44310

CAFE RESTAURANT DE LA BOULOGNE
(Mr Jean-Luc Hervouet) 11, place de l'Abbatiale
TEL: 02.40.78.70.55
DIRECTIONS: RD18bis, between Nantes and Challans.
MENU: 49 Frs.
ROOMS: 100 to 125 Frs
RESTAURANT: Snacks from 9.00, lunch 12.00-14.30
CLOSED: Sat and Sun.
SPECIALITIES: home-cooking.
HOTEL: 6 rooms
OTHER POINTS: bar.
9thC abbey-churches (abbatiales); Lac de Grand-Lieu.

SAINT PIERRE DES LANDES
Mayenne, 53500

LA RABINE
(Mlle Véronique Jouvin) Route Nationale 12 – La Rabine
TEL: 02.43.05.15.02
DIRECTIONS: RN 12, RN12, between Ernée and Fougères.
MENU: 55 Frs (drink included).
RESTAURANT: Snacks from 6.30, lunch 11.30-14.30, dinner 19.00-21.30
CLOSED: Sat, Sun and from 20th Dec to 5th Jan.
SPECIALITIES: home-cooking.
OTHER POINTS: credit cards accepted.

SAINT PIERRE DU FRESNE
Calvados, 14260

CHEZ DOUDOU
(Mr Loïc Lelègard) Les Haies Tigards
TEL: 02.31.77.80.89
DIRECTIONS: RN175, between Rennes and Dinan.
LANGUAGES: English.
MENU: 50 to 70 Frs.
RESTAURANT: Snacks from 5.00, lunch 11.00-15.00, dinner 19.00-23.00
CLOSED: Sun.
SPECIALITIES: home-cooking.
OTHER POINTS: credit cards accepted.

SAINT PIERRE LANGERS
Manche, 50530

LA GRILLADE
(Mr Marc Johan) Hameau de la Havaudière
TEL: 02.33.48.12.63
DIRECTIONS: RD973, between Cherbourg and Avranches.
LANGUAGES: English.
MENU: 50 to 60 Frs.
ROOMS: 120 to 150 Frs.
RESTAURANT: Snacks from 6.30
CLOSED: Sun (out of season), and between Christmas Day and New Year's Day.
SPECIALITIES: choucroute, couscous.
HOTEL: 8 rooms.
FACILITIES: shower, bath, private bathroom
OTHER POINTS: credit cards accepted.
Abbaye de la Lucerne; Granville; Avranches: jardin des plantes; Mont-Saint-Michel.

SAINT POL DE LEON
Finistère, 29250

LE PASSIFLORE – Les Routiers
(Mr Jean-Louis Floch) 28, rue Pen Ar Pont
TEL: 02.98.69.00.52

DIRECTIONS: Morlaix train station.
LANGUAGES: English.
MENU: 55 to 150 Frs.
ROOMS: 180 to 230 Frs.
RESTAURANT: Snacks from 7.00, lunch 12.00-15.00, dinner 19.00-23.00
CLOSED: Sun evening.
SPECIALITIES: fruits de mer (to order), home-cooking.
HOTEL: ☆ 18 rooms.
FACILITIES: shower, bath, private bathroom, television
OTHER POINTS: credit cards accepted.
Roscoff: cathedral, port.

SAINT QUENTIN LES ANGES
Mayenne, 53400

LE RELAIS
(Mme Marie-Annick Trottier) Le Bourg
TEL: 02.43.06.10.62 **FAX:** 02.43.06.08.41
DIRECTIONS: the Rennes/Angers road, between Craon and Segré.
LANGUAGES: English.
MENU: 52 to 117 Frs.
ROOMS: 90 to 150 Frs.
RESTAURANT: Snacks from 7.00, lunch 11.45-15.00, dinner 19.30-21.30
CLOSED: Sun afternoon (1/11 to 30/03) and 3 first weeks in Aug.
SPECIALITIES: filet de canard à la craonnaise, filet de sandre (fish) au beurre blanc, regional menu, home-cooking.
HOTEL: 11 rooms.
FACILITIES: shower, private bathroom
OTHER POINTS: credit cards accepted.
châteaux at Craon and Mortiercrolles; la Mine Bleue; musée Robert Tatin.

SAINT REMY DE SILLE
Sarthe, 72140

LA COQUE
(Mme Marie-Laure Vincent) 11bis, route du Mans
TEL: 02.43.20.11.84
DIRECTIONS: RD304, between Le Mans and Sillé-le-Guillaume.
MENU: 55 Frs.
RESTAURANT: Snacks from 7.00, lunch 11.30-14.00
CLOSED: Sun, public holidays, 1 week mid-Aug and last week in Dec.
SPECIALITIES: home-cooking.
OTHER POINTS: bar.
lake and forêt de Sillé-le-Guillaume; Sault-du-Cerf.

SAINT REMY SUR ORNE
Calvados, 14570

AU BON ACCUEIL
(Mme Josette Benoit)
TEL: 02.31.69.43.87
DIRECTIONS: RD562, between Condé-sur-Noireau and Thury-Harcourt.
MENU: 55 Frs.
RESTAURANT: Snacks from 6.30
CLOSED: Sun (out of season).
SPECIALITIES: home-cooking,
OTHER POINTS: credit cards accepted.
La Suisse normande; Saint-Rémy: musée de la mine (mining).

SAINT ROMAIN DE COLBOSC
Seine-Maritime, 76430

LE FRESCOT
(Mr Pascal Ledoult) 18, route Nationale 15
TEL: 02.35.20.15.09
DIRECTIONS: RN15, on the road to Le Havre.
LANGUAGES: English.
MENU: 55 Frs, dish of the day at 38 Frs.
ROOMS: 60 Frs.
RESTAURANT: Snacks from 6.00, lunch 11.30-14.15, dinner 19.15-20.45
CLOSED: Sat afternoon, Sun and in Aug.
SPECIALITIES: home-cooking.
HOTEL: 4 rooms
OTHER POINTS: bar.

SAINT SAMSON DE LA ROQUE
Eure, 27680

RELAIS NORD BRETAGNE
(Mr Marcel Poiraud) Route du Pont de Tancarville
TEL: 02.32.57.67.30
DIRECTIONS: RN815A.
LANGUAGES: English, Spanish.
RESTAURANT: Dinner -23.00
CLOSED: Sat and Sun.
OTHER POINTS: bar.

SAINT SAUVEUR D'EMALLEVILLE
Seine-Maritime, 76110

LE RELAIS DE SAINT SAUVEUR
(Mr Philippe Holstaine) Route Départementale 925 – Lieu dit : La Forge
TEL: 02.35.27.21.56
DIRECTIONS: CD925, between Le Havre and Fécamp.
MENU: 52.50 Frs (drink included).

RESTAURANT: Snacks from 7.00, lunch 11.30-14.00, dinner 19.00-21.00
CLOSED: Sat.
SPECIALITIES: home-cooking.
OTHER POINTS: bar.
Etretat cliffs; Fécamp.

SAINT THEGONNEC
Finistère, 29223

RESTAURANT DU COMMERCE – Les Routiers
(Mr Alain Mevel) 1, rue de Paris
TEL: 02.98.79.61.07
DIRECTIONS: RN12 to Brest, on the expressway.
LANGUAGES: English.
MENU: 54 Frs (drink included).
RESTAURANT: Snacks from 7.30, lunch 11.30-14.00
CLOSED: Sat, Sun, and beginning of Aug.
SPECIALITIES: home-cooking.
OTHER POINTS: credit cards accepted.
the 'enclos' circuit.

SAINT VIGOR LE GRAND
Calvados, 14400

CHEZ PEPONNE
(Mme Marie-Annick Victoire) 3, rue du Pont Trubert
TEL: 02.31.92.28.39
DIRECTIONS: Cherbourg.
MENU: 52 Frs.
RESTAURANT: Snacks from 6.00, lunch 11.30-16.00, dinner 18.00-23.00
CLOSED: Sun.
SPECIALITIES: home-cooking.
OTHER POINTS: bar.
Bayeux tapestry; landing beaches and museum; cathedral.

SAINT VINCENT STERLANGES
Vendée, 85110

A L'ACCUEIL VENDEEN – Chez Dudu
(Mr Auguste Baty) Route Nationale 137
TEL: 02.51.40.23.21 **FAX:** 02.51.40.22.51
DIRECTIONS: RN137, the Nantes/La Rochelle road.
MENU: 40 Frs to 150 Frs
ROOMS: 140 to 160 Frs.
RESTAURANT: Snacks from 6.30, lunch 11.30-14.30, dinner 19.00-22.00
CLOSED: Sun afternoon, and 1st to 8th Oct.
SPECIALITIES: home-cooking,
HOTEL: ☆ 6 rooms.
FACILITIES: shower, private bathroom, television
OTHER POINTS: credit cards accepted.
le Puy du Fou; lakes.

SAINTE FOY DE MONTGOMMERY
Calvados, 14140

LE RELAIS DE MONTGOMERY
(Mme Planckeel)
TEL: 02.31.63.53.02
DIRECTIONS: RN179.
HOTEL: 4 rooms
OTHER POINTS: bar.

SAINTE LUCE SUR LOIRE
Loire-Atlantique, 44980

LA BOUGRIERE
(Mr Pierre Pertue) 4, rue du Pavillon
TEL: 02.40.25.60.84
DIRECTIONS: CD68, A11 – exit at Thouaré-Sainte-Luce Centre.
LANGUAGES: English, Spanish.
MENU: 51.40 to 179 Frs.
RESTAURANT: Snacks from 6.30, lunch 12.00-14.30, dinner 19.00-22.30
CLOSED: Fri evening, Sat, Sun (except for functions), in Aug, and from Christmas Day to New Year's Day.
SPECIALITIES: fruits de mer, poissons au beurre blanc, grenouilles, anguilles (eels), grillades (grills), regional menu, home-cooking.
OTHER POINTS: credit cards accepted.
Nantes: château des ducs de Bretagne, jardin des plantes; tour de Bretagne (du Bouffay district with pedestrianized streets); vineyards; banks of the Loire; zoo at Port-Saint-Père.

SAINTENY
Manche, 50500

LE RELAIS DES FORGES
(Mme Francine Cousin) Les Forges
TEL: 02.33.42.39.36
MENU: 52 Frs.
RESTAURANT: Snacks from 7.00, lunch 12.00-14.30, dinner 19.00-20.00
CLOSED: Tues, and in Aug.
SPECIALITIES: home-cooking.
OTHER POINTS: credit cards accepted.

SAUMUR
Maine-et-Loire, 49400

RESTAURANT DE LA GARE
(Mme Thérèse Loison) 16, avenue David d'Angers
TEL: 02.41.67.34.24
DIRECTIONS: opposite the SNCF station.
MENU: 68 to 150 Frs.
ROOMS: 110 to 230 Frs.
RESTAURANT: Snacks from 7.00, lunch 12.00-15.00, dinner 19.00-22.00

CLOSED: Sun 13.00 to Mon 18.00 (out of season) and 15th Oct to 7th Nov.
SPECIALITIES: cuisses de poulet 'bonne femme', rôti à la saumuroise, sandre (fish) au beurre blanc, magrets de canard sauce roquefort, regional menu, home-cooking.
HOTEL: ☆☆ 18 rooms.
FACILITIES: shower, bath, private bathroom, television, telephone
OTHER POINTS: credit cards accepted.
the banks of the Loire; Saumur: château and countryside, troglodyte dwellings; musée des champignons (mushrooms); musée des blindés (armoured tanks); wine-cellars; zoo at Doué-la-Fontaine.

SEES
Orne, 61500

CAFE DE LA GARE
(Mr Jacques Vallée) 15, rue Edouard Paysan
TEL: 02.33.27.80.05
DIRECTIONS: RN 138, RN138, on the Le Mans/Alenáon road.
LANGUAGES: English.
MENU: 55 Frs (wine and coffee included).
RESTAURANT: Snacks from 6.30
CLOSED: Sun (out of season).
SPECIALITIES: regional menu, home-cooking.
OTHER POINTS: credit cards accepted.

SEGRE
Maine-et-Loire, 49500

LE RELAIS DU COMMERCE
(Mr Emile Georget) 1, place de la Gare
TEL: 02.41.92.22.27
DIRECTIONS: RN775, the Cholet road.
RESTAURANT: Snacks from 6.30
SPECIALITIES: home-cooking.
HOTEL: 6 rooms
OTHER POINTS: bar.
la Mine Bleue; Noyant-la-Gravoyère.

SENE
Morbihan, 56860

RELAIS ROUTIERS
(SA Penru) 46, route de Vannes – Le Poulfanc
TEL: 02.97.47.47.97
DIRECTIONS: between Vannes and Lorient.
LANGUAGES: English.
MENU: 48 to 165 Frs.
RESTAURANT: Snacks from 6.00, lunch 11.30-15.30, dinner 19.00-22.30
CLOSED: 24th Dec to 2nd Jan.
SPECIALITIES: fruits de mer, home-cooking.
HOTEL: ☆ 42 rooms.
FACILITIES: shower, bath, private bathroom, television
OTHER POINTS: credit cards accepted.
Gulf of Morbihan; marina and beaches.

SERQUEUX
Seine-Maritime, 76440

RESTAURANT DU CENTRE
(Mr Jean-Paul Lefébvre) 1004, route de Neufchâtel
TEL: 02.35.09.84.72
DIRECTIONS: between Neufchâtel-en-Bray and Forges-les-Eaux.
LANGUAGES: German.
MENU: 55 Frs (wine included).
ROOMS: 80 to 110 Frs.
RESTAURANT: Snacks from 8.30, lunch 12.00-14.00, dinner 19.00-22.30
CLOSED: Sun and the last 2 weeks in Aug.
SPECIALITIES: home-cooking.
HOTEL: 5 rooms
OTHER POINTS: credit cards accepted.

SIZUN
Finistère, 29450

HOTEL RESTAURANT DES VOYAGEURS
(Mr Joseph Corre) 2, rue de l'Argoat
TEL: 02.98.68.80.35 **FAX:** 02.98.24.11.49
LANGUAGES: English.
MENU: 65 to 120 Frs.
ROOMS: 160 to 260 Frs.
RESTAURANT: Snacks from 7.30, lunch 12.00-13.45, dinner 19.15-20.45
CLOSED: Sat evening (out of season), and from 6th to 29th Sept.
SPECIALITIES: terrine de lapin, mousseline de truite, fruits de mer, regional menu, home-cooking.
HOTEL: ☆☆ 28 rooms.
FACILITIES: shower, bath, private bathroom, television, telephone
OTHER POINTS: credit cards accepted.
the 'enclos' circuit; parc régional d'Armorique.

SOMZEE
Morbihan, 5651

LE VIEUX SOMZEE
(Mr Michel Parmentier) 15, grand Rue
TEL: 071.213.012
DIRECTIONS: RN 5, RN5, on the Charleroi/Philippeville axis.
LANGUAGES: English, Dutch.
MENU: 290 to 690 FB.
RESTAURANT: Snacks from 10.00, lunch 11.30-15.00, dinner 18.30-22.30
SPECIALITIES: tartare, canard crèbe, Angus Beef.
OTHER POINTS: credit cards accepted.

SORINIERES (LES)
Loire-Atlantique, 44840

LE RELAIS – Chez Pierrette et Jean-Louis
(Mr Jean-Louis Benoît) 16, rue du Général de Gaulle
TEL: 02.40.31.22.91
DIRECTIONS: RN137 and 178, on the road to La Roche-sur-Yon.
MENU: 47 to 125 Frs.
ROOMS: 100 Frs.
RESTAURANT: Snacks from 6.30, lunch 11.30-15.00, dinner 19.30-22.00
CLOSED: Sat evening, Sun, and 20th Dec to 15th Jan.
SPECIALITIES: couscous, entrecôte, grillades (grills), home-cooking.
HOTEL: 7 rooms
OTHER POINTS: credit cards accepted.

SOUDAN
Loire-Atlantique, 44110

CAFE DE LA POSTE
(Mr Claude Fruchard) 7, place Talhouët
TEL: 02.40.28.62.36
DIRECTIONS: RN171, the Laval/Paris road.
MENU: 50 Frs (wine included).
RESTAURANT: Snacks from 7.00
CLOSED: Mon, Wed afternoon, and in Aug.
SPECIALITIES: home-cooking.
OTHER POINTS: bar.
Châteaubriant.

SOURDEVAL
Manche, 50150

AU BON ACCUEIL – Les Routiers
(Mr Daniel Delaunay) 1, place du Champ de Foire
TEL: 02.33.59.62.91
DIRECTIONS: RD977, the Caen/Vire road.
LANGUAGES: English.
MENU: 47 to 100 Frs.
ROOMS: 80 to 120 Frs.
RESTAURANT: Snacks from 6.00, dinner -22.00
CLOSED: Sun (except bookings).
SPECIALITIES: home-cooking.
HOTEL: 5 rooms
OTHER POINTS: credit cards accepted.
Mont-Saint-Michel; Avranches: musée du granit.

SOURDEVAL LES BOIS
Manche, 50450

CHEZ COLETTE
(Mme Colette Dufour) Lieu dit "La Croix"
TEL: 02.33.61.77.99
DIRECTIONS: RN799, Abbaye d'Hambye.
MENU: 45 Frs.
RESTAURANT: Snacks from 7.00, lunch 12.00-15.00
SPECIALITIES: home-cooking.
OTHER POINTS: bar.
Abbaye d'Hambye (2km); Villedieu-les-Poëles.

SUZAY
Eure, 27420

LE RELAIS DE SUZAY
(Mme Claire Carric) Route Nationame 14
TEL: 02.32.55.65.01
DIRECTIONS: RN14, the Paris/Rouen road.
MENU: 53 Frs (1/4 wine included).
RESTAURANT: Snacks from 6.00, lunch 11.00-15.00, dinner 19.00-21.00
CLOSED: Sun and in Aug.
SPECIALITIES: regional menu, home-cooking.
OTHER POINTS: credit cards accepted.

TALMONT SAINT HILAIRE
Vendée, 85440

HOTEL DU CENTRE
(Mr Michel Le Blond) 1 rue du Centre
TEL: 02.51.90.60.35
DIRECTIONS: RD949, les Sables d'Olonne/Luáon road.
ROOMS: 100 to 180 Frs.
RESTAURANT: Dinner -21.00
CLOSED: Sat, and in Oct.
SPECIALITIES: fruits de mer, regional menu, home-cooking.
HOTEL: 12 rooms.
FACILITIES: shower, bath, private bathroom, television, telephone
OTHER POINTS: credit cards accepted.
Talmont: château, automobile museum.

TESSY SUR VIRE
Manche, 50420

LES ROUTIERS
(Mr Denis Fouquet) 24, place du Marché
TEL: 02.33.56.35.25
DIRECTIONS: RD13, Granville.
MENU: 53 Frs.
RESTAURANT: Snacks from 7.00, lunch 11.30-15.00, dinner 19.00-21.00
CLOSED: Thurs afternoon.
SPECIALITIES: pieds de veau, home-cooking.
OTHER POINTS: credit cards accepted.

Vire river gorges; chapel at Vire; Saint-Lô; Villedieu-les-Poëles; Coutances.

THOMER LA SOGNE
Eure, 27240

RELAIS 154
(Mme Nicole Vandecandelaere) Route d'Orléans
TEL: 02.32.67.41.00
DIRECTIONS: RN154, between Evreux and Dreux.
LANGUAGES: English.
MENU: 52 Frs.
RESTAURANT: Snacks from 5.00, lunch 11.00-15.00, dinner 19.00-22.00
CLOSED: Sat, Sun and 2 weeks mid-Aug..
SPECIALITIES: home-cooking.
OTHER POINTS: credit cards accepted.
cathedral at Evreux.

TIVOLY
Eure, 27320

LE RELAIS EUROPEEN
Route Nationale 154
TEL: 02.32.58.31.75
DIRECTIONS: RN154, the Evreux/Dreux road.
LANGUAGES: English.
MENU: 55 to 60 Frs.
RESTAURANT: Snacks from 5.00, dinner 19.00-22.30
CLOSED: Sat afternoon and Sun.
SPECIALITIES: fruits de mer, tartes maison, home-cooking.
OTHER POINTS: credit cards accepted.
Center Parc; Verneuil-sur-Avre.

TOLLEVAST
Manche, 50470

LES CHEVRES
(Mr Claude Yssambourg) Route Nationale 13
TEL: 02.33.43.77.92
DIRECTIONS: RN13.
LANGUAGES: English.
MENU: 50 Frs.
RESTAURANT: Open 24h.
SPECIALITIES: pieds de veau, home-cooking.
OTHER POINTS: credit cards accepted.
dockyard; port; Cap de la Hague.

TOTES
Seine-Maritime, 76890

LE NORMANDY
(Mr Alain Montier) Route d'Yvetôt
TEL: 02.35.32.99.54
DIRECTIONS: RN27.
MENU: 55 to 100 Frs.
RESTAURANT: Snacks from 7.00, lunch 11.45-13.45, dinner 19.15-21.15
CLOSED: Sat, Sun, and the 3 first weeks in Aug.
SPECIALITIES: home-cooking.
OTHER POINTS: credit cards accepted.
zoo at Clères; Bocasse amusement park; Dieppe; Rouen.

TRAIT (LE)
Seine-Maritime, 76580

LE JEAN BART – Les Routiers
(Mr Jean Mahier) 488, rue Jean Bart
TEL: 02.35.37.22.47
DIRECTIONS: RD982, between Duclair and Caudebec-en-Caux.
LANGUAGES: English, German.
MENU: 45 Frs.
ROOMS: 80 Frs.
RESTAURANT: Snacks from 5.00, lunch 11.00-15.30, dinner 18.00-21.00
CLOSED: Sun (except functions), and last 3 weeks in Aug.
SPECIALITIES: langue sauce piquante, boudin noir maison, onglet (beef) à l'échalotte, tripes maison, pâtés and rillettes maison, regional menu, home-cooking.
HOTEL: 3 rooms.
FACILITIES: shower, bath, private bathroom, television, telephone
OTHER POINTS: credit cards accepted.
Abbaye de Saint-Wandrille; pont de Brotonne; pont de Tancarville; silver cutlery factory.

TREFFENDEL
Ille-et-Villaine, 35380

LE RN 24
(Mr René Pestel) La Gare
TEL: 02.99.61.00.62
DIRECTIONS: RN24, between Rennes and Lorient.
MENU: 52 Frs.
RESTAURANT: Snacks from 5.30, lunch 11.45-14.30, dinner 19.00-22.30
SPECIALITIES: home-cooking.
OTHER POINTS: credit cards accepted.
Brocéliande valley; l'arbre en or.

TREMBLAY
Ille-et-Villaine, 35460

AUBERGE BRETONNE
(Mr Stéphane Louvet) La Gare
TEL: 02.99.98.26.11
DIRECTIONS: RN155, between Antrain and Fougères.
LANGUAGES: English.
MENU: 45 to 85 Frs.
ROOMS: 110 to 185 Frs.
RESTAURANT: Snacks from 7.00

SPECIALITIES: fruits de mer, home-cooking.
HOTEL: 10 rooms.
FACILITIES: shower
OTHER POINTS: bar.
Mont-Saint-Michel; château at Fougères; Saint-Malo.

TREMONT
Maine-et-Loire, 49310

AUBERGE DES 3 MONTS
(Mme Marie-Hélène Beau) 6, rue du Livier – Lieu dit : Pont de Trémont
TEL: 02.41.59.69.37 FAX: 02.41.59.96.64
DIRECTIONS: between Saumur and Chôlet.
MENU: from 52 Frs.
RESTAURANT: Snacks from 7.30, lunch 11.30-14.30, dinner 18.30-20.30
CLOSED: Wed afternoon, and 2 weeks in Aug.
SPECIALITIES: home-cooking.
OTHER POINTS: credit cards accepted.
zoo at Doué-la-Fontaine; Saumur.

TREMOREL
Côtes-d'Armor, 22230

LES ROUTIERS – Chez Simone
(Mr Simone Sohier) Le Bourg
TEL: 02.96.25.21.70 FAX: 02.96.25.23.48
DIRECTIONS: RN164 bis, between Rennes and Loudéac.
MENU: 50 to 53 Frs.
RESTAURANT: Snacks from 7.00, lunch 11.00-16.00, dinner 19.00-21.00
CLOSED: Mon afternoon and 12th to 26th Aug.
SPECIALITIES: home-cooking.
OTHER POINTS: credit cards accepted.

TRONQUAY (LE)
Calvados, 14490

AU ROUTIER SYMPA
(Daniel et Christine Meriel) La Commune
TEL: 02.31.92.38.68
DIRECTIONS: RD572, between Bayeux and Saint-Lô.
RESTAURANT: Snacks from 5.00, lunch 11.30-14.00, dinner 18.30-21.30
CLOSED: Sat evening and Sun.
SPECIALITIES: home-cooking.
OTHER POINTS: credit cards accepted.
Balleroy: château; musée des ballons; Bayeux: cathedral and tapestry; landing museum; pottery; musée de la mine (mining) at Le Molay-Littry.

ULMES (LES)
Maine-et-Loire, 49700

LES ROUTIERS – Chez Liline
(Mme Sergeline Dorard) Le Moulin Cassé
TEL: 02.41.67.86.16
DIRECTIONS: between Saumur and Doué-la-Fontaine.
MENU: 53 Frs (drink included) to 69 Frs.
RESTAURANT: Snacks from 7.00, lunch 11.20-15.00, dinner 19.00-21.30
CLOSED: Sun.
SPECIALITIES: home-cooking, fritures d'anguilles (fry of eels in summer), home-made desserts.
OTHER POINTS: credit cards accepted.

UROU ET CRENNES
Orne, 61200

LE CLOS FLEURI
(Mr Gilbert Estelle) Route de Paris
TEL: 02.33.67.08.85 FAX: 02.33.67.08.85
DIRECTIONS: RN26, the Paris/Argenton road.
LANGUAGES: English, German.
MENU: 55 Frs.
ROOMS: 85 Frs.
RESTAURANT: Snacks from 6.30, lunch 12.00-14.30, dinner 19.00-22.00
CLOSED: Sat evening and Sun.
SPECIALITIES: regional menu, home-cooking.
HOTEL: 9 rooms.
FACILITIES: shower, private bathroom
OTHER POINTS: credit cards accepted.
haras (stud-farrn) du Pin; Bagnoles-de-l'Orne.

VALLET
Loire-Atlantique, 44330

RESTAURANT DE LA GARE
(Mr Michel Jouy) 43, rue Saint Vincent
TEL: 02.40.33.92.55 FAX: 02.40.36.39.66
DIRECTIONS: RD756 and 763, on the bypass round the centre of Vallet.
LANGUAGES: English.
MENU: 52 to 240 Frs.
ROOMS: 160 to 220 Frs.
RESTAURANT: Snacks from 6.00, lunch 11.30-14.30, dinner 19.00-21.30
CLOSED: Sun (except the hotel).
SPECIALITIES: fruits de mer, poisson au beurre blanc, navarin au muscadet, regional menu, home-cooking.
HOTEL: ☆☆ 25 rooms.
FACILITIES: shower, bath, private bathroom, television, telephone

OTHER POINTS: credit cards accepted.
Nantes; château de Clisson; zoo at La Boissière; musée Pierre Abelliard at Le Vallet.

VALOGNES
Manche, 50700

AU PETIT MONT ROUGE
(Mme Monique Le Blond) 14, boulevard de la Victoire
TEL: 02.33.40.11.80
DIRECTIONS: RN13.
RESTAURANT: Snacks from 7.00
CLOSED: Sat, Sun, and in Aug.
SPECIALITIES: home-cooking.
OTHER POINTS: bar.

VANNES
Morbihan, 56190

L'AUBERGE VIEILLE FONTAINE
(Mr Didier Le Ray) La Vieille Fontaine – La Trinité Surzur
TEL: 02.97.42.01.01
DIRECTIONS: the Nantes/Vannes road.
LANGUAGES: English.
MENU: 47 to 135 Frs.
ROOMS: 120 to 200 Frs.
RESTAURANT: Snacks from 7.00, lunch 11.30-14.30, dinner 19.00-22.00
SPECIALITIES: fruits de mer, regional menu, home-cooking.
HOTEL: ☆☆ 11 rooms.
FACILITIES: shower, bath, private bathroom, telephone
OTHER POINTS: credit cards accepted.
Presqu'île de Rhys; Vannes; Gulf of Morbihan.

LE RELAIS DE LUSCANEN
(Mr Yves Casabianca) ZA de Luscanen – Ploeren
TEL: 02.97.63.15.77
DIRECTIONS: RN165, Vannes/Lorient and Nantes/Quimper.
LANGUAGES: English, German.
MENU: 50 Frs.
ROOMS: 145 to 185 Frs.
RESTAURANT: Snacks from 6.00, lunch 11.30-15.00, dinner 19.00-22.30
CLOSED: Sat after 4pm and Sun.
SPECIALITIES: sea-food specialities, regional menu, home-cooking.
HOTEL: ☆☆ 24 rooms.
FACILITIES: shower, bath, private bathroom, television, telephone
OTHER POINTS: credit cards accepted.
Golfe du Morbihan; Carnac (dolmens); Quiberon; La Trinité-sur-Mer.

VARVANNES
Seine-Maritime, 76890

LE CLOS DE VARVANNES
(Mr Georges Quesnel) Le Clos de Varvannes
TEL: 02.35.32.16.52
DIRECTIONS: RN29, between Le Havre and Tôtes.
MENU: 55 Frs.
RESTAURANT: Snacks from 6.30, lunch 11.30-14.30, dinner 19.00-21.30
CLOSED: Sun and Aug.
SPECIALITIES: regional menu, home-cooking.
OTHER POINTS: credit cards accepted.
Normandy.

VERN SUR SEICHE
Ille-et-Villaine, 35770

LE WELCOME BAR
(Mr Michel Clinard) Le Clos Berquet
TEL: 02.99.62.83.18
DIRECTIONS: RD163, between Angers and Châteaubriant.
LANGUAGES: English, German.
MENU: 55 Frs.
RESTAURANT: Snacks from 7.30, lunch 11.30-15.00, dinner 19.00-21.00
CLOSED: Sat afternoon, Sun and 2 weeks in Aug.
SPECIALITIES: home-cooking,
OTHER POINTS: credit cards accepted.
Rennes.

VERNON
Eure, 27200

LA BUISSONNIERE
(Mme Michelle Bourgault) Le Petit Val
TEL: 02.32.51.08.41
DIRECTIONS: the Vernon/Paris axis.
RESTAURANT: Snacks from 6.30
CLOSED: Sun.
SPECIALITIES: home-cooking,
OTHER POINTS: credit cards accepted.

VERTOU
Loire-Atlantique, 44120

RESTAURANT DE LA GARE
(Mr Noël Gohaud) 10, avenue de la Gare
TEL: 02.40.34.08.74
DIRECTIONS: RN149, between Clisson and Nantes – near Vertou station.
MENU: 51 Frs.
RESTAURANT: Snacks from 6.00, lunch 12.00-14.30, dinner 19.00-21.00
CLOSED: Sat, Sun and in Aug.
SPECIALITIES: home-cooking.
OTHER POINTS: bar.

Nantes: château des Ducs de Bretagne; zoo at Doué-la-Fontaine.

VILDE GUINGALAN
Côtes-d'Armor, 22980

LA BORGNETTE
(Mr Alain Lambard – SARL Mélodie) La Borgnette
TEL: 02.96.27.61.10
DIRECTIONS: the Dinan/Saint-Brieuc road, 9km from Dinan.
MENU: 51 Frs.
RESTAURANT: Lunch 11.00-15.00, dinner 19.00-22.00
CLOSED: Sat and SUn.
SPECIALITIES: home-cooking.
OTHER POINTS: credit cards accepted.
Dinan (9km).

VILLEBAUDON
Manche, 50410

CHEZ TINTIN ET NICOLE
(Mme Nicole Goutte) Le Bourg
TEL: 02.33.61.20.52
DIRECTIONS: Cherbourg-Avranche/Caen-Granville.
MENU: 55 Frs (drink and coffee included).
RESTAURANT: Snacks from 6.00
SPECIALITIES: home-cooking, regional menu.
OTHER POINTS: credit cards accepted.

VILLEDIEU LES POELES
Manche, 50800

HOTEL DES VOYAGEURS
(Mr Bernard Magusto) 36, avenue du Maréchal Leclerc
TEL: 02.33.51.08.98
DIRECTIONS: between Caen and Avranches.
MENU: 50 Frs.
ROOMS: 120 to 140 Frs.
RESTAURANT: Snacks from 6.00
CLOSED: Sun (out of season).
SPECIALITIES: home-cooking.
HOTEL: 6 rooms
OTHER POINTS: children's menu.
Villedieu: bell-foundry, cycling and furniture museums, zoo; Granville; Mont-Saint-Michel.

VILLERS BOCAGE
Calvados, 14310

LA GRANDE COUR
(Mme Martine Echivard) 6, rue Foch
TEL: 02.31.77.39.00
DIRECTIONS: RN175, the Vire/Caen road.
LANGUAGES: Spanish.
MENU: 50 to 100 Frs.
ROOMS: 100 to 180 Frs.
RESTAURANT: Snacks from 5.00, lunch 11.00-15.00, dinner 19.00-22.00
CLOSED: Sun.
SPECIALITIES: home-cooking.
HOTEL: 9 rooms.
FACILITIES: shower, bath, private bathroom
OTHER POINTS: credit cards accepted.
zoo at jurques; Normandy landing beaches; Bayeux: musée de la 2ème guerre mondiale (Second World War).

VIMOUTIERS
Orne, 61120

HOTEL DE LISIEUX
(Mme Yvette Larivière) 37, avenue Lyautey
TEL: 02.33.39.02.62
DIRECTIONS: RN179, Camembert.
MENU: 54 Frs.
ROOMS: 85 to 115 Frs.
RESTAURANT: Snacks from 7.00, dinner 19.00-21.00
CLOSED: Sat afternoon to Sun evening, and last 2 weeks in Aug.
SPECIALITIES: home-cooking.
HOTEL: 5 rooms.
FACILITIES: shower
OTHER POINTS: bar.
Camembert region.

VIRE
Calvados, 14500

HOTEL DE FRANCE
(Mr Roger Carnet) 4, rue d'Aignaux
TEL: 02.31.68.00.35 FAX: 02.31.68.22.65
DIRECTIONS: the Caen/Rennes or Paris/Granville road.
LANGUAGES: English.
MENU: 58 to 220 Frs.
ROOMS: 165 to 350 Frs.
RESTAURANT: Snacks from 7.00, lunch 12.00-14.00, dinner 19.00-21.00
CLOSED: from 20th Dec to 10th Jan.
SPECIALITIES: home-cooking, ris de veau Vallée d'Auge, tarte aux pommes flambée au Calvados, escalope normande, regional menu.
HOTEL: ☆☆ 20 rooms.
FACILITIES: shower, bath, private bathroom, television, telephone
OTHER POINTS: credit cards accepted
Lac de la Dathée; leisure park; forêt de Saint-Sever; zoo at Jurques; la Suisse normande.

VIVY
Maine-et-Loire, 49680

HOTEL RESTAURANT SAINT PAUL
(Mme Marie-Louise Bidet) 30, rue Nationale
TEL: 02.41.52.50.13 FAX: 02.41.52.58.96

DIRECTIONS: RN147, between Saumur and Le Mans via Baugé.
LANGUAGES: English.
MENU: 58 to 170 Frs.
ROOMS: 125 to 235 Frs.
RESTAURANT: Snacks from 7.00, lunch 12.00-14.30, dinner 17.30-22.00
SPECIALITIES: home-cooking, brochet ou sandre de Loire (fish) au beurre blanc, regional menu.
HOTEL: ☆ 27 rooms.
FACILITIES: shower, bath, private bathroom, television, telephone
OTHER POINTS: credit cards accepted.
Saumur: château, museums, wine-cellars, riding school; Loire châteaux.

VOIVRES (LES)
Sarthe, 72210

RELAIS LE TAMARIS
(Mr Patrick Leguy) Route de la Suze
TEL: 02.43.88.52.60
DIRECTIONS: RD23, exit Le Mans Sud (South).
MENU: 63.50 Frs.
ROOMS: 103 Frs.
RESTAURANT: Snacks from 6.30, lunch 12.00-15.00, dinner 18.00-22.00
CLOSED: Sat afternoon, Sun and in Aug.
SPECIALITIES: home-cooking.
HOTEL: 4 rooms.
FACILITIES: shower, bath, private bathroom, telephone
OTHER POINTS: credit cards accepted.
old Le Mans; racing circuit; bird park at Spay.

YERVILLE
Seine-Maritime, 76760

L'ESCALE
(Mr Alain Benoit) Avenue Charles de Gaulle
TEL: 02.35.96.78.06
DIRECTIONS: RN29, Yvetot/Tôtes axis.
MENU: 59 to 89 Frs.
RESTAURANT: Snacks from 6.30
CLOSED: Sat and Sun.
SPECIALITIES: regional menu, home-cooking.
OTHER POINTS: credit cards accepted.
Clères: zoologique park, museum.

ZARAGOZA
Manche, 50692

BP OIL ESPANA SA
(BP TRUCKSTOPS) Carretera Nacional 232 km 257 – Autovia de Logrono
TEL: 976.65.10.00 FAX: 976.65.11.15
DIRECTIONS: between Barcelona and "le Pays Basque".
LANGUAGES: English.
RESTAURANT: Lunch 13.00-16.00, dinner 20.00-24.00
SPECIALITIES: regional menu, home-cooking, migas à la Aragonesa, ternasco, fabada.
OTHER POINTS: credit cards accepted.

The Loire

The following départments are included in this chapter:

Charente (16)
Charente-Maritime (17)
Cher (18)
Deux-Sèvres (79)
Eure-et-Loire (28)
Indre (36)
Indre-et-Cher (41)
Loire-et-Cher (41)
Loiret (45)
Vienne (86)

ABSIE (L')
Deux-Sèvres, 79240

RESTAURANT DE LA POSTE
(Mr Eugène Bignon) 21 Rue de la Poste
TEL: 05.49.95.90.21
DIRECTIONS: Bressuire/Parthenay
MENU: 50 to 68 Frs.
RESTAURANT: Snacks from 8.00, lunch 11.30-14.30, dinner 17.00-20.00
CLOSED: Sun and 1 week in Sept.
SPECIALITIES: home-cooking,
OTHER POINTS: bar.

AIRVAULT
Deux-Sèvres, 79600

LES CHENES VERTS
(Mr Alain Rousseau) La Maucarrière
TEL: 05.49.69.71.11
DIRECTIONS: RD938, between Parthenay and Thouars.
MENU: 50 to 92 Frs.
ROOMS: 70 to 150 Frs.
RESTAURANT: Snacks from 6.30, lunch 12.00-14.00, dinner 19.00-21.00
CLOSED: Sun, and 15th Sept to 15th Oct.
SPECIALITIES: home-cooking.
HOTEL: 10 rooms
OTHER POINTS: credit cards accepted.
Airvault: church, museum, dam.

ALLOGNY
Cher, 18110

CAFE RESTAURANT DE LA MAIRIE
(Mr Noël Hellegouarch) Place de la Mairie
TEL: 02.48.64.00.71
DIRECTIONS: RD944, between Salbris and Bourges.
LANGUAGES: English.
MENU: 58 Frs.
RESTAURANT: Snacks from 7.00, lunch 12.00-14.30, dinner 19.00-22.00
CLOSED: Thurs.
SPECIALITIES: game (according to season), coq au vin, regional menu, home-cooking.
OTHER POINTS: credit cards accepted.
Bourges cathedral; pottery.

ANGLIERS
Vienne, 86330

LE SAINT HUBERT DE SCEVOLLES
(Mr Jean-Pierre Fritschy) Route nationale 147
TEL: 05.49.98.19.15
DIRECTIONS: RN147, Loudun/Poitiers road.
MENU: 58 Frs (wine included).
RESTAURANT: Snacks from 6.00, lunch 11.00-15.00, dinner 19.00-21.30
CLOSED: Wed afternoon.
SPECIALITIES: home-cooking.
OTHER POINTS: credit cards accepted.
Loudun.

ARDENTES
Indre, 36120

CAFE DES SPORTS
(Mr Dominique Millault) 21, avenue de Verdun
TEL: 02.54.36.21.19
DIRECTIONS: the Châteauroux/Montluáon road.
LANGUAGES: English, Spanish, Portuguese.
MENU: 55 to 130 Frs.
ROOMS: 130 Frs.
RESTAURANT: Snacks from 6.00
SPECIALITIES: home-cooking.
HOTEL: 5 rooms.
FACILITIES: shower, bath, private bathroom
OTHER POINTS: credit cards accepted.
Georges Sand's château at Nohant (15km); château at Mers-sur-Indre (15km).

LE RELAIS DE CLAVIERES
(Mme Pascale Portrait) Route de Montluáon – Clavières
TEL: 02.54.26.98.46
DIRECTIONS: Montiuáon.

MENU: 48 to 68 Frs.
ROOMS: 75 to 100 Frs.
RESTAURANT: Snacks from 7.00, lunch 12.00-13.30, dinner 20.00-20.30
CLOSED: Sun.
SPECIALITIES: home-cooking.
HOTEL: 4 rooms.
FACILITIES: shower
OTHER POINTS: bar.
Georges Sand's château.

ARGENT SUR SAULDRE
Cher, 18410

AUBERGE DES BRUYERES
(Mr Jean-Yves Muelle) 10, rue Nationale
TEL: 02.48.73.60.20
RESTAURANT: Snacks from 9.00, lunch 12.00-14.00, dinner 19.00-21.00
CLOSED: Mon evening and in Oct.
SPECIALITIES: home-cooking.
OTHER POINTS: credit cards accepted.
Musée des métiers (trades/crafts).

ATHEE SUR CHER
Indre-et-Loire, 37270

L'ESCALE
(Mr Henry Le Roy)
TEL: 02.47.50.67.29
DIRECTIONS: RN76, between Tours and Vierzon.
MENU: 55 Frs (wine included).
RESTAURANT: Snacks from 6.30, lunch 11.00-15.00, dinner 18.30-21.30
CLOSED: Sun.
SPECIALITIES: galette de pomme de terre, home-cooking.
OTHER POINTS: credit cards accepted.
Tours; Bléré; Loire châteaux.

AUBIGNY SUR NERE
Cher, 18700

LES ROUTIER
(Mr Bernard Ollier) 17, avenue Charles Lefèbvre
TEL: 02.48.58.01.42
DIRECTIONS: RN940, the Gien/Vierzon road.
MENU: 52 Frs.
ROOMS: 80 to 104 Frs.
RESTAURANT: Snacks from 7.00, lunch 12.00-14.00, dinner 19.00-21.30
CLOSED: Sun and in Aug.
SPECIALITIES: sanglier (boar), chevreuil (venison) (in season), regional menu.
HOTEL: 9 rooms.
FACILITIES: shower
OTHER POINTS: credit cards accepted.
châteaux; Sancerre vineyards.

AUNEAU
Eure-et-Loir, 28700

AUX TROIS MARCHES
(Régine et Christian Séttaoui-Gasnier) 2, rue Emile Labiche
TEL: 02.37.31.70.49
DIRECTIONS: A11 (Ablis exit) or A10 (Allainville exit).
MENU: 54 to 58.50 Frs.
ROOMS: 120 to 180 Frs.
RESTAURANT: Snacks from 6.00, lunch 11.00-14.30, dinner 19.00-20.30
CLOSED: Sat evening, Sun, in Aug and last week in Dec.
SPECIALITIES: home-cooking.
HOTEL: 8 rooms
OTHER POINTS: credit cards accepted.
château at Auneau.

AUSSAC VADALLE
Charente, 16560

LA BELLE CANTINIERE
(Mme Murielle Judes) Route Nationale 10
TEL: 05.45.20.66.89 FAX: 05.45.20.71.99
DIRECTIONS: RN10, the Poitiers/Bordeaux road.
RESTAURANT: Snacks from 5.00
CLOSED: Sat evening and Sun.
SPECIALITIES: fruits de mer, home-cooking.
OTHER POINTS: credit cards accepted.

AZAY LE FERRON
Indre, 36290

LA RENAISSANCE
(Mr Philippe Morvant) Place de l'Eglise
TEL: 02.54.39.21.75
DIRECTIONS: between Châteauroux and Chatellerault.
LANGUAGES: English, Spanish.
MENU: 59 Frs (drink included) to 135 Frs.
RESTAURANT: Snacks from 7.00
CLOSED: the first 2 weeks in Jan.
SPECIALITIES: regional menu, home-cooking, feuilletés, poissons.
OTHER POINTS: credit cards accepted.

AZAY LE RIDEAU
Indre-et-Loire, 37190

RESTAURANT DE LA GARE
(Mr Didier Chevallier) 63, avenue de la Gare
TEL: 02.47.45.40.60
DIRECTIONS: between Chinon and Tours.
MENU: 52 Frs (wine included) to 200 Frs.
RESTAURANT: Snacks from 7.30, lunch 12.00-14.30, dinner 19.00-22.00
CLOSED: Sun.
SPECIALITIES: home-cooking.

OTHER POINTS: credit cards accepted.
Chinon; Musée Dufresne; Cadillac museum.

BARBEZIEUX
Charente, 16360

LA CAMBROUSSE
(Mr Jean-Claude Pichon) Le Pont du Noble – La Tatre
TEL: 05.45.78.52.83
DIRECTIONS: RN10, between Angoulème and Bordeaux.
MENU: 57 Frs.
ROOMS: 90 to 110 Frs.
RESTAURANT: Open 24h.
CLOSED: Sat 10am to Sun 11pm.
SPECIALITIES: home-cooking.
HOTEL: 13 rooms.
FACILITIES: shower, bath, private bathroom
OTHER POINTS: credit cards accepted.

BARBEZIEUX SAINT HILAIRE
Charente, 16120

RELAIS DE LA BILLETTE
(Mme Danielle Houdusse) Ladiville
TEL: 05.45.78.57.09 FAX: 05.45.78.35.33
DIRECTIONS: RN10, 20km south of Angoulème, 10km north of Barbezieux.
LANGUAGES: Spanish.
MENU: 70 Frs.
RESTAURANT: Open 24h.
CLOSED: Sun, and 1 week in Aug.
SPECIALITIES: confit de canard, escalope à la charentaise, magret de canard, lapin au pineau des Charentes, escalope à la charentaise, filet de canard, regional menu, home-cooking.
OTHER POINTS: credit cards accepted.
church at Ladiville; château at Barbezieux; Angoulème: hôtel-de-ville and old quarters, le Maine Girand.

BAZOCHE GOUET (LA)
Eure-et-Loir, 28330

LA BONNE AUBERGE
(Mr Jean-Paul Thierry) 54, avenue du Général Leclerc
TEL: 02.37.49.21.61
DIRECTIONS: RD927, the Chartres/Le Mans road.
MENU: 45 to 75 Frs.
RESTAURANT: Snacks from 7.00
CLOSED: Sun, 2 weeks in Feb and 2 weeks in Sept.
SPECIALITIES: regional menu, home-cooking.
OTHER POINTS: bar.
Perche hills; château at Nogent-le-Rotrou; open-air centre at Brou; numerous étangs (ponds).

BAZOCHES EN DUNOIS
Eure-et-Loir, 28140

AU BON ACCUEIL
(Mme Marie-Claude Boucher) 7, rue de l'Eglise
TEL: 02.37.22.08.30
DIRECTIONS: RN927, Chartres/Orléans/Châteaudun.
MENU: 52 to 56.50 Frs (coffee included).
RESTAURANT: Snacks from 7.30, lunch 11.00-15.00, dinner 19.00-22.00
CLOSED: 8 days in June or Sept.
SPECIALITIES: truites à l'oignon, potée beauceronne, rognons (kidneys) au vin rouge, pot-au-feu sauce tomate, tarte à la rhubarbe, home-cooking.
OTHER POINTS: bar.
Chartres cathedral; Châteaudun; Orléans; Loire châteaux; grottes (caves) du Foulon.

BEAUNE LA ROLANDE
Loiret, 45340

HOTEL DE LA GARE
(Mme Jacqueline Todesco) Gare d'Auxy
TEL: 02.38.96.70.44 FAX: 02.38.96.70.44
DIRECTIONS: the Orléans/Paris road.
LANGUAGES: English.
MENU: 55 Frs (wine and coffee included) to 98 Frs.
ROOMS: 100 to 150 Frs.
RESTAURANT: Snacks from 7.00, lunch 12.00-15.00, dinner 19.00-22.00
SPECIALITIES: regional menu, home-cooking.
HOTEL: 10 rooms
OTHER POINTS: credit cards accepted.
Montargis; Pithiviers; Nemours; Gien.

BEAUVOIR SUR NIORT
Deux-Sèvres, 79360

L'ETAPE
(Mme Annick Duverne) 7, place de l'Hôtel de Ville
TEL: 05.49.09.70.17
DIRECTIONS: RN150, between Saint-jean d'Angély and Niort.
LANGUAGES: English.
MENU: 53 Frs (wine and coffee included) and 70 Frs.
RESTAURANT: Lunch 12.00-14.00, dinner 19.00-21.00
CLOSED: Sun afternoon.
SPECIALITIES: regional menu, home-cooking.
OTHER POINTS: bar.
zoo at Chizé (10km); Rimbaud's windmill (1km); churches (10km).

BLERE
Indre-et-Loire, 37150

LE RELAIS
(Mme Paulette Rossignol) 48 Rue de Tours
TEL: 02.47.57.92.31

DIRECTIONS: RN76, the Tours/Vierzon road.
MENU: 60 to 85 Frs.
RESTAURANT: Snacks from 8.00, lunch 12.00-14.30, dinner 19.00-21.30
SPECIALITIES: home-cooking.
OTHER POINTS: credit cards accepted.
châteaux at Chenonceaux, Amboise and Loches; musée des poids-lourds (HGVs); abbey at Pontlevoy.

BLOIS
Loir-et-Cher, 41000

BAR DE LA CITE
(Mr Didier Moreau) 55, avenue de Vendôme
TEL: 02.54.43.48.54
DIRECTIONS: RD951, Vendôme.
MENU: 50 Frs (wine and coffee included).
RESTAURANT: Snacks from 5.00, lunch 12.00-14.30, dinner 19.00-21.00
CLOSED: Sat and Sun.
SPECIALITIES: home-cooking.
OTHER POINTS: bar.
Loire châteaux at Blois, Chambord, Cheverny; the town of Blois.

BOIS DE FEUGERES
Eure-et-Loir, 28800

RELAIS ROUTIER DU BOIS DE FEUGERES
(Mr Alain Laurent) 26, route Nationale
TEL: 02.37.96.33.01 **FAX:** 02.37.96.30.75
DIRECTIONS: RN10, between Chartres and Châteaudun.
LANGUAGES: English, German.
MENU: 58 to 71 Frs.
RESTAURANT: Snacks from 4.00
CLOSED: Sat evening and Sun.
SPECIALITIES: home-cooking.
OTHER POINTS: credit cards accepted.
Chartres cathedral.

BORDS
Charente-Maritime, 17430

CAFE DU CENTRE
(Mr Evelyne Perrocheau) Place de l'Eglise
TEL: 05.46.83.84.31
DIRECTIONS: RN137, between Rochefort and Saintes.
MENU: 55 Frs.
RESTAURANT: Snacks from 6.30, lunch 12.00-14.00
CLOSED: Sat after 13.30.
SPECIALITIES: home-cooking.
OTHER POINTS: bar.

BOSSEE
Indre-et-Loire, 37240

AUX DELICES ANTILLAIS
(Mme Nicole Le Lain) Route Départementale 760
TEL: 02.47.92.88.27
DIRECTIONS: RN10, between Loches and Chinon.
LANGUAGES: English, Spanish.
MENU: 56 Frs (wine included) to 135 Frs.
RESTAURANT: Snacks from 7.00, lunch 12.00-15.00, dinner 19.00-1.00
CLOSED: Mon, and in Feb.
SPECIALITIES: dishes from the Antilles, regional menu, home-cooking.
OTHER POINTS: credit cards accepted.
Loire châteaux; cellars at Nourray, Montlouis and Chinon.

BOURRAS
Charente, 16200

RELAIS DES VIGNES
(Mme Monique Delavoie)
TEL: 05.45.35.81.62
DIRECTIONS: RN141, between Cognac and Royan.
MENU: 51 to 55 Frs.
RESTAURANT: Snacks from 7.30, lunch 11.30-14.30, dinner 19.30-22.00
CLOSED: Sun, and 15th Aug to 15th Sept.
SPECIALITIES: home-cooking.
OTHER POINTS: credit cards accepted.
distillery buildings, cooper's workshop.

BRECHES
Indre-et-Loire, 37330

RESTAURANT ROUTIERS
(Mme Anita Vaillant) Lieu dit : Le Bel Air
TEL: 02.47.24.13.03
DIRECTIONS: RD766, between Angers (80km) and Blois (75km).
MENU: 59.50 Frs.
RESTAURANT: Snacks from 6.00
CLOSED: Sat, Sun, and in Aug.
SPECIALITIES: home-cooking.
OTHER POINTS: credit cards accepted.
Loire châteaux.

BREUIL CHAUSSE
Deux-Sèvres, 79300

CHEZ MARINETTE
(Mme Marie-Reine Vignaud) 22, route de Bressuire
TEL: 05.49.65.16.31
DIRECTIONS: Bressuire/La-Roche-sur-Yon.
LANGUAGES: English, Spanish, Italian.

MENU: 50 Frs (drink included).
RESTAURANT: Snacks from 6.30
SPECIALITIES: home-cooking.
OTHER POINTS: credit cards accepted.

BRIARE
Loiret, 45250

LE RELAIS
(Mr Eric Bourgoin) Gare de Chatillon sur Loire
TEL: 02.38.31.44.42
DIRECTIONS: RN7.
MENU: 55 to 65 Frs.
ROOMS: 75 to 85 Frs.
RESTAURANT: Snacks from 5.00
CLOSED: Sat evening and Sun.
SPECIALITIES: home-cooking.
HOTEL: 9 rooms.
FACILITIES: shower
OTHER POINTS: bar.

BRIE
Charente, 16590

L'AUBERGE DES ROUTIERS
(Dominique Doré) Les Rassats
TEL: 05.45.65.90.24
DIRECTIONS: RN141, the Limoges/Bordeaux road.
MENU: 57 to 68 Frs.
RESTAURANT: Snacks from 4.30, lunch 11.00, dinner - 23.00
CLOSED: Sat evening, Sun, and 3 weeks in Aug.
SPECIALITIES: Charentais dishes, home-cooking.
OTHER POINTS: credit cards accepted.
château at La Rochefoucauld; Angoulême; Cognac.

BRION PRÈS THOUET
Deux-Sèvres, 79290

LE RELAIS DE BRION
(Mr Patrice Poussin) 39, rue Principale
TEL: 05.49.67.73.34
DIRECTIONS: RD938, the Saumur/Thouars road.
MENU: 54.50 Frs (wine included, 60 Frs with coffee).
ROOMS: 110 Frs.
RESTAURANT: Snacks from 6.30, lunch 11.30-14.30, dinner 19.00-21.00
CLOSED: Sat, Sun and public holidays.
SPECIALITIES: magret de canard (duck) à l'orange, home-cooking.
HOTEL: 2 rooms.
FACILITIES: shower
OTHER POINTS: credit cards accepted.
Saumur (25km); Montreuil-Bellay (7km); Thouars (old town).

BRIOUX SUR BOUTONNE
Deux-Sèvres, 79170

AUBERGE DU CHEVAL BLANC
(Mme Pierrette André) 23, place du Champ de Foire
TEL: 05.49.07.52.08
DIRECTIONS: between Poitiers and Saint-Jean d'Y (d'Angély).
MENU: 55 Frs to 150 Frs.
ROOMS: 100 to 180 Frs.
RESTAURANT: Snacks from 7.00, lunch 12.00-15.00, dinner 19.30-21.00
CLOSED: Sun.
SPECIALITIES: pigeonneau au pineau, chevreau (kid) aux oignons, farci, home-cooking.
HOTEL: 6 rooms.
FACILITIES: shower, bath, private bathroom
OTHER POINTS: credit cards accepted.
Niort; Melle; silver mines.

BROU
Eure-et-Loir, 28160

HOTEL DE LA GARE
(Mr Alain Duparc) 76, avenue du Général de Gaulle
TEL: 02.37.47.00.81
DIRECTIONS: RD955, between Alenáon and Orléans.
MENU: 51.50 Frs.
ROOMS: 130 to 148 Frs.
RESTAURANT: Snacks from 6.00, lunch 11.30-14.00, dinner 19.00-21.00
CLOSED: Sat, Sun, and in Dec.
SPECIALITIES: home-cooking.
HOTEL: 8 rooms.
FACILITIES: shower
OTHER POINTS: bar.
châteaux at Nogent and Châteaudun.

CELLE SAINT AVANT (LA)
Indre-et-Loire, 37160

LA CARAVANE
(Mr Jacky Baudouin) Route Nationale 10
TEL: 02.47.65.07.82
DIRECTIONS: RN10, between Poitiers and Tours.
MENU: 55 (wine included) to 65 Frs.
ROOMS: 60 to 150 Frs.
RESTAURANT: Snacks from 5.00, lunch 11.30-15.00, dinner 19.00-23.00
SPECIALITIES: home-cooking.
HOTEL: 8 rooms
OTHER POINTS: credit cards accepted.
Loire châteaux; Futuroscope.

CELON
Indre, 36200

LES ROUTIERS
(Mr Maurice Dufour)
TEL: 02.54.25.32.08
DIRECTIONS: RN20, the Paris/Toulouse road.
MENU: 60 to 90 Frs.
SPECIALITIES: sauté de veau à l'ancienne, regional menu, home-cooking.
OTHER POINTS: credit cards accepted.
Vallée de la Creuse; lac d'Eguzon.

CHAINGY
Loiret, 45161

LE RELAIS DU FOURNEAUX
(Mr Carlos De Sousa) Route Nationale 152
TEL: 02.38.80.69.12
LANGUAGES: English.
OTHER POINTS: bar.

CHAMPAGNE MOUTON
Charente, 16350

HOTEL PLAISANCE
(Mme Nathalie Cambien) Place du Château
TEL: 05.45.31.80.52
DIRECTIONS: RN740, between Confolens and Ruffec.
LANGUAGES: English, German, Spanish.
MENU: 60 to 250 Frs.
ROOMS: 120 to 220 Frs.
RESTAURANT: Snacks from 7.00, lunch 12.00-14.00, dinner 19.00-21.00
CLOSED: Sun evening.
SPECIALITIES: daube en croute, cassoulet, raviole de Saint-Jacques (scallops), petit salé (pickled pork) aux lentilles, regional menu, home-cooking.
HOTEL: 15 rooms.
FACILITIES: shower, bath, private bathroom, telephone
OTHER POINTS: credit cards accepted.
Confolens; Nanteuil-en-Vallée; Angoulême.

CHANIERS
Charente-Maritime, 17610

AUBERGE DE LA BOISERIE
(Mr Jean-Pierre Lorillon) Route Nationale 141 – Le Maine Allain
TEL: 05.46.91.11.78 **FAX:** 05.46.91.08.03
DIRECTIONS: RN141, Cognac/Saintes road.
LANGUAGES: English.
MENU: 59 Frs (wine included) to 155 Frs.
ROOMS: 100 to 155 Frs.
RESTAURANT: Snacks from 7.00, lunch 12.00-14.00, dinner 19.30-21.30
SPECIALITIES: fricassées d'anguilles (eels), écrevisses (cray-fish) au cognac, regional menu, home-cooking.
HOTEL: ☆ 11 rooms.
FACILITIES: shower, private bathroom
OTHER POINTS: credit cards accepted.
Saintes.

CHAPELLE SAINT LAURENT (LA)
Deux-Sèvres, 79430

CAFE DES SPORTS
(Louisette et André Guérin) 6 Route de Bressuire
TEL: 05.49.72.05.64
DIRECTIONS: RD748, between Niort and Angers.
MENU: 51 Frs.
RESTAURANT: Snacks from 7.00, lunch 12.00-14.00, dinner 19.00-20.30
CLOSED: Sat (restaurant only), and a few days in Aug.
SPECIALITIES: regional menu, home-cooking.
OTHER POINTS: credit cards accepted.
Futuroscope; Le Puy du Fou; Poitou marshlands; moulin (windmill) des Mothes.

CHARENTON DU CHER
Cher, 18210

LA BONNE TABLE
(Mme Antoinette Frège) 36, rue Nationale
TEL: 02.48.60.72.73
DIRECTIONS: RN151 bis.
RESTAURANT: Snacks from 6.30, dinner up to 22.00
CLOSED: Tues evening, and in Aug.
SPECIALITIES: home-cooking.
OTHER POINTS: bar.

LE FAISAN DORE
(Mme Carmen Ville) Laugère
TEL: 02.48.60.75.38
DIRECTIONS: Châteauroux/Bourges/Moulins.
LANGUAGES: Spanish.
MENU: 60 to 120 Frs.
RESTAURANT: Snacks from 7.00, lunch 11.00-14.30, dinner 19.00-21.00
CLOSED: Sat morning.
SPECIALITIES: home-cooking.
OTHER POINTS: credit cards accepted.
forêt de Tronáais; étang (pond) de Gould.

CHARSONVILLE
Loiret, 45130

LES ROUTIERS
(Mr Patrick Billard) 15, rue de la Libération
TEL: 02.38.74.23.00
DIRECTIONS: RN157, the Orléans/Le Mans road.
MENU: 48 Frs.
RESTAURANT: Snacks from 5.00, lunch 11.45-14.00

CLOSED: Sun, Mon afternoon.
SPECIALITIES: regional menu, home-cooking.
OTHER POINTS: credit cards accepted.
Loire châteaux.

CHARTRES
Eure-et-Loir, 28000

RELAIS BEAUCERON
(Mr Lucien Lichet) Route Nationale 10 – Mignières
TEL: 02.37.26.46.21 **FAX:** 02.37.26.30.64
DIRECTIONS: RN10, the Chartres/Tours road, Thivars exit A11.
MENU: 69 to 138 Frs.
ROOMS: 190 Frs.
RESTAURANT: Snacks from 5.00, lunch 11.45-15.00, dinner 18.45-23.00
CLOSED: Sat evening (out of season) and Sun.
SPECIALITIES: oeufs à la Chartres, côte de boeuf au gris meunier, home-cooking.
HOTEL: ☆☆ 30 rooms.
FACILITIES: shower, bath, private bathroom, television, telephone
OTHER POINTS: credit cards accepted.
Chartres cathedral; moulin du bois de Feugère; church at Meslay-le-Grenet; banks of the river Loir; Loire and Châteaudun châteaux.

CHASSENEUIL SUR BONNIEURE
Charente, 16260

CHEZ NICOLE
(Mme Nicole Bardet) 25, avenue de la République
TEL: 05.45.39.61.50 **FAX:** 05.45.22.52.64
DIRECTIONS: RN 141, RN141, on the Angoulême/Limoges axis.
LANGUAGES: English.
MENU: 55 Frs (wine included).
RESTAURANT: Snacks from 7.30, lunch 11.30-15.00, dinner 19.00-21.00
SPECIALITIES: home-cooking.
OTHER POINTS: credit cards accepted.

CHATEAU GAILLARD SANTILLY
Eure-et-Loir, 28310

RELAIS CHEZ LILI
(Mme Liliane Boldiou) 1, rue Charles Péguy
TEL: 02.37.90.07.03
DIRECTIONS: RN20.
LANGUAGES: Polish, Russian.
RESTAURANT: Snacks from 3.30
CLOSED: Sun., and 2 weeks in Aug
SPECIALITIES: home-cooking.
OTHER POINTS: credit cards accepted.
sugar refinery; Artenay.

LE RELAIS 20
(Mrs Dahmani Frères) 33, rue Charles Peguy – Route Nationale 20
TEL: 02.37.90.07.33 **FAX:** 02.37.90.02.14
DIRECTIONS: RN20, between Toury and Artenay.
LANGUAGES: English, Spanish, Portuguese, Arabic.
MENU: 56 Frs.
RESTAURANT: Snacks from 4.00
CLOSED: Sat afternoon and Sun.
SPECIALITIES: home-cooking, couscous (Thurs and Fri).
OTHER POINTS: credit cards accepted.
Toury.

CHATEAU LA VALLIERE
Indre-et-Loire, 37330

LE GRAND CERF
(Mr Jean Meunier) La Porerie
TEL: 02.47.24.11.06 **FAX:** 02.47.24.18.95
DIRECTIONS: RD959, the Tours/Laval road between Le Lude and Château-la-Vallière.
LANGUAGES: English.
MENU: 55 to 160 Frs.
ROOMS: 130 to 250 Frs.
RESTAURANT: Snacks from 7.00, lunch 12.00-14.00, dinner 19.00-21.00
CLOSED: Sat (in winter), Sun evening, and from 25th Oct to 15th Nov. Specialaies: rillette de]a Sarthe, ris
SPECIALITIES: regional menu, home-cooking,
HOTEL: ☆☆ 23 rooms.
FACILITIES: shower, bath, private bathroom, television, telephone
OTHER POINTS: credit cards accepted.
Lude châteaux, lac de Rille; zoo; La Flèche.

CHATEAUBERNARD
Charente, 16100

PENSION DU CAMP
(Mr Jean-Louis Bruno) Route de Barbezieux
TEL: 05.45.82.09.47
DIRECTIONS: between Barbezieux and Bordeaux.
LANGUAGES: English.
MENU: 60 to 85 Frs.
ROOMS: 100 to 200 Frs.
RESTAURANT: Snacks from 6.00, lunch 12.00, dinner up to 24.00
CLOSED: Fri after 15.00, Sat and Sun.
SPECIALITIES: home-cooking.
HOTEL: 3 rooms.
FACILITIES: shower, private bathroom, television, telephone
OTHER POINTS: credit cards accepted.
Cognac; Saint-Gobin.

CHATEAUNEUF SUR LOIRE
Loiret, 45110

HOTEL DE LA PLACE
(Jacky Maillard) 2, route de Châteauneuf – Germigny des Prés
TEL: 02.38.58.20.14 **FAX:** 02.38.58.21.33
DIRECTIONS: RN60, between Orléans and Montargis.
MENU: 59 to 140 Frs.
ROOMS: 150 to 220 Frs.
RESTAURANT: Snacks from 00.30, lunch 12.00-14.00, dinner 20.00-21.30
CLOSED: Fri (out of season).
SPECIALITIES: fricassee de pintade (guinea-fowl) angevine, home-cooking.
HOTEL: 11 rooms.
FACILITIES: shower, bath, private bathroom, television, telephone
OTHER POINTS: credit cards accepted.
valley of kings; Carlovingian church; Saint-Benoit monastery, château at Sully-sur-Loire; Gien; musée de la marine (maritime museum) at Châteauneuf-sur-Loire.

CHATEAUROUX
Indre, 36000

BAR DE L'AVENUE
(Mr Laurent Guillot) 1 avenue de la Manufacture
TEL: 02.54.34.09.27
DIRECTIONS: RN20.
LANGUAGES: English.
OTHER POINTS: bar.

CHATILLON SUR INDRE
Indre, 36700

AUBERGE DE LA PROMENADE
(Mr Pascal Bouquin) 88, rue Grande
TEL: 02.54.38.80.79
DIRECTIONS: RN143, between Tours and Châteauroux.
LANGUAGES: English.
MENU: 56.50 Frs.
ROOMS: 150 to 190 Frs.
RESTAURANT: Snacks from 6.15, lunch 11.00-14.00, dinner 18.00-21.00
CLOSED: Sat, Sun, last week of Oct and first week of Nov.
SPECIALITIES: home-cooking.
HOTEL: 7 rooms.
FACILITIES: shower, bath, private bathroom, telephone
OTHER POINTS: bar.
Loire châteaux; wildlife park at La Brenne; nature reserve at La Haute-Touche.

LE RELAIS DU MAIL
(Mme Huguette Soret) Boulevard du Général Leclerc
TEL: 02.54.38.71.21
DIRECTIONS: RN143.
MENU: 52 to 70 Frs.
ROOMS: 90 to 190 Frs.
RESTAURANT: Lunch 12.00, dinner 19.00-21.00
CLOSED: for 10 days in early Nov.
SPECIALITIES: home-cooking.
HOTEL: 5 rooms.
FACILITIES: shower, bath
OTHER POINTS: bar.
château at Azay-le-Ferron (20km).

CHATRE (LA)
Indre, 36400

LE RELAIS DU CHAMP DE FOIRE
(Mr Patrick Lecuyer) 2, rue Eugène Delacroix
TEL: 02.54.48.01.57
DIRECTIONS: on the Poitiers/Montluáon axis.
LANGUAGES: English, German.
MENU: 59 Frs (wine included).
RESTAURANT: Snacks from 7.00, lunch 11.30-14.00, dinner 19.00-20.30
CLOSED: Sun.
SPECIALITIES: home-cooking, "Vieille France" coq au vin, bourguignon, blanquette.
OTHER POINTS: bar.

CHAUNAY BOURG
Vienne, 86510

LE COMMERCE
(Mr Le Roux Patrick)
TEL: 05.49.59.02.71
DIRECTIONS: RN10, the Poitiers/Bordeaux road, 40km from Poitiers.
LANGUAGES: English.
MENU: 58 Frs (wine included) to 120 Frs.
ROOMS: 160 to 220 Frs.
RESTAURANT: Snacks from 6.00, lunch 12.00-14.30, dinner 19.00-22.30
SPECIALITIES: regional menu, home-cooking.
HOTEL: ☆ 8 rooms.
FACILITIES: shower, bath
OTHER POINTS: credit cards accepted.
Civray, Ruffec.

CHAUVIGNY
Vienne, 86300

RESTAURANT DU MARCHE
(Mr Joël Torsat) 8, place du Marché
TEL: 05.49.46.32.34
DIRECTIONS: RN151, the Poitiers/Châteauroux road.

MENU: 52 to 67 Frs.
RESTAURANT: Snacks from 7.30, lunch 12.00-14.00, dinner 19.30-21.00
CLOSED: Thurs, and from 15th Sept to 15th Oct.
SPECIALITIES: home-cooking.
OTHER POINTS: credit cards accepted.
Chauvigny (medieval city); Civaux (Merovingian cemetery).

CHOUZE SUR LOIRE
Indre-et-Loire, 37140

AUBERGE DE PORT BOULET
(SARL Adeline) 50, route de Tours
TEL: 02.47.95.00.39 **FAX:** 02.47.95.04.52
DIRECTIONS: RN152 et RD 749, RN152 et RD749, Tours/Saumur and Bourgueil/Chinon.
LANGUAGES: English.
MENU: 54 Frs (wine included) to 120 Frs.
ROOMS: 128 to 195 Frs.
RESTAURANT: Snacks from 6.00, lunch 11.00-18.00, dinner 19.00-23.00
CLOSED: Sun evening.
SPECIALITIES: regional menu, traditionnal et marocan recipes.
HOTEL: ☆ 11 rooms.
FACILITIES: shower, bath, private bathroom, television, telephone
OTHER POINTS: credit cards accepted.

CIVRAY
Vienne, 86400

LE RELAIS DES USINES
(Mme Brigitte Nicoulaud) 19, rue Norbert Portejoie
TEL: 05.49.87.04.33
DIRECTIONS: the Niort/Limoges road.
MENU: 53 Frs.
RESTAURANT: Snacks from 6.45, lunch 11.30-15.00, dinner 19.00-21.30
CLOSED: Sat afternoon and Sun.
SPECIALITIES: home-cooking.
OTHER POINTS: bar.
church at Civray; Saint-Nicolas; Charroux.

CIVRAY DE TOURAINE
Indre-et-Loire, 37150

LE MARECHAL
(Mr Jean Jabveneau) 1, rue de Bléré
TEL: 02.47.23.92.16
DIRECTIONS: RN76, the Tours/Vierzon road.
MENU: 60 to 68 Frs.
RESTAURANT: Snacks from 6.00, lunch 12.00-14.00, dinner 19.00-22.00
CLOSED: Sat afternoon, Sun, public holidays and 26th Aug to 15th Sept.
SPECIALITIES: regional menu.
OTHER POINTS: credit cards accepted.
châteaux at Chenonceaux, Amboise and Loches.

CLION SUR INDRE
Indre, 36700

AUBERGE DU PIED DE BOURGES
(Mme Nicole Chamton) 31 Rue Nationale
TEL: 02.54.38.60.90
DIRECTIONS: on theTours/Châteauroux axis.
MENU: 57 Frs (wine included).
ROOMS: 100 Frs (30% for extra bed).
RESTAURANT: Snacks from 6.00, lunch 11.00-13.30, dinner 19.00-21.00
SPECIALITIES: home-cooking.
HOTEL: 6 rooms.
FACILITIES: shower, private bathroom
OTHER POINTS: credit cards accepted.
châteaux.

CLUIS
Indre, 36340

CHEZ VALERIE
(Mme Valérie Mazure) 6, rue des Parc
TEL: 02.54.31.26.06
LANGUAGES: English.
MENU: 55 Frs.
SPECIALITIES: escargots.
OTHER POINTS: credit cards accepted.

CONFOLENS
Charente, 16500

RELAIS DES CIGOGNES
(Mr Saïd Yassa) Brillac
TEL: 05.45.89.45.90
DIRECTIONS: CD951, between Bellac and Angoulême.
MENU: 60 to 70 Frs.
RESTAURANT: Snacks from 6.00, lunch 11.00-14.00, dinner 18.00-22.00
CLOSED: Mon.
SPECIALITIES: home-cooking.
OTHER POINTS: credit cards accepted.
Ouradour-sur-Glane; château at Saint-Germain-de-Confolens.

CORMENON
Loir-et-Cher, 41170

AUBERGE DU PARC
(Mme Andrée Touffu) 86, rue de la Poterie
TEL: 02.54.80.92.04
DIRECTIONS: RN157, Le Mans.
MENU: 53 and 80 Frs.
RESTAURANT: Snacks from 7.00
CLOSED: Sun and last 2 weeks in Aug.
SPECIALITIES: home-cooking.

OTHER POINTS: credit cards accepted.
Mondoubleau; Loir valley; musée des poids-lourds (HGVs).

COURTENAY
Loiret, 45320

LE RELAIS DES SPORTS
(Mr Gérard Martin) 38, rue de Villeneuve
TEL: 02.38.97.32.37
DIRECTIONS: RD60, between Sens and Montargis.
LANGUAGES: English, German.
MENU: 57 Frs, dish of the day at 42 Frs.
ROOMS: 70 to 120 Frs.
RESTAURANT: Snacks from 7.30, lunch 12.00-14.00, dinner 19.00-21.00
CLOSED: Sat evening, Sun, 15th to 30th March and 15th Aug to 7th Sept.
SPECIALITIES: home-cooking.
HOTEL: 6 rooms.
FACILITIES: shower, bath, private bathroom
OTHER POINTS: credit cards accepted.

COZES
Charente-Maritime, 17120

LE RELAIS BEL AIR
(Mr Pédro Crespo) Route de Royan – Grezac
TEL: 05.46.90.84.24
DIRECTIONS: between Mirambeau and Royan.
LANGUAGES: Spanish.
MENU: 59 Frs (wine and coffee included) to 130 Frs.
RESTAURANT: Snacks from 7.00, lunch 11.00-14.30, dinner 19.00-21.00
CLOSED: Mon afternoon and Sun evening.
SPECIALITIES: home-cooking,
OTHER POINTS: credit cards accepted.

CRECHE (LA)
Deux-Sèvres, 79260

LES PYRAMIDES
(Mr Robert Reveillaud) Centre Routier
TEL: 05.49.25.03.37 FAX: 05.49.25.02.86
DIRECTIONS: A10, A10, Autoroute A10, junction 32.
LANGUAGES: English.
MENU: 60 Frs (wine included).
RESTAURANT: Snacks from 6.30, lunch 11.45-14.30, dinner 19.00-22.30
CLOSED: Sat and Sun.
SPECIALITIES: home-cooking.
OTHER POINTS: credit cards accepted.

CREVANT-MONTIERCHAUME
Indre, 36130

AU CHEZ SOI
(Mme Yvonne Belouin-Ferré) Route Nationale 151
TEL: 02.54.26.00.19
DIRECTIONS: RN151, between Châteauroux and Bourges.
MENU: 45 Frs (drink and coffee included).
RESTAURANT: Snacks from 11.00, lunch 11.00-15.00
CLOSED: Sat, Sun, and in Aug.
SPECIALITIES: home-cooking.
OTHER POINTS: children's menu.

DAMPIERRE EN CROT
Cher, 18260

LES TILLEULS
(Mr André Paris) Route Départementale 923
TEL: 02.48.73.81.04
DIRECTIONS: RD923, between Aubigny and Cosnes.
MENU: 58 to 130 Frs (wine included).
ROOMS: 80 to 120 Frs.
RESTAURANT: Snacks from 5.30, lunch 12.00-14.30, dinner 18.30-21.00
SPECIALITIES: home-cooking.
HOTEL: 5 rooms
OTHER POINTS: bar.
Sancerre; musée de la sorcellerie (sorcery); châteaux.

DEOLS
Indre, 36130

AIRE L'ESCALE VILLAGE
(Mr Jean-Claude Sergent) Route Nationale 20 – Déols-Châteauroux-Nord sortie n¯12
TEL: 02.54.22.03.77 FAX: 02.54.22.56.70
DIRECTIONS: RN20, the Paris/Limoges road.
LANGUAGES: English, Spanish.
MENU: 52.50 to 130 Frs.
RESTAURANT: Open 24h.
SPECIALITIES: fruits de mer, regional menu.
OTHER POINTS: credit cards accepted.
château at Valenáay; Georges Sand's château; nature reserve at La Haute-Touche; region of 1,000 étangs (ponds).

LE RELAIS DE L'INTER
(Mr Boubekeur Abderrahmane) Route d'Issoudun
TEL: 02.54.27.20.07
LANGUAGES: English, Spanish, Arabic.
MENU: 49.50 to 98.50 Frs.
RESTAURANT: Snacks from 5.00, lunch 10.30-15.30, dinner 18.30-23.30
SPECIALITIES: couscous, grillades (grills), regional menu, home-cooking.
OTHER POINTS: credit cards accepted.

DIGNY
Eure-et-Loir, 28250

AUBERGE DE LA VALLEE
(Mr Dominique Royant) 35, rue du Maréchal Leclerc
TEL: 02.37.29.01.04
DIRECTIONS: RD928, Le Mans/Rouen.
MENU: 58 Frs (drink and coffee included).
RESTAURANT: Snacks from 6.30
SPECIALITIES: couscous, paella, choucroute, home-cooking.
OTHER POINTS: credit cards accepted.
Chartres cathedral; La Ferté-Vidaure (château and museum); museum of miniatures.

DREUX
Eure-et-Loir, 28100

LE MARCEAU
(Mr Jean-Pierre Parent) 40-42, avenue du Général Marceau
TEL: 02.37.46.05.57
DIRECTIONS: RN12 and 154, between Chartres and Le Mans.
MENU: 54 Frs.
RESTAURANT: Snacks from 6.30, lunch 12.00-14.00
CLOSED: Sun, and in Aug.
SPECIALITIES: home-cooking.
OTHER POINTS: credit cards accepted.
royal chapel, ancient belfry.

EGLISES D'ARGENTEUIL (LES)
Charente-Maritime, 17400

CHEZ VEVETTE
(Mr Joël Pillot)
TEL: 05.46.59.94.21
DIRECTIONS: CD950, the Poitiers/Saintes road.
MENU: 65 Frs.
ROOMS: 100 to 180 Frs.
RESTAURANT: Snacks from 7.00, lunch 12.00-14.00, dinner 19.30-21.00
CLOSED: Fri and Sat evenings, Sun and from 15th Aug to 1st Sept.
SPECIALITIES: home-cooking.
HOTEL: 6 rooms
OTHER POINTS: bar.

ENNORDRES
Cher, 18380

CHEZ BOUDUCHE
(Mr Jean-Louis Breton) Route Départementale 940
TEL: 02.48.58.40.18
DIRECTIONS: D940, Bourges/Montargis/Paris.
MENU: 60 Frs.
RESTAURANT: Snacks from 5.00, dinner 19.00-22.00
CLOSED: Sat and Sun.
SPECIALITIES: home-cooking.
OTHER POINTS: credit cards accepted.
Château; cathedral.

EPANNES
Deux-Sèvres, 79270

LE RELAIS SUISSE OCEAN
(M Jacky)
TEL: 05.49.04.80.01
DIRECTIONS: RN11, the Niort/La Rochelle road, exit 23.
MENU: 58 to 140 Frs.
ROOMS: 100 to 150 Frs.
RESTAURANT: Snacks from 6.30, lunch 11.30-14.30, dinner 19.00-21.00
CLOSED: Sat evening, Sun, and first 2 weeks in Sept.
SPECIALITIES: fruits de mer, poissons, regional menu, home-cooking.
HOTEL: 9 rooms.
FACILITIES: shower, bath, private bathroom, television
OTHER POINTS: bar.
Poitou marshlands; forêt de Chizé; La Rochelle.

EPERNON
Eure-et-Loir, 28230

LA GUINGUETTE
(Mme Gislaine Das Dores) 47, rue du Grand Pont
TEL: 02.37.83.51.25
DIRECTIONS: RD306, between Chartres and Rambouillet.
MENU: 55 to 90 Frs.
RESTAURANT: Snacks from 8.00, lunch 11.30-14.00, dinner 19.00-21.00
SPECIALITIES: home-cooking.
OTHER POINTS: credit cards accepted.
château at Maintenon; wine-presses at Epernon.

ESVRES SUR INDRE
Indre-et-Loire, 37520

LE SAINT MALO
(Mme Marie-Claire Bouvard) La Pommeraie – Route Nationale 143
TEL: 02.47.65.77.58
DIRECTIONS: RN143.
LANGUAGES: English.
MENU: 52 Frs.
RESTAURANT: Snacks from 6.00
CLOSED: Sat and Sun.
SPECIALITIES: home-cooking.
OTHER POINTS: bar.
Loire châteaux.

FLEURE
Vienne, 86340

AUX AMIS DE LA ROUTE
(Mr Michel Saulai) 8, route de Poitiers – Route Nationale 147
TEL: 05.49.42.60.25
DIRECTIONS: RN147, the Poitiers/Limoges road.
LANGUAGES: English.
MENU: 50 Frs (wine included).
RESTAURANT: Snacks from 6.00, lunch 11.30-15.00, dinner 19.00-22.00
CLOSED: Sun afternoon.
SPECIALITIES: home-cooking.
OTHER POINTS: credit cards accepted.
Futuroscope; le Puy du Fou.

FONDETTES
Indre-et-Loire, 37230

LE BEAU MANOIR
(Mme Edith Bourreau) 6, quai de la Guignière
TEL: 02.47.42.01.02
DIRECTIONS: RN152, the Angers/Nantes road.
MENU: 52 Frs.
RESTAURANT: Snacks from 7.00, lunch 12.00-14.00, dinner 19.00-21.30
CLOSED: Sat afternoon, Sun and public holidays.
SPECIALITIES: home-cooking.
OTHER POINTS: credit cards accepted.
Loire châteaux (radius 10-30km).

FONTAINE EN SOLOGNE
Loir-et-Cher, 41250

LE RELAIS DE SOLOGNE
(Mr Guy Normand) Route Départementale 765 – La Chaucherie
TEL: 02.54.79.98.85
DIRECTIONS: RD765, the Blois/Romorantin/Vierzon road.
MENU: 58 Frs (wine included) to 75 Frs.
RESTAURANT: Snacks from 6.30, lunch 11.30-14.30, dinner 19.00-22.00
CLOSED: Sat afternoon, Sun and last 2 weeks in Aug.
SPECIALITIES: home-cooking.
OTHER POINTS: credit cards accepted.
châteaux at Cheverny and Chambord.

FONTAINE LE COMTE
Vienne, 86240

AUBERGE DE LA GARENNE
(Mr Jacky Boireau) 1, allée des Cerfs
TEL: 05.49.57.01.22
DIRECTIONS: the Niort/Bordeaux road, the Poitiers Sud exit.
MENU: 56 Frs (drink included).
RESTAURANT: Snacks from 6.00, lunch 11.30-14.30, dinner 19.00-22.00
CLOSED: Sun evening.
SPECIALITIES: regional menu, home-cooking.
OTHER POINTS: credit cards accepted.
Futuroscope(10km).

FONTENAY SUR LOING
Loiret, 45210

LES 100 BORNES
(Mr Guy Martin) Route Nationale 7
TEL: 02.38.95.82.06
DIRECTIONS: RN7, between Montargis and Dordives.
MENU: 58 Frs (weekdays) to 110 Frs (weekend).
RESTAURANT: Open 24h.
CLOSED: 1 or 2 weeks in Aug.
SPECIALITIES: home-cooking.
OTHER POINTS: credit cards accepted.

FOSSE
Loir-et-Cher, 41330

BAR DE L'ESPERANCE
(Mme Brigitte Chauvin-Sala) 7, rue de Saint Sulpice
TEL: 02.54.20.01.77
DIRECTIONS: RN153, between Vendôme and Le Mans.
MENU: 58 Frs.
RESTAURANT: Snacks from 7.30, lunch 11.30-14.30
CLOSED: Sat and Sun.
SPECIALITIES: home-cooking.
OTHER POINTS: credit cards accepted.

FRETEVAL
Loir-et-Cher, 41160

SARL LE PLESSIS
(Mlle Isabelle Thebault) Route Nationale 10
TEL: 02.54.82.64.28
DIRECTIONS: RN1 0, between Vendôme (20km) and Châteaudun (24km).
LANGUAGES: English, German, Spanish.
MENU: 67 to 145 Frs.
RESTAURANT: Open 24h.
CLOSED: from Sat 10am to Sun 10am, and 1 week at Christmas.
SPECIALITIES: home-cooking.
OTHER POINTS: credit cards accepted.
Vendôme; Loir valley.

GIEN
Loiret, 45500

CAFE DU NORD
(Mme Suzanne Botineau) 51 Place de la Victoire
TEL: 02.38.67.32.98
DIRECTIONS: RN140 and CD952.
LANGUAGES: English.

OTHER POINTS: bar.

LE RELAIS NORMAND
(Mr Pierre Montceau) 64, place de la Victoire
TEL: 02.38.67.28.56
DIRECTIONS: opposite the faïencerie (pottery).
LANGUAGES: English.
MENU: 56 Frs.
ROOMS: 130 to 180 Frs.
RESTAURANT: Snacks from 5.45, lunch 11.00-14.30, dinner 19.00-21.00
CLOSED: Sun.
SPECIALITIES: home-cooking.
HOTEL: 12 rooms.
FACILITIES: shower, private bathroom
OTHER POINTS: credit cards accepted.
Gien: pottery, musée de la chasse (hunting).

GIEVRES
Loir-et-Cher, 41130

SARL RELAIS DE NORAY
(Mme Christiane Laithier) Route de Vierzon
TEL: 02.54.98.64.00
DIRECTIONS: RN76, Vierzon.
MENU: 58 Frs.
RESTAURANT: Snacks from 7.00, lunch 11.00-14.30, dinner 19.00-22.30
CLOSED: Sat evening, Sun, and in Aug.
SPECIALITIES: home-cooking.
OTHER POINTS: bar.
château at Selles-sur-Cher.

GRACAY
Cher, 18310

LA PLAISANCE
(Mr Richard Paget) Autoroute A.20 – sortie n¯9
TEL: 02.54.49.77.15 FAX: 02.54.49.82.42
DIRECTIONS: A20/RN20, Paris/Toulouse.
LANGUAGES: English.
MENU: 58 Frs (wine included) and from 98 to 133 Frs (tourist menu).
RESTAURANT: Snacks from 5.30
SPECIALITIES: regional menu, home-cooking.
OTHER POINTS: credit cards accepted.

HUISSEAU EN BEAUCE
Loir-et-Cher, 41310

LES PLATANES
(Mr Hubert Breton) Route Nationale 10
TEL: 02.54.82.81.46
DIRECTIONS: RN10, between Vendôme and Châteaurenault.
MENU: 62 Frs.
RESTAURANT: Snacks from 6.30, lunch 12.00-15.00, dinner 19.00-22.30
CLOSED: Sat, Sun and public holidays.
SPECIALITIES: home-cooking.
OTHER POINTS: credit cards accepted.
Loir valley.

INTVILLE LA GUETARD
Loiret, 45300

LE RELAIS D'INTVILLE
(Mr Philippe Robillard)
TEL: 02.38.39.71.70
DIRECTIONS: between Etampes and Pithiviers.
LANGUAGES: English.
MENU: 58 Frs (wine included).
RESTAURANT: Snacks from 5.30
CLOSED: Sun.
SPECIALITIES: home-cooking.
OTHER POINTS: credit cards accepted.
Pithiviers.

ISDES
Loiret, 45620

HOTEL DU DAUPHIN
(Mr Lucien Laurent) 11 grande Rue
TEL: 02.38.29.10.29
DIRECTIONS: RD83, between La Motte-Beuvron and Sully.
MENU: 55 to 120 Frs.
ROOMS: 60 to 120 Frs.
RESTAURANT: Snacks from 6.30, lunch 11.30-14.00, dinner 19.00-20.30
CLOSED: Mon afternoon.
SPECIALITIES: regional menu, home-cooking.
HOTEL: 11 rooms.
FACILITIES: shower
OTHER POINTS: bar.
château at Sully; musée de la chasse (hunting) at Gien; canal bridge at Briare; château at Chambord; Jeanne d'Arc's house at Orléans.

ISSOUDUN
Indre, 36100

LE RELAIS ISSOLDUNOIS
(Mr Hervé De Sa) 8, route de Bourges
TEL: 02.54.03.04.05 FAX: 02.54.03.01.00
DIRECTIONS: RN151, between Châteauroux (27km) and Bourges (27km).
LANGUAGES: English, German.
MENU: 53 Frs.
ROOMS: 165 to 235 Frs.
RESTAURANT: Snacks from 6.00, lunch 11.45-14.30, dinner 19.00-22.30
CLOSED: Sun evening.
SPECIALITIES: regional menu, home-cooking.
HOTEL: 16 rooms.
FACILITIES: shower, bath, private bathroom,

television, telephone
OTHER POINTS: credit cards accepted.
Issoudun; Bourges.

JARNAC
Charente, 16200

LES ROUTIERS
(Mme Maryse Bouffinie) 77, rue Pasteur
TEL: 05.45.81.02.40
DIRECTIONS: RN141, between Angoulême and Royan.
MENU: 55 Frs.
RESTAURANT: Snacks from 7.00, lunch 12.00-14.00, dinner 19.00-22.00
CLOSED: Sun (except bookings).
SPECIALITIES: home-cooking.
OTHER POINTS: bar.
Cognac distillery buildings (Courvoisier).

LA CHAPELLE D ANGILLON
Cher, 18380

LE RELAIS DES ROUTIERS
(Mme Georgette Champion) Route Départementale 30
TEL: 02.48.58.06.36
DIRECTIONS: RN30
OTHER POINTS: bar.

LADON
Loiret, 45270

LE RELAIS DE LADON
(Mr Pierre Guillaumin) 400, avenue du 24 Novembre
TEL: 02.38.95.51.32
DIRECTIONS: RN60, between Montargis and Orléans.
MENU: 50 to 70 Frs.
ROOMS: 92 to 147 Frs.
RESTAURANT: Snacks from 5.30
CLOSED: Sun, 23rd June to 14th July, 2 weeks after Christmas.
SPECIALITIES: home-cooking.
HOTEL: 7 rooms.
FACILITIES: shower
OTHER POINTS: bar.
windmill.

LAGEON
Deux-Sèvres, 79200

LE SAMPIERO
(Mr Christian Garandeau) Route Départementale 938
TEL: 05.49.69.82.11
DIRECTIONS: RD938, between Partlienay and Thouars.
LANGUAGES: English, Italian.
MENU: 55 Frs (wine included) to 175 Frs.
RESTAURANT: Snacks from 6.15, lunch 11.30-15.00, dinner 19.30-23.00
CLOSED: Sun evening.
SPECIALITIES: regional menu, home-cooking.
OTHER POINTS: bar.
Partenay; Thouars; Poitou marshlands.

LENCLOITRE
Vienne, 86140

AU 14 ANNE ANDRE
(Mr André Pernelle) 2, place du Champ de Foire
TEL: 05.49.90.71.29
DIRECTIONS: between Châtellerault and Nantes.
MENU: 50 to 60 Frs.
RESTAURANT: Snacks from 7.00, lunch 11.00-15.00, dinner 19.00-23.00
CLOSED: Sun.
SPECIALITIES: couscous (to order), home-cooking.
OTHER POINTS: credit cards accepted.
Futuroscope; Poitou marshlands; Loire châteaux: Azay-le-Rideau, Villanciry, Chinon, Saumur.

LORRIS
Loiret, 45260

AUBERGE DE LA CROIX ROUGE
(Mme Lisiane Berlin) 28, rue Guillaume
TEL: 02.38.92.47.03
DIRECTIONS: RD961.
RESTAURANT: Snacks from 8.00
CLOSED: Sun afternoon.
SPECIALITIES: home-cooking.
OTHER POINTS: bar.

LOULAY
Charente-Maritime, 17330

CHEZ JO
(Mr Georges Mahdid) 10 place du Général de Gaulle
TEL: 05.46.33.80.59
DIRECTIONS: RN150, between Saint-Jean d'Angély and Niort.
MENU: 55 to 65 Frs.
ROOMS: 100 to 145 Frs.
RESTAURANT: Snacks from 8.00, lunch 12.00-14.00, dinner 19.30-21.00
CLOSED: Sun.
SPECIALITIES: home-cooking.
HOTEL: 5 rooms.
FACILITIES: shower, private bathroom
OTHER POINTS: bar.
La Rochelle (40km); Poitou marshlands; forêt de Chizé; Neolithic museum; châteaux.

LUCAY LE MALE
Indre, 36360

LE DAUPHIN
(Mr Patrick Bruneau) 7, place de Verdun
TEL: 02.54.40.41.17
DIRECTIONS: between Valenáay and Loches.
MENU: 55 to 82 Frs.
RESTAURANT: Snacks from 8.00, lunch 11.30-15.00, dinner 19.30-23.00
CLOSED: Wed, and the last 2 weeks in Aug.
SPECIALITIES: home-cooking.
OTHER POINTS: credit cards accepted.
Valenáay.

LUNERY
Cher, 18400

BAR DU CENTRE
(Mr Michel Porcheron) 1, place Jacques Georges
TEL: 02.48.68.98.71
DIRECTIONS: RD27, Saint-Florent, between Bourges and Châteauneuf-sur-Cher.
MENU: 52 Frs (with wine and coffee included) to 100 Frs.
RESTAURANT: Snacks from 7.00, lunch 12.00-13.30, dinner 19.00-21.00
CLOSED: Tues, 2 weeks in Feb and 2 weeks in Sept.
SPECIALITIES: paté aux pommes de terre, magret de canard, home-cooking.
OTHER POINTS: credit cards accepted.
Bourges (20km).

LUPLANTE
Eure-et-Loir, 28360

LE LAPIN BARBU
(Mr Alain Penilleau) 9, rue de l'Europe
TEL: 02.37.26.60.72
DIRECTIONS: RD 28, RD28, between Thivars and Bonneval.
MENU: 57 Frs (wine and coffee included).
RESTAURANT: Snacks from 8.00, lunch 12.00-14.30, dinner 19.30-21.00
CLOSED: Thurs afternoon.
SPECIALITIES: home-cooking.
OTHER POINTS: bar.

LUSSAC LES CHATEAUX
Vienne, 86320

LE CHENE VERT
(Mme Nadia Homaërt) 14, route de Limoges
TEL: 05.49.48.40.30 FAX: 05.49.84.94.62
DIRECTIONS: RN147, the Poitiers/Limoges road.
MENU: 62 Frs.
RESTAURANT: Snacks from 6.00, lunch 12.00-15.00, dinner 19.00-22.00
CLOSED: Sun.
SPECIALITIES: magrets, confits, salade landaise, home-cooking.
OTHER POINTS: credit cards accepted.
Vienne valley; La Rigaudière dungeon at Bouresse; caves and prehistory museums.

LUTZ EN DUNOIS
Eure-et-Loir, 28200

LA RENCONTRE
(Mr Francis Berrier)
TEL: 02.37.45.18.08
DIRECTIONS: D955, between Châteaudun and Orléans.
MENU: 58 Frs.
ROOMS: 60 Frs.
RESTAURANT: Snacks from 5.30, lunch 11.00-15.00, dinner 19.00-21.00
CLOSED: Sat evening, Sun, public holidays and mid-Feb to 1st March.
SPECIALITIES: home-cooking.
HOTEL: 5 rooms.
FACILITIES: shower, bath, private bathroom
OTHER POINTS: credit cards accepted.
Châteaudun: château, caves, windmills; Loir valley.

MARANS
Charente-Maritime, 17230

LE POINT DU JOUR
(Sylviane et Joël Morice) 2, rue des Moulins
TEL: 05.46.01.14.54
DIRECTIONS: RN137, Nantes.
MENU: 49 to 59 Frs.
RESTAURANT: Snacks from 5.30, lunch 12.00-15.00, dinner 19.00-21.00
CLOSED: Sat and Sun.
SPECIALITIES: mouclade (mussels in curry sauce), home-cooking.
OTHER POINTS: credit cards accepted.
Poitou marshlands; La Rochelle.

MARENNES
Charente-Maritime, 17320

BAR DE LA CASERNE
(Mme Michelle Bachelard) 54, avenue du Maréchal Leclerc
TEL: 05.46.85.06.74
DIRECTIONS: RD123, between Saintes and l'Ile d'Oléron.
MENU: 56 Frs.
RESTAURANT: Snacks from 8.00, lunch 11.30-14.30, dinner 19.00-21.00
CLOSED: Sun (from 15 Jan to 1st May).

SPECIALITIES: moules marinières, lapin au cidre, oysters, home-cooking.
OTHER POINTS: bar.

MAROLLES
Eure-et-Loir, 28260

LE RELAIS DE MAROLLES
(Mr Norbert Lopez – SARL SOMALO) 44, rue Georges Bréant
TEL: 02.37.43.20.50
DIRECTIONS: RN12, on the Dreux/Houdan axis.
LANGUAGES: English, Spanish.
MENU: 57 Frs (drink included).
RESTAURANT: Snacks from 5.00, lunch 11.00-16.00, dinner 18.00-22.30
CLOSED: Sat and Sun.
SPECIALITIES: home-cooking, escalope normande, omelette aux pleurottes, grillades (grills).
OTHER POINTS: credit cards accepted.

MERY SUR CHER
Cher, 18100

LE RELAIS BERRY SOLOGNE
(Mr Claude Carré) Route Nationale 76
TEL: 02.48.75.20.34
DIRECTIONS: RN76, between Vierzon and Tours.
MENU: 65 Frs.
ROOMS: 85 to 145 Frs.
RESTAURANT: Snacks from 5.00, dinner 19.00-22.00
CLOSED: Sat and Sun.
SPECIALITIES: Berry regional dishes, home-cooking.
HOTEL: 11 rooms.
FACILITIES: shower
OTHER POINTS: credit cards accepted.
Loire châteaux.

MEZIERES EN BRENNE
Indre, 36290

LES ROUTIERS – Chez Sylviane
(Mr Henri Peuvion) 11, rue de l'Ouest
TEL: 02.54.38.11.62
DIRECTIONS: RD925, at the entrance to Mézières coming from Leblanc.
LANGUAGES: English.
MENU: 55 to 80 Frs.
ROOMS: 90 to 220 Frs.
RESTAURANT: Snacks from 7.30, lunch 11.30-14.30, dinner 19.00-21.00
SPECIALITIES: home-cooking.
HOTEL: 6 rooms.
FACILITIES: shower, bath
OTHER POINTS: bar.
La Brenne nature reserve; les 1,000 étangs (ponds).

MIGNERES
Loiret, 45490

LE RELAIS DE MIGNERES
(Mr Romain Cousin) 3, rue de la Gare
TEL: 02.38.87.85.57
DIRECTIONS: RD94, between Auxy and Montargis.
MENU: 59 Frs (wine and coffee included) to 100 Frs.
ROOMS: 80 to 120 Frs.
RESTAURANT: Snacks from 6.30, lunch 11.00-14.00, dinner 19.00-20.00
CLOSED: Sun and mid-Feb.
SPECIALITIES: regional menu, home-cooking.
HOTEL: 7 rooms.
FACILITIES: shower, private bathroom, telephone
OTHER POINTS: bar.

MONNAIE
Indre-et-Loire, 37380

LA BONNE ETAPE
(Mr Didier Gauthier) 67, rue Nationale
TEL: 02.47.56.10.64
DIRECTIONS: RN10, Tour/Château Renault.
MENU: 54 to 95 Frs.
ROOMS: 150 to 175 Frs.
RESTAURANT: Snacks from 6.45, lunch 11.30-14.30, dinner 19.00-21.00
SPECIALITIES: home-cooking,
HOTEL: 6 rooms
OTHER POINTS: credit cards accepted.

MONTBAZON
Indre-et-Loire, 37250

LA GRANGE BARBIER
(Mr William Laborde) Route Nationale 10
TEL: 02.47.26.01.69
DIRECTIONS: RN10, Montbazon southern exit, towards Poitiers.
MENU: 54 to 110 Frs.
ROOMS: 100 to 150 Frs.
RESTAURANT: Snacks from 7.15, lunch 12.00-14.00, dinner 19.00-21.30
CLOSED: Sun evening, and the last 2 weeks in Aug.
SPECIALITIES: home-cooking.
HOTEL: 5 rooms.
FACILITIES: shower
OTHER POINTS: credit cards accepted.
Loire châteaux.

MONTILS (LES)
Loir-et-Cher, 41120

LES DEUX ROUES
(Mr Jean-Pierre Levaux) 28, rue de Bel Air
TEL: 02.54.44.02.40
DIRECTIONS: RN764, between Blois and Montrichard.

RESTAURANT: Snacks from 7.00, lunch 11.30-14.00, dinner 19.30-20.30
CLOSED: Sun.
SPECIALITIES: home-cooking.
OTHER POINTS: bar.
tower and ancient porchway at Les Montils.

MONTLOUIS SUR LOIRE
Indre-et-Loire, 37270

LE RELAIS 140
(Mr Michel Mercier) La Gravelle
TEL: 02.47.50.78.08
DIRECTIONS: RD140, the Tours/Bléré axis.
LANGUAGES: English, Italian.
MENU: 55 Frs (drink included).
RESTAURANT: Snacks from 6.30, lunch 11.00-15.00, dinner 18.30-22.00
CLOSED: Sat afternoon and Sun.
SPECIALITIES: home-cooking.
OTHER POINTS: credit cards accepted.

MORNAY SUR ALLIER
Cher, 18600

LE RELAIS DE LA ROUTE
(Mlle Jacqueline Chevrot) Route Nationale 76
TEL: 02.48.74.53.54
DIRECTIONS: RN76.
LANGUAGES: English, German.
MENU: 52 to 90 Frs.
ROOMS: 60 to 90 Frs.
RESTAURANT: Open 24h.
CLOSED: from Sat 15.00 to Mon 1.00.
SPECIALITIES: home-cooking.
HOTEL: 5 rooms.
FACILITIES: bath, private bathroom
OTHER POINTS: credit cards accepted.
Apremont (15km); parc de Saint-Augustin (7km).

MOULISMES
Vienne, 86500

LA TABLE OUVERTE
(SARL Gransagne-Baudet) Route Nationale 147
TEL: 05.49.91.90.68
DIRECTIONS: RN147, between Poitiers (50km) and Limoges (70km).
MENU: 54 to 120 Frs.
ROOMS: 125 to 205 Frs.
RESTAURANT: Snacks from 6.00, lunch 12.00-14.30, dinner 19.30-21.30
CLOSED: Sat and Sun afternoon (out of season).
SPECIALITIES: home-cooking.
HOTEL: ☆ 7 rooms.
FACILITIES: shower, bath, private bathroom, television, telephone
OTHER POINTS: credit cards accepted.
Gartempe and Vienne valleys; Futuroscope; Oradour-sur-Clane; nuclear power station at Civaux.

NAINTRE
Vienne, 86530

LA HALTE
(Henni Houas) Nationale 10
TEL: 05.49.90.09.69
DIRECTIONS: RN10, Châtellerault southern exit, on Aquitaine autoroute.
LANGUAGES: English, German, Spanish, Arabic.
OTHER POINTS: bar.

NEUVY
Loir-et-Cher, 41250

LA CHEMINEE
(Mr Philippe Masclet) Le Bourg
TEL: 02.54.46.42.70
DIRECTIONS: RD923, the Paris/Angoulême road.
LANGUAGES: English.
MENU: 65 Frs (with wine and coffee included) to 140 Frs.
ROOMS: 180 to 270 Frs.
RESTAURANT: Snacks from 7.00, lunch 12.00-14.00, dinner 19.00-21.00
CLOSED: Wed, and 2 weeks in Sept.
SPECIALITIES: escargots, salade de gésiers (chicken gizzards), feuilleté de chêvre, rognons de veau, filet de canard, dame de saumon, coquille Saint-Jacques, cuisses de grenouilles, regional menu, home-cooking.
HOTEL: 9 rooms.
FACILITIES: shower, private bathroom
OTHER POINTS: credit cards accepted.
Cliambord (10km); Cheverny (15km); Blois (20km); Villesavin (10km).

NEUVY BOUIN
Deux-Sèvres, 79300

BAR DES SPORTS
(Mr Bernard Denechère) 20, rue du Commerce
TEL: 05.49.63.76.22
DIRECTIONS: RD948, between Bressuire and Niort.
MENU: 50 Frs (wine included)
RESTAURANT: Snacks from 7.30, lunch 12.00-14.00, dinner 19.00-21.00
CLOSED: Mon afternoon one week in Aug.
SPECIALITIES: home-cooking.
OTHER POINTS: bar.
Niort; Bressuire.

NEUVY SAINT SEPULCRE
Indre, 36230

LA CHARRETTE
(Mr Nicolas Pavlicevic) 21, place du Champ de Foire
TEL: 02.54.30.84.77
DIRECTIONS: RD927, between La Châtre and Montluáon.
LANGUAGES: Italian, Polish, Russian.
MENU: 64.50 and 80 Frs.
ROOMS: 140 to 190 Frs.
RESTAURANT: Lunch 12.30-14.00, dinner 19.00-22.00
SPECIALITIES: coq au vin, boeuf bourguignon, blanquette de veau (to order), home-cooking.
HOTEL: 7 rooms.
FACILITIES: shower
OTHER POINTS: bar.
Georges Sand's château; château de Nohan-Vic, château de Sarsay; basilica.

NIORT
Deux-Sèvres, 79000

AU BON ACCUEIL
(Mme Thérèse Denibaud) 424, avenue St Jean d'Angély
TEL: 05.49.79.27.60
DIRECTIONS: RN150, the Niort/Bordeaux road.
MENU: 58.50 to 75 Frs.
RESTAURANT: Snacks from 6.00, lunch 12.00-14.00, dinner 19.30-22.30
CLOSED: Sat afternoon, Sun, 3 weeks in Aug and 2 weeks at Christmas.
SPECIALITIES: home-cooking.
OTHER POINTS: credit cards accepted.
Poitou marshlands (15km); zoo; forêt de Chizé (20km).

NOGENT LE PHAYE
Eure-et-Loir, 28630

LE RELAIS DU MOULIN ROUGE
(Mme Marie-Pierre Drezet) Route Nationale 10
TEL: 02.37.31.62.68
DIRECTIONS: RN10, Chartres exit, towards Paris.
LANGUAGES: English.
MENU: 61 Frs (wine and coffee included).
RESTAURANT: Snacks from 4.00, lunch 11.00, dinner up to 23.00
CLOSED: Sat.
SPECIALITIES: home-cooking.
OTHER POINTS: credit cards accepted.

NOHANT EN GOUT
Cher, 18390

RELAIS DU BERRY
(Sarl Ligot) Route Nationale 151
TEL: 02.48.30.42.90
DIRECTIONS: RN151, the La Charité-sur-Loire/Auxerre road.
LANGUAGES: English, German, Spanish.
MENU: 50 to 110 Frs.
RESTAURANT: Lunch 11.00-15.30, dinner 19.00-23.00
CLOSED: Mon from 15.00, and 2 weeks in Feb.
SPECIALITIES: Berry regional dishes, feuilleté, de ris de veau, regional menu, home-cooking.
OTHER POINTS: credit cards accepted.
Bourges and environs.

NOHANT VIC
Indre, 36400

LA BERRIAUDE
(Mme Christine Bahi) Le Bourg
TEL: 02.54.31.02.64 **FAX:** 02.54.31.02.64
DIRECTIONS: RD 943, RD943, on the Châteauroux/Montluáon axis.
MENU: 55 Frs (wine included).
RESTAURANT: Snacks from 7.00, lunch 12.00-14.00, dinner 19.00-21.30
CLOSED: Sun evening, Mon and Oct.
SPECIALITIES: regional menu, home-cooking, Berrichonnes.
OTHER POINTS: credit cards accepted.

NOYANT DE TOURAINE
Indre-et-Loire, 37800

CHEZ MIMI
(Mme Annick Giret) Route de Chinon
TEL: 02.47.65.82.26
DIRECTIONS: l'île Bouchard.
LANGUAGES: English.
MENU: 54 Frs.
RESTAURANT: Snacks from 5.00
CLOSED: Sat from 14.00 and Sun.
SPECIALITIES: rillons maisons, rognons flambés au cognac, fruits de mer, gratin de fruits rouges au Sabayon, home-cooking.
OTHER POINTS: credit cards accepted.
châteaux at Chinon and Azay-le-Rideau (44km); Maillé.

PARANCAY
Charente-Maritime, 17330

LE RELAIS D'AUNIS
(Mr Jean-Paul Ferru)
TEL: 05.46.33.94.67
LANGUAGES: English.

MENU: 52.50 to 118 Frs.
RESTAURANT: Lunch 11.30-14.30, dinner 19.30-21.00
CLOSED: Sat, and the last 2 weeks in Dec.
SPECIALITIES: escargots, anguilles (eels).
OTHER POINTS: bar.

PELLEVOISIN
Indre, 36180

LE RELAIS DES ROUTIERS – Chez Babette
(Mme Elisabeth Petit) 30, rue Jean Giraudoux
TEL: 02.54.39.03.78
DIRECTIONS: RD11, between Buzanáais and Ecueillé.
MENU: 60 Frs.
RESTAURANT: Snacks from 9.00, lunch 12.00-14.00
CLOSED: 3 first weeks in Aug and 1 week for Christmas.
SPECIALITIES: salade de chêvre chaud, salade de gésiers (chicken gizzards), grillades, home-cooking.
OTHER POINTS: credit cards accepted.
châteaux at Valenáay and Argy.

PERRUSSON
Indre-et-Loire, 37600

LES ROUTIERS
(Mr Kléber Lanchais) 3, rue de l'Indre
TEL: 02.47.59.04.34
DIRECTIONS: RN143, the Tours/Châteauroux road.
MENU: 60 Frs (coffee included).
RESTAURANT: Snacks from 7.30, lunch 12.00-15.00, dinner 19.00-22.00
CLOSED: Sun evening, and 2 weeks in Aug.
SPECIALITIES: home-cooking,
HOTEL: 7 rooms.
FACILITIES: shower, bath
OTHER POINTS: credit cards accepted.
château at Loches.

PEZOU
Loir-et-Cher, 41100

RELAIS D'ARGENTEUIL
(Mr Pierre Hauville) Lieu dit "Fontaine"
TEL: 02.54.23.42.47
DIRECTIONS: RN10, the "Fontaine" crossroad.
MENU: 66 Frs.
ROOMS: 96 to 200 Frs.
RESTAURANT: Snacks from 5.00, lunch 11.30-14.00, dinner 18.30-22.00
CLOSED: Sat after 11am, Sun, public holidays, Aug, and 1 week at end of Dec.
SPECIALITIES: home-cooking.
HOTEL: 6 rooms.
FACILITIES: shower
OTHER POINTS: credit cards accepted.

POMPAIRE
Deux-Sèvres, 79200

LA CLE DES CHAMPS
(Mme Yolande Dubin) Route de Saint Maixent
TEL: 05.49.95.20.75
DIRECTIONS: in the commercial centre.
MENU: 52 to 110 Frs.
RESTAURANT: Snacks from 7.00, lunch 11.00-15.00, dinner 19.00-21.30
CLOSED: Sun (except groups).
SPECIALITIES: cuisses de grenouilles, anguille (eel) provenáale, plateau de fruits de mer, regional menu, home-cooking.
OTHER POINTS: credit cards accepted.
Parthenay (medieval city); Poitou marshlands.

PRESSAC
Vienne, 86460

LE RELAIS ROUTIER
(Mme Francine Bouyer) Place de l'Eglise
TEL: 05.49.48.56.99
DIRECTIONS: RN148, Niort/Poitiers/Limoges/Guéret.
MENU: 54 Frs (wine and coffee included).
RESTAURANT: Snacks from 5.00, lunch 10.00-16.00, dinner 19.00-24.00
CLOSED: Sat, and last 2 weeks in Aug.
SPECIALITIES: farcis poitevin, home-cooking.
OTHER POINTS: bar.
Futuroscope; driving tours of the Vienne and Vigeant rivers; Clain valley.

PRUNAY LE GILLON
Eure-et-Loir, 28360

LA GERBE D'OR
(Mr Henri Gosset) 20, rue du Pavillon – Lieu dit : Frainville
TEL: 02.37.25.72.38
DIRECTIONS: RN154, between Chartres and Orléans.
MENU: 55 Frs to 120 Frs.
ROOMS: 160 to 180 Frs.
RESTAURANT: Snacks from 7.00, lunch 11.00-15.00, dinner 18.00-22.00
CLOSED: Sat evening and Sun evening (in winter).
SPECIALITIES: home-cooking.
HOTEL: 10 rooms.
FACILITIES: shower, private bathroom, television, telephone
OTHER POINTS: credit cards accepted.
Chartres cathedral; museum.

REIGNAC
Indre-et-Loire, 37310

CAFE DE LA GARE
(Mme Claudine Rousselet) Route Nationale 143

TEL: 02.47.94.12.01
DIRECTIONS: RN143, Tours/Châteauroux road.
MENU: 48 Frs (wine included).
RESTAURANT: Snacks from 6.20, lunch 11.00-15.00, dinner 19.00-21.00
SPECIALITIES: home-cooking.
OTHER POINTS: bar.

RHODES
Indre, 36170

RELAIS ROUTIERS DE RHODES
(Mr Jean-Pierre Pérez) Mouhet
TEL: 02.54.47.65.26 FAX: 02.54.47.65.82
DIRECTIONS: RN20, between Limoges and Châteauroux.
MENU: 58 Frs.
RESTAURANT: Snacks from 6.00
CLOSED: Sat, Sun, and in Aug.
SPECIALITIES: home-cooking.
OTHER POINTS: bar.
Gallo-Roman sites; Lac d'Eguzon; Creuse valley.

ROCHELLE (LA)
Charente-Maritime, 17000

L'AQUARELLE
(Mme Muriel Parente) 26, boulevard du Maréchal Lyautey
TEL: 05.46.43.00.27
DIRECTIONS: Ile de Ré/La Pallice.
LANGUAGES: Portuguese.
MENU: 54 Frs.
ROOMS: 135 to 185 Frs.
RESTAURANT: Snacks from 7.30, dinner 20.00-21.30
CLOSED: Sat.
SPECIALITIES: home-cooking.
HOTEL: ☆ 10 rooms.
FACILITIES: shower, bath, private bathroom, television
OTHER POINTS: credit cards accepted.
La Rochelle; the Ile de Ré.

LE DELMAS BAR
(Mme Jeanine Francson) 32, boulevard Emile Delmas
TEL: 05.46.42.60.23
DIRECTIONS: between La Rochelle and Ile de Ré.
OTHER POINTS: bar.
Ile d'Oléron; Aix; Ré; Poitou marshlands.

LE GOELAND
(Mr Jacques Durandeau) 15, rue du Docteur Bigois
TEL: 05.46.42.05.29
LANGUAGES: English, Spanish.
MENU: 55 Frs.
ROOMS: 150 to 200 Frs.
RESTAURANT: Snacks from 6.30, lunch 11.30-15.00, dinner 19.00-22.30
CLOSED: Sat.
SPECIALITIES: home-cooking.
HOTEL: 6 rooms.
FACILITIES: shower, private bathroom, television, telephone
OTHER POINTS: credit cards accepted.
La Rochelle (port); Ile de Ré; maritime museum; museum of automata.

LES EMBRUNS
(René et Fabienne Poultier) 413 avenue Jean Guiton
TEL: 05.46.42.61.88
DIRECTIONS: port de la Pallice, head of the bay.
LANGUAGES: English.
MENU: 48 to 120 Frs.
RESTAURANT: Snacks from 6.00, lunch 11.30-15.00, dinner 19.00-21.00
CLOSED: Sat and Sun.
SPECIALITIES: couscous, paella, choucroute (every Fri) Portuguese and Spanish dishes, fruits de mer, regional menu, home-cooking.
OTHER POINTS: credit cards accepted.
Port de la Pallice (new fishing port).

CHEZ NANOU
(Mlle Véronique Chasseau) 413, avenue Guiton la Pallice
TEL: 05.46.42.17.89
DIRECTIONS: between La Pallice and La Rochelle.
LANGUAGES: English.
MENU: 58 Frs (wine and coffee included).
RESTAURANT: Snacks from 6.00, lunch 12.00-14.00, dinner 19.00-21.00
CLOSED: Sat, Sun afternoon (in winter) and between Christmas and New Year.
SPECIALITIES: home-cooking, fruits de mer, poisson.
OTHER POINTS: credit cards accepted.

ROCHELLE PALLICE (LA)
Charente-Maritime, 17000

CHEZ ANNIE
(Mme Annie Bernelas) Rue de l'Ile de Ré
TEL: 05.46.42.53.61
MENU: 56 Frs.
RESTAURANT: Snacks from 6.00, lunch 12.00-15.00, dinner 19.00-21.30
CLOSED: Sun, and 1st 2 weeks in Aug.
SPECIALITIES: home-cooking.
OTHER POINTS: credit cards accepted.
the Ile de Ré; La Rochelle (commercial and fishing port).

ROMORANTIN LANTHENAY
Loir-et-Cher, 41200

LES AUBIERS
(Mme Guy Boivin) 1, avenue de Blois
TEL: 02.54.76.05.59 FAX: 02.54.76.08.44
DIRECTIONS: RN722 and 765, town centre.
MENU: 54 to 180 Frs.
ROOMS: 150 to 200 Frs.
RESTAURANT: Snacks from 6.30, lunch 12.00-14.00, dinner 19.30-21.00
CLOSED: Sun evening.
SPECIALITIES: home-cooking.
HOTEL: ☆ 19 rooms.
FACILITIES: shower, bath, private bathroom, television, telephone
OTHER POINTS: bar.
châteaux at Chambord, Romorantin, Lassay and Blois.

RELAIS DE L'AVENIR
(Mme Jocelyne Breton) 44, avenue de Villefranche
TEL: 02.54.76.14.28
DIRECTIONS: between Villefranche-sur-Cher and Romorantin.
MENU: 55 Frs.
RESTAURANT: Snacks from 7.15, lunch 11.45-15.00
CLOSED: Sat, Sun, and 2 weeks in Aug.
SPECIALITIES: home-cooking.
OTHER POINTS: bar.

RORTHAIS
Deux-Sèvres, 79700

LE MILLE PATTES
(Mme Isabelle Guette) Route nationale 149
TEL: 05.49.81.44.42
DIRECTIONS: RN149, the Poitiers/Nantes road.
LANGUAGES: English, Spanish.
MENU: 45 Frs (wine included).
RESTAURANT: Snacks from 5.00, lunch 11.00-14.00, dinner 18.00-20.00
CLOSED: Sun (out of season)
SPECIALITIES: home-cooking.
OTHER POINTS: credit cards accepted.

ROUILLAC
Charente, 16170

LA BOULE D'OR
(Mme Elisabeth Lhermite) 56, rue du Général de Gaulle
TEL: 05.45.96.50.45
DIRECTIONS: RN939, between La Rochelle and Angoulême.
LANGUAGES: English, German.
MENU: 53 Frs (wine and coffee included).
ROOMS: 150 to 200 Frs.
RESTAURANT: Snacks from 7.00, lunch 11.30-14.00, dinner 19.00-21.30
CLOSED: Sun, incl 2 weeks in Aug.
SPECIALITIES: regional menu, home-cooking.
HOTEL: 9 rooms.
FACILITIES: shower, private bathroom
OTHER POINTS: credit cards accepted.
château at Lignière (5km); Cognac (25km); Angoulême (25km).

ROUILLE
Vienne, 86480

CHEZ MARYSE
(Mme Maryse Tellier) Le Grand Breuil
TEL: 05.49.43.93.75
DIRECTIONS: RD950, between Poitiers and Royan.
MENU: 60 Frs.
ROOMS: 120 Frs.
RESTAURANT: Snacks from 7.00, lunch 12.00-14.00, dinner 19.00-21.00
CLOSED: Sun, and the last 2 weeks in May.
SPECIALITIES: home-cooking.
HOTEL: 6 rooms.
FACILITIES: shower, bath, private bathroom
OTHER POINTS: credit cards accepted.
Gallo-Roman ruins; Futuroscope at Poitiers.

ROULLET SAINT ESTEPHE
Charente, 16440

LES VALLEES
(Mr Jean-Jacques Faudry) Les Vallées
TEL: 05.45.66.30.31
DIRECTIONS: RN10, the Paris/Bordeaux road.
MENU: 59 to 95 Frs.
ROOMS: 110 to 150 Frs.
RESTAURANT: Snacks from 7.00, lunch 11.00-15.00, dinner 19.00-22.00
CLOSED: Sat evening and Sun evening (out of season).
SPECIALITIES: terrine maison au cognac, lapin (rabbit) au pineau des charentes, regional menu, home-cooking.
HOTEL: 4 rooms.
FACILITIES: shower
OTHER POINTS: bar.
cognac distillery; Angoulême (ramparts, hôtel-de-ville, cathedral), chocolate making factory.

ROUMAZIERES
Charente, 16370

LES ROUTIERS
(Mr Bruneau – Société Brittany) 122, route nationale
TEL: 05.45.71.10.88
DIRECTIONS: RN141, between Limoges and

Angoulême.
MENU: 50 Frs (wine included).
RESTAURANT: Snacks from 6.00, lunch 11.00-16.00, dinner 19.00-22.00
CLOSED: Sat and Sun.
SPECIALITIES: home-cooking.
OTHER POINTS: credit cards accepted.
La Rochefoucauld; Confolens; dam at Lavaud.

ROUMAZIERES LOUBERT
Charente, 16270

LES ROUTIERS LES 3 CHENES
(Mr Raymond Bissérier)
TEL: 05.45.71.71.83
DIRECTIONS: Angoulême/Montluáon.
MENU: 59 to 75 Frs.
ROOMS: 100 Frs.
RESTAURANT: Snacks from 5.00, lunch 10.30-15.00, dinner 18.30-23.00
CLOSED: Sat, Sun, and the last 2 weeks in Aug.
SPECIALITIES: home-cooking.
HOTEL: 7 rooms.
FACILITIES: shower, bath, private bathroom
OTHER POINTS: bar.
châteaux at Nieul and Confolens; Angoulême; La Rochefoucauld.

ROYAN
Charente-Maritime, 17200

LE SYMPATIC
(Mr Yves Boinard) 30, avenue de la Libération
TEL: 05.46.05.67.21 **FAX:** 05.46.05.26.30
DIRECTIONS: on the outskirts of Royan, coming from Bordeaux.
MENU: 55 to 77 Frs.
ROOMS: 160 to 220 Frs.
RESTAURANT: Snacks from 6.00, lunch 12.00-14.00, dinner 19.00-21.00
CLOSED: Sun.
SPECIALITIES: home-cooking.
HOTEL: 15 rooms.
FACILITIES: shower, bath, private bathroom, television
OTHER POINTS: credit cards accepted.
museums; zoological gardens; forests.

ROZIERES EN BEAUCE
Loiret, 45130

LA BAGATELLE
(Mme Sylvie Bihel) 1, rue Bagatelle
TEL: 02.38.74.22.03
DIRECTIONS: RN157, between Orléans and Le Mans.
MENU: 50 to 70 Frs.
ROOMS: 120 to 150 Frs.
RESTAURANT: Snacks from 6.00, lunch 11.00-15.00, dinner 18.30-23.00
CLOSED: Sat.
SPECIALITIES: home-cooking.
HOTEL: 4 rooms.
FACILITIES: shower, bath, private bathroom
OTHER POINTS: credit cards accepted.
Orléans; Loire châteaux.

RUFFEC
Charente, 16700

LE LANDAIS
(Mr Jean-Michel Lapegue) 34, avenue Célestin Sieur
TEL: 05.45.31.04.16
DIRECTIONS: at the Ruffec exit, towards Angoulême.
MENU: 58 to 100 Frs.
RESTAURANT: Snacks from 6.00, lunch 12.00-14.30, dinner 19.00-21.30
CLOSED: Sun, and 2 weeks in Dec.
SPECIALITIES: home-cooking.
OTHER POINTS: credit cards accepted.
old Angoulême; Futuroscope at Poitiers.

RUFFEC LE CHATEAU
Indre, 36300

CHEZ P'TIT JEAN
(Mme Micheline Marandon) Route Nationale 151
TEL: 02.54.37.70.05 **FAX:** 02.54.37.91.96
DIRECTIONS: RN151, the Châteauroux/Poitiers road.
MENU: 55 to 130 Frs.
ROOMS: 140 to 250 Frs.
RESTAURANT: Snacks from 6.00, lunch 12.00-14.00, dinner 19.00-21.00
SPECIALITIES: regional menu, home-cooking.
HOTEL: 5 rooms.
FACILITIES: shower, private bathroom
OTHER POINTS: credit cards accepted.
La Brenne wildlife park; Futuroscope.

SAINT AGNANT
Charente-Maritime, 17260

AU RENDEZ-VOUS DES AMIS
(Mme Muriel Chautard) Le Pont
TEL: 05.46.83.30.36
LANGUAGES: English, German.
MENU: 60 Frs (wine and coffee included).
RESTAURANT: Lunch 11.30-14.00, dinner 19.00-22.00
SPECIALITIES: home-cooking, marmite de poissons aux petits légumes.
OTHER POINTS: bar.

SAINT AIGNAN LE JAILLARD
Loiret, 45600

LES ROUTIERS SAINT AIGNAN
(Mme Claudine Gasnier) 78, rue Nationale
TEL: 02.38.36.38.21

DIRECTIONS: between Sully and Gien.
MENU: 55 to 120 Frs.
RESTAURANT: Snacks from 7.30, lunch 11.30-15.00, dinner 19.00-23.00
CLOSED: Wed, Feb school holiday, last 2 weeks in Aug.
SPECIALITIES: coq au vin, couscous, choucroute, grillades (grills), home-cooking.
OTHER POINTS: bar.
châteaux at Gien, Chambord and Sully; La Sologne; Saint-Benoist basilica; pottery at Gien; trout-breeding.

SAINT ARNOULT DES BOIS
Eure-et-Loir, 28190

LE TY KORN
(Mr Frédéric Lepleux) 40, grande rue
TEL: 02.37.22.53.17
DIRECTIONS: between Chartres and Senonches.
LANGUAGES: English.
MENU: 50 Frs (drink included).
ROOMS: 130 Frs.
RESTAURANT: Snacks from 6.30, lunch 11.30-14.30, dinner 20.00-21.30
CLOSED: Sun.
SPECIALITIES: regional menu, home-cooking.
HOTEL: 5 rooms
OTHER POINTS: credit cards accepted.

SAINT AUBIN DES BOIS
Eure-et-Loir, 28300

AUBERGE DE LA MORICERIE
(Mr Claude Millet) Route Nationale 23
TEL: 02.37.32.99.25
DIRECTIONS: RN23, Chartres/Le Mans axis.
LANGUAGES: Italian.
MENU: 52 Frs.
ROOMS: 130 to 140 Frs.
RESTAURANT: Snacks from 4.00, lunch 11.30-15.00, dinner 19.00-21.00
CLOSED: Sat evening and Sun.
SPECIALITIES: home-cooking.
HOTEL: 18 rooms
OTHER POINTS: credit cards accepted.

SAINT ETIENNE DE CHIGNY
Indre-et-Loire, 37230

LA POELE A FRIRE
(Mr Serge Saint Jalmes) 1, quai de la Loire
TEL: 02.47.55.55.88
DIRECTIONS: RN 152, RN152, on the Tours/Saumur road.
LANGUAGES: English.
MENU: 55 Frs (drink included).
RESTAURANT: Snacks from 6.00, lunch 11.30-14.30, dinner 19.00-21.30
CLOSED: Sun evening and Mon.
SPECIALITIES: home-cooking.
OTHER POINTS: credit cards accepted.

SAINT EUGENE
Charente-Maritime, 17520

LES DEUX CHARENTES
(Mme Marcelle Blanchard) Lieu dit : La Maison de Bois
TEL: 05.46.49.13.28
DIRECTIONS: RD731, Cognac/Royan/Barbezieux.
MENU: 55 to 180 Frs.
RESTAURANT: Snacks from 6.30, lunch 11.00-14.30, dinner 19.15-21.00
CLOSED: Wed afternoon, and mid-Feb.
SPECIALITIES: regional menu, home-cooking.
OTHER POINTS: credit cards accepted.
distilleries at Brie and Archiac; dolmen at Saint-Fort; Cognac; Jarnac.

SAINT FLORENT SUR CHER
Cher, 18400

L'IMPREVU
(Mr Bernard Ruellan) 60, avenue Jean Jaurès
TEL: 02.48.55.12.00
DIRECTIONS: RN151, between Bourges and Châteauroult.
MENU: 60 Frs (coffee included).
RESTAURANT: Snacks from 5.00, dinner 19.00-21.30
CLOSED: Sun.
SPECIALITIES: galettes bretonnes, home-cooking.
OTHER POINTS: credit cards accepted.

SAINT GEORGES SUR EURE
Eure-et-Loir, 28190

AU RENDEZ-VOUS DES PECHEURS
(Henri et Monique Hubert) 9, rue Raymond Bataille
TEL: 02.37.26.81.90
DIRECTIONS: RN23, between Chartres and Le Mans.
LANGUAGES: English.
MENU: 50 Frs.
ROOMS: 130 to 170 Frs.
RESTAURANT: Snacks from 6.30, lunch 12.00-14.00, dinner 19.00-20.30
CLOSED: Sun, and 1 week at Christmas.
SPECIALITIES: home-cooking, coq au vin, pieds panés, choucroute, cassoulet, horne-cooking.
HOTEL: 9 rooms.
FACILITIES: shower, bath, private bathroom, television
OTHER POINTS: credit cards accepted.
Chartres: cathedral (8km); sailing lakes.

SAINT GERMAIN LA GATINE
Eure-et-Loir, 28300

LE RELAIS SAINT GERMAIN
(SARL Lassalle) 1 et 3, route de Chartres
TEL: 02.37.22.87.88 **FAX:** 02.37.22.84.26
DIRECTIONS: RN154, between Dreux and Chartres.
LANGUAGES: English, German.
MENU: 55 Frs (wine included).
ROOMS: 150 to 190 Frs.
RESTAURANT: Snacks from 4.30, lunch 11.30-15.00, dinner 18.30-22.30
CLOSED: Sun.
SPECIALITIES: home-cooking.
HOTEL: 15 rooms
OTHER POINTS: credit cards accepted.
Chartres cathedral.

SAINT HILAIRE DE VILLEFRANCHE
Charente-Maritime, 17770

A LA FORTUNE DU POT
(Mr Antoine Ferrutti) Avenue de Saint Jean d'Angély
TEL: 05.46.95.35.44
DIRECTIONS: RN 150, RN150, on the Saintes/Niort road.
MENU: 55 Frs (drink included).
RESTAURANT: Snacks from 7.00, lunch 11.00
CLOSED: between Christmas and New Year.
SPECIALITIES: home-cooking, grillades.
OTHER POINTS: bar.

SAINT HILAIRE LA GRAVELLE
Loir-et-Cher, 41160

AUBERGE DU LOIR
(Mr Sylvain Pierdos) 10, rue Léon Cibié
TEL: 02.54.82.65.00
DIRECTIONS: RD19, the Orléans/Le Mans road.
LANGUAGES: English.
MENU: 65 Frs.
ROOMS: 235 Frs.
RESTAURANT: Snacks from 7.00, lunch 12.00-14.00, dinner 19.00-22.00
CLOSED: Wed, and in Sept.
SPECIALITIES: home-cooking,
HOTEL: 2 rooms.
FACILITIES: shower
OTHER POINTS: credit cards accepted.

SAINT JEAN SAINT GERMAIN
Indre-et-Loire, 37600

RELAIS SAINT JEAN
(Mr Christian Ledoux) Route Nationale 143 – Le Bourg
TEL: 02.47.94.86.88
DIRECTIONS: RN143, Tours/Châteauroux.
LANGUAGES: English.
MENU: 53 Frs (wine included).
ROOMS: 130 Frs.
RESTAURANT: Snacks from 6.15, dinner up to 23.00
CLOSED: Sun.
SPECIALITIES: home-cooking.
HOTEL: 5 rooms.
FACILITIES: shower
OTHER POINTS: credit cards accepted.
Château de Loches and Châteaux de la Loire.

SAINT MAURICE SUR FESSARD
Loiret, 45700

CAFE DE LA GARE
(Mme Colette Jehl) Route Nationale 60
TEL: 02.38.97.81.00
DIRECTIONS: RN60, the Paris/Orléans road.
LANGUAGES: English.
MENU: 58 to 65 Frs.
RESTAURANT: Snacks from 6.30, lunch 11.30-14.00, dinner 19.00-21.00
CLOSED: Sat afternoon and Sun (out of season).
SPECIALITIES: home-cooking,
OTHER POINTS: credit cards accepted.

LE RELAIS DE SAINT MAURICE
(Mr Pascal Crouvisier) Route Nationale 60
TEL: 02.38.97.80.59
DIRECTIONS: RN60, the Montargis/Orléans road.
MENU: 58.50 Frs.
RESTAURANT: Snacks from 6.30, lunch 12.00-14.00, dinner 19.15-21.30
CLOSED: Sat evening and Sun.
SPECIALITIES: regional menu, home-cooking.
OTHER POINTS: credit cards accepted.

SAINT NICOLAS DE BOURGUEIL
Indre-et-Loire, 37140

LE RELAIS
(Mr Joël Joulin) Place de l'Eglise
TEL: 02.47.97.75.39
DIRECTIONS: RD35, the Tours/Angers road, via Bourgueil.
MENU: 53 to 78 Frs.
ROOMS: 135 to 190 Frs.
RESTAURANT: Snacks from 6.45, lunch 11.30-14.00, dinner 19.30-20.30
CLOSED: Sat, Sun, public holidays, and in Aug.
SPECIALITIES: home-cooking.
HOTEL: 3 rooms.
FACILITIES: shower, bath, private bathroom
OTHER POINTS: credit cards accepted.

SAINT PARDOUX
Deux-Sèvres, 79130

LA CROIX DES VIGNES
(Mr Olivier Hivert)
TEL: 05.49.63.44.22
DIRECTIONS: between Partenay and Niort.
MENU: 53 Frs (wine and coffee included).
RESTAURANT: Snacks from 5.30, lunch 11.30-15.00, dinner 19.30-22.00
CLOSED: Sat evening and Sun.
SPECIALITIES: home-cooking.
OTHER POINTS: credit cards accepted.

SAINT PIERRE DES CORPS
Indre-et-Loire, 37700

LE GRILLON
(Mr Patrick Vitel) 9, quai de la Loire
TEL: 02.47.44.74.90
DIRECTIONS: Ambroise.
MENU: 58 to 100 Frs.
RESTAURANT: Snacks from 6.00, lunch 12.00-14.00, dinner 19.00-22.00
CLOSED: Sun.
SPECIALITIES: home-cooking.
OTHER POINTS: credit cards accepted.
châteaux at Tours, Amboise and Chenonceau; numerous museums.

SAINT PORCHAIRE
Deux-Sèvres, 79300

LA POTERIE
(Mme Emmanuelle Hemon) 5, rue de Chambroutet
TEL: 05.49.74.10.31
DIRECTIONS: between Thouars and Bresuire.
LANGUAGES: English.
MENU: 52 to 75 Frs.
RESTAURANT: Snacks from 7.00, lunch 12.00, dinner up to 22.00
SPECIALITIES: home-cooking.
OTHER POINTS: credit cards accepted.

SAINT SATUR
Cher, 18300

CHEZ NORA
(Mr Aouda Belhadj) 8-10, rue Paul Cannier
TEL: 02.48.54.22.05
DIRECTIONS: on the Nevers/Bourges axis.
MENU: 60 Frs (drink included) to 100 Frs.
RESTAURANT: Snacks from 8.00
CLOSED: Sun afternoon.
SPECIALITIES: home-cooking, couscous, choucroute.
OTHER POINTS: bar.

SAINT SAVINIEN
Charente-Maritime, 17350

LE SAINT SAVINIEN
(Mlle Elisabeth Dieu) 27, rue de Champeroux
TEL: 05.46.90.20.33
DIRECTIONS: RD18, between Saintes (12km) and Saint-Jean d'Angély (10km).
MENU: 60 Frs (wine included).
ROOMS: 130 to 265 Frs.
RESTAURANT: Snacks from 7.00, lunch 12.00-14.00, dinner 19.30-21.30
CLOSED: Wed afternoon (except bookings), Sun evening and end-Dec.
SPECIALITIES: regional menu, home-cooking.
HOTEL: 9 rooms
OTHER POINTS: credit cards accepted.
Saintes (12km); Saint-Jean d'Angély (10km); miniature port; Saint-Savinien (visitor site).

SAINT SORNIN
Charente, 16220

LES ROUTIERS
(Mr Thérèse Dubois) Le Bourg
TEL: 05.45.23.12.83
DIRECTIONS: between La Rochefoucauld and Montbron.
MENU: 58 Frs.
RESTAURANT: Snacks from 6.30, lunch 12.00-14.00, dinner 19.00-21.00
CLOSED: Mon after 14.00, and 2 weeks in Aug.
SPECIALITIES: home-cooking.
OTHER POINTS: bar.

SAINT SYMPHORIEN
Eure-et-Loir, 28700

LE RELAIS DES ESSARS
(Mr Alain Nau) Route Nationale 10 – Essars
TEL: 02.37.31.18.30 FAX: 02.37.90.96.44
DIRECTIONS: RN10, between Rambouillet and Chartres.
LANGUAGES: English.
MENU: 61 Frs.
RESTAURANT: Snacks from 5.00, lunch 11.00-15.30, dinner 18.00-22.30
CLOSED: Sun.
SPECIALITIES: home-cooking.
OTHER POINTS: credit cards accepted.
château at Maintenon; Rambouillet (18km).

SAINTE MAURE DE TOURAINE
Indre-et-Loire, 37800

L'ETOILE DU SUD
(Mr Norhislem Medjahed) Route Nationale 10
TEL: 02.47.65.40.61

DIRECTIONS: RN10, the Tours/Poitiers road.
LANGUAGES: English, Spanish, Arabic.
MENU: 60 Frs (wine included).
ROOMS: 100 to 250 Frs.
RESTAURANT: Snacks from 5.00, lunch 12.00-14.30, dinner 18.30-22.30
SPECIALITIES: oriental dishes, regional menu, home-cooking.
HOTEL: ☆ 25 rooms.
FACILITIES: shower, bath, private bathroom
OTHER POINTS: credit cards accepted.
Chinon; Azay-le-Rideau; caves at Savonnières; Villandry.

SAINTES
Charente-Maritime, 17100

L'OASIS
(Mr Guy Fumoleau) Route de Rochefort
TEL: 05.46.93.07.20
DIRECTIONS: RN137, Saintes centre.
MENU: 45 to 95 Frs.
RESTAURANT: Snacks from 6.00, lunch 12.00-14.00, dinner 19.15-21.15
CLOSED: Sat, Sun, from 3rd to 25th Aug and 1 week at Christmas.
SPECIALITIES: home-cooking.
OTHER POINTS: bar.
Gallo-Roman town, with arenas, baths, châteaux, museums.

SALIGNAC SUR CHARENTE
Charente-Maritime, 17800

LE RELAIS DU PERAT
(Mme Denise Millot) 1, rue du Relais
TEL: 05.46.96.49.88
DIRECTIONS: RN 732, RN732, between Pons and Cognac.
MENU: 58 to 115.50 Frs.
ROOMS: 148.50 Frs.
RESTAURANT: Snacks from 6.00, lunch 11.30-14.30, dinner 18.30-21.00
SPECIALITIES: home-cooking.
HOTEL: 5 rooms.
FACILITIES: shower, private bathroom, television, telephone
OTHER POINTS: credit cards accepted.

SANCERGUES
Cher, 18140

LE BON LABOUREUR
(Mme Martine Dubois) 54, Grande Rue
TEL: 02.48.72.76.13
DIRECTIONS: RN151, between La Charité-sur-Loire and Bourges.
LANGUAGES: German, Italian.
MENU: 60 to 250 Frs.
ROOMS: 100 to 120 Frs.
RESTAURANT: Snacks from 7.00, lunch 11.30-13.30
CLOSED: Tues afternoon, and from 5th July to 5th Aug.
SPECIALITIES: fruits de mer, poissons, choucroute, home-cooking,
HOTEL: 4 rooms.
FACILITIES: shower, bath, private bathroom, telephone
OTHER POINTS: bar.
Sancerre (25km); Bourges cathedral (40km); abbey at Noirlac (60km), floral park at Apremont.

SAUJON
Charente-Maritime, 17600

HOTEL DE LA GARE
(Mme Jocelyne Mellot) 2, rue Clémenceau
TEL: 05.46.02.80.33 FAX: 05.46.02.42.90
DIRECTIONS: RN150, between Saintes and Royan.
LANGUAGES: English.
MENU: 35 to 60 Frs.
ROOMS: 140 to 210 Frs.
RESTAURANT: Snacks from 6.30, lunch 12.00-14.00, dinner 19.30-21.00
CLOSED: Sun, and end Dec.
SPECIALITIES: home-cooking.
HOTEL: ☆ 12 rooms.
FACILITIES: shower, bath, private bathroom, television, telephone
OTHER POINTS: credit cards accepted.
Saujon environs and beach.

SAUZE VAUSSAIS
Deux-Sèvres, 79190

LE RELAIS DES ROUTIERS
(Mr Joël Quintard) Chaignepain
TEL: 05.49.29.34.61
DIRECTIONS: RD948.
MENU: 50 Frs.
RESTAURANT: Snacks from 7.00, lunch 11.30-14.00, dinner 19.00-21.30
CLOSED: Sat, and in Aug.
SPECIALITIES: home-cooking.
OTHER POINTS: credit cards accepted.

SAZILLY
Indre-et-Loire, 37220

RELAIS DE LA PROMENADE
(Mme Jocelyne Bigot) Le Bourg
TEL: 02.47.58.55.50
DIRECTIONS: RN760, towards Chiron.
MENU: 55 Frs.
RESTAURANT: Snacks from 7.00, lunch 11.45-14.00, dinner 19.00-20.30

CLOSED: Sun.
SPECIALITIES: home-cooking.
OTHER POINTS: bar.
Loire châteaux.

SCOURY
Indre, 36300

LE CHASSE MAREE LES ROUTIERS
(Mr Laurent Léo)
TEL: 02.54.37.98.09 **FAX:** 02.54.37.91.18
DIRECTIONS: RN151, between Châteauroux and Poitiers.
LANGUAGES: Italian.
MENU: 59 Frs.
ROOMS: 100 to 190 Frs.
RESTAURANT: Snacks from 5.00, lunch 5.00, dinner up to 22.00
CLOSED: Sat afternoon, Sun, the week of the 15th Aug national holiday, and Christmas
SPECIALITIES: home-cooking.
HOTEL: 6 rooms.
FACILITIES: shower, bath, private bathroom, television
OTHER POINTS: credit cards accepted.
La Brenne wildlife park (20km).

SECONDIGNY
Deux-Sèvres, 79130

LES ROUTIERS
(Mr Noël Duranceau) 43, rue de la Vendée
TEL: 05.49.95.61.35
DIRECTIONS: RD949, La Roche-sur-Yon.
LANGUAGES: English.
MENU: 55 to 150 Frs.
ROOMS: 120 to 180 Frs.
RESTAURANT: Snacks from 7.00, lunch 11.30-14.00, dinner 19.00-21.00
CLOSED: Sun evening, Mon, 1 week in Feb and 1 week in Sept.
SPECIALITIES: farcis poitevin, moules marinières, escargots farcis, salade gourmande, regional menu, home-cooking.
HOTEL: 5 rooms.
FACILITIES: shower, private bathroom, television, telephone
OTHER POINTS: credit cards accepted.
Romanesque churches, château at Saint-Loup; Mervent (forest); Futuroscope at Poitiers.

SERAZEREUX
Eure-et-Loir, 28170

MOTEL DE PEAGE AU BON ACCEUIL
(Mme Eliane Hérisson) Zone Industrielle du Bois de Brou
TEL: 02.37.65.22.49
DIRECTIONS: RN154, between Chartres and Dreux.
LANGUAGES: English.
MENU: 55 to 90 Frs.
ROOMS: 160 to 240 Frs.
RESTAURANT: Snacks from 4.00
CLOSED: Sun.
SPECIALITIES: home-cooking.
HOTEL: 12 rooms.
FACILITIES: shower, private bathroom, television
OTHER POINTS: credit cards accepted.
Chartres cathedral.

SERIGNY
Charente-Maritime, 17230

CHEZ JOHAN
(Mr Johan Mercier) Route Nationale 137
TEL: 05.46.01.40.43
DIRECTIONS: Nantes.
RESTAURANT: dinner up to 24.00
CLOSED: Sun.
OTHER POINTS: bar.

SOLTERRE
Loiret, 45700

AUBERGE DE LA ROUTE BLEUE
(Mr Claude Baudouin) Route Nationlae 7 – La Commodité
TEL: 02.38.94.90.04
DIRECTIONS: RN7, the Paris/Nevers/Bourges/ Lyon road.
MENU: 56 Frs (wine and coffee included) to 84 Frs.
RESTAURANT: Snacks from 4.30, lunch 12.00-14.00, dinner 19.00-21.30
CLOSED: Sat afternoon, sun and 2 weeks in Feb
SPECIALITIES: ris de veau normand, escalope cordon bleu, escargots roquefori, home-cooking.
OTHER POINTS: credit cards accepted.
Gien; Montargis; Briare; Rogny-les-Sept-Ecluses.

SUEVRES
Loir-et-Cher, 41500

LE RELAIS DE LA PROVIDENCE
(Mr Michel Grosse) 1, place de la Mairie
TEL: 02.54.87.80.88
DIRECTIONS: RN152, between Orléans and Tours.
LANGUAGES: Spanish.
MENU: 60 to 125 Frs.
ROOMS: 100 to 210 Frs.
RESTAURANT: Snacks from 6.00, lunch 12.00-14.30, dinner 19.00-22.00
CLOSED: Sat evening, Sun and 3 weeks Aug/Sept.
SPECIALITIES: home-cooking.
HOTEL: 7 rooms.
FACILITIES: shower
OTHER POINTS: credit cards accepted.
Loire châteaux; Poulain chocolate-making

factory; nuclear power station at Saint-Laurent; wine-making cellars.

SULLY SUR LOIRE
Loiret, 45600

CHEZ LIONEL
(Mr Lionel Funten) 47-49, avenue de la Gare
TEL: 02.38.36.26.11
DIRECTIONS: Train station/Gendarmerie.
MENU: 58.50 Frs (wine included).
ROOMS: 100 to 190 Frs.
RESTAURANT: Snacks from 6.00, dinner up to 21.30
CLOSED: Sat afternoon, Sun, and from 8th to 23rd Aug.
SPECIALITIES: rognons à l'ancienne, lapin aux moutardes, home-cooking.
HOTEL: ☆ 10 rooms.
FACILITIES: shower, bath, private bathroom
OTHER POINTS: credit cards accepted.
château Sully; Saint-Benoît basilica; 9thc church at Germiny.

LE SAINT GERMAIN – Le Cercle d'Or
(Bernard et Patricia Schwartz) 2, place Saint Germain
TEL: 02.38.36.27.02
DIRECTIONS: RN152, as you leave Sully, in the direction of Orléans.
LANGUAGES: English, Spanish.
MENU: 53 to 104 Frs.
ROOMS: 130 to 155 Frs.
RESTAURANT: Snacks from 6.30, lunch 11.30-13.45, dinner 19.00-21.00
CLOSED: Fri evening, Sun evening, and the last 2 weeks in Dec.
SPECIALITIES: andouillette de Jargeou, coq au vin maison, fish, regional menu.
HOTEL: 6 rooms.
FACILITIES: shower
OTHER POINTS: bar.
château at Sully-sur-Loire, Saint-Benoît basilica; Gien: pottery; musée de la chasse (hunting); Vallley of kings.

SURY AUX BOIS
Loiret, 45530

LE RELAIS DU PONT DES BEIGNERS
(Mr Jean-Pierre Gueru) Pont des Beigners
TEL: 02.38.55.97.72 FAX: 02.38.55.91.27
DIRECTIONS: RN60, between Orléans and Montargis.
MENU: 63 to 72 Frs.
RESTAURANT: Snacks from 6.00, lunch 11.30-14.30, dinner 18.30-22.00
CLOSED: Sat afternoon, Sun, and from mid-Aug to mid-Sept.
SPECIALITIES: coq au vin de l'Orléanais, poulet sauté à la provenáale, home-cooking.
OTHER POINTS: credit cards accepted.
Sully-sur-Loire; Montargis.

TAILLEBOURG
Charente-Maritime, 17350

L'AUBERGE DU CHATEAU
(Mr Jean-Philippe Lequivard)
TEL: 05.46.91.70.23
DIRECTIONS: between Saintes and Saint Savinien.
LANGUAGES: English, Spanish.
MENU: 60 to 120 Frs.
RESTAURANT: Snacks from 8.30, lunch 12.00-14.30, dinner 19.00-21.30
CLOSED: Mon (in winter).
SPECIALITIES: home-cooking, anguilles (eels).
OTHER POINTS: bar.

TENDU
Indre, 36200

LE RELAIS
(Mr André Luneau) Route Nationale 20
TEL: 02.54.24.14.10
MENU: 65 to 160 Frs.
ROOMS: 130 to 190 Frs.
RESTAURANT: Snacks from 7.30, lunch 11.30-14.00, dinner 19.30-20.30
CLOSED: Tues afternoon and Wed (out of season), 2 weeks Sept/Oct and last 10 days in June.
SPECIALITIES: regional menu, home-cooking.
HOTEL: 9 rooms.
FACILITIES: shower
OTHER POINTS: credit cards accepted.
dam at Eguzon (25km); La Brenne (25km); Creuse valley, Argenton.

THEILLAY
Loir-et-Cher, 41300

RELAIS DE LA LOGE
(Mr Guy Paillaud) Route Nationale 20
TEL: 02.54.83.37.20
DIRECTIONS: RN20, 13km from Vierzon.
LANGUAGES: English.
ROOMS: 100 to 150 Frs.
SPECIALITIES: game (in season), home-cooking.
HOTEL: ☆ 35 rooms.
FACILITIES: shower, bath, private bathroom
OTHER POINTS: credit cards accepted.

THIVARS
Eure-et-Loir, 28630

LE RESTAURANT DU STADE
(Mr Patrick Petit) 15, route Nationale
TEL: 02.37.26.40.05

DIRECTIONS: RN10, 5km from Chartres.
MENU: 55 Frs.
ROOMS: 140 Frs (+ 35 Frs for extra bed).
RESTAURANT: Snacks from 6.30, lunch 12.00-14.30, dinner 19.00-21.30
CLOSED: Sat evening and Sun, and 1st 3 weeks in Aug.
SPECIALITIES: home-cooking.
HOTEL: 8 rooms.
FACILITIES: shower, bath, private bathroom
OTHER POINTS: credit cards accepted.
Chartres cathedral.

THOU
Loiret, 45420

AU LIT ON DORT
(Mr Solange Bertrand)
TEL: 02.38.31.62.07
DIRECTIONS: RD965.
MENU: 55 to 140 Frs
RESTAURANT: Snacks from 8.00, lunch 12.00-15.00
CLOSED: Mon afternoon, and in Aug.
SPECIALITIES: vol-au-vent, filet de boeuf and charlotte au chocolat, home-cooking.
OTHER POINTS: bar.

TONNAY CHARENTE
Charente-Maritime, 17430

L'OASIS
(Mme Geneviève Vachon) 27, rue de Lattre de Tassigny
TEL: 05.46.88.70.84
DIRECTIONS: between Rochefort-sur-Mer and Saintes.
RESTAURANT: Snacks from 8.00, lunch 12.00-14.00
CLOSED: Sun.
SPECIALITIES: couscous, home-cooking.
OTHER POINTS: bar.

LES FONTAINES
(Mr Jean-Paul Revelaud) 110 Avenue d'Aunis
TEL: 05.46.83.79.11
DIRECTIONS: RN137, between Nantes and Bordeaux, Rochefort exit.
MENU: 50 Frs.
RESTAURANT: Lunch 11.30-14.30, dinner 19.00-21.00
CLOSED: Sun.
SPECIALITIES: home-cooking,
OTHER POINTS: bar.

TOURY
Eure-et-Loir, 28390

LE RELAIS DE LA CHAPELLE
(Mme Claudine Comarlot) 60, avenue de la Chapelle
TEL: 02.37.90.64.96
DIRECTIONS: RN20.
MENU: 60 to 68 Frs.
RESTAURANT: Snacks from 4.00, lunch 12.00-14.30, dinner 19.00-23.00
CLOSED: Sat, Sun, 1 week in May, 3 weeks in Aug and 1 week at Christmas.
SPECIALITIES: home-cooking.
OTHER POINTS: bar.

TOUVERAC
Charente, 16360

LE BOIS VERT
(Mr Daniel Bertrand) Route Nationale 10
TEL: 05.45.78.43.77
DIRECTIONS: on the Angoulême/Bordeaux axis.
LANGUAGES: English, Spanish.
MENU: 57 Frs (drink included).
ROOMS: 100 to 135 Frs.
RESTAURANT: Snacks from 5.30, lunch 11.00, dinner up to 23.00
CLOSED: Sun lunchtime and between Christmas and New Year.
SPECIALITIES: home-cooking, couscous, paëlla (Thursday), barbecue (summer).
HOTEL: 6 rooms
OTHER POINTS: credit cards accepted.

TREON
Eure-et-Loir, 28500

LE RELAIS DE TREON
(Mme Paulette Cuvellier) 20, rue de Châteauneuf
TEL: 02.37.82.62.35
DIRECTIONS: RN928, between Le Mans and Nogent-le-Rotrou.
MENU: 57.50 Frs.
RESTAURANT: Snacks from 6.30, lunch 11.30-14.30, dinner 19.30-21.00
CLOSED: Sat, Sun and 2 weeks in Aug.
SPECIALITIES: home-cooking.
HOTEL: 8 rooms.
FACILITIES: shower, bath, private bathroom, television
OTHER POINTS: credit cards accepted.
Chartres cathedral; royal chapel at Dreux; château at Maintenon.

TRIMOUILLE (LA)
Vienne, 86290

L'AUBERGE FLEURIE
(Mme Monique Dufour) 30, rue Octave Bernard
TEL: 05.49.91.60.64
DIRECTIONS: RN675, towards Blois/Périgueux.
MENU: 55 Frs.
ROOMS: 100 to 200 Frs.
RESTAURANT: Snacks from 7.00, lunch 12.00-14.00
CLOSED: Sun and public holidays after lunch.

SPECIALITIES: moules au vert, médaillon de ris de veau à la Trimouillaise, home-cooking.
HOTEL: 5 rooms.
FACILITIES: shower, private bathroom
OTHER POINTS: bar.
Futuroscope (70km); abbey at Villesalem; church at Saint-Savin; château/town of Archambault-Guillaume.

VERGNE
Charente-Maritime, 17330

CHEZ PAPOU ET NADINE
(Mr et Mme Sabourin) Route Nationale 150 – Tout y Faut
TEL: 05.46.24.62.05
DIRECTIONS: RN150, the Niort/Bordeaux road.
LANGUAGES: English.
MENU: 60 Frs (wine included).
RESTAURANT: Snacks from 5.00, lunch 11.00-15.30, dinner 19.30-23.00
CLOSED: Sun (out of season).
SPECIALITIES: home-cooking.
OTHER POINTS: bar.
Dampierre; Saint-Jean d'Y (d'Angély); Niort.

VERRUE
Vienne, 86420

LA BALBINIERE
(Paulette et Rémy Nativelle) La Balbinière
TEL: 05.49.22.84.01
DIRECTIONS: RN147, the Poitiers/Angers road.
MENU: 57 to 85 Frs.
ROOMS: 130 to 220 Frs.
RESTAURANT: Snacks from 7.30, lunch 12.00-14.00, dinner 19.30-22.00
CLOSED: Sun evening, Mon, mid-Jan to mid-Feb and one week in Aug.
SPECIALITIES: home-cooking.
HOTEL: 8 rooms.
FACILITIES: shower, bath
OTHER POINTS: credit cards accepted.
futuroscope at Poitiers.

VIENNAY
Deux-Sèvres, 79200

LE RELAIS DE VIENNAY
(Mr Moustapha Belhadj Salem) 46, route de Thouars
TEL: 05.49.95.18.84
DIRECTIONS: between Parthenay and Thouars.
LANGUAGES: English.
MENU: 60 Frs (drink and coffee included).
RESTAURANT: Snacks from 6.45, lunch 12.00-14.00, dinner 19.00-22.00
CLOSED: Sun.
SPECIALITIES: home-cooking, couscous.
OTHER POINTS: credit cards accepted.

VIERZON
Cher, 18100

AUX MILLE PATTES
(Mr Ludwig Jakubik) 85, route de Tours
TEL: 02.48.75.46.38
DIRECTIONS: RN76, the Vierzon/Tours road.
MENU: 53 Frs.
RESTAURANT: Snacks from 7.00
CLOSED: Sun.
OTHER POINTS: bar.
Bourges.

MODERN'SPORT
(Mme Jeanine Madeleine) 141, avenue Edouard Vaillant
TEL: 02.48.75.13.63
DIRECTIONS: RN20, Vierzon town centre.
MENU: 58 to 60 Frs (coffee included).
RESTAURANT: Snacks from 6.30, lunch 12.00-14.00, dinner 19.00-22.00
CLOSED: Sat, and in Aug.
SPECIALITIES: home-cooking.
OTHER POINTS: bar.

VILLEDOMER
Indre-et-Loire, 37110

LE GAI PRINTEMPS
(Mme Luce Mounissens) Route Nationale 10
TEL: 02.47.55.02.02
LANGUAGES: English.
MENU: 50 to 150 Frs.
RESTAURANT: Snacks from 6.00
CLOSED: Sat, Sun, public holidays in Aug.
SPECIALITIES: home-cooking.
OTHER POINTS: credit cards accepted.
Loire châteaux.

LES GRANDS VINS DE TOURAINE
(Mr Claude Romian) Route Nationale 10 – La Grand'Vallée
TEL: 02.47.55.01.05
DIRECTIONS: RN10, between Châteaurenault and Monnaie.
MENU: 58 to 130 Frs.
ROOMS: 90 to 200 Frs.
RESTAURANT: Snacks from 7.00, lunch 11.45-14.00, dinner 19.00-21.30
CLOSED: Wed, and the last 2 weeks in July.
SPECIALITIES: andouillette and cuisse de lapin au Vouvray, cuisses de grenouille, coq au vin, home-cooking.
HOTEL: 4 rooms.
FACILITIES: shower

OTHER POINTS: credit cards accepted.
châteaux at Amboise and Tours; wine-cellars at Vouvray.

VILVORDE
Cher, 1800

MONICO
(Mr Philippe Pollet) 548 Schaarbeecklei
TEL: 022.520.685
DIRECTIONS: Ring/Brussels axis.
MENU: 60 Frs.
RESTAURANT: Snacks from 7.30, lunch 12.00-14.00, dinner 19.00-22.00
CLOSED: Sat, Sun and in July.
SPECIALITIES: regional menu, home-cooking.
OTHER POINTS: credit cards accepted.

VIVONNE
Vienne, 86370

LES ROUTIERS
(Mr Serge Judes) Route Nationale 10
TEL: 05.49.43.41.03 **FAX:** 05.49.43.42.36
DIRECTIONS: RN10, the Paris/Bordeaux road.
LANGUAGES: Spanish.
MENU: 60 Frs (wine included) to 100 Frs.
RESTAURANT: Open 24h.
SPECIALITIES: entrecôtes aux échalottes, home-cooking.
OTHER POINTS: credit cards accepted.
Futuroscope at Poitiers.

YMONVILLE
Eure-et-Loir, 28150

LE RELAIS DE BEAUCE
(Mme Martine Millochau) Lieu-dit "La Michellerie" – Route Nationale 154
TEL: 02.37.32.26.34
DIRECTIONS: RN154, the Orléans/Chartres road.
MENU: 58 Frs.
RESTAURANT: Snacks from 5.30, lunch 11.30-14.30, dinner 19.00-22.00
CLOSED: Sat, Sun, public holidays, and in Aug.
SPECIALITIES: home-cooking.
OTHER POINTS: credit cards accepted.
Chartres: cathedral, maison de Picassiette; windmill.

Central France

The following départments are included in this chapter:

Allier (03)
Cantal (15)
Corrèze (19)
Creuse (23)
Haute-Loire (43)
Haute-Vienne (87)
Puy-de-Dôme (63)

AIXE SUR VIENNE
Haute-Vienne, 87700

LA CHAUMIERE
(Mme Josette Péchalat) 5, avenue de la Gare
TEL: 05.55.70.12.12
DIRECTIONS: RN21, Limoges/Périgueux road.
MENU: 55 to 120 Frs.
ROOMS: 10 to 140 Frs.
RESTAURANT: Snacks from 7.00, lunch 12.00-14.00
CLOSED: Wed evening, Sun evening and the last 2 weeks in Aug.
SPECIALITIES: coq au vin, confit de canard, entrecôte bordelaise, regional menu, home-cooking.
HOTEL: 5 rooms.
FACILITIES: shower
OTHER POINTS: bar.
Limoges (12km); Oradour-sur-Glane (20km); porcelain factory tours.

ARFEUILLES CHATELUS
Allier, 03640

LES CHEVREAUX
(Mr Amar Kaouani) Route Nationale 7
TEL: 04.70.55.00.79
DIRECTIONS: RN7.
LANGUAGES: English, Arabic.
MENU: 58 to 70 Frs.
RESTAURANT: Open 24h.
SPECIALITIES: home-cooking.
OTHER POINTS: credit cards accepted.
château at Lapalisse; leisure park.

ARGENTAT
Corrèze, 19400

CHEZ RAYMOND
(Mme Monique Pouzaud) Place du 14 juillet
TEL: 05.55.28.01.97
DIRECTIONS: Tulle.
MENU: 65 to 100 Frs (wine included).
ROOMS: 120 to 220 Frs.
RESTAURANT: Snacks from 6.00, lunch 12.00-14.00, dinner 19.00-21.00
CLOSED: Sun (except bookings).
SPECIALITIES: home-cooking.
HOTEL: 7 rooms.
FACILITIES: shower, bath
OTHER POINTS: bar.

AUBUSSON
Creuse, 23200

LE RELAIS VERT ET BLEU
(Mme Murielle Magnat) Z.I. du Mont
TEL: 05.55.83.85.45
DIRECTIONS: between Montluáon and Ussel.
MENU: 58 Frs (wine included) to 95 Frs.
RESTAURANT: Snacks from 7.00
SPECIALITIES: regional menu, home-cooking.
OTHER POINTS: credit cards accepted.
Aubusson.

AURILLAC
Cantal, 15000

BAR L'ESCUDILLIERS
(Mr Robert Montourcy) Place du 8 Mai
TEL: 04.71.63.79.30
DIRECTIONS: between Rodez and Brive-la-Gaillarde.
MENU: 55 Frs (wine and coffee included).
RESTAURANT: Snacks from 6.00, lunch 11.00-14.00
CLOSED: Sun.
SPECIALITIES: coq au vin, regional menu, home-cooking.
OTHER POINTS: bar.
Saint-Flour; Salers; Conques.

L'ETAPE DE LA MAISON NEUVE
(Mr Muller) Lavaurs Giou de Mamou
TEL: 04.71.64.58.42
DIRECTIONS: RN122, 4km from Aurillac, towards Clermont-Ferrand.
MENU: 52 Frs (wine included) to 65 Frs.
ROOMS: 130 to 160 Frs.

RESTAURANT: Snacks from 6.30, lunch 11.30-14.00, dinner 19.00-22.00
CLOSED: Sun (except in July and Aug).
SPECIALITIES: regional menu, home-cooking.
HOTEL: 10 rooms
OTHER POINTS: credit cards accepted.
Puy Mary; Super Lioran.

LE RELAIS DE LA SABLIERE
(Mme Jeanine Delort) Route Nationale 122 – La Sablière
TEL: 04.71.64.51.80
DIRECTIONS: RN122, Montauban/Toulouse.
LANGUAGES: English, Spanish.
MENU: 58 Frs.
RESTAURANT: Snacks from 7.00, lunch 12.00-14.30, dinner 18.30-21.00
CLOSED: Sun, and in Aug.
SPECIALITIES: regional menu, home-cooking.
OTHER POINTS: bar.

BEAUNE LES MINES
Haute-Vienne, 87280

LA TERRASSE DE BEAUNE
(Mme Janine Malterre)
TEL: 05.55.39.90.58 FAX: 05.55.39.47.55
DIRECTIONS: RN20, at the limoges exit.
LANGUAGES: English.
MENU: 52 Frs.
ROOMS: 140 to 260 Frs.
RESTAURANT: Snacks from 6.30, lunch 11.30-15.00, dinner 19.00-22.30
CLOSED: Sun, and 2 weeks in Aug.
SPECIALITIES: home-cooking.
HOTEL: 9 rooms.
FACILITIES: shower, bath, private bathroom
OTHER POINTS: credit cards accepted.
Limoges.

BOURGANEUF
Creuse, 23400

LA BERGERIE
(Mr Christian Pérucaud) Route Nationale 141 – Montboucher
TEL: 05.55.64.11.64
DIRECTIONS: RN141, between Limoges and Clermont-Ferrand.
MENU: 58 Frs (wine included).
RESTAURANT: Snacks from 5.30, lunch 11.00-15.00, dinner 19.30-22.00
SPECIALITIES: civet de gibier (game stew), fish, home-cooking.
OTHER POINTS: bar.
Lac de Vassivière (25km); Aubusson tapestries (30km); Oradour-sur-Glane; museum at L'évêché.

BRIOUDE
Haute-Loire, 43100

LES ROUTIERS DES SPORTS
(Mr Pierre Pichot) Route de Clermont Ferrand
TEL: 04.71.50.14.39
DIRECTIONS: RN102, Le Puy-en-Velay/Clermont road.
MENU: 60 Frs.
RESTAURANT: Snacks from 5.30, lunch 12.00-14.30, dinner 19.00-21.00
CLOSED: Sat evening and Sun evening.
SPECIALITIES: home-cooking.
OTHER POINTS: credit cards accepted.
Basilica; maison du saumon; the Allier valley.

BRIVE
Corrèze, 19100

LE NOUVEL HOTEL
(Mr Jean-Luc Ferrer) 2, avenue Desgenettes
TEL: 05.55.86.01.66
DIRECTIONS: RN89, between Périgueux and Clermont-Ferrand.
LANGUAGES: English.
MENU: 57 to 60 Frs.
ROOMS: 90 to 140 Frs.
RESTAURANT: Snacks from 6.30, lunch 12.00-14.30, dinner 19.00-21.30
CLOSED: Sat and Sun.
SPECIALITIES: home-cooking.
HOTEL: 12 rooms
OTHER POINTS: credit cards accepted.
Caves of Lascaux; Les Eyziers de Tayac; Rocamadour; Padirac.

BRIVES CHARENSAC
Haute-Loire, 43700

LE RELAIS DU COMMERCE
(Mme Elie Masson-Ferret) 2, route de Lyon
TEL: 04.71.09.16.16
DIRECTIONS: Valence/Saint-Etienne road.
MENU: 55 to 65 Frs.
ROOMS: 90 to 130 Frs.
RESTAURANT: Snacks from 6.00, lunch 11.30-14.00, dinner 19.00-21.00
SPECIALITIES: home-cooking.
HOTEL: 10 rooms.
FACILITIES: shower
OTHER POINTS: credit cards accepted.
Le Puy-en-Velay (3Km); Loire châteaux (25Km); source of the Loire (45km).

BROMONT LAMOTHE
Puy-de-Dôme, 63230

LE RELAIS DES DOMES
(Mr Guy Tixeron) Route nationale 941B

TEL: 04.73.88.76.24
DIRECTIONS: RD941B, between Clermont-Ferrand and Limoges.
MENU: 55 Frs.
RESTAURANT: Snacks from 7.00, lunch 12.00-16.00, dinner 19.00-22.30
SPECIALITIES: home-cooking.
OTHER POINTS: bar.

BROUT VERNET
Allier, 03110

SARL CENTRE ROUTIER
(Mme Georgette Roux) Route Nationale 9
TEL: 04.70.58.24.61 **FAX:** 04.70.58.25.16
DIRECTIONS: RN9, between Gannat and Saint-Pourcain-sur-Sioule.
MENU: 60 to 65 Frs.
ROOMS: 120 to 150 Frs.
RESTAURANT: Snacks from 5.30, lunch 12.00-14.30, dinner 19.00-23.30
CLOSED: Sat and Sun.
SPECIALITIES: home-cooking.
HOTEL: 9 rooms
OTHER POINTS: credit cards accepted.
La Sioule.

CHAMBORET
Haute-Vienne, 87140

LA BERGERIE
(SARL Albenque/Moreau)
TEL: 05.55.53.44.16 **FAX:** 05.55.53.57.41
DIRECTIONS: RN147, between Limoges and Poitiers,
MENU: 58 to 125 Frs.
RESTAURANT: Snacks from 6.00, lunch 12.00-14.00, dinner 19.00-23.00
CLOSED: Sun.
SPECIALITIES: home-cooking.
OTHER POINTS: credit cards accepted.
Oradour-sur-Glane; lac de Saint-Pardoux; le Mont de Blond.

CHAPELLE D'AUREC (LA)
Haute-Loire, 43120

LE RELAIS DE LA CHAPELLE
La Mioulaterre
TEL: 04.71.66.53.55
DIRECTIONS: RN88, Le Puy-en-Velay.
MENU: 60 to 135 Frs.
ROOMS: 100 to 180 Frs.
RESTAURANT: Snacks from 6.30, lunch 12.00-14.00, dinner 19.30-21.00
SPECIALITIES: home-cooking.
HOTEL: 4 rooms.
FACILITIES: shower, bath, private bathroom
OTHER POINTS: credit cards accepted.

CHATEAUNEUF LA FORET
Haute-Vienne, 87130

AUX CEPS
(Mr Philippe Le Corbelec) La Veytisou
TEL: 05.55.69.33.38
DIRECTIONS: RD979, between Limoges and Eymoutiers.
LANGUAGES: English.
MENU: 53 Frs (wine included) to 80 Frs.
ROOMS: 85 to 150 Frs.
RESTAURANT: Snacks from 6.30
SPECIALITIES: potée limousine, ceps, poissons, home-made desserts, home-cooking.
HOTEL: 8 rooms.
FACILITIES: shower
OTHER POINTS: bar.
Vassivière; Montgargon.

CLERMONT FERRAND
Puy-de-Dôme, 63000

AUVERGNE PYRENEES – Les Routiers
(Mme Marie-Louise Laborde) 12bis, place des Carmes
TEL: 04.73.92.35.73
DIRECTIONS: RN9, in town centre.
LANGUAGES: English, Spanish.
MENU: 54 to 95 Frs.
ROOMS: 145 to 270 Frs.
RESTAURANT: Snacks from 7.00, lunch 12.00-14.00, dinner 19.30-21.00
SPECIALITIES: coq au vin, regional menu, home-cooking.
HOTEL: ☆☆ 15 rooms.
FACILITIES: shower, bath, private bathroom, telephone
OTHER POINTS: bar.
Puy de Dôme; Chamalières; Royat; Montferrand, lakes; châteaux.

COSNE D'ALLIER
Allier, 03430

L'ESCALE
(Mme Marie-Joseph Sauvat-Majdoub) 2, place de la Liberté
TEL: 04.70.07.21.10
DIRECTIONS: A74, between Montluáon and Villefranche-d'Allier.
LANGUAGES: English, Spanish.
MENU: 55 Frs (wine and coffee included)
ROOMS: 100 Frs.
RESTAURANT: Snacks from 6.45, lunch 11.00-15.30, dinner 17.00-22.30
SPECIALITIES: regional menu, home-cooking.
HOTEL: 6 rooms.

FACILITIES: shower
OTHER POINTS: credit cards accepted.
châteaux and forest.

COSTAROS
Haute-Loire, 43490

LES ROUTIERS
(Mme Thérèse Rossello) Rue Principale
TEL: 04.71.57.16.04
DIRECTIONS: RN88, Le Puy-en-Velay/Marseille road.
LANGUAGES: Spanish.
MENU: 60 Frs
ROOMS: 100 Frs.
RESTAURANT: Snacks from 7.00, lunch 12.00-14.30, dinner 19.30-21.00
CLOSED: Sat (out of season), and from end Dec to mid-Jan.
SPECIALITIES: grenouilles, mousse de brochet, avocat farci, lapin chasseur, truite meunière, caille flambée, rognons au madère, regional menu.
HOTEL: 17 rooms.
FACILITIES: shower, television
OTHER POINTS: bar.

CREUZIER LE VIEUX
Allier, 03300

LA MERE RIBOULIN
(Mr Louis Camensuli) 10, allée des Ailes
TEL: 04.70.98.44.88
MENU: 58 to 90 Frs.
ROOMS: 100 to 120 Frs.
RESTAURANT: Snacks from 5.30, lunch 11.30-15.00, dinner 19.30-22.30
SPECIALITIES: regional menu, home-cooking, cuisses de grenouilles, friture, gambas.
HOTEL: 14 rooms.
FACILITIES: shower, private bathroom
OTHER POINTS: credit cards accepted.

CROUZILLE (LA)
Haute-Vienne, 87240

HOTEL DU LAC
(Mme Monique Barberon)
TEL: 05.55.71.30.65
DIRECTIONS: A20, A20, on the Limoges/Châteauroux axis.
LANGUAGES: English.
MENU: 58 Frs (wine and coffee included) to 150 Frs.
ROOMS: 100 to 150 Frs.
RESTAURANT: Snacks from 7.00, lunch 10.00-15.00, dinner 19.00-22.00
SPECIALITIES: regional menu, home-cooking, viandes limousines.
HOTEL: ☆ 12 rooms.
FACILITIES: shower, private bathroom
OTHER POINTS: credit cards accepted.

CUSSAC
Haute-Vienne, 87150

BAR RESTAURANT HOTEL TABAC
(Mme Denise Barrière) Route Départementale 699 – Le Bourg
TEL: 05.55.70.94.84
DIRECTIONS: RD699, Limoges/Angoulème road.
MENU: 50 Frs (wine included) to 90 Frs.
ROOMS: 120 to 160 Frs.
RESTAURANT: Snacks from 7.00, lunch 11.00-15.00, dinner 18.30-21.30
SPECIALITIES: ris de veau, omelette aux cèpes, regional menu, home-cooking.
HOTEL: 10 rooms.
FACILITIES: shower, bath, private bathroom
OTHER POINTS: credit cards accepted.
Richard Coeur de Lion circuit; châteaux.

CUSSET
Allier, 03300

HOTEL DE LA GARE
(Mr Jean Laroque) 1, route de Paris
TEL: 04.70.98.26.10
MENU: 60 Frs.
RESTAURANT: Snacks from 6.30, lunch 12.00-13.30
CLOSED: Sun, and in July.
SPECIALITIES: home-cooking.
OTHER POINTS: bar.

LES MONTAGNARDS
(Mr Jean Pierre Corre) 20, rue du Général Raynal
TEL: 04.70.98.38.60
DIRECTIONS: at the Cusset exit, towards Lapalisse.
MENU: 58 Frs.
RESTAURANT: Snacks from 7.00, lunch 12.00-14.30
CLOSED: Sun.
SPECIALITIES: home-cooking.
OTHER POINTS: bar.
Bourbonnais mountains (20km); Vichy (3km).

Allier, 03240

LE RELAIS DE L'AMITIE
(Mme Brigitte Bordier) Route Nationale 145
TEL: 04.70.47.14.83 FAX: 04.70.47.01.79
DIRECTIONS: RN145, between Moulins and Bellac.
LANGUAGES: English, Spanish, Italian.
MENU: 59 to 110 Frs.
RESTAURANT: Snacks from 4.30
CLOSED: Sat afternoon, Sun.
SPECIALITIES: home-cooking.
OTHER POINTS: credit cards accepted.

DOMPIERRE SUR BESBRE
Allier, 03290

LE RELAIS DE LA BESBRE
(Mr Jean-Pierre Marossa) 207, avenue de la Gare
TEL: 04.70.34.53.69
DIRECTIONS: RN79, between Moulins and Mâcon.
MENU: 54 to 68 Frs.
RESTAURANT: Snacks from 6.15, lunch 12.00-14.00, dinner 19.00-21.00
CLOSED: Sat afternoon, Sun, and from mid-Sept to beginning of Oct.
SPECIALITIES: home-cooking.
OTHER POINTS: bar.
Besbre valley.

DOYET
Allier, 03170

CAFETERIA LE BOURBONNAIS
(Mr Christophe Ozenne) A71 – Aire de l'Allier Accessible dans les deux sens
TEL: 04.70.07.70.13 FAX: 04.70.07.73.69
OTHER POINTS: credit cards accepted.

DURDAT LAREQUILLE
Allier, 03310

RESTAURANT DES SPORTS – Chez Gérard et Nathalie
(Gérard et Nathalie Lombardi) Route Nationale 144
TEL: 04.70.51.07.28
DIRECTIONS: RN144, Montluáon/Clermont-Ferrand road.
LANGUAGES: English, Spanish, Italian.
MENU: 65 Frs.
RESTAURANT: Snacks from 6.00, lunch 11.30-14.30
CLOSED: Sun.
SPECIALITIES: home-cooking.
OTHER POINTS: bar.
Sioule gorges (30km); château at Chouvigny (35km).

EYMOUTIERS
Haute-Vienne, 87120

LE SAINT PSALMET
(Mr Michel Le Petit) Place du Champ de Foire
TEL: 05.55.69.10.06 FAX: 05.55.69.23.92
DIRECTIONS: CD940 and 941, Limoges/Ussel or Guéret/Tulle roads.
LANGUAGES: English, Spanish.
MENU: 45 (wine included) to 120 Frs.
ROOMS: 125 to 180 Frs.
RESTAURANT: Snacks from 6.00, lunch 12.00-15.00, dinner 19.00-22.00
SPECIALITIES: gigot de lotte aux cèpes, regional menu, home-cooking.
HOTEL: ☆☆ 38 rooms.
FACILITIES: shower, bath, private bathroom, telephone
OTHER POINTS: credit cards accepted.
Lac de Vassivière.

ISSOIRE
Puy-de-Dôme, 63500

AU REPOS DES ROUTIERS
(Mme Ginette Clauzin) Veneix
TEL: 04.73.96.62.01
DIRECTIONS: A75, Clermont/Montpellier road, junction 9.
MENU: 55 Frs.
ROOMS: 100 to 185 Frs.
RESTAURANT: Snacks from 6.00
SPECIALITIES: home-cooking.
HOTEL: 7 rooms.
FACILITIES: shower, private bathroom
OTHER POINTS: bar.
Issoire; Montpeyrou.

LE CHAPEAU ROUGE
(Mme Christine Chambefort) 113, route de Saint Germain – Sortie 14 de l'autoroute
TEL: 04.73.89.14.74
DIRECTIONS: exit 14, for aerodrome.
MENU: 58 Frs.
RESTAURANT: Snacks from 5.00, lunch 11.30-15.00, dinner 19.00-22.00
CLOSED: Sat 16.00 to Mon 5.00.
SPECIALITIES: home-cooking.
OTHER POINTS: credit cards accepted.
Auvergne volcanic park.

JOURGNAC
Haute-Vienne, 87800

LE RELAIS SAINT ROCH
(Mme Adrienne Yazgi) Le Bourg
TEL: 05.55.58.11.02
DIRECTIONS: RN 704, RN704, between Limoges and Nexon.
LANGUAGES: English.
MENU: 55 Frs (drink and coffee included) to 110 Frs.
ROOMS: 220 Frs.
RESTAURANT: Snacks from 8.00
CLOSED: Wed evening.
SPECIALITIES: regional menu, home-cooking.
HOTEL: 3 rooms
OTHER POINTS: credit cards accepted.

LAFEUILLADE EN VEZIE
Cantal, 15130

LE RETREO
(Mme Sylvia Laurissergues) Le Bourg

TEL: 04.71.62.58.66
DIRECTIONS: on the Aurillac/Rodez road.
LANGUAGES: English.
MENU: 55 to 90 Frs.
RESTAURANT: Snacks from 7.30, lunch 12.00-14.30, dinner 19.00-21.30
SPECIALITIES: regional menu, home-cooking, poissons en sauce.
OTHER POINTS: bar.

LAPALISSE
Allier, 03120

LE CHAPON DORE
(Mr Jean-Luc Lalauze) 1, avenue du 8 Mai 1945
TEL: 04.70.99.09.51
DIRECTIONS: RN7, Vichy/Paris/Moulins road.
MENU: 60 to 140 Frs.
ROOMS: 95 to 200 Frs.
RESTAURANT: Snacks from 7.00, lunch 12.00-14.00, dinner 19.00-21.00
CLOSED: Sat evening and Sun.
SPECIALITIES: home-cooking.
HOTEL: ☆ 8 rooms.
FACILITIES: shower, bath
OTHER POINTS: bar.
Zoo; châteaux; amusement and leisure parks.

LAPTE
Haute-Loire, 43200

LE RELAIS DU LIGNON
(Mme Marie-France Gianneti) La Chambertière
TEL: 04.71.59.38.41 **FAX:** 04.71.65.81.58
DIRECTIONS: CD 105, CD105, Yssingeau/Annonay/Valence.
MENU: 60 Frs (wine and coffee included).
RESTAURANT: Snacks from 7.00, lunch 12.00-14.30, dinner 19.00-21.30
CLOSED: Tues afternoon.
SPECIALITIES: home-cooking.
OTHER POINTS: credit cards accepted.

LIMOGES
Haute-Vienne, 87000

CHEZ BICHON
(Mr Roland Houard) 60 avenue du Maréchal de Lattre de Tassigny
TEL: 05.55.30.68.83
DIRECTIONS: RN20, Toulouse/Lyon road.
LANGUAGES: English, Spanish.
MENU: from 55 Frs (children under 10 half-price).
RESTAURANT: Snacks from 6.00, lunch 12.00-14.00, dinner 18.00-21.00
CLOSED: Sat.
SPECIALITIES: specialities to order, home-cooking.
OTHER POINTS: bar.
Cathedral; factory and museum of porcelain; Oradour-sur-Glane (20km).

MALEMORT
Corrèze, 19360

CHEZ PAULETTE
(Mme Marie-Paulette Vergne) 2, avenue Pierre et Marie Curie
TEL: 05.55.92.28.14
DIRECTIONS: RN89, Clermont-Ferrand road.
MENU: 55 to 70 Frs.
RESTAURANT: Snacks from 7.00, lunch 12.00-14.30
CLOSED: Sun and in Aug.
SPECIALITIES: petit salé, (pickled pork), choux farci, pâté de pommes de teirre, home-cooking.
OTHER POINTS: bar.
Collonge-la-Rouge; tower at Brénige-Malemont.

MAURIAC
Cantal, 15200

LES ROUTIERS – Chez Brigitte
(SARL Laroche-Rongier) 27, rue Saint Mary
TEL: 04.71.68.00.79
DIRECTIONS: RD678, Ussel.
MENU: 50 to 120 Frs.
ROOMS: 100 to 140 Frs.
RESTAURANT: Snacks from 7.00, lunch 12.00-13.30, dinner 19.00-21.00
CLOSED: Sun (out of season).
SPECIALITIES: Auvergnat specialities, home-cooking.
HOTEL: 10 rooms.
FACILITIES: shower, bath, private bathroom
OTHER POINTS: credit cards accepted.
Puy Mary; château at Val; Salers; Dordogne valley; golf-course at Saint-Jean; Val-Saint-Jean pool at Mauriac.

MEZIERES SUR ISSOIRE
Haute-Vienne, 87330

LA BERGERIE
(Mme Liliane Rousseau) 5, rue Ovin
TEL: 05.55.60.09.21 **FAX:** 05.55.60.09.22
DIRECTIONS: RN 951, RN951, on the Angoulème/Gueret axis.
MENU: 55 Frs (wine and coffee included).
RESTAURANT: Snacks from 6.30, lunch 12.00-15.00, dinner 19.00-22.30
CLOSED: Sun.
SPECIALITIES: home-cooking, Bavette d'aloyeau.
OTHER POINTS: credit cards accepted.

MOLOMPIZE
Cantal, 15500

HOTEL DU CENTRE
(Mme Franáoise Dubois)
TEL: 04.71.73.61.97
LANGUAGES: English.
MENU: 50 to 80 Frs.
ROOMS: 100 to 150 Frs.
RESTAURANT: Snacks from 7.00, lunch 12.00-13.30, dinner 19.30-21.00
SPECIALITIES: regional menu, home-cooking.
HOTEL: 15 rooms.
FACILITIES: bath, private bathroom
OTHER POINTS: credit cards accepted.
Garabit (viaduc); Chaudes-Aigues; Salers; Saint-Flour.

MONTMARAULT
Allier, 03390

RELAIS DE L'ETAPE
(Mr Michel Favrichon) Route de Moulins
TEL: 04.70.07.36.03
DIRECTIONS: RN145 expressway; 100 metres from exit A71.
MENU: 66 Frs (coffee included) to 87 Frs.
RESTAURANT: Snacks from 5.00
CLOSED: Sat evening and Sun.
SPECIALITIES: home-cooking.
OTHER POINTS: credit cards accepted.

MOULINS
Allier, 03000

LES TROIS RUBANS
(Mr Pierre Molinie) Route de Paris
TEL: 04.70.44.08.51
DIRECTIONS: RN7, Lyon.
MENU: 60 Frs (wine included).
RESTAURANT: Snacks from 6.30, lunch 11.30-14.30
CLOSED: Sat afternoon, Sun and in Aug.
SPECIALITIES: home-cooking.
OTHER POINTS: bar.

NEUSSARGUES
Cantal, 15170

AUBERGE DES BRANQUES
(Mme Jeanine Terrisse) Rue du Calvaire
TEL: 04.71.20.53.92
DIRECTIONS: RN122, between Aurillac and Clermont-Ferrand.
MENU: 50 to 70 Frs.
RESTAURANT: Snacks from 7.00, lunch 12.00-15.00, dinner 19.00-22.00
CLOSED: Sun.
SPECIALITIES: home-cooking.
OTHER POINTS: bar.
Garabit viaduct; Saint-Flour; Puy Mary.

NOAILLES
Corrèze, 19600

RELAIS D'ANTAN
(Mr Patrick Lomey) Route Nationale 20
TEL: 05.55.85.85.76 **FAX:** 05.55.85.15.82
DIRECTIONS: RN20, between Brive-la-Gaillarde and Toulouse.
MENU: 64 to 89 Frs.
ROOMS: 120 to 150 Frs.
RESTAURANT: Snacks from 6.00, lunch 11.30-14.00, dinner 19.00-22.00
CLOSED: Sat evening and Sun,
SPECIALITIES: home-cooking.
HOTEL: 12 rooms.
FACILITIES: shower
OTHER POINTS: credit cards accepted.
Turenne; Rocamadour; Padirac; Souilliac.

OLLIERGUES
Puy-de-Dôme, 63880

LA SAPINIERE
(Mr Bernard Somma) Route Départementale 906 – Giroux Gare
TEL: 04.73.53.56.58
DIRECTIONS: RD906, between Thiers and Ambert.
MENU: 50 Frs (wine and coffee included).
RESTAURANT: Snacks from 7.00
SPECIALITIES: home-cooking.
OTHER POINTS: bar.
Olliergues.

PERIGNY
Allier, 03120

LE RELAIS DE PERIGNY
(Mr Patrice Cardinaud) Le Bourg
TEL: 04.70.99.84.57
DIRECTIONS: RN7, 3km from Lapalisse.
LANGUAGES: English.
MENU: 60 Frs.
ROOMS: 100 to 120 Frs.
RESTAURANT: Open 24h.
CLOSED: Sat and Sun.
SPECIALITIES: regional menu, home-cooking.
HOTEL: ☆ 6 rooms.
FACILITIES: shower, private bathroom, television
OTHER POINTS: credit cards accepted.
Vichy; château at Lapalisse.

PERTUIS (LE)
Haute-Loire, 43260

LE RELAIS DU COL
(Mme Odile Diétrich) Route Nationale 88
TEL: 04.71.57.60.06
DIRECTIONS: RN79, between Moulins (50km) and Mâcon (100km).
MENU: 60 to 80 Frs.
ROOMS: 100 to 200 Frs.
RESTAURANT: Snacks from 5.00, lunch 12.00-14.30, dinner 19.00-22.00
CLOSED: Sat afternoon and Sun.
SPECIALITIES: home-cooking.
HOTEL: 8 rooms
OTHER POINTS: bar.

PINOLS
Haute-Loire, 43300

HOTEL DES VOYAGEURS
(Mme Jacqueline Cornet)
TEL: 04.71.74.11.42
DIRECTIONS: RN590.
MENU: 65 to 80 Frs.
ROOMS: 60 to 75 Frs.
RESTAURANT: Snacks from 7.00, dinner 19.00-21.00
SPECIALITIES: potée auvergnate, ris de veau aux champignons, home-cooking.
HOTEL: 6 rooms.
FACILITIES: shower, bath
OTHER POINTS: bar.
Le Puy-en-Velay; le Mont Mouchet.

PONT DE MENAT
Puy-de-Dôme, 63560

CHEZ ROGER
(Mme Marie Pinel) Menat
TEL: 04.73.85.50.17
DIRECTIONS: RN144, Montluáon/Clermont-Ferrand road.
MENU: 60 to 140 Frs
ROOMS: 110 to 180 Frs.
RESTAURANT: Snacks from 9.00, lunch 12.00-14.00, dinner 19.00-21.00
CLOSED: Tues.
SPECIALITIES: tampon d'Auvergne, potée auvergnate, trout, regional menu, home-cooking.
HOTEL: 8 rooms.
FACILITIES: shower, bath, private bathroom
OTHER POINTS: bar.

PONTAUMUR
Puy-de-Dôme, 63380

CHEZ LUCETTE
(Mme Lucette Condon) Puy Maury
TEL: 04.73.79.00.40
DIRECTIONS: between Pontaumur et Aubusson.
MENU: 65 to 120 Frs.
RESTAURANT: Snacks from 7.00, lunch 12.00-14.30, dinner 19.30-21.00
CLOSED: August.
SPECIALITIES: home-cooking.
OTHER POINTS: bar.
summit of the Puy-de-Dôme (50km); viaduct at Fades; dam at Sauret-Bessève; Auvergne regional volcanic park.

PUY EN VELAY (LE)
Haute-Loire, 43000

LA TAVERNE
(Mr René Rolland) 50, boulevard Carnot
TEL: 04.71.09.35.16
MENU: 65 to 80 Frs.
ROOMS: 130 to 220 Frs.
RESTAURANT: Snacks from 7.00, lunch 12.00-14.00, dinner 19.00-21.00
CLOSED: in Sept.
SPECIALITIES: regional menu, home-cooking.
HOTEL: 10 rooms.
FACILITIES: shower
OTHER POINTS: credit cards accepted.
Cathedral.

RIOM
Puy-de-Dôme, 63200

AU STAND
(Mme Janine Dassaud) 24, avenue de Clermont
TEL: 04.73.38.04.06
DIRECTIONS: RN9, Riom Sud (South).
LANGUAGES: English.
MENU: 60 to 85 Frs.
RESTAURANT: Snacks from 7.00, lunch 11.30-14.00
CLOSED: Sun, public holidays, and in Aug.
SPECIALITIES: home-cooking.
OTHER POINTS: credit cards accepted.
Auvergne regional volcanic park; museums and monuments at Rioni.

RIS
Puy-de-Dôme, 63290

HOTEL DE LA GARE
(Mr Thierry Pérard) Ris Gare
TEL: 04.73.94.69.38
DIRECTIONS: CD906, between Vichy and Thiers.
MENU: 60 Frs (wine and coffee included).
RESTAURANT: Snacks from 5.00, lunch 11.00-15.00, dinner 19.00-22.00
CLOSED: Sun.
SPECIALITIES: home-cooking.

HOTEL: 6 rooms.
FACILITIES: shower, bath, private bathroom
OTHER POINTS: bar.
Vichy; Thiers; Clermont-Ferrand; mountains of the Bourbonnais; park at Livradois; Auvergne regional volcanic park.

ROFFIAC
Cantal, 15100

AUBERGE DE LA VALLEE
(Mr Pierre Farges)
TEL: 04.71.60.04.50
DIRECTIONS: RD826, St-Flour, towards Aurillac.
MENU: 55 to 150 Frs.
RESTAURANT: Snacks from 6.45, lunch 12.00-14.00, dinner 19.00-23.00
CLOSED: January.
SPECIALITIES: regional menu, home-cooking.
OTHER POINTS: credit cards accepted.

SAINT BONNET DE BELLAC
Haute-Vienne, 87300

L'ETAPE
(Mlle Catherine Garnotel) Route Nationale 147
TEL: 05.55.60.09.47
DIRECTIONS: RN 147, RN147, on the Poitiers/Limoges axis.
LANGUAGES: English, Spanish.
MENU: 58 Frs (drink included).
RESTAURANT: Snacks from 5.00
SPECIALITIES: home-cooking.
OTHER POINTS: credit cards accepted.

SAINT BONNET PRES RIOM
Puy-de-Dôme, 63200

LE BON COIN
(Mr Jean Levadoux) 2, rue de la République
TEL: 04.73.63.31.14
DIRECTIONS: RN143.
MENU: 50 Frs, (full-board 165 Frs).
OTHER POINTS: bar.

SAINT FLOUR
Cantal, 15100

LE PROGRES
(Mr Alain Mourgues) 61, rue des Lacs
TEL: 04.71.60.03.06
LANGUAGES: English, Spanish.
MENU: 55 to 220 Frs.
ROOMS: 150 to 220 Frs.
RESTAURANT: Snacks from 7.00, lunch 12.00-14.00, dinner 19.30-22.00
SPECIALITIES: Ativergnat specialities, regional menu.
HOTEL: ☆☆ 10 rooms.
FACILITIES: shower, bath, private bathroom, television, telephone
OTHER POINTS: credit cards accepted.
Garabit viaduct; circus at Mallet; cascade at Le Sailhant; plentiful rambling.

LES ROUTIERS
(Mme Liliane Teissèdre) 49, place de la Liberté
TEL: 04.71.60.23.00 FAX: 04.71.60.41.81
DIRECTIONS: RN9.
LANGUAGES: English, Spanish.
MENU: 60 to 100 Frs.
ROOMS: from 100 Frs.
RESTAURANT: Snacks from 7.30, lunch 12.00-16.00, dinner 19.00-22.00
CLOSED: Mon (out of season), and in Jan and Feb.
SPECIALITIES: tripoux de Saint-Flour, regional menu, home-cooking.
HOTEL: 7 rooms.
FACILITIES: shower
OTHER POINTS: credit cards accepted.
Garabit viaduct; circus at Mallet; Chaudes-Aigues; château at Alleuze-du-Sailbant; Desierres; Mont-Mouchet; cathedral at Saint-Flour.

SAINT GENCE
Haute-Vienne, 87510

LE CAMPANELLE
(Mr Albert Denardou) Campanelle
TEL: 05.55.48.02.83
DIRECTIONS: between Limoges and Bellegarde.
MENU: 60 Frs.
RESTAURANT: Snacks from 8.00, lunch 12.00-14.00, dinner 19.00-21.00
CLOSED: Sat, and in Aug.
SPECIALITIES: home-cooking.
OTHER POINTS: bar.

SAINT GEORGES D'AURAC
Haute-Loire, 43230

LES TILLEULS
(Mr Eric Crouzet) Route Nationale 102
TEL: 04.71.77.50.75
DIRECTIONS: RN102, between Le Puy-en-Velay and Clermont-Ferrand.
MENU: 52 Frs (wine and coffee included).
ROOMS: 90 to 100 Frs.
RESTAURANT: Snacks from 6.00, lunch 11.30-14.30, dinner 19.00-22.00
SPECIALITIES: home-cooking.
HOTEL: 8 rooms
OTHER POINTS: bar.
château at Chavagniac-la-Fayette.

SAINT JULIEN CHAPTEUIL
Haute-Loire, 43260

AUBERGE DU MEYCAL
(Mr René Chapuis) Boussoulet
TEL: 04.71.08.71.03
DIRECTIONS: RD15, Le Puy-en-Velay/Valence road.
MENU: 52 to 92 Frs.
ROOMS: 120 to 150 Frs.
RESTAURANT: Snacks from 8.00, lunch 12.00-13.15, dinner 19.00-20.30
SPECIALITIES: home-cooking,
HOTEL: ☆ 12 rooms.
FACILITIES: shower, bath, private bathroom, telephone
OTHER POINTS: bar.
château; 4 lakes (25km).

SAINT JUNIEN
Haute-Vienne, 87200

L'ETOILE
(Mr Alain Noble) 8, avenue Henri Barbusse
TEL: 05.55.02.15.19 FAX: 05.55.02.92.64
DIRECTIONS: RN141, Angoulème/Limoges road.
LANGUAGES: English.
MENU: 55 to 180 Frs.
ROOMS: 130 to 220 Frs (overnight stop 170 Frs).
RESTAURANT: Snacks from 6.30, lunch 11.00-16.00, dinner 19.30-22.00
CLOSED: Sun and 20th Dec to 6th Jan.
SPECIALITIES: home-cooking.
HOTEL: 10 rooms.
FACILITIES: shower, bath, private bathroom
OTHER POINTS: credit cards accepted.

SAINT JUST LE MARTEL
Haute-Vienne, 87590

LE PETIT SALE
(Mr Jean-Pierre Teyti) Les Chabanes
TEL: 05.55.09.21.14
DIRECTIONS: RD141, Clermont-Ferrand.
MENU: 60 to 170 Frs
ROOMS: 140 to 280 Frs.
RESTAURANT: Snacks from 7.00, lunch 12.00-15.00, dinner 19.00-22.00
SPECIALITIES: truite meunière aux amandes, saumon à l'oseille, raie aux câpres, magret de canard au poivre, pintade rotie, ris de veau sauce madère, boeuf limousin, regional menu.
HOTEL: ☆☆ 10 rooms.
FACILITIES: shower, bath, private bathroom, television, telephone
OTHER POINTS: credit cards accepted.
Limoges; porcelain factories; Aubusson tapestries; Saint-Léonard; Lac de Vassivière; château at Peyrat.

SAINT SORNIN LEULAC
Haute-Vienne, 87290

HOTEL DU CENTRE
(Mr Patrick Gaillac)
TEL: 05.55.76.32.54
DIRECTIONS: RN145, between La Croisière and Beltac.
LANGUAGES: English.
MENU: 50 Frs (wine and coffee included).
RESTAURANT: Snacks from 7.00
SPECIALITIES: home-cooking.
OTHER POINTS: credit cards accepted.
Lac de Saint-Pardoux; Le Dordat.

SAINT VICTURNIEN
Haute-Vienne, 87420

LE PUIS MALAIS
(Mr Mouh – SARL MBR) Route Nationale 141 – La Malaise
TEL: 05.55.03.87.03
DIRECTIONS: RN141, Limoges/Angoulème road.
MENU: 57 Frs (wine included) to 130 Frs.
RESTAURANT: Snacks from 6.00
SPECIALITIES: regional menu, home-cooking.
HOTEL: 8 rooms.
FACILITIES: shower
OTHER POINTS: credit cards accepted.
Oradour-sur-Glane (8km).

SAINT YORRE
Allier, 03270

NOUVEL HOTEL
(Mr Hubert Chesnel) 17, avenue de Vichy
TEL: 04.70.59.41.97 FAX: 04.70.59.47.30
DIRECTIONS: CD906, between Thiers and Vichy.
LANGUAGES: English.
MENU: 48 to 130 Frs.
ROOMS: 100 to 150 Frs.
RESTAURANT: Snacks from 6.30, lunch 11.45-14.30, dinner 17.45-21.30
CLOSED: Sat, and in Feb.
SPECIALITIES: home-cooking.
HOTEL: 12 rooms.
FACILITIES: shower, bath, private bathroom, television
OTHER POINTS: credit cards accepted.
château at Busset; Vichy: spa, park; crystallery; butterfly farm.

SOUTERRAINE (LA)
Creuse, 23300

LES ROUTIERS
(Mr Raymond Boutet) La Croisière Saint Maurice
TEL: 05.55.63.77.55
DIRECTIONS: RN145, between Limoges and Guéret.

MENU: 55 Frs.
ROOMS: 90 to 130 Frs.
RESTAURANT: Snacks from 5.30, lunch 12.00-15.00, dinner 19.00-22.00
CLOSED: Sun, public holidays and from 24th Dec to 2nd Jan.
SPECIALITIES: rognons au porto, coq au vin, potée auvergnate, home-cooking.
HOTEL: 11 rooms.
FACILITIES: shower
OTHER POINTS: credit cards accepted.
étang de la Cazine; étang du Cheix.

TOULON SUR ALLIER
Allier, 03400

LE RELAIS FLEURI
(Mr Alain Belain) Route Nationale 7
TEL: 04.70.20.40.18
DIRECTIONS: RN7, Lyon/Moulins.
MENU: 65.50 to 68 Frs.
RESTAURANT: Snacks from 7.00, lunch 12.00-14.00, dinner 19.00-22.00
CLOSED: Sun.
SPECIALITIES: home-cooking,
OTHER POINTS: credit cards accepted.

VARENNES SUR ALLIER
Allier, 03150

LA RENAISSANCE
(Mme Rose Gardel) Bellevue
TEL: 04.70.45.62.86
DIRECTIONS: RN7.
LANGUAGES: Portuguese.
RESTAURANT: Dinner -21.00
OTHER POINTS: bar.

VERNET LA VARENNE
Puy-de-Dôme, 63580

HOTEL DU COMMERCE
(Mme Raymonde Dégieux) Place Saint Roch
TEL: 04.73.71.31.73
DIRECTIONS: RD999, RD999, Issoire/Ambert/La-Chaise-Dieu.
LANGUAGES: English.
ROOMS: 150 to 200 Frs.
RESTAURANT: Snacks from 7.30
CLOSED: Mon afternoon (in winter).
SPECIALITIES: regional menu, home-cooking, jambon au champagne, écrevisses bordelaises, poularde aux morilles.
HOTEL: ☆ 20 rooms
OTHER POINTS: credit cards accepted.

VERNET LA VARENNE (LE)
Puy-de-Dôme, 63580

HOTEL DU CHATEAU
(Bernard et Denis – SNC Charnay-Magaud)
TEL: 04.73.71.31.79
DIRECTIONS: RD999, Issoire.
LANGUAGES: English.
MENU: 50 to 100 Frs.
ROOMS: 90 to 130 Frs.
RESTAURANT: Snacks from 7.30, lunch 12.00-14.00, dinner 19.30-21.00
CLOSED: Tues afternoon (from 3pm).
SPECIALITIES: potée auvergnate, terrines maison, regional menu, home-cooking.
HOTEL: 7 rooms.
FACILITIES: shower, bath, private bathroom
OTHER POINTS: credit cards accepted.
La Chaise-Dieu; Ambert; amethyst mines.

VICHY
Allier, 03200

RELAIS DE LA PASSERELLE
(Mr Jean-Pierre Pesce) 1, rue de Bordeaux
TEL: 04.70.98.57.70
DIRECTIONS: towards Thiers and Le Puy-en-Velay.
MENU: 50 Frs.
ROOMS: 80 to 140 Frs.
RESTAURANT: Snacks from 6.30, lunch 12.00-14.00, dinner 19.00-20.00
CLOSED: Sun, and in Aug.
SPECIALITIES: home-cooking.
HOTEL: 4 rooms.
FACILITIES: shower, telephone
OTHER POINTS: bar.
Vichy: spa and parks; pool; dam; salmon ladders.

VIEILLE BRIOUDE
Haute-Loire, 43100

LES GLYCINES
(Mme Viviane Chardonnal) Avenue de Versailles
TEL: 04.71.50.91.80 FAX: 04.71.50.92.90
DIRECTIONS: RN102, between Clermont-Ferrand and Le Puy-en-Velay.
LANGUAGES: English, Spanish.
MENU: 68 to 260 Frs.
ROOMS: 195 to 320 Frs.
RESTAURANT: Snacks from 7.00, lunch 12.00-14.00, dinner 19.30-21.00
CLOSED: in January.
SPECIALITIES: saumon, gibier (game) (in season).
HOTEL: ☆☆☆ 13 rooms.
FACILITIES: shower, bath, private bathroom, television, telephone

OTHER POINTS: credit cards accepted.
valley of the Allier; basilica; house of salmon; museum of lace-making; abbey at Lavandieu.

VOLVIC
Puy-de-Dôme, 63530

HOTEL DE LA NUGERE
(Mme Elisabeth Ternisien-Bourdon) Le Cratère
TEL: 04.73.33.50.47
DIRECTIONS: between Clermont-Ferrand and Limoges.
MENU: 55 to 85 Frs.
ROOMS: 80 to 110 Frs.
RESTAURANT: Snacks from 6.00, lunch 12.00-14.30, dinner 19.00-22.30
SPECIALITIES: specialities of Périgord, couscous, paella, regional menu, home-cooking.
HOTEL: 16 rooms.
FACILITIES: shower, bath
OTHER POINTS: bar.
the Puy de Dôme; maison de la pierre; château at La Tour Noël.

VOREY SUR ARZON
Haute-Loire, 43800

RESTAURANT DE LA BASCULE
(Mr Serge Hilaire) Place des Moulettes
TEL: 04.71.03.41.67
DIRECTIONS: RN103, between Saint-Etienne and Le Puy-en-Velay.
LANGUAGES: Italian.
ROOMS: 80 to 100 Frs.
RESTAURANT: Snacks from 6.30, lunch 11.45-15.00, dinner 19.00-21.30
SPECIALITIES: home-cooking.
HOTEL: 5 rooms
OTHER POINTS: bar.
Loire valley; Le Puy-en-Velay.

YSSINGEAUX
Haute-Loire, 43200

LA PETITE AUBERGE
(Mr Yves Drevet) Lieu dit "La Guide"
TEL: 04.71.65.57.75
DIRECTIONS: RN88, Saint-Etienne/Le Puy-en-Velay road.
MENU: 55 to 130 Frs.
ROOMS: 130 to 200 Frs.
RESTAURANT: Snacks from 6.00, lunch 12.00-15.00, dinner 19.30-21.30
CLOSED: Sat afternoon and Sun afternoon.
SPECIALITIES: regional menu, home-cooking.
HOTEL: 4 rooms
OTHER POINTS: credit cards accepted.
Le Puy-en-Velay; volcanic mountains in the Velay region; forêt du Meygal; dams; châteaux.

South-West France

The following départments are included in this chapter:

Ariège (09)
Aude (11)
Aveyron (12)
Dordogne (24)
Gard (30)
Gers (32)
Gironde (33)
Haute-Garonne (31)
Hautes-Pyrénnés (65)
Hérault (34)
Landes (40)
Lot (46)
Lot-et-Garonne (47)
Lozère (48)
Pyrénnés-Atlantiques (64)
Pyrénnés-Orientales (66)
Tarn (81)
Tarn-et-Garonne (82)

ABZAC
Gironde, 33230

LE GAULOIS
(Mr Jacques Lacoux) Tripoteau
TEL: 05.57.49.07.34
DIRECTIONS: RN84, road to Lyon.
MENU: 50 to 75 Frs.
RESTAURANT: Snacks from 5.00
SPECIALITIES: regional menu, home-cooking.
OTHER POINTS: credit cards accepted.
Saint-Emilion; Pomerol.

AGUESSAC
Aveyron, 12520

LE BALLON ROND
(Mr Guy Pailhas) Route Nationale 9
TEL: 05.65.59.80.18
DIRECTIONS: Millau/Gorges du Tarn.
MENU: 55 to 110 Frs.
ROOMS: 120 to 180 Frs.
RESTAURANT: Snacks from 7.30, lunch 12.00-14.00, dinner 19.30-21.00
SPECIALITIES: tripoux, daube, regional menu.
HOTEL: 6 rooms
OTHER POINTS: credit cards accepted.
gorges of the Tarn; Millau; Roquefort; La Couvertoirade; grottes (caves) de l'Aven Armand and Dargilan; lac du Levezou.

ALBAN
Tarn, 81250

RESTAURANT DU MIDI
(Mr Patrick Daurelle) 9, place des Tilleuls
TEL: 05.63.55.82.24 FAX: 05.63.55.89.73
DIRECTIONS: RD999, between Albi ind Millau.
LANGUAGES: Spanish.
MENU: 67 Frs (wine included).
RESTAURANT: Snacks from 7.00, lunch 12.00-14.00, dinner 19.00-21.00
CLOSED: Tues after 15.00, last week in Aug.
SPECIALITIES: daube, tripoux, regional menu, home-cooking.
OTHER POINTS: credit cards accepted.
Roquefort; Albi; Cistres; Cordes; gorges of the Tarn.

ALBI
Tarn, 81000

LE RELAIS CATALAN
(Mme Virginie Campin) Barrière de Montplaisir - Route de Millau
TEL: 05.63.60.27.00
DIRECTIONS: RD999, the Albi/Millau road.
LANGUAGES: English.
MENU: 65 Frs.
ROOMS: 110 Frs.
RESTAURANT: Snacks from 6.00, lunch 11.30-14.30, dinner 19.00-21.30
CLOSED: Sat, Sun and between Christmas and New Year.
SPECIALITIES: home-cooking.
HOTEL: 8 rooms
OTHER POINTS: credit cards accepted.
Albi; Cordes-sur-Ciel; Monesties; Ambialet.

LE RELAIS FLEURI
(Mr Pédro Casado) 25, avenue Franáois Verdier
DIRECTIONS: RN88, on the outskirts of Albi, coming from Toulouse.
LANGUAGES: Spanish.
MENU: 55 to 120 Frs.
ROOMS: 120 to 150 Frs.
RESTAURANT: Snacks from 7.30, lunch 11.00-15.00, dinner 19.00-22.00
CLOSED: Sun.
SPECIALITIES: regional menu, home-cooking,
HOTEL: 3 rooms.
FACILITIES: shower, bath, private bathroom
OTHER POINTS: bar.
cathedrals; musée Toulouse-Lautrec; musée de cire (wax); gorges of the Tarn.

AMBRES
Tarn, 81500

AUBERGE LES POMMIERS
(Mr Roland Leclerc) Le Grès
TEL: 05.63.58.05.56
DIRECTIONS: RD87, Toulouse/Albi motorway, Rabastens exit towards Lavaur.
LANGUAGES: English, Spanish.
MENU: 59 to 100 Frs.
ROOMS: 110 to 200 Frs.
RESTAURANT: Snacks from 7.00, lunch 11.30-15.00, dinner 19.00-21.00
SPECIALITIES: regional menu, home-cooking.
HOTEL: ☆ 8 rooms.
FACILITIES: shower
OTHER POINTS: credit cards accepted.

ANTONNE ET TRIGONANT
Dordogne, 24420

LE RELAIS DE LAURIERE
(Mr Jean-Claude Condaminas) Laurière
TEL: 05.53.06.17.92
DIRECTIONS: RN21, between Périgueux and Limoges.
LANGUAGES: English.
MENU: 58 Frs (wine and coffee included).
ROOMS: 80 Frs.
SPECIALITIES: terrine, rillette maison, petit salé (pickled pork), regional menu, home-cooking.
HOTEL: 4 rooms
OTHER POINTS: credit cards accepted.
Périgueux (10km): Renaissance château (1kM); Hautefort (20km).

ARDOISE (L')
Gard, 30290

LE CHALET
(Mme Sylvie Barrez) Route Nationale 580
TEL: 04.66.50.22.22
LANGUAGES: English, Spanish, Italian.
MENU: 95 Frs.
ROOMS: 150 to 190 Frs.
RESTAURANT: Snacks from 6.30
CLOSED: Sat evening, Sun evening.
SPECIALITIES: croñte morille, poulet au sang (vin de Bourgogne), regional menu.
HOTEL: 8 rooms.
FACILITIES: shower
OTHER POINTS: bar.
gorges of the Ardèche (3Okm); Nîmes (35km); Avignon (25km).

ASPIRAN
Hérault, 34800

LE RELAIS DE LA GARE
(Mr Gilles Duffours) Route Nationale 9
TEL: 04.67.96.55.48
DIRECTIONS: RN9.
MENU: 63 Frs.
RESTAURANT: Snacks from 7.00, lunch 11.30-15.00, dinner 19.00-22.00
CLOSED: Sun.
SPECIALITIES: regional menu, home-cooking.
OTHER POINTS: credit cards accepted.
Lake at Salagou; Pézenas; Le Pont du Diable (the Devil's Bridge).

ASTAFFORT
Lot-et-Garonne, 47220

LE RELAIS DES PYRENEES
(Mr Claude Parma) Barbonvièle
TEL: 05.53.67.14.57
DIRECTIONS: RN21, the Agen/Lourdes road.
LANGUAGES: Spanish, Italian.
MENU: 62 Frs.
RESTAURANT: Snacks from 5.30, lunch 9.00, dinner up to 20.00
CLOSED: Sun.
SPECIALITIES: magrets de canard aux cêpes (to order), regional menu, home-cooking.
OTHER POINTS: credit cards accepted.
châteaux; Armagnac cellars (25-km radius).

AUCAMVILLE
Haute-Garonne, 31140

LE TOIT
(Mr Jean-Pierre Lablanche) 50, chaussée des Mazuries
TEL: 05.61.70.46.37
LANGUAGES: Spanish.
RESTAURANT: dinner up to24.00
OTHER POINTS: bar.

AUSSILLON MAZAMET
Tarn, 81200

CHEZ PHILOU - LE COMMERCE
(Mr Philippe Barreau) 21, avenue Charles Sabatier
TEL: 05.63.61.26.16
DIRECTIONS: RN112, the Albi/Beziers road.
LANGUAGES: English, Spanish.
MENU: 60 Frs.
RESTAURANT: Snacks from 6.15, lunch 12.00-15.00, dinner 20.00-22.00
CLOSED: Sun.

SPECIALITIES: regional menu, home-cooking.
OTHER POINTS: credit cards accepted.
la montagne noire.

AUZITS
Aveyron, 12390

IGUE DU MOULIN
(Mr Bruno Nogaret) Route Nationale 140
TEL: 05.65.63.90.90
DIRECTIONS: RN140, the Brive/Mediterranean road.
MENU: 60 Frs.
RESTAURANT: Snacks from 6.00, lunch 12.00 14.00, dinner 19.00-21.00
CLOSED: Sat.
SPECIALITIES: stockfish, soupe an fromage, regional menu, home-cooking.
OTHER POINTS: bar.
Conques; Decazeville; 'la Découverte' mine.

AVIGNONET LAURAGAIS
Haute-Garonne, 31290

LA PERGOLA
(Mr Etienne Batan) Route Nationale 113
TEL: 05.61.81.63.54 FAX: 05.61.27.82.76
DIRECTIONS: RN113, between Villefranche and Castelnaudary.
LANGUAGES: English, Spanish.
MENU: 60 to 135 Frs.
ROOMS: 115 to 185 Frs.
RESTAURANT: Snacks from 7.00, lunch 12.00-14.30, dinner 19.30-21.30
CLOSED: Sat evening, Sun evening, and in Feb (school holidays).
SPECIALITIES: cassoulet, confits, regional menu, home-cooking.
HOTEL: 6 rooms.
FACILITIES: shower
OTHER POINTS: credit cards accepted.
Port Lauragais: musée Pierre-Paul Riquet; canal du Midi watershed.

AZERAT
Dordogne, 24210

LE RELAIS D'AZERAT - Chez Annie
(Mme Annie Debord)
TEL: 05.53.05.21.05
DIRECTIONS: RN89, between Périgueux and Brive-la-Gaillarde.
RESTAURANT: Snacks from 6.00, lunch 12.00, dinner 19.00
CLOSED: the last 2 weeks in Aug.
SPECIALITIES: home-cooking.
HOTEL: 4 rooms
OTHER POINTS: bar.
grottes (caves) de Lascaux (12km); château d'Hautefort (20km).

BACCARETS (LES)
Haute-Garonne, 31550

LA CHAUMIERE
(Mr Daniel Laroche) Route Nationale 20 - Cintegabelle
TEL: 05.61.08.90.70
DIRECTIONS: RN20, the Toulouse/Foix road.
MENU: 55 Frs.
ROOMS: 85 to 115 Frs.
RESTAURANT: Snacks from 6.00
CLOSED: Sun, and one week from Christmas Day.
SPECIALITIES: home-cooking.
HOTEL: 12 rooms
OTHER POINTS: credit cards accepted.

BAGNAC SUR CELE
Lot, 46270

RELAIS ROUTIERS LA PLANQUETTE
(Mme Micheline Claudon) Route d'Aurillac
TEL: 05.65.34.93.50
DIRECTIONS: RN122, between Aurillac and Figeac.
MENU: 55 to 65 Frs.
ROOMS: 120 to 140 Frs.
RESTAURANT: Snacks from 7.00, lunch 11.30-14.00, dinner 19.00-21.00
CLOSED: Mon afternoon.
SPECIALITIES: home-cooking.
HOTEL: 4 rooms
OTHER POINTS: bar.

BAIGTS DE BEARN
Pyrénées-Atlantiques, 64300

LE RELAIS DE BAIGTS
(Mme Danièle Austruy)
TEL: 05.59.62.32.42
DIRECTIONS: RN117.
LANGUAGES: English, Spanish.
MENU: 56 to 120 Frs.
ROOMS: 130 to 220 Frs.
RESTAURANT: Snacks from 6.30, lunch 12.00-14.30, dinner 19.00-22.00
SPECIALITIES: regional menu,
HOTEL: 13 rooms.
FACILITIES: private bathroom, television
OTHER POINTS: credit cards accepted.

BAIGTS EN CHALOSSE
Landes, 40380

LE CARREFOUR
(Mr Jean Bonnot) Le Carrefour
TEL: 05.58.98.63.05
DIRECTIONS: RD2, between Dax and Saint-Sever.

MENU: 55 to 190 Frs.
ROOMS: 90 Frs.
RESTAURANT: Snacks from 7.00, lunch 12.00-14.00, dinner 20.00-21.00
CLOSED: Mon.
SPECIALITIES: Burgundian dishes, home-cooking.
HOTEL: 4 rooms.
FACILITIES: shower, bath, private bathroom
OTHER POINTS: credit cards accepted.

BALARUC LE VIEUX
Hérault, 34540

LA SOURCE
(Mr Paul Amidieu) Lieu dit : Issanka
TEL: 04.67.78.72.85 **FAX:** 04.67.78.65.19
DIRECTIONS: RN113, Gigean, the Sète/Poussan axis.
LANGUAGES: English, German, Spanish.
MENU: 62 Frs.
RESTAURANT: Snacks from 5.00, lunch 12.00-14.30, dinner 19.00-22.00
CLOSED: Sat evening and Sun.
SPECIALITIES: rouille sétoise, bourride de merlu, regional menu, home-cooking.
HOTEL: 9 rooms.
FACILITIES: shower, bath, private bathroom
OTHER POINTS: credit cards accepted.
étang de Thau; Mont Saint-Clair; cimetière marin (sailors' cemetery); musée George-Brassens; abbaye de Valimagne; parc à huitres (oyster beds).

BANYULS DELS ASPRES
Pyrénées-Orientales, 66300

LA TOUR CATALOGNE
(Mr Vincent Oltra) Village Catalan Aire de repos A.9
TEL: 04.68.21.74.81
DIRECTIONS: A9/N9.
LANGUAGES: English, Spanish.
MENU: 62 Frs.
RESTAURANT: Snacks from 11.00, lunch 11.00-16.00, dinner 18.00-23.00
SPECIALITIES: regional menu.
OTHER POINTS: credit cards accepted.

BARAQUEVILLE
Aveyron, 12160

LE PALOUS
(Mrs Cluzel, Druilhe et Palous) 184, avenue du Centre
TEL: 05.65.69.01.89 **FAX:** 05.65.69.10.80
DIRECTIONS: at the crossroads of the Albi/Montauban/Millau/Rodez roads.
LANGUAGES: English.
MENU: 60 Frs.
ROOMS: 215 to 235 Frs.
RESTAURANT: Snacks from 6.30
CLOSED: public holidays and for 1 Week at Christmas
SPECIALITIES: tripoux, magret, confit de canard, foie gras, regional menu.
HOTEL: ☆☆ 16 rooms.
FACILITIES: shower, bath, private bathroom, television, telephone
OTHER POINTS: credit cards accepted.
Sauveterre-de-Rouergue; viaduct at Le Viaur; lac de Pareloup; Conques.

BASTIDE L'EVEQUE (LA)
Aveyron, 12200

RELAIS DE L'HERMET
(Mr Yvan Bourdoncle) Route Départementale 911
TEL: 05.65.65.61.41
DIRECTIONS: RD911.
OTHER POINTS: bar.

BEAUCHALOT
Haute-Garonne, 31360

AU BEARNAIS
(Mr René Fréchou) Saint Martory
TEL: 05.61.98.01.01
DIRECTIONS: RN117, 10Km from St-Gaudens towards Tarbes on the the Toulouse/Bayonne road.
LANGUAGES: English, Spanish.
MENU: 60 to 200 Frs.
ROOMS: 120 to 170 Frs.
RESTAURANT: Snacks from 7.00, lunch 12.00-14.00, dinner 19.00-20.30
CLOSED: Mon, and in Sept.
SPECIALITIES: garbure (thick soup) béarnaise, foie gras, confit de canard, civet de chevreuil (venison), regional menu, home-cooking.
HOTEL: 5 rooms.
FACILITIES: shower, private bathroom
OTHER POINTS: bar.
Saint-Bernard-de-Comminges.

BERCHEM
Gironde, 3325

L'ARCHE DE LUXEMBOURG BERCHEM
AE25 - Aire de Berchem Ouest - Accessible sens Bruxelles/Metz
OTHER POINTS: credit cards accepted.

BERCHEM BETTEMBOURG
Gers, 3201

L'ARCHE DE BERCHEM
(Mr Aimé Henry) Autoroute E25 Aire de berchem Ouest BP 72
TEL: (352) 52.17.40 **FAX:** (352) 52.17.41

DIRECTIONS: autoroute E25, autoroute E25, in the Brussels/Metz direction.
RESTAURANT: Open 24h.
OTHER POINTS: children's menu.

BERNOS BEAULAC

Gironde, 33430

LE RESTORELAIS

(SARL Lamy-Lefèvre) Bois de Fond
TEL: 05.56.25.45.05
DIRECTIONS: RD932, Pau.
MENU: 56.50 to 67 Frs.
RESTAURANT: Snacks from 5.00, lunch 11.00-15.00, dinner 19.00-22.30
CLOSED: Sat afternoon and Sun.
SPECIALITIES: confit de canard, entrecôte, foie gras, regional menu, home-cooking.
OTHER POINTS: credit cards accepted.
châteaux de Roquetaillade and de Préchacq.

BERTHOLENE

Aveyron, 12310

HOTEL BANCAREL

(Mr Jean Brun) Route Nationale 88
TEL: 05.65.69.62.10 **FAX:** 05.65.70.72.88
DIRECTIONS: RN88, between Rodez and Millau.
MENU: 55 to 150 Frs.
ROOMS: 150 to 240 Frs.
RESTAURANT: Snacks from 7.00, lunch 12.00-14.00, dinner 19.00-21.00
CLOSED: from 25th Sept to 15th Oct, and last 2 weeks in Jan.
SPECIALITIES: choux farci à la paysanne, confit de canard, feuilleté au roquefort, regional menu.
HOTEL: ☆ 13 rooms.
FACILITIES: shower, bath, private bathroom, television
OTHER POINTS: credit cards accepted.
lac du Levezou; trou de Bozouls; gorges of the Tarn and the Lot; lac de Pareloup; forêt des palanges; rivers (fishing).

BEZIERS

Hérault, 34000

L'OPPIDUM

(Mr Alain Cherrier) Route Nationale 113
TEL: 04.67.28.30.34
DIRECTIONS: RN113, exit Béziers Ouest (West) (3km).
LANGUAGES: English.
MENU: 65 Frs.
ROOMS: 90 to 160 Frs.
RESTAURANT: Snacks from 6.30, dinner 19.00-22.00
CLOSED: Sat afternoon and Sun.
HOTEL: 16 rooms.
FACILITIES: shower
OTHER POINTS: bar.
Sète; Roman site; les 7 écluses (locks).

LA VITARELLE

(Mr Christophe Comandini) Route Nationale 112 - La Vitarelle - Portiragnes
TEL: 04.67.90.88.90
DIRECTIONS: RN112, between Béziers and Sète.
LANGUAGES: English, German, Spanish, Italian.
MENU: 60 Frs (wine included) to 198 Frs.
ROOMS: 100 to 250 Frs.
RESTAURANT: Snacks from 6.45, lunch 11.45-15.00, dinner 18.45-22.00
CLOSED: Sun evening (out of season).
SPECIALITIES: paella, couscous, regional menu, home-cooking.
HOTEL: 28 rooms.
FACILITIES: shower, bath, private bathroom, television, telephone
OTHER POINTS: credit cards accepted.
Greco-Roman churches at Agde and Béziers; les 9 écluses (locks) (unique in Europe); Cap d'Agde; Sète; étang (pool) de Thau.

RELAIS ROUTIER LE CANTAGAL

(Mr Christian Mourier) Route de Pézenas - Route Nle 113
TEL: 04.67.31.25.47
DIRECTIONS: RN113, Pezenas/Millau/Montpellier road.
LANGUAGES: Spanish.
MENU: 65 Frs.
RESTAURANT: Snacks from 6.30, lunch 11.30-14.30, dinner 19.00-22.00
CLOSED: Sat evening and Sun.
SPECIALITIES: regional menu, home-cooking.
OTHER POINTS: credit cards accepted.
Canal du Midi; Oppidum; beaches; Agde; Valras.

BIARS SUR CERE

Lot, 46130

CHEZ ALAIN

(Mr Alain Cavalhac) 16, avenue de la République
TEL: 05.65.38.42.30
DIRECTIONS: RN140.
RESTAURANT: Lunch 12.00-15.00, dinner 19.00-22.30
CLOSED: Sun, and in Aug.
SPECIALITIES: home-cooking.
HOTEL: 4 rooms
OTHER POINTS: bar.
Rocamadour; gouffre de Padirac; château at Castelnau.

BLAYE LES MINES

Tarn, 81400

LE RELAIS SAINTE MARIE

(Mme Marie-Louise Bernier) 53, avenue d'Albi

TEL: 05.63.76.53.81
DIRECTIONS: RN88, Toulouse/Rodez road.
MENU: 65 Frs.
ROOMS: 90 to 180 Frs.
RESTAURANT: Snacks from 7.00
CLOSED: Sat and Sun.
SPECIALITIES: regional menu.
HOTEL: 7 rooms.
FACILITIES: shower, bath, private bathroom
OTHER POINTS: bar.
open-cast mines.

BORDEAUX
Gironde, 33800

L'INTER DES ROUTIERS
(Mme Marie-Thérèse Dubesset) 295, cours Balguerie Stuttenber
TEL: 02.56.43.15.47
DIRECTIONS: RN10
LANGUAGES: Spanish, Portuguese.
RESTAURANT: Snacks from 6.30, lunch 11.30-15.00, dinner 19.00-23.00
CLOSED: Sat afternoon and Sun, and public holidays.
SPECIALITIES: home-cooking,
OTHER POINTS: bar.

RESTAURANT DE L'UNION
(Mr Dominique Depeyris) 116, rue Lucien Faure
TEL: 05.56.50.05.77
DIRECTIONS: RN10, Bordeaux centre.
LANGUAGES: English.
MENU: 54 Frs.
RESTAURANT: Snacks from 6.00
CLOSED: Sat, Sun, and in Aug.
SPECIALITIES: home-cooking.
OTHER POINTS: bar.

LE RELAIS D'AUVERGNE
(Mr Djamel Chouar) 131bis, quai des Chartrons
TEL: 05.56.39.27.78
LANGUAGES: Dutch, Arabic.
MENU: 55 Frs (wine and coffee included).
RESTAURANT: Snacks from 10.00, lunch 12.00, dinner 19.30-24.00
SPECIALITIES: home-cooking, couscous.
OTHER POINTS: bar.

AU BON ACCUEIL
(Mr Fidel Gonzalez) 12, quai de la Monnaie
TEL: 02.56.91.05.26
LANGUAGES: Spanish, Italian.
MENU: 49 to 95 Frs.
RESTAURANT: Snacks from 8.30, lunch 12.00-14.15, dinner 19.00-23.00
CLOSED: Sat evening, Sun and in Aug.
SPECIALITIES: home-cooking.
OTHER POINTS: bar.

BORDEAUX BASTIDE
Gironde, 33100

LE PORTO
(Mme Rosa-Maria Pereira) 202bis, quai de Brazza
TEL: 02.56.86.15.93
DIRECTIONS: RN10, Bordeaux right bank, towards Lormont.
LANGUAGES: Spanish, Portuguese.
MENU: 57.50 to 65 Frs.
RESTAURANT: Snacks from 6.30, lunch 11.30, dinner up to 22.30
CLOSED: Sat, Sun, public holidays and in Aug.
SPECIALITIES: Portuguese dishes, home-cooking.
HOTEL: 12 rooms.
FACILITIES: shower, bath, private bathroom
OTHER POINTS: credit cards accepted.
Bordeaux: place des Quinconces, cathedral, grand théâtre.

BOUCOIRAN
Gard, 30190

LE TAHURE
(Mme Yolande Martin) Route Nationale 106 - Pont de Ners
TEL: 04.66.83.36.36
DIRECTIONS: RN 106, RN106, on the Nîmes/Alès axis.
LANGUAGES: English, Spanish.
MENU: 55 Frs.
RESTAURANT: Snacks from 4.00
SPECIALITIES: home-cooking.
OTHER POINTS: credit cards accepted.

BRAM
Aude, 11150

CHEZ ALAIN
(Mr Alain Albecq) Route Nationale 113
TEL: 04.68.76.53.16
DIRECTIONS: RN113, between Carcassonne and Toulouse.
LANGUAGES: Spanish.
MENU: 67 Frs.
ROOMS: 150 Frs.
RESTAURANT: Snacks from 5.00, lunch 11.00-15.00, dinner 19.00-23.00
CLOSED: Sat, Sun, and in Aug.
SPECIALITIES: cassoulet, escargots, tripes, blanquettes, civets (game stew), regional menu, home-cooking.
HOTEL: 11 rooms.
FACILITIES: shower, bath, private bathroom, television, telephone
OTHER POINTS: credit cards accepted.
Carcassonne; cathedral at Montréal (8km); Ariège; Andorra.

BROUZET LES ALES
Gard, 30580

AUBERGE DES CAMBONS
(Mr Joseph Mastrosimone)
TEL: 04.66.83.15.13
DIRECTIONS: RD6, between Alès and Bagnols-sur-Cèze.
MENU: 60 Frs.
RESTAURANT: Snacks from 6.30
CLOSED: Sat lunchtime out of season.
SPECIALITIES: escargots, couscous, choucroute, home-cooking.
OTHER POINTS: children's menu.

CAHORS PERN
Lot, 46170

LE RELAIS DES CIGALES
(Mr José-Manuel Fernandez) Route Nationale 20 - Saint Barthelemy
TEL: 05.65.21.97.49 FAX: 05.65.21.86.66
DIRECTIONS: RN20, the Cahors/Toulouse road.
LANGUAGES: English, Spanish.
MENU: 58 to 128 Frs.
ROOMS: 150 Frs.
RESTAURANT: Snacks from 5.00, lunch 12.00-15.00, dinner 19.00-23.00
CLOSED: Sun.
SPECIALITIES: magrets, cassoulet au confit d'oie, foie gras, regional menu, home-cooking.
HOTEL: 14 rooms.
FACILITIES: shower, bath, private bathroom, television
OTHER POINTS: credit cards accepted.
Cahors; Lot valley; caves at Rocamadour; gouffre de Padirac; gorges of the Aveyron.

CALMETTE (LA)
Gard, 30190

LE RELAIS DE L'ESCALETTE
(Mr Georges Apostolakis) Route Nationale 6
TEL: 04.66.63.13.63
DIRECTIONS: RN6.
LANGUAGES: English.
RESTAURANT: dinner up to 24.00
CLOSED: Sun.
OTHER POINTS: bar.

CAMPAGNAC
Aveyron, 12560

LA FERME DE BONSECOURS
(Mme Corinne Vayssie) A.75 - sortie 41
TEL: 05.65.47.64.77 FAX: 05.65.47.67.96
MENU: 65 to 170 Frs.
RESTAURANT: Snacks from 6.00
CLOSED: Sat evening (except bookings).
SPECIALITIES: regional menu, home-cooking.
OTHER POINTS: credit cards accepted.
medieval château de Séverac; gorges of the Tarn; medieval village; cave (cellar) de Roquefort.

CAMPSEGRET
Dordogne, 24140

LES TAMARIS
(Mr Alain Thomas) La Croix - Route Nationale 32
TEL: 05.53.24.21.75
DIRECTIONS: RN21, between Bergerac and Périgueux.
LANGUAGES: English.
MENU: 55 to 150 Frs.
ROOMS: 150 to 180 Frs.
RESTAURANT: Snacks from 6.00, dinner 19.00-23.00
CLOSED: Sun evening (out of season).
SPECIALITIES: foie gras mi-cuit, salade du Périgord, noix de Saint-Jacques à la crème de crevettes, filet de saumon, magret aux trois poivres, tournedos aux cêpes, regional menu, home-cooking.
HOTEL: ☆ 11 rooms.
FACILITIES: shower, bath, private bathroom, television, telephone
OTHER POINTS: credit cards accepted.

CAP DE PIN
Landes, 40210

AU ROUTIER
(Mr Jean-Pierre Fortinon) Escource
TEL: 05.58.07.20.54
DIRECTIONS: RN10, Sabres, exit 15.
MENU: 70 to 230 Frs.
ROOMS: 150 to 250 Frs.
RESTAURANT: Snacks from 6.30, lunch 12.00-14.30, dinner 19.30-22.30
CLOSED: Sun, and 3 weeks from 23th Dec to 16th Jan.
SPECIALITIES: salade de foie de canard frais, ris de veau madère, magret grillé, regional menu.
HOTEL: 15 rooms.
FACILITIES: shower
OTHER POINTS: credit cards accepted.
musée de Marquèze (18km); beach at Mimizan (30km).

CASSEUIL
Gironde, 33190

LE RELAIS DE CASSEUIL
(Mr René Boudeyron) Route Nationale 113
TEL: 05.56.71.10.65
DIRECTIONS: RN 113, RN113, between Langon and La Réole.
MENU: 55 to 75 Frs.
RESTAURANT: Snacks from 6.00, lunch 12.00-14.00, dinner 19.30-22.00

CLOSED: Sun.
SPECIALITIES: home-cooking.
OTHER POINTS: credit cards accepted.

CASTELNAU RIVIERE BASSE
Hautes-Pyrénées, 65700

LE RELAIS DE MADIRAN
(Mr Michel Ducasse) Route de Bordeaux
TEL: 05.62.31.97.99
DIRECTIONS: RD935, between Aire-sur-l'Adour and Tarbes.
LANGUAGES: Spanish, Italian, Portuguese.
MENU: 55 to 105 Frs.
RESTAURANT: Snacks from 6.30, lunch 11.30-14.00, dinner 19.30-21.00
CLOSED: Sun (out of season) evenings in summer, and in Aug.
SPECIALITIES: gambas à la crème, magret grillé, regional menu, home-cooking.
OTHER POINTS: bar.
vine-growing region; Madiran; Pachrenc; les courses landaises (entertaining and bloodless mock bullfights).

CASTELSARRASIN
Tarn-et-Garonne, 82100

CHEZ MAURICE
(Mr Jean-Pierre Boissier) 35, route de Toulouse
TEL: 05.63.32.30.83
DIRECTIONS: RN113, the Toulouse/Bordeaux road.
MENU: 63 to 90 Frs.
ROOMS: 100 to 140 Frs.
RESTAURANT: Snacks from 5.00, lunch 12.00-15.00, dinner 19.00-23.00
CLOSED: Sat evening, Sun, and 3 weeks in Aug.
SPECIALITIES: cassoulet, magrets de canard, confits, foie gras maison, blanquette de veau, regional menu, home-cooking.
HOTEL: 15 rooms.
FACILITIES: shower
OTHER POINTS: bar.
Moissac; Auvillar; canal du Midi; Saint-Antonin-Noble-Val.

CASTETS
Landes, 40260

CENTRE ROUTIER
(Mr Fernand Judes)
TEL: 05.58.55.01.67 FAX: 05.58.55.01.69
DIRECTIONS: RN10.
MENU: 60 Frs (wine included).
RESTAURANT: Snacks from 5.00
SPECIALITIES: regional menu, home-cooking.
OTHER POINTS: credit cards accepted.

CASTETS DES LANDES
Landes, 40260

LE STUC
(Mme Danielle Calleja)
TEL: 05.58.89.40.62
DIRECTIONS: RN10.
LANGUAGES: Spanish, Portuguese.
MENU: 50 Frs.
RESTAURANT: Snacks from 7.00, lunch 12.00-14.30
CLOSED: Sun (out of season), and 15th Oct to 15th Nov.
SPECIALITIES: home-cooking.
OTHER POINTS: credit cards accepted.
lakes.

CASTRES
Tarn, 81100

AUX AMIS DE LA ROUTE
(Mr Michel Labessouille) 247, avenue Charles de Gaulle
TEL: 05.63.35.54.38
DIRECTIONS: RN622, the Mazamet road.
MENU: 65 Frs.
RESTAURANT: Snacks from 6.00, lunch 12.00-15.00, dinner 19.30-22.00
SPECIALITIES: couscous, cassoulet, home-cooking.
OTHER POINTS: credit cards accepted.
Sidobre region; musée Goya; jardin de l'Exéché.

CAUNEILLE
Landes, 40300

AU HAOU
(Mme Henriette Lalanne) Route Nationale 117
TEL: 05.58.73.04.60
DIRECTIONS: RN117.
RESTAURANT: dinner up to 23.00
CLOSED: from 20th Dec for 2 weeks.
OTHER POINTS: bar.

CAUSSADE
Tarn-et-Garonne, 82300

LE RELAIS D'AUVERGNE
(Mr Pierre Saint-Paul) Z.I. de Meaux
TEL: 05.63.93.03.89
DIRECTIONS: RN20, between Montauban and Cahors.
MENU: 55 to 108 Frs.
ROOMS: 95 to 165 Frs.
RESTAURANT: Snacks from 6.00, lunch 11.30-14.30, dinner 19.00-21.00
CLOSED: Sun.
SPECIALITIES: cassoulet, grillades (grills), confit de canard, home-cooking.
HOTEL: 15 rooms.
FACILITIES: shower, bath, private bathroom

OTHER POINTS: credit cards accepted.
gorges of the Tarn; Saint-Antonin; Bruniquel.

CENAC
Dordogne, 24250

LA PROMENADE
(Mr Pascal Thomas) Route Nationale 703
TEL: 05.53.28.36.87
DIRECTIONS: RN703, Sarlat/Domme.
MENU: 55 to 150 Frs.
ROOMS: 120 to 170 Frs.
RESTAURANT: Snacks from 7.00, lunch 12.00-14.00, dinner 19.00-21.00
SPECIALITIES: regional menu.
HOTEL: 4 rooms
OTHER POINTS: credit cards accepted.
the heart of 'Périgord noir'.

CESTAS
Gironde, 33610

CHEZ NANOU
(Mme Anne-Marie Marcon) 101, avenue de Tassigny
TEL: 05.56.68.02.44
DIRECTIONS: RN250, Bordeaux/Arcachon axis.
LANGUAGES: English, Spanish.
MENU: 55 Frs (wine and coffee included).
RESTAURANT: Snacks from 7.00, lunch 11.30-14.30, dinner 19.00-21.30
CLOSED: Sun.
SPECIALITIES: home-cooking.
OTHER POINTS: credit cards accepted.
Arcachon.

CHAUDEYRAC
Lozère, 48170

HOTEL DE FRANCE
(Mr Yves Trémoulet) Route Nationale 88
TEL: 04.66.47.91.00 **FAX:** 04.66.47.93.29
DIRECTIONS: RN88, the Lyon/Toulouse road.
LANGUAGES: Spanish.
MENU: 50 to 150 Frs.
ROOMS: 180 to 230 Frs.
RESTAURANT: Snacks from 6.00, lunch 12.00-15.00, dinner 18.00-22.00
SPECIALITIES: regional menu, home-cooking.
HOTEL: ☆ 12 rooms.
FACILITIES: shower, bath, private bathroom, television, telephone
OTHER POINTS: credit cards accepted.
lac de Naussac; Notre-Dame-des-Neiges; gorges of the Tarn.

COLOMBIERS
Hérault, 34440

LA GRILLADE
(Mr Lionel Gilhodes) Route de Narbonne
TEL: 04.67.37.26.01 **FAX:** 04.67.37.66.94
DIRECTIONS: RN113, Narbonne.
LANGUAGES: English.
MENU: 59.50 Frs (wine and coffee included) to 128 Frs.
ROOMS: 175 to 225 Frs.
RESTAURANT: Snacks from 6.00, lunch 12.00-14.00, dinner 19.30-22.00
CLOSED: Sun.
SPECIALITIES: home-cooking.
HOTEL: ☆☆ 30 rooms.
FACILITIES: shower, bath, private bathroom, television, telephone
OTHER POINTS: credit cards accepted.
canal du Midi; beach (14km).

CONILHAC CORBIERES
Aude, 11200

LE CERS
(Mr Antoine Mata) Route Nationale 113
TEL: 04.68.27.07.64
DIRECTIONS: RN113, the Toulouse/Narbonne axis.
LANGUAGES: Spanish.
MENU: 55 to 70 Frs.
RESTAURANT: Snacks from 6.00, lunch 11.30-15.00, dinner 19.00-23.00
CLOSED: Sun out of season.
SPECIALITIES: cassoulet, paëlla, calamars à la provenáale, regional menu, home-cooking.
OTHER POINTS: bar.

L'ONCLE ET LE NEVEU
(Mr Gilbert Delbourg) Route Nationale 113
TEL: 04.68.27.44.51
DIRECTIONS: RN 113, RN113, between Narbonne and Carcassonne.
LANGUAGES: Spanish.
MENU: 55 Frs.
ROOMS: 100 Frs.
RESTAURANT: Snacks from 5.00
SPECIALITIES: home-cooking.
HOTEL: 7 rooms
OTHER POINTS: credit cards accepted.

COQUILLE (LA)
Dordogne, 24450

LES PORTES DU PERIGORD VERT
(Mr Jean-Pierre Deyts) Route Nationale 21
TEL: 05.53.52.83.46
DIRECTIONS: the Périgueux/Limoges road.
MENU: 55 to 120 Frs (wine included).

RESTAURANT: Snacks from 5.30
SPECIALITIES: Périgord dishes, regional menu, home-cooking.
OTHER POINTS: bar.
grottes (eaves) de Villard; Jumilhac-le-Grand; Puiguilham.

COUX ET BIGAROQUE (LE)
Dordogne, 24220

LE PETIT CHAPERON ROUGE
(Mr Fabrice Constant) La Faval
TEL: 05.53.29.37.79 FAX: 05.53.29.46.63
DIRECTIONS: Saint Cyprien/Périgueux.
LANGUAGES: English, German.
MENU: 60 Frs (wine included) to 200 Frs.
ROOMS: 130 to 240 Frs.
RESTAURANT: Snacks from 8.00, lunch 12.00-14.00, dinner 19.30-22.00
SPECIALITIES: regional menu, home-cooking, magret à la gelée de Pécharmant, fricassée de gambas et de calamars, brochet farci à l'Oseille, gibiers (in season).
HOTEL: 12 rooms
OTHER POINTS: credit cards accepted.

CRAYSSAC
Lot, 46150

LE BIENVENUE
(Mme Idalia Campos Ferreira) Mas de Costes
TEL: 05.65.30.97.06 FAX: 05.65.30.79.22
DIRECTIONS: RD911, between Cahors and Fumel.
LANGUAGES: English, Spanish, Portuguese.
MENU: 60 Frs (wine and coffee included) to 80 Frs.
RESTAURANT: Snacks from 7.00, lunch 11.30-14.00, dinner 19.00
SPECIALITIES: mique, tourin, confits de canard, regional menu, home-cooking.
OTHER POINTS: credit cards accepted.

CUQ TOULZA
Tarn, 81470

LE RELAIS CHEZ ALAIN
(Mr Alain Pratviel) La Bombardière
TEL: 05.63.75.70.36
DIRECTIONS: RD621, Between Toulouse and Castres.
LANGUAGES: English, Spanish.
MENU: 65 to 300 Frs.
ROOMS: 120 to 240 Frs.
RESTAURANT: Snacks from 5.00, lunch 11.00-15.00, dinner 19.00-22.00
SPECIALITIES: home-cooking, bouillabaisse, regional menu.
HOTEL: ☆ 9 rooms.
FACILITIES: shower, bath, private bathroom, television, telephone
OTHER POINTS: credit cards accepted.
lac de Saint-Ferréol; Sidobre region; château and circuit de Pastel.

CUXAC CABARDES
Aude, 11390

LA MONTAGNE NOIR - Chez Jojo
(Mr Harry Hovinga) Route Départementale 118
TEL: 04.68.26.50.03
DIRECTIONS: RD118, between Carcassonne and Mazamet.
LANGUAGES: English, German, Dutch.
RESTAURANT: Lunch 12.00-14.00
SPECIALITIES: home-cooking.
OTHER POINTS: credit cards accepted.
Carcassonne; grottes (caves) du Limousis; Catharist châteaux.

DAX
Landes, 40100

AUBERGE DE LA CHALOSSE
(Mr Christian Richaud) 157, avenue Georges Clémenceau
TEL: 05.58.74.23.08
DIRECTIONS: D117/D134, Orthez/Pau axis.
MENU: 54 Frs.
ROOMS: 120 to 180 Frs.
RESTAURANT: Snacks from 6.00, lunch 12.00-14.00, dinner 20.00-22.00
CLOSED: Sun, public holidays and in Aug.
SPECIALITIES: home-cooking.
HOTEL: 6 rooms.
FACILITIES: shower
OTHER POINTS: bar.
hot springs; museum.

DECAZEVILLE
Aveyron, 12300

A L'AUBERGE DE SAINT JULIEN
(Mme Yvette Carrière) Route Départementale 963 - Saint Julien de Piganiol
TEL: 05.65.64.05.92 FAX: 05.65.64.05.92
DIRECTIONS: the Aurillac/Rodez road.
MENU: 45 to 100 Frs.
RESTAURANT: Snacks from 8.30, lunch 12.00-14.00
CLOSED: Mon
SPECIALITIES: stockfish, aligot, poule farcie, regional menu.
OTHER POINTS: bar.

DENGUIN
Pyrénées-Atlantiques, 64230

AUBERGE DENGUINOISE
(Mr Claude Arriulou) Route Nationale 117

TEL: 05.59.68.85.32
DIRECTIONS: RN117.
LANGUAGES: Spanish.
MENU: 55 to 110 Frs.
ROOMS: 95 to 130 Frs.
RESTAURANT: Snacks from 6.00, lunch 12.00-15.00, dinner 19.00-23.00
CLOSED: Sun evening.
SPECIALITIES: regional menu, home-cooking.
HOTEL: ☆ 14 rooms.
FACILITIES: shower
OTHER POINTS: credit cards accepted.

DOUZENS
Aude, 11700

LES ROUTIERS
(Mme Monique Hulin) 98, avenue des Corbières
TEL: 04.68.79.19.99
DIRECTIONS: RD2113, between Narbonne and Carcassonne.
LANGUAGES: English.
MENU: 53 to 150 Frs.
ROOMS: 120 to 200 Frs.
SPECIALITIES: regional menu, home-cooking.
HOTEL: 8 rooms.
FACILITIES: shower, bath, private bathroom
OTHER POINTS: credit cards accepted.
musée des oiseaux (birds); numerous abysses (gouffres) and abbeys in a radius of 50km.

ESPALION
Aveyron, 12500

RELAIS DES QUATRE ROUTES
(Mr Michel Molinier) Les Quatre Routes - Route Départementale 920
TEL: 05.65.44.05.14
DIRECTIONS: RD920, Clermont-Ferrand.
MENU: 58 to 85 Frs.
ROOMS: 80 to 130 Frs.
RESTAURANT: Snacks from 6.00, lunch 12.00-14.00, dinner 19.30-22.00
CLOSED: Sat evening and Sun.
SPECIALITIES: regional menu, home-cooking.
HOTEL: ☆ 4 rooms.
FACILITIES: shower, bath, private bathroom
OTHER POINTS: bar.
Lot valley; château de Calmont; historic monuments.

ESPERE
Lot, 46090

AUBERGE DE L'ESPERANCE
(Mme Paulette Bourdarie) D.911 Plaine de Marty
TEL: 05.65.30.95.72
DIRECTIONS: D911, Cahors/Villeneuve-sur-Lot.
MENU: 42 Frs (plat du jour) to 63 Frs (wine and coffee included).
RESTAURANT: Snacks from 7.00, lunch 11.30-14.30, dinner 19.00-21.00
CLOSED: Sat evening and Sun, 2 weeks in Aug and 10 days at the end of the year.
SPECIALITIES: home-cooking.
OTHER POINTS: bar.
Cahors (10km).

FABREGUES
Hérault, 34690

RESTAURANT LE 113
(Mme Josette Avignon)
TEL: 04.67.85.12.86
DIRECTIONS: RN113.
MENU: 45 to 60 Frs.
RESTAURANT: Snacks from 6.00
CLOSED: Sun, and in Oct.
SPECIALITIES: regional menu, home-cooking.
OTHER POINTS: credit cards accepted.
Bouzique; Saint-Guilhem-le-Desert; le Grau-du-Roi.

FAUILLET
Lot-et-Garonne, 47400

L'ETOILE DU SUD
(Mr Jean-Marie Lefèbvre) Route Nationale 113 - Zone Industrielle du Mayne
TEL: 05.53.88.19.68
DIRECTIONS: RN 113, RN113, between Marmande and Tonneins.
LANGUAGES: English, Spanish, Portuguese.
MENU: 60 Frs (wine included).
RESTAURANT: Snacks from 6.00, lunch 11.30
CLOSED: Sun.
SPECIALITIES: home-cooking.
OTHER POINTS: credit cards accepted.

FIGEAC
Lot, 46100

LE RELAIS DES CHASSEURS
(Mme Véronique Noyer) Route de Capdenac - La Vayssière
TEL: 05.65.34.12.33
DIRECTIONS: RN140, the Brive/Montpellier road, Figeac exit towards Rodez.
LANGUAGES: English.
MENU: 60 Frs (wine and coffee included).
ROOMS: 120 to 170 Frs.
RESTAURANT: Snacks from 6.00, lunch 11.30-14.00, dinner 19.00-21.00
CLOSED: Sun.
SPECIALITIES: regional menu, home-cooking.
HOTEL: 8 rooms.

FACILITIES: shower, private bathroom, television, telephone
OTHER POINTS: credit cards accepted.
Figeac; Capdenac-le-Haut; valleys of the Lot and Célé.

FIRBEIX
Dordogne, 24450

RELAIS DES SPORTS
(Mr René Beaubatit) Route Nationale 21
TEL: 05.53.52.82.53
DIRECTIONS: RN21.
OTHER POINTS: bar.

FITOU
Aude, 11510

LA GARRIGUE
(Mr Christian Marsan) 17, route Nationale 9
TEL: 04.68.45.68.07
DIRECTIONS: RN 9, RN9, between Perpignan and Narbonne.
LANGUAGES: German, Spanish.
MENU: 60 Frs.
RESTAURANT: Snacks from 4.00, lunch 11.00, dinner up to 22.30
SPECIALITIES: home-cooking.
HOTEL: 46 rooms.
FACILITIES: shower
OTHER POINTS: credit cards accepted.

FOIX
Ariège, 09000

LE SOLEIL D'OR
(Mr Jean Coumes) 57, avenue du Général Leclerc
TEL: 05.61.65.01.33
DIRECTIONS: RN20.
LANGUAGES: Spanish.
MENU: 40 to 70 Frs.
ROOMS: 90 to 130 Frs.
RESTAURANT: Snacks from 6.30, lunch 12.00-14.00, dinner 20.00-21.00
CLOSED: Sat and Sun (except bookings).
SPECIALITIES: home-cooking.
HOTEL: 6 rooms.
FACILITIES: shower, private bathroom
OTHER POINTS: bar.
château de Foix; grottes (caves).

FUMEL
Lot-et-Garonne, 47500

BAR ROUTIER DE LA SOIERIE
(Mme Liliane Lafon) 88 avenue de l'Usine
TEL: 05.53.71.34.22
MENU: 50 Frs.
RESTAURANT: Snacks from 6.00, dinner 18.00-20.00
CLOSED: Sun.
SPECIALITIES: home-cooking.
OTHER POINTS: bar.
château de Bonaguil; Périgord.

GAGES
Aveyron, 12630

LE RELAIS DE LA PLAINE
(Mme Yvonne Dallo)
TEL: 05.65.42.29.03
DIRECTIONS: RN88, the Brive/Mediterrancan road, 10km from Rodez.
LANGUAGES: English.
MENU: 55 to 100 Frs.
ROOMS: 100 to 200 Frs.
RESTAURANT: Snacks from 6.30, lunch 12.00-14.00, dinner 19.30-21.30
CLOSED: weekends (out of season), 2 weeks in Nov and 1 week-at New Year.
SPECIALITIES: tripoux, confit de canard, salade de gésiers (chicken gizzards), regional menu, home-cooking.
HOTEL: 22 rooms.
FACILITIES: shower, bath, private bathroom
OTHER POINTS: credit cards accepted.
gorges of the Tarn; Lot valley; grottes (caves) de l'Aubrac; lacs de Pareloup; Rodez: cathedral.

GARANOU LUZENAC
Ariège, 09250

LES ROUTIERS
(Mme Marie Pirès) Avenue de la Gare
TEL: 05.61.64.47.13 FAX: 05.61.44.47.13
DIRECTIONS: RN20, between Toulouse and Andorra.
LANGUAGES: Spanish, Portuguese.
MENU: 60 Frs.
ROOMS: from 160 Frs.
RESTAURANT: Snacks from 8.00, lunch 12.00-14.00, dinner 20.00-22.00
CLOSED: Sun, Aug.
SPECIALITIES: home-cooking.
HOTEL: 9 rooms.
FACILITIES: shower, bath, private bathroom
OTHER POINTS: credit cards accepted.
soapstone quarries; caves and subterranean streams; château de Foix, Andorra.

GER
Pyrénées-Atlantiques, 64530

A LA CLE D'OR
(Mr Alain Coudert) Route Nationale 117
TEL: 05.62.31.50.56
DIRECTIONS: RN117, the Pau (28km)/Tarbes (12km) road.

LANGUAGES: Spanish.
MENU: 58 Frs.
ROOMS: 75 to 100 Frs.
RESTAURANT: Snacks from 6.00, lunch 12.00-14.00
CLOSED: Sat, Sun, and 3 weeks from 15th Aug.
SPECIALITIES: home-cooking.
HOTEL: 4 rooms
OTHER POINTS: bar.
Pau; Lourdes; the Pyrenees.

GRAMAT
Lot, 46500

HOTEL DU CENTRE
(Mr André Grimal) Place de la République
TEL: 05.65.38.73.37 FAX: 05.65.38.73.66
DIRECTIONS: RN140, between Brive-la-Gaillarde and Rodez.
LANGUAGES: English.
MENU: 78 to 200 Frs.
ROOMS: 230 to 350 Frs.
RESTAURANT: Snacks from 7.00, lunch 12.00-14.00, dinner 19.30-21.00
CLOSED: Sat (out of season), 3rd week of Nov and Feb school holidays.
SPECIALITIES: foie gras, confits de canard, cêpes, tripoux, gésiers (chicken gizzards), cassoulet, regional menu, home-cooking.
HOTEL: ☆☆ 14 rooms.
FACILITIES: shower, bath, private bathroom, television, telephone
OTHER POINTS: credit cards accepted.
Rocamadour; gouffre de Padirac, gorges of the Antoire.

GRAYAN L'HOPITAL
Gironde, 33590

LE COQ ROUGE
(Mme Jocelyne Lavigne) Route de Soulac sur Mer
TEL: 05.56.09.48.65
DIRECTIONS: RD101, Pointe de Grave, Bordeaux.
MENU: 55 Frs (wine included) to 140 Frs.
RESTAURANT: Snacks from 7.30
SPECIALITIES: confits, fruits de mer, home-cooking.
OTHER POINTS: credit cards accepted.
the Médoc region; pointe de Grave.

HENDAYE
Pyrénées-Atlantiques, 64700

RELAIS ROUTIERS - Chez Mongobert
(Mr Alain Mongobert) 11, avenue d'Espagne
TEL: 05.59.70.78.95
DIRECTIONS: RN10, near the Spanish border.
LANGUAGES: German.
MENU: 58 Frs.
RESTAURANT: Snacks from 7.00
CLOSED: Sun, Aug.
SPECIALITIES: home-cooking.
OTHER POINTS: bar.

ISLE JOURDAIN (L')
Gers, 32600

L'OLYMPIA - Les Routiers
(Mr Michel Amour) 5, rue de la République
TEL: 05.62.07.01.35
DIRECTIONS: RN124, between Toulouse and Auch.
MENU: 50 to 78 Frs.
RESTAURANT: Snacks from 9.00, lunch 11.00-14.30, dinner 18.30-21.00
CLOSED: Sun, public holidays, and in Aug.
SPECIALITIES: regional dishes according to season, home-cooking.
OTHER POINTS: credit cards accepted.
Auch: (ancient city) cathedral; numerous châteaux and lakes.

ISSANKA
Hérault, 34540

LE GARRIGOU
(Mme Danyelle Hohmann) Le Garrigou
TEL: 04.67.78.71.30
DIRECTIONS: RN113, Sète exit, towards Gigean.
MENU: 61 to 120 Frs.
ROOMS: 110 to 160 Frs.
RESTAURANT: Snacks from 5.30, lunch 10.00-15.00, dinner 18.00-23.00
CLOSED: Sun in winter.
SPECIALITIES: seiche à la rouille, poissons, regional menu, home-cooking.
HOTEL: ☆☆ 8 rooms.
FACILITIES: shower, bath, telephone
OTHER POINTS: children's menu.
Mont Saint-Clair; abbaye de Saint-Félix.

JUGAZAN
Gironde, 33420

LA CHARRETTE
(Mr René Tesson) Le Bourg
TEL: 05.57.84.01.37
LANGUAGES: English.
MENU: 60 Frs (wine and coffee included).
RESTAURANT: Snacks from 6.45, lunch 11.45-14.00, dinner 19.45-21.30
CLOSED: Sat, from 1st to 15th Sept and from 24th Dec to 2nd Jan.
SPECIALITIES: regional menu, home-cooking, soups, salads, coq au vin, navarin, boeuf mode, choucroute.
OTHER POINTS: credit cards accepted.

LABATUT
Landes, 40300

LA GUINGUETTE
(Mr Christian Begu) Route Nationale 117
TEL: 05.58.98.18.82
DIRECTIONS: RN117, between Toulouse and Bayonne.
LANGUAGES: English, Spanish.
MENU: 65 to 195 Frs.
ROOMS: 140 to 260 Frs.
RESTAURANT: Snacks from 7.00, lunch 11.30-14.30, dinner 18.30-21.30
CLOSED: Sat (out of season) and Sun evening.
SPECIALITIES: garbure (thick soup), salade landaise, foie gras, confits, salade de kiwi, regional menu.
HOTEL: 5 rooms.
FACILITIES: shower, bath
OTHER POINTS: credit cards accepted.
lake; le Gave-de-Pau.

LACAPELLE MARIVAL
Lot, 46120

LA MARMITE
(Mme Muriel Mivielle) Place de Larroque
TEL: 05.65.40.98.07
DIRECTIONS: RN140, between Brive-la-Gaillarde and Figeac.
LANGUAGES: English, Spanish.
MENU: 50 (wine included) to 75 Frs.
RESTAURANT: Snacks from 7.30, lunch 11.00-15.00, dinner 18.30-23.00
CLOSED: Sat.
SPECIALITIES: home-cooking.
OTHER POINTS: bar.
Rocamadour; Padirac, Gramat.

LACAUNE
Tarn, 81230

LE CHALET
(Mr Joseph Delpino) 14, rue André Theron
TEL: 05.63.37.08.91
DIRECTIONS: RN81, the Albi/Castres road.
LANGUAGES: Spanish.
MENU: 45 to 180 Frs.
ROOMS: 140 to 180 Frs.
RESTAURANT: Snacks from 9.00, lunch 12.00-14.30, dinner 19.30-22.00
CLOSED: Sun and from 23rd Dec to 5th Jan.
SPECIALITIES: paella, couscous, cassoulet, home-cooking.
HOTEL: 8 rooms.
FACILITIES: shower, bath, private bathroom
OTHER POINTS: credit cards accepted.
Sidobre region; cave de Roquefort; leisure activities: walks, fishing, sailboarding.

LACEPEDE
Lot-et-Garonne, 47360

AUBERGE DU PAYS DE SERRES
(Mme Marie-France Fournier)
TEL: 05.53.95.00.78
DIRECTIONS: between Villeneuve-sur-Lot and Aiguillon.
LANGUAGES: English, German.
MENU: 65 Frs (wine and coffee included).
ROOMS: 220 to 250 Frs.
RESTAURANT: Snacks from 8.00, lunch 12.00-14.00, dinner 19.00-21.00
CLOSED: Mon (except bookings) and in Feb.
SPECIALITIES: regional menu, home-cooking.
HOTEL: ☆☆ 7 rooms.
FACILITIES: shower, private bathroom, television, telephone
OTHER POINTS: credit cards accepted.

LAFITTE SUR LOT
Lot-et-Garonne, 47320

LES AMIS DE LA ROUTE
(Mr Max Briot) Route de Villeneuve
TEL: 05.53.84.08.98
DIRECTIONS: RD666, Villeneuve-sur-Lot.
LANGUAGES: English, Spanish.
RESTAURANT: Snacks from 7.00, lunch 12.00-14.00, dinner 19.00-21.00
CLOSED: in August.
SPECIALITIES: home-cooking.
OTHER POINTS: credit cards accepted.

LAFOX
Lot-et-Garonne, 47270

LES ROUTIERS - Le Toulousain
(Mr René André) Route Nationale 113
TEL: 05.53.68.54.83
DIRECTIONS: RN113, the Bordeaux/Toulouse road.
LANGUAGES: Spanish, Italian.
MENU: 60 to 110 Frs.
ROOMS: 118 to 138 Frs.
RESTAURANT: Snacks from 4.30, dinner up to 19.30
CLOSED: from 15th to 30th Aug.
SPECIALITIES: regional menu, home-cooking.
HOTEL: ☆ 27 rooms.
FACILITIES: shower, bath, private bathroom, television
OTHER POINTS: credit cards accepted.

LAGARRIGUE
Tarn, 81090

RESTAURANT BIGUES
(Mme Josiane Bigues) 2, avenue de Mazamet
TEL: 05.63.35.12.25
DIRECTIONS: RN112, between Castres and Mazamet.

MENU: 65 Frs.
ROOMS: 190 to 200 Frs.
RESTAURANT: Snacks from 7.00, lunch 12.00-14.00, dinner 19.30-21.00
CLOSED: Sat evening, Sun, and in Aug.
SPECIALITIES: cassoulet, soupe au fromage, regional menu, home-cooking.
HOTEL: 8 rooms.
FACILITIES: shower, bath, private bathroom, television, telephone
OTHER POINTS: credit cards accepted.
Castres, Sidobre region,

LALOUBERE
Hautes-Pyrénées, 65310

HOTEL DES PYRENEES
(Mme Michèle Cazamayou) 13, rue du Maréchal Foch
TEL: 05.62.45.29.62
DIRECTIONS: RD135, between Bagnères-de-Bigorre and La Mongie.
LANGUAGES: English, Spanish.
MENU: 70 to 90 Frs.
ROOMS: 120 to 160 Frs.
RESTAURANT: Snacks from 7.00, lunch 12.00-14.00, dinner 19.30-21.00
CLOSED: Sun, and in Aug.
SPECIALITIES: home-cooking, regional menu.
HOTEL: 13 rooms.
FACILITIES: shower, bath
OTHER POINTS: credit cards accepted.
Lourdes (17km); Pic du Midi; cirque de Gavarnie.

LAMAGISTERE
Tarn-et-Garonne, 82360

CHEZ BOMPA
(Mr Gilbert Bompa) 56, avenue Saint-Michel
TEL: 05.63.39.91.56
DIRECTIONS: RN113, the Bordeaux/Toulouse road.
LANGUAGES: Spanish.
MENU: 55 to 80 Frs.
RESTAURANT: Snacks from 6.00, lunch 12.00-15.00, dinner 19.00-22.00
CLOSED: Sat, and 2 weeks in Aug.
SPECIALITIES: regional menu, home-cooking,
OTHER POINTS: credit cards accepted.
Centrale (powerstation) Golfech; Auvillar; échelles à poisons (fish-ladders).

LANGON
Gironde, 33210

HOTEL RESTAURANT DARLOT
(Mr Jean-Paul Darlot) 10, rue Dotézac
TEL: 05.56.63.01.36
DIRECTIONS: RN113, A62 autoroute, Langon exit.
LANGUAGES: English, Spanish.
MENU: 60 to 200 Frs.
ROOMS: 130 to 170 Frs.
RESTAURANT: Snacks from 7.00, lunch 12.00-15.00, dinner 19.00-22.00
CLOSED: Sun, and in Aug.
SPECIALITIES: civet de lièvre, cêpes à la bordelaise, salmis de palombe (dove), regional menu, home-cooking.
HOTEL: 11 rooms.
FACILITIES: shower, bath, private bathroom
OTHER POINTS: bar.
Verdelais basilica and calvary; grottes (caves) de Sainte-Croix-du-Mont; château de Roquetaillade; Bazas: cathedral; Saint-Macaire; Montesquieu's château de la Brède; Graves wines (30km).

LE PASSAGER
(Mr Gérard Barcelonna) Route de Pau - Mazère
TEL: 05.56.63.15.22
DIRECTIONS: at the Langon exit (3km), towards Pau.
MENU: 62.50 Frs (drink and coffee included).
RESTAURANT: Snacks from 5.00, lunch 11.30-14.30, dinner 19.30-22.00
CLOSED: Sat and Sun.
SPECIALITIES: home-cooking.
OTHER POINTS: credit cards accepted.

LANNEMEZAN
Hautes-Pyrénées, 65300

HOSTELLERIE DU CHATEAU
(Monique et Virginio Vassiliou-Rodriguez) 133, place du Château
TEL: 05.62.98.06.29
DIRECTIONS: between Auch (70km) and Tarbes (35km).
LANGUAGES: Spanish.
MENU: 56 Frs (wine and coffee included) to 100 Frs.
ROOMS: 80 to 120 Frs.
RESTAURANT: Snacks from 7.00, lunch 11.30-14.30, dinner 18.30-21.00
CLOSED: Sun and last 2 weeks in Dec.
SPECIALITIES: paella, regional menu, home-cooking.
HOTEL: 7 rooms
OTHER POINTS: credit cards accepted.
caves; châteaux.

LAPALME
Aude, 11480

LE CALYPSO
(Mme Rosie Guiraud) Aire de Lapalme
TEL: 04.68.45.65.00 **FAX:** 04.68.45.65.03
DIRECTIONS: A9 autoroute, accessible in both directions.
LANGUAGES: English, German, Spanish, Italian.

MENU: 65 Frs.
RESTAURANT: Snacks from 7.00
SPECIALITIES: home-cooking.
OTHER POINTS: credit cards accepted.

LES TAMARIS
(Mr Jean-Michel Marchand - SARL La Plaine du Sud) Route Nationale 9
TEL: 04.68.45.66.60 **FAX:** 04.68.45.61.45
DIRECTIONS: RN9, RN9, between Narbonne and Perpignan.
MENU: 55 Frs.
RESTAURANT: Snacks from 5.00
SPECIALITIES: home-cooking.
OTHER POINTS: credit cards accepted.

LAPANOUSE DE SEVERAC
Aveyron, 12150

LES ROUTIERS
(Mr Roger Arnal) Route de Rodez
TEL: 05.65.71.60.44
DIRECTIONS: RN88, in the centre of the village.
MENU: 50 to 60 Frs.
ROOMS: 80 to 120 Frs.
RESTAURANT: Snacks from 8.00, lunch 12.00-15.00, dinner 19.00-23.00
CLOSED: Sun.
SPECIALITIES: tripoux, regional menu, home-cooking.
HOTEL: 5 rooms.
FACILITIES: shower, bath, private bathroom, television
OTHER POINTS: bar.
lacs du Levézoti; gorges of the Tarn; medieval château de Séverac; cave de Rquefort; ski pistes 'Laguiole-Brameloup'.

LARDIN SAINT LAZARE (LE)
Dordogne, 24570

LE RELAIS SAINT LAZARE
(Mme Ginette Westwood) Route Nationale 89
TEL: 05.53.51.37.45
DIRECTIONS: RN89, between Périgueux (47km) and Brive-la-Gaillarde (20km).
LANGUAGES: English, Dutch.
MENU: 60 (wine and coffee included).
ROOMS: 120 to 150 Frs.
RESTAURANT: Snacks from 6.30
CLOSED: Sun.
SPECIALITIES: home-cooking.
HOTEL: 10 rooms
OTHER POINTS: bar.
Montignac; Les Eyzies; Roc Saint-Christophe; Sarlat.

LE VEZERE
(Mme Marie-Claire Semprez) Route Nationale 89
TEL: 05.53.51.28.21
DIRECTIONS: RN89, the Périgueux/Brive-la-Gaillarde road.
MENU: 50 Frs (wine and coffee included) to 100 Frs.
ROOMS: 70 to 100 Frs.
RESTAURANT: Snacks from 5.00, lunch 12.00-15.00, dinner 19.00-24.00
CLOSED: Sun.
SPECIALITIES: home-cooking.
HOTEL: 6 rooms
OTHER POINTS: bar.
'Périgord noir'; the Dordogne and Vezère valleys.

LARUSCADE
Gironde, 33620

LE CHAT HUANT
(Mr Ange Portela - SARL La Corogne) Route Nationale 10 - Le Chavan
TEL: 05.57.68.54.16
DIRECTIONS: RN10, the Bordeaux/Angoulème road.
LANGUAGES: Spanish, Portuguese.
MENU: 57 Frs (wine ind coffee included).
RESTAURANT: Snacks from 6.00
SPECIALITIES: home-cooking, honie-cooking.
OTHER POINTS: credit cards accepted.

LAUSSEIGNAN BARBASTE
Lot-et-Garonne, 47230

LES PALMIERS
(SNC Gineste & Fils)
TEL: 05.53.65.55.02
DIRECTIONS: RN655, the Agen/Bayonne road.
MENU: 48 to 155 Frs.
RESTAURANT: Snacks from 7.00, lunch 12.00-14.00, dinner 19.30-21.15
CLOSED: Sat (out of season), Mon evening (in season) and in Jan.
SPECIALITIES: paupiette de veau (grand prix d'honneur in the French 1992 championships), regional menu.
OTHER POINTS: credit cards accepted.
moulin (windmill) des tours; Henri IV's château; Vianne: bastide (country house), verrerie (glassworks); la cave (wine-cellar) de Buzet; chocolate-making at Nérac.

LECTOURE
Gers, 32700

LE GALIS
(Mme Claudette Labat) ZI des Galis
TEL: 05.62.68.88.28 **FAX:** 05.62.68.88.27
LANGUAGES: English, Spanish.
MENU: 65 Frs (wine and coffee included).
RESTAURANT: Snacks from 5.30, lunch 12.00-14.00,

dinner 19.30-22.00
SPECIALITIES: regional menu, home-cooking, confits, foie gras, cassoulet.
OTHER POINTS: credit cards accepted.

LEDENON
Gard, 30210

LE RELAIS DE LEDENON
(Mr Corhodin) Route Nationale 86
TEL: 04.66.37.34.84 FAX: 04.90.91.45.84
DIRECTIONS: RN86, the Avignon/Remoulins/Nimes road
MENU: 50 to 90 Frs.
RESTAURANT: Snacks from 5.00, lunch 12.00-16.00, dinner 19.00-24.00
CLOSED: Sun.
SPECIALITIES: regional menu, home-cooking.
OTHER POINTS: credit cards accepted.
Pont du Gard; Nînes.

LESCAR
Pyrénées-Atlantiques, 64230

LE QUATRO
(Mme Nathalie Senger) Rue du Souvenir Franáais
TEL: 05.59.81.37.52
DIRECTIONS: RN 117, RN117, on the Pau/Bayonne axis.
LANGUAGES: English, German.
MENU: 60 Frs.
RESTAURANT: Snacks from 6.00, lunch 11.30-15.00, dinner 18.30-23.00
CLOSED: Sun.
SPECIALITIES: home-cooking.
OTHER POINTS: credit cards accepted.

LIBOURNE
Gironde, 33500

LE MOULIN BLANC
(Mme Geneviève Fernandez) 132, avenue Georges Clémenceau
TEL: 05.57.25.06.27
DIRECTIONS: RN89, the Libourne/Périgueux road.
LANGUAGES: Spanish, Italian.
MENU: 60 to 120 Frs.
ROOMS: 120 to 200 Frs.
RESTAURANT: Snacks from 7.30, lunch 12.00-15.00, dinner 19.00-21.30
SPECIALITIES: couscous, paella, home-cooking.
HOTEL: ☆ 10 rooms.
FACILITIES: shower, bath, private bathroom
OTHER POINTS: bar.
Bordeaux wine-growing region: Saint-Emilion (8km), Pomerol (3km), Fronsac (3km).

LIGARDES
Gers, 32100

RELAIS CHEZ DUDULE
(Mr Francis Dulong) Route d'Agen
TEL: 05.62.28.85.76
DIRECTIONS: RD931, the Agen/Pau road.
RESTAURANT: Snacks from 7.30, lunch 12.00, dinner 19.00
SPECIALITIES: regional menu, home-cooking.
OTHER POINTS: credit cards accepted.
La Romieu; Seviac; Flardan; Condom.

LIPOSTHEY
Landes, 40410

CHEZ ALINE
(Mme Aline Gros)
TEL: 05.58.82.30.30
DIRECTIONS: RN10, exit 17.
MENU: 60 to 150 Frs.
RESTAURANT: Snacks from 6.00, lunch 12.00-14.00, dinner 19.30-21.30
CLOSED: Sat, and from Christmis Day to mid-Jan.
SPECIALITIES: Landes dishes, home-cooking.
OTHER POINTS: bar.

LODEVE
Hérault, 34700

RELAIS DE LA CROIX
(Mr Jean-Denis Roig) Cartels
TEL: 04.67.44.00.72
DIRECTIONS: RN9, from Millau junction 54 or from Montpellier junction 55.
MENU: 60 Frs.
ROOMS: 100 Frs.
RESTAURANT: Snacks from 7.00, lunch 12.00-15.00, dinner 19.30-22.00
CLOSED: Sat and Sun.
SPECIALITIES: home-cooking.
HOTEL: 5 rooms.
FACILITIES: shower, bath, private bathroom
OTHER POINTS: credit cards accepted.

RELAIS ESCALETTE
(Mr Gilbert Cavalier) Route Nationale 9
TEL: 04.67.44.01.14 FAX: 04.67.44.43.93
DIRECTIONS: RN9.
LANGUAGES: English, German, Italian.
MENU: 70 to 220 Frs.
ROOMS: 100 to 170 Frs.
RESTAURANT: Snacks from 4.00, lunch 12.00-13.30, dinner 19.00-22.00
SPECIALITIES: boeuf Saint-Fulcran, grillade au feu de bois, canard aux olives, regional menu.
HOTEL: 20 rooms.
OTHER POINTS: credit cards accepted.

cirque de Navacelle and de Maureze; lac du Salagou; grottes (caves) de l'Abeil.

LOMBEZ
Gers, 32220

LE RELAIS DES PYRENEES
(Mme Michelle Mula) Route de Samatan
TEL: 05.62.62.32.11
DIRECTIONS: the Auch/Toulouse/Tarbes road.
LANGUAGES: Spanish.
MENU: 50 Frs (wine and coffee included) to 145 Frs.
ROOMS: 80 to 100 Frs.
SPECIALITIES: confits, magrets, foie gras, regional menu, home-cooking.
HOTEL: 8 rooms
OTHER POINTS: credit cards accepted.

LONS
Pyrénées-Atlantiques, 64140

MIDI / MINUIT
(Mr Jean-Jacques Philibert) Au Larregain - Zone Monthaubat
TEL: 05.59.32.07.57
MENU: 55 Frs.
RESTAURANT: Snacks from 6.30, lunch 12.00-16.00, dinner 19.00-23.00
CLOSED: Sun.
SPECIALITIES: home-cooking.
OTHER POINTS: credit cards accepted.

LUBBON
Landes, 40240

CHEZ MAMY
(Mme Martine Laurens)
TEL: 05.58.93.60.47
DIRECTIONS: RD933, between Casteljaloux and Mont-de-Marsan.
MENU: 65 Frs.
ROOMS: 100 Frs.
RESTAURANT: Snacks from 5.00, lunch 12.00-15.00, dinner 19.00-21.00
CLOSED: Sat evening, and in Oct.
SPECIALITIES: foie gras, confits, cêpes, poulet farcie, regional menu, home-cooking.
HOTEL: 10 rooms.
FACILITIES: shower
OTHER POINTS: credit cards accepted.
Barbotan; old Nérac: chocolate-makers; Puydesseau.

MAGES (LES)
Gard, 30960

RESTO 104
(Mme Sylvette Groshens) Rte départementale 904
TEL: 04.66.25.67.00
DIRECTIONS: RD904, Aubenas/Nîmes road.
MENU: 60 Frs (wine and coffee included).
ROOMS: from 120 Frs.
RESTAURANT: Snacks from 7.00, lunch 12.00-14.00, dinner 19.30-21.00
CLOSED: Sat and Sun.
SPECIALITIES: couscous, home-cooking.
HOTEL: 15 rooms.
FACILITIES: shower
OTHER POINTS: credit cards accepted.
the Cèze valley.

MAGNANAC
Haute-Garonne, 31340

LES ROUTIERS
(Mme Franáoise Rossi)
TEL: 05.61.09.01.87
DIRECTIONS: RN630, between Montauban and Castres.
MENU: 62 Frs.
ROOMS: 120 Frs.
RESTAURANT: Snacks from 6.30, lunch 12.00-14.00, dinner 19.30-21.00
CLOSED: Fri evening, Sun, public holidays, last 2 weeks in Aug.
SPECIALITIES: home-cooking.
HOTEL: 4 rooms.
FACILITIES: shower, bath, private bathroom
OTHER POINTS: credit cards accepted.

MANCIET
Gers, 32370

CHEZ MONIQUE
(Mme Monique Oxoby) Route Nationale 124
TEL: 05.62.08.56.40
DIRECTIONS: RN124, between Auch and Mont de Marsan.
LANGUAGES: Spanish.
MENU: 60 Frs (wine and coffee included).
ROOMS: 150 Frs.
RESTAURANT: Snacks from 7.00, lunch 11.30-15.00, dinner 19.00-21.30
CLOSED: Mon afternoon.
SPECIALITIES: home-cooking.
HOTEL: 5 rooms
OTHER POINTS: credit cards accepted.

MARGUERITTES
Gard, 30320

LE RELAIS D'AVIGNON
(Mr Yves Debrie) Route Nationale 86
TEL: 04.66.26.02.20
DIRECTIONS: Avignon.
MENU: 60 to 120 Frs.

ROOMS: 150 to 200 Frs.
RESTAURANT: Snacks from 6.00
CLOSED: Sun.
SPECIALITIES: regional menu, home-cooking.
HOTEL: 15 rooms.
FACILITIES: shower, bath, private bathroom
OTHER POINTS: credit cards accepted.

MARSAN AUBIET
Gers, 32270

RELAIS 124
(Mr Fernand Castaing)
TEL: 05.62.65.63.43
DIRECTIONS: RN124, the Toulouse/Auch road, 15km from Auch.
LANGUAGES: English.
MENU: 60 Frs (wine included).
RESTAURANT: Snacks from 7.00, lunch 11.30-15.00, dinner 19.00-22.00
CLOSED: Sat, Sun, one week in Aug and one week at end of Dec.
SPECIALITIES: home-cooking, horne-cooking.
OTHER POINTS: credit cards accepted.

MARSAS
Gironde, 33620

RESTAURANT DE LA RENAISSANCE
(Patrice et Sylvie Elie) 2, rue des Terriers
TEL: 05.57.68.08.04 **FAX:** 05.57.68.02.94
DIRECTIONS: D18/RN10, 1km from RN10, near Cavignac towards Libourne.
LANGUAGES: Spanish.
MENU: 60 to 195 Frs.
RESTAURANT: Snacks from 6.30
CLOSED: Sun evening.
SPECIALITIES: regional menu, home-cooking.
OTHER POINTS: credit cards accepted.
Blaye: citadel; vineyards: Saint-Emilion.

MARSEILLAN PLAGE
Hérault, 34340

LE CREOLE
(Mr Gilles Lepinette) 5, avenue de la Méditerranée
TEL: 04.67.21.98.25
DIRECTIONS: Sète exit, towards Mèze.
MENU: 50 to 120 Frs.
RESTAURANT: Snacks from 9.30, lunch 12.00-15.00, dinner 19.00-22.00
CLOSED: Wed (out of season).
SPECIALITIES: regional menu, home-cooking.
OTHER POINTS: credit cards accepted.
Agde (Greek town) (6km); Minerve (medieval town) (45km); Bouzigues: étang de Thau (15km); Pézenas (Molière's medieval city) (20km).

MASSEUBE
Gers, 32140

CHEZ MARTINE
(Mme Martine Delrieu) 22 avenue Elysée Duffréchou - Route Nationale
TEL: 05.62.66.02.14
DIRECTIONS: RN129, Lamezan.
MENU: 55 Frs.
RESTAURANT: Snacks from 6.30, lunch 11.30-14.00
CLOSED: Public holidays and in Aug.
SPECIALITIES: home-cooking,
OTHER POINTS: credit cards accepted.

MAUBOURGUET
Hautes-Pyrénées, 65700

BAR RELAIS DES AUTOBUS
(Mme Nicole Dauba) 87, place de la Libération
TEL: 05.62.96.38.78
MENU: 35 to 165 Frs.
RESTAURANT: Snacks from 6.00, lunch 11.00-14.30, dinner 19.00-21.30
SPECIALITIES: regional menu, home-cooking.
OTHER POINTS: bar.

MAVALEIX
Dordogne, 24800

LES JARDINS DE LA TUILIERE
(Mme Suzette Deschamps) Route Nationale 21
TEL: 05.53.52.03.85 **FAX:** 05.53.62.54.44
DIRECTIONS: RD710, between Fumel and Siorac.
LANGUAGES: English, Spanish.
MENU: 59 to 130 Frs.
ROOMS: 120 to 160 Frs.
RESTAURANT: Snacks from 6.00, lunch 11.30-15.00, dinner 19.00-22.00
SPECIALITIES: regional menu, couscous, paella, chili con carne, home-cooking.
HOTEL: 3 rooms.
FACILITIES: shower, bath, private bathroom
OTHER POINTS: credit cards accepted.
Belves; Monpazier; Les Eyzies; Sarlat; Dordogne valley.

MILLAU LARZAC
Aveyron, 12230

RELAIS ESPACE
(Mr Vincent Gineste) Aérodrôme Millau-Larzac
TEL: 05.65.62.76.22 **FAX:** 05.65.62.79.02
DIRECTIONS: RN9, the Clermont-Ferrand/Béziers road.
LANGUAGES: English, Spanish.
MENU: 40 to 100 Frs.
ROOMS: 200 Frs.
RESTAURANT: Snacks from 6.00, lunch 11.00-15.00, dinner 18.30-21.30

SPECIALITIES: terrine de foie gras, langue de boeuf sauce piquante, loup (bass) au basilic, regional menu, home-cooking.
HOTEL: ☆☆ 10 rooms.
FACILITIES: shower, bath, private bathroom, television, telephone
OTHER POINTS: credit cards accepted.
gorges of the Tarn; cirque Navacelle; La Couvertoirade; Roquefort.

MIRAMONT D'ASTARAC
Gers, 32300

LE RELAIS DES TROUETTES
(Mr Frédéric Normand) Route Nationale 21
TEL: 05.62.66.60.50
DIRECTIONS: RN21, the Agen/Auch/Tarbes road.
LANGUAGES: English, Spanish.
MENU: 58 to 85 Frs.
RESTAURANT: Snacks from 6.00, lunch 12.00-14.00, dinner 19.30-22.30
CLOSED: Sat, and end of Dec.
SPECIALITIES: home-cooking.
HOTEL: 8 rooms.
FACILITIES: shower
OTHER POINTS: bar.
Auch (15km); Mirande (5km).

MOISSAC
Tarn-et-Garonne, 82200

RELAIS AUVERGNAT
(Mr Jacques Ginisty) 31, boulevard Camille Delthil
TEL: 05.63.04.02.58
DIRECTIONS: RN927, Montauban.
LANGUAGES: English, Spanish.
MENU: 50 to 80 Frs.
ROOMS: 130 to 200 Frs.
RESTAURANT: Snacks from 7.00, lunch 12.00-14.00, dinner 19.30-22.00
CLOSED: Sun afternoon.
SPECIALITIES: cassoulet, confit, grillades (grills), regional menu, home-cooking.
HOTEL: ☆ 9 rooms.
FACILITIES: shower, bath, television
OTHER POINTS: credit cards accepted.
sites de Boudou (viewing point); Montauban (30km): cathedral, museum; Larrazet (15km); Moissac: château, park.

MONASTIER (LE)
Lozère, 48100

LES AJUSTONS
(Mr Guy Gibelin) Lieu dit : Les Ajustons
TEL: 04.66.32.70.35
DIRECTIONS: RN9, the Millau road.
MENU: 65 to 130 Frs.
ROOMS: 100 and 180 Frs.
RESTAURANT: Snacks from 7.00, lunch 12.00-14.00, dinner 19.30-21.00
CLOSED: Sat, and in Jan and Feb.
SPECIALITIES: truite, tripoux auvergnat, regional menu, home-cooking.
HOTEL: ☆ 15 rooms.
FACILITIES: shower, bath, private bathroom, telephone
OTHER POINTS: credit cards accepted.
gorges of the Tarn; Aubrac plateau.

MONDAVEZAN
Haute-Garonne, 31220

LA FERMIERE
(Mme Alexine Ferrage) Route Nationale 117
TEL: 05.61.97.01.52
DIRECTIONS: RN117, the Toulouse/Saint-Gaudens road.
LANGUAGES: Spanish.
MENU: 58 to 110 Frs.
ROOMS: 70 to 195 Frs.
RESTAURANT: Snacks from 6.00, lunch 11.00-14.00, dinner 19.00-22.00
CLOSED: Sun, and last 2 weeks in Aug.
SPECIALITIES: confit de canard, cassoulet, regional menu, home-cooking.
HOTEL: 21 rooms.
FACILITIES: shower
OTHER POINTS: credit cards accepted.

MONT DE MARSAN
Landes, 40000

BAR DES SPORTS
(Mme Josiane Ledoux) Place des Arènes
TEL: 05.58.75.05.08
LANGUAGES: Spanish.
MENU: 50 to 120 Frs.
ROOMS: 100 to 180 Frs.
RESTAURANT: Snacks from 6.30, lunch 12.00-14.00, dinner 19.30-22.00
CLOSED: Sun.
SPECIALITIES: home-cooking.
HOTEL: 22 rooms
OTHER POINTS: bar.

MONTAREN
Gard, 30700

LES ROUTIERS - Chez Régine
(Mme Régine Hangard) 7 Route d'Ales
TEL: 04.66.22.25.26
DIRECTIONS: RN981.
HOTEL: 9 rooms
OTHER POINTS: bar.

MONTDRAGON
Tarn, 81440

AUBERGE LA FERME
(SARL Danaroc) La Sagnette
TEL: 05.63.42.15.54
DIRECTIONS: RD631, Réalmont/Graulhet.
MENU: 60 to 135 Frs.
RESTAURANT: Snacks from 7.00, lunch 11.30-14.00, dinner 19.00-22.00
SPECIALITIES: foie gras, confits, magrets, home-cooking.
OTHER POINTS: credit cards accepted.
Albi; Lautrec; Graulhet.

MONTECH
Tarn-et-Garonne, 82700

RELAIS DE L'AVENUE
(Mr Georges Taupiac) 7, boulevard Lagal
TEL: 05.63.64.72.26
DIRECTIONS: RD928, between Montauban and Auch.
MENU: 54 to 100 Frs.
RESTAURANT: Snacks from 7.00, lunch 11.30-14.00, dinner 19.00-20.30
CLOSED: Sun, public holidays, and 2 weeks from 20th Dec.
SPECIALITIES: regional menu, home-cooking.
OTHER POINTS: bar.

MONTREDON DES CORBIERES
Aude, 11100

LE STEPHANOIS
(Mr Gilles Pasquet) Route Nationale 113
TEL: 04.68.42.08.41 **FAX:** 04.68.41.37.51
DIRECTIONS: RN113.
LANGUAGES: Spanish.
RESTAURANT: Snacks from 4.00, lunch 11.30-14.30, dinner 19.00-24.00
CLOSED: Sun.
OTHER POINTS: bar.
abbaye de Fontfroide (15km).

MONTVALENT
Lot, 46600

LA BERGERIE DE POULOT
(Mme Ginette Gigleux-Magnier) Route Nationale 140 - Lieu dit : Poulot
TEL: 05.65.37.41.04
DIRECTIONS: RN140, between Brive-la-Gaillarde and Rodez.
MENU: 55 (wine included) to 160 Frs.
RESTAURANT: Snacks from 5.00, lunch 11.00, dinner up to 22.00
CLOSED: Sat evening, Sun and 10 days from Christmas to the new year
SPECIALITIES: Périgord dishes, regional menu, home-cooking.
OTHER POINTS: bar.
Rocamadour; Padirac; Gramat.

MURET
Haute-Garonne, 31600

LE MARCLAN
(Mme Régine Soler) 22bis, rue de Marclan - Z.I. Marclan
TEL: 05.61.56.82.93
DIRECTIONS: RN117, between Toulouse and Saint-Caudens.
MENU: 55 Frs (coffee included).
RESTAURANT: Snacks from 7.00, lunch 11.30-14.30
CLOSED: Sat and Sun.
SPECIALITIES: soupe de poissons, home-cooking.
OTHER POINTS: credit cards accepted.

MUSSIDAN
Dordogne, 24400

RELAIS LE PERIGORD
(Mme Annie Callens) 37, avenue Gambetta
TEL: 05.53.81.05.85
DIRECTIONS: RN89, between Bordeaux and Périgueux.
MENU: 50 to 170 Frs.
ROOMS: 170 to 240 Frs.
RESTAURANT: Snacks from 7.00, lunch 12.00-14.30, dinner 19.00-22.00
CLOSED: 1st Nov.
SPECIALITIES: foie gras, cou d'oie (goose-neck) farci, confit, ris de veau, magrets de canard, regional menu, home-cooking.
HOTEL: 6 rooms.
FACILITIES: shower, bath, private bathroom, television
OTHER POINTS: credit cards accepted.
château de Montréal; musée artisanal (crafts); wine-cellars; caves; spring.

NARBONNE
Aude, 11100

LA CAILLE QUI CHANTE
(Mr Alain Garcies - SARL G2G) Montredon des Corbières
TEL: 04.68.42.04.36 **FAX:** 04.68.42.42.85
DIRECTIONS: RN113, exit at Narbonne Sud (South), towards Carcassonne.
LANGUAGES: English, German, Spanish.
MENU: 55 to 160 Frs.
ROOMS: 120 to 185 Frs.
RESTAURANT: Snacks from 5.00, lunch 11.00-15.00, dinner 18.30-24.00
SPECIALITIES: grillades (grills), fruits de mer, paella, regional menu.
HOTEL: ☆☆ 20 rooms.

FACILITIES: shower, bath, private bathroom, television, telephone
OTHER POINTS: credit cards accepted.
abbaye de Fontfroide; ranch offering 'promenades à cheval'(riding); Catharist château.

LE NOVELTY

(Claude et Louis Strazzera) 33, avenue des Pyrénées
TEL: 04.68.42.24.28 FAX: 04.68.42.13.37
LANGUAGES: English, Spanish, Italian, Arabic.
MENU: 58 to 100 Frs.
ROOMS: 90 to 120 Frs.
RESTAURANT: Snacks from 7.00, lunch 12.00-14.00, dinner 19.30-22.30
CLOSED: Sun (in winter).
SPECIALITIES: poulet à la narbonnaise, cassoulet, choucroute, paella, couscous (Thurs), regional menu, home-cooking.
HOTEL: 20 rooms.
FACILITIES: shower
OTHER POINTS: credit cards accepted.
cathedral; museums; ponds (étangs); beaches.

RESTAURANT DES 2 MERS

(Mr Franco Mattei) Route de la Nautique - Complexe Routier International
TEL: 04.68.41.00.21
DIRECTIONS: RN9, exit at Narbonne Sud (South).
LANGUAGES: English, Italian.
MENU: 62 to 72 Frs.
RESTAURANT: Snacks from 5.30, lunch 11.00-15.00, dinner 18.00-24.00
CLOSED: Sat evening and Sun.
SPECIALITIES: poissons, viandes en sauce, home-cooking.
OTHER POINTS: credit cards accepted.
abbaye de Fontfroide; route des Corbières; cathedral at Saint-lust; musée des vins.

L'AIGRE DOUX

(Mme Chantal Vilar) Route Nationale 9
TEL: 04.68.65.11.01
DIRECTIONS: RN 9, RN9, between Beziers and Narbonne.
LANGUAGES: Spanish.
MENU: 62 Frs.
RESTAURANT: Snacks from 5.30, lunch 11.30-14.30, dinner 19.00-23.30
CLOSED: Sun.
OTHER POINTS: credit cards accepted.

NICOLE

Lot-et-Garonne, 47190

LE PLAISANCE

(Mr Bernard Lambert) Route Nationale 113 - Aiguillon
TEL: 05.53.79.64.07 FAX: 05.53.79.64.07
DIRECTIONS: RN113.
LANGUAGES: Spanish.
MENU: 54 to 100 Frs.
ROOMS: 85 to 110 Frs.
RESTAURANT: Snacks from 7.00, lunch 12.00-14.00, dinner 19.00-22.00
CLOSED: Sat, Aug.
SPECIALITIES: home-cooking, confit, magret de canard, tête de veau ravigotte, regional menu.
HOTEL: 6 rooms.
FACILITIES: shower, bath, television
OTHER POINTS: credit cards accepted.
Lot and Garonne valleys; site du Pech de Berre.

NIMES

Gard, 30900

LE CHANTECLER

(Mr Vincent Savorit) Route de Montpellier - Marché Gare
TEL: 04.66.84.86.79
DIRECTIONS: RN113.
LANGUAGES: English, Spanish.
MENU: 44 to 89 Frs.
RESTAURANT: Snacks from 5.00
CLOSED: Sun and public holidays.
SPECIALITIES: home-cooking.
OTHER POINTS: credit cards accepted.

ONET LE CHATEAU

Aveyron, 12850

LA ROCADE

(Mr Francis Gayraud) La Roquette
TEL: 05.65.67.17.12 FAX: 05.65.78.29.15
DIRECTIONS: RN88, between Sévérac-le-Château and Millau.
MENU: 54 to 120 Frs.
ROOMS: 130 to 200.
RESTAURANT: Snacks from 7.00, lunch 12.00-14.00, dinner 19.30-21.00
CLOSED: Fri evening, Sat, I st 2 weeks in July, 2 weeks from 24th Dec.
SPECIALITIES: confit de canard, civet (stew) d'oie (goose), tripoux, grillades au feu de bois (charcoal grills), regional menu.
HOTEL: ☆ 14 rooms.
FACILITIES: shower, bath, private bathroom, television, telephone
OTHER POINTS: credit cards accepted.
Conques; gorges of the Tarn; Rodez.

LE CRYSTAL

(Mr Yvan Dissac) Route d'Espalion
TEL: 05.65.74.91.49
DIRECTIONS: CD935, the Rodez/Clermont-Ferrand road.

MENU: 52 Frs.
ROOMS: 90 to 150 Frs.
RESTAURANT: Snacks from 7.00, lunch 11.30-14.00, dinner 19.00-21.00
CLOSED: Sat, SUn and Aug.
SPECIALITIES: regional menu, home-cooking.
HOTEL: 16 rooms.
FACILITIES: shower, bath, private bathroom
OTHER POINTS: credit cards accepted.
Rodez, Conques, Bozouls, Espalion, gorges of the Tarn.

PAU
Pyrénées-Atlantiques, 64000

LE BELLEVUE
(Mme Marcelle Lorry) Belair - Buziet
TEL: 05.59.21.76.03
DIRECTIONS: the Pau/Oloron road.
LANGUAGES: Spanish.
MENU: 62 Frs (wine and coffee included).
ROOMS: 170 to 200 Frs.
RESTAURANT: Snacks from 9.00, lunch 12.00-15.00, dinner 19.30-21.30
CLOSED: Sat, and one week at Christmas.
SPECIALITIES: confit, garbure béarnaise, regional menu, home-cooking.
HOTEL: 6 rooms.
FACILITIES: shower
OTHER POINTS: bar.
Pyrenees; Ossau and Aspe valleys; Lourdes; Pau; wine route; juranáon.

PAUILLAC
Gironde, 33250

LE YACHTING
(Mme Louisette Puyfourcat) 12 Port de Plaisance - Quai Lèon Perrier
TEL: 02.56.59.06.43
DIRECTIONS: RD2.
LANGUAGES: English.
MENU: 52 to 122 Frs.
ROOMS: 130 to 320 Frs.
SPECIALITIES: regional menu, entrecôte bordelaise, home-cooking.
HOTEL: ☆ 16 rooms.
FACILITIES: shower, bath, private bathroom
OTHER POINTS: bar.
numerous châteaux.

PERPIGNAN
Pyrénées-Orientales, 66000

LA CHAUMIERE
(Mr Philippe Chevallier) Avenue de Bruxelles Z.I. Saint Charles
TEL: 04.68.56.57.69 FAX: 04.68.56.95.46
DIRECTIONS: exit autoroute sud direction Marché-Saint-Charles
MENU: 60 Frs.
SPECIALITIES: paella, grillades à la Plancha, parillades, home-cooking.
OTHER POINTS: credit cards accepted.

PESSAC
Gironde, 33600

RESTAURANT LE RELAIS
(Mr Yannick Boucher) 374, avenue de Lattre de Tassigny
TEL: 05.56.68.04.34
DIRECTIONS: RD250, Bordeaux/Arcachon road.
LANGUAGES: English.
MENU: 50 Frs (wine included) to 76 Frs.
RESTAURANT: Snacks from 8.30, lunch 11.00-15.00, dinner 18.00-21.00
CLOSED: Sat and Sun.
SPECIALITIES: home-cooking.
OTHER POINTS: credit cards accepted.
Arcachon; Bordeaux.

PEYREHORADE
Landes, 40300

FINS GOURMETS
(Mr Bernard Dupouy) Rue du Fronton
TEL: 05.58.73.00.68
MENU: 50 to 85 Frs.
ROOMS: 150 to 200 Frs.
RESTAURANT: Snacks from 8.00, lunch 12.00-14.30, dinner 18.00-22.00
CLOSED: Sun.
SPECIALITIES: home-cooking.
HOTEL: 6 rooms
OTHER POINTS: bar.

PUJAUT
Gard, 30131

LES GRAVIERES
(Mme Odette Quiquemelle) Les Gravières - Route de Bagnols sur Cèze
TEL: 04.90.25.19.70
DIRECTIONS: RN580, Bagnols-sur-Cèze.
MENU: 62 Frs.
RESTAURANT: Snacks from 6.30, lunch 12.00-14.30, dinner 19.00-22.30
CLOSED: Sat, Sun and in Aug.
SPECIALITIES: home-cooking.
OTHER POINTS: credit cards accepted.
Pont du Gard; Avignon: Palais des Papes; Théâtre Antique at Orange; Tavel vineyards; La Chartreuse.

QUILLAN
Aude, 11500

L'ESPEQUI
(Marilyne et Guy Gabens) 69, avenue de Carcassonne
TEL: 04.68.20.03.51
DIRECTIONS: RD118, the Carcassonne/Perpignan road.
LANGUAGES: Spanish.
MENU: 60 Frs (wine and coffee included).
RESTAURANT: Snacks from 7.30, lunch 11.00, dinner up to 21.00
CLOSED: Mon evening, Sun evening, and the 1st week of Jan.
SPECIALITIES: cassoulet, couscous (winter), paella, regional menu, home-cooking.
OTHER POINTS: bar.

REALMONT
Tarn, 81120

LES ROUTIERS
(Mr Richard Duarte) 27, boulevard Armengaud
TEL: 05.63.55.65.44
DIRECTIONS: RN112, between Aibi and Béziers.
LANGUAGES: Spanish, Portuguese.
MENU: 60 to 99 Frs.
RESTAURANT: Snacks from 8.00, lunch 11.30-14.00, dinner 19.00-21.00
CLOSED: Sun Lunch.
SPECIALITIES: foie gras, magrets, regional menu.
OTHER POINTS: credit cards accepted.
Albi; Castres; barrage (dam) de la Bancalie.

REBENACQ
Pyrénées-Atlantiques, 64260

CHEZ PALU
(Mr Alain Palu) Place de la Mairie
TEL: 05.59.05.54.11
DIRECTIONS: RD936, the lourdes road.
MENU: 50 to 90 Frs.
RESTAURANT: Snacks from 7.00, lunch 10.00-15.00, dinner 19.00-21.00
CLOSED: Mon evening, Sun evening.
SPECIALITIES: garbure (thick soup), confits, pipérade, fromage du pays, regional menu, home-cooking.
OTHER POINTS: credit cards accepted.
Ossau valley; ancient church; Spanish frontier.

REOLE (LA)
Gironde, 33190

LE FLAUTAT
(Mr Jean-Paul Daldoss) Route Nationale 113 - Le FlaÅtat
TEL: 05.56.71.00.37
LANGUAGES: English.
MENU: 50 Frs (wine included).
RESTAURANT: Snacks from 6.00, lunch 11.00-15.00, dinner 19.00-22.00
CLOSED: Sat, Sun and public holidays.
SPECIALITIES: home-cooking.
OTHER POINTS: credit cards accepted.

RIBERAC
Dordogne, 24600

SNACK BAR RESTAURANT LAKANAL
(Mr Jean-Marie Lagarde) 1, avenue Lakanal
TEL: 05.53.90.04.77
DIRECTIONS: the Angoulème/Agen road.
LANGUAGES: English.
MENU: 50 to 100 Frs.
RESTAURANT: Snacks from 6.30, lunch 11.30-14.30, dinner 17.30-22.00
CLOSED: Thurs afternoon.
SPECIALITIES: regional menu, Périgord dishes.
OTHER POINTS: credit cards accepted.
Brantôme; grotte (cave) at Villars; Dordogne valley.

RIEUPEYROUX
Aveyron, 12240

CHEZ PASCAL
(Mr Claude Bou) Rue de l'Hom
TEL: 05.65.65.51.13
DIRECTIONS: RD605, between Rodez (38km) and Villefranche-de-Rouergue (23km).
MENU: 65 to 130 Frs.
ROOMS: 120 to 210 Frs.
RESTAURANT: Snacks from 7.00, lunch 12.00-14.00, dinner 19.00-21.00
CLOSED: Sun evening (out of season), and 1st to 15th Oct and 2nd to 18th March.
SPECIALITIES: home-cooking, tripoux, confits, magrets, regional menu.
HOTEL: ☆ 8 rooms.
FACILITIES: shower, bath, private bathroom, television, telephone
OTHER POINTS: credit cards accepted.
château de Belcastel (15km); château du Bosc; grottes (caves) at Foissac (30km); viaduct at Le Viaur (30km); Rodez: cathedral (38km); Albi; gorges of the Tarn.

RIEUTORT DE RANDON
Lozère, 48700

RELAIS DE LA POSTE
(Mme Annie Magne) Place de la Poste
TEL: 04.66.47.34.67
DIRECTIONS: RN106, between Saint-Chély-d'Apcher and Mende.

MENU: 60 to 80 Frs.
RESTAURANT: Snacks from 6.30, lunch 11.00-14.00
CLOSED: Sat and Sun.
SPECIALITIES: home-cooking.
OTHER POINTS: bar.

RISCLE
Gers, 32400

RELAIS DE L'AUBERGE
(Mme Elisabeth Portes) Place de la Mairie
TEL: 05.62.69.70.49
ROOMS: 65 to 80 Frs.
HOTEL: 10 rooms
OTHER POINTS: bar.

RIVIERE (LA)
Gironde, 33126

LA RIVIERE
(Mme Laurence Cazenave) Route Départementale
TEL: 05.57.24.94.26
DIRECTIONS: RD670, between Libourne and Saint-André-de-Cubzac.
LANGUAGES: English.
MENU: 55 Frs (wine included) to 75 Frs.
RESTAURANT: Snacks from 6.30, lunch 11.30-15.00, dinner 19.00-23.00
SPECIALITIES: home-cooking.
OTHER POINTS: credit cards accepted.
Fronsac; the Bordeaux vineyards.

ROQUEFORT DES CORBIERES
Aude, 11540

RELAIS DES COTES DE ROQUEFORT
(Mr René Carbonnel) Route Nationale 9
TEL: 04.68.48.45.51 **FAX:** 04.68.48.32.88
DIRECTIONS: RN9.
LANGUAGES: German, Spanish.
MENU: 55 to 85 Frs.
RESTAURANT: Snacks from 7.00, lunch 11.30-15.00, dinner 19.00-22.00
CLOSED: Sun (out of season).
OTHER POINTS: bar.

LE ROMARIN
(Mr Jean-Charles Parant) Route Nationale 9
TEL: 04.68.48.65.22 **FAX:** 04.68.48.65.22
DIRECTIONS: RN9, Perpignan/Narbonne.
MENU: 70 to 180 Frs.
RESTAURANT: Snacks from 5.00
CLOSED: Sun (in winter).
SPECIALITIES: fishes and sea-food specialities, regional menu, home-cooking.
OTHER POINTS: credit cards accepted.
Village Portel: wine testing; african reserve; promenade à cheval (horse riding); beaches; Port La Nouvelle and forest.

ROUFFILLAC DE CARLUX
Dordogne, 24370

AUX POISSONS FRAIS
(Mr Jean-Noël Cayre)
TEL: 05.53.29.70.24 **FAX.** 05.53.31.16.36
DIRECTIONS: RD703, between Sarlat and Souillac.
LANGUAGES: English.
MENU: 75 to 220 Frs.
ROOMS: 250 to 365 Frs.
RESTAURANT: Snacks from 8.00, lunch 12.30-14.00, dinner 19.30-21.00
CLOSED: in Oct.
SPECIALITIES: confit de canard, cou d'oie farci (stuffed goose-neck), tête de veau ravigotte, large choice of desserts on Sun and public holidays, regional menu, home-cooking.
HOTEL: ☆☆ 18 rooms.
FACILITIES: shower, bath, private bathroom, television, telephone
OTHER POINTS: credit cards accepted.
grottes (caves) de Lascaux; Rocamadour; Padirac; Cognac; Les Eyzies; Sarlat; manoir d'Eyrignac.

ROUSSON
Gard, 30340

BAR RESTAURANT PIZZERIA LE RELAIS DU CHENE
(Mme Franáoise Oliver) Pont d'Avène
TEL: 04.66.85.81.21
DIRECTIONS: RD 904, RD904, Aubenas/Saint-Ambroix/Ales.
MENU: 58 (lunch), 60 (dinner) to 120 Frs.
SPECIALITIES: home-cooking.
OTHER POINTS: bar.

SAINT ANTOINE DE BREUILH
Dordogne, 24230

CAFE DE FRANCE - Chez Kiki
(Mme Valérie Patti)
TEL: 05.53.24.78.97
DIRECTIONS: RD936, between Bergerac and Libourne.
LANGUAGES: English, Spanish, Polish.
MENU: 57 Frs to 80 Frs.
RESTAURANT: Snacks from 6.00, lunch 6.00-14.00, dinner 19.30-23.00
SPECIALITIES: regional menu, home-cooking.
OTHER POINTS: credit cards accepted.
Bergerac vineyards; Saint-Emilion.

SAINT AUBIN DE BLAYE
Gironde, 33820

LE RELAIS DE ROUBISQUE
(Mr Olivier Devesa) Route Nationale 137
TEL: 05.57.64.72.62
DIRECTIONS: RN137, the Bordeaux/Saintes/Royan road.
LANGUAGES: English, Spanish.
MENU: 59 Frs (wine and coffee included).
RESTAURANT: Snacks from 7.00, lunch 11.30-14.30, dinner 19.00-22.00
CLOSED: Sun.
SPECIALITIES: plateau de fruits de mer, regional menu, home-cooking.
OTHER POINTS: bar.
centrale (power station) de Blaye.

SAINT CERE
Lot, 46400

HOTEL RESTAURANT DU QUERCY
(Mme Colette Gibbe) 21, avenue Anatole de Monzie
TEL: 05.65.38.04.83
DIRECTIONS: between Gramat and Rocamadour.
MENU: 52 to 180 Frs.
ROOMS: 130 to 200 Frs.
RESTAURANT: Snacks from 7.00, lunch 12.00-14.00, dinner 19.00-21.00
CLOSED: Fri afternoon (out of season).
SPECIALITIES: salade de gésiers, confit de canard forestier, foie gras, regional menu, home-cooking.
HOTEL: 10 rooms.
FACILITIES: shower
OTHER POINTS: credit cards accepted.
châteaux de Luráat, Castelneau and Montal; grottes (caves) de Padirac (gouffre); Saint-Céré: old town.

SAINT CHELY D'APCHER
Lozère, 48200

LE BARCELONE
(Mme Monique Vitré) 33, avenue de la Gare
TEL: 04.66.31.01.22
DIRECTIONS: RN9, Montpellier or Clermont-Ferrand.
MENU: 55 Frs.
ROOMS: 100 to 140 Frs.
RESTAURANT: Snacks from 9.00, lunch 12.00-13.30, dinner 19.30-21.00
CLOSED: Sun evening (out of season).
SPECIALITIES: home-cooking.
HOTEL: 5 rooms.
FACILITIES: shower, bath, private bathroom, telephone
OTHER POINTS: credit cards accepted.
Garabit viaduct; gorges of the Tarn; parc des loups du Gévaudan; les bisotis de La Margeride; Lozère region.

SAINT CREPIN D'AUBEROCHE
Dordogne, 24330

LE RELAIS DES ILES
(Mme Marie-Rosine Pouwels) Route Nationale 89
TEL: 05.53.54.73.49
DIRECTIONS: RN 89, RN89, on the Brive/Périgueux road.
LANGUAGES: English.
MENU: 55 Frs (wine included).
RESTAURANT: Snacks from 6.00, lunch 11.45-15.00, dinner 19.00-22.00
SPECIALITIES: regional menu, home-cooking, Mauriciennes (creole and sino-indian).
OTHER POINTS: bar.

SAINT ETIENNE DU VALDONNEZ
Lozère, 48000

LE RELAIS DE MONTMIRAT
(Mlle Géraldine Lavaud et Mr Arnaud Lacan) Route Nationale 106
TEL: 04.66.48.01.91
DIRECTIONS: RN 106, RN106, between Mende and Florac.
MENU: 55 to 120 Frs.
ROOMS: 150 to 250 Frs.
RESTAURANT: Snacks from 8.00, lunch 11.30-14.00, dinner 18.30-21.30
CLOSED: from 18th to 30th Dec and 1 week in Jan.
SPECIALITIES: regional menu, home-cooking.
HOTEL: 13 rooms.
FACILITIES: shower, bath, private bathroom, telephone
OTHER POINTS: credit cards accepted.

SAINT FELIX LAURAGAIS
Haute-Garonne, 31540

LE GRILLON
(Mme Aliette Bonnes) Route de Castelnaudary - Revel
TEL: 05.61.27.65.27
DIRECTIONS: RN622, between Toulouse and Casteinaudary.
MENU: 70 Frs.
ROOMS: 150 to 200 Frs.
RESTAURANT: Snacks from 7.00, lunch 12.00-14.00
CLOSED: Sun, public holidays and last 2 weeks in Aug.
SPECIALITIES: cassoulet au confit de canard, couscous, regional menu, home-cooking.
HOTEL: 5 rooms.
FACILITIES: shower
OTHER POINTS: credit cards accepted.

montagne noire; lac de Saint-Féréol; village de cuivres (cooper); Carcassonne.

SAINT GENIES DE MALGOIRES
Gard, 30190

L'OASIS
(Mme Fabienne Rouif) Route Nationale 106
TEL: 04.66.81.63.18
DIRECTIONS: RN106, Nîmes/Alès.
MENU: 66 Frs (wine and coffee included).
RESTAURANT: Snacks from 5.00, lunch 12.00-14.30, dinner 20.00-22.00
CLOSED: Sat and Sun out of season.
SPECIALITIES: home-cooking.
OTHER POINTS: credit cards accepted.

SAINT GERMAIN D'ESTEUIL
Gironde, 33340

LE RELAIS
(Mr André Destruel) Route Nationale 215
TEL: 05.56.73.06.28
DIRECTIONS: RN215, the Bordeaux/Le Verdon road.
MENU: 55 to 82 Frs.
RESTAURANT: Snacks from 7.30, lunch 11.30-15.00, dinner 19.00-20.00
CLOSED: Sun, last week in Aug and 1 week for Christmas/New Year.
SPECIALITIES: regional menu, magrets, confits, gambas, home-cooking.
OTHER POINTS: bar.
Pauillac; Le Verdon; Hourtiti: lakes; vineyards; extensive beaches.

SAINT JULIEN LES ROSIERS
Gard, 30340

LE MISTRAL
(Mr Yves Galéra) Route de Saint Ambroix
TEL: 04.66.86.15.29 FAX: 04.66.86.15.29
DIRECTIONS: RD904.
MENU: 55 Frs.
ROOMS: 100 to 150 Frs.
RESTAURANT: Snacks from 6.30, lunch 12.00-15.00, dinner 19.00-22.00
SPECIALITIES: tripoux, paella, rouille du pêcheur, regional menu, home-cooking.
HOTEL: 10 rooms.
FACILITIES: shower
OTHER POINTS: bar.
grottes Cocalières (20km); grottes Trabuc (20km); Pont du Gard (40km).

SAINT LON LES MINES
Landes, 40300

HOTEL DU FRONTON
(Mr Daniel Laffitte) Au Bourg
TEL: 05.58.57.80.45
DIRECTIONS: RN117, between Dax and Peyrehorade.
LANGUAGES: Spanish.
ROOMS: 130 to 200 Frs.
RESTAURANT: Snacks from 7.00, lunch 12.00-14.00, dinner 19.00-21.00
CLOSED: Fri evening, Sat lunch, and in Feb.
SPECIALITIES: foie gras, confits, magrets, regional menu, home-cooking.
HOTEL: ☆ 10 rooms.
FACILITIES: telephone
OTHER POINTS: credit cards accepted.
château de Peyrehorade; hot springs at Dax.

SAINT MARTIN DE SEIGNANX
Landes, 40390

LES ROUTIERS
(Mr Bernard Dupouy)
TEL: 05.59.56.52.25
DIRECTIONS: N117.
MENU: 55 Frs to 85 Frs.
ROOMS: 150 to 200 Frs.
RESTAURANT: Snacks from 7.30, lunch 11.30-15.00, dinner 20.00-23.00
CLOSED: Sun.
SPECIALITIES: home-cooking.
HOTEL: 5 rooms.
FACILITIES: shower, private bathroom, telephone
OTHER POINTS: bar.

SAINT NAUPHARY
Tarn-et-Garonne, 82370

LES ROUTIERS
(Mr Patrick Monruffet)
TEL: 05.63.67.85.09
DIRECTIONS: RD999, between Albi and Castres.
MENU: 50 to 62 Frs.
ROOMS: 90 to 130 Frs.
RESTAURANT: Snacks from 7.00, lunch 12.00-14.00, dinner 19.30-21.30
CLOSED: from Fri 17.00 to Mon 9.00, and in Aug.
SPECIALITIES: confits, home-cooking.
HOTEL: 11 rooms.
FACILITIES: shower, bath, private bathroom
OTHER POINTS: bar.
Saint-Antonin-Noble-Val; gorges of the Tarn.

SAINT NAZAIRE
Gard, 30200

LES TERAILLES
(Mme Nicole Menu) Route Nationale 86
TEL: 04.66.89.66.14
DIRECTIONS: RN86, between Bagnols-sur-Cèze and Pont-St-Esprit.

SPECIALITIES: home-cooking,
HOTEL: ☆ 12 rooms
OTHER POINTS: bar.

SAINT PARDOUX ISAAC
Lot-et-Garonne, 47800

LE BOSQUET - Chez Milord
(Mr Jean-Pierre Saby) Route de Bergerac
TEL: 05.53.93.49.59
DIRECTIONS: RD933, between Bayonne and Limoges.
LANGUAGES: Spanish.
MENU: 55 Frs (wine included) to 115 Frs.
ROOMS: 100 to 130 Frs.
RESTAURANT: Snacks from 5.30, lunch 11.30-15.00, dinner 19.30-23.00
SPECIALITIES: regional menu, home-cooking.
HOTEL: 7 rooms
OTHER POINTS: credit cards accepted.
châteaux de Duras and de Lauzun; Eymet; musée de la préhistoire; Miramont-de-Guyenne.

SAINT PAUL CAP DE JOUX
Tarn, 81220

LES GLYCINES
(Mr Claude Peyrard) Rue Philippe Pinel
TEL: 05.63.70.61.37
DIRECTIONS: RN112, between Montauban and Toulouse.
MENU: 65 Frs.
RESTAURANT: Snacks from 9.00, lunch 12.00-14.30, dinner 19.00-21.30
CLOSED: Mon.
SPECIALITIES: home-cooking.
OTHER POINTS: bar.

SAINT PAUL DE LOUBRESSAC
Lot, 46170

RELAIS DE LA MADELEINE
(Mr Bernard Devianne) Route Nationale 20
TEL: 05.65.21.98.08
DIRECTIONS: 100m from the RN 20 on RD 83 bis towards La Madeleine.
LANGUAGES: English, Spanish.
MENU: 60 to 150 Frs.
ROOMS: 140 to 250 Frs.
RESTAURANT: Snacks from 7.30, lunch 12.00-13.45, dinner 19.30-21.00
CLOSED: Sat all year, Sun (out of season), 1 week in early Nov and 2 weeks at Christmas.
SPECIALITIES: Quercy dishes: foie gras, confit, magret, regional menu, home-cooking.
HOTEL: ☆ 15 rooms.
FACILITIES: shower, bath, private bathroom, television, telephone
OTHER POINTS: credit cards accepted.

SAINT PERDON
Landes, 40090

LE RELAIS DE LA LANDE
(Mme Christiane Labarrière)
TEL: 05.58.75.08.25
DIRECTIONS: between Mont-de-Marsan and Dax.
LANGUAGES: English, Spanish.
MENU: 60 to 120 Frs.
ROOMS: 140 to 250 Frs.
RESTAURANT: Snacks from 7.30, lunch 12.00-14.00, dinner 17.30-21.30
CLOSED: Sat ou Sun (out of season).
SPECIALITIES: confits, magrets, gambas, foie gras, jambon de Bayonne, regional menu, home-cooking.
HOTEL: ☆ 10 rooms.
FACILITIES: shower, bath, private bathroom, television, telephone
OTHER POINTS: credit cards accepted.
Mont-de-Marsan: museum, amphitheatre, animal park.

SAINT PEY D'ARMENS
Gironde, 33330

RELAIS DE GASCOGNE
(Mr Eric Samson) Route Départementale 936
TEL: 02.57.47.15.02
DIRECTIONS: RD936, the Bergerac road.
LANGUAGES: English.
MENU: 55 Frs.
RESTAURANT: Snacks from 7.00, lunch 11.30-14.30, dinner 19.30-22.00
CLOSED: Sat evening and Sun.
SPECIALITIES: grillades, entrecôte, côte bordelaise, magret, regional menu, home-cooking.
OTHER POINTS: credit cards accepted.
Saint-Emilion; wine route; excavations.

SAINT PRIVAT DES VIEUX
Gard, 30340

L'ESCALE
(Mr Jean-Marc Calcat) 59, route de Bagnols
TEL: 04.66.30.54.14
DIRECTIONS: RD216, between Alès and Bagnols-sur-Cèze
LANGUAGES: English.
MENU: 60 Frs.
ROOMS: 110 to 160 Frs.
RESTAURANT: Snacks from 6.00, lunch 12.00-14.00, dinner 20.00-24.00
SPECIALITIES: regional menu, home-cooking.
HOTEL: 8 rooms.
OTHER POINTS: credit cards accepted.
Bambouseraie; mine témoin (mining exhibition) at Alès.

SAINT ROME DE CERNON
Aveyron, 12490

LES ROUTIERS
(Mr Philippe Sanchez) Avenue de Millau
TEL: 05.65.62.33.56
DIRECTIONS: RD999, the Millau/Saint-Affrique/Albi road.
MENU: 45 to 120 Frs.
ROOMS: 120 to 140 Frs.
RESTAURANT: Snacks from 7.00, lunch 12.00-14.30, dinner 19.00-22.00
CLOSED: Sun evening (restaurant).
SPECIALITIES: regional menu, home-cooking
HOTEL: 6 rooms
OTHER POINTS: credit cards accepted.
gorges of the Tarn; caves (cellars) de Roquefort.

SAINT SEURIN SUR L'ISLE
Gironde, 33660

BRASSERIE DE LA GARE
(Mr Roland Douin) RN 89 La Gare
TEL: 05.57.49.71.58
DIRECTIONS: RN89, Bordeaux/Périgueux road.
MENU: 53 Frs (wine included).
RESTAURANT: Snacks from 5.00
SPECIALITIES: home-cooking.
OTHER POINTS: credit cards accepted.
the Isle valley; Saint-Emillion.

SAINT VINCENT DE PAUL
Landes, 40990

AUX PLATANES
(Mr Roger Vicente)
TEL: 05.58.73.90.13
DIRECTIONS: RN124.
LANGUAGES: Spanish.
OTHER POINTS: bar.

SAINTE GEMME
Tarn, 81190

HOTEL DE LA TERRASSE
(Mr Jean-Christophe Carcenac) Route Nationale 88 - Les Farguettes
TEL: 05.63.76.66.97
DIRECTIONS: RN 88, RN88, on the Toulouse/Rodez axis.
LANGUAGES: German.
MENU: 60 Frs.
ROOMS: 85 to 135 Frs.
RESTAURANT: Snacks from 7.00, lunch 11.30-14.30, dinner 19.00-21.00
CLOSED: Fri evening.
HOTEL: 3 rooms
OTHER POINTS: bar.

SAINTE LIVRADE
Lot-et-Garonne, 47110

AU BON ACCUEIL
(Mme Roberdeau) Route de Villeneuve
TEL: 05.53.01.02.34
DIRECTIONS: RN111, Tonnein/Villeneuve sur Lot.
LANGUAGES: English, Spanish.
MENU: 57 Frs (wine included).
ROOMS: 110 to 150 Frs.
RESTAURANT: Snacks from 6.30, lunch 12.00-14.00, dinner 19.30-21.30
CLOSED: Fri, Sat and Sun evening.
SPECIALITIES: regional menu, home-cooking,
HOTEL: 8 rooms
OTHER POINTS: credit cards accepted.

SAINTE MARIE DE GOSSE
Landes, 40390

LES ROUTIERS
(Mr Marc Deloube) Route Nationale 117
TEL: 05.59.56.32.02 **FAX:** 05.59.56.36.06
DIRECTIONS: RN117, between Bayonne and Pau.
LANGUAGES: English, Spanish.
MENU: 50 to 150 Frs.
ROOMS: 120 to 180 Frs.
RESTAURANT: Snacks from 6.00, lunch 12.00-14.30, dinner 19.30-22.00
CLOSED: Fri evening and Sat (out of season), and from mid-Oct to mid-Nov.
SPECIALITIES: confits, foie gras, poissons régionaux (in season), salade landaise, foie en terrine et foie frais, regional menu, home-cooking.
HOTEL: ☆ 15 rooms.
FACILITIES: shower, bath, private bathroom, telephone
OTHER POINTS: credit cards accepted.
Landes and Basque coasts; caves; abbeys.

SARLAT
Dordogne, 24200

CAFETERIA DU PONTET
(Mr Jean-Pierre Bouy) Route de Bergerac
TEL: 05.53.31.05.36 **FAX:** 05.53.29.46.14
DIRECTIONS: RN21, the Bergerac road.
LANGUAGES: English, Spanish.
MENU: 35 Frs. Dish of the day at 25 Frs.
RESTAURANT: Snacks from 8.00, lunch 11.30-15.00, dinner 19.00-22.00
CLOSED: New Year's Eve and New Year's Day.
SPECIALITIES: gibiers (game), sanglier (boar), magret sauce au poivre, regional menu, home-cooking.
OTHER POINTS: credit cards accepted.
Sariat; Rocamadour; gouffre de Padirac; Castelnaud; Les Eyzies; grottes de Lascaux.

SEILH
Haute-Garonne, 31840

LES ROUTIERS
(Mme Nelly Gouyou) Les Tricheries
TEL: 05.61.59.90.17
DIRECTIONS: Blagnac or Grenoble.
MENU: 55 to 120 Frs.
RESTAURANT: Snacks from 6.30, dinner 18.30-20.30
SPECIALITIES: cassoulet, daube, pot au feu, home-cooking.
OTHER POINTS: credit cards accepted.

SERRES CASTET
Pyrénées-Atlantiques, 64121

LES ROUTIERS
(Mr Léon Salis)
TEL: 05.59.33.91.06
DIRECTIONS: RN134, the Bordeaux road.
LANGUAGES: Spanish.
MENU: 60 Frs.
ROOMS: 100 Frs.
RESTAURANT: Snacks from 6.00
CLOSED: Sun, and in Aug.
SPECIALITIES: B6arn dishes, regional menu, home-cooking.
HOTEL: 5 rooms.
FACILITIES: shower, private bathroom
OTHER POINTS: bar.
Pau: museum, château; Lourdes.

SETE
Hérault, 34560

LE 7 SUR SETE
Route Nationale 113 - Poussan
TEL: 04.67.78.33.29 FAX: 04.67.78.36.07
DIRECTIONS: between Sète and Béziers.
RESTAURANT: Snacks from 6.00, lunch 11.30-14.30, dinner 19.30-22.00
CLOSED: Sat evening and Sun evening.
SPECIALITIES: regional menu, home-cooking.
OTHER POINTS: credit cards accepted.
Bouziques: oyster beds; Montpellier; the Camargue.

LA REGENCE - Les Isles
(Mme Savita Barthe) 1, place de Lille
TEL: 04.67.74.32.92
DIRECTIONS: RN108, on the Montpellier road, at the entrance to the port.
MENU: 65 Frs (wine included).
RESTAURANT: Snacks from 8.30, lunch 9.00-16.00, dinner 19.00-23.00
SPECIALITIES: moules farcies, paella, encornets farcis (seafood), poulet au curry, couscous, regional menu.
OTHER POINTS: bar.
the sea; pool (étang); mountains; grave of George Brassens.

LA PENICHE - Resto Routiers
(Mme Pâquerette Dupuy) 1, quai des Moulins
TEL: 04.67.48.64.13
DIRECTIONS: RN108; as you reach Sète, coming from Montpeliier.
LANGUAGES: English, Spanish.
MENU: 62 Frs.
RESTAURANT: Lunch 12.00-14.00, dinner 19.00-22.00
CLOSED: Sat lunch.
SPECIALITIES: rouille sétoise, bourride sétoise, coquelet aux écrevisses, moules, regional menu, home-cooking.
OTHER POINTS: credit cards accepted.
Mont Saint-Clair; espace Georges-Brassens.

SOTURAC
Lot, 46700

LA TABLE AUX AMIS
(Mme Bernadette Bessou) Route Départementale 911
TEL: 05.53.40.97.78
DIRECTIONS: RD911, between Cahors and Fumel.
MENU: 55 Frs (wine included) to 90 Frs.
RESTAURANT: Snacks from 6.00, lunch 11.30-15.00, dinner 19.00-22.00
CLOSED: Mon evening (out of season), and 2 weeks in Feb.
SPECIALITIES: poule au pot, raviolis frais, mique, home-cooking.
OTHER POINTS: credit cards accepted.
Fumel; Duravel.

SOUILLAC
Lot, 46200

RELAIS DE L'ESCALE
(Mr Alain Fage) 39 Avenue Louis Jean Malvy
TEL: 05.65.37.82.65
DIRECTIONS: RN20.
OTHER POINTS: bar.

SOUMOULOU
Pyrénées-Atlantiques, 64420

HOTEL RESTAURANT BEARNAIS
(Mme Anne-Marie Delroise) 5, rue des Platanes
TEL: 05.59.04.60.45 FAX: 59.04.64.54
DIRECTIONS: between Tarbes and Lourdes.
MENU: 50 to 65 Frs.
ROOMS: 80 to 120 Frs.
RESTAURANT: Snacks from 6.00, lunch 11.00-16.00, dinner 18.00-22.00
CLOSED: Sat, and 3 weeks in Aug.

SPECIALITIES: confit de canard, poissons, regional menu, home-cooking.
HOTEL: 5 rooms
OTHER POINTS: bar.
grottes (caves) de Betharan; Lourdes; Pau: château; the Pyrenees.

TARBES
Hautes-Pyrénées, 65000

LE RELAIS DES PYRENEES
(Mr Jean-Louis Perez et Jacques Duvin) Autoport des Pyrénées Boulevard Kennedy
TEL: 05.62.93.26.06 **FAX:** 05.62.93.28.88
DIRECTIONS: the Bayonne/Toulouse road, via boulevard périphérique.
LANGUAGES: Spanish.
MENU: 50 to 90 Frs.
RESTAURANT: Snacks from 6.30, lunch 11.45-14.15, dinner 19.30-21.30
CLOSED: Sat evening and Sun (except groups).
SPECIALITIES: tripes, cassoulet, confits, couscous, home-cooking.
OTHER POINTS: credit cards accepted.
Lourdes; ski resorts; mountains; lakes.

LE VICTOR HUGO
(Mme Patricia Jouanlong) 52, rue Victor Hugo
TEL: 05.62.93.36.71
DIRECTIONS: RN117, Gare SNCF.
LANGUAGES: English, Spanish.
MENU: 50 to 100 Frs.
ROOMS: 80 to 120 Frs.
RESTAURANT: Snacks from 7.00, lunch 11.00-15.00, dinner 18.00-21.30
CLOSED: Sun.
SPECIALITIES: confit de canard maison, magret de canard, gambas flambées, moules marinières, brochettes, regional menu, home-cooking.
HOTEL: 8 rooms
OTHER POINTS: bar.
Lourdes; La Mongie and Cauterets (ski); grottes (caves) de Bétharam; le 'donjon des aigles'.

TAURIAC DE NAUCELLE
Aveyron, 12800

LE RELAIS DU VIADUC
(Mme Jacqueline Leduc) Pont de Tanus
TEL: 05.65.69.23.81 **FAX:** 05.65.72.04.61
DIRECTIONS: RN 88, RN88, Rodez-Albi-Toulouse.
MENU: 60 to 125 Frs.
RESTAURANT: Snacks from 6.30, lunch 11.30, dinner up to 23.00
CLOSED: Sun evening.
SPECIALITIES: home-cooking, Normandes.
OTHER POINTS: credit cards accepted.

TEMPLE SUR LOT (LE)
Lot-et-Garonne, 47110

LE VAL DU LOT
(Mr Lionel Hutrel) Gouneau
TEL: 05.53.84.90.26
DIRECTIONS: RD91 1, the Villeneuve-sur-Lot/Bordeaux/Agen/Bergerac road.
LANGUAGES: English.
MENU: 47 Frs to 125 Frs.
ROOMS: 100 to 120 Frs.
RESTAURANT: Snacks from 7.00, lunch 12.00-14.30, dinner 19.00-22.00
CLOSED: Sat and from mid-Aug to mid-Sept.
SPECIALITIES: confits, magrets, regional menu, home-cooking.
HOTEL: 5 rooms.
FACILITIES: shower, bath
OTHER POINTS: credit cards accepted.
naval base; abbaye des automates (automata); musée du pruneau (prunes/plums), caves (wine-cellars) de Buzet.

THENON
Dordogne, 24210

CHEZ SERGE - LES TOURNISSOUS
(Mr Serge Leymarie) Les Tournissous
TEL: 05.53.05.20.31
DIRECTIONS: RN89, between Brive-la-Gaillarde and Périgueux.
LANGUAGES: English, Portuguese.
MENU: 40 to 76 Frs.
ROOMS: 90 to 180 Frs.
RESTAURANT: Snacks from 4.00
SPECIALITIES: foie gras, confit de canard, entrecôte, home-cooking.
HOTEL: 12 rooms.
FACILITIES: shower, bath, private bathroom, television, telephone
OTHER POINTS: credit cards accepted.
grottes de Lascaux (15km); Sarlat (40km).

TOULOUSE
Haute-Garonne, 31300

LE PROGRES
(Mr Félix Ober) 185, route de Bayonne
TEL: 05.61.49.22.75
DIRECTIONS: RN124, Auch.
MENU: 60 to 220 Frs.
RESTAURANT: Snacks from 7.00, lunch 12.00-14.00, dinner 19.00-22.00
CLOSED: Sun, and in Aug.
SPECIALITIES: regional menu.
OTHER POINTS: credit cards accepted.
Toulouse.

TOURNAY
Hautes-Pyrénées, 65190

CAFE DE LA GARE
(Mme Yasmina Marchand) 14, rue du Général Leclerc
TEL: 05.62.35.70.15
DIRECTIONS: between Tarbes and Lannemezan.
MENU: 55 to 60 Frs.
ROOMS: 120 to 150 Frs.
RESTAURANT: Snacks from 7.00, lunch 12.00-14.00, dinner 19.00-21.00
CLOSED: Sun.
SPECIALITIES: home-cooking.
HOTEL: 5 rooms.
FACILITIES: shower, bath, private bathroom
OTHER POINTS: credit cards accepted.

TREBES
Aude, 11800

LE RELAIS DES CAPUCINS
(Mr Gilbert Laffont) 34, route de Narbonne
TEL: 04.68.78.70.07
DIRECTIONS: RN113, 2km from the Carcassonne Est (East) exit, towards Narbonne.
LANGUAGES: English, Spanish.
MENU: 64 Frs (wine included).
ROOMS: 95 to 130 Frs.
RESTAURANT: Snacks from 6.00, lunch 11.30, dinner up to 23.00
CLOSED: Sat, Sun, 1 week in July and 1 week from Christmas Day.
SPECIALITIES: cassoulet au confit, couscous, regional menu, home-cooking.
HOTEL: 13 rooms.
FACILITIES: shower, private bathroom
OTHER POINTS: credit cards accepted.
Carcassonne; Catharist châteaux.

TRIE SUR BAISE
Hautes-Pyrénées, 65220

CAFE RESTAURANT DE LA PAIX
(Mr Jacky Cenac) 37, rue des Monts de Bigorre
TEL: 05.62.35.61.11 FAX: 05.62.35.65.66
DIRECTIONS: RD632.
LANGUAGES: Spanish.
MENU: 55 Frs (wine included).
RESTAURANT: Snacks from 7.00, lunch 10.00-15.00, dinner 19.30-22.00
CLOSED: Wed afternoon (after 3pm).
SPECIALITIES: home-cooking.
OTHER POINTS: credit cards accepted.
Lourdes.

VALERGUES
Hérault, 34130

RELAIS DE VALERGUES
(Mr Claude Bernabé) Route Nationale 113
TEL: 04.67.86.75.27
DIRECTIONS: RN113.
LANGUAGES: Spanish.
RESTAURANT: dinner up to 23.00
CLOSED: Sun.
OTHER POINTS: bar.

VENSAC
Gironde, 33590

RESTAURANT CHEZ NICOLE
(Mme Nicole Figerou) 24, grand'rue
TEL: 05.56.09.44.05
MENU: 60 Frs.
ROOMS: 120 to 180 Frs.
RESTAURANT: Snacks from 8.00, lunch 12.00-14.00, dinner 19.00-21.00
CLOSED: Mon (out of season).
SPECIALITIES: foie gras, confits maison, cèpes, regional menu, home-cooking.
HOTEL: 5 rooms.
FACILITIES: shower
OTHER POINTS: credit cards accepted.
windmill; châteaux.

VIAZAC
Lot, 46100

LE BUZAC
(Mr Jean-Luc Lacambre) Route d'Aurillac
TEL: 05.65.34.20.02
DIRECTIONS: RN 122, RN122, between Figeac and Aurillac.
LANGUAGES: English, Spanish, Italian.
MENU: 58 Frs (drink and coffee included).
ROOMS: 90 to 140 Frs.
RESTAURANT: Snacks from 6.00, lunch 11.30-14.30, dinner 19.00-22.00
CLOSED: Sat.
SPECIALITIES: regional menu, home-cooking, grillades (June-Septembre).
HOTEL: 9 rooms
OTHER POINTS: credit cards accepted.

VIC EN BIGORRE
Hautes-Pyrénées, 65500

LE RANCH
(Mr Bernard Griffon) Route de Rabastens de Bigorre
TEL: 05.62.96.72.32
DIRECTIONS: the Auch road.
MENU: 55 to 120 Frs.

RESTAURANT: Snacks from 7.00, lunch 12.00-15.00, dinner 20.00-22.00
CLOSED: Sat, and in Oct.
SPECIALITIES: regional menu, home-cooking.
OTHER POINTS: credit cards accepted.
Lourdes; the Pyrenees.

VIC LE FESQ
Gard, 30260

RELAIS DE LA NOUVELLE
(Mr Hubert Tani)
TEL: 04.66.77.82.81
DIRECTIONS: between Montpeliier and Alès.
MENU: 65 Frs.
RESTAURANT: Snacks from 6.00, lunch 11.00-14.00, dinner 19.00-20.30
CLOSED: Sat evening, Sun and public holidays (out of season), 2 weeks end Aug and 1 week end Dec.
SPECIALITIES: regional menu, home-cooking.
OTHER POINTS: credit cards accepted.
gateway to the Cévennes; caves (wine-cellars); museums.

VILLEFRANCHE DE ROUERGUE
Aveyron, 12200

RELAIS DES CABRIERES
(Mr Alain Toulouse) Route de Montauban
TEL: 05.65.81.16.99
DIRECTIONS: RD926, the Montauban/Toulouse road.
MENU: 45 to 60 Frs.
RESTAURANT: Snacks from 8.00, lunch 11.00-15.00
CLOSED: Sun.
SPECIALITIES: tripes, tripoux, home-cooking.
OTHER POINTS: bar.
grottes (caves) de Foisac; Villefranche: bastide (country house); château (ruins) at Najac.

VILLENEUVE D'AVEYRON
Aveyron, 12260

AUBERGE DE LA TOUR - Chez Rosy et Francis
(Mme Rose-Mary Scudier-Laval) Faubourg Saint Roch
TEL: 05.65.81.75.62
DIRECTIONS: in the suburb of Saint-Roch.
MENU: 55 to 140 Frs.
RESTAURANT: Snacks from 7.00, lunch 11.30-14.00, dinner 19.00-20.30
CLOSED: Sat, and 2 weeks in Aug.
SPECIALITIES: home-cooking.
OTHER POINTS: credit cards accepted.

VILLENEUVE DE RIVIERE
Haute-Garonne, 31800

L'ESCALE
(Mr Gérard Valentin) Route Nationale 117
TEL: 05.61.89.39.05 FAX: 05.61.95.08.83
DIRECTIONS: RN117, between Toulouse and lrun (Spanish border).
LANGUAGES: Spanish.
MENU: 60 to 75 Frs.
ROOMS: 100 to 150 Frs.
RESTAURANT: Snacks from 5.15
CLOSED: Sun.
SPECIALITIES: confits de canard, foie gras mi-cuit, regional menu, home-cooking.
HOTEL: 10 rooms.
FACILITIES: shower, television
OTHER POINTS: credit cards accepted.
Luchon; Lourdes; the Pyrenees.

VILLENEUVE SUR LOT
Lot-et-Garonne, 47300

RELAIS DE GASCOGNE
(Mr Alain Guiraud) 31, avenue du Général Leclerc
TEL: 05.53.70.06.48
DIRECTIONS: RN21, Agen.
LANGUAGES: Spanish.
MENU: 54 to 110 Frs.
ROOMS: 120 to 160 Frs.
RESTAURANT: Lunch 11.45-14.00, dinner 19.00-22.00
CLOSED: Sun (except bookings).
SPECIALITIES: Gascon dishes, regional menu.
HOTEL: 8 rooms.
FACILITIES: shower, private bathroom, television
OTHER POINTS: credit cards accepted.

VILLETELLE
Hérault, 34400

BOUQUET RESTAURATION
(Bouquet SA) A.9 Aire d'Ambrusson Nord
TEL: 04.67.86.87.88 FAX: 04.67.86.87.89
DIRECTIONS: A9, between Nimes and Montpellier.
LANGUAGES: English, Spanish, Italian.
MENU: 64 Frs (1/4 wine and coffee included).
RESTAURANT: Snacks from 5.00
SPECIALITIES: boeuf gardiane, seiche (cuttlefish) provenáale, regional menu.
OTHER POINTS: credit cards accepted.
Ambrusson; Gallo-Roman bridge.

VIRAZEIL
Lot-et-Garonne, 47200

LE RALLYE
(Mr Louis Le Gall) Route Départementale 933
TEL: 05.53.20.18.77
DIRECTIONS: D933, the Périgueux/Mont-de-Marsan axis.
LANGUAGES: English.
MENU: 58 Frs.
RESTAURANT: Snacks from 6.00, lunch 12.00-14.00, dinner 19.00-21.30
CLOSED: Mon afternoon.
SPECIALITIES: home-cooking.
OTHER POINTS: credit cards accepted.
Château de Duras; Garonne valley; musée de la Roue (museum of the wheel).

South-East France

The following départments are included in this chapter:

Ain (01)
Alpes-de-Haute-Provence (04)
Alpes Maritime (06)
Ardèche (07)
Bouches-du-Rhône (13)
Drôme (26)
Haute-Savoie (74)
Hautes Alpes (05)
Isère (38)
Loire (42)
Rhône (69)
Savoie (73)
Var (83)
Vaucluse (84)

ALBENC (L')
Isère, 38470

AUBERGE DU VERCORS
(Mme Claudette Torri) Place Jean Vinay
TEL: 04.76.64.75.17
DIRECTIONS: RN92, the Grenoble and Valence road.
RESTAURANT: Snacks from 6.30, lunch 12.00-14.00, dinner 19.00-21.00
CLOSED: Sun, and the 1st week of Aug.
SPECIALITIES: home-cooking.
OTHER POINTS: bar.
Le Vercors; wine-cellars at Choranche; Voiron: La Grande Chartreuse.

ALBON
Drôme, 26140

RELAIS DE LA TOUR D'ALBON
(Mr Camille Bertrand) Route Nationale 7
TEL: 04.75.03.11.22
DIRECTIONS: RN7, either Chanas Sud (South) exit or Valence Nord (North) exit.
LANGUAGES: English.
MENU: 63 Frs.
ROOMS: 130 to 200 Frs.
RESTAURANT: Snacks from 6.00, lunch 11.00-15.00, dinner 19.00-22.30
CLOSED: Sun (except to order).
SPECIALITIES: home-cooking.
HOTEL: 13 rooms. FACILITIES: shower
OTHER POINTS: credit cards accepted.
Auterive: palais idéal du Facteur Cheval (fantasy shell palace); Peaugres: safari park; tour d'Albon; cave (wine-cellar) de Saint-Donat.

ALIXAN
Drôme, 26300

HOTEL ALPES PROVENCE
(Mr Jean-Claude Bocaud) Aire de Bayanne
TEL: 04.75.47.02.84 FAX: 04.75.47.11.72
DIRECTIONS: RN532, Valence Nord (North) exit, towards Grenoble.
LANGUAGES: English, German.
MENU: 58 to 200 Frs.
ROOMS: 140 to 300 Frs,
RESTAURANT: Snacks from 6.00, lunch 12.00-14.00, dinner 19.30-21.30
SPECIALITIES: regional menu.
HOTEL: ☆☆ 22 rooms. FACILITIES: shower, bath, private bathroom, television, telephone
OTHER POINTS: credit cards accepted.
Rornans: musée de]a chaussure (shoes); Auterive: palais du Facteur Cheval; excursions into Le Vercors; Upie: jardin des oiseaux (bird garden).

ALLEX
Drôme, 26400

LE DAUPHINOIS
(Mr Marcel Pisano) Quartier de la Butte
TEL: 04.75.62.61.69
DIRECTIONS: RN7 and RD93, between Fiancey and Crest.
MENU: 60 to 65 Frs.
SPECIALITIES: home-cooking.
OTHER POINTS: credit cards accepted.
site des Rainières; Le Vercors (60km); Auterive: patais idéal du Facteur Cheval (60km); aquarium and bird gardens.

AMBERIEU EN BUGEY
Ain, 01500

LE RELAIS DU BUGEY HUBERT - Chez Denise
(Mme Denise Hubert) 84, avenue Jules Pellaudin
TEL: 04.74.38.10.27
DIRECTIONS: RN504.
RESTAURANT: Dinner -24.00
CLOSED: Sun, Aug.
OTHER POINTS: bar.

AMPUIS
Rhône, 69420

AUX PORTES DE PROVENCE
(Mr Maurice Terpend) Route Nationale 86 - Les Allées
TEL: 04.74.56.10.31 **FAX:** 04.74.56.19.10
DIRECTIONS: RN86, Nimes.
ROOMS: 80 to 150 Frs.
RESTAURANT: Snacks from 7.00, lunch 12.00-14.30, dinner 19.00-22.00
CLOSED: Wed.
SPECIALITIES: home-cooking,
HOTEL: 9 rooms. **FACILITIES:** shower, bath
OTHER POINTS: credit cards accepted.
Peaugres: safari park.

ARBRESLE (L')
Rhône, 69210

RELAIS DES ROUTIERS
(Mme Marie-Antoinette Durix-Michaud) 91, rue Gabriel Péri
TEL: 04.74.01.05.81
DIRECTIONS: RN89, Clermont-Ferrand.
MENU: 60 Frs.
RESTAURANT: Snacks from 6.30
CLOSED: Sat afternoon and Sun.
SPECIALITIES: home-cooking.
OTHER POINTS: bar.

ARCS SUR ARGENS (LES)
Var, 83460

HOTEL DE L'AVENIR
(Mme Marie-Jeanne Hortal) Rue Jean Jaurès
TEL: 04.94.73.30.58
MENU: 55 to 100 Frs.
ROOMS: 100 to 215 Frs.
RESTAURANT: Lunch 12.00-14.30, dinner 19.00-21.30
CLOSED: Sat (out of season).
HOTEL: 29 rooms
OTHER POINTS: bar.

ARLES
Bouches-du-Rhône, 13200

LE RELAIS DU PASSAGE A NIVEAU
(Antoine et Laurence Pech-Faure) Route de Tarascon - 31, avenue de la Libération
TEL: 04.90.96.06.64
DIRECTIONS: RN113.
LANGUAGES: English, German, Spanish, Italian.
HOTEL: 8 rooms
OTHER POINTS: bar.

LE PALMIER
(Mme Chantal Volle) Route de Saint Gilles - Quartier de la Furanne
TEL: 04.90.96.04.06
DIRECTIONS: RN 572, RN572, Arles-Saint Gilles-Montpellier.
MENU: 58 Frs (wine included).
RESTAURANT: Snacks from 7.00
CLOSED: Sun afternoon.
SPECIALITIES: regional menu, home-cooking.
OTHER POINTS: credit cards accepted.

AUBAGNE
Bouches-du-Rhône, 13400

LES PALMIERS
(Mr Gérard Cannistraro) 24, route Nationale 8 - Saint Mitre
TEL: 04.42.03.12.14
DIRECTIONS: RN 8, RN8, between La Penne and Aubagne.
LANGUAGES: English.
MENU: 55 to 100 Frs.
RESTAURANT: Snacks from 6.00, lunch 11.30-14.30, dinner 19.00-22.00
CLOSED: Sun.
SPECIALITIES: regional menu, home-cooking.
OTHER POINTS: credit cards accepted.

AUBIGNAS
Ardèche, 07400

CAFE TABAC DE LA GARE - Les Routiers
(Mlle Elisabeth Borne) Quartier de la Gare
TEL: 04.75.52.43.89
DIRECTIONS: RN102, between Montélimar and Le Puy-en-Velay.
LANGUAGES: English.
MENU: from 60 Frs.
ROOMS: 75 to 200 Frs.
RESTAURANT: Snacks from 6.30, lunch 11.30-15.00, dinner 18.50-21.00
CLOSED: Sat and Sun (out of season).
SPECIALITIES: regional menu, home-cooking.
HOTEL: 5 rooms. **FACILITIES:** shower, bath, private bathroom
OTHER POINTS: credit cards accepted.
gorges of the Ardèche; Ardèche canoe trips; Vallon-Pont-d'Arc; Vals-les-Bains (thermal resort).

AVIGNON
Vaucluse, 84140

RELAIS D'AVIGNON
(Mrs Daniel et Laurent Savry) La Petite Castelette - Montfavet
TEL: 04.90.84.18.28 **FAX:** 04.90.84.17.60
DIRECTIONS: RN7, exit at Avignon Sud (South).
RESTAURANT: Snacks from 5.00

s: toro à la gardiane, regional menu.
19 rooms. FACILITIES: shower, bath, private bathroom, television, telephone
OTHER POINTS: credit cards accepted.
Avignon; Saint-Rémy; Les Baux-de-Provence; Pont du Card; Nîmes; Arles; the Camargue.

BALAN LA VALBONNE
Ain, 01360

LE FRONT DE BANDIERE
(Mr André Voussatiouk-Koval) Route de Balan
TEL: 04.78.06.35.61
MENU: 53 Frs.
ROOMS: 80 to 100 Frs.
RESTAURANT: Lunch 11.45-15.00, dinner 19.45-22.00
SPECIALITIES: home-cooking.
HOTEL: 10 rooms. FACILITIES: shower
OTHER POINTS: bar.
Pérouges: medieval city; Port-Galan.

BALMONT COMMUNE DE SEYNOD
Haute-Savoie, 74600

L'AUBERGE
(Mr Pierre Carlioz) 1152, route d'Aix les Bains
TEL: 04.50.46.71.02
DIRECTIONS: RN201, Annecy/Aix-les-Bains axis.
MENU: 60 to 120 Frs.
ROOMS: 120 to 150 Frs.
RESTAURANT: Snacks from 6.00, lunch 11.30-15.00, dinner 19.00-23.00
CLOSED: Sat (out of season) and Sun.
SPECIALITIES: home-cooking.
HOTEL: 8 rooms
OTHER POINTS: credit cards accepted.

BARCELONNETTE
Alpes-de-Haute-Provence, 04400

LES SEOLANES
(Mr Hubert Maure) Les Thuiles
TEL: 04.92.81.07.37
DIRECTIONS: Gap.
LANGUAGES: English, Italian.
MENU: 68 to 120 Frs.
ROOMS: 115 to 220 Frs.
RESTAURANT: Snacks from 7.00, lunch 12.00-13.30, dinner 19.00-21.00
CLOSED: Sat and Sun (out of season).
SPECIALITIES: raviolles, home-cooking.
HOTEL: 6 rooms. FACILITIES: shower
OTHER POINTS: credit cards accepted.
valJée de l'Ubaye; fort; musée de Barcelonnette; parc national de Mercantour.

BARNAS
Ardèche, 07330

A L'ETOILE 102
(Mme Joëlle Dupuis) Route Nationale 102
TEL: 04.75.36.40.78
DIRECTIONS: RN102, RN102, Montélimar/Le Puy/Clermont-Ferrand.
MENU: 60 to 100 Frs.
ROOMS: 130 to 170 Frs.
RESTAURANT: Snacks from 7.00, lunch 12.00-14.30, dinner 19.00-22.00
SPECIALITIES: home-cooking.
HOTEL: 12 rooms. FACILITIES: shower, bath
OTHER POINTS: bar.

BARQUE (LA)
Bouches-du-Rhône, 13710

LE RELAIS DES 4 CHEMINS
(Mr Girardi - SARL Lauvir)
TEL: 04.42.58.60.03
MENU: 60 Frs.
RESTAURANT: Snacks from 4.00, lunch 11.30-15.00
CLOSED: Sat and Sun.
SPECIALITIES: regional menu, home-cooking.
OTHER POINTS: credit cards accepted.

BEAUCROISSANT
Isère, 38140

LES ROUTIERS DU CHAMP DE FOIRE
(Mme Marie-Thérèse Blain) Le Bain
TEL: 04.76.91.05.17
DIRECTIONS: RD159.
MENU: 55 to 60 Frs.
RESTAURANT: Lunch 11.00-14.30, dinner 19.00-21.00
CLOSED: Sun, 2 weeks in May and 2 weeks in Oct.
SPECIALITIES: couscous, poulet aux écrevisses and rognons à la portugaise, home-cooking.
OTHER POINTS: credit cards accepted.
couvent (convent) at La Chartreuse (30km); distillery (10km).

BEAUSSET (LE)
Var, 83330

LE RESTAURANT DE L'AERODROME DU CASTELLET
(Mme Marie-France Gautier) Route Nationale 8
TEL: 04.94.90.71.48
LANGUAGES: English, Portuguese.
RESTAURANT: Lunch 11.30-15.00
CLOSED: Sat, and in Aug.
SPECIALITIES: couscous, aioli, home-cooking.
OTHER POINTS: bar.

BELLEVILLE
Rhône, 69220

RESTAURANT BELLERIVE
(Mr Lucien Pages) 6, avenue du Port
TEL: 04.74.66.33.82 FAX: 04.74.66.39.81
DIRECTIONS: RD17, exit Belleville, towards Châtillon.
MENU: 58 to 100 Frs.
RESTAURANT: Snacks from 8.00, lunch 11.00-15.00, dinner 19.00-22.30
CLOSED: Sun evening (from Oct to March).
SPECIALITIES: fritures (whitebait) de Saône, grenouilles, coq au vin, regional menu, home-cooking.
OTHER POINTS: bar.
Villars: bird park; museums; Beaujolais wine-cellars; Roche de Solutré; Pérouge: medieval village.

BELLEY
Ain, 01300

RESTAURANT DE LA GARE
(Mme Elisabeth Bavu) Avenue de la Gare
TEL: 04.79.81.06.60
DIRECTIONS: RN504.
LANGUAGES: Italian.
MENU: 40 Frs.
ROOMS: 80 to 150 Frs.
RESTAURANT: Snacks from 6.30, lunch 12.00-14.00, dinner 20.00-22.00
CLOSED: last 2 weeks in Dec.
SPECIALITIES: gibiers (game), poissons, grenouilles, escargots, regional menu, home-cooking.
HOTEL: 5 rooms
OTHER POINTS: bar.

BELLIGNAT
Ain, 01810

LA BONNE AUBERGE - Les Routiers
(Mr Michel Detouillon) 11, avenue Oyonnax
TEL: 04.74.77.24.18
DIRECTIONS: RN840, exit Saint-Martin-du-Frêne, towards Lyon/Nantua.
MENU: 55 Frs.
RESTAURANT: Snacks from 6.30, lunch 11.30-14.00, dinner 19.30-20.30
CLOSED: Sun, and in Aug.
SPECIALITIES: regional menu, home-cooking.
HOTEL: 4 rooms. FACILITIES: shower, telephone
OTHER POINTS: credit cards accepted.

BELLIGNEUX
Ain, 01360

LE JATHANIEL
(Mr Jacques Jarrier) Route Nationale 84 - La Grande Dangereuse
TEL: 04.78.06.09.86
DIRECTIONS: on the Lyon/Genève axis.
LANGUAGES: English.
MENU: 65 Frs.
SPECIALITIES: home-cooking.
OTHER POINTS: credit cards accepted.

BERRE L'ETANG
Bouches-du-Rhône, 13130

RESTAURANT L'ENTENTE
(Mme Marie-Thérèse Le Guennec) Route du Moulin Vieux
TEL: 04.42.85.37.44
DIRECTIONS: RN113, Marseille.
MENU: 55 Frs (wine included).
RESTAURANT: Snacks from 6.30
CLOSED: Sat, Sun, and in Aug.
SPECIALITIES: home-cooking.
OTHER POINTS: traditional decor.

BLYES
Ain, 01150

AUBERGE DE BLYES
(Mr Patrice Astier) Lieu dit "La Plaine de l'Ain"
TEL: 04.74.61.50.15
DIRECTIONS: exit Pérouges/Lagnieu.
LANGUAGES: English.
MENU: 60 to 138 Frs.
RESTAURANT: Snacks from 7.00, lunch 11.30-14.30, dinner 19.00-21.00
CLOSED: Sat and Sun.
SPECIALITIES: Périgord dishes, regional menu, home-cooking.
OTHER POINTS: credit cards accepted.
Pérouges; medieval city; grottes (caves); de La Balme; Cerdon (wines); centrale (power station) at Le Bugey.

BOLLENE
Vaucluse, 84500

LE RELAIS DE LA CROISIERE
(Mr Serge Bacon) Route Nationale 7 - La Croisière
TEL: 04.90.30.08.53
DIRECTIONS: RN7, exit at Bollène, towards Orange.
LANGUAGES: English.
MENU: 60 to 63 Frs.
ROOMS: 100 to 180 Frs.
RESTAURANT: Snacks from 4.30, lunch 11.30-14.30, dinner 19.00-23.00
CLOSED: Sat evening, Sun and first 2 weeks in Aug.
SPECIALITIES: home-cooking.
HOTEL: 15 rooms
OTHER POINTS: credit cards accepted.
gorges of the Ardèche; Orange; Avignon.

BONSON
Loire, 42160

RESTAURANT DES SPORTS
(Mr Alain Chazelle) 14, avenue de Saint Rambert
TEL: 04.77.55.20.12
DIRECTIONS: RN198, between Andrézieu and Bouthéon or Saint-just and Saint-Rambert.
LANGUAGES: English.
MENU: 58 to 200 Frs.
ROOMS: 115 to 150 Frs.
RESTAURANT: Snacks from 7.00, lunch 12.00-14.30, dinner 19.00-20.30
CLOSED: Sun and in Aug.
SPECIALITIES: home-cooking.
HOTEL: 7 rooms. FACILITIES: shower, bath, television
OTHER POINTS: credit cards accepted.
Bonson: chapel; musée de Saint-Rambert; Saint-Etienne.

BORMES LES MIMOSAS
Var, 83230

LE RELAIS DES 4 SAISONS
(Mr Aldo Aldrighettoni) Avenue Lou Mistraou - Quartier La Verrerie
TEL: 04.94.71.87.05 FAX: 04.94.71.87.05
DIRECTIONS: between Toulon and Saint-Tropez.
LANGUAGES: English, Spanish, Italian.
MENU: 65 Frs.
RESTAURANT: Snacks from 7.00, lunch 11.30-15.00, dinner 19.00-23.00
CLOSED: Sun (out of season).
SPECIALITIES: regional menu, home-cooking.
OTHER POINTS: bar.

BOUC BEL AIR
Bouches-du-Rhône, 13320

AUBERGE DES MURIERS
(Mr Frédéric Dhilly) Plan Marseillais
TEL: 04.42.22.08.04
DIRECTIONS: RN8, between Marseille and Aix.
MENU: 58 Frs.
ROOMS: 100 to 120 Frs.
RESTAURANT: Snacks from 5.30, lunch 11.30-14.30, dinner 19.30-21.00
CLOSED: Sat and Sun in summer.
SPECIALITIES: regional menu, home-cooking.
HOTEL: 12 rooms. FACILITIES: shower, television
OTHER POINTS: bar.

LES ROUTIERS DE LA MALLE
(Mr Jean-Louis Zanon) Lieu dit : La Malle
TEL: 04.42.22.08.84
DIRECTIONS: RN8.
MENU: 50 Frs.
RESTAURANT: Snacks from 6.00
CLOSED: Sat, Sun.
SPECIALITIES: Provenáal dishes, home-cooking.
OTHER POINTS: bar.

BOURG D'OISANS
Isère, 38520

HOTEL BELLEDONNE
(Mme Mireille Esposito) Rochetaillée
TEL: 04.76.80.07.04
DIRECTIONS: RD91, between Brianáon and l'Alpe-d'Huez.
MENU: 70 Frs
ROOMS: 125 to 340 Frs.
RESTAURANT: Snacks from 6.30, lunch 12.00-14.00, dinner 19.00-21.00
CLOSED: Sat and Sun (out of season).
SPECIALITIES: regional specialities to order, home-cooking.
HOTEL: ☆ 21 rooms. FACILITIES: shower, bath
OTHER POINTS: credit cards accepted.
various ski resorts (stations de ski), incl. l'Alpe-d'Huez, from 3-50km.

BOURG DE PEAGE
Drôme, 26300

RELAIS ROUTIER DU VERCORS SARL
L'Ecancière
TEL: 04.75.48.83.44
DIRECTIONS: RN532, between Pizanáon and Saint-Nazaire-en-Royan.
MENU: 60 Frs.
RESTAURANT: Snacks from 5.00, lunch 11.45-14.00, dinner 19.30-22.00
CLOSED: Sun.
SPECIALITIES: home-cooking.
OTHER POINTS: credit cards accepted.
Le Vercors.

BOURG EN BRESSE
Ain, 01440

SARL RELAIS DE BRESSAN
(Mme Patricia Vadot) 8, rue de la Charolaise - Viriat
TEL: 04.74.45.29.22
DIRECTIONS: RN84, Autoroute A40 exit and North entrance 5km.
MENU: 60 Frs.
ROOMS: 120 to 160 Frs.
RESTAURANT: Snacks from 6.00, lunch 12.00-15.00, dinner 19.00-21.00
CLOSED: Sat and Sun.
SPECIALITIES: regional menu, home-cooking.
HOTEL: ☆☆ 12 rooms. FACILITIES: shower, bath, private bathroom, television, telephone
OTHER POINTS: credit cards accepted.

Eglise de Bron, ornithology park at Villar-les-Dombes; the Ain valley.

BOURGOIN JALLIEU
Isère, 38300

RELAIS DE LA MAISON BLANCHE
(Mr André Piloz) Route Nationale 85 Nivolas Vermelle
TEL: 04.74.27.92.86
DIRECTIONS: RN85, exit Bourgoin, towards Grenoble.
MENU: 60 Frs.
RESTAURANT: Snacks from 5.00, lunch 11.15-14.00
CLOSED: Sat, Sun, 3 weeks in Aug and 1 week at Christmas.
SPECIALITIES: home-cooking.
OTHER POINTS: bar.
lac de Charavines; the Alps.

BREUIL (LE)
Rhône, 69620

CAFE DE L'ESPERANCE
(Marc et Sylvie Thivin) Le Gélicain - Route Nationale 485
TEL: 04.74.71.64.82
DIRECTIONS: RD485, between Lyon and Charolies.
LANGUAGES: English, Spanish.
MENU: 60 Frs.
RESTAURANT: Snacks from 6.30, lunch 12.00-13.30
CLOSED: Mon.
SPECIALITIES: home-cooking.
OTHER POINTS: credit cards accepted.
Beaujolais wine-cellars; route des Pierres Dorées; le bois d'Oingt; Lyon.

BRIANCON
Hautes-Alpes, 05100

LA LANTERNE
(Mr René Parisot) Chamandrin
TEL: 05.92.21.12.33
DIRECTIONS: RN94, the Gap road.
LANGUAGES: English, German, Spanish.
MENU: 65 Frs.
RESTAURANT: Snacks from 9.00, lunch 11.00-14.00, dinner 18.00-21.30
SPECIALITIES: home cooking.
OTHER POINTS: credit cards accepted.
Brianáon: old town; forts built by Vauban.

BRULY DE COUVIN
Hautes-Alpes, 05660

CHEZ PIERRE
(Zina et Marc Lefèvre) 61, rue Grande
TEL: 060.377.202 FAX: 060.377.202
DIRECTIONS: RN5, between Charleville Mézières and Charleroi (Belgique).
MENU: 55 Frs.
RESTAURANT: Snacks from 5.00, lunch 11.00, dinner - 1.30
SPECIALITIES: regional menu.
OTHER POINTS: credit cards accepted.
Grottes (caves) at Neptune; abbaye at Chimay; lake at Virelles; musée Rimbaud; ardoiseries (slate-making factories); fortifications at Rocroi; lake at Witaker.

CANNET DES MAURES (LE)
Var, 83340

AUBERGE LES QUATRE VENTS
(Mme Antonia Iannella) Route Nationale 7
TEL: 04.94.60.96.41
DIRECTIONS: RN7, exit Le Luc, towards Vidauban.
LANGUAGES: Spanish, Italian.
MENU: 60 Frs.
RESTAURANT: Snacks from 5.00, lunch 11.30-17.00, dinner 18.30-24.00
SPECIALITIES: home-cooking.
OTHER POINTS: credit cards accepted.
Var plain and hinterland; village des tortues (tortoises).

CARNOULES
Var, 83660

CHEZ DOUDOU
(Mr Adrien Piasco) 20, rue Pierre Sémard
TEL: 04.94.28.33.15
DIRECTIONS: RN97, between Touion and Nice via Le Luc.
LANGUAGES: Italian.
MENU: 58 to 170 Frs.
ROOMS: 110 Frs.
RESTAURANT: Snacks from 6.15, lunch 11.30-14.00, dinner 19.30-21.00
CLOSED: Sat, and 2 weeks in Aug/Sept.
SPECIALITIES: Provenáal dishes, home-cooking.
HOTEL: 5 rooms
OTHER POINTS: credit cards accepted.

CARPENTRAS
Vaucluse, 84200

RESTAURANT DU MARCHE GARE
(Mr Bernard Gil) Route de Velleron (à l'intérieur du marché)
TEL: 04.90.63.19.00
DIRECTIONS: RN538.
LANGUAGES: Spanish.
MENU: 60 Frs (wine included)
RESTAURANT: Snacks from 5.00, lunch 12.00-14.30
CLOSED: Sun.
SPECIALITIES: home-cooking.

OTHER POINTS: credit cards accepted.
Mont-Ventoux; Fontaine-de-Vauclusel; Gordes.

CHABEUIL
Drôme, 26120

LE RELAIS DU SOLEIL
(Mme Bernard Rigollet) 44, avenue de Romans
TEL: 04.75.59.15.32 FAX: 04.75.59.11.82
DIRECTIONS: RD 538, RD538, on the Romans/Crest, axis.
LANGUAGES: English, German, Spanish.
MENU: 50 to 120 Frs.
ROOMS: 120 to 140 Frs.
RESTAURANT: Snacks from 7.00
SPECIALITIES: regional menu, home-cooking.
HOTEL: 5 rooms
OTHER POINTS: credit cards accepted.

CHAMPAGNEUX
Savoie, 73240

RELAIS DES TROIS PROVINCES - Chez Nicole
(Mme Nicole Curtillat) La Tuilière
TEL: 04.76.31.86.97
DIRECTIONS: RN516, between Yenne and Saint-Genix-sur-Guiers.
MENU: 62 Frs.
RESTAURANT: Snacks from 7.00, lunch 12.00-14.00
CLOSED: Sat.
SPECIALITIES: fondue savoyarde, fondue bourguignonne, home-cooking.
OTHER POINTS: bar.
château de Montfleury; musée d'Aoste (Gallo-Roman); Glandieu: waterfall.

CHAPELLE (LA)
Savoie, 73220

LE VORNAY
(Mr Jean-Marc Fedezyszyn) Route Nationale 6
TEL: 04.79.36.12.05
DIRECTIONS: RN6, Chambéry or Grenoble/Turin.
LANGUAGES: English, Italian.
MENU: 64 Frs (drink included) to 84 Frs.
RESTAURANT: Open 24h.
SPECIALITIES: regional menu, home-cooking.
OTHER POINTS: credit cards accepted.
La Maurienne valley; ski resorts.

CHARVIEU CHAVAGNEU
Isère, 38230

RELAIS DE LA LECHERE
(Mr Paul Maunand) Route de Lyon - Lieu dit : La Léchère
TEL: 04.72.46.04.89
DIRECTIONS: Route de Lyon, Crémieu.
MENU: 62 Frs (wine and coffee included) to 110 Frs.
RESTAURANT: Snacks from 6.30, lunch 11.30-14.30, dinner 19.00-21.00
CLOSED: Sat and Sun.
SPECIALITIES: grenouilles, fritures, home-cooking.
OTHER POINTS: credit cards accepted.
Crémieu: medieval city; grotte (cave) de La Balme.

CHASSE SUR RHONE
Isère, 38670

CENTRAL BAR - Chez Babeth
(Mme Elisabeth Marotte) 5, rue Pasteur
TEL: 04.78.73.10.82
DIRECTIONS: the Lyon/Valence road.
MENU: 62 Frs.
RESTAURANT: Snacks from 5.45, lunch 11.30-14.30, dinner 18.30-22.00
CLOSED: Sat afternoon, Sun and public holidays.
SPECIALITIES: couscous, cassoulet, choucroute, home-cooking.
OTHER POINTS: bar.
Vienne: ancient city.

CHATEAUNEUF DE GADAGNE
Vaucluse, 84470

RESTAURANT DU MARCHE
(Mr Claude Micheletti) Place du Marché
TEL: 04.90.22.41.14
LANGUAGES: Spanish.
RESTAURANT: Snacks from 6.30
CLOSED: Sun.
OTHER POINTS: bar.

CHATTE
Isère, 38160

LE SIROCCO
(Mr Maurice Moyroud) Quartier Saint Ferreol
TEL: 04.76.64.43.41 FAX: 04.76.64.45.95
DIRECTIONS: RN92, between Romans and Grenoble.
MENU: 60 Frs.
RESTAURANT: Snacks from 6.00, lunch 11.30-14.30
CLOSED: Sat afternoon, Sun, 1st 2 weeks in Aug and 1 week at Christmas.
SPECIALITIES: home-cooking.
OTHER POINTS: credit cards accepted.
jardin ferroviaire (railways); abbaye de Saint-Antoine; 'Royans-Vercors' paddle-boat,

CHAUFFAYER
Hautes-Alpes, 05800

TOURISME HOTEL
(Mr Robert Reynaud) Route Nationale 85

TEL: 04.92.55.22.74
DIRECTIONS: RN85.
LANGUAGES: English.
MENU: 65 Frs.
ROOMS: 100 to 165 Frs.
RESTAURANT: Snacks from 6.00, lunch 11.00-15.00, dinner 19.15-22.00
CLOSED: 10 days in June and 2 weeks in Sept.
SPECIALITIES: regional menu, home-cooking.
HOTEL: 10 rooms. FACILITIES: shower
OTHER POINTS: credit cards accepted.

CHONAS L'AMBALLAN
Isère, 38121

RELAIS ROUTIERS LA TRUFFE NOIRE
(Mr Bernard Mortier) Route Nationale 7
TEL: 04.74.58.81.51
DIRECTIONS: RN7, between Lyon and Valence.
LANGUAGES: English, Italian.
MENU: 65 Frs.
RESTAURANT: Snacks from 6.30, lunch 12.00-15.00, dinner 19.00-23.00
CLOSED: Sat afternoon and Sun (mid-Sept till April).
SPECIALITIES: home-cooking.
OTHER POINTS: credit cards accepted.

CHORGES
Hautes-Alpes, 05230

STATION ELF
(Mr Didier Boccone) La Grande Ile RN 94
TEL: 04.92.50.65.76 FAX: 04.92.50.65.76
DIRECTIONS: RN94, Gap/Brianáon/Italie.
LANGUAGES: English, Spanish, Italian.
MENU: 60 Frs.
RESTAURANT: Snacks from 5.00
SPECIALITIES: home-cooking.
OTHER POINTS: credit cards accepted.
Lake at Serre-Ponáon; snow and ski ressort.

COGOLIN
Var, 83310

AUBERGE DU GISCLET
(Mme Nicole Vialenc) Route Nationale 98
TEL: 04.94.56.40.39
DIRECTIONS: RN98.
MENU: 62 to 78 Frs.
RESTAURANT: Snacks from 8.00
CLOSED: Sun.
SPECIALITIES: home-cooking.
OTHER POINTS: credit cards accepted.
Saint-Tropez.

CONTES
Alpes-Maritimes, 06440

LE RELAIS CAMPAGNARD
(Mr Jean-Luc Foulon) Route Nationale - Blausasc
TEL: 04.93.91.13.14
LANGUAGES: English, German, Italian.
MENU: 62 Frs, dish of the day at 45 Frs.
RESTAURANT: Snacks from 5.30
CLOSED: Sun.
SPECIALITIES: regional menu, home-cooking.
OTHER POINTS: credit cards accepted.

CORPS
Isère, 38970

RESTAURANT DU TILLEUL
(Mr Claude Jourdan) Rue des Fossés
TEL: 04.76.30.00.43 FAX: 04.76.30.06.12
DIRECTIONS: RN85, between Grenoble and Gap.
LANGUAGES: English, German.
MENU: 70 to 145 Frs
ROOMS: 180 to 310 Frs.
RESTAURANT: Snacks from 7.00, lunch 12.00-14.00, dinner 19.00-21.00
CLOSED: in Nov and the 1st 2 weeks in Dec.
SPECIALITIES: gratin dauphinois, civet de porcelet, poulet aux écrevisses, regional menu, home-cooking.
HOTEL: ☆☆ 10 rooms. FACILITIES: shower, bath, private bathroom, television, telephone
OTHER POINTS: credit cards accepted.
barrage (clam) de Sautel; sanctuaire de La Salette.

COUCOURDE (LA)
Drôme, 26740

RELAIS DES ROCHES
(Mr Yvon Larsonnier) Route Nationale 7
TEL: 04.75.53.70.02
DIRECTIONS: Valence-Montélimar
MENU: 58 Frs.
RESTAURANT: Snacks from 5.00, lunch 11.00-5.00, dinner 19.00-22.00
CLOSED: Sat and Sun (from Oct to Apr).
SPECIALITIES: home-cooking.
OTHER POINTS: credit cards accepted.

CREST
Drôme, 26400

LE CHAMP DE MARS
(Mr Bernard Genthon) 8, place de la Liberté
TEL: 04.75.40.61.06
LANGUAGES: German.

RESTAURANT: Snacks from 6.00, lunch 12.00-14.00, dinner 19.00
SPECIALITIES: home-cooking.
OTHER POINTS: credit cards accepted.
Crest: old town, tower.

RESTAURANT DE L'ETAPE
(Mme Martine Jorand) Quartier La Plaine
TEL: 04.75.40.65.01 FAX: 04.75.40.64.93
DIRECTIONS: RD93, Valence/Gap.
MENU: 60 to 90 Frs.
RESTAURANT: Snacks from 6.00, lunch 12.00-14.30, dinner 19.00-22.00
CLOSED: Sun.
SPECIALITIES: regional menu, home-cooking.
OTHER POINTS: credit cards accepted.
La Tour de Crest (the highest dungeon in Europe); Le Diois; le Vercors: historical sites; le jardin des oiseaux (birds garden) at Upie.

CROIX VALMER (LA)
Var, 83420

LA CIGALE
(Mr Frédéric Suma)
TEL: 04.94.79.60.41
DIRECTIONS: RD559, between La Foux/Cavalaire.
MENU: 60 to 128 Frs.
ROOMS: 130 to 200 Frs.
RESTAURANT: Snacks from 6.00, lunch 11.45-14.00, dinner 19.00-21.00
CLOSED: Sun evening.
SPECIALITIES: regional menu, bouillabaisse faáon pêcheur, bourride véritable, daurade royale, chapon farci, home-cooking.
HOTEL: 7 rooms
OTHER POINTS: credit cards accepted.

CRUAS
Ardèche, 07350

RELAIS ROUTIER
(Mme Sylvie Madeira) La Devière
TEL: 04.75.51.41.12
DIRECTIONS: RN86.
MENU: 50 to 130 Frs.
RESTAURANT: Snacks from 6.00, lunch 10.00-17.00, dinner 17.00-23.00
SPECIALITIES: home-cooking.
OTHER POINTS: bar.
medieval châteaux; church; nuclear power station.

CUZIEU
Loire, 42330

RESTAURANT DE LA MAIRIE
(Mme Janine Dard) Route Nationale 82 - Le Bourg
TEL: 04.77.54.88.21 FAX: 04.77.54.42.07
DIRECTIONS: RN82, coming from Saint-Etienne, exit at Veauche.
LANGUAGES: English, German, Spanish, Italian.
MENU: 60 Frs.
ROOMS: 120 to 180 Frs.
RESTAURANT: Snacks from 6.00, lunch 11.00-15.00, dinner 18.00-23.00
CLOSED: Sat afternoon, Sun, and in Aug.
SPECIALITIES: regional menu, home cooking.
HOTEL: 12 rooms. FACILITIES: shower, bath, private bathroom, television
OTHER POINTS: credit cards accepted
barrages (clams) de Villerest and Grangent-sur-la-Loire Mont-Pilat; Saint-Romain-le-Puy: priory; la Bâtie d'Urfé; musée de la mine (mining).

DARDILLY
Rhône, 69570

AUBERGE POLONAISE : CRACOVIE
(Mr Jean-Jacques Sadeski) 22, route Nationale 7
TEL: 04.78.48.01.39
DIRECTIONS: old RN7.
LANGUAGES: English, Italian, Polish.
MENU: 60 Frs.
ROOMS: 110 to 130 Frs.
RESTAURANT: Lunch 11.30-14.00, dinner 19.00-21.30
CLOSED: Sun.
SPECIALITIES: Polish dishes, home-cooking.
HOTEL: 8 rooms
OTHER POINTS: credit cards accepted.
Marcy-l'Etoile: musée national de la Poupée (dolls); Courzier: wildlife park (eagles).

LE CHENE ROND
(Mr Emile Lagoutte) 87 Route Nationale 7
TEL: 04.78.87.15.48
DIRECTIONS: RN7, the Lyon/Roanne road.
MENU: 65 Frs.
ROOMS: 60 to 120 Frs.
RESTAURANT: Snacks from 6.00, lunch 12.00-14.00, dinner 20.00-21.00
CLOSED: Sat afternoon, Sun, public holidays, and in Aug.
SPECIALITIES: home-cooking.
HOTEL: 6 rooms. FACILITIES: shower
OTHER POINTS: bar.

LE RELAIS DE LA BASCULE
(Mr Claude Renaud) Route nationale 6
TEL: 04.78.35.56.30
DIRECTIONS: RN6, 23km after the toll at Villefranche-sur-Saône.
MENU: 65 Frs.
RESTAURANT: Snacks from 6.00, lunch 11.30-15.00, dinner 19.00-24.00
CLOSED: Sat afternoon and Sun.

SPECIALITIES: home-cooking.
OTHER POINTS: credit cards accepted.
Lyon (Gallic capital): museums, monuments, parc de la Tête d'Or, basilicas.

DONZERE
Drôme, 26290

LA MARGELLE FLEURIE
(Mr Claude Jeannaux) Route Nationale 7
TEL: 04.75.51.75.11 **FAX:** 04.75.51.58.11
DIRECTIONS: RN7, Montélimar.
LANGUAGES: English, German.
MENU: 65 to 120 Frs
ROOMS: 105 to 140 Frs.
RESTAURANT: Snacks from 5.30, lunch 11.30-14.00, dinner 19.00-22.00
CLOSED: Sun (out of season), Last week in Aug and in Dec.
SPECIALITIES: Savoy dishes, home-cooking.
HOTEL: 9 rooms. **FACILITIES:** shower, bath
OTHER POINTS: credit cards accepted.
gorges of the Ardèche; Pierrelatte.

RELAIS DE DONZERE
(Mr Jean Bertrand) Route Nationale 7
TEL: 04.75.51.64.58 **FAX:** 04.75.51.56.76
DIRECTIONS: RN7.
MENU: 70 Frs.
ROOMS: 100 to 125 Frs.
RESTAURANT: Open 24h.
CLOSED: Sat to Sun night, and 1 week from 25th Dec.
SPECIALITIES: poulet aux écrevisses, waterzooi (Belgian speciality), home-cooking.
HOTEL: 10 rooms. **FACILITIES:** shower, bath, private bathroom
OTHER POINTS: credit cards accepted.
the Ardèche region.

RELAIS LE BOLO
(Mr José Da Fonseca) Route Nationale 7
TEL: 04.75.51.61.48 **FAX:** 04.75.51.57.54
DIRECTIONS: RN7, exit Montélimar Sud (South).
LANGUAGES: English, Spanish, Portuguese.
MENU: 62 to 70 Frs.
ROOMS: 100 to 200 Frs.
RESTAURANT: Open 24h.
HOTEL: ☆ 22 rooms. **FACILITIES:** shower, bath, private bathroom
OTHER POINTS: credit cards accepted.

DRAGUIGNAN
Var, 83300

LE PENALTY
(Mr Guy Chabrand) 1, avenue de la 1ère Armée - Quartier Saint Léger
TEL: 04.94.68.11.28
DIRECTIONS: in the Saint-Léger quarter.
MENU: 55 to 65 Frs.
RESTAURANT: Snacks from 5.30, lunch 12.00-14.00, dinner 19.00-20.00
CLOSED: Sun and public holidays.
SPECIALITIES: regional menu, home-cooking.
OTHER POINTS: bar.

EYGUIANS
Hautes-Alpes, 05300

HOTEL DE LA GARE
(Mme Michelle Robert)
TEL: 04.92.66.20.08 **FAX:** 04.92.66.29.93
DIRECTIONS: RN75, exit A51, 20km north of Sisteron.
LANGUAGES: English.
MENU: 60 to 100 Frs.
ROOMS: 110 to 220 Frs.
RESTAURANT: Snacks from 6.00, lunch 12.00-14.00, dinner 20.00-21.30
CLOSED: Sat (out of season), and in Jan.
SPECIALITIES: gigot d'agneau de pays, pieds et paquets (mutton tripe and trotters), daube, gratin dauphinois, regional menu, home-cooking.
HOTEL: ☆ 15 rooms. **FACILITIES:** shower, bath, private bathroom, television, telephone
OTHER POINTS: credit cards accepted.
gorges of the Méouge; Prieuré (priory) de Saint-André; Sisteron: citadel; Orpierre: Provenáal village (7km).

FEISSONS SUR ISERE
Savoie, 73260

LE RELAIS ROUTIERS
(Mr Michel Ruffier)
TEL: 04.79.22.50.97
DIRECTIONS: RN90, between Albertville and Moutiers, exit 36.
MENU: 60 Frs.
RESTAURANT: Snacks from 5.45, lunch 11.45-14.15
CLOSED: Sat afternoon, Sun, last 2 weeks in Aug and 1 week at Christmas.
SPECIALITIES: home-cooking.
OTHER POINTS: credit cards accepted.
'circuit de la Tarentaise'.

FELINES
Ardèche, 07340

LE RELAIS DE LA REMISE
(Mme Annie-France Goichot) Route Nationale 82 - La Remise
TEL: 04.75.34.82.22
DIRECTIONS: RN82, the Annonay/Saint-Etienne/Le Puy-en-Velay road.
MENU: 65 Frs.

RESTAURANT: Snacks from 6.00, lunch 11.00-13.30
CLOSED: Sat and Sun, public holidays and Aug.
SPECIALITIES: home-cooking.
OTHER POINTS: bar.
Peaugres: safari park.

FIANCEY
Drôme, 26250

ROUVEYROL
(Mr Roland Rouveyrol) Route Nationale 7
TEL: 04.75.61.62.06
DIRECTIONS: RN7, exit Valence Sud (South), towards Montélimar.
RESTAURANT: Snacks from 5.30, lunch 12.00-14.30, dinner 19.30-22.30
CLOSED: Sat, Sun, last 2 weeks in Aug and last week in Dec.
SPECIALITIES: home-cooking.
HOTEL: 13 rooms
OTHER POINTS: credit cards accepted.
palais idéal du Facteur Cheval (fantasy shell palace); tour (tower) de Crest; Le Vercors.

FLAVIAC
Ardèche, 07000

LES ROUTIERS
(Mr Didier Garayt) Place Emile Crémière
TEL: 04.75.65.77.57
DIRECTIONS: RN104, exit Loriol, towards Aubenas.
MENU: 58 to 80 Frs.
RESTAURANT: Snacks from 6.30
CLOSED: Sat, Sun, last week in Aug and first week in Sept.
SPECIALITIES: regional menu, rognons au madère, home-cooking,
OTHER POINTS: credit cards accepted.
gorges of the Ardèche (55km); Eyrieux valley (20km).

FLEURIEUX SUR L'ARBRESLE
Rhône, 69210

RELAIS LA BONBONNE SARL
(Mr Franck Asinari) 105, route de Paris
TEL: 04.74.01.26.99
DIRECTIONS: RN7, Roanne/Lyon.
MENU: 65.50 Frs (1/4 wine included).
RESTAURANT: Snacks from 6.30, lunch 11.30-14.30, dinner 19.00-22.00
CLOSED: Sun.
SPECIALITIES: home-cooking.
OTHER POINTS: credit cards accepted.
Le Corbusier à Eveux-sur-L'Arbresle (architecture); Lyon.

FOS SUR MER
Bouches-du-Rhône, 13270

LE MOULIN
(Mr Jean-Bernard Lefèbvre) Place du Cavaou
TEL: 04.42.05.48.38
DIRECTIONS: crossroads at Ma Campagne, towards Les Plages.
LANGUAGES: English.
RESTAURANT: Dinner -22.00
OTHER POINTS: bar.

MA CAMPAGNE - SARL LE TRIDENT
(Mr Bernard Silhol) 50, avenue Jean Jaurès
TEL: 04.42.05.01.66 **FAX:** 04.42.05.53.67
DIRECTIONS: the Aries/Marseille expressway.
LANGUAGES: English, Spanish, Italian.
MENU: 50 to 98 Frs.
ROOMS: 100 to 150 Frs.
RESTAURANT: Snacks from 6.00, lunch 11.00-15.00, dinner 19.00-22.00
CLOSED: Sun.
SPECIALITIES: poissons, regional menu, home-cooking.
HOTEL: 25 rooms. **FACILITIES:** shower, bath
OTHER POINTS: credit cards accepted.
the Camargue.

LA CAMARGUE
(Mr Jean-Paul Godart) 25, avenue de la Gare
TEL: 04.42.06.22.25
DIRECTIONS: between Port-de-Bare and Fos (Fos station).
MENU: 57 Frs.
RESTAURANT: Snacks from 6.00, lunch 11.30-14.30, dinner 19.00-21.30
CLOSED: Sun.
SPECIALITIES: home-cooking.
OTHER POINTS: credit cards accepted.

FREJUS
Var, 83600

LES TROIS CHENES
(Mme Monique Laurent) Route de Cannes
TEL: 04.94.53.20.08
DIRECTIONS: RN7, exit 38 at Fréjus, towards Cannes.
LANGUAGES: English, German, Italian.
MENU: 65 Frs.
ROOMS: 200 to 260 Frs.
RESTAURANT: Snacks from 7.00, lunch 12.00-14.00, dinner 19.00-21.00
SPECIALITIES: bouillabaisse, paella, bourride, regional menu, home-cooking.
HOTEL: ☆ 29 rooms. **FACILITIES:** shower, bath, private bathroom, television
OTHER POINTS: credit cards accepted.
Indochina memorial; gorges of the Verdon;

lakes at Saint-Cassien; grotte (cave) de Saint-Cezaire; Cannes.

LE TROQUET
(Mme Gisèle Ciantar) Z.I. La Palud
TEL: 04.94.40.15.93
DIRECTIONS: RN7, Puget/Le Muy.
LANGUAGES: English.
MENU: 65 Frs.
RESTAURANT: Snacks from 6.00, lunch 11.30-14.30
CLOSED: Sun and public holidays (except bookings).
SPECIALITIES: regional menu, home-cooking.
OTHER POINTS: credit cards accepted.

GAP
Hautes-Alpes, 05000

LE BOCAGE
(Mr Vincent Médili) 39, avenue d'Embrun
TEL: 04.92.51.03.67
DIRECTIONS: Brianáon.
LANGUAGES: Italian.
MENU: 65 Frs.
RESTAURANT: Snacks from 4.00, lunch 12.00-15.00
CLOSED: Sun.
SPECIALITIES: home-cooking.
OTHER POINTS: credit cards accepted.
barrage (dam) de Serre-Ponáon; Saint-Véran; Corps; Notre-Dame-de-la-Salette; Route Napoléon.

GENAY
Rhône, 69730

LA PETITE RIVE
(SARL AGFK) Zone Industrielle Nord - Chemin de Halage
TEL: 03.78.91.34.02
DIRECTIONS: A46.
LANGUAGES: English.
MENU: 60 to 115 Frs.
ROOMS: 135 Frs.
RESTAURANT: Snacks from 6.30, lunch 12.00-14.30, dinner 19.00-21.30
SPECIALITIES: regional menu, home-cooking.
HOTEL: ☆ 8 rooms. FACILITIES: shower, bath, private bathroom, television, telephone
OTHER POINTS: credit cards accepted.
Rochetaillee: musée de l'automobile; Ars; Lyon.

GRANONS (LES)
Alpes-de-Haute-Provence, 04110

LE RELAIS DES GRANONS
(Mme Patricia Dolidier) Route Nationale 100
TEL: 04.92.76.46.01
MENU: 68 Frs.
RESTAURANT: Snacks from 8.00, lunch 11.30-15.00, dinner 19.00-21.00
CLOSED: Tues evening and Thurs evening (out of season).
SPECIALITIES: regional menu, home-cooking.
OTHER POINTS: bar.

GRENOBLE
Isère, 38000

LE CATALPA
(Mme Denise Brisset) 8, boulevard de l'Esplanade
TEL: 04.76.47.38.03
DIRECTIONS: Grenoble Bastille.
LANGUAGES: Italian.
MENU: 68 Frs (wine and coffee included).
RESTAURANT: Snacks from 7.00, lunch 12.00-15.00, dinner 19.00-22.00
CLOSED: Sun afternoon.
SPECIALITIES: gratin dauphinois, regional menu, home-cooking.
OTHER POINTS: credit cards accepted.
Bastille; le musée dauphinois (museum of the Dauphinée region); old Grenoble; fortifications.

GRIMAUD
Var, 83310

LE RESTAUROUTE
(Mr Bernard Gentile) Route Nationale 98 - Saint Pons les Mñrs
TEL: 04.94.56.03.75
DIRECTIONS: RN98, Saint-Tropez.
LANGUAGES: English, Italian.
RESTAURANT: Snacks from 6.00, lunch 12.00-14.00, dinner 19.00-21.45
CLOSED: Sun, and in Dec.
SPECIALITIES: bouillabaisse, paella, home-cooking.
OTHER POINTS: credit cards accepted.
Port-Grimaud (1km); Saint-Tropez (6km); Cogolin: musée Raimu, manufacture of pipes and carpets (6km).

GUEREINS
Ain, 01090

LA CROISEE
(Mr Michel Manains) La Croisée
TEL: 04.74.66.14.93
DIRECTIONS: RD17, Belleville, towards Châtillon.
MENU: 60 to 105 Frs.
RESTAURANT: Snacks from 6.15, lunch 11.00-15.00, dinner 19.00-21.30
CLOSED: Tues evening, Sun evening, 3 weeks in Aug.
SPECIALITIES: grenouilles, home-cooking.
OTHER POINTS: credit cards accepted.
the Beaujolais region; Pérouges: medieval city; Dombes.

GUILLESTRE
Hautes-Alpes, 05600

HOTEL DE LA GARE
(SNC Lacour) Montdauphin Gare
TEL: 04.92.45.03.08 **FAX:** 04.92.45.40.09
DIRECTIONS: RN94.
LANGUAGES: English.
MENU: 78 to 180 Frs
ROOMS: 160 to 300 Frs.
RESTAURANT: Snacks from 7.00, lunch 12.00-13.45, dinner 19.00-21.00
CLOSED: Sat (May and June and Sept to Dec).
SPECIALITIES: truites aux morilles, filet de boeuf grillé, côte d'agneau, regional menu.
HOTEL: ☆☆ 44 rooms. **FACILITIES:** shower, bath, private bathroom, television, telephone
OTHER POINTS: credit cards accepted.
Montdauphin-Fort; la vallée du Queyras; le col d'Izoard; Saint-Véran.

HEYRIEUX
Isère, 38540

LE GLOBE TROTTER
(Mme Henriette Meslati) 1, place Jules Ferry
TEL: 04.78.40.00.29 **FAX:** 04.78.40.02.78
DIRECTIONS: on the bypass Est (East), the Lyon/Grenoble/Chambéry autoroute.
LANGUAGES: English.
MENU: 60 Frs (wine and coffee included) to 85 Frs.
ROOMS: 130 to 150 Frs.
RESTAURANT: Snacks from 6.15, lunch 11.30-14.30, dinner 19.00-22.00
CLOSED: Sun.
SPECIALITIES: regional menu, home-cooking.
HOTEL: 10 rooms. **FACILITIES:** shower, private bathroom, television
OTHER POINTS: credit cards accepted.
Lyon region; Eurespo.

HOPITAL SOUS ROCHEFORT (L')
Loire, 42130

CHEZ SYLVIANNE ET JEANNOT
(Mr Jean Devanne) Route Nationale 89 Boen-sur-Lignon
TEL: 04.77.24.55.52
DIRECTIONS: RN89.
LANGUAGES: English.
RESTAURANT: Dinner -23.00
OTHER POINTS: bar.

ISLE D'ABEAU
Isère, 38080

L'ARCHE DE L'ISLE D'ABEAU
(Mr Thierry Sauvage) A43 - Aire de l'Isle d'Abeau
Accessible dans les deux sens
TEL: 04.74.27.10.14 **FAX:** 04.74.27.08.28
RESTAURANT: Snacks from 6.00
OTHER POINTS: credit cards accepted.

JARRIE
Isère, 38560

LE RELAIS DU PONT
(Mr André Nucci) Champ sur Drac
TEL: 04.76.68.85.38
DIRECTIONS: RN85, between Grenoble and Brianáon
LANGUAGES: Italian.
MENU: 50 to 70 Frs.
RESTAURANT: Snacks from 6.00, lunch 11.30-14.00, dinner 19.00-20.30
CLOSED: Sat evening and Sun evening.
SPECIALITIES: home-cooking.
OTHER POINTS: bar.
Le Vercors; Vizille; Le Bourg-d'Oisans.

JOYEUSE
Ardèche, 07260

LES CEVENNES
(Mme Colette Reynouard) Rosières
TEL: 04.75.39.52.07
DIRECTIONS: Loriol.
MENU: 60 to 100 Frs.
ROOMS: 140 to 180 Frs.
RESTAURANT: Snacks from 7.00, lunch 12.00-14.00, dinner 20.00-22.00
CLOSED: 2 weeks in Oct.
SPECIALITIES: home-cooking.
HOTEL: 14 rooms
OTHER POINTS: credit cards accepted.
Vallon-Pont d'arc; gorges of the Ardèche; grottes (caves) Cocalières; Orgnac.

LABEGUDE
Ardèche, 07200

SARL AUX QUATRE SAISONS
(Mr Didier Ollier) 64, route Nationale
TEL: 04.75.37.40.25
DIRECTIONS: RN102, Montélimar/Le Puy.
LANGUAGES: English.
MENU: 55 to 89 Frs.
RESTAURANT: Snacks from 7.30, lunch 11.30-14.30, dinner 19.00-21.30
SPECIALITIES: home-cooking.
OTHER POINTS: credit cards accepted.
Aven d'Orgnac; lac d'Issarlès.

RESTAURANT LE MALPAS
(Mr Eric Laurent)
TEL: 04.75.37.41.77
DIRECTIONS: RN102, Montélimar/Le Puy road.

MENU: 60 to 120 Frs.
RESTAURANT: Snacks from 7.00, lunch 12.00-14.30, dinner 19.00-22.00
SPECIALITIES: regional menu, home-cooking.
OTHER POINTS: credit cards accepted.
Station Thermale (baths); Vals-les-Bains; Vallon Pont d'Arc.

LAMBESC
Bouches-du-Rhône, 13410

LE RELAIS DE LA GARE
(Mme Germaine Lansac) Boulevard des Coopératives
TEL: 04.42.92.97.60
DIRECTIONS: RN7.
LANGUAGES: Italian.
OTHER POINTS: bar.

LAMOTTE DU RHONE
Vaucluse, 84840

L'ESCALE
(Annick et Bernard Duminy) Quartier Santi
TEL: 04.90.30.90.15
DIRECTIONS: RN 994, RN994, between Pont-Saint-Esprit and Bollène.
MENU: 60 to 80 Frs.
RESTAURANT: Snacks from 8.00
CLOSED: Sun.
SPECIALITIES: regional menu, home-cooking.
OTHER POINTS: bar.

LANCON DE PROVENCE
Bouches-du-Rhône, 13680

AUBERGE DU MOULIN
(Mme Monique Eymard) Route Nationale 113
TEL: 04.90.42.71.14
DIRECTIONS: RN113, between Salon-de-Provence and Marseille.
MENU: 55 Frs.
ROOMS: 100 Frs.
RESTAURANT: Snacks from 5.00, lunch 11.30-15.00, dinner 19.00-21.00
CLOSED: Afternoons on Sat and Sun.
SPECIALITIES: regional menu, home-cooking.
HOTEL: 6 rooms. **FACILITIES:** shower
OTHER POINTS: credit cards accepted.
château Cempeni; zoo at La Barben; musée Grévin (wax figures).

L'ARCHE DE LANCON DE PROVENCE
(Mr Marcel Prioul) A7 - Aire de Lanáon - Accessible dans les deux sens
TEL: 05.90.42.88.88 FAX: 05.90.42.83.60
RESTAURANT: Open 24h.
OTHER POINTS: credit cards accepted.

LE RELAIS DES FOURCHES
(Mr Marc Gonela) Route Nationale 113 - Quartier des Ferrages
TEL: 04.90.42.71.21
DIRECTIONS: RN113.
LANGUAGES: Italian.
MENU: 59 Frs.
RESTAURANT: Snacks from 6.00, lunch 11.00, dinner - 21.30
CLOSED: Sat evening and public holidays.
SPECIALITIES: paella, couscous, regional menu, home-cooking.
OTHER POINTS: credit cards accepted.
Salon-de-Provence; Arles; l'Etang de Berre.

LEYMENT
Ain, 01150

LE RELAIS DE LA GARE
(Mr Marcel Bessière) 34, rue de la Gare
TEL: 04.74.34.94.30
DIRECTIONS: RN84.
HOTEL: 7 rooms
OTHER POINTS: bar.

LIGNANE
Bouches-du-Rhône, 13540

LE RELAIS DE LIGNANE
(Mr Christian Mondin) Route Nationale 7
TEL: 04.42.92.51.15
DIRECTIONS: RN7, the Aix-en-Provence/Avignon/Salon road.
MENU: 60 to 70 Frs
RESTAURANT: Snacks from 6.00, lunch 11.00-14.30, dinner 19.00-23.00
CLOSED: Sun, and in mid-Aug.
SPECIALITIES: pieds et paquets (mutton tripe and trotters), boeuf en daube, alouettes sans tête (beef or veal strips), civet de porcellet, regional menu, home-cooking.
OTHER POINTS: bar.
Aix-en-Provence; La Barben: château; Lauris.

LIVRON
Drôme, 26250

AUBERGE RELAIS MACAMP
(Mme Josiane Vocanson) Route Nationale 7 - Fiancey
TEL: 04.75.61.73.91
DIRECTIONS: RN7.
RESTAURANT: Snacks from 6.30
CLOSED: Sun, and in Aug.
SPECIALITIES: regional menu, home-cooking.
HOTEL: 17 rooms. **FACILITIES:** shower, bath, private bathroom, television

OTHER POINTS: credit cards accepted.
the Ardèche region; Le Vercors.

LONDE DES MAURES (LA)
Var, 83250

LE PETIT BOIS
(Mr Guy Silvi) Route de Maramar
TEL: 04.94.66.80.12
MENU: 55 Frs (1/4 wine included).
RESTAURANT: Snacks from 7.00, lunch 12.00-15.00, dinner 19.30-22.00
OTHER POINTS: bar.

LORIOL
Drôme, 26270

LE RELAIS DE SAINT PAUL
(Mr Jacques Plessis) Route Nationale 7
TEL: 04.75.61.76.31
DIRECTIONS: RN7, betwwen Valence and Montélimar.
MENU: 60 Frs.
RESTAURANT: Snacks from 5.45, lunch 11.30-14.30, dinner 19.00-21.30
CLOSED: Sun (out of season).
SPECIALITIES: home-cooking.
OTHER POINTS: credit cards accepted.

LUS LA CROIX HAUTE
Drôme, 26620

TOURING HOTEL
(Mme Monique Brouttier) Route Nationale 75
TEL: 04.92.58.50.01 FAX: 04.92.58.55.21
DIRECTIONS: RN 75, RN75, Grenoble/Gap/Sisteron.
LANGUAGES: English.
MENU: 65 to 160 Frs.
ROOMS: 120 to 195 Frs.
RESTAURANT: Snacks from 6.00
SPECIALITIES: regional menu, home-cooking.
HOTEL: 28 rooms. FACILITIES: shower, bath
OTHER POINTS: credit cards accepted.

LYON
Rhône, 69002

LES ROUTIERS
(Mr Pierre Sala) 21, quai Perrache
TEL: 04.78.37.75.86
DIRECTIONS: via Fourvière tunnel, towards Perrache.
MENU: 75 Frs (wine included).
RESTAURANT: Snacks from 7.00, lunch 12.00-15.00, dinner 19.30-24.00
CLOSED: Sat, Sun, and in Aug.
SPECIALITIES: home-cooking.
OTHER POINTS: bar.
Lyon.

BRASSERIE DU MARCHE GARE
(Mr Roger Martins) 36, rue Casimir Perrier
TEL: 04.72.77.50.25
DIRECTIONS: Quai Perrache, wholesale market (marché au gros).
LANGUAGES: Spanish, Italian, Portuguese.
MENU: 65 Frs.
RESTAURANT: Snacks from 5.00, lunch 12.00-14.30, dinner 19.00-22.30
CLOSED: Sat and Sun.
SPECIALITIES: home-cooking.
OTHER POINTS: credit cards accepted.

LYON MIONNAY
Rhône, 69000

L'ARCHE DE MIONNAY
(Mr Edouard Rozes) A46 - Aire de Mionnay - Accessible dans les deux sens
OTHER POINTS: credit cards accepted.

LYON SAINT PRIEST
Rhône, 69000

CAFETERIA DE SAINT PRIEST
(Mr Stéphane Andriot) A43 - Aire de Saint Priest - Accessible sens Lyon/Chambéry.
TEL: 04.78.90.16.82 FAX: 04.78.90.16.82
OTHER POINTS: credit cards accepted.

MARCILLY LE CHATEL
Loire, 42130

RELAIS DU CHATEL
(Mme Josianne Béal) Au bourg
TEL: 04.77.97.44.36
DIRECTIONS: RD8, between Boén and Montbrison.
MENU: 60 to 80 Frs.
RESTAURANT: Snacks from 7.00, lunch 12.00-14.00, dinner 19.00-21.00
CLOSED: Mon evening and the last 3 weeks in Aug.
SPECIALITIES: home-cooking.
OTHER POINTS: bar.
château de Sainte-Anne (voleric du Forez); la Bâtie d'Urfé.

MARSEILLE
Bouches-du-Rhône, 13016

BAR DE LA GARE D'ARENC - Chez Pilou
(Mr Philippe Chiaramonte) 25, rue d'Anthoine
TEL: 04.91.91.23.07
LANGUAGES: English, Italian.
MENU: 50 Frs.
RESTAURANT: Snacks from 5.00
CLOSED: Sun.
OTHER POINTS: bar.

LE RELAIS DES AMIS
(Mr Raymond Servière) 110, boulevard de Paris
TEL: 04.91.62.60.76
DIRECTIONS: RN8.
MENU: 40 Frs (choice of 8 main courses).
RESTAURANT: Snacks from 5.00
CLOSED: Sat, Sun, and in Aug.
SPECIALITIES: regional menu, home-cooking.
OTHER POINTS: bar.
Marseille.

MEGEVE
Haute-Savoie, 74120

CHALET DES FLEURS
(Mr Georges Roussel) Pont d'Arbon
TEL: 04.50.21.21.46
DIRECTIONS: RN21 2, from Sallanches, first building on the left as you enter Megève.
LANGUAGES: English.
MENU: 70 to 170 Frs.
ROOMS: 150 to 270 Frs.
RESTAURANT: Snacks from 7.00, lunch 12.00-14.30, dinner 19.30-22.00
CLOSED: from Apr to mid-June, and from Oct to mid-Dec.
SPECIALITIES: truite à la crème et aux amandes, escalope normande garnie, quenelles (meatballs) de brochet à la crème, foie gras des Landes à l'Armagnac, regional menu, home-cooking.
HOTEL: ☆☆ 22 rooms. FACILITIES: shower, bath, private bathroom, television, telephone
OTHER POINTS: credit cards accepted.
Mont-Blanc; Mont d'Arbois; Rochebrune; Le Jaillet; gorges of the Arlly; numerous lakes.

MEYTHET
Haute-Savoie, 74960

LE RELAIS
(Mr Claude Gallay) 22, route de Frangy
TEL: 04.50.22.02.93
ROOMS: 120 to 150 Frs.
RESTAURANT: Dinner -22.00
CLOSED: Sun, 1 week at Christmas, and in May.
HOTEL: 17 rooms
OTHER POINTS: bar.

MEYZIEU
Rhône, 69330

LE RELAIS DE L'INDUSTRIE - PMU
(Mr Gérard Dumont) 104, rue de la République - Les Plantées
TEL: 04.78.31.78.31
DIRECTIONS: RD517, Lyon.
MENU: 65 Frs (1/4 wine and coffee included)
RESTAURANT: Snacks from 6.30, lunch 11.30-15.00, dinner 19.00-21.30
CLOSED: Sun afternoon.
SPECIALITIES: home-cooking,
OTHER POINTS: credit cards accepted.

MEZEL
Alpes-de-Haute-Provence, 04270

HOTEL RESTAURANT DE LA PLACE
(Mme Christiane Sarracanie et Fils) Place Victor Arnaux
TEL: 04.92.35.58.10
DIRECTIONS: RN85, between Digne and Nice.
LANGUAGES: English, Spanish.
MENU: 65 to 115 Frs.
ROOMS: 145 to 210 Frs.
RESTAURANT: Snacks from 6.30, lunch 12.00-14.00, dinner 19.30-21.00
CLOSED: Mon (out of season), and from 15th Dec to 15th Jan.
SPECIALITIES: regional menu, home-cooking,
HOTEL: 11 rooms. FACILITIES: shower, bath, private bathroom, television, telephone
OTHER POINTS: credit cards accepted.
gorges of the Verdon; Col d'Allos; lac de Sainte-Croix; geological storehouse.

MEZERIAT
Ain, 01660

LE RELAIS DE MEZERIAT
(Mr Alain Darbon) Les Pigots
TEL: 04.74.30.25.87
DIRECTIONS: RN79, A40 autoroute, exit Mâcon Est (East), towards the town (bourg).
MENU: 71 to 105 Frs.
RESTAURANT: Snacks from 6.45, lunch 12.00-14.30, dinner 19.30-22.30
CLOSED: Sat evening, Sun and in Aug.
SPECIALITIES: grenouilles, poulet à la crème, fricassé de volatile à la crème, regional menu.
OTHER POINTS: credit cards accepted.

MIONNAY
Ain, 01390

LE RELAIS BRESSAN
(Monique Millet et Christian Desmaris) Route Nationale 83
TEL: 04.78.91.05.23 FAX: 04.78.91.05.23
DIRECTIONS: RN83, Les Echets exit,
LANGUAGES: English.
MENU: 60 Frs, dish of the day from 44 Frs.
RESTAURANT: Snacks from 5.00, lunch 11.00-15.00, dinner 19.00-22.00
CLOSED: Sat, Sun, 3 weeks in Aug and one week in winter.
SPECIALITIES: home-cooking.

OTHER POINTS: credit cards accepted.
Pérouges; parc des oiseaux (bird park) at Villars-les-Dombes; musée du caimion (HGVs) at Villars; musée de l'automobile at Rochetaillée.

MIRABEAU
Vaucluse, 84120

RELAIS DE LA DILIGENCE
(Mr Alain Michel) Route Nationale 96
TEL: 04.90.77.00.90 **FAX:** 04.90.77.05.10
DIRECTIONS: RN96, the Manosque/Sisteron road.
LANGUAGES: English, Italian.
ROOMS: 80 to 100 Frs.
RESTAURANT: Snacks from 5.00
CLOSED: Sun (out of season).
SPECIALITIES: paella, couscous, bouillabaisse, cassoulet, home-cooking.
HOTEL: 5 rooms. **FACILITIES:** shower, bath, private bathroom, television, telephone
OTHER POINTS: credit cards accepted.
châteaux at Mirabeau and Peyrolles; la Tour d'Aigues.

MOIDIEU DETOURBE
Isère, 38440

CHEZ DEDE
(Mr André Seigle)
TEL: 04.74.58.13.02
DIRECTIONS: RD502, the Vienne/Grenoble road.
MENU: 60 Frs.
RESTAURANT: Snacks from 5.00, lunch 11.00-14.00, dinner 19.00-21.30
CLOSED: Sat afternoon, Sun afternoon, 2 weeks in Aug, 1 week at Christmas.
SPECIALITIES: home-cooking.
OTHER POINTS: bar.

LES CERISIERS
(Mr Ferdinant Vaudot) La Détourbe
TEL: 04.74.58.14.02
DIRECTIONS: RN502, Vienne/Grenoble axis.
LANGUAGES: Italian.
MENU: 65 Frs (1/4 wine and coffee included).
RESTAURANT: Snacks from 6.00, lunch 12.00-15.00, dinner 19.00-22.30
CLOSED: Sun.
SPECIALITIES: home-cooking.
OTHER POINTS: bar.
La Côte St-André; Berlioz native city; Vienne la Romaine.

MOIRANS
Isère, 38430

LE RELAIS DU VIADUC
(Mr Fernand Barral-Poulat) 4, route de Grenoble
TEL: 04.76.35.31.01
DIRECTIONS: RN85, the Lyon/Crenoble road.
MENU: 55 Frs.
ROOMS: 70 Frs.
RESTAURANT: Snacks from 6.00, lunch 11.30-15.00, dinner 19.30-22.00
CLOSED: Sat and Sun.
SPECIALITIES: home-cooking.
HOTEL: 4 rooms
OTHER POINTS: credit cards accepted.
lakes; dams; grottes (caves) de Sassenage; Chartreuse liqueur cellars.

MONTAUROUX
Var, 83440

LE RELAIS DU LAC
(Nicole et Jean Hernandez) Route Départementale 562
TEL: 05.94.76.43.65 **FAX:** 05.94.47.60.13
DIRECTIONS: RN562, between Grasse and Draguignan.
LANGUAGES: English, Spanish.
MENU: 60 to 195 Frs.
ROOMS: 90 to 230 Frs.
RESTAURANT: Snacks from 6.30, lunch 12.00-14.30, dinner 19.00-21.30
SPECIALITIES: home-cooking, paella, couscous.
HOTEL: ☆☆ 37 rooms. **FACILITIES:** shower, private bathroom, television, telephone
OTHER POINTS: credit cards accepted.

MONTBRISON
Loire, 42600

LE RELAIS DE LA GARE
(Mr Jean-Pierre Gacon) 2, place de la Gare
TEL: 04.77.58.30.33
MENU: 60 to 110 Frs.
ROOMS: 99 to 120 Frs.
RESTAURANT: Snacks from 6.30, dinner -22.00
CLOSED: Sun, and in Aug.
SPECIALITIES: home-cooking.
HOTEL: 8 rooms. **FACILITIES:** shower, bath, private bathroom, telephone
OTHER POINTS: bar.

MONTELIMAR
Drôme, 26200

ESPACE TESTE ANIMATION
(Mr Jacques Teste) Zone sud Nationale 7
TEL: 04.75.01.44.43 **FAX:** 04.75.51.05.13
DIRECTIONS: Montélimar/Avignon motorway (Autoroute du Soleil) exit Nord/Sud.
MENU: 60 Frs.
RESTAURANT: Snacks from 7.30, lunch 11.30-14.00
CLOSED: Sat and Sun.
SPECIALITIES: home-cooking.

OTHER POINTS: credit cards accepted.
Château de Grignan; musée de la Miniature; usine de Nougat (sweet factory).

MONTFAVET
Vaucluse, 84140

RELAIS DE BONPAS
(Mr Alain Laugier) Route Nationale 7
TEL: 04.90.23.07.01
DIRECTIONS: RN7, between Avignon and Marseille, exit Avignon Sud (South).
LANGUAGES: English, Spanish.
ROOMS: 120 to 180 Frs.
RESTAURANT: Snacks from 6.00, lunch 11.30-14.30, dinner 19.00-23.00
SPECIALITIES: home-cooking.
HOTEL: ☆ 15 rooms. FACILITIES: shower
OTHER POINTS: credit cards accepted.
Fontaine-de-Vaucluse; Avignon; Les Baux-de-Provence; the Lubéron and Camargue regions; Saint-Rémy-de-Provence.

MONTFORT
Alpes-de-Haute-Provence, 04600

LE RELAIS FLEURI DE MONTFORT
(Mr Robert Estournet) Route Nationale 96
TEL: 04.92.64.11.91
DIRECTIONS: RN96, between Peyruis and Saint-Auban.
MENU: 65 Frs.
RESTAURANT: Snacks from 7.00, lunch 11.30-15.00, dinner 19.00-22.00
CLOSED: Sun evening.
SPECIALITIES: home-cooking.
OTHER POINTS: credit cards accepted.
pénitents des Mées; station de Lurs.

MONTREVEL EN BRESSE
Ain, 01340

LE MONTREVEL - Chez Gilles et Christelle
(Mr Gilles Marche) 21, rue de la Gare
TEL: 04.74.30.86.47
DIRECTIONS: RD 975, RD975, Bourg/Chalon-sur-Saone/Mâcon.
LANGUAGES: English, German.
MENU: 60 Frs.
RESTAURANT: Snacks from 7.00, lunch 12.00-14.30, dinner 19.00-22.00
CLOSED: Sun evening.
SPECIALITIES: home-cooking.
OTHER POINTS: credit cards accepted.

MONTROND LES BAINS
Loire, 42210

BAR RESTAURANT LE 82
(Mr Patrice Pereira) 37, route de Roanne
TEL: 04.77.54.89.88
DIRECTIONS: RN82, the Saint-Etienne/Roanne road.
LANGUAGES: Spanish, Portuguese.
MENU: 58 Frs (1/4 wine and coffee included).
RESTAURANT: Snacks from 6.00, lunch 11.30-15.00, dinner 19.00-23.00
SPECIALITIES: regional menu, home-cooking.
OTHER POINTS: credit cards accepted.
casino at Montrond; thermal spring.

LES OMBRELLES
(Mr Laurent Thouant) Route Nationale 82 - Lieu dit : Meylieu
TEL: 04.77.54.52.44
DIRECTIONS: RN82, between Saint-Etienne and Clermont-Ferrand.
LANGUAGES: English.
MENU: 57 Frs.
RESTAURANT: Snacks from 4.00, lunch 11.45-15.00, dinner 19.00-21.30
CLOSED: Sat, Sun, mid-Apr to mid-May, and one week at Christmas.
SPECIALITIES: cuisses de grenouilles (in July/Aug), home-cooking.
OTHER POINTS: credit cards accepted.
château de Montrond.

MORANCE
Rhône, 69480

RESTAURANT DE LA MAIRIE
(Mr Rémy Dorier) Le Bourg
TEL: 04.78.43.60.82
DIRECTIONS: RD100, the Anse/Larbresle/Feurs road.
ROOMS: 120 to 150 Frs.
RESTAURANT: Snacks from 7.00, lunch 11.30-14.30, dinner 19.00-21.00
SPECIALITIES: home-cooking.
HOTEL: 5 rooms
OTHER POINTS: bar.
Beaujolais wine circuit; Villefranche-sur-Saône.

MORNANT
Rhône, 69440

LE RELAIS DE BELLEVUE
(Mr Patrick Coupard) Route Départementale 42 - Bellevue
TEL: 04.78.81.22.26
DIRECTIONS: RD42, between Brignais and Rive-de-Gier.

LANGUAGES: Spanish.
MENU: 60 to 150 Frs.
RESTAURANT: Snacks from 6.30, lunch 11.30-15.00
CLOSED: Sun and in Aug.
SPECIALITIES: poulet aux écrevisses, loup (bass) l'américaine, regional menu.
OTHER POINTS: credit cards accepted.
Mornant; monts du Lyonnais.

MORNAS
Vaucluse, 84420

L'ARCHE DE MORNAS
(Mr Philippe Vaché) A7 - Aire de Mornas Village - Accessible sens Lyon/Marseille
TEL: 05.90.37.03.09 FAX: 05.90.37.05.29
RESTAURANT: Open 24h.
OTHER POINTS: credit cards accepted.

LA CASCADE
(Mme Jeanne Bretagnolle) Route Nationale 7
TEL: 04.90.37.02.67
DIRECTIONS: RN7, the Avignon road.
MENU: 60 Frs.
RESTAURANT: Snacks from 5.00, lunch 11.30-14.00, dinner 19.00-22.30
CLOSED: Sat, Sun and 3 weeks in Aug.
SPECIALITIES: regional menu,
OTHER POINTS: credit cards accepted.
Mornas: medieval château.

MUY (LE)
Var, 83490

LA CHAUMIERE
(Mr Claude Brunasso-Cattarello) Quartier de la Gare - Route Nationale 7
TEL: 04.94.45.10.81
DIRECTIONS: RN7.
LANGUAGES: Italian.
MENU: 50 to 80 Frs.
ROOMS: 120 to 170 Frs.
RESTAURANT: Snacks from 6.00, lunch 11.30-14.30, dinner 19.00-21.30
CLOSED: Sat evening, Sun and public holidays.
SPECIALITIES: regional menu, home-cooking,
HOTEL: 8 rooms
OTHER POINTS: credit cards accepted.

NEAUX
Loire, 42470

CHEZ PATOU
(Mr Patrick Prast) Route Nationale 7 - La Croix
TEL: 04.77.62.70.32
DIRECTIONS: RN7, between Lyon and Roanne.
MENU: 60 to 80 Frs.
RESTAURANT: Snacks from 5.00, lunch 11.30-14.30, dinner 19.00-21.30
CLOSED: Mon afternoon.
SPECIALITIES: home-cooking.
OTHER POINTS: credit cards accepted.
Loire: gorges and châteaux.

NOVES
Bouches-du-Rhône, 13550

RELAIS DE LA BASSAQUE
(Mr Joseph Masi) Route Nationale 7
TEL: 04.90.94.26.84
DIRECTIONS: RN7.
LANGUAGES: Italian.
RESTAURANT: Snacks from 5.00
CLOSED: Sat evening, Sun and 2 weeks end Aug.
OTHER POINTS: bar.

NOYAREY
Isère, 38360

AU BON ACCUEIL
(Mr Jean-Claude Compe) Rue du Maupas
TEL: 04.76.53.95.61
DIRECTIONS: RN532, the Grenoble/Valence road.
LANGUAGES: German, Spanish, Italian.
MENU: 61 to 85 Frs.
ROOMS: 90 to 140 Frs.
RESTAURANT: Snacks from 5.30, lunch 11.30-14.00
CLOSED: Sat and Sun.
SPECIALITIES: home-cooking.
HOTEL: 11 rooms. FACILITIES: shower
OTHER POINTS: bar.
Le Vercors; La Chartreuse massif.

ORGON
Bouches-du-Rhône, 13660

AU BEC FIN
(Mme Arlette Sault) Route Nationale 7
TEL: 04.90.73.30.38 FAX: 04.90.73.30.50
DIRECTIONS: RN7, between Aix-en-Provence and Marseille.
LANGUAGES: English, Spanish.
MENU: 57 Frs.
RESTAURANT: Snacks from 5.00
CLOSED: Sat evening, Sun.
SPECIALITIES: couscous, paella, gratin du chef, regional menu, home-cooking.
OTHER POINTS: bar.
Les Baux-de-Provence; Cordes; Fontaine-de-Vaucluse.

BRASSERIE BELLEVUE
Route Nationale 7
TEL: 04.90.73.00.24
DIRECTIONS: RN7, the Marseille/Lyon road.
MENU: 55 to 95 Frs.

RESTAURANT: Snacks from 6.00, lunch 11.00-15.00, dinner 18.30-23.00
SPECIALITIES: Provetial dishes, regional menu, home-cooking.
OTHER POINTS: credit cards accepted.
Les Baux-de-Provence; the Lubéron region.

RELAIS DES FUMADES
(Mr Jean Etcheverry)
TEL: 04.90.73.00.81 **FAX:** 04.90.73.30.69
DIRECTIONS: RN7, between Avignon and Aix-en-Provence.
LANGUAGES: English, German, Spanish, Italian.
ROOMS: 110 to 150 Frs.
RESTAURANT: Snacks from 6.00, lunch 12.00-14.00, dinner 19.30-24.00
SPECIALITIES: home-cooking.
HOTEL: ☆ 11 rooms. **FACILITIES:** shower, bath
OTHER POINTS: credit cards accepted.
Saint-Rémy-de-Provence; Salon; Cordes; Fontaine-de-Vaucluse.

ORLIENAS
Rhône, 69530

BAR RESTAURANT CHEZ CHAPELLE
(Mme Annie Chapelle) Lieu dit : Les 7 Chemins
TEL: 04.78.05.21.54
DIRECTIONS: RN86, the Lyon/Saint-Etienne road.
MENU: 60 Frs.
RESTAURANT: Snacks from 6.00, lunch 12.00-15.00
CLOSED: Sat and Sun.
SPECIALITIES: cuisses de grenouilles, couscous, paella, home-cooking.
OTHER POINTS: bar.
Lyon: aqueducts, wine-cellars of côteau du Lyonnais, with tasting (caveau de dégustation), at Millery and Taluyers.

PAJAY
Isère, 38260

MA PETITE AUBERGE
(Mme Huguette Vivier) La Côte Saint André
TEL: 04.74.54.26.06
DIRECTIONS: RD73, between Beaurepaire and La-Côte-Saint-André.
LANGUAGES: English, German
MENU: 60 to 150 Frs
ROOMS: 110 to 240 Frs.
RESTAURANT: Snacks from 6.00, lunch 12.00-14.00, dinner 19.00-21.00
CLOSED: 1st 2 wks Sept.
SPECIALITIES: home-cooking, grenouilles, lotte (monkfish) l'américaine, gratin dauphinois, regional menu.
HOTEL: 7 rooms. **FACILITIES:** shower, bath, private bathroom, television
OTHER POINTS: credit cards accepted.
Côte Saint-André; Berlioz museum; route du tabac; Auterive: palais idéal du Facteur Cheval; Voiron: la Chartreuse.

PARIGNY LE COTEAU
Loire, 42120

RELAIS LE PARIGNY
(Mme Christine Favre) Route Nationale 7 - Le Bas de Rhins
TEL: 04.77.62.06.18
DIRECTIONS: RN7.
MENU: 55 Frs.
ROOMS: 90 to 120 Frs.
RESTAURANT: Snacks from 6.00, lunch 11.30-14.30, dinner 19.00-21.30
CLOSED: Sat afternoon, Sun and 1st 2 weeks in Aug.
SPECIALITIES: home-cooking.
HOTEL: 7 rooms. **FACILITIES:** shower
OTHER POINTS: bar.

PEIPIN
Alpes-de-Haute-Provence, 04200

AUX BONS ENFANTS - LE MISTRAL
(Mr Jean-Louis Decome) Route Nationale 85
TEL: 04.92.62.44.11
DIRECTIONS: RN85, between Marseille and Sisteron.
MENU: 65 to 90 Frs.
ROOMS: 140 to 180 Frs.
RESTAURANT: Snacks from 5.30, lunch 12.00-15.00, dinner 20.00-22.00
CLOSED: Sun evening.
SPECIALITIES: regional menu, home-cooking.
HOTEL: 10 rooms. **FACILITIES:** shower, private bathroom
OTHER POINTS: credit cards accepted.

PERTUIS
Vaucluse, 84120

LE VICTOR HUGO
(Mr Jacky Chalot) 143, boulevard Victor Hugo
TEL: 04.90.79.12.29
DIRECTIONS: on the Cavaillon road.
LANGUAGES: English, Italian.
MENU: 56 Frs (wine included).
RESTAURANT: Snacks from 7.00, lunch 11.30-15.00
CLOSED: Sun and 2 weeks over Christmas and the New Year.
SPECIALITIES: home-cooking.
OTHER POINTS: bar.
châteaux d'Ansouis, de Lourmarin and de la Tour-d'Aigues; étang (pond) de la Bonde.

PIOLENC
Vaucluse, 84420

LE COMMERCE
(Mr Roger Sambucini) Place Cours Corsin
TEL: 04.90.29.60.14 FAX: 04.90.29.60.14
DIRECTIONS: RN7.
LANGUAGES: English, Italian.
MENU: 58 to 130 Frs.
RESTAURANT: Snacks from 7.00, lunch 12.00-14.00, dinner 19.00-21.00
CLOSED: Wed, Dec.
SPECIALITIES: filet de boeuf aux morilles, poulet, écrevisses, pieds et paquets (mutton tripe and trotters), galantine de canard, home-cooking.
OTHER POINTS: credit cards accepted.
Orange: arc de triomphe (5km); Avignon: Palais des Papes, pont Saint-Bénézet.

PLAN D'ORGON
Bouches-du-Rhône, 13750

RESTAURANT DU PONT
(Mr Dominique Balloy) ZI du Pont
TEL: 04.90.73.20.62 FAX: 04.90.73.20.57
MENU: 60 to 80 Frs.
RESTAURANT: Snacks from 6.00
CLOSED: Sat evening and Sun.
SPECIALITIES: home-cooking.
OTHER POINTS: children's menu.

PONT D'AIN
Ain, 01160

RESTAURANT DE LA GARE - LE CRISNO
(Mr Christian Sanchez) 56, rue Saint Expéry
TEL: 04.74.39.01.22 FAX: 04.74.39.18.48
MENU: 60 to 90 Frs.
RESTAURANT: Snacks from 6.00, lunch 11.30-15.00, dinner 19.00-23.00
OTHER POINTS: credit cards accepted.
Cerdon; château d'Ambronay; Le Bugey: centrate électrique (power station).

PONT DE CHERUY
Isère, 38230

LE ROUTIER
(Mme Marie-Paule Blanc) 30, rue Giffard
TEL: 04.78.32.20.02
DIRECTIONS: RN517, the Loyettes road.
LANGUAGES: Italian.
MENU: 60 Frs (wine and coffee included).
ROOMS: 80 to 180 Frs.
RESTAURANT: Snacks from 5.00, lunch 11.30-15.00, dinner 19.00-22.00
CLOSED: Sun.
SPECIALITIES: home-cooking.
HOTEL: 30 rooms. FACILITIES: shower, private bathroom
OTHER POINTS: credit cards accepted.
Cremieu; Le Bugey.

PONT DE L'ISERE
Drôme, 26600

L'ARCHE DE VALENCE LATITUDE 45
(Mr Eric Arnaud) A7 - Aire de Latitude 45 - Accessible sens Orange/Lyon
TEL: 04.75.84.50.37 FAX: 04.75.84.79.09
RESTAURANT: Snacks from 6.00
OTHER POINTS: credit cards accepted.

PONTCHARRA
Isère, 38530

RELAIS DU PONT DE LA GACHE
(Mr Jean-Pierre Rubatat) La Gache
TEL: 04.76.97.30.08 FAX: 04.76.97.30.08
DIRECTIONS: RN90, between Grenoble and Chambéry.
LANGUAGES: English, Italian.
MENU: 60 to 65 Frs.
RESTAURANT: Snacks from 6.30, lunch 11.00-15.00, dinner 19.00-22.00
CLOSED: Sat and the last 2 weeks in Aug.
SPECIALITIES: gratin dauphinois à la crème, regional menu, home-cooking.
OTHER POINTS: credit cards accepted.
La Chartreuse massif.

PONTET (LE)
Vaucluse, 84130

L'OSERAIE
(Mr Guy Cherpin) Quartier de l'Oseraie - Route Nationale 7
TEL: 04.90.31.04.55
DIRECTIONS: RN7.
MENU: 60 Frs.
ROOMS: 100 to 120 Frs.
RESTAURANT: Snacks from 6.30, lunch 12.00-15.00, dinner 19.00-21.00
CLOSED: Sat, Sun, Aug.
SPECIALITIES: home-cooking.
HOTEL: 5 rooms. FACILITIES: shower
OTHER POINTS: credit cards accepted.
Avignon.

POURRIERES
Var, 83910

LE PROVENCE
(Nadine et Gérard Magne) Route Nationale 7
TEL: 04.94.78.41.28
DIRECTIONS: between Aix and Saint-Maximin.

LANGUAGES: English, Spanish, Italian.
MENU: 65 Frs.
RESTAURANT: Snacks from 6.00
CLOSED: Sun.
SPECIALITIES: regional menu, home-cooking.
OTHER POINTS: credit cards accepted.

POUZIN (LE)
Ardèche, 07250

LES ROUTIERS
(Mme Juliette Vialatte) 64, rue Olivier de Serres
TEL: 04.75.63.83.45
DIRECTIONS: between Loriol and Privas.
MENU: 55 to 65 Frs.
ROOMS: 85 to 120 Frs.
RESTAURANT: Snacks from 7.00, lunch 12.00-14.00, dinner 19.00-21.00
CLOSED: Sun, Aug.
SPECIALITIES: home-cooking.
HOTEL: 5 rooms. FACILITIES: shower, private bathroom
OTHER POINTS: bar.
the Ardèche region.

LE PROVENCAL
(Anny Delubac) 14, rue Marcel Seignobus
TEL: 04.75.63.82.29
DIRECTIONS: RN 86, RN86, on the Lyon/Montpelier axis.
LANGUAGES: English, Italian.
MENU: 60 Frs.
ROOMS: 90 to 150 Frs.
RESTAURANT: Snacks from 6.00, lunch 12.00-14.00, dinner 19.30-21.00
CLOSED: Sat evening, Sun, public holidays, in Aug and 1 week for Christmas.
HOTEL: 5 rooms. FACILITIES: shower
OTHER POINTS: bar.

PRIVAS
Ardèche, 07000

LA RENAISSANCE
(Mr Jean-Pierre Monteil) Place du Champ de Mars
TEL: 04.75.64.21.60
DIRECTIONS: RN104, between Pouzin and Aubenas.
MENU: 50 to 60 Frs.
RESTAURANT: Snacks from 7.30, lunch 11.15-14.00, dinner 19.15-20.30
CLOSED: Sun, Aug.
SPECIALITIES: home-cooking.
OTHER POINTS: bar.

PUYRICARD
Bouches-du-Rhône, 13540

LE TOURANGEAU
(Mme Danielle Roccia) Route Nationale 7 - Lieu dit : La Petite Calale
TEL: 04.42.21.60.65
DIRECTIONS: RN7.
LANGUAGES: Italian.
RESTAURANT: Dinner -23.00
CLOSED: Sat evening, Sun and in Aug.
HOTEL: 14 rooms
OTHER POINTS: bar.

REYRIEUX
Ain, 01600

RESTAURANT DE LA GARE
(Mme Yvonne Ortiz) Rue de la Gare
TEL: 04.74.00.03.04
DIRECTIONS: RD933, between Neuville and Trévoux.
LANGUAGES: English, Spanish.
MENU: 65 Frs (wine and coffee incl.); Sun 80-140 Frs.
RESTAURANT: Snacks from 6.30, lunch 11.00-15.30, dinner 19.00-21.00
CLOSED: Sun (out of season).
SPECIALITIES: grenouilles fraiches, home-cooking.
OTHER POINTS: credit cards accepted.
Ars: basilica; Trévoux and Pérouges: medieval cities.

RIVE DE GIER - LA MADELEINE
Loire, 42800

RESTAURANT LE BARBECUE
(Mme Marie-Claude Gonon) 70, rue des Martyrs de la Résistance
TEL: 04.77.75.59.70
DIRECTIONS: RN88, the Lyon/Saint-Etienne road.
MENU: 55 to 110 Frs.
RESTAURANT: Snacks from 7.00, lunch 12.00-14.30, dinner 19.00-21.00
CLOSED: Mon afternoon (out of season).
SPECIALITIES: cuisses de grenouilles, fritures (whitebait), regional menu, home-cooking.
OTHER POINTS: bar.
zoo at Saint-Martin-ia-Plaine; la Chartreuse de Sainte-Croix-en-Jarez; le Mont-Pilat.

ROCHEMAURE
Ardèche, 07400

RELAIS DE LA CONDAMINE
(Mme Josiane Sicoit)
TEL: 04.75.52.96.26
DIRECTIONS: RN86, the Lyon/Marseille road.
MENU: 48 Frs.
RESTAURANT: Snacks from 6.00, lunch 11.00-14.00, dinner 19.00-20.30
CLOSED: Sun.
SPECIALITIES: home-cooking.
OTHER POINTS: terrace.

ROQUE D'ANTHERON (LA)
Bouches-du-Rhône, 13640

AU RELAIS FLEURI
(Mr Guy Auguste) Hameau de Saint-Christophe
TEL: 04.42.50.20.24
DIRECTIONS: CD543 and 561, at the intersection of CD 561 and 543.
LANGUAGES: English, German.
MENU: 60 to 95 Frs.
ROOMS: 120 to 150 Frs.
RESTAURANT: Snacks from 7.00, lunch 12.00-14.00, dinner 19.30-22.00
SPECIALITIES: home-cooking.
HOTEL: 9 rooms. **FACILITIES:** shower, private bathroom
OTHER POINTS: credit cards accepted.
the Lubéron region; château de Lourmariti.

SABLONNIERES
Isère, 38460

BAR RESTAURANT DE LA PLACE
(Mme Noelle Mailler)
TEL: 04.74.92.80.19
DIRECTIONS: RD522 and 517.
MENU: 55 (75 Frs on Sun).
RESTAURANT: Snacks from 6.30, lunch 12.00-14.30, dinner 19.30-21.00
CLOSED: Sat, Aug.
SPECIALITIES: home-cooking.
OTHER POINTS: bar.

SAILLANS
Drôme, 26340

LE NATIONAL - PMU
(Mme Jeanine Chauvet) Grande Rue
TEL: 04.75.21.51.33
DIRECTIONS: RN93, between Crest and Cap.
MENU: 65 to 85 Frs.
ROOMS: 170 to 200 Frs.
RESTAURANT: Snacks from 8.00, lunch 12.30-14.00, dinner 19.30-21.00
CLOSED: Wed, and 5 weeks in Sept/Oct.
SPECIALITIES: gigot d'agneau, daube provenáale, gratin dauphinois, regional menu, home-cooking.
HOTEL: 6 rooms. **FACILITIES:** shower
OTHER POINTS: bar.
Drôme valley; 11thC church; Le Vercors.

SAINT AGATHE LA BOUTERESSE
Loire, 42130

LE PETIT RELAIS
(Mme Malise Maréchal) La Bouteresse
TEL: 04.77.24.17.20
DIRECTIONS: RN89, the Feurs/Boën axis.
MENU: 58 Frs.
RESTAURANT: Snacks from 7.00, lunch 11.30-15.30, dinner 19.00-21.00
CLOSED: Sat, Sun and the last 2 weeks in August.
SPECIALITIES: home-cooking.
OTHER POINTS: bar.

SAINT BONNET LES OULES
Loire, 42330

LE GORDON
(Mme Marie-Thérèse Munier) Lapra
TEL: 04.77.94.93.30
MENU: 50 to 100 Frs.
RESTAURANT: Snacks from 9.00, lunch 12.00-14.00, dinner 18.30-21.30
SPECIALITIES: lapin au whisky, home-cooking.
OTHER POINTS: credit cards accepted.
musée ferme agricole (farming).

SAINT CHAMOND
Loire, 42400

AUBERGE DES SAULES
39, route de la Varizelle
TEL: 04.77.22.10.43
DIRECTIONS: the Lyon/Saint-Etienne road.
MENU: 55 Frs (80 Frs on Saturday).
RESTAURANT: Snacks from 8.00, lunch 12.00-20.00
CLOSED: Sun.
SPECIALITIES: home-cooking,
OTHER POINTS: bar.
Saint-Etienne.

SAINT CLAIR DU RHONE
Isère, 38370

LE RELAIS FLEURI
(Tonino et Colette Tognoloni) 3, rue du Commandant l'Herminier
TEL: 04.74.56.43.12
DIRECTIONS: RN516.
LANGUAGES: Italian.
RESTAURANT: Open 24h.
CLOSED: the last 2 weeks in Aug.
SPECIALITIES: home-cooking,
HOTEL: 12 rooms. **FACILITIES:** shower, private bathroom, television
OTHER POINTS: credit cards accepted.

SAINT CYR DE FAVIERES
Loire, 42132

RELAIS ALSACIEN
(Mr Marcel Terrier)
TEL: 04.77.64.81.01
DIRECTIONS: RN7, the Paris/Lyon road.
RESTAURANT: Snacks from 6.00, lunch 11.30-14.30,

dinner 19.30-22.00
CLOSED: Sat, Sun, July.
SPECIALITIES: home-cooking.
OTHER POINTS: bar.
dam at Villerest.

RELAIS ROUTIERS LAGOUTTE
(Mr Yves Jonard) L'Hôpital sur Rhins
TEL: 04.77.64.80.13
DIRECTIONS: from the autoroute, exit at L'Hôpital-sur-Rhins.
LANGUAGES: English.
MENU: 60 to 130 Frs.
ROOMS: 105 Frs.
RESTAURANT: Snacks from 5.00, lunch 12.00-14.00, dinner 19.00-22.00
CLOSED: Sat, and in Aug.
SPECIALITIES: regional menu.
HOTEL: 3 rooms
OTHER POINTS: credit cards accepted.
dam at Villerest.

SAINT CYR SUR MENTHON
Ain, 01380

L'AUBERGE DE SAINT CYR
(Mme Marie-Odile Chêne) Route Nationale 79 - Le Logis
TEL: 03.85.36.30.69
DIRECTIONS: RN79.
MENU: 62 to 135 Frs.
RESTAURANT: Snacks from 6.30, lunch 11.30-14.30, dinner 19.00-22.30
CLOSED: Sun afternoon.
SPECIALITIES: couscous.
OTHER POINTS: credit cards accepted.

SAINT DIDIER SUR BEAUJEU
Rhône, 69430

LE RELAIS DES DEPOTS
(Mme Pascale Batteur) Les Dépots
TEL: 04.74.69.50.75
DIRECTIONS: RN 37, RN37, between Belelville-sur-Saone and Charolles.
MENU: 59 Frs.
ROOMS: 110 Frs.
RESTAURANT: Snacks from 6.00, lunch 12.00-14.30, dinner 19.00-22.00
SPECIALITIES: home-cooking.
HOTEL: 4 rooms
OTHER POINTS: credit cards accepted.

SAINT ETIENNE
Loire, 42000

LE MISTRAL
(Mme Christiane Durif) 4, rue Jean Neyret
TEL: 04.77.32.95.39
DIRECTIONS: RN82, Douanes/Marché de gros (customs/wholesale market).
LANGUAGES: Italian.
MENU: 55 Frs.
RESTAURANT: Snacks from 6.00, lunch 11.30-15.00, dinner 19.00-22.00
CLOSED: Sat and Sun.
SPECIALITIES: couscous, pizza, home-cooking.
OTHER POINTS: bar.

LE POISSON ROUGE
(Mme Monique Coquard) 134, rue Florent Evrard - Quartier de la Béraudière
TEL: 04.77.81.30.52
DIRECTIONS: near the western bypass (la rocade).
MENU: 49 to 95 Frs.
RESTAURANT: Snacks from 9.00, lunch 11.00-15.00, dinner 18.30-21.30
CLOSED: Sun (except bookings) and 2 weeks in Aug.
SPECIALITIES: regional menu, home-cooking.
OTHER POINTS: credit cards accepted.
musée de la mine (mining); le Mont-Pilat (ski piste); zoo at Saint-Martin-de-la-Plaine.

SAINT FIRMIN
Hautes-Alpes, 05800

LA TRINITE
(Mr Gérard Marletta) Route Nationale 85 - Route Napoléon
TEL: 04.92.55.21.64
DIRECTIONS: RN85, between Grenoble and Cap.
MENU: 60 to 150 Frs.
ROOMS: 130 to 220 Frs.
RESTAURANT: Snacks from 6.00, lunch 12.00, dinner - 23.00
SPECIALITIES: oreille d'ane, magret de canard, regional menu, home-cooking,
HOTEL: ☆ 12 rooms. FACILITIES: shower, bath, private bathroom
OTHER POINTS: credit cards accepted.
vallée de Valgodemard; Notre-Dame-de-la-Salette.

SAINT GENIX SUR GUIERS
Savoie, 73240

AUBERGE CAMPAGNARDE AILLOUD
(Mme Reine Ailloud) Hameau de Joudin - Sortie Bourg en Bresse sur autoroute.
TEL: 04.76.31.80.19
DIRECTIONS: RD916, Le Pont-de-Beauvoisin, between Saint-Genix and Pont-de-Beauvois.
MENU: 55 to 110 Frs.
RESTAURANT: Snacks from 6.00
CLOSED: Sat, and Sept and Oct.
SPECIALITIES: grenouilles, home-cooking.

OTHER POINTS: bar.
château de Montfleury-sur-Auressieux; musée d'Aoste; abbaye en Chartreuse.

SAINT HILAIRE DU ROSIER
Isère, 38840

LE RELAIS - Chez Tony
(Mr Tony Lopez)
TEL: 04.76.64.53.84
DIRECTIONS: RN92, between Saint-Marcellin and Romans.
MENU: 55 to 90 Frs.
ROOMS: 145 Frs.
RESTAURANT: Snacks from 7.00, lunch 12.00-15.00, dinner 19.00-23.00
CLOSED: Sat, Sun, and in Sept.
SPECIALITIES: regional menu, home-cooking,
HOTEL: 5 rooms. FACILITIES: shower, bath, private bathroom
OTHER POINTS: credit cards accepted.
Le Vercors.

SAINT JEAN D'ARDIERES
Rhône, 69220

SARL LE NATIONAL
(Mme Martine Guilland) 175, route Nationale 6
TEL: 04.74.66.10.55
DIRECTIONS: RN6, Macon-Lyon and Belleville-sur-Saône/Mâcon axis.
MENU: 59 Frs (1/4 wine and coffee included).
RESTAURANT: Snacks from 5.00, lunch 12.00-14.30, dinner 19.00-21.00
CLOSED: Sun and public holidays.
SPECIALITIES: home-cooking.
OTHER POINTS: credit cards accepted.
Le vignoble du Beaujolais (Beaujolais wineyards); zoological park; Romaneche Thorin.

SAINT JEAN DE CHEVELU
Savoie, 73170

LES QUATRE CHEMINS
(Mr Jean Rubod) Lieu dit "Les Quatre Chemins"
TEL: 04.79.36.80.06 FAX: 04.79.36.78.07
DIRECTIONS: RN504, between Lyon and Chambéry.
LANGUAGES: English.
MENU: 64 to 126 Frs.
ROOMS: 105 to 140 Frs.
RESTAURANT: Snacks from 4.00, lunch 11.30-14.15, dinner 19.00-22.15
CLOSED: Sat evening, Sun, 2 weeks in Aug and 1 week end Dec.
SPECIALITIES: home-cooking.
HOTEL: 9 rooms. FACILITIES: shower, bath, private bathroom
OTHER POINTS: credit cards accepted.
abbaye de Hautecombe (12km); cru Jongieux wine-cellars.

SAINT JUST DE CLAIX
Isère, 38680

BAR RESTAURANT LE DAUPHINOIS
(Mme Arlette Doncques) Le Village
TEL: 04.75.48.49.49
DIRECTIONS: RN532, the Valence/Grenoble road.
MENU: 60 Frs.
RESTAURANT: Snacks from 6.00, lunch 12.00-14.30, dinner 19.00-22.00
SPECIALITIES: home-cooking.
OTHER POINTS: bar.
grottes (caves) de Choranche and de Thaïs; Le Vercors.

SAINT LAURENT DU VAR
Alpes-Maritimes, 06700

LE PROVENCE
(Mme Suzanne Desrumeaux) Zone industrielle
TEL: 04.93.31.60.55
DIRECTIONS: Parallel to the A8
MENU: 65 Frs.
RESTAURANT: Snacks from 6.30, lunch 11.30-15.00
CLOSED: Sat, Sun and public holidays.
SPECIALITIES: regional menu, home-cooking.
OTHER POINTS: credit cards accepted.
Nice; Cannes.

LE RELAIS ROUTIER
(Mme Torrente) Allée des Cableurs - Secteur B Z.I.
TEL: 04.93.31.26.47
LANGUAGES: English, German, Spanish.
MENU: 57 Frs.
RESTAURANT: Lunch 12.00-14.00, dinner 19.00-21.30
CLOSED: Sun.
SPECIALITIES: paella, couscous, cassoulet, home-cooking.
OTHER POINTS: bar.

SAINT MARCEL DE FELINES
Loire, 42122

LA REVOUTE
(Mr Didier Rey) Lieu dit : La Revoute
TEL: 04.77.64.61.60
DIRECTIONS: RN82, between Roanne and Saint-Etienne.
LANGUAGES: English.
MENU: 59 to 125 Frs.
RESTAURANT: Snacks from 7.30, lunch 11.45-14.00, dinner 19.00-21.00
CLOSED: Mon evening, and 2 weeks in Sept.
SPECIALITIES: home-cooking.
OTHER POINTS: credit cards accepted.

château de Saint-Marcel-de-Félines; barrage (dam) at Villerest; banks of the Loire.

SAINT MARCEL LES VALENCE
Drôme, 26320

LA PRAIRIE
(Mr Michel Montusclat - SARL La Prairie) 8, rue de la Liberté
TEL: 04.75.58.70.38
DIRECTIONS: RN532, between Valence and Romans.
MENU: 60 to 115 Frs.
RESTAURANT: Snacks from 7.00
CLOSED: in Aug.
SPECIALITIES: poissons, regional menu, home-cooking.
OTHER POINTS: credit cards accepted.

SAINT MARTIN DE CLELLES
Isère, 38930

MON REGAL
(Mme Monique Flandin) Route Nationale 75
TEL: 04.76.34.42.84
DIRECTIONS: RN75.
RESTAURANT: Dinner -21.00
CLOSED: every evening from Nov to Feb.
SPECIALITIES: home-cooking.
OTHER POINTS: children's menu.

SAINT MARTIN DE CRAU
Bouches-du-Rhône, 13310

LA CABANE BAMBOU
(Jacques Giraud & Fils) Route Nationale 113
TEL: 04.90.50.67.36 FAX: 04.90.50.62.52
DIRECTIONS: RN113, between Salon and Aries.
LANGUAGES: English, Spanish, Italian.
RESTAURANT: Open 24h.
CLOSED: Sun (out of season).
SPECIALITIES: daube de toro, regional menu.
HOTEL: 10 rooms
OTHER POINTS: credit cards accepted.
the Camargue; Les Baux-de-Provence; Saint-Rémy-de-Provence; la plaine de la Crau.

LE RELAIS DES SPORTS - La Dynamite
(Mr Daniel Nivaggioli) La Dynamite
TEL: 04.90.47.05.24 FAX: 04.90.47.05.24
DIRECTIONS: RN113, Salon/Arles, Arles/Fos.
LANGUAGES: Spanish, Italian.
MENU: 50 to 80 Frs.
RESTAURANT: Snacks from 6.00, lunch 12.00-14.15, dinner 19.30-22.00
CLOSED: Sun evening.
SPECIALITIES: regional menu, home-cooking,
OTHER POINTS: bar.

RESTAURANT DE LA GARE
(Mr Pascal Selva) Route de la Dynamite
TEL: 04.90.47.05.18
DIRECTIONS: in the station area.
MENU: 55 Frs.
ROOMS: 100 Frs.
RESTAURANT: Snacks from 5.30, lunch 11.30-14.30
CLOSED: Sun.
HOTEL: 7 rooms
OTHER POINTS: bar.

SAINT PAUL LE JEUNE
Ardèche, 07460

RELAIS DE CHEYRES
(Mme Marie-Thérése Vernede) Banne
TEL: 04.75.39.30.09
DIRECTIONS: RD104.
RESTAURANT: Snacks from 8.00
CLOSED: Sun.
SPECIALITIES: escargots, regional menu, home-cooking.
OTHER POINTS: credit cards accepted.
grottes (caves) Cocali6res; Vallon-Pont-d'Arc; Orgnac; gorges of the Ardèche.

SAINT RAPHAEL
Var, 83700

BEL AZUR
(Mr Robert Magnani) 247, boulevard de Provence
TEL: 04.94.95.14.08
LANGUAGES: Italian.
MENU: 65 Frs (wine and coffee included).
ROOMS: 150 to 250 Frs.
RESTAURANT: Snacks from 7.00
CLOSED: Sat, Sun evening (out of season), and from 24th Dec to 4th Jan.
SPECIALITIES: bouillabaisse, aioli, paella, marmite du pêcheur, soupe de poisson maison, home-cooking.
HOTEL: ☆ 20 rooms. FACILITIES: shower, bath, private bathroom, telephone
OTHER POINTS: credit cards accepted.
gorges of the Verdon and the Loup; Roman remains; Fréjus: Roman arena.

SAINT ROMAIN LA MOTTE
Loire, 42640

AU BON ACCUEIL
(Mme Lucienne Galichon) Les Baraques -
TEL: 04.77.72.00.01
DIRECTIONS: RN7, the Paris/Roanne road.
MENU: 60 to 80 Frs.
ROOMS: 120 to 160 Frs.
RESTAURANT: Snacks from 4.30, lunch 11.00-15.00,

dinner 19.00-22.00
CLOSED: Sat afternoon and in Aug.
SPECIALITIES: grenouilles (in summier), fritures (whitebait), home-cooking.
HOTEL: 3 rooms. **FACILITIES:** shower, private bathroom
OTHER POINTS: credit cards accepted.
lac de Villeré; barrage (dam) de La Toiche.

SAINT SAUVEUR DE MONTAGUT
Ardèche, 07190

LES COPAINS
(Mme Micheline Bauer) Le Moulinon
TEL: 04.75.65.49.12
MENU: 60 to 85 Frs.
ROOMS: 150 to 180 Frs.
RESTAURANT: Snacks from 7.30, lunch 12.00-14.30, dinner 19.00-22.00
CLOSED: Wed after 15.00.
SPECIALITIES: home-cooking.
HOTEL: 6 rooms. **FACILITIES:** shower, private bathroom, television
OTHER POINTS: credit cards accepted.

SAINT SERNIN
Ardèche, 07200

BAR RESTAURANT DE LA GARE
(Mme Lisette Véra) Quartier Saint Paul
TEL: 04.75.93.37.33
DIRECTIONS: RN104, Aubenas-Vallon/Pont d'Arc or Alès roads.
MENU: 60 to 95 Frs.
RESTAURANT: Snacks from 7.30, lunch 12.00-15.00, dinner 19.00-21.30
CLOSED: Mon evening (October to end of May)
SPECIALITIES: home-cooking.
OTHER POINTS: credit cards accepted.
Gorges de l'Ardèche.

SAINTE FOY L'ARGENTIERE
Rhône, 69610

AUBERGE DE LA PLACE - Chez Nadine et Christian
(Mlle Nadine Aime) 49, Grande Rue
TEL: 04.74.70.00.51
DIRECTIONS: RN89, the main Lyon/Clermont-Ferrand road.
LANGUAGES: English, Italian.
MENU: 52 to 65 Frs.
RESTAURANT: Snacks from 6.30
CLOSED: Sat.
SPECIALITIES: home-cooking.
OTHER POINTS: bar.
wildlife park at Courzier; millinery museum at Chazelle-sur-Lyon; mining museum at Saint-Pierre-de-la-Palud.

SAINTE FOY LES LYON
Rhône, 69110

LE POT DES GONES
(Mr Patrice Lachard) 66, route de la Libération
TEL: 04.78.59.03.05
DIRECTIONS: RD42, Tassin/Saint-Etienne road.
LANGUAGES: English.
MENU: 62 Frs (1/4 wine included).
RESTAURANT: Snacks from 6.00, lunch 12.00-14.00
CLOSED: Sun afternoon.
SPECIALITIES: home-cooking.
OTHER POINTS: credit cards accepted.
Beaunart aqueducts.

SALAISE SUR SANNE
Isère, 38150

RELAIS DE LA SANNE
(Mr Marc Giraud) Route Nationale 7
TEL: 04.74.86.37.91
DIRECTIONS: RN7, the Lyon/Valence road, Chanas exit.
LANGUAGES: English, German.
MENU: 62 to 88 Frs.
RESTAURANT: Snacks from 6.00, lunch 11.45-14.30, dinner 19.15-22.30
CLOSED: Sun.
SPECIALITIES: home-cooking,
OTHER POINTS: credit cards accepted.
Peaugres: safari park; musée animalier at Ville-sous-Anjou.

SARCEY
Rhône, 69490

RELAIS DES MARRONNIERS
(Mr Patrick Parisi) Place de l'Eglise
TEL: 04.74.26.86.65
DIRECTIONS: RN7, between L'Arbresle and Tarare.
LANGUAGES: English.
MENU: 53 to 80 Frs.
RESTAURANT: Snacks from 6.00, lunch 12.00-13.30
CLOSED: Wed afternoon.
SPECIALITIES: home-cooking.
OTHER POINTS: bar.
the Beaujolais region.

SATOLAS ET BONCE
Isère, 38290

RELAIS ROUTIERS DU CHAFFARD
(Mr Marc Seguin) Le Chaffard
TEL: 04.74.94.46.35
MENU: 65 Frs (wine and coffee included).
RESTAURANT: Snacks from 6.00, lunch 12.00-14.30, dinner 19.00-22.00
CLOSED: the weekend .

SPECIALITIES: home-cooking.
OTHER POINTS: credit cards accepted.

SAULCE
Drôme, 26270

LE DISQUE BLEU
(Mr Jacques Brillo) Quartier des Blâches - Cliousclat
TEL: 04.75.63.00.08
DIRECTIONS: RN7 and RD26, autoroute exits at Loriol and Montélimar Nord (North).
MENU: 64 Frs.
ROOMS: 80 to 110 Frs.
RESTAURANT: Dinner -24.00
CLOSED: Sun.
SPECIALITIES: home-cooking.
HOTEL: 8 rooms
OTHER POINTS: credit cards accepted.

SAUVAGES (LES)
Rhône, 69170

HOTEL SAINT PIERRE
(Mr Jean Gouttenoire)
TEL: 04.74.89.10.49
DIRECTIONS: RD8.
ROOMS: 120 to 280 Frs.
RESTAURANT: Snacks from 7.00, lunch 12.00-13.30, dinner 19.00-20.30
CLOSED: Wed, end of Aug and one week at Christmas.
SPECIALITIES: grenouilles, home-cooking.
HOTEL: 7 rooms. FACILITIES: shower, bath, private bathroom, television
OTHER POINTS: credit cards accepted.
Notre-Dame-de-Rohe; le lac des Sapins.

SAVASSE
Drôme, 26740

RELAIS DE LA TETE NOIRE
(Mlle Raymonde Rochette) Hameau de l'Horme d'Arme - Route Nationale 7
TEL: 04.75.51.17.14
DIRECTIONS: RN7, Valence/Montélimar - motorway north exit.
MENU: 60 Frs.
ROOMS: 120 to 180 Frs.
RESTAURANT: Snacks from 4.30, lunch 11.30-14.30, dinner 19.00-22.00
CLOSED: Sat afternoon and Sun.
SPECIALITIES: home-cooking.
HOTEL: 8 rooms
OTHER POINTS: credit cards accepted.
Magnificient region at the south of the Drôme.

SENAS
Bouches-du-Rhône, 13560

L'ETAPE
(SNC Veyrier Frères) Route Nationale 7
TEL: 04.90.59.22.81
MENU: 54 Frs.
RESTAURANT: Snacks from 6.00
CLOSED: Sat and Sun.
SPECIALITIES: home-cooking.
OTHER POINTS: credit cards accepted.

SERVAS
Ain, 01000

LE RELAIS POSTILLON - Chez Marcelle
(Mr Kaddour Lastab) Route Nationale 83
TEL: 04.74.52.79.10
DIRECTIONS: RN83.
MENU: 57 Frs (wine and coffee included).
ROOMS: 100 to 120 Frs.
RESTAURANT: Snacks from 6.00, lunch 11.30-14.00, dinner 19.00-21.30
CLOSED: Sat evening and Sun.
SPECIALITIES: home-cooking.
HOTEL: 5 rooms. FACILITIES: bath, private bathroom
OTHER POINTS: credit cards accepted.
Villard-les-Dombe: bird park; Gourg: église de Brou.

SEYNE SUR MER (LA)
Var, 83500

RELAIS DE BREGAILLON
(Mr Robert Montesino) Route de Toulon
TEL: 04.94.94.86.56
DIRECTIONS: Route de Toulon.
LANGUAGES: English, Spanish, Italian.
ROOMS: (half board and full board only).
RESTAURANT: Snacks from 6.00
CLOSED: Sun.
SPECIALITIES: canard aux olives, paella, couscous, regional menu, home-cooking.
HOTEL: 9 rooms
OTHER POINTS: credit cards accepted.
the port; the beaches.

SEYNOD
Haute-Savoie, 74600

RELAIS SAINTE CATHERINE
(Mr Lucien Zerbola) 181, route d'Aix
TEL: 04.50.69.00.86 FAX: 04.50.52.07.49
DIRECTIONS: RN201, exit Annecy Sud (South), towards Chambéry.
LANGUAGES: English, German.
MENU: 60 to 100 Frs.

ROOMS: 120 to 160 Frs.
RESTAURANT: Snacks from 6.00, lunch 12.00-13.30, dinner 19.30-21.00
CLOSED: Sat and Sun, and in Aug.
SPECIALITIES: steack aux morilles, fondue savoyarde, cuisses de grenouilles, regional menu, home-cooking.
HOTEL: ☆ 10 rooms. **FACILITIES:** shower, bath, private bathroom
OTHER POINTS: credit cards accepted.
lac dannecy; Albertville; Chamonix; gorge du Fier; Mont-Blanc; châteaux.

SIGOTTIER
Hautes-Alpes, 05700

LE PONT LA BARQUE
(Mr Willy Malandrone) Pont la Barque
TEL: 04.92.67.04.15
DIRECTIONS: RN75, between Sisteron and Grenoble.
MENU: 65 to 110 Frs.
RESTAURANT: Snacks from 7.30, lunch 12.00-14.00, dinner 19.30-20.45
CLOSED: Sun (out of season), and from 25th Dec to 7th Jan.
SPECIALITIES: gibiers (game), home-cooking.
OTHER POINTS: credit cards accepted.

SISTERON
Alpes-de-Haute-Provence, 04200

LE CHALET DE L'EUROPE
(Mr Jean-Marie Estèves) 1, allée des Romarins - Parc d'activité de Sisteron
TEL: 04.92.61.26.55 FAX: 04.92.61.26.55
DIRECTIONS: in the 'parc d'activité de Sisteron'.
MENU: 65 Frs.
RESTAURANT: Snacks from 5.00, lunch 11.30-15.00, dinner 19.30-22.00
CLOSED: Sat evening and Sun.
SPECIALITIES: regional menu, home-cooking.
OTHER POINTS: credit cards accepted.

SURY LE COMTAL
Loire, 42450

RESTAURANT DE LA TERRASSE
(Mme Georgette Cote) Rue Jordan
TEL: 04.77.30.81.38
DIRECTIONS: RD8, between Saint-Etienne and Montbrison.
MENU: 55 Frs.
RESTAURANT: Snacks from 7.00, lunch 11.45-15.00, dinner 19.00-21.00
CLOSED: Sun, and the week of 15th Aug.
SPECIALITIES: home-cooking.
OTHER POINTS: credit cards accepted.
medieval château and church.

TAIN L'HERMITAGE
Drôme, 26600

RELAIS DE LA MULE BLANCHE
(Mr James Perdreau)
TEL: 04.75.08.52.75
DIRECTIONS: RN7.
MENU: 60 Frs (1/4 wine and coffee included).
ROOMS: 110 to 130 Frs.
RESTAURANT: Snacks from 5.00, lunch 12.00-14.00, dinner 19.00-22.00
CLOSED: from Fri 3pm to Mon 5am, and in August.
HOTEL: 5 rooms
OTHER POINTS: credit cards accepted.
Ardèche and Vercors.

TEIL (LE)
Ardèche, 07400

AU BON COIN
(Mme Marie Gineste) 11 rue Henri Barbusse
TEL: 04.75.49.02.61
DIRECTIONS: RN86.
MENU: 50 to 65 Frs.
RESTAURANT: Lunch 12.00-14.00, dinner 19.00-21.00
CLOSED: Sun evening.
SPECIALITIES: home-cooking,
OTHER POINTS: bar.

L'ETAPE
(Mr Christophe Vantouroux) 40, avenue Paul Langevin
TEL: 04.75.49.09.19
DIRECTIONS: RN96.
LANGUAGES: English, German.
MENU: 55 Frs.
ROOMS: 100 to 120 Frs.
RESTAURANT: Snacks from 6.30, lunch 11.30-14.00, dinner 19.00-21.30
SPECIALITIES: home-cooking,
HOTEL: 7 rooms
OTHER POINTS: bar.
gorges of the Ardèche; Drôme châteaux.

THONES
Haute-Savoie, 74230

L'HERMITAGE
(Mr Pierre Bonnet) Avenue du Vieux Pont
TEL: 04.50.02.00.31 FAX: 04.50.02.04.86
DIRECTIONS: RN509.
LANGUAGES: English.
MENU: 65 to 160 Frs.
ROOMS: 120 to 200 Frs.
RESTAURANT: Snacks from 7.00, lunch 12.00-14.00, dinner 19.00-21.00
CLOSED: Mon (out of season), 1st week of May, and from 20th Oct to 15th Nov.

SPECIALITIES: papillote de saumon, feuilleté d'escargots, foie gras, magrets, pithiviers de Saint-jacques, poularde landaise, sole belle meunière, fricassé de canette, regional menu, home-cooking.
HOTEL: ☆ 42 rooms. FACILITIES: shower, bath, private bathroom, television, telephone
OTHER POINTS: credit cards accepted.
col des Aravis; ski resorts; museum.

TIGNIEU
Isère, 38230

AUBERGE DES CHARMILLES
(Mme Josiane Renon) 71 route de Bourgoin
TEL: 04.78.32.23.57
DIRECTIONS: RD18.
MENU: 55 to 110 Frs (plat du jour 36 Frs).
RESTAURANT: Snacks from 7.00, lunch 12.00-14.30
CLOSED: August
SPECIALITIES: grenouilles, gratin dauphinois, home-cooking.
OTHER POINTS: bar.

TOULON
Var, 83000

RESTAURANT DE L'ESCAILLON
(Mr Bernard Lemaire) 2, rue Chateaubriand
TEL: 04.94.24.21.02
DIRECTIONS: RN8, the Toulon/Marseille road.
MENU: 62 Frs (1/4 wine included).
RESTAURANT: Snacks from 6.00, lunch 12.00-14.00, dinner 19.30-21.00
CLOSED: last 2 weeks of Aug.
SPECIALITIES: home-cooking.
OTHER POINTS: credit cards accepted.

TOUR DU PIN (LA)
Isère, 38110

CHEZ BABETH
(Mme Elisabeth Rostaing) Saint Didier de la Tour
TEL: 04.74.97.15.87
DIRECTIONS: RN6, bebveen La Tour-du-Pin and Les Abrets, on the main road.
MENU: 58 to 98 Frs.
RESTAURANT: Snacks from 5.30, lunch 12.00-14.00, dinner 19.00-21.00
CLOSED: Sun evening.
SPECIALITIES: grenouilles, home-cooking.
OTHER POINTS: credit cards accepted.
Walibi: leisure park; lac de Charavines; medieval cities of Saint Chef and Crémieu.

TOURRETTES
Var, 83440

LE GRILLON
(Mr José Deshayes) Route Départementale 562 - Les Terrassonnes
TEL: 04.94.76.09.36 FAX: 04.94.76.01.02
DIRECTIONS: RD 562, RD562, between Grasse and Draguignan.
LANGUAGES: English, German, Spanish.
MENU: 55 to 90 Frs.
ROOMS: 150 to 169 Frs.
RESTAURANT: Snacks from 7.00, lunch 11.30-14.30, dinner 19.00-21.00
CLOSED: Sun evening.
SPECIALITIES: regional menu, home-cooking, Normandes.
HOTEL: 12 rooms. FACILITIES: shower, private bathroom, television, telephone
OTHER POINTS: credit cards accepted.

TULLINS FURES
Isère, 38210

RESTAURANT DU CENTRE
(Mme Monique Duclos) 110, boulevard Michel Perret
TEL: 04.76.07.93.08
DIRECTIONS: RN92, the Grenoble/Valence road.
LANGUAGES: English.
MENU: 55 Frs (wine and coffee included).
RESTAURANT: Snacks from 8.00, lunch 12.00-14.30, dinner 19.00-24.00
CLOSED: Wed afternoon.
SPECIALITIES: (to order) regional menu, home-cooking.
OTHER POINTS: bar.
Grenoble; Le Vercors; La Chartreuse massif.

VALLON PONT D'ARC
Ardèche, 07150

BAR RESTAURANT DE LA POSTE
(Mr Bernard Garrido) 6, rue Jean Jaurès
TEL: 04.75.88.02.11
DIRECTIONS: D579, RN 86 Bourg St Andéol Le Puy.
LANGUAGES: English, German, Spanish.
MENU: 50 Frs.
RESTAURANT: Snacks from 7.00, lunch 12.00-14.00, dinner 19.00-21.00
CLOSED: Sun and in December.
SPECIALITIES: pizzas, home-cooking.
OTHER POINTS: bar.
Gorges de l'Ardèche, source de l'Ardèche (spring of the Ardèche river) au Mont Gerbier des Joncs.

VAUX EN BUGEY
Ain, 01150

LE RAMEQUIN
(Mme Michelle Gallon) Route Nationale 75
TEL: 04.74.35.95.09
DIRECTIONS: RN75, the Grenoble road.
RESTAURANT: Snacks from 6.00, lunch 11.45-14.30, dinner 19.15-21.30
CLOSED: Sat, Sun, 2 weeks in Aug and 2 weeks in Dec.
SPECIALITIES: home-cooking.
OTHER POINTS: credit cards accepted.

VENISSIEUX
Rhône, 69200

LES ROUTIERS
(Mr Hervé Ligier) 66, boulevard Joliot Curie
TEL: 04.78.76.49.94
DIRECTIONS: the Saint-Etienne/Marseille road.
LANGUAGES: Spanish.
MENU: 66 Frs (wine and coffee included).
RESTAURANT: Snacks from 6.00, lunch 11.30-15.00, dinner 19.00-21.00
CLOSED: Sat, Sun, and in Aug.
SPECIALITIES: home-cooking.
OTHER POINTS: bar.

VEYRINS THUELLIN
Isère, 38630

L'OUSTAL
(Mr Raymond Belingheri) Le Bourg
TEL: 04.74.33.94.27
DIRECTIONS: RN75, Bourg Grenoble.
LANGUAGES: English, Italian.
MENU: 55 to 110 Frs.
ROOMS: 130 to 170 Frs.
RESTAURANT: Snacks from 6.30, lunch 12.00-14.30, dinner 19.00-22.00
CLOSED: 1st 2 weeks in Oct.
SPECIALITIES: regional menu, home-cooking.
HOTEL: ☆ 9 rooms. FACILITIES: shower, bath
OTHER POINTS: bar.
Walibi: leisure park; centrale nucléaire (nuclear power station) at Crest-Malville.

VILLEFRANCHE SUR SAONE
Rhône, 69400

LE RELAIS CALADOIS
(Mr Denis Gimaret) 300, rue Joseph Léon Jacquemaire
TEL: 04.74.60.69.88 FAX: 04.74.60.34.09
DIRECTIONS: RN6, Mâcon.
LANGUAGES: English, Spanish.
RESTAURANT: Snacks from 5.30, lunch 11.30-14.30, dinner 19.00-22.30
CLOSED: Sat and Sun.
SPECIALITIES: regional menu, home-cooking.
OTHER POINTS: credit cards accepted.
caveaux (vaults) du Beaujolais.

VILLENEUVE
Alpes-de-Haute-Provence, 04180

RELAIS ROUTIERS - Chez Roger
(Mr Pierre Curri) Route Nationale 96
TEL: 04.92.78.42.47 FAX: 04.92.78.46.88
DIRECTIONS: RN96, between Aix and Sisteron.
MENU: 62 Frs.
ROOMS: 120 Frs.
RESTAURANT: Snacks from 4.00, lunch 12.00-15.00, dinner 20.00-22.00
CLOSED: Sun, public holidays and in Aug.
SPECIALITIES: home-cooking.
HOTEL: 7 rooms. FACILITIES: shower, bath, private bathroom
OTHER POINTS: credit cards accepted.
Manosque region; Sisteron; the Lubéron; gorges of the Verdon.

VILLEREVERSURE
Ain, 01250

LE RECITAL
(Mr José Reyes) La Gare
TEL: 04.74.30.65.98 FAX: 04.74.30.65.98
DIRECTIONS: RD 42, RD42, between Lons-le-Saunier and Pont-d'Ain.
LANGUAGES: English, Spanish.
MENU: 60 to 150 Frs.
ROOMS: 90 to 140 Frs.
RESTAURANT: Snacks from 7.00, lunch 11.30-14.30, dinner 19.00-22.00
CLOSED: Wed afternoon.
SPECIALITIES: regional menu, home-cooking, sur commande.
HOTEL: 8 rooms. FACILITIES: shower, bath, private bathroom
OTHER POINTS: credit cards accepted.

VINEZAC
Ardèche, 07110

AUBERGE DES COTES
(Mr Serge Zagar) Les Côtes
TEL: 04.75.36.80.10
DIRECTIONS: RD104, between Aubenas and Alès.
MENU: 70 Frs.
ROOMS: 70 to 100 Frs.
RESTAURANT: Snacks from 5.30, lunch 12.00-14.00, dinner 19.00-20.00
CLOSED: Sat, Sun, public holidays and in Sept.
SPECIALITIES: home-cooking.

HOTEL: 3 rooms. FACILITIES: shower, private bathroom
OTHER POINTS: credit cards accepted.
Vinezac; Balazuc.

VITROLLES
Bouches-du-Rhône, 13127

LA TAVERNE
(Mme Nadine Ramero) Route Nationale 113
TEL: 04.42.87.00.39
DIRECTIONS: RN113, Marseille/Avignon road.
LANGUAGES: Spanish, Italian.
MENU: 60 Frs (wine included).
RESTAURANT: Snacks from 6.00
CLOSED: Sat evening and Sun evening.
SPECIALITIES: fishes and sea-food specialities, home-cooking.
OTHER POINTS: credit cards accepted.
Etang de Berre (Berre pond).

FRANCE

KEY TO MAP PAGES

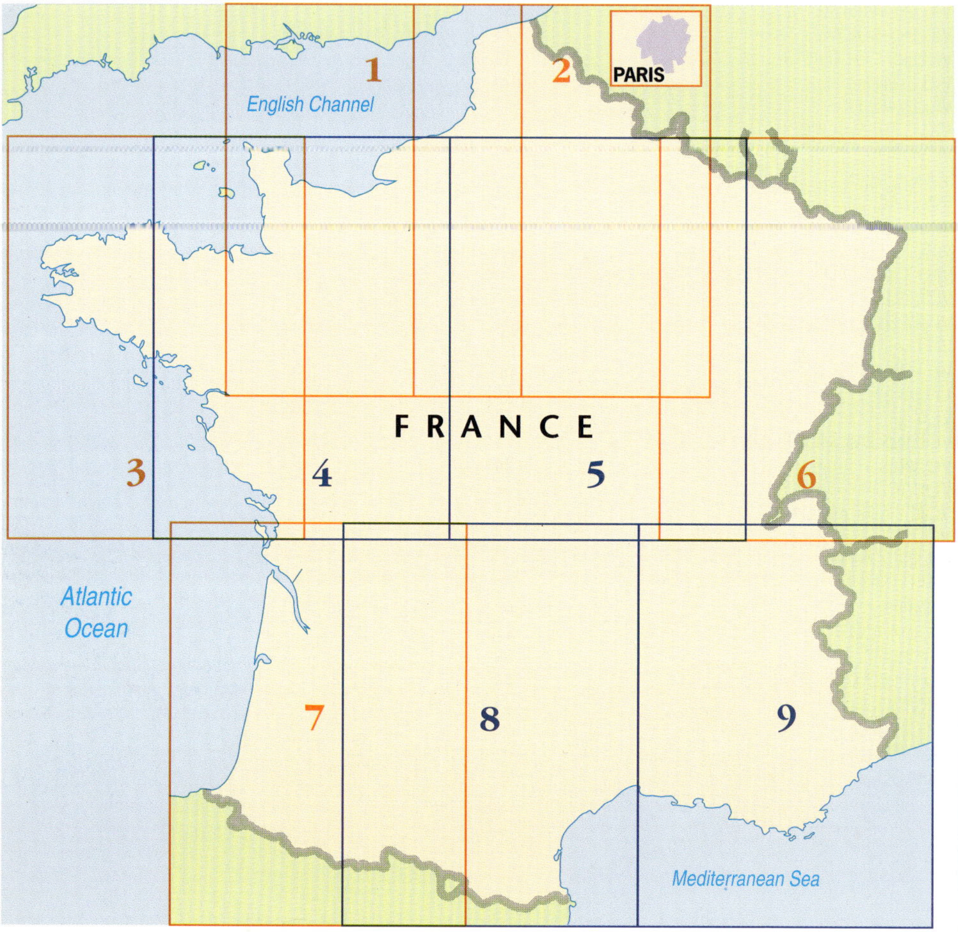

KEY TO MAP SYMBOLS

Autoroute	
Route Nationale	
Route Départementale	
National boundary	
Airport	
PARIS	City
Calais	Large town
Gravelines	Small town
St.-Inglevert	City/town/village with one or more Les Routiers establishments

Scale

0 50 100 km

0 50 100 miles

ced by E.S.H. Ltd., Byfleet, Surrey
1
ENGLAND
Strait of Dove
Calais
Gravelines
St.-Inglevert
C. Griz-Nez
Marquise
Boulogne-sur-Mer
Colembert
St.-Omer
Desvres
Lumbres
Le Touquet Paris-Plage
Étaples
Merlimont
Berck-sur-Mer
Berck
Humières
Hesdin
Authie
Labroye
2
ENGLISH CHANNEL
Cayeux
St.-Requier
Abbeville
Le Tréport
Pont-Remy
Chépy
Eu
Somme
Dieppe
Blangy
Dreuil-lès-Amiens
Amiens
St.-Valery-en-Caux
St.-Aubin-sur-Scie
Fourcarmont
Neuchâtel-en-Bray
Aumale
Poix
Hague
Pte. de Barfleur
Étretat
Fécamp
Grémonville
Varvannes
Yvetot
Totes
Béthune
Breteuil
Cherbourg-Tourlaville
Quettehou
La Glacerie
St.-Sauveur-d'Émalleville
Bolbec
Abbeville-St.-Lucien
Couville
Valognes
Baie de la Seine
St.-Romain-de-Colbosc
Le Havre
Lillebonne
Notre-Dame-de-Gravenchon
Croisy-sur-Andelle
Ferrières-en-Bray
Emondeville
Le Trait
Gournay
Beavais
Laversines
Arromanches
Honfleur
Seine
St.-Samson-de-la-Roque
Rouen
Piccauville
St.-Côme-de-Fresné
Trouville
Deauville
Beuzeville
Grainville
Sérifontaine
La Houssoye
Osmanville
Mosles
Mathieu
Pont-Audemer
Rougemontiers
Caudebec-lès-Elbeuf
Richeville
Gisors
Carentan
Bayeux
Carcagny
Cabourg
St.-Denis-de-Monts
Elbeuf
Amblainville
Le Molay-Littry
Ouistreham
Colombelles
Louviers
Les Andelys
Courcelles-lès-Gisors
St.-Fromond
Rots
Caen
Cagny
Goustranville
Tremblay-Omonville
Saintenay
Hottot-les-Bagues
Fleury-sur-Orne
Corbon
Duranville
Bernay-Carsix
Le Goulet
Pont-Herbert
St.-Lô
Lisieux
Bernay
Autheuil-Authouillet
Vernon
Cléry-en-Vixen
Chambly
Coutances
Villers Bocage
May-sur-Orne
Bellengreville
Le Mesnil Durand
Nassandres
Pontoise
St.-Pierre-du-Fresne
Magny-la-Campagne
St.-Denis-de-Mailloc
Gravigny
Chaignes
Hyenville
Guilberville
Croisilles
Bretteville-sur-Dives
Orbec
Broglie
Evreux
Limay
St.-Martin-des-Bascaces
St.-Remy-sur-Orne
Chaufaur-les-Bonnières
Mantes
Villebaudon
Tessy-sur-Vire
Vimoutiers
La Neuve-Lyre
La Bonneville-sur-Iton
Sourdeval-les-Bois
St.-Denis-de-Méré
Falaise
Monnai
Thomer-la-Sôgne
Epône
Villedieu
Vire
Ambenay
Bueil
Normandie
Caligny
St.-Evroult-de-Montfort
Breteuil-sur-Iton
Crespières
Rouffigny
Rônai
Urou et Crennes
Gacé
Ezy-sur-Eure
Versailles
Avranches
St.-Martin-des-Champs
Argentan
Aube
Tivoly
Marolles
Sourdeval
Exmes
L'Aigle
Dreux
Houdan
Trappes
Mt. St.-Michel
Romagny
Verneuil
Tréon
Les Essarts-le-Roi
Rambouillet
Rânes
Mortrée
Serazereux
Briis-sous-Forges
Juilley
Lapenty
Domfront
Châteauneuf-en-Thimerais
Epernon
Sées
Boissy-sous-St.-Yon
St.-Georges-de-Rouelley
Joué-du-Bois
Antrain
Bagnoles-de-l'Orne
St.-Langis-lès-Mortagne
Mortagne
Digny
St.-Germain-la-Gâtine
Ablis
Tremblay
Ceuce
La Loupe
Chartres
Brecé
Huisne
Auneau
Étampes
Fougères
Montaudin
St.-Cyr-en-Pail
Pacé
Alençon
Sarthe
Le Gue-de-la-Chaine
Bellême
St.-Georges-sur-Eure
Thivars
Guillerval
Beauce
Oisseau-le-Petit
Mamers
Nogent-le-Rotrou
La Chapelle-St.-Aubert
Mayenne
Piacé
La Chapelle-du-Bois
Malé
Luplanté
Bois-de-Feugères
Maine
Montreuil-le-Chétif
Bonnétable
La Ferté-Bernard
Bonneval
Toury
Pithiviers
Noyale-sur-Vilaine
Vitré
Change
Conile
Châteaudun
Bazoches-en-Dunois
Château-Gaillard-Santilly
St.-Berthevin
Laval
Chassile
Champagne
Connerré
La Bazouche-Gouet
Artenay
Vern-sur-Seiche
Le Mans
St.-Mars-la-Brière
Cormenon
Lutz-en-Dunois
La Guerche-de-Bretagne
Cloyes
Janzé
St.-Calais
St.-Hilaire-la-Gravelle
Orléans
Ecorpain
Charsonville
La Chapelle-Craonnaie
Château-Gontier
Sablé-sur-Sarthe
Bessé-sur-Braye
Pezou
Châteauneuf-sur-Loire
Martigné-Ferchaud
Marigné-Laillé
Orléanais
Vendôme
Beaugency
St.-Quentin-les-Agnes
Clermont-Créans
St.-Jean-de-la-Mothe
Loir
Loire
La-Ferté-St.-Aubin
Erbray
Segré
La Flèche
Luceau
La Chartre-sur-le-Loir
Huisseau-en-Beauce
Suèvres
Mayenne
Fossé
Isdes
Loire
La Croix-Beauchêne
Châteaurenault
Blois
Fontaine-en-Sologne
Riaillé
Candé
Bauge
4
Château-la-Vallière
Villedômer
Erdre
Angers
Corné
Monnaie
Les Montils
Beuvron
Salbris
Anetz
Loire
Cuon
Fondettes
Amboise
St. Pierre-des-Corps

2
Strait of Dover
C. Griz-Nez
Calais
St.-Inglevert
Marquise
Boulogne-sur-Mer
Colembert
Desvres
Dunkerque
Gravelines
Quaëdypre
Wormhout
Steenvoorde
Bailleul
St.-Omer
Lumbres
Armentières
Croix
Halluin
Tourcoing
Roubaix
Lille
Locon
Verdin-lès-Béthune
Béthune
Mazingarbe
Bruay-en-Artois
Lens
Avelin
Capelle-en-Pèvelle
Beuvry-la-Forêt
Douai
Scarpe
Valenciennes
Bavay
Maubeuge
Le Touquet Paris-Plage
Étaples
Merlimont
Berck-sur-Mer
Berck
Hesdin
Humières
St. Pol
Artois
Labroye
Authie
Arras
L'Arbet
Bailleulval
Louvignies-Quesnoy
Eclaibes
Cambrai
Landrecies
Avesnes
Etroeungt
Cayeux
Abbeville
St.-Requier
Doullens
Bapaume
Le Tréport
Chépy
Eu
Pont-Remy
Ovillers-la-Boisselle
Albert
Le Cateau
La Groise
Dieppe
Blangy
Somme
Poulainville
Picardie
Dreuil-lès-Amiens
Amiens
Péronne
St.-Quentin
Guise
Hirson
Rocroi
Fumay
Revin
St.-Aubin-sur-Scie
Fourcarmont
Boves
Omiécourt
Ham
Oise
St.-Quentin-Urvillers
Vervins
Auvillers-les-Forges
Tremblois-lès-Rocroi
Nouzonville
Neuchâtel-en-Bray
Aumale
Poix
Flavy-le-Martel
Thiérache
Charleville Mézières
Sedan
Yvetot
Totes
Béthune
Breteuil
Monididier
Chauny
Noyon
Laon
Montcornet
Dizy-le-Gros
Poix-Terran
Abbeville-St.-Lucien
Rollot
Cuvilly
Sissonne
Rethel
Novion-Porcein
Croisy-sur-Andelle
Ferrières-en-Bray
Coucy-le-Château
Attigny
Rouen
Gournay
Beauvais
Laversines
Compiègne
Aisne
Soissons
Le Châtelet-sur-Retourne
Grainville
Sérifontaine
La Houssoye
Clermont
Trosly-Breuil
Fismes
Vouziers
Forêt d'Argonne
Caudebec-lès-Elbeuf
Richeville
Gisors
Courcelles-lès-Gisors
Amblainville
St.-Leu
Villers-Cotterêts
Reims
Louviers
Les Andelys
Seine
Le Goulet
Bernes-sur-Oise
Chambly
Senlis
Chantilly
Bourneville-Marolles
Beaumont-sur-Vesle
Prosnes
Champagne
Autheuil-Authouillet
Vernon
Cléry-en-Vexin
Pontoise
Beaumont
Survilliers
Epinay-Champlâtreux
Marne
St.-Menehould
Évreux
Gravigny
Chaignes
Limay
Ile de France
Château-Thierry
La Bonneville-sur-Iton
Chaufour-les-Bonnières
Mantes
PARIS
Meaux
Athis
Châlons-sur-Marne
Thomer-la-Sôgne
Bueil
Épône
Claye-Souilly
Lagny
Sablonnières
Montmirail
Étoges
Ezy-sur-Eure
Crespières
Coulommiers
La Ferté-Gaucher
Voisins-par-Mouroux
Sommesous
Bar-le-Duc
Ivoly
Marolles
Versailles
Dreux
Houdan
Trappes
Pontault-Combault
Esternay
Sézanne
Vitry-le-François
Tréon
Les Essarts-le-Roi
Courgivaux
Mailly-le-Camp
Châteauneuf-en-Thimerais
Serazereux
Eure
Rambouillet
Briis-sous-Forges
Quincy-sous-Senart
Viry-Chatillon
Corbeil-Essonnes
Montlhéry
Epernon
Boissy-sous-St.-Yon
Provins
Romilly
Arcis-sur-Aube
Digny
St.-Germain-la-Gâtine
Melun
Ablis
Nogent-sur-Seine
Mesgrigny
Gumery
St.-Georges-sur-Eure
Chartres
Auneau
Étampes
Fontainebleau
Varennes-sur-Seine
Montereau-faut-Yonne
Brienne-le-Château
Rachecourt-sur-Marne
Lupiante
Thivars
Guillerval
La Chapelle-la-Reine
La Brosse-Montceaux
Troyes
Creney
Unienville
Bois-de-Feugères
Malesherbes
Aube
Brou
Ymonville
Intville-la-Guétard
Nemours
Nonville
La Rivière-de-Corps
Lusigny-sur-Barse
Bar-sur-Aube
Bonneval
Sens
Subligny
Bouilly
Toury
Aufferville
Châteaudun
Bazoches-en-Dunois
Château-Gaillard-Santilly
Pithiviers
Beaune-la-Rolande
Arces
Villeneuve-au-Chemin
Bar-sur-Seine
Artenay
Villeneuve-sur-Yonne
Villevallier
Fontenay-sur-Loing
St.-Florentin
Neuvy-Sautour
Lutz-en-Dunois
Mignères
Courtenay
Brienon-sur-Armançon
Germigny
Cloyes
Sury-aux-Bois
Ladon
Montargis
Joigny
Canal de Bourgogne
Armançon
Mussy
St.-Hilaire-la-Gravelle
Orléans
Epineau-les-Voves
Charsonville
Châteauneuf-sur-Loire
Solterre
Seneu
Dannemoine
Tonnerre
Châtillon-sur-Seine
Pezou
Orléanais
Lorris
Loing
Vendôme
Beaugency
Auxerre
Chablis
Serein
Loire
La-Ferté-St.-Aubin
Sully-sur-Loire
Gien
Fossé
Suèvres
Isdes
Briare
St.-Fargeau
Coursen-les-Carrières
Montbard
Cussy-les-Forges
Blois
Fontaines-en-Sologne
Argent-sur-Sauldre
Thou
Bonny
Yonne
Avallon
Les Montils
Beuvron
Clamecy
Aubigny-sur-Nère
Dampierre-en-Crat
Salbris
La Celle-sur-Loire
Vézelay
Vitteaux
Digitally produced by E.S.R. Ltd., Byfleet, Surrey
PARIS inset
Domont
Deuil-la-Barre
St.-Gratien
Pierrefitte-sur-Seine
St.-Denis
Le Bourget
Le Blanc Mesnil
La Courneuve
Clichy
Les Pavillons-sous-Bois
Aubervilliers
St.-Ouen
Chelles
Montreuil
Charenton-le-Pont
St.-Maur-des-Fossés
Alfortville
Antony

oduced by E.S.R. Ltd., Byfleet, Surrey

4
C. de la Hague
Auderville
1
Pte. de Barfleur
Cherbourg
Equeudreville
Cherbourg-Tourlaville
Quettehou
La Glacerie
Couville
Valognes
Emondeville
Carteret
Piccauville
Baie de la Seine
Channel Islands (Îles Normandes) (U.K.)
La Haye-du-Puits
Carentan
Osmanville
Mosles
Arromanches
St.-Côme-de-Fresné
Le Molay-Littry
Bayeux
Carcagny
Ouistreham
Mathieu
Saintenay
St.-Fromond
Rots
Caen
Colombelles
Cagny
Goustranville
Pont-Hébert
St.-Lô
Hottot-les-Bagues
Fleury-sur-Orne
Coutances
Villers Bocage
May-sur-Orne
Bellengreville
St.-Pierre-du-Fresne
Guilberville
Magny-la-Campagne
Montmartin-sur-Mer
Hyenville
Villebaudon
Tessy-sur-Vire
St.-Martin-des-Besaces
Croisilles
St.-Remy-sur-Orne
St. Denis-de-Méré
Falaise
de Ialbert
3
Goudeville
Granville
Sourdeval-les-Bois
Villedieu
Vire
La Haye-Pesnel
Rouffigny
Golfe de St.-Malo
St.-Pierre-Langers
C. Fréhel
Avranches
St.-Martin-des-Champs
Sourdeval
Dinard
St.-Malo
La Mt. St.-Michel
Romagny
La Gouesnière
Pontorson
Plouër-sur-Rance
Juilley
Lapenty
St.-Georges-de-Rouelley
Domfront
Landébia
Lamballe
Dinan
Dol-de-Bretagne
Antrain
St.-Brieuc
Plaintel
St.-Brandan
St.-Igneuc
Vildé-Guingalan
St.-Helen
Combourg
Tremblay
Brecé
Ceuce
Moncontour
Plené-Jugon
Romazy
Fougeres
Montaudin
Loudéac
Rance
Montauban-de-Bretagne
La Chapelle-St.-Aubert
Beauce
Mayenne
Trémorel
Bedee
Gaël
St.-Gregoire
Noyale-sur-Vilaine
Mauron
Montfort-sur-Meu
L'Hermitage
Rennes
Vitré
Change
Josselin
Treffendel
St.-Jacques-de-la-Lande
St.-Berthevin
Laval
Bréal-sous-Montfort
Vern-sur-Seiche
La Guerche-de Bretagne
Moréac
Ploërmel
Janzé
Colpo
La Chapelle-Caro
Poligné
La Chapelle-Craonnaie
Château-Gontier
Sablé-sur-Sarthe
Pipriac
Bain-de-Bretagne
Martigné-Ferchaud
Landes de Lanvaux
Oust
Vilaine
Elven
Châteaubriant
St.-Quentin-les-Agnes
Vannes
Bains-sur-Oust
Redon
St.-Nicolas-de-Redon
Derval
Erbray
Segré
Séné
Nozay
Marzan
Loire
Mayenne
Sarthe
St.-Gildas-de-Rhuys
La Roche-Bernard
St.-Gildas-des-Bois
Riaillé
Candé
Blain
Erdre
Angers
Pontchâteau
Héric
Anetz
Le Croisic
La Baule
Montoir-de-Bretagne
Ancenis
Bourgneuf-en-Mauges
La Jumellière
St.-Nazaire
Donges
Ste.-Luce-sur-Loire
St.-Brevin-l'Ocean
Nantes
Jallais
Chemillé
Chéméré
Bouguenais
Rezé
Vallet
St.-Germain-sur-Moine
Trémont
Pte. de St.-Gildas
Pornic
Les Sorinières
Pont-St.-Martin
Chateau-Thébaud
Clisson
Lac de Grand-Lieu
Noirmoutier
St.-Philbert-de-Grand-Lieu
St.-Hilaire-de-Loulay
Mortagne-sur-Sèvre
Cholet
Île de Noirmoutier
Montaigu
Beauvoir-sur-Mer
Chambretaud
Rorthais
L'Herbergement
Sèvre Nantaise
Bressuire
Challans
Falleron
St.-Jean-de-Monts
Les Essarts
Pouzauges
St.-Mesmin
Aizenay
St.-Vincent-Sterlanges
La Chapelle-St.-Laurent
Île d'Yeu
St.-Gilles-Croix-de-Vie
L'Aiguillon-sur-Vie
La Roche-sur-Yon
Chantonnay
Bournezau
L'Absie
St.-Mathurin
Nieul-le-Dolent
St.-Etienne-de-Brillouet
Les Sables-d'Olonne
Talmont-St.-Hilaire
Lay
Luçon
Mouzeuil-St.-Martin
Fontenay-le-Comte
Chaillé-les-Marais
Sèvre Noirtaise
Pertuis Breton
Marans
Niort
Île de Ré
7
La Rochelle
Epannes
Surgères
Beauvoir-sur-Noirt
Brioux-sur-Boutonne
Chef-Boutonne
Loulay
Digitally produced by E.S.R. Ltd., Byfleet, Surrey
Normandie
Maine
Bretagne
Anjou
Poitou
Touraine
St. Valery-en-Caux
St.-Aubin-sur-Scie
Étretat
Fécamp
Yvetot
St.-Sauveur-d'Émalleville
Bolbec
St.-Romain-de-Colbosc
Le Havre
Lillebonne
Notre-Dame-de-Gr
Seine
Le Trait
Rou
Honfleur
St.-Samson-de-la-Roque
Trouville
Deauville
Beuzeville
Pont-Audemer
Cabourg
Elbeuf
St.-Denis-de-Monts
Risle
Corbon
Duranville
Bernay-Carsix
Lisieux
Bernay
Le Mesnil Durand
St.-Denis-de-Mailloc
Nassandres
Bretteville-sur-Dives
Orbec
Broglie
Vimoutiers
La Neuve-Lyre
Monnai
Ambenay
Breteuil-sur-Iton
Rônai
Urou et Crennes
Gacé
St.-Evroult-de-Montfort
Argentan
Aube
L'Aigle
Caligny
Exmes
Rânes
Mortrée
Joué-du-Bois
Sees
Bagnoles-de-l'Orne
St.-Langis-lès-Mortagne
Mortagne
La Loupe
Pacé
Alençon
Sarthe
Le Gue-de-la-Chaine
Bellême
Huisne
St.-Cyr-en-Pail
Oisseau-le-Petit
Mamers
Nogent
Piacé
La Chapelle-du-Bois
Malé
St.-Remy-de-Sillé
Montreuil-le-Chétif
Bonnétable
La Ferté-Berr
Conile
La Bazouche
Chassile
Champagne
Connerré
Le Mans
St.-Mars-la-Brière
St.-Calais
Ecorpain
Marigné-Laillé
Bessé-sur-Braye
Clermont-Créans
St.-Jean-de-la-Mothe
La Flèche
Luceau
La Chartre-sur-le-Loir
Loir
La Croix-Beauchêne
Bauge
Château-la-Vallière
Corné
Cuon
Longué
Fondettes
St.-Pierre-des-Corps
Tours
Vivy
Montbazon
Saumur
St.-Nicholas-de-Bourgueil
Azay-le-Rideau
Chinon
Doué-la-Fontaine
Ste.-Maure-de-Touraine
Bossée
Brion-près-Thouet
Vienne
Sazilly
La Celle-St.-Avan
Loudun
Thouars
Creuse
Châtillon-sur
Verrue
Lencloître
Châtellerault
Airvault
Thouet
Mirabeau
Naintré
Lageon
Parthenay
Poitiers
Chauvigny
St.-Pardoux
Fontaine-le-Comte
Lusignan
Fleuré
Vivonne
Rouillé
St.-Maixent-l'Ecole
Lussac-les-Château
Clain
Melle-sur-Bretonne
Chaunay-Bourg
Civray
Pressac
Mézières-sur-Issoire
Vienne

5
2
6
6
8
Fourcarmont
Amiens
Boves
Omiécourt
Péronne
St.-Quentin
Guise
Vervins
Tremblois-lès-Rocroi
Nouzonville
Aumale
Poix
Ham
St.-Quentin-Urvillers
Flavy-le-Mantel
Auvillers-les-Forges
Thiérache
Charleville Mézières
Sedan
Blagny
Breteuil
Monididier
Noyon
Chauny
Laon
Montcornet
Dizy-le-Gros
Sissonne
Poix-Terran
Montmédy
Abbeville-St.-Lucien
Rollot
Cuvilly
Coucy-le-Château
Rethel
Novion-Porcein
Stenay
Ferrières-en-Bray
Attigny
Gournay
Beauvais
Laversines
Compiègne
Soissons
Aisne
Le Châtelet-sur-Retourne
Sérifontaine
La Houssoye
Clermont
Trosly-Breuil
Fismes
Vouziers
Consenvoye
Richeville
Gisors
Forêt d'Argonne
Andelys
Courcelles-lès-Gisors
Amblainville
St.-Leu
Oise
Villers-Cotterêts
Reims
Meuse
Aire
Bernes-sur-Oise
Senlis
Beaumont-sur-Vesle
Prosnes
Verdun
Chambly
Chantilly
Bourneville-Marolles
Vernon
Cléry-en-Vixen
Beaumont
Survilliers
Marne
St.-Menehould
Epinay-Champlâtreux
Château-Thierry
Limay
Pontoise
Ile de France
Athis
Mantes
Meaux
Étoges
Châlons-sur-Marne
Epône
Claye-Souilly
Sablonnières
Montmirail
PARIS
Lagny
Coulommiers
Crespières
Voisins-par-Mouroux
La Ferté-Gaucher
Bar-le-Duc
Versailles
Sommesous
Houdan
Trappes
Esternay
Sézanne
Vitry-le-François
Pontault-Combault
Champagne
Les Essarts-le-Roi
Courgivaux
Mailly-le-Camp
St.-Dizier
Rambouillet
Briis-sous-Forges
Quincy-sous-Senart
Eure
Viry-Châtillon
Ancerville
Epernon
Montlhéry
Corbeil-Essonnes
Provins
Romilly
Arcis-sur-Aube
Rachecourt-sur-Marne
Boissy-sous-St.-Yon
Melun
Abbis
Gumery
Nogent-sur-Seine
Mesgrigny
Seine
Chartres
Auneau
Étampes
Fontainebleau
Varennes-sur-Seine
Montereau-faut-Yonne
Brienne-le-Château
Joinville
Marne
Prez-sous-Lafauche
La Chapelle-la-Reine
La Brosse-Montceaux
Aube
Troyes
Creney
Unienville
Guillerval
Malesherbes
La Rivière-de-Corps
Lusigny-sur-Barse
Bar-sur-Aube
Ymonville
Intville-la-Guétard
Nemours
Nonville
Sublign
Sens
Toury
Aufferville
Bouilly
Bazoches-en-Dunois
Château-Gaillard-Santilly
Pithiviers
Beaune-la-Rolande
Villeneuve-sur-Yonne
Arces
Villeneuve-au-Chemin
Bar-sur-Seine
Chaumont
Artenay
Fontenay-sur-Loing
Villevallier
St.-Florentin
Neuvy-Sautour
Mignères
Courtenay
Joigny
Brienon-sur-Armançon
Germigny
Mussy
Sury-aux-Bois
Ladon
Montargis
Epineau-les-Voves
Armançon
Canal de Bourgogne
Orléans
Châteauneuf-sur-Loire
Solterre
Sens
Dannemoine
Châtillon-sur-Seine
Langres
Charsonville
Loing
Tonnerre
Lorris
Auxerre
Chablis
Longeau
Sully-sur-Loire
La Ferté-St.-Aubin
Serein
Loire
Suèvres
Gien
Montbard
Cussy-les-Forges
Isdes
Briare
St.-Fargeau
Coursan-les-Carrières
Til-Châtel
Bourgogne
Fontaine-en-Sologne
Argent-sur-Sauldre
Thou
Bonny
Yonne
Avallon
St.-Seine-l'Abbaye
Beuvron
Clamecy
Aubigny-sur-Nère
La Celle-sur-Loire
Vézelay
Vitteaux
Romorantin Lanthenay
Salbris
Dampierre-en-Crat
Cosne-sur-Loire
Dijon
Ennordres
Vaizy
Theillay
Nivernais
Corbigny
Saulieu
Morey-St.-Denis
Méry-sur-Cher
Sancerre
Gièvres
Vierzon
Allogny
Prémery
Nuits-St.-Georges
Chelsey
Valençay
Graçay
Sancergues
La Charité
Comblanchien
Arnay-le-Duc
Luçay-le-Mâle
Nohant-en-Goût
Château Chinon
Beaune
Tronsanges
Guérigny
Bourges
Berry
Seurre
Navilly
Autun
Chagny
Lunery
Nevers
Issoudun
Challuy
Cher
Le Creusot
Mercurey
Arnon
Decize
Chalon-sur-Saône
Déols
Mornay-sur-Allier
Devay
Torcy
St.-Eusèbe
Arroux
La Nocle-Mauxlaix
Varennes-le-Grand
St.-Pierre-le-Moûtier
Loire
Ardentes
St.-Amand-Montrond
Charenton-du-Cher
Montceau-les-Mines
Bourbon-l'Archambault
Neuvy-St.-Sépulchre
Génelard
Jouvençon
Seille
Tournus
Le Châtre
Moulins
St.-Aubin-sur-Loire
Toulon-sur-Allier
Bourbonnais
Digoin
Charolles
Lugny
Cluny
Cluis
Cosne-d'Allier
Dompierre-sur-Besbre
Vitry-en-Charollais
Cambrai
La Roche-Vineuse
Mts. du Lyonnais
St.-Cyr-sur-Menthon
Boussac
Doyet
Montmarault
Varennes-sur-Allier
Montluçon
St.-Pourçain
Lapalisse
Marcigny
Varennes-les-Mâcon
Creuse
Durdat-Larequille
Mézériat
Périgny
La Souterraine
Sioule
Servas
Loire
Brout-Vernet
St.-Romain-la-Motte
Saône
Guéret
Evaux-les-Bains
Pont-de-Menat
Gannat
Vichy
Besbre
Roanne
Belleville
Guéreins
Marche

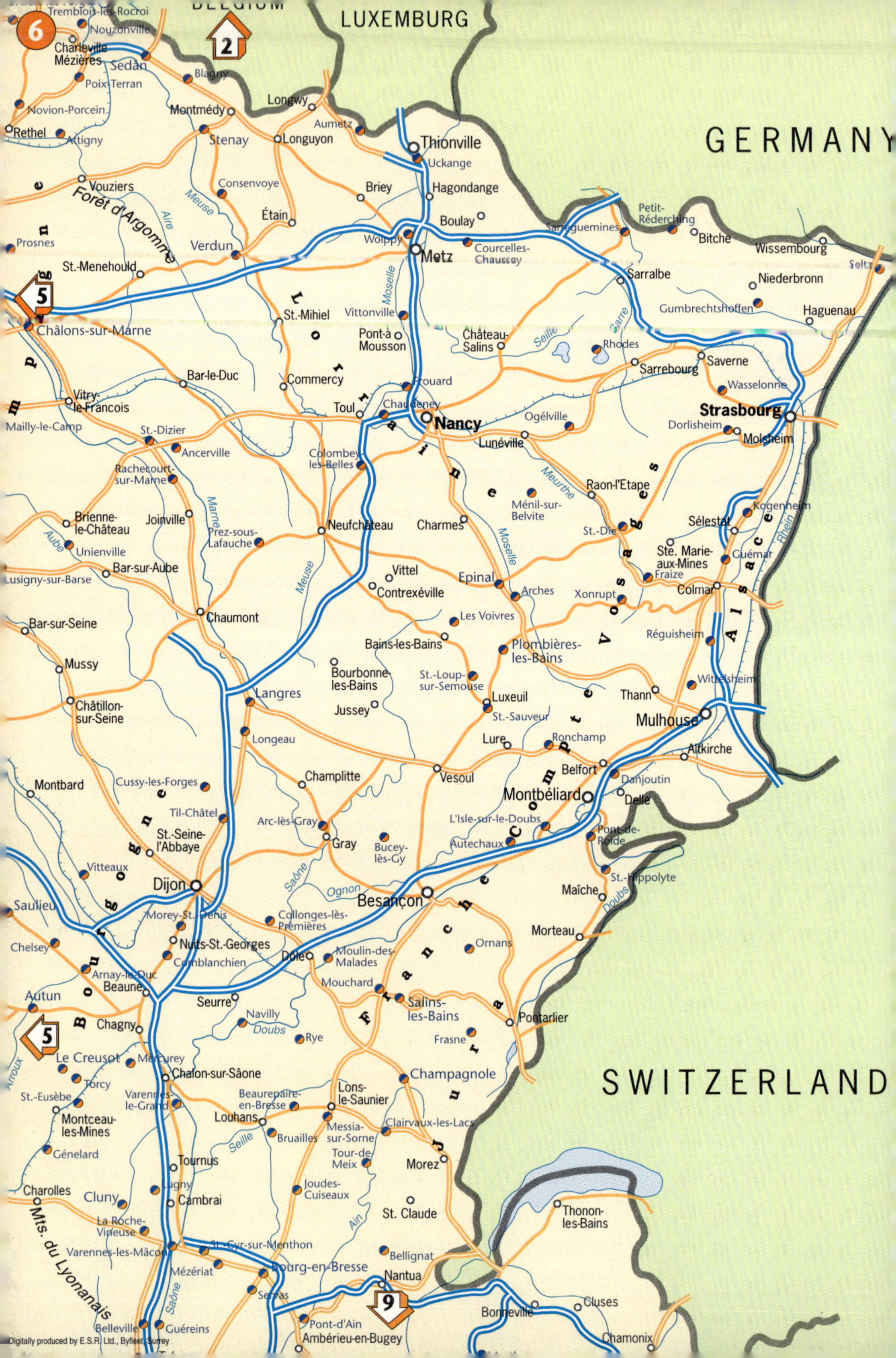

6
BELGIUM
2
LUXEMBURG
GERMANY
SWITZERLAND
Tremblois-lès-Rocroi
Nouzonville
Charleville Mézières
Sedan
Blagny
Poix-Terran
Novion-Porcein
Montmédy
Longwy
Rethel
Attigny
Stenay
Longuyon
Aumetz
Thionville
Uckange
Vouziers
Forêt d'Argonne
Consenvoye
Briey
Hagondange
Meuse
Aire
Étain
Boulay
Prosnes
Verdun
Woippy
Metz
Courcelles-Chaussoy
Sarreguemines
Petit-Réderching
Bitche
Wissembourg
Seltz
St.-Menehould
5
St.-Mihiel
Moselle
Vittonville
Sarralbe
Niederbronn
Gumbrechtshoffen
Haguenau
Châlons-sur-Marne
Pont-à-Mousson
Château-Salins
Seille
Sarre
Rhodes
Saverne
Bar-le-Duc
Commercy
Frouard
Sarrebourg
Wasselonne
Vitry-le-François
Toul
Chaudeney
Nancy
Ogélville
Strasbourg
Mailly-le-Camp
Dorlisheim
Molsheim
St.-Dizier
Ancerville
Lunéville
Colombey-les-Belles
Rachecourt-sur-Marne
Meurthe
Raon-l'Etape
Ménil-sur-Belvite
Kogenheim
Brienne-le-Château
Joinville
Marne
Sélestat
Aube
Prez-sous-Lafauche
Neufchâteau
Charmes
St.-Dié
Rhein
Unienville
Ste. Marie-aux-Mines
Guémar
Bar-sur-Aube
Vittel
Epinal
Fraize
Lusigny-sur-Barse
Contrexéville
Arches
Colmar
Xonrupt
Chaumont
Les Voivres
Bar-sur-Seine
Bains-les-Bains
Plombières-les-Bains
Réguisheim
Mussy
Bourbonne-les-Bains
St.-Loup-sur-Semouse
Wittelsheim
Châtillon-sur-Seine
Langres
Jussey
Luxeuil
Thann
St.-Sauveur
Mulhouse
Longeau
Lure
Ronchamp
Altkirche
Montbard
Champlitte
Vesoul
Belfort
Danjoutin
Cussy-les-Forges
Montbéliard
Delle
Til-Châtel
Arc-lès-Gray
L'Isle-sur-le-Doubs
St.-Seine-l'Abbaye
Gray
Bucey-lès-Gy
Autechaux
Pont-de-Roide
Vitteaux
Saône
St.-Hippolyte
Dijon
Ognon
Besançon
Maîche
Saulieu
Morey-St.-Denis
Collonges-lès-Premières
Nuits-St.-Georges
Morteau
Chelsey
Comblanchien
Dole
Moulin-des-Malades
Ornans
Doubs
Arnay-le-Duc
Beaune
Mouchard
Autun
Seurre
Salins-les-Bains
Pontarlier
Navilly
Chagny
Rye
Frasne
Le Creusot
Mercurey
Chalon-sur-Saône
Champagnole
Torcy
Beaurepaire-en-Bresse
Lons-le-Saunier
St.-Eusèbe
Varennes-le-Grand
Louhans
Montceau-les-Mines
Messia-sur-Sorne
Clairvaux-les-Lacs
Bruailles
Génelard
Tour-de-Meix
Morez
Tournus
Lugny
Charolles
Cluny
Cambrai
Joudes-Cuiseaux
St. Claude
Thonon-les-Bains
Mts. du Lyonanais
La Roche-Vineuse
Ain
Varennes-les-Mâcon
St.-Cyr-sur-Menthon
Bellignat
Mézériat
Bourg-en-Bresse
Nantua
Servas
9
Bonneville
Cluses
Belleville
Guéreins
Pont-d'Ain
Ambérieu-en-Bugey
Chamonix
Digitally produced by E.S.R. Ltd., Byfleet, Surrey

ced by E.S.R. Ltd., Byfleet, Surrey

igitally produced by E.S.R. Ltd., Byfleet, Surrey

9
6
ITALY
MEDITERRANEAN SEA
Savoie
Dauphin
Alpes du Dauphiné
Alpes Maritimes
Provence
Belleville
Guéreins
Villefranche-sur-Saone
Trévoux
Reyrieux
Pont-d'Ain
Ambérieu-en-Bugey
Bonneville
Cluses
Chamonix
Annecy
Meythet
Seynod
Thônes
Megève
Les Sauvages
Genay
Mionnay
Balan-la-Valbonne
Le Breuil
Sarcey
Morancé
Dardilly
Meyzieu
Blyes
Charvieu-Chavagnieux
Rhône
Belley
St.-Jean-de-Chevelu
Aix-les-Bains
Albertville
Ste.-Foy-lès-Lyon
Villeurbanne
Lyon
Satolas-en-Bonce
Vénissieux
Veyrins-Thuellin
L'Isle-d'Abeau
Bourgoin-Jallieu
St.-Genix-sur-Guïers
Feissons-sur-Isère
Mornant
Givors
Rive-de-Gier
Heyrieux
Marennes
Chasse-sur-Rhône
La-Tour-du-Pin
Chambéry
Vienne
Moidieu-Détourbe
Allevard
La Chapelle
Courchevel
St.-Chamond
Chonas-l'Amballan
St.-Étienne
St.-Clair-du-Rhône
Pajay
Beaucroissant
Voiron
Lanslebourg
St. Jean-de-Maurienne
Salaise-sur-Sanne
Beaurepaire
Tullins-Fures
Moirans
Félines
Annonay
Albon
Noyarey
L'Albenc
Chatte
Grenoble
Tain-l'Hermitage
St.-Hilaire-du-Rosier
St.-Marcellin
Isère
Jarrie
Alp-d-Huez
Tournon
Romans-sur-Isere
Vif
Le Bourg-d'Oisans
St.-Marcel-lès-Valence
Alixan
Drac
Château-Bernard
Lamastre
Briançon
Valence
St.-Martin-de-Clelles
Le Pouzin
Flaviac
Loriol
Die
Corps
Chauffayer
Crest
Saillans
Drôme
Guillestre
Privas
Labegude
Savasse
Cruas
Le Teil
Gap
Chorges
Embrun
Vinezac
Mantélimar
Donzère
Sigottier
Aspres-sur-Buech
Serres
Barcelonnette
Nyons
Vallons-Pont-d'Arc
Eyguians
Durance
Aigues
Lamotte-du-Rhône
Bollène
Ambroix
Bourg-St. Andéol
Mornas
Orange
Sisteron
Colmars
Brouzet-lès-Alès
L'Ardoise
Peipin
Montfort
Digne
St. Martin-Vésubie
Tende
Carpentras
Montaren
Uzès
Pujaut
Mézel
Pugat-Théniers
Sospel
Lédenon
Remoulins
Le Pontet
Châteauneuf-de Gadagne
Forcalquier
Villeneuve
Avignon
Montfavet
Apt
Castellane
Contes
Beaucaire
Noves
Plan-d'Orgon
Tarascon
Orgon
Cavaillon
Sénas
Manosque
Verdon
St-Laurent-Du-Var
Menton
Monte-Carlo
Nice
Antibes
La Roque-d'Anthéron
Ampus
Montauroux
Grasse
Arles
Lambesc
St.-Gilles
St.-Martin-de-Crau
Salon-de-Provence
Salernes
Draguignan
Cannes
Puyricard
Istres
Lançon-de-Provence
Aix-en-Provence
Argens
Les Arcs-sur-Argens
Le Muy
St.-Raphael
Etang de Berre
Bouc-Bel-Air
La Barque
St. Maximim
Fréjus
Stes.-Maries-de-la-Mer
Berre-l'Etang
Vitrolles
Fos-sur-Mer
Brignoles
Le Luc
Le Cannet-des-Maures
Ste. Maxime
Port-St. Louis
Martigues
Carnoules
Grimaud
St. Tropez
C. Couronne
Marseille
Aubagne
Le Castellet
Bormes-les-Mimosas
La Croix-Valmer
Le Cietat
Hyères
Le Lavandou
C. Croisette
Toulon
La Londe-des-Maures
Bandol
La Seyne-sur-Mer
Îles d'Hyères